Law and Education

CONTEMPORARY ISSUES AND COURT DECISIONS

Fifth Edition

H. C. HUDGINS, JR.
Professor of Educational Leadership, Emeritus
East Carolina University

RICHARD S. VACCA
Professor of Education
Virginia Commonwealth University

LEXIS® Publishing

1176011

This book is lovingly dedicated to the memory of Edward C. and Hazel Bolmeier. They were largely responsible for our interest in education law as young graduate students at Duke University. Both served as role models and mentors as we grew in the discipline, and our admiration and appreciation of them remain unabated.

It is also dedicated to all of our graduate students at the master's and doctoral degree level. Their interest, hard work, and enthusiasm in the study of law have sustained us over the years.

TABLE OF CONTENTS

v

TABLE OF CONTENTS

PART II

LAW AND LOCAL BOARDS OF EDUCATION

vi

TABLE OF CONTENTS

TABLE OF CONTENTS

TABLE OF CONTENTS

PART III

LAW AND PROFESSIONAL STAFF

TABLE OF CONTENTS

PART IV

LAW AND STUDENTS

TABLE OF CONTENTS

TABLE OF CONTENTS

TABLE OF CONTENTS

TABLE OF CONTENTS

Page

INTRODUCTION

Since the original publication of this book in 1979, the authors have experienced two matters of interest. The first has been the very positive reception of people throughout the country to this text. Individual purchasers and professors who have adopted the book for their courses have invariably remarked very favorably about the book's scope, its treatment of issues important to them, and its readability. Based on these reactions, the authors feel that their original intent in writing such a book has been achieved.

The second matter of interest is the authors' realization that law constantly changes. That in itself is not a revelation; however this realization becomes acutely obvious when one attempts to keep abreast of court decisions that affect in some way what has already been written. The authors decided that five years is long enough before revising the book.

In considering the various options for bringing the book up-to-date, the authors chose not to undertake what would probably have been the easiest route: adding a supplement. Instead, we decided to revise the contents more comprehensively and, accordingly, have added nearly 300 new court opinions to each of the succeeding editions. These opinions represented a variety of topics that have variously modified previous law, supplemented what courts formerly held, and treated new issues.

In this fifth edition, the authors have again attempted to bring the material up-to-date with the current state of law as it affects public education. As in the four previous editions, the strategy has been to identify issues that affect the daily operation of schools. These issues affect boards of education, administrators, teachers, and students. It is hoped that the treatment of these matters will help readers to understand their various roles in the education system and perform those roles consistently with law and sound educational practice.

The preparation of revised editions is no small task. For two authors who have worn the dual hats of professor and college administrator, the task can be very challenging, particularly with respect to time, or lack of it. The assistance, as well as encouragement, of others has helped us reach our objective. Professor Hudgins wishes to thank several people who, through the years, have supported and encouraged his research and writing. They include Deans Jay Scribner (Temple University), John Johansen (Northern Illinois University), and Charles Coble (East Carolina University). In addition, Phyllis Fleming's adept secretarial skills provided valuable assistance.

Professor Vacca wishes to thank Dean John S. Oehler of the School of Education, who values research, encourages faculty to engage in it, and creates a climate where it can be done. He is also grateful to Mrs. Sue Goins, whose pleasant personality and efficient and effective skills helped bring each project to conclusion; Dr. Louis M. Millhouse for his valuable research contributions; Dr. Cheryl C. Magill for her assistance with the up-date of special education law; and, most of all, his wife Nancy Turner Vacca and their children and grandchildren, for their love, encouragement, and support.

H. C. H.
R. S. V.

PART I

LAW: SOURCES AND RESOURCES

Chapter One

SOURCES OF EDUCATION LAW

§ 1.0. The American Legal System.

The American legal system is not a monolithic structure. Born of the United States Constitution and bound by a common set of principles, this nation's legal system is nevertheless very complex and multifaceted. As one observer commented, "[t]he legal systems of the United States baffle most foreign visitors. And not a few American citizens stand in awe of them. There is such a multiplicity of courts, laws and jurisdictions that even the perceptive nonprofessional observer can become lost in the legal maze . . . ."[1]

Basically, our nation is organized into one federal legal system and fifty separate state legal systems. Each of the latter is unique, in that each one is created by individual state constitutional and legislative enactment. Subsequent sections of this chapter will discuss the federal and state legal systems in more detail.

---

1. A.A. MORRIS, THE CONSTITUTION AND AMERICAN EDUCATION (Durham: Carolina Academic Press, 1989).

1

§ 1.1. Sources of Law.

Law may be defined as a body of principles, standards, and rules that govern human behavior by creating obligations as well as rights, and by imposing penalties. Different from *equity* (i.e., the system of justice and fairness intended to supplement and complement the legal relief granted by courts of law), law in our nation is made up of constitutional provisions, legislative enactments, court precedents, lawyers' opinions, and evolving customs.[2]

Our current, complex Anglo-American system of law (its concepts, principles, and procedures) is the result of over 800 years of development.[3] In our present society, elements of law can be found in every aspect of our daily lives. One writer has said that law

> guides our relations with each other. It tells us how we may be punished for our crimes; it makes us pay when, by our fault, we injure others; it says what we must do if we want our promises to be endorsed as contracts; it makes us pay our taxes; it requires us to take out licenses in order to engage in business, to get married, and even to practice such a pastoral pastime as the art of angling.[4]

Suffice it to say, public school systems are not immune from the law; in fact, they are actually creatures of the law. Because schools are created by state constitutional and legislative mandate, most of what is done in carrying out the daily affairs of a public school possesses a legal dimension.

§ 1.2. Forms of American Law.

This nation's body of law (federal and state), manifests itself in three forms or types. These forms of law are statutory law, common law, and administrative law.

---

2. For a more nearly complete and formal definition of law, see BLACK'S LAW DICTIONARY 884-85 (6th ed. 1990).

3. F.G. KEMPLIN, HISTORICAL INTRODUCTION TO ANGLO-AMERICAN LAW IN A NUTSHELL 2 (St. Paul, Minnesota: West Publishing Co., 1973).

4. *Id.*

Statutory law is written law and includes formal acts of a legally constituted body. Examples of statutory law are the federal and state constitutions, acts of the United States Congress, state codes, and city ordinances.

Common law is unwritten law and emerges from custom (the ways that things are done over a period of time), and from the decrees and judgments of courts of law. Some legal experts refer to common law as "judge-made law." Examples of common law are the body of precedents set by court decisions, the body of opinions rendered by attorneys general (federal and state), and the decisions of various chief state school officers (*e.g.,* the State Commissioners of New Jersey and New York).

Administrative law is comprised of the formal regulations and decisions of various governmental agencies, as well as decisions made by administrative judges. Examples of administrative law are the regulations and decisions of the Interstate Commerce Commission, the National Labor Relations Board, the Federal Communications Commission, the Federal Securities and Exchange Commission and (one that is well known to public school officials) the Equal Employment Opportunity Commission (E.E.O.C.).

With the exception of the State of Louisiana (where the historical development of that state's legal system stemmed from the French legal system of the European Continent), our nation's legal system is a common law system (growing out of the legal system of England).

Because our legal system is dependent upon decided (precedent) cases, it is imperative that students of the law seek out and examine the opinions of courts of record interpreting the written law. Generally, constitutional provisions, federal or state statutes, and city ordinances lack practical meaning and remain legal abstractions until they are interpreted by a court of law and are made to apply in a given situation. To put it another way, even though statutes control all situations legally contested, the interpretations

3

of statutes by judges in courts of law are what give meaning and force to written legislative pronouncements.[5]

§ 1.3. The Adjudication Process and Conflict Resolution.

At the very core of the American legal system is the principle that for every *wrong* (violation of a right) done to an individual by government or by any other individual, there should be a *remedy* (some form of compensation or relief) provided. A citizen must be protected from injustice and must also have some place to go (when all else fails) to seek justice. In our social structure the courts of this nation exist for such purposes. However, while the purpose of taking a lawsuit is to gain remedy for a wrong done, a court might subsequently determine that any remedy available is found exclusively in a specific statute and, as such, the court will not add to or in any other way supplement that law. A good example of this *exclusivity doctrine* can be found in controversies involving the Individuals with Disabilities Education Act (IDEA).

In our system of justice there are acts or failures to act enumerated in statutes (federal and state). These violations of statutory law are known technically as *crimes,* the commission of which will result in government prosecution and in government-imposed punishments. In *criminal* courts, the government (federal or state) is always the plaintiff. On the other hand, our system of justice also includes a mechanism for allowing one person to seek remedy when wronged by another individual. The *civil* courts exist for this purpose, and do not involve matters of government-imposed sanctions.

Where a controversy exists, the parties to that matter have the option of settling their dispute without going to court. Options are available for reaching mutually agreed upon settlements of a variety of conflicts involving property rights, financial agreements, employment disputes and domestic difficulties.

---

5. *Id.* at 12-16.

In our country there are several formal, rational means available to citizens to settle disputes. For example, *arbitration* (the settlement of a dispute through the intercession and decision of an impartial third party) has brought many disputes to a final determination, as has the process of *mediation* (where a neutral third party facilitates decision-making by the parties). In recent years, however, individuals and groups of citizens have increasingly resorted to *adjudication* for settling disputes. Complaining parties have taken their conflicts to courts of law for the application of pre-existing rules and precedents to their conflict in search of a just settlement.

Bound by strict rules of procedure, courts do not solicit their business; petitioners must seek their help. As such, courts of law "do not act on their own initiative. They assume jurisdiction only of controversies and other legal matters referred to them for decision. Once a controversy is before the courts, they are relatively free to effectuate complete justice as they deem it to be."[6]

Individuals seeking redress of their grievances must make certain that their matter is taken to the appropriate court. A formal petition must be filed, and the matter must be accepted for adjudication (a decision that is the court's alone to make). To successfully initiate and maintain their lawsuit, parties must possess *standing* to sue. The *standing doctrine* holds that an individual (or individuals) must have a real and legally protected interest at stake in the controversy. Lawsuits have been disposed of at various stages (from the initial pleading stage through the appellate stage) where a lack of standing on the part of the moving party has been demonstrated.

Generally, school controversies do not result in petitions for redress filed in a court of law. Mechanisms to resolve conflicts exist at all administrative levels within state education systems. Generally, grievance and appeals channels are available to professional employees, parents, and students. What is more, state stat-

---

6. E.E. REUTTER, JR., THE LAW OF PUBLIC EDUCATION (4th ed. Mineola, New York: The Foundation Press, 1994).

utes often provide vehicles of grievance and appeal from the lowest administrative level within a school building up through the highest level in the educational system (*e.g.,* the state board of education and chief state school officer). In some states (*e.g.,* Virginia) the decisions of fact-finding panels (hearing teacher grievances) are not binding on local school boards. There are occasions, however, when someone alleges that the actions of a school board, an administrator, or a teacher are in some way a violation of constitutional or statutory law and that such actions go beyond the channels available. As a general rule, aggrieved persons should exhaust all administrative channels prior to going to court. However, the exhaustion doctrine is not a hard and fast rule. For example, where a question of law exists, and not a question requiring administrative findings of fact, the doctrine may not apply. Here an individual may not be required to exhaust all administrative channels prior to initiating a lawsuit. Such matters more often than not culminate in adjudication.

§ 1.4. Federal Government and Public Education.

Historically, the absence of specific language in the United States Constitution regarding education and schools, coupled with the application of the tenth amendment, placed the direct responsibility for establishing and maintaining public school systems in the hands of state governments. Each state assumed complete control of education within its boundaries. Thus, in this country today, there is no single, national public school system; rather, public education exists in fifty different state public school systems. To understand fully the legal aspects of public education the researcher must study the school codes and related court decisions from each state.

In the past and up to the present, however, the federal government has exercised growing influence in educational matters, primarily through congressional enactment, agency regulations and guidelines, and federal court decree.

All three branches of the federal government exercise significant influence on the day-to-day operation of public school systems. Matters of finance, curriculum, personnel, and student control have each felt the influence of Congress, the President, and federal judges.

a. *Congress and the Schools.* Article I, § 1 of the United States Constitution provides: "All legislative powers herein granted shall be vested in a Congress of the United States . . . ."[7] Over the years, Congress has passed numerous laws having direct impact on public education. From the early years of this nation the national government has taken steps to ensure an important place for education in our society, and to stimulate the growth of education in the states. For example, as early as 1787, Congress (in establishing the Northwest Territory) expressed the following belief: "Religion, morality, and knowledge being necessary to good government and the happiness of mankind, schools and the means of education shall be forever encouraged."[8]

Article I, § 8 of the United States Constitution grants Congress the power to tax and to "provide for the common defense and general welfare of the United States." This constitutional provision has served as a legal foundation for the passage of specific education laws, each of which has funneled billions of federal tax dollars into school programs within the states. Federal laws have provided extensive programs in such areas as adult education, vocational and technical education, multicultural education, special education, science education, foreign language education, and others. Congressional actions have even made it possible to reimburse public school systems for providing their children with milk, with breakfasts, and with lunches served at school. Bills in Congress that would grant funds to attract more qualified students into teaching in public schools, and granting funds to assist with asbestos clean-up in school buildings, are other examples of contin-

---

7. U.S. CONST. art. I, § 1, ratified 1789.

8. N. EDWARDS & H.G. RICHEY, THE SCHOOL IN THE AMERICAN SOCIAL ORDER 216 (Boston, Massachusetts: Houghton Mifflin Co., 1963).

ued federal legislative involvement in public education in the states.

A 1975 Act of Congress having direct impact on the day-to-day operation of public schools is Public Law 94-142 (codified at 20 U.S.C. § 1401 et seq.), the Education for All Handicapped Children Act. Referred to as a "Bill of Rights for the Handicapped Children," P.L. 94-142 went into effect in November, 1976.

Public Law 94-142 (in 1990 retitled as the Individuals with Disabilities Education Act (I.D.E.A.)) mandated that states provide a free public education for all handicapped children between the ages of three years and twenty-one years. Penalty for failure to comply with this mandate may involve the loss of all current federal funding, and disqualification from eligibility to receive future federal funding.

Among other things, I.D.E.A. requires that an individualized educational program (IEP) be written for each child covered by the statute. Moreover, a major goal of the Act[9] is that all such children be placed in general education classes to the "maximum extent" possible.

The above law, coupled with § 504 of the Rehabilitation Act of 1973,[10] caused public school systems and public higher educational institutions to take immediate action to remove all forms of exclusion and discrimination involving students with disabilities.

Another excellent example of the impact of Congress on the day-to-day operation of schools is the passage of Public Law 93-380. Named the Family Educational Rights and Privacy Act of 1974, and coupled with emerging state statutes, this law served not

---

9. For a detailed summary of the provisions of P.L. 94-142, see L.V. Goodman, *A Bill of Rights for the Handicapped,* AMERICAN EDUCATION (July, 1976). This law was retitled by the passage of P.L. 101-476 (1990), its scope was expanded, and it is now referred to as IDEA (INDIVIDUALS WITH DISABILITIES EDUCATION ACT).

10. P.L. 93-112, 29 U.S.C. § 794. This law mandates that "no otherwise handicapped individual . . . shall, solely by reason of his handicap, be excluded from participation, be denied the benefits of, or be subjected to discrimination under any program or activity receiving federal financial assistance."

only to protect the confidentiality of student records from scrutiny by unauthorized third parties, but opened free access to school records by parents or guardians and students (within certain age limitations) with the prerogative to challenge the accuracy and authenticity of the information contained in that record.

Following the passage of this Act, state after state enacted statutes and implementing regulations governing access to student records. As a result, contemporary public school systems maintain carefully planned procedures for collecting, keeping, reevaluating, and using student information. It can be said that rather than produce a flood of new court cases, the 1974 Act of Congress has greatly reduced the vulnerability of school officials to lawsuits regarding school records.

b. *The Executive Branch and Schools.* Of the three branches of our national government (legislative, executive, and judicial), it is difficult to see at first glance just where and how the President of the United States has an effect on public education.[11] Unlike Congress and the federal courts, the President's involvement in public school matters tends to be more indirect; yet, several responsibilities of our nation's chief executive do have direct impact on school matters.

The President, through public pronouncements, messages to Congress, and interagency communications voices his opinions and beliefs on education and school-related matters. Generally, these oral and written remarks help set a level of "national priority" for education. Former President Reagan continued support of student prayer in public schools and academic excellence. President Bush emphasized giving parents more choice in where their children go to school (elementary and secondary), and initiated America 2000, a statement of education goals that this nation should achieve by the beginning of the twenty-first century. President Clinton continued support of those goals by signing into law the Goals 2000: Educate America Act (P.L. 103-227, 1994).

---

11. U.S. Const. art. II, ratified 1789.

9

Another point of impact on education is found in the President's *veto* power. Federal programs and ultimate funding (after passing Congress) must have the President's signature in order to be implemented.

The power of appointment also represents a significant source of executive involvement in matters of education and schools, especially as it concerns appointments of certain cabinet officers and the appointment of federal judges. The two most significant cabinet positions affecting schools are the Secretary of Education (Department of Education) and the Attorney General (United States Department of Justice).

The Department of Education is responsible for administering most federal education projects. Guidelines written by the Department of Education staff members for the implementation and administration of federal funds and federal projects are published in the *Federal Register*. These published guidelines set forth procedures for school officials to follow regarding the application for, the receipt of, and the expenditure of federal funding through a particular federal law.

The Department of Justice (the Attorney General's responsibility) often gets involved in public school matters when claims of discrimination and other injustices are brought by parties against public school systems and institutions of higher education. In recent years the Department of Justice and its attorneys have investigated several such complaints from citizens in all sections of the country.

Federal judges are appointed by the President. As will be shown in subsection c. below, and in subsequent sections of this book, much of what is done and cannot be done in American public schools (and to a more limited degree in private schools) in matters of finance, governance, curriculum, personnel, parent involvement, and student control is a direct result of federal court decree.

c. *The Federal Courts and Schools.* Article III, § 1 of the United States Constitution provides that "[t]he judicial power of the United States shall be vested in one Supreme Court, and in such inferior courts as the Congress may from time to time ordain and establish."[12] These courts have authority to adjudicate all cases in law and equity arising out of the Constitution, Acts of Congress, and United States treaties and, among other things, to decide controversies to which the United States shall be a party, or which are between one state and citizens of another state.[13]

The United States Supreme Court, in addition to having original jurisdiction in certain matters, has jurisdiction to review: "(1) all cases in lower federal courts, and (2) all cases in state courts in which there is involved a question of the meaning or effect of a federal statute or a constitutional provision . . . ."[14]

The Supreme Court's mandatory appeal jurisdiction was limited when, in 1988, the President signed P.L. 100-352. Effective on September 25, 1988, obtaining a *writ of certiorari* became the major path to the high court from lower federal courts and the state courts. Granting *certiorari* is within the sole discretion of the Justices of the Supreme Court.

While state courts have *general jurisdiction* (the presumption is that they have authority to hear all cases that involve the state's constitution and state law, unless a showing is made to the contrary), federal courts have *limited jurisdiction.* The presumption is that a federal court lacks jurisdiction unless a plaintiff can show the court that the problem presented for judicial review involves a federal question (issue arising under the United States Constitution or federal law.)[15]

Traditionally, the judges at all levels are reluctant to encroach upon the law-making prerogatives of the legislative branch of government (local, state, and federal). Judges have the discretion to abstain in such matters. However, occasions arise where courts, by invoking the doctrine of judicial review, declare acts of legisla-

---

12. U.S. CONST. art. III, § 1, ratified 1789.

13. *Id.* at § 2.

14. E.C. BOLMEIER, SCHOOL IN THE LEGAL STRUCTURE 55, 56 (2d ed. Cincinnati, Ohio 1973).

15. C.A. WRIGHT, LAW OF FEDERAL COURTS 15 (2d ed. St. Paul, Minnesota: West Publishing Co., 1970).

tive bodies to be unconstitutional, or in some other way nullify a legislative initiative.

The federal court system is structured into three levels. The United States Supreme Court is at the highest level. The *thirteen* United States Courts of Appeals are intermediate courts of appeal and function at the next level down from the Supreme Court. The third level, below the Courts of Appeals, houses the ninety-plus United States District Courts, the trial courts of the federal structure. Additionally, there are some specialized courts to hear such matters as customs, patents, and taxes. The chart below outlines the current federal court structure.

Chart 1[16]

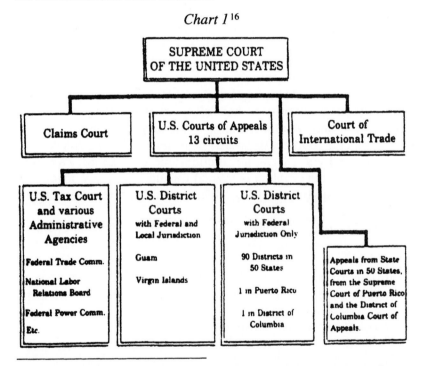

---

16. This chart was originally taken directly from *The United States Courts,* Report of the Committee on the Judiciary, House of Representatives 3 (Washington, D.C., 1975), and has been updated to reflect changes since that date. See also *A Guide to the Federal Courts* (Rev. ed. Wash. D.C.: WANT Pub'g Co. 1984).

As shown above, the federal court structure contains 90-plus United States District Courts (federal trial courts). Each state has at least one such court, with large states like California, New York, and Texas having as many as four.[17]

Each possessing a lifetime Presidential appointment, there are several hundred United States District Court judges, with each district having a varying number of judges.[18] Generally, *one* judge sits (presides) in a United States District Court. However, special situations often warrant that a panel of district court judges sit to hear a case. A trial may be by jury or by the judge (or judges) hearing the case.

One receiving an adverse decision in a United States District Court has an automatic right to appeal to the Federal Circuit Court of Appeals for the circuit wherein that trial court is located. The United States is divided into thirteen *circuits* for the purpose of hearing these appeals.[19] More often than not a public school case does not go beyond this intermediate level to the United States Supreme Court. The chart on the following page shows the division of the nation into the thirteen judicial circuits.

---

17. *Id.* at 7.

18. *Id.*

19. *Id.* at 5. Eleven circuits plus the District of Columbia Circuit comprise the conventional twelve circuits. The Thirteenth Circuit is composed of specialized courts such as the Court of Claims, and the Court of Military Appeals.

Chart 2[20]

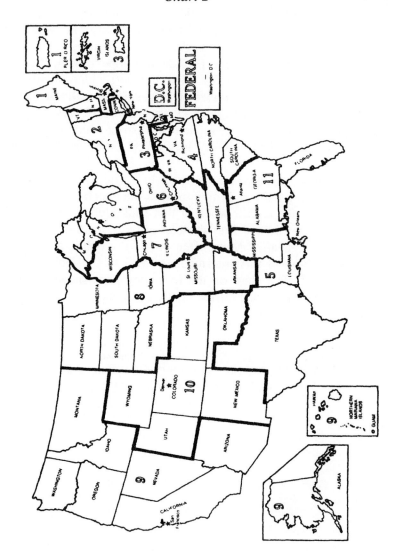

---

20. *Id.* at 6.

Mainly possessing appellate jurisdiction, the United States Courts of Appeals for the circuits also have jurisdiction to review orders issued by federal administrative agencies.

Federal Circuit Court judges are appointed by the President (with advice and consent of the Senate), and serve lifetime terms. The number of judges on each circuit court varies from *five* (in the *First* Circuit) to *twenty-one* (in the *Ninth* Circuit). The chart below shows the names of the circuit courts of appeals, their geographical jurisdictions, and the number of authorized judgeships in each circuit court.

Chart 3[21]

FEDERAL CIRCUIT COURTS OF APPEALS

Court of Appeals	Number of authorized judgeships	Location and postal address
District of Columbia Circuit (District of Columbia)	11	Washington, D.C. 20001.
1st Circuit (Maine, Massachusetts, New Hampshire, Rhode Island, and Puerto Rico)	6	Boston, Mass. 02109.
2d Circuit (Connecticut, New York, and Vermont)	12	New York, N.Y. 10007.
3d Circuit (Delaware, New Jersey, Pennsylvania, and the Virgin Islands)	12	Philadelphia, Pa. 19107.
4th Circuit (Maryland, North Carolina, South Carolina, Virginia, and West Virginia)	13	Richmond, Va. 23219.
5th Circuit (Louisiana, Mississippi, and Texas)	16	New Orleans, La. 70130.
6th Circuit (Kentucky, Michigan, Ohio, and Tennessee)	15	Cincinnati, Ohio 45202.
7th Circuit (Illinois, Indiana, and Wisconsin)	11	Chicago, Ill. 60604.

21. *Id.* at 5.

Court of Appeals	Number of authorized judgeships	Location and postal address
8th Circuit (Arkansas, Iowa, Minnesota, Missouri, Nebraska, North Dakota, and South Dakota)	10	St. Louis, Mo. 63101.
9th Circuit (Alaska, Arizona, California, Hawaii, Idaho, Montana, Nevada, Oregon, Washington, and Guam)	21	San Francisco, Calif. 94101.
10th Circuit (Colorado, Kansas, New Mexico, Oklahoma, Utah, and Wyoming)	12	Denver, Colo. 80202.
11th Circuit (Alabama, Georgia, Florida)	12	Atlanta, Ga. 30303.
Federal Circuit	11	Washington, D.C. 20001.

Of the few school-related conflicts heard by federal courts, only a small percentage ever reaches the Supreme Court. When school cases are heard, however, certain provisions of the United States Constitution are involved more than others and might be regarded as foundations for seeking relief in federal court. These provisions are the first, fourth, sixth, eighth, and eleventh amendments, with the primary vehicle for taking school cases into federal court being the provisions of the fourteenth amendment, both the due process clause and the equal protection clause.

Even though the Supreme Court maintains a reluctant attitude toward hearing school cases, it has nevertheless rendered several decisions altering the daily operation of public school systems across the country. Such issues as school integration, student rights, religion in schools, school finance, and teachers' rights offer excellent examples of this phenomenon and are discussed in subsequent sections of this book.

§ 1.5. State Government and Public Education.

The silence of the Federal Constitution, coupled with the language of the tenth amendment ("powers not delegated to the United States by the Constitution, nor prohibited by it to the States, are reserved to the States respectively, or to the people"), bestowed upon state government the legal responsibility for the establishment of public school systems. Thus, as the nation grew, and our population increased, individual states assumed complete authority to provide public education for their children, only restricted in action by the provisions of the United States Constitution and by subsequent acts of that state's legislature.[22]

a. *State Legislatures and Schools.* Generally, the constitution of each state contains a mandate for the establishment of public education.[23] Typically, this constitutional mandate places the legal authority to establish and to maintain a public school system directly in the hands of the state legislature. The following provision from the Constitution of the Commonwealth of Virginia offers an excellent example of such a mandate: "The General Assembly shall provide for a system of free public elementary and secondary schools for all children of school age throughout the Commonwealth, and shall seek to ensure that an educational program of high quality is established and continually maintained."[24]

Not every state constitution includes such a detailed mandate as does Virginia's. For example, the Pennsylvania Constitution states very simply that: "The General Assembly shall provide for maintenance and support of a thorough and efficient system of public schools to serve the needs of the Commonwealth."[25]

Despite the fact that legislatures generally have constitutional authority to construct a state's system of education through statutory enactment, their authority is not without legal boundaries. Historically, federal courts, through their application of fourteenth

---

22. REUTTER, *supra* note 6.
23. BOLMEIER, *supra* note 14, at 88-99.
24. VA. CONST. art. VIII, § 1, effective July 1, 1971.
25. PA. CONST. art. III, § 14, enacted.

17

amendment guarantees and through their interpretations of federal statutes, have conditioned the exercise of state authority over educational matters. As early as 1923, in deciding the first case to reach it in which state authority over public school curriculum was involved, the United States Supreme Court suggested: "That the State may do much, go very far, indeed, in order to improve the quality of its citizens, physically, mentally, and morally, is clear; but the individual has certain fundamental rights."[26] Two years later, the High Court went one step further in an Oregon case and made it clear that children are not mere "creatures of the State."[27]

Down through the years federal courts have consistently limited state authority over education as cases were decided challenging several aspects of public school operation. Decisions on such state matters as compulsory attendance, compulsory flag salutes, prayer and Bible reading in schools, teachers' rights, and others all placed state authority over public school matters under a federal constitutional overlay.

Over the past twenty years a child's chance to become involved in public education provided by a state has (primarily through court action) become a matter of legal *entitlement.* This judicial trend began with the United States Supreme Court's benchmark decision in *Brown v. Board of Education.*[28] In that decision the high court established the notion that "[t]oday, education is perhaps the most important function of state and local governments. . . . Such an opportunity, where the State has undertaken to provide it, is a right which must be made available to all on equal terms." The judicial mold was thus set for a series of landmark decisions to follow. Through such cases as *Tinker v. Des Moines Independent Community School District,*[29] *P.A.R.C. v. Common-*

---

26. Meyer v. Nebraska, 262 U.S. 390, 43 S. Ct. 625, 67 L. Ed. 1042 (1923).

27. Pierce v. Society of Sisters, 268 U.S. 510, 45 S. Ct. 510, 69 L. Ed. 1070 (1925).

28. 347 U.S. 483, 74 S. Ct. 686, 98 L. Ed. 873 (1954).

29. 393 U.S. 503, 89 S. Ct. 733, 21 L. Ed. 2d 731 (1969).

wealth of Pennsylvania,[30] *Mills v. Board of Education*,[31] *Goss v. Lopez*,[32] and others, the legal *entitlement* of children to be included in public schools became a reality.

State courts themselves have rendered decisions limiting the educational authority of legislatures. As early as 1926, for example, the State Supreme Court of Appeals for Virginia said, in *Flory v. Smith*, that "[t]he legislature . . . has the power to enact any legislation in regard to the conduct, control, and regulation of the public free schools, which does not deny to the citizen the constitutional right to enjoy life and liberty, to pursue happiness and to acquire property."[33] Contemporary state courts have continued to check and balance the educational authority of state legislatures.

Since state legislators themselves cannot possibly assume actual supervisory responsibility for public schools, the general supervision and administrative control over a state's public school system is generally placed in the hands of a state board of education. As Bolmeier pointed out almost thirty years ago:

> Although the legislature is usually charged with the responsibility of organizing, providing for, and administering a state system of education, it is obvious that the legislature cannot perform these functions directly by itself . . . accordingly most state legislatures have delegated a good share of the responsibility of policy making, as well as other school matters, to state boards of education.[34]

Thus, whether they be called State Regents or State Boards, these high level policymakers still exercise considerable regulatory authority over all public school matters in a state.

To understand completely the legal nature of a state school board of education, one must examine the specific constitutional and statutory provisions of each state. Subsequent chapters of this

---

30. 334 F. Supp. 1257 (E.D. Pa. 1971), final consent agreement at 343 F. Supp. 279 (E.D. Pa. 1972).

31. 348 F. Supp. 866 (D.D.C. 1972).

32. 419 U.S. 565, 95 S. Ct. 729, 42 L. Ed. 2d 725 (1975).

33. 145 Va. 164, 134 S.E. 360 (1926).

34. BOLMEIER, *supra* note 14, at 115.

book will delve more deeply into issues related to state board action in matters of public education.

b. *The Governor and Schools.* Much like the President of the United States, each state's governor has impact on education and schools. Limited in authority by state constitutional and statutory law, governors nevertheless may have a substantial effect on public education and schools within their state's boundaries.

Governors, as their state's chief executive, through official messages to the legislature and through other public pronouncements, help chart the state's course for education. In the past, some governors gained a reputation as "education governors" because of the high priority they placed on education during their terms of office. In recent history several states have experienced significant growth and development in post-secondary education through the efforts of a particular governor. Whole, statewide community college systems have developed, in states where no community college system existed, because of a governor's efforts.

In some states the governor appoints all state level education officials. For example, in Virginia all high level state education officials are appointed by the governor, with approval of the General Assembly. Members of the State Board of Education, the State Superintendent of Public Instruction, the State Secretary of Education (in the Governor's cabinet), the State Community College Board, the State Council of Higher Education, the Boards of Visitors of each four-year state college and university, and several other high officials are appointed by the Governor of Virginia.

A state governor, as chief executive, also exercises the power of *veto* over all legislation. Thus, statewide programs and program funding for education and schools in most states are affected by a stroke of the governor's pen.

Some state statutes grant to a governor the authority to appoint local and state level judges to courts. Suffice it to say, the kind and caliber of judicial appointee may have an effect on the conduct of the schools and the quality of education produced as school cases are adjudicated in state court.

c. *The State Judiciary and Schools.* As emphasized in previous sections of this chapter, public education is an entity of state law. Thus, what a particular state's courts say about education and schools is most important. One cannot possibly understand the legalities of public education by simply reading a state's education code, or by studying the regulations of a state board of education. State court decisions must be analyzed and interpreted if meaning and understanding are to be found.

Although similarities exist among the fifty state judicial systems, each state does have its own unique court structure. The more populous states (*e.g.,* California, New York, and Texas) tend to have complicated court structures with several levels of trial courts, intermediate courts, and appellate courts, while the less populous states (*e.g.,* Virginia) tend to have very simple court structures. Additionally, the names for courts with similar jurisdictions often differ from state to state. The researcher must, therefore, examine the court structure of particular states to understand the route taken by a school-related issue in litigation. Examples of different state court systems follow.

In Maryland, the state's highest court is called the Court of Appeals. An intermediate court of appeals, called the Court of Special Appeals, sits between the Court of Appeals and the Circuit Courts of the various counties (having original jurisdiction over all civil and criminal cases). The Maryland court structure also contains District Courts, People's Courts (in some counties and cities), Orphan's Courts, and a Superior Court and a Court of Common Pleas for the City of Baltimore.

The highest court in the State of Illinois is the Supreme Court of Illinois. There are District Appellate Courts (intermediate appellate courts), and Circuit Courts (possessing original jurisdiction) that exist in the various counties and cities of the State. Cook County has a Superior Court functioning as its Circuit Court.

The Supreme Court of Pennsylvania is that Commonwealth's highest court. The Superior Court of Pennsylvania is an intermediate-level appellate court and beneath it is a statewide court (Commonwealth Court) with original and appellate jurisdiction in criminal and civil cases. The lower-level courts are called Courts of Common Pleas, while the City of Philadelphia has Municipal and Traffic Courts.

In the Commonwealth of Virginia, the Virginia Supreme Court is the state's highest court. At the intermediate level sits the Virginia Court of Appeals, possessing appellate jurisdiction in both criminal cases (except for the death penalty) and civil cases (including domestic relations). In Virginia, the Circuit Courts of the various cities and counties are the trial courts of record, while at the basic level matters are heard by the General District Courts, which include juvenile and domestic relations.

Generally, state courts assume the same attitude of "nonintervention in school matters" as is evident among the federal judiciary. School matters heard by state courts are usually settled at the trial court level, with the state courts of appeals (intermediate or supreme court level) functioning as the courts of last resort.

d. *State Attorneys General and Schools.* The state attorney general may also become involved in public school matters. Although the school law student may neglect to search the opinions of state attorneys general for material concerning the legal aspects of public school operation, such opinions are vitally important sources to explore when looking for the interpretations of state statutes.

Typically, a state's attorney general will issue an official opinion only to another state or local official (for example, a local school board chairman can request an opinion, but not a local school principal). The request for an attorney general's opinion must be made on the official stationery of the individual or the governmental organization requesting the opinion, and the request must state a specific legal question to be answered. After researching the question by drawing upon statutory law, case law precedents (state and federal), and state board policy, the attorney general will send his official answer back, on letterhead paper, to the individual who requested it. The opinion-letter will bear the signature of the attorney general.

Not all experts in school law agree on the importance of formal opinions from state attorneys general. Basically, there are two schools of thought regarding their impact on legal matters. One school of thought sees the opinion of an attorney general as having the same weight of importance as a court decision. A second group sees the opinion of an attorney general as no more important than is the opinion of any other attorney. These latter individuals will most probably challenge the attorney general if and when an opinion adverse to their cause is written and published.

Whatever their true importance, opinions of a state's attorney general do, from time to time, interpret state education law, school board policy, and the pronouncements and actions of school administrators and teachers. Thus, these official pronouncements of the state's chief legal counsel represent another vital area to explore when searching for sources of school law.

§ 1.6. Summary.

Public education in the year 2000 remains a function of federal, state and local government. Public school systems are creations of state law. Thus, students of education law must constantly strive to gain a more thorough understanding of the American legal system and the position of public education and schools in that complex setting.

Additionally, a need has grown in recent years for professionals in public schools to become more knowledgeable about the interplay of courts with the day-to-day operation of schools and school systems. Once thought to be the sole concern of school board attorneys, school board members, and school administrators, education-related legal problems have, in recent years, become problems of supervisors, counselors, and teachers, as well.

To comprehend the impact and ramifications of emerging court decrees and legislative enactments affecting public education, the student of school law must study the complex legal nature of public school problems. The remaining chapters of this book are planned to help the reader accomplish that objective.

Chapter Two

TOOLS OF LEGAL RESEARCH

§ 2.0. Law Libraries.

Increasingly, educators are involved in problems that have their resolution in law. For example, a teacher debates whether law and academic freedom clash in teaching a controversial short story in literature class. A principal studies whether law applies in searching a student's locker for stolen library books and narcotics. A superintendent reviews "due process" procedures when he rates a teacher as being unsatisfactory and subject to dismissal. A school board member reminds himself that he may now be sued for damages under a statute over 100 years old if he violates a constitutional right of one employed in the school district.

Not only have educators become more aware of law, but law itself has become more complex. Problems that were previously resolved easily and without a challenge from the affected party may well now get to court. This is particularly true when decisions are made without an understanding and application of what current law is.

Why should one study law? The superintendent who, ten years ago, only occasionally called on his board attorney for advice, may today hold daily discussions with him. Today's educator is also dealing with an electorate better informed than ever. The public at large is more likely to challenge an educator's decision. Further, courts have increasingly entertained legal suits, and, as a result of judges' decisions, people have been encouraged to challenge school authority in court. If one is familiar with law, not only is he more likely to behave legally, he is also better prepared for preventing problems.

How does one become familiar with law? That is the basic question of this chapter. One becomes familiar with law by studying it — by mastering basic legal principles from which specific issues are more readily resolved. In order to achieve this purpose, one must first become familiar with techniques and tools of legal research. This study should be done systematically rather than haphazardly.

An educator who has become familiar with a general education library, and made frequent use of it, soon finds himself comfortable in being able to locate and isolate materials appropriate for a research topic. That same educator, in being introduced to a law library, may initially find the experience to be confusing. Legal materials are assimilated and organized differently from educational materials. In law, constitutions, statutes, and court decisions comprise much of basic research, and the way these materials are organized, so that one can get at them, means that the neophyte researcher must learn a new research system. Although learning to do legal research may appear at first to be overwhelming, one learns by familiarizing himself step by step while spending a number of sessions in a law library.

This chapter introduces the reader to materials that are basic to law libraries and useful to one researching in education law. By necessity, the legal tools identified here are selective rather than exhaustive; there are others that a more advanced legal scholar will become familiar with. Those that are identified in this chapter will, however, provide the reader with a comprehensive, basic knowledge of legal tools.

§ 2.1. Statutes.

a. *In General.* A statute refers to a legislative law; it is derived from the action of a legislature. It may refer to a state or a federal law. The law of a local legislative body is referred to as an ordinance. In engaging in legal research, one should examine first the statutes that may govern the legal issue before proceeding to other sources, including case law or the decisions of judges. Either a state or a federal statute, or both, may bear on the topic.

The official designation of federal laws is *Statutes at Large.* After a term of Congress or a state legislature is concluded, the laws are then published in bound form. They become a chronological arrangement of laws on the various subjects with which a legislative body has dealt.

The terms "codes," "compilations" and "revisions" are used interchangeably. They designate topical breakdowns of legislative acts, as, for example, the laws treating education are organized into a school code. Codes are organized further by specific subject.

A code may or may not reflect the elimination of laws that have been superseded or become obsolete. Since organizing and publishing a code is often by a commercial body not otherwise authorized by the legislature, it is viewed as not having official sanction. Nonetheless, the use of it is authoritative in legal research.

Many codes are published in annotated editions. Accompanying each section of law is a statement of the legislative history as well as citations to court decisions treating that section. These annotations are a very valuable service to legal researchers.

One may locate a statute by using one of three methods: the descriptive word method, the topic method, or the popular name method.

The Descriptive Word Method. This method involves using the index of a code similarly to the way one would use an index to a textbook. In classifying sections of the code, editors select significant words or phrases that identify the subject of the specific law. These words and phrases are then arranged alphabetically. In the index to codes, one may find not only the appropriate word or phrase, but also the section number of the law from which it was derived, and the title or chapter of the law. From that information, one can then proceed directly to the appropriate statute.

The Topic Method. This method involves use of the classified subject or title arrangement of the code similar to the way one would use the contents page of a textbook. For the novice researcher, this method may be more difficult than the descriptive word method, for it presumes familiarity with the organization and topics of the code. A more experienced researcher may go directly to the title or chapter of a code and study the outline of topics. He would then identify his specific subject by the appropriate section of the code and proceed to locate it in the text.

The Popular Name Method. If a researcher knows a statute only by its popular name, he may find its official name and citation. Federal statutes may be identified in one of several sources, among them the following: *United States Code Annotated, United States Supreme Court Digest,* and *Federal Code Annotated Popular Name Table for Acts of Congress.* Popular names for state statutes may be located through *Shepard's Citations* for the states or through the State Codes and their Popular Names of State Acts.

b. *Federal.* Supreme over any federal statute, state constitution, or state law is the Constitution of the United States. Not only is the text of the Constitution significant in legal research, but also of particular importance is its construction as determined by court decisions. The Constitution, as construed by court decisions, is available in several sources, among them the following: *United States Code Annotated, Federal Code Annotated, United States Supreme Court Reports Digest,* and *United States Supreme Court Digest.*

28

Prior to their publication in bound volumes, Congressional laws are referred to as "slip laws." As each law is enacted, it is printed on a separate piece of paper (a slip of paper, hence the name). Later, the "slip laws" are cited according to the number of the Congress enacting them and the order of enactment. For example, Public Law 94-142 was enacted by the 94th Congress, and it was the 142nd law passed by that Congress and signed by the President. One may cite a slip law by its number until the bound volumes appear, at which point one then cites from the Statutes at Large.

Statutes at Large is the designation of the permanent form of federal statutes. Its titles are the official source for laws of Congress. They are now published after each session of Congress. The volumes are numbered consecutively as they are published from session to session. Each volume contains a numerical and chronological list of the laws contained within it as well as a subject index.

A different publication from the Statutes at Large is the United States Code (U.S.C.). This work grew out of a perceived need of Congress to accumulate and bring up to date the permanent laws of Congress. It was felt that, instead of having to go through each session of the Statutes at Large to find appropriate statutes on a topic, one should be able to go to a source in which the statutes were organized cumulatively around subjects. For this monumental work, Congress sought the assistance of a commercial publisher who initially classified the subject matter into 50 general subjects called "Titles," number 20 being Education. The titles, in turn, were divided into sections. There were gaps in the numbering of sections to provide for future expansion.

The editors made some minor modifications in the wording of the statutes without attempting to change the meaning or intent of them.

The United States Code Annotated is organized like the United States Code with one valuable added feature. It contains annotations of various court decisions which have construed sections of the code, historical notes, cross references, and other editorial aids.

It is kept current by both temporary and annual cumulative supplements. A subject index of several volumes, individual title indexes, and a table of acts by popular names are also features.

A competing work of the United States Code Annotated is the Federal Code Annotated. It is organized similarly to the U.S.C.A. and provides the same kind of information.

Two loose leaf services may aid the researcher with statutory research. *United States Law Week,* treated elsewhere in this chapter, publishes the text of significant federal legislation. *Commerce Clearing House, Congressional Index,* gives current references to pending and new legislation. It is a useful guide to the status of pending legislation as well as that already enacted.

c. State. Just as the Federal Constitution is supreme over any federal law, so is the constitution of a given state supreme over any of its laws. When researching a topic peculiar to any state, it is necessary to examine the state's constitution to determine if it has a provision applicable to that law. It may or may not have a provision on a given topic but, since some state constitutions contain very specific provisions, one should check its content. Next, one should also examine the state statutes applicable to that topic.

Although laws of states differ considerably, the classification of those laws is similar. Thus, if one is able to research statutory law in one state, he should also be able to do it in another.

Like federal laws, the laws of a state legislature are synonymously known as "codes," "compilations," or "revisions." Their subdivisions are called either "titles," "chapters," or "subdivisions." Pennsylvania's school code is organized by titles, number 24 being Education. These titles are further divided into 15 chapters and then into sections. For example, under Title 24, § 15-1512 refers to "Courses of study adapted to age, etc., of pupils."

Similarly, Chapter 122 of the Illinois statutes is the state's school code. The chapter is divided into articles and further into sections. For example, in the citation, ch. 122, § 27-20.1, the 122 refers to the chapter, 27 to the article, and 20.1 to the section. The codes are broken down by subject matter, contain annotations about their legislative history, and have court decisions construing the law. Annual pocket-part supplements keep the codes current. In North Carolina, the public school laws are found in Chapter 115C of the General Statutes.

If one wished to research the laws of the fifty states on a given topic, he might try one of two sources. The Law Digest volume of the *Martindale-Hubbell Law Directory,* published annually, contains a brief digest of the laws of the fifty states. Its classification plan allows for all laws on a given topic to be organized around the same general topic. After building a bibliography of case law, one must then go to the statutes of the various states that have a law on that subject.

Shepard's Citations covers statutes for every state. The citator indicates whether a given statute has been amended or repealed, and it gives references to state and federal court decisions which cited that statute. In order to use *Shepard's* for legislative research, one must know the title and section number of a given statute. (See discussion of *Shepard's,* § 2.6).

§ 2.2. Legal Digests.

a. *In General.* Digests are indexes to case law, the law growing out of court decisions. They provide the researcher with a system for identifying case law on a given problem. These works contain, in a systematic fashion, a concise summary of the facts and the court decision in a case. They identify the point or points of law in which a case is classified and give the case citation. One uses the digests to build a bibliography of court citations from which one may proceed directly to a study of the cases themselves.

Digests serve a variety of courts. They may appear for courts for a single state, a group of states, a single court, or court systems. The best known and most comprehensive is the American Digest System, to be treated later in this chapter.

The material in a digest is classified according to topics. Analytical notes in both the American Digest System and the National Reporter System are identical.

One may begin his preliminary research in the digests by using one of three methods: the descriptive word method, the topic method, and the table of cases method. These three methods do not have to be used in isolation but may complement each other as a need arises. As in the previous section, each method will be treated here briefly.

The Descriptive Word Method. One would use this method just as he would an index in any textbook. He would select a word or term that is descriptive of his problem and locate it in the index. The descriptive words in the index come from actual court opinions that help describe the facts of the case. These descriptions are arranged in volumes of the American Digest System called the *Descriptive Word Index.* These indexes contain not only the words describing the points of law, but also refer the researcher, in bold type, to the topic and a key number. The topic is the classification of the subject matter; the key number denotes the more specific point of law around which the case is decided. Having this information, the researcher can then refer to the specific volume in the digest that contains his topic and key number.

The Topic Method. A second method of beginning legal research in the digest is through the topic method. The American. Digest System contains over 400 major topics, and one cannot possibly readily master all of them. Further, legal problems can usually be classified under more than one topic. Since it would be unwieldy to classify each problem under every conceivable topic, the editors instead resolved this matter by placing a problem under one topic and then cross-referencing it. If one begins research through this method, he should survey the total topical classification in order to become familiar with it. From the Law Chart of over 400 topics, one would be likely to find his appropriate topic. When he has identified the topic, he is referred to a key number, which he uses in seeking an analysis of that topic. Preceding the actual analysis are scope notes which alert the reader as to whether the subject matter digested is within the ambit of his topic.

The Table of Cases Method. A third method of engaging in legal research is through the table of cases method. In order to use this method, one must first have the name of a case treating his topic. In locating the case, one identifies the key number for that topic and then proceeds to find other citations appropriate for that topic. One can locate a key number from the table of cases in both the state digests and the regional reporters.

A table of cases serves several functions. It gives the correct title of the cases. It gives parallel citations to the National Reporter System, the State Reports, and the Annotated Reports. It gives the history of the case. It also gives the topics and key numbers under which the points of law have been classified. With this resource, after one has a case citation and has located it in the table of cases, he can identify his topic, key number, and then proceed in locating other relevant case citations on the subject.

b. *State Digests.* There is also a state digest for reported decisions for all courts of record of a given state. Many of these state digests use the key number system. They are constructed in the same manner and are identical in organization so that a point of law, having been searched in a local digest, does not need to be researched in the American Digest System for that same jurisdiction.

The names of the state digests often follow the name of the state, as for example, *The New Jersey Digest* or *The Illinois Digest.* The digest for Pennsylvania is known as *Vale's Pennsylvania Digest.*

Some state and local digests have classification systems of their own. However, their use as well as their special features are similar to the organization of the American Digest System. They have a topical arrangement with a fact index to all cases.

§ 2.3. The American Digest System.

The American Digest System is the most comprehensive and most used of the digests. It contains digests of court decisions that may be found in the National Reporter System, discussed more fully in § 2.5 of this chapter. It is so organized that one can locate relatively easily any court decision, provided one has even limited information.

The American Digest System has over 400 major topics. The number may change in that, as new issues arise, new topics are added. A complete list of topics is found in the front of every volume of the *Decennial Digest*. The major topic in which educators should begin is "Schools and School Districts." It contains 183 subtopics. Under the subsection of "Pupils, and Conduct and Discipline of Schools," the following partial list appears:

(H.) Pupils, and Conduct and Discipline of Schools.

    148. Nature of right to instruction in general.

    148½. Aid to indigent children.

    149. Eligibility.

    150. — In general.

    151. — Race or color.

    152. — Age.

    153. — Residence.

    154. — Assignment or admission to particular schools.[1]

Each decennial digest also has a table of cases. These digests contain the full citation to the official reports and the key number for the case. These cases are arranged alphabetically. The following is an example of a citation: *Deutsch v. Teel,* 400 F. Supp. 598 (E.D. Wis. 1975). The citation reveals that Deutsch was the plaintiff or the one who initiated the suit; Teel was the defendant. The case is reported in volume 400 of the *Federal Supplement,* the case begins on page 598, and it was decided in 1975 by the federal court for the Eastern District in Wisconsin.

Its indexes contain decisions of American courts of record, beginning in 1658 and continuing to the present. A court of record is viewed as being the first-level appellate court and all other appeals courts at the state level. Included at the federal level are

---

1. *The American Digest System* is published by the West Publishing Company, St. Paul, Minnesota. The example here was taken from Vol. 27 of the *Seventh Decennial Digest,* page 461.

cases heard by the district courts, circuit courts, and the Supreme Court.

Within the digests, the cases are arranged according to ten-year periods. An exception is the *Century Digest*, which contains in its 50 volumes the decisions of courts from 1658 to 1896.

The digests for the ten-year periods are referred to as decennial digests. They cover the following time periods:

First Decennial Digest	*1897-1906*
Second Decennial Digest	*1907-1916*
Third Decennial Digest	*1917-1926*
Fourth Decennial Digest	*1927-1936*
Fifth Decennial Digest	*1937-1946*
Sixth Decennial Digest	*1947-1956*
Seventh Decennial Digest	*1957-1966*
Eighth Decennial Digest	*1967-1976*
Ninth Decennial Digest	*1977-1986*
Tenth Decennial Digest	*1987-1996*

In addition to the above digests, a general digest keeps the decennial digests current. It includes, after the latest decennial digest, a pamphlet issued once a month and a bound volume every four months. For one to locate a complete list of all relevant court citations since the issuance of the latest decennial digest, it is necessary to go through each of the general digests. Each of these general digests is complete within itself; each has a table of cases. A separate *Descriptive Word Index* is issued for each volume. It contains all the topics arranged alphabetically and the key number under which that topic is digested.

a. *The Key Number System.* The standard plan of legal classification of subject matter in the American Digest System is the key number system. Developed by West Publishing Company, it is a system of classification of all sections of topics found in the American Digest System. It is organized so that all cases that refer to a point of law are classified according to key numbers. The following are examples of three key numbers under the subsection of "Teachers."

35

145. — Actions.
146. Pensions.
147. Duties and liabilities.[2]

The value of the key number is that all past, present, and future legal authority is classified according to the key number. Once one has located a topic and a key number, he then has access to all the cases decided in American courts of record on this issue. The key number system is thus, in effect, a system for indexing case law.

The key number system treats seven major categories: persons, property, contracts, torts, crimes, remedies, and government. These seven categories, in turn, are divided into over 400 topics. One of the topics under the category of government, "Schools," is the one in which educators do most of their legal research. Those searching in higher education would begin their research in "Colleges and Universities."

Each of the subtopics is numbered separately, beginning with 1 and continuing as far as necessary. Under "Schools," the subtopics run from 1 to 183. If new legal points are added since the original listing of subtopics, decimals or fractions are used to divide a numbered subtopic further. This preserves consistency in the numbering of subtopics as well as in grouping them according to subject matter. Under subtopic 133, "Employment (of teachers) in general," fifteen other subtopics have been added. "Transportation of pupils" became subtopic 159½ after it was separated from 159, "Payment for tuition."

Each point of law in each court decision is digested under one of the key numbers. A specific key number refers to only one point of law, but one case may include several key numbers since it may contain more than one point of law. The *Century Digest* does not contain key numbers since the use of the key number system antedates that digest. However, if one knows the key number of his topic and wishes to research it in the *Century Digest,* he may look up the key number in either the First or Second *Decennial Digests*

---

2. *Id.* at 461.

where a reference is made to the corresponding classification of the *Century Digest.*

b. *The National Reporter System.* The National Reporter System is a set of thousands of volumes containing all cases from all courts of record, including all state and all federal courts. It also gives the actual court opinion in each case.

For ease in finding court opinions in appropriate volumes, a numbering system has been devised. Each of the reporters began with a first series and continued until 200 volumes appeared, as in the following reporters: Atlantic, North Eastern, South Eastern, and Southern. The numbering then began anew and the series was designated as a second series with the abbreviation "2d." The following reporters in the first series ran from 1 to 300: South Western, Pacific, and North Western.

Several bound volumes of the reporters appear each year. The number of volumes varies according to the workload of the various courts and the length of the judges' opinions. Bound volumes appear on the shelf of a law library several months after a decision has been handed down. Prior to publication of each bound volume, preliminary reports, also called advance sheets, are issued. These preliminary reports contain several court opinions, bound in paper. Slip sheets are also issued. These are single opinions and are generally available within one week of the decision.

Each volume of the reporters contains, in addition to the court opinion, information of assistance to the researcher. At the front of each volume is a list of judges for the courts in the region reported within the volume. A contents page identifies the cases reported, and they are organized by states. Each volume also contains a digest of the cases in the volume. A table of cases lists citations to all decisions in the volume. That table includes references to statutes, constitutions, court rules, municipal ordinances and session laws. A section on words and phrases contains terms judicially defined in the volume. In addition to regional reporters which contain state court opinions, many, but not all, states also have reporters which contain opinions that are covered in the regional reporters. Thus, the same court opinion may be found in two places. For example, *Ayala v. Philadelphia Board of Public Education,* 453 Pa. 584 (1973), may also be found at 305 A.2d 877 (1973). When citing a court decision, one should cite both reporters; if only one citation is available, the regional reporter is considered as being the authoritative one. Federal court decisions are reported in the volumes of the National Reporter System according to the level of the federal court. Supreme Court decisions are reported in the United States Supreme Court Reporter (S. Ct.);[3] the decisions of the Courts of Appeal are reported in the Federal Reporter (F., F.2d, F.3d); and the decisions of the district courts are reported in the Federal Supplement (F. Supp. and F. Supp. 2d).

The National Reporter System also reports other kinds of decisions. The Federal Rules Decisions (F.R.D.) covers the opinions of the federal district courts that are not designated for publication in the Federal Supplement. These kinds of decisions typically involve federal rules covering civil and criminal procedure. The National Reporter System also reports decisions of the Court of Claims (Ct. Cl.), and the Court of Customs and Patent Appeals (C.C.P.A.).

For ease in reporting, the system of volumes covering state court opinions is divided into nine regions. The following are the regions and the states they serve, the name of the set of volumes, the abbreviation for that set, and the states included in the region:

Atlantic (A. or A.2d) Connecticut, Delaware, Maine, Maryland, New Hampshire, New Jersey, Pennsylvania, and Vermont.

California (Cal. Rptr. or Cal. Rptr. 2d) California.[4]

---

3. Decisions of the Supreme Court of the United States are reported in two other places. The Court's official reports appear in United States Reports (U.S.). The third source is the United States Supreme Court Reports, Lawyer's Edition (L. Ed.). This last source includes parts of attorneys' briefs and numerous annotations not found in the other two sources.

4. The California Reporter, begun in 1960, contains all decisions of the California Supreme Court and approved decisions of lower California appellate courts no longer published in the Pacific Reporter since 347 P.2d. The California Reporter duplicates the state reports beginning with 53 Cal. 2d and 177 Cal. App. 2d.

New York Supplement (N.Y.S. or N.Y.S.2d) New York.[5]

North Eastern (N.E. or N.E.2d) Illinois, Indiana, Massachusetts, New York, Ohio, and Rhode Island.

North Western (N.W. or N.W.2d) Iowa, Michigan, Minnesota, Nebraska, North Dakota, South Dakota, and Wisconsin.

Pacific (P. or P.2d) Alaska, Arizona, California, Colorado, Hawaii, Idaho, Kansas, Montana, Nevada, New Mexico, Oklahoma, Oregon, Utah, Washington, and Wyoming.

South Eastern (S.E. or S.E.2d) Georgia, North Carolina, South Carolina, Virginia, and West Virginia.

Southern (So. or So.2d) Alabama, Florida, Louisiana, and Mississippi.

South Western (S.W. or S.W.2d) Arkansas, Kentucky, Missouri, Tennessee, and Texas.

Preceding each court opinion is the syllabus of the decision. It also contains information helpful to the researcher. It gives the title of the decision (the parties to the case), the court deciding the case, the date the case was argued and decided, the date a rehearing was granted or denied, and a synopsis of the case. The synopsis contains the following information: the facts and summary of the decision, digest paragraphs (references to points of law that are keyed to the American Digest System by a key number), and a list of attorneys arguing the case. Headnotes (the digest paragraphs) are numbered consecutively to correspond to the subject matter in the text of the opinion.

The headnotes of the court opinion are broken down by sections, and each section is given a number: a key number. That number identifies the subject matter of the opinion around which the major point of law was resolved. The summaries should not be used in lieu of an actual reading of the court opinion which follows the headnotes.

---

5. The New York Supplement, begun in 1888, contains all decisions of the state's highest court, the Court of Appeals, since 1847, and many lower court decisions.

Beginning in 1982, West Publishing Company, which publishes the court opinions found in the National Reporter System, expanded its coverage of education law decisions. It began to publish *West's Education Law Reporter,* a series of volumes which include decisions of courts of record solely from the field of education. These cases have been litigated in both federal and state courts. The *Reporter* contains *verbatim* the full court opinion with the pagination identical to the opinion as published in the *National Reporter System.* Approximately five or six volumes of the *Reporter* are issued each year.

The *Reporter* also contains commentary on significant court decisions. This commentary is written by authorities and treats not only an analysis of the actual court opinion, but also guidelines for administrators and educators.

West also publishes its reporters in a compact disk (CD rom) format. The benefit of case searching on CD rom is that it allows a law student to use simple queries while rapidly searching through a number of reporter volumes.

§ 2.4. Shepard's Citations.

Shepard's Citations is a system that provides a history of a reported court decision and a treatment of that decision. In like manner, it provides a history of a statute and indicates court decisions having an effect on that statute. The value of *Shepard's* is that it gives up-to-date authority on both court decisions and statutes so that a researcher may rely on the applicable court holding.

Shepard's Citations has a number of units which cover legal reporting systems. Each of the states has a unit, each of the regional reporters has a unit, and each of the three levels of federal courts has a unit. There are also *Shepard's* units for specialized practice areas, including bankruptcy and intellectual property law.

In addition to the history and treatment of a court decision, *Shepard's* is also useful for finding similar decisions to a case under consideration.

The process of checking the status of cases or statutes by using *Shepard's* is known as Shepardizing®. References in *Shepard's* are to case citations as reported by official and unofficial publishers, including the various reporters in the National Reporter System. One secures the appropriate unit of *Shepard's* that corresponds to the page of the opinion in the reporter and turns to the page in *Shepard's* that treats the case. The following is a partial treatment of the case *West Virginia State Board of Education v. Barnette*, 319 U.S. 624, 63 S. Ct. 1178, 87 L. Ed. 1628 (1943):

-624-
(87LE1628)
(63SC1178)
(147ALR674)
s47FS251
319US588
320US708
j321US113
321US165
j321US174
321US665
322US86
323US527
323US545[6]
etc.

With the aid of the History and Treatment Abbreviations at the front of the volume, one can interpret the various entries. The following abbreviations are used in the analysis:

HISTORY of CASE

a (affirmed)	Citing case affirms cited case on appeal or rehearing.
cc (connected case)	Citing case related to cited case, involving same subject matter or parties.
D (dismissed)	Citing case dismisses appeal from cited case.

---

6. SHEPARD'S CITATIONS. Colorado Springs: Shepard's Company. The example was taken from page 1557 of the volume covering the above citation.

HISTORY of CASE

m (modified)	Citing case modifies cited case on appeal.
r (reversed)	Citing case reverses cited case on appeal.
s (same case)	Citing case involves same litigation as cited case but at different stage of proceeding.
S (superseded)	Citing case supersedes or is substituted for cited case on appeal or rehearing.
v (vacated)	Citing case vacates or withdraws cited case.
US app pndg	Certiorari pending before Supreme Court.
US cert den	Certiorari denied by Supreme Court.
US cert dis	Certiorari dismissed by Supreme Court.
US cert gran	Certiorari granted by Supreme Court.
US reh den	Rehearing denied by Supreme Court.
US reh dis	Rehearing dismissed by Supreme Court.

TREATMENT of CASE

c (criticised)	Citing opinion disagrees with reasoning or result of cited case, but may not affect precedential value.
d (distinguished)	Citing case differs from cited case in law or fact for reasons given.
e (explained)	Citing opinion interprets or clarifies cited case in a significant way.
f (followed)	Citing opinion relies on cited case as controlling or persuasive authority.
h (harmonized)	Citing case differs from cited case but reconciles differences in reaching decision.
j (dissenting opinion)	A dissenting opinion cites the cited case.
L (limited)	Citing opinion restricts application of cited case to specific circumstances.
o (overruled)	Citing opinion overrules or disapproves all or part of cited case.
p (parallel)	Citing case substantially alike or on all fours with cited case in its law or facts.
q (questioned)	Citing opinion questions precedential value of cited case due to intervening circumstances, including judicial or legislative overruling.[7]

---

7. This example was taken from the explanatory material on the use of *Shepard's Citations.*

Through the above use of *Shepard's,* one can learn about the history of the case, including subsequent appeals and the disposition of those appeals. The treatment of a decision includes cases which have had some effect on it: whether followed, rejected, modified, expanded, or merely cited.

The treatment of statutes in *Shepard's* varies somewhat from the arrangement of court decisions. Constitutions are arranged by article and section, or amendment; legislative acts are arranged by date of enactment, chapter and section.

It may not be necessary to Shepardize each court decision in a lengthy research paper; however, one must not overlook the necessity of being certain that he is dealing with the most current applicable law.

An electronic (CD rom) version of *Shepard's Citations* allows law students to quickly Shepardize a case without searching through several bound volumes. In addition to *Shepard's* standard notation, a graphic signal provides an at-a-glance indicator of the precedential status of the case. A red signal indicates that there is a negative treatment of the case in subsequent decisions, a green signal means that there is positive treatment, and yellow indicates that there is possible negative treatment. *Shepard's* may also be researched on-line from a PC with modem by subscribers to Lexis-Nexis research services and may also be accessed on the Internet at *lexis.com.*

§ 2.5. United States Law Week.

United States Law Week (U.S.L.W.) is a loose-leaf weekly publication that provides two main kinds of services. It supplies information about Congress and legislation in its General Law Section and about the United States Supreme Court in its Supreme Court Sections. Its value is in providing up-to-date information of the subjects it treats.

The General Law Section is a source for "slip laws" of Congress. It reproduces verbatim, in full, laws passed by Congress that are of general interest or importance. It has a section that contains

[handwritten margin note: Congressional Laws prior to their publication in bound volumes]

short summaries and developments about recent legislation and court decisions. Finally, it contains quotations from very recent court decisions not yet reported elsewhere. The usefulness of this service is its being up-to-date in the selected areas it treats.

The second part, Supreme Court Sections, is divided further into two sections. One section covers the proceedings of the Court. It lists the cases filed with the Court, the cases docketed, a calendar of hearings scheduled, and a summary of the Court's orders. It frequently has supplementary articles on the work and decisions of the court.

The second section contains "slip" decisions of the Supreme Court. Since these decisions are mailed within a day of their being announced, subscribers such as libraries have access to the actual court decision within a week of its being handed down.

§ 2.6. Legal Encyclopedias.

Students of law may find two reference encyclopedias helpful in starting legal research. They are *Corpus Juris Secundum* (second body of law) (C.J.S., C.J.S.2d) and *American Jurisprudence* (Am. Jur., Am. Jur. 2d, Am. Jur. 3d). These works are useful in that they provide an overview of a legal issue and support it with case citations.

The value of *Corpus Juris Secundum* is two-fold. It gives the researcher a notion of the state of law on a given issue and citations from which one can build a bibliography on that topic. The case citations are the specific cases from which the principles are derived.

Major content topics are arranged alphabetically in 101 volumes. An educator would refer to the major topic, "Schools and School Districts," which is covered in volumes 78 and 78a. Under this topic there are 818 subtopics, each of which is discussed and analyzed.

Below are listed several topics from the subtopic, "Pupils, and Conduct and Discipline of Schools."

3. Control of Pupils and Discipline

Each volume contains a word index for each major topic in it. In addition, a four-volume index accompanies the entire series. Cumulative annual pocket parts keep the citations up-to-date. It is necessary to refer to these annual supplements in order to collect the latest case citations that have accumulated since the original publication of the bound volume.

One may begin his research in *Corpus Juris Secundum* in one of two ways. He may go directly to the major topic, "Schools and School Districts," find the appropriate subtopic with the number to the left of it and, using the number, locate the topic in the text. A second way is by going to the index, finding the topic and subtopic there, and then proceeding to the topic in the text.

Within the text itself, the upper part of each page contains an analysis of the topic and relevant legal principles. The raised numbers in the text refer to footnotes at the bottom of the page. These footnotes come directly from the cases that support the principle of law. Since these principles are identified by the editors of *Corpus Juris Secundum* rather than by the courts, the researcher is advised

---

8. CORPUS JURIS SECUNDUM. Brooklyn: The American Law Book Co. The example here was taken from Vol. 78, page 604.

to read the actual court opinion rather than rely exclusively on the comment in *Corpus Juris Secundum.*

Unlike *Corpus Juris Secundum,* its competitor, *American Jurisprudence,* is based upon selected rather than all court cases. It is a complete revision of its predecessor, *Ruling Case Law.* Its 83 volumes are organized similarly to *Corpus Juris Secundum.* It contains an index at the end of each volume with references to material in that volume. There is also a four-volume index to the entire set with cumulative pocket parts.

The topics in *American Jurisprudence* are arranged under the major heading of "Schools" in Volume 68. An example of the treatment of the subject of discipline follows.

F. DISCIPLINE AND PUNISHMENT

1. In General

§ 256. Generally; rights of parents and school authorities
§ 257. Punishable offenses
§ 258. Corporal punishment
§ 259. Detention after school hours

2. Suspension and Expulsion

§ 260. Generally
§ 261. Power of school authorities and directors
§ 262. Teacher's power
§ 263. Grounds; generally
§ 264. — Use of profanity
§ 265. — Default in educational requirements
§ 266. — Conduct out of school
§ 267. — Miscellaneous
§ 268. Remedies for wrongful exclusion
§ 269. Procedural rights of students in suspension or expulsion proceedings
§ 270. — Preliminary hearing prior to suspension[9]

---

9. AMERICAN JURISPRUDENCE 2d. Rochester: The Lawyer's Co-Operative Publishing Co. This example was taken from Vol. 68, page 357. *See also* WEST'S ENCYCLOPEDIA OF AMERICAN LAW. St. Paul: West Group, 1998.

Because either of these two works is adequate for the educational researcher, it is not necessary to use both of them. One may, in fact, bypass them and begin research in the legal digests.

If one is researching a topic that involves only a state or local matter, he may prefer to rely on a state rather than a general encyclopedia. The *Pennsylvania Law Encyclopedia* is typical of a state encyclopedia. It has 57 volumes, three of which are a general index. Education topics are organized under "Schools," which is divided further into 177 subtopics. These subtopics are similar, but do not correspond exactly, to those listed under "Schools and School Districts" in the American Digest System. Another typical state law encyclopedia is *Illinois Law and Practice*, for the state of Illinois.

§ 2.7. American Law Reports Annotated.

American Law Reports is a series of volumes that contains commentary on selected decisions and topics by legal authorities. The decisions and topics are selected for their general, broad interest. Topics of purely local or individual interest are not covered. Of the cases that are reviewed and analyzed, A.L.R. concentrates on topics in which there is difference of opinion. This source is useful in supplementing court decisions, for the subject matter is treated by authorities who present balanced arguments on a legal issue. An example of an entry from the index follows:

RIGHT OF STUDENT TO HEARING ON CHARGES BEFORE
SUSPENSION OR EXPULSION FROM EDUCATIONAL
INSTITUTION

§ 1. Introduction and scope, p. 904

Marriage or pregnancy of public school student as ground for expulsion or exclusion, or of restriction of activities. 11 ALR3d 996.

Validity of regulation by public school authorities as to clothes or personal appearance of pupils. 14 ALR3d 1201.

Participation of student in demonstration on or near campus as warranting expulsion or suspension from school or college. 32 ALR3d 864.

Liability of college or university to student enrolled in course of instruction terminated prior to completion. 51 ALR3d 1003.

Right to discipline pupil for conduct away from school grounds or not immediately connected with school activities. 53 ALR3d 1124.[10]

The indexes to A.L.R. are referred to as "Red Books." The entries are alphabetical, and the key lead word or subject identifies all references to an annotation on that subject. Topics in education are listed under "Schools."

A supplement service keeps the annotations current.

The following are features of the American Law Reports Annotated: (1) It contains a report of the entire court decision. (2) It gives the court opinion. (3) It gives a summary of the briefs of parties to the case. (4) It contains an annotation. The annotation supplements legal points covered in the opinion, treats lines of reasoning not covered by the courts, and identifies seemingly contrary decisions.

Approximately six volumes appear each year. Each digest covers its own arrangement of topics and subtopics. The annotations are not cumulative; that is, they do not repeat material covered in earlier volumes.

A.L.R. is issued in a series of companion sets of annotations of legal topics. The earliest one is A.L.R., which covered reports from 1919 to 1948. The second set, A.L.R.2d, ran from 1948 to 1965. A.L.R.3d also covered material from 1965 to 1980. A.L.R.4th covered reports from 1980-1991. A.L.R.5th covers reports from 1991 to the present.

---

10. AMERICAN LAW REPORTS 2d. Rochester: The Lawyer's Co-Operative Publishing Co. This example was taken from the Later Case Service (covering Vols. 56-63 of A.L.R.3d), page 235.

In addition to A.L.R., there is a series which treats only federal court decisions. It is known as A.L.R. Fed. and has been published since 1969. Approximately four volumes in this series are issued annually.

§ 2.8. Legal Dictionaries.

As one engages in legal research, he realizes that words often have meanings other than when used in nonlegal circumstances. That is, law often has a vocabulary of its own. Not only should the researcher be aware of this, but he should also have access to and use terms as they are legally defined. There are a number of legal dictionaries that serve this purpose.

The most comprehensive of the legal dictionaries is *Words and Phrases*. It includes in its many volumes any word or phrase that has been defined in any case in American courts. Like the American Digest System, it covers reported cases from 1658 to the present.

Organizationally, definitions are arranged alphabetically. A word or phrase is defined by giving a digest paragraph followed by the citation to the case. The definition is in the court's own language except where it might be preferable to modify the language for ease in clarity and publishing.

Words and Phrases has a complete alphabetical index by subject headings. It contains numerous cross references and is kept up-to-date with annual cumulative pocket parts.

In addition to supplying definitions, *Words and Phrases* serves an additional function in legal research. One can locate pertinent cases through case citations to a definition. Seven paragraphs are devoted to the term "expulsion." Paragraph three is listed below:

> "Expulsion" means to eject, banish, or cut off from the privileges of an institution or society permanently. *John B. Stetson University v. Hunt,* 102 So. 637, 639, 88 Fla. 510.[11]

---

11. WORDS AND PHRASES (permanent ed. St. Paul, Minn.: West Publishing Co., 1952). This example was taken from Vol. 15A, page 593.

In addition to *Words and Phrases,* there are several excellent legal dictionaries in one or two volumes. These dictionaries are frequently revised and brought up to date since law constantly undergoes change. Among the standard dictionaries are *Ballentine, The Self-Pronouncing Law Dictionary; Black's Law Dictionary;* and *Bouvier's Law Dictionary and Concise Encyclopedia.*

Bouvier's first definition of "expulsion" is as follows:

> EXPULSION (Lat. expellere, to drive out). The act of depriving a member of a body politic or corporate, or of a society, of his right of membership therein, by the vote of such body or society, for some violation of his duties as such, or for some offense which renders him unworthy of longer remaining a member of the same.[12]

In addition to the general legal dictionaries, there are also those for very specialized fields in law.

§ 2.9. Index to Legal Periodicals.

Many, if not most, law schools publish journals, typically referred to as law reviews. They contain leading articles on topical issues, notes and comments, case notes, and book reviews. The articles are typically scholarly, comprehensive treatments of current subjects. They are often written by a law professor, a lawyer, a judge, or a specialist on that subject. Somewhat like articles, the notes and comments are briefer and are often written by the abler law students in the host publishing school. Case notes involve treatment of a specific court decision, usually by a law student. Law books are reviewed in the book review section.

In order to identify periodical articles on legal subjects, one should refer to the *Index to Legal Periodicals,* the best known and most widely used source in its field. It corresponds to the *Reader's Guide to Periodical Literature* for those researching in education, and each of these publications has the same format. *Index to Legal*

---

12. BOUVIER'S LAW DICTIONARY (3d rev., 8th ed., Kansas City: Vernon Law Book Co., 1914).

Periodicals contains a table of contents, an index, and a table of cases. It has references to legal journal articles plus a few other publications. It refers to printed material not only in the United States but also in Canada, England, Scotland, Ireland, Northern Ireland, Australia, and New Zealand.

The Index is published monthly except September. A permanent bound volume appears every three years. In between, there are periodically cumulative issues as well as an annual cumulative volume.

The Index consists of three parts. The first is a combined subject and author index. Subjects are arranged alphabetically and correspond similarly, but not exactly, to those used by the Key Number System. Thus, one may look under the author index if he knows the author's last name or under the appropriate subject entry. The following are two entries from the September, 1973 — August, 1976 issue under "Schools and School Districts."

> Academic freedom in the public schools: the right to teach. NYU L Rev 48:1176-99 D '73
> Alternative schools for minority students: the constitution, the civil rights act and the Berkeley experiment. Calif L Rev 61:858-918 My '73[13]

The second part is a table of cases. It lists court decisions for which there are case notes or case comments. It is organized on the plaintiff-defendant format.

The third part is a book review section. Books are listed under the last name of the author, followed by the title of the book and its publication date. Periodical citations of reviews then follow under each entry.

An electronic (CD rom) version of the *Index to Legal Periodicals* is a service of the H.W. Wilson Company, and works much the same way as the traditional bound reference source. Unlike the bound version, however, the CD rom version presents a law student with ready access to author and subject information. In addi-

---

13. INDEX TO LEGAL PERIODICALS. New York: The H. W. Wilson Co. The examples were taken from the September 1973 to August 1976 volume, page 983.

tion, the electronic version searches the entirety of over 620 legal periodicals and 2500 books without the need to look through multiple bound volumes.

The use of the *Index to Legal Periodicals,* as well as the *Reader's Guide to Periodical Literature,* should give the researcher a comprehensive bibliography of journal articles on a given subject.

§ 2.10. ELA.

A useful source in the study of education law is the Education Law Association (ELA). The ELA houses an array of legal materials and disseminates current legal matter.

Founded in 1954 at Duke University, ELA (at that time called the National Organization on Legal Problems of Education (NOLPE)) was organized by Edward C. Bolmeier, mentor of the coauthors of this book, for the purpose of providing "broad unbiased information about current issues in school law." In the four decades of its existence, it has grown to the point where it includes members from each of the fifty states, the territories, and a number of foreign countries as well. Its membership rolls are open to individuals and organizations interested in law and education.

Through its publications, conferences, and seminars, ELA has reached a large audience. It offers the following services:

ELA School Law Reporter: a loose-leaf publication containing all education law decisions of state and federal courts of record in the United States. Cases are digested by authorities in school law. Issued monthly.

ELA Notes: a loose-leaf publication highlighting current developments in education law. It contains reviews of publications and announcements of school law conferences in addition to reporting selected court opinions of interest. Issued monthly.

Yearbook of School Law: a publication containing a review and analysis of education law decisions for the previous year. Authorities in the field contribute to the book's various chapters. The book also contains a table of cases decided by courts of record in that year's time. Issued annually.

Other publications include papers given at the annual convention; monographs and mini-monographs on specialized topics in school law; bibliographies of case citations on restricted subject areas; and books on selected topics.

In addition to its annual convention, ELA sponsors a series of seminars on topics of interest to both attorneys and educators. Its clearinghouse acts as a referral agency by providing its membership with information and assistance in specific matters.

The value of ELA is in its range of services, particularly in disseminating information about education law. Its members are provided with up-to-date information and assistance on the entire gamut of subjects involving courts and the law.

§ 2.11. Computer Research.

Computer assisted legal research (CALR) in law school and in the practice of law has evolved to become an essential skill for law student and lawyer alike. Legal researchers can now devote more time to analyzing and evaluating the results of their legal research because computers and legal databases have made finding the law a less laborious process. However, the precision that CALR brings to legal research requires researchers to be even more precise in developing a research methodology.

Two of the best known providers of CALR systems are LEXIS Publishing and WEST Group. Each of these legal publishers offers comprehensive computer accessible research systems. Both services can be accessed via the World Wide Web or by loading proprietary communications software available from the vendor. Regardless of which method a user chooses to access these services, a wealth of information is only a few keystrokes or mouse clicks away. Users have access to case law, statutes, law review articles, model codes and laws, court rules, a variety of secondary legal materials, news and other information.

The traditional method of accessing these materials involves a three-step approach:

1. Users select a database (sometimes referred to as a library) in which to conduct their search. This has the effect of immediately narrowing a user's search. Databases can be selected based on jurisdiction (the case law or statutes from a particular state for example) or by legal topic (searching only labor law or torts cases).
2. Users then enter a keyword search using Boolean connectors to express the relationship between the words. Basic connectors (*and* and *or*) work the same on both vendors' products. Each vendor offers several additional connectors that help researchers craft sophisticated searches that will let the experienced user retrieve the desired documents with great precision. Detailed information about using either system is available directly from each publisher.
3. The final step is reading and analyzing the search results. Both systems provide tools to narrow the search results in useful ways or let the researcher craft a new search and try again.

Both companies also provide an alternate method of searching known as "natural language" searching. After selecting a database to search, users enter key words or plain English questions as their search. The research systems' search engines apply sophisticated algorithms to the search request and try to return appropriate search results. New users sometimes gravitate to natural language searching because it seems easier to learn. However, experienced researchers almost always use Boolean searching because it offers more precision and provides a more comprehensive answer set. Users who only know how to use natural language search tools cannot lay claim to being proficient computer researchers. Legal research demands the accuracy that is achievable only with Boolean searching. That said, natural language is a great way to get started understanding an unfamiliar legal issue or finding one good case on point to use as a starting point for additional research.

One of the most often used features is the rapid retrieval of case, statutes and other legal documents and law review articles when the researcher already knows the cite. Both services let users enter the citation and retrieve the document directly without having to select and search a database.

Perhaps the biggest distinction between the two vendors' research systems is the citator tools offered by each. Currently, the traditional tool for cite checking, SHEPARD'S®, is available only from the online research systems offered by LEXIS Publishing. The West Group has fielded their own proprietary cite checking tool, KeyCite™. Researchers should contact the appropriate vendor to obtain current information on how each of these cite checking tools works, and to understand the differences between them.

§ 2.12. Researching a Topic.

A major objective in undertaking a study of education law is to achieve an awareness of what law actually is. The methodology used in many education law classes is like that in most courses in a law school: the case study method. It involves an analysis of many court decisions from which legal principles are derived. Study of case law is augmented with an analysis of statutory law — state and federal, where applicable.

Statutes and court decisions are considered to be primary sources; these are the references that one should use initially. They may be supplemented later with secondary sources: annotations, legal encyclopedias, law reviews, educational articles, and books. Researchers who do not have access to a law library may have to undertake their study in secondary sources.

One begins his research by framing a problem as a legal issue. In framing the problem, one must necessarily define and possibly refine it to make it manageable. In the process of limiting the topic, one determines whether it has national or local import. If it has national implications, the research must be extended beyond the laws and court decisions of a given state. An example of such a problem is the extent to which the first amendment protects students in publishing a school-sponsored newspaper. If the problem is restricted to only one state, one then works with more limited resources. An example of a state or local topic is the maximum distance a student may be required to walk from his home to a school bus stop.

In treating an issue, one looks first to the statutes that may be controlling. In doing this, one also examines the federal and state constitutions to determine if either has any provisions on the topic. After collecting the appropriate statutes, one then builds a bibliography of court decisions. As noted in previous sections of this chapter, one may begin this search in several places.

Each court decision should be read and analyzed with care. A systematic approach will work to the researcher's advantage. One plan is to organize the study around four major areas: the facts, the question, the decision and rationale, and implications. Each is considered briefly below.

The facts. Who are the parties to the case? Who is suing whom? What factual situation occurred that precipitated a suit? What does the plaintiff base his case on — constitutional or statutory law, or something else? What is the defendant's response to the plaintiff's charge? What remedy is the plaintiff seeking?

The question. What is the court asked to decide? If one or more issues are involved, reduce the questions to their simplest form.

The decision and rationale. What is the court's actual decision? What are its reasons for deciding the way it did? Were there concurring and/or dissenting opinions? What was the reasoning of these judges?

Implications. Does the decision have local or general applicability? Is it consistent with previous rulings on the same subject? Does it set a precedent? What effect will it be likely to have on a school or school system?

After one has researched, analyzed, and begun to synthesize all relevant statutes and court decisions, he should examine secondary sources. Then, after synthesizing the primary and secondary sources, he should be able to state a definitive position on the given legal issue.

Since a court holding today may be overturned tomorrow, law is never static. Thus, law should be viewed as being controlling at a

56

given point in time. It is consequently necessary for one to review constantly the state of law on an issue in order to be certain of being up-to-date.

PART II

LAW AND LOCAL BOARDS OF EDUCATION

Chapter Three

LOCAL SCHOOL DISTRICTS AND BOARDS OF EDUCATION

§ 3.0. Introduction.

According to a shibboleth, education is of national interest, a function of state government, and subject to local control. That statement is an over-simplification in that the three spheres of government are all very much involved in education and controls over it are found at all three levels. The truism exists, nonetheless, that much control of education still remains at the local level. The controlling body in the local school district is usually called a board of education, school committee, or board of trustees. Its primary function is the enactment of policy for the district.

The approximately 16,000 local school districts in this country are very diverse. They may include an entire state as in Hawaii, or they may be created out of counties, townships, municipalities, or by some other means. In size they vary from less than fifty to thousands of square miles; in school population, from none (an inoperative district) to several hundred thousand pupils. Beyond what a state requires, programs may vary greatly among districts, for policies and regulations covering local matters depend on the will of the people and, specifically, on the decisions made by the board of education.

What these districts and school boards have in common under law is the focus of this chapter. Since there is no national system of education, the powers and duties of these local school districts are determined, for the most part, by the laws of a given state. In that respect, one should not assume that the laws of one state apply to another. What is to be found in this chapter are general principles, illustrated with case law, that apply to the organization and governance of education at the local level.

§ 3.1. Status of Local School Districts.

It was indicated in Chapter One that, under our constitutional system, state governments were clothed with the legal responsibility for establishing and maintaining a system of public education. Thus, with two exceptions, a state has complete power with respect to determining the organization and control of local school systems. The two exceptions are conflicting constitutional provisions at the federal and state levels and conflicting legislative provisions at the federal level. It is fundamental that a constitutional provision is controlling over any other kind of law, and a federal statute is controlling over any constitutional provision or legislative law of a state.

Although the plenary power of states over education is considerable, state legislatures do not actually operate schools; rather, they provide for the operation of schools. The authority for this operation is delegated to a local governmental body. The name of the local body may vary from state to state and even within a state, but it takes the structure of a local school district. It is to this body that the state has given specified powers and duties in discharging a state function: education of young people. In delegating this responsibility, a state does not relinquish its control over education in general as well as over school districts in particular. This point was made almost fifty years ago by the acknowledged founder of the field of school law as an area of study, Newton Edwards:

> Whatever agencies the legislature may select as the instruments for the execution of its educational policies, these agencies are completely subject to its control within constitutional limits. Since school districts are purely creatures of the state, they possess no inherent local rights — no rights at all in fact, except those with which they are endowed by the legislature. Their powers and the mode of exercise of these powers are defined by legislative act and may be added to, diminished, or destroyed as the legislature may determine.[1]

Since local school districts derive their power from the state, they have no inherent power of their own. Whatever powers they possess are those which the state has delegated to them. That delegated power may be enlarged, modified, or withdrawn if the state decides.

A local school district is both a political and a geographical entity. It is political in that it operates as an agency of the state, carries on a state function, has an organizational structure, and must rely on the will of the electorate it serves in order to achieve its purposes. It is geographical in that it has territorial boundaries which are, in fact, subdivisions of the state. The school boundaries are defined only for the purpose of establishing a school system,

---

1. EDWARDS, THE COURTS AND THE PUBLIC SCHOOLS 84 (rev. ed. Chicago: University of Chicago Press, 1955).

although they may or may not be coterminous with any other political subdivision.

The relationship of the school district to the state is explained in another statement by Edwards:

> [T]he state may create new districts without regard to existing political boundaries or subdivisions, or it may use existing subdivisions, such as counties, townships, or cities. If a school district is carved out of the same geographical boundaries as a political subdivision, it should be recognized that the two perform different functions. The local political agency is created for the purpose of local self-government; the district is an instrument of state policy. It was not created to perform a local function.[2]

The legislature is the source of control of education at the state level. As was stated previously, the legislature is limited, within the state, only by the constitution. In the exercise of its control, a state legislature can create, alter, consolidate, or abolish a school district. It can, with or without the approval of the voters, determine the taxing unit, impose special taxes, or order special elections. It can determine the number of school board members, their terms of office, and the manner of their election. It can require that specified subjects be taught or not taught. In short, the state's power is nearly complete. The extent to which it exercises that power or delegates it to a local school district depends on a given state and more particularly on the will of the legislators. Thus, in some states there is a highly centralized system of education while in others, local school districts have considerable power.

§ 3.2. Powers of Local School Boards.

A local school board has no power of its own. The powers it does possess are those conferred upon it by the legislature. A school board cannot divest itself of any power or duty specifically authorized to it. Conversely, it cannot grant itself any power which

---

2. *Id.* at 93.

it otherwise does not possess. Where school board members derive any powers from the state's constitution, that power can be altered only by an amendment to the constitution. Similarly, where power is derived from the legislature, that power can be changed only by an act of the legislature.

Two cases serve as examples of a school board's abrogating its power. In one, a New Jersey board of education and the teachers' association entered into an agreement that delegated to an individual teacher or the teachers' association decisions about discussing controversies in the classroom. The court negated the agreement, for it noted that the legislature had mandated that the board was responsible for courses of study. This responsibility, the court held, could not be bargained away.[3] In the other case, an Iowa court held that a school board cannot delegate its rule-making power to a state high school athletic association.[4] An athlete had been declared ineligible for competition under the association's rules because he had knowingly ridden in a car that contained alcoholic beverages.

Similarly, a school board cannot delegate its specific powers to the superintendent, even if the board of education subsequently ratifies the actions of the superintendent. In particular, only a board of education can actually terminate an employee; the superintendent can, however, recommend to the board employees to be terminated.[5]

The laws that spell out the power and authority of school boards are often stated in general terms, for it would be impossible to forsee all the possible acts in which boards may engage. Even if they could be foreseen, it would be impractical to list all of them.

---

3. Board of Educ. v. Rockaway Twp. Educ. Ass'n, 120 N.J. Super. 564, 295 A.2d 380 (1972).

4. Bunger v. Iowa High Sch. Athletic Ass'n, 197 N.W.2d 555 (Iowa 1972).

5. Gallegos v. Los Lunas Consol. Sch. Bd. of Educ., 619 P.2d 836 (N.M. App. 1980). In addition, in a case out of the Seventh Circuit, a successor school board was not obligated to honor a decision made by a previous board involving a real estate acquisition. Perritt Ltd. Pt'ship v. Kenosha Unified Sch. Dist., 153 F.3d 489 (7th Cir. 1998).

a. *Expressly Granted and Implied Powers.* In discharging its duties, a local school board can exercise those powers only expressly granted it, those powers implied from the ones expressly granted, and those necessary for accomplishing the purposes for which the board was created. Courts do not normally question the action of a school board in exercising its expressly granted powers, unless there is an abuse of them, for they are rather clearly spelled out by the legislature. School boards are more often challenged in the exercise of implied powers, for it is easier to allege that a board exceeded its power where it was not specifically stated that the board possessed it.

An expressly granted power is one that is stated in legislative acts. Examples of such powers include levying taxes, establishing an extracurricular activity program, and bargaining with a teachers' association. An implied power is one not spelled out in legislative acts, but considered necessary for a board to assume in order to perform duties legally imposed on it. The employment of an architect may be an implied power; building a school building may be an expressly granted power. Hiring a teacher is an expressly granted power; using funds in recruiting teachers may be an implied power.

Confusion sometimes exists as to whether or not a power is expressly granted or is implied. For example, the authority to "make all necessary and reasonable provisions for the best interests of the school system" provides for considerable interpretation of the exercise of that power. Generally, such a provision would not clothe the board with unlimited power; for where a board is given a large grant of power, the exercise of it is determined, not in light of the large grant but in specifically enumerated grants of power.

School boards may exercise their grants of power only as a corporate body. That is, school board action is legal only when the board members act in concert, as a unit, in a meeting. As individuals, its members possess no power.[6] When a board is not in session, its members possess no authority; their legal status within the district is like that of any other citizen. An order or pronouncement by an individual board member is without legality.

If school boards go beyond their duly constituted authority, they act *ultra vires,* that is, beyond the scope of law. Their action is viewed as being that of individuals and not legal; hence, it is not binding on the board. If challenged successfully, board action may be merely nullified, or board members may be sued as individuals. Courts have traditionally given board members benefit of the doubt when their actions actually exceeded their authority, unless there was a clear indication that their behavior was motivated by malice, greed, personal benefit, attempt to injure, or clear disregard of the law.

b. *Discretionary and Ministerial Acts.* Like power, actions by local boards of education may be classified into two categories. They consist of discretionary or ministerial acts.

A discretionary act is one which requires judgment of the board. Such action involves debate and discussion, and it is expected that a board deliberate fully before agreeing on an issue. Most of the board's actions fall within this category. Discretionary action cannot be delegated to a committee of the board, to subordinate educators, or to other agencies. Discretionary action includes such matters as selecting a school site, employing professional personnel, approving courses of study, and authorizing expenditures of funds. A school board may call on other people for assistance in considering discretionary matters, but the action involving approval or disapproval of such matters must be its own.

Courts are reluctant to interfere with school boards in the exercise of discretionary action. When it is recognized that a school

---

6. This point is emphasized in Thermo Prods. Co. v. Chilton Indep. Sch. Dist., 647 S.W.2d 726 (Tex. Civ. App. 1983). *See, e.g.,* State v. Whittle Commun., 402 S.E.2d 556 (N.C. 1991) in which the Supreme Court of North Carolina held that the State Board of Education did not have authority to prevent a local school system from entering into a contract with a private corporation for showing on television twelve minutes of news each day.

board has such authority, the exercise of it in the normal course of events will not be challenged unless, of course, there is evidence of its abuse.

A ministerial act is one which does not involve judgment of the board. It is considered as being routine or mechanical. A board can delegate this action to another person. For example, the employment of professional personnel requires action by a full board — a discretionary action; the actual execution of the contract is mechanical — a ministerial act which may be exercised by the board chairman, for instance. Preparation of a budget may be a ministerial act, but board approval of it is discretionary.

Many court cases dealing with discretionary and ministerial actions focus on personnel matters. The issues have often centered on procedural rather than substantive issues. Two cases are included here as examples. A California court held that the revocation of a teacher's license was a ministerial act; moreover, it was a duty in this instance. The teacher had earlier been convicted of a sex crime; the contract had been revoked by the state board of education. The court held that the state board had acted properly in maintaining the integrity of the schools.[7]

In a case decided the following year, the question involved the procedure used in dismissing a teacher. Here, the court ruled against the school board, for it had failed to give reasons and provide procedural due process for the employee. The court ruled that, by failing to supply both reasons and procedural due process, the board had failed in a ministerial act that could lead to members' liability.[8]

Challenges have been made to school boards' discretionary powers over a number of issues. These challenges have been evi-

---

7. Purifoy v. State Bd. of Educ., 30 Cal. App. 3d 187, 106 Cal. Rptr. 201 (1973).

8. Van Buskirk v. Bleiler, 77 Misc. 2d 272, 354 N.Y.S.2d 93 (1974). *See also* Michigan City Educ. Ass'n v. Board of Sch. Trustees of the Michigan Area Schs., 597 N.E.2d 1004 (Ind. App. 1991) in which an Indiana School Board was not upheld for delegating the dismissal of a teacher to an arbitrator through a collective bargaining agreement.

dent in such recent issues as a board's decision regarding building construction specifications,[9] the setting of attendance boundaries,[10] and school closings.[11] Courts generally favor boards in such litigation, when their actions are reasonable, and neither arbitrary nor capricious.

§ 3.3. Meetings of School Boards.

In order for any action by a school board to be considered as being legal, it must transpire in an official board meeting. The meeting itself must conform to law. Where there are statutory provisions that require specifically that certain conditions exist at a meeting, those provisions must be met. Although laws of the fifty states vary, some general statements may be made concerning the legality of school board meetings. One would need to examine the statutes of his given state to ascertain if they apply here.

a. *Notice of Regular Meetings.* It is a fundamental principle that every board member shall be entitled to notice of meetings. That serves to alert the member that a meeting will transpire as well as to allow him opportunity to prepare for it. Courts have held that notice is for the benefit of board members rather than the public, and unless a statute authorizes it, the public is not entitled to notice. Some states require that public notice shall be given of meetings, as, for example, in a local newspaper.

If the meeting is a regularly scheduled one and the board, in its rules of organization, has established a fixed date, time, and place for all its meetings, further notice is not necessary. If there is any deviation from the standard schedule, notice is required for that meeting.

The meeting may be held anywhere within the school district, unless statutes authorize otherwise. Unless statutes specifically provide for it, a meeting cannot be held outside the district.

---

9. Byrne v. Alexander, 424 A.2d 602 (Pa. Commw. 1981).

10. Plantation Residents Ass'n v. School Bd., 424 So. 2d 879 (Fla. App. 1982).

11. Cortese v. School Bd., 425 So. 2d 554 (Fla. App. 1982).

b. *Notice of Special Meetings.* In addition to its regular meetings, boards of education often have special meetings. They, too, must conform to law. A special meeting requires special notice in that it has been called for a special purpose. Generally, notice must include date, time, place, and the business to be transacted. Any business transacted other than what was stated in the notice would not be considered as being legal.

Some states specify the number of days' notice that a board member must have prior to a special meeting. Where statutes are silent on this question, courts have ruled that a reasonable period of time is all that is required. That time may be variable in consideration of a number of factors, such as ease in communicating with the members and the amount and complexity of items for consideration.

The notice may be written or otherwise, depending on the statutes. In the absence of a law, written notice is not required.

There are three exceptions to the notice requirement for special board meetings. If all board members are together and agree to act, notice would not be necessary in that it had already been served. However, if one board member objects, the board could not act under such terms of notice. Similarly, after a meeting has begun, a board member could not object and have his action sustained.

The second exception is when it would be physically impossible for a board member to attend. For example, if one were hospitalized with a serious illness or on an African safari, rendering one impossible to attend, in either case, on one or two days' notice, a special meeting would not otherwise be invalidated.

A third exception is when there is an emergency. When an attempt to get board members together would exacerbate the problem, the action of one or two board members, on behalf of the entire board, would be upheld. This kind of action constitutes an exception also to the requirement that the board act as a whole or a corporate body. Such action is rarely exercised.

c. *Closed Meetings.* Many states have statutes which require that all school board meetings be open, that is, that the public be allowed to attend. The thinking is that a school board is a public body which transacts public business; consequently, this business should be conducted openly rather than secretly. This holds true for most, but not all, school board action.

Some deliberations by a school board do not lend themselves to open meetings; therefore, closed meetings may be allowed, unless they are forbidden by law. Statutes typically specify what kinds of business can be transacted in a closed meeting. For instance, it would be unwise for a school board to decide publicly that it had four school sites under consideration, for it could lead to land speculation, forcing up prices, and political pressure on board members to select a given site. This point was made by an Illinois court on a challenge to a school board that had met secretly in deciding to purchase land. In ruling that the meeting was legal, the court stated:

> To hold otherwise would either greatly handicap the ability of school boards to deal for real estate or would drive the boards to informal get-togethers instead of regular meetings. Public knowledge of board intentions and actions resulting from compulsory public deliberative sessions when considering the purchase of real estate would destroy any advantage to be gained from negotiation and would work a severe detriment upon the board and the public they represent.[12]

Similarly, some personnel transactions are better handled in a closed session. A morals charge against a teacher, without merit, could well damage that individual's reputation beyond repair. It would be better to have the hearing privately.

Attempts to avoid compliance of open meeting laws by various innovations usually fail when challenged in the courts. One such method involved a superintendent who met individually with each of his board members to discuss school business and then relayed the comments of the other board members; thus, in effect, the

---

12. Collinsville Community Unit Sch. Dist. No. 10 v. White, 5 Ill. App. 3d 500, 283 N.E.2d 718 (1972). *See also* Save Our Springs v. Austin Indep. Schs., 973 S.W.2d 378 (Tex. App. 1998).

board transacted board business without public knowledge of what was transacted.[13]

As long as no official business is transacted, it is permissible for all board members to attend a state or national school board convention, without violating open meeting laws. Conducting private administrative/board workshops which involve pertinent school district issues, such as the discussion of alternative plans to school closings, does violate open meeting laws.[14] In New York a court ruled that board subcommittees are also subject to open meeting laws.[15]

In light of the strict monitoring of school board activities and the intent behind open meeting legislation, the practice of outside socialization among board members, and, in particular, school board retreats, should be practiced with caution.

d. *Executive Sessions.* Unlike a closed meeting, an executive session is a conference by the board in private. It is held for the purpose of discussion only and not for formal action. The general rule is that matters considered in an executive session must be formally ratified in an open meeting. Even if a board agrees on a matter in an executive session, the matter must still be acted upon in an open meeting. The degree of action taken in an executive session may be subject to challenge. In a North Dakota school district, a school board met in an executive session, in violation of the state's "sunshine law" and voted not to renew a teacher's contract. At a subsequent open meeting, the board affirmed, without

---

13. Blackford v. School Bd., 375 So. 2d 578 (Fla. App. 1979). In Shirley v. Beauregard Parish Sch. Bd., 615 So. 2d 17 (La. App. 3d Cir. 1993), the court held that notice of a public meeting indicating that one item on the board's agenda was to hear recommendations for an assistant principal position was sufficient to satisfy the public notice requirement of the Louisiana statutory requirement.

14. St. Cloud Newspapers, Inc. v. District 742 Community Schs., 332 N.W.2d 1 (Minn. 1983).

15. *In re* Dombroske, 462 N.Y.S.2d 146 (A.D. 1983).

discussion, its earlier action. The court held that the dismissal was void in that it was the product of an earlier illegal meeting.[16]

In an executive session, another school board voted not to renew a teacher's contract. The board did not officially act, however, on the matter at the open meeting, and it sent a letter of dismissal to the teacher. Later, the board ratified its action, but the court held that the board had acted improperly.[17]

In a North Carolina case, a school board, in a work session, selected an agent to pick a school site. The board was challenged for holding an illegal meeting, but the court held that the briefing session was legal, for the board had formally ratified its action at an open meeting.[18]

A question of a school board's legality in purchasing land was considered in the previous subsection. The court held that the state's public meeting law contained an exception for considering the acquisition and sale of land:

> All official meetings at which any legal action is taken by the governing bodies of . . . school districts . . . shall be public meetings except . . . meetings where the acquisition or sale of property is being considered, provided that no other portion of such meetings shall be closed to the public.[19]

In what seems to be a consensus of what courts have held concerning holding closed sessions, a Louisiana court ruled that a

---

16. Peters v. Bowman Pub. Sch. Dist. No. 1, 231 N.W.2d 817 (N.D. 1975). Note that where a school board discussed personnel matters in an executive session that were not later identified in an open meeting, it acted in violation of the state's Open Meetings Act. Floyd Cty. Bd. of Educ. v. Ratcliff, 955 S.W.2d 921 (Ky. 1997). In Church v. Steller, 35 F. Supp. 2d 215 (N.D.N.Y. 1999), the fact that a school district's attorney had knowledge of an employment matter discussed in executive session did not subject the contents of the meeting to public disclosure.

17. Kerns v. School Dist. No. 6, 515 P.2d 121 (Colo. 1973).

18. Eggiman v. Wake Cty. Bd. of Educ., 22 N.C. App. 459, 206 S.E.2d 754 (1974).

19. *Collinsville, supra* note 12.

school board may hold informal sessions without notice to the public for the purpose of exchanging ideas rather than making binding commitments requiring board action.[20]

e. *Rules of Procedure*. When states require that specific rules of procedure be followed in conducting school board business, these rules must be followed. Although many states prescribe some operating rules, they are not often all-inclusive. As a result, local school boards are free to supplement with their own rules. The general rule of law is that, in the absence of controlling statutes and rules, strict adherence to technical rules of procedure is not required. The reason for this is that it is not so important to have a board comprised of strict parliamentarians or to be the best possible adherent to Robert's Rules of Order, but rather to have an orderly system for the transaction of business. Thus, a board has considerable autonomy in determining the extent to which it wishes to be formal or informal, rigid or flexible. It should be made clear, however, that when a board adopts its own rules of procedure, they are as binding as statutes. Failure to follow them can, if challenged, nullify board action. This was made clear in an Ohio case.[21] A school board had approved a rule providing that school bus drivers involved in five accidents that resulted in police investigation would be dismissed. A driver, after little sleep the previous night, was involved in an accident. Although there were no injuries, the board dismissed him. The court held for the driver, citing the board regulation. The judge observed that it might be the better part of wisdom if the driver were relieved of his responsibilities, but to do so would be a violation of established procedure.

---

20. Reeves v. Orleans Parish Sch. Bd., 281 So. 2d 710 (La. 1973).

21. State *ex rel.* Edmundson v. Board of Educ., 2 Ohio Misc. 137, 201 N.E.2d 729 (1964). Of course, these rules may be subject to challenge. For example, in Leventhal v. Vista Unified Sch. Dist., 973 F. Supp. 951 (S.D. Cal. 1997), a school board's policy restricting private citizens from airing complaints or charges against school district employees at open board meetings violated a citizen's right of freedom of speech.

In a teacher dismissal case, a state statute regarding board procedure was cited as controlling the issue.[22] At a meeting in which a teacher was dismissed, a roll call vote was not held, and members' votes were not recorded, both violations of state law. The statute provided:

> [A]ny vote or action thereon (employment, hiring, etc. of any public employee) must be taken in public meeting with the vote of each member (of the school board) publicly cast and recorded.
>
> Any other action taken in violation of the above provisions shall be invalid.[23]

The court held that the board's failure to record the votes as prescribed was more than harmless error; it constituted invalid action.

In a New Hampshire case, the court upheld school board action where parliamentary procedure was not followed.[24] The court pointed out that no statutes were violated. A board meeting was invalidated in a Missouri school district when two members got together and decided to have a meeting without notifying a third member. They called for a special election which, the court held, was invalidated.[25]

In the final case in this subsection, a board was called to task for violation of a technical matter on the general procedures it had approved.[26] Louisiana statutes give a school board the right to adopt its own rules of order, and the board adopted Robert's Rules of Order. They were violated in a meeting involving the election of a superintendent. At one board meeting, fourteen of fifteen members were present, and Broussard was elected by a seven to six vote, with apparently one abstention. The board chairman ruled that Broussard was not elected in that he needed eight votes, or a

---

22. Oldham v. Drummond Bd. of Educ., 542 P.2d 1309 (Okla. 1975).

23. OKLA. STAT. tit. 25, § 201 (1972).

24. Lamb v. Danville Sch. Bd., 102 N.H. 569, 162 A.2d 614 (1960).

25. Stewart v. Consolidated Sch. Dist., 281 S.W.2d 511 (Mo. 1955).

26. State *ex rel.* Broussard v. Gauthe, 262 La. App. 105, 265 So. 2d 828 (1972).

majority of the total board. At a later meeting in which all fifteen members were present, Broussard was removed by an eight to seven vote and a replacement was elected.

The court held that Robert's Rules of Order provide that, normally, when a quorum is present, a majority vote is usually sufficient to carry any motion. According to Robert's Rules, a quorum is a majority of the members, and a quorum was present at the first meeting when Broussard was elected by a seven to six vote. The vote to remove him was invalid since he could be removed only for cause.

In order for a board meeting to be legal, a quorum must be present. State statutes generally specify what constitutes a quorum; it is usually a simple majority. Where a quorum does not exist, a board cannot act, otherwise its actions would be deemed as being that of individuals rather than of a board. When vacancies exist on a board, that does not reduce the number needed for a quorum.

f. Voting. Rules governing voting in school board meetings are included in statutes or rules of procedure. These rules often prescribe the method for voting as well as the number of votes required to approve an action.

Individual roll call votes may or may not be required in all kinds of voting. When they are required, they should identify the name of each board member and how he voted on the specific question. Where roll call votes are not required, the number of affirmative and negative votes cast is sufficient.

When a quorum is present, a majority vote is usually sufficient except for special, designated situations, such as the dismissal of professional personnel, in which case a larger number than a simple majority is usually required. Many people feel that when a school board decides a matter unanimously, the better it is for the district. It may be sound thinking in terms of politics or psychology, but it is not a legal consideration.

A board member attending a meeting has a duty to vote; failure to do so is an abrogation of his responsibility. There are some cases on record of a member in attendance not voting on an issue. According to prevailing law, his vote is viewed as acceding to the decision of the majority. An example of this situation occurred in an early case.[27] Of a seven-member board, three voted in favor of a contract, two opposed it, and two did not vote. The court held that the motion carried by a vote of five to two.

In a case from Missouri, a three-member board was considering an annexation issue. One voted for it, one against it, and one refused to vote. The court held that the issue was approved. It observed:

> There were two of the three members of the School Board present and by their presence constituted a quorum for the transaction of business, and it became and was the duty of each member to vote for or against any proposition which was presented to them. Mr. Eveland voted in favor of submitting the question of annexation and Mr. Williams did not vote. . . . [I]t was his duty to vote for or against the question submitted. . . . [W]hen a member of a school board sits silently by when given an opportunity to vote, he is regarded as acquiescing in, rather than opposing, the measure, and is regarded in law as voting with the majority . . . .[28]

Bolmeier notes one exception to the general rule of one acquiescing with the majority when he fails to vote and that exception is "when a statute *requires* the affirmative vote of all members present."[29]

School board members cannot delay their voting by leaving the room while remaining in the vicinity. Various courts have held that, technically, those members are still viewed as being in attendance.

g. *Minutes.* Evidence of what a school board has decided is revealed through the records the board has kept. The minutes provide legal evidence of the matters that were transacted. Not only

---

27. Collins v. Janey, 147 Tenn. 477, 249 S.W. 801 (1923).

28. Mullins v. Eveland, 234 S.W.2d 639 (Mo. 1950).

29. E. C. BOLMEIER, THE SCHOOL IN THE LEGAL STRUCTURE 167 (2d ed. Cincinnati: W. H. Anderson Co., 1973).

do the minutes supply evidence but, if necessary, they also reveal the intent of the board.

Board members cannot, as individuals, speak for the board itself. It is only through the minutes that a board actually speaks. The minutes serve several purposes: to reveal what a board has done, to provide guidance for the present board, to serve as a resource for future boards, and to serve as a record for citizen or public inquiry. In short, minutes indicate what a board actually did and how it acted.

Most school boards keep rather sophisticated forms of minutes. While desirable, it is not legally required. So long as they reflect what a board of education actually did, minutes need not be formal or technical. The major objective is accuracy and clarity. A full statement on what should be included in minutes, given more than three decades ago, is still applicable today:

> Generally, business to be covered in minutes should include names of all those present, including those who come late, with arrival noted, actions upon all communications to the board, reports of all standing and special committees and action taken thereon, business manager's report, including therein a financial statement of the general account, building fund, sinking fund, monthly vouchers, bids, purchases, the superintendent's report, including therein personnel changes, those employees hired and discharged or retiring, curriculum changes or suggestions, changes in policy to be discussed, future meeting sites and dates.
>
> When policy is to be changed, minutes should include a copy of the old and new policy, complete salary schedules when adopted, names of all visitors giving presentations, and recording of board action of all resolutions, including recording by name the number of ayes and nays.[30]

---

30. Brown, *Records of School Board Meetings,* ch. 2 in LEGAL PROBLEMS OF SCHOOL BOARDS (Arthur A. Rezny ed., Cincinnati: W. H. Anderson Co., 1966).

A school board can amend or correct its minutes. Although it does not have to take place at the next meeting, it should be done within a reasonable period of time. The amending or correcting cannot be done to satisfy the whims of a member or even the entire board; rather, the content must reflect actual board action. Minutes cannot be altered after a meeting on the basis of information by or political pressure from citizens unless the change reflects actual board decisions.

School board minutes become official when formally approved by the board. Courts have held that the notes of minutes do not constitute board minutes. States vary with respect to requirements for the actual execution of the minutes. In some states all board members must sign them; in others, the signature of the president and the secretary is sufficient. After formal approval and the required signatures, minutes are then considered as being public documents and may be inspected by interested persons.

Several states have recently permitted filming, televising, and tape recording of trials and other official activities, despite a long tradition against this practice. Technology has been a major factor in the change. Equipment is no longer very cumbersome or distracting. Taping of a school board meeting will generate a more accurate record of what was transacted than resorting to memory or relying on notes made during the meeting.

§ 3.4. Office-Holding of Board Members.

a. *Selection of Board Members*. There is no uniformity among the states with respect to requirements for becoming a local school board member. Even within some states, requirements vary.

The number of board members varies from three to over twenty. The modal number is usually from five to nine. The larger the total school district population, the greater the tendency to have large school boards; thus, large city school systems tend to have large school boards.

Board members are selected in a variety of ways. Over four-fifths of the local school board members in this country are elected, most often in a nonpartisan election. In some states, however, board members run in a partisan election. Where board members are appointed, it is by a variety of ways: by local judges, grand jury, city council, mayor, governor, or by the legislature.

Qualifications for office are minimal. Among the requirements are citizenship, a minimum age, and residency within the district. Other more general requirements might state that a candidate be of good character and have an interest in education.

Most board members serve without pay. Traditionally, they have been viewed as rendering a public or civic service, and a salary would be inimical to that thinking. Although they receive no salary, some board members have received modest expense allowances. More recently, however, some larger affluent school districts have begun to pay board members a salary of several thousand dollars a year and some state legislatures have mandated specific amounts of compensation for service on local school boards.

Terms of office vary among, and sometimes within, states. A typical term is from two to six years with members serving overlapping terms. The member with the most seniority does not automatically accede to the presidency or chairmanship of the board.

b. *Restrictions on Office-Holding.* When one becomes a school board member, he may have to forego some opportunities that he might otherwise be entitled to. He may, for example, be restricted in the employment of his relatives; he may be ineligible for another office; and he may not do business with the school district. Each of these three restrictions will be examined briefly.

1. *Employment of Relatives.* Common sense dictates that a school board member should not employ his relatives in a school district that he serves. To do otherwise would be to create a conflict of interest or the possibility of a conflict of interest. Statutes often specify the classes of relatives ineligible for employment, or in more lenient states, statutes may specify that so long as the related board member disqualifies himself from voting on the employment of his relative, the individual may, on getting a favorable vote, be employed.

In a 1977 decision from West Virginia, a court held that a superintendent was not disqualified from holding office simply because he and a board member were married to sisters.[31]

A New York law forbade more than one member of a family from serving on the same board of education. A wife sought a seat on the Albany school board; her husband was already a member. The court held that the law was sound in that it provided for a broader representation of the school community and it allowed individual members to debate issues with their fellow board members objectively and independent of intimate relationships.[32]

2. Dual Office-Holding. Most states have provisions in their constitutions or statutes that forbid the holding of two offices simultaneously. Since board members are viewed as being officers, they are thus ineligible to hold a second office which would be in conflict with the first one. Incompatibility exists when a superordinate-subordinate relationship exists or when the offices are in different branches of government. For example, one could not be a board member as well as a local judge who would rule on school controversies; one could not be a board member and a member of city council which appoints board members and acts on the school's budget.

It has often been held that when one holding a public office accepts another one incompatible with the first one, he automatically resigns the first office. The general principle was modified, however, by a New Jersey court in 1971.[33] The mayor appointed a teacher to fill a vacancy on the school board. The appointment was challenged, and the defendant argued that his acceptance of the board position vacated his teacher's position. The court responded that "Here, defendant teacher was bound by his teaching contract for the school term and was not legally free to abandon one public job for another."

---

31. State *ex rel.* Anderson v. Board of Educ., 233 S.E.2d 703 (W. Va. 1977).
32. Rosenstock v. Scaringe, 387 N.Y.S.2d 716 (A.D. 1976).
33. Visotcky v. City Council, 113 N.J. Super. 263, 273 A.2d 597 (1971).

In Pennsylvania the question of the legality of a supervisor's being a member of a school board was litigated.[34] The supervisor was employed by an intermediate school district (a conglomerate of a number of local school districts) and served as a board member for one of the constituent districts. The court held that the two positions were not incompatible in that an intermediate school district is not a school district. The law prohibited only the executive director and the assistant executive director from serving on the intermediate board.

Teachers are considered as being employees, not officers. Even so, they are ineligible to serve as a board member in the district in which they work. They may be eligible, however, to serve as a board member in the district in which they reside but do not work.

In Illinois, in 1977, a court held that a generally worded statute did not forbid wives of board members from being employed as teachers in that district.[35] Although it appeared that the issue was moot, the court elected to rule on the matter because of the public interest in it. It relied on a provision of the state's Corrupt Practices Act that provides:

> No person holding any office, either by election or appointment under the laws or constitution of this state, may be in any manner interested, either directly or indirectly, in his own name or in the name of any other person, association, trust or corporation, in any contract or the performance of any work in the making or letting of which such officer may be called upon to act or vote.[36]

The court also relied on a statute that provided that a married woman has the right to contract as if she were single and a right to her earnings as her own separate property.

---

34. Commonwealth *ex rel.* Waychoff v. Tekavec, 456 Pa. 521, 319 A.2d 1 (1974). In a 1994 opinion the Supreme Court of Wyoming ruled that a maintenance worker for the school district could not also serve on the local board of education. *See* Thomas v. Dremmel, 868 P.2d 263 (Wy. 1994).

35. Hollister v. North, 50 Ill. App. 3d 56, 365 N.E.2d 258 (1977).

36. ILL. REV. STAT. ch. 102, § 104 (1973).

3. *Conflict of Interest.* Another fundamental principle of law is that a school board member cannot have an interest in a contract with an agency he administers. Were he to do so, he would tend to profit from the association. For example, a school board member who was also an insurance broker wrote a contract for the school district with his firm. His action was inconsistent with the statutes which forbade any school board member from having an interest in any contract made by the board. The court held that the member's action constituted a basis for removal from office.[37]

In another case, a conflict of interest was found to exist in Kentucky when two school board members were declared ineligible for continuing in office.[38] One had sold $55.06 of supplies to the home economics department; the other had continued briefly after his election to supply transportation to the school system. Both were in violation of the statute that provided that no person shall be eligible for office as a school board member, who at the time of election, was involved in the sale of any property, supplies, or services for which school funds were spent.

c. *Disqualification for Office.* When a school board member has been appointed for an indefinite or non-fixed term, he may be removed arbitrarily without cause and without notice. Incident to the power of appointment is the power of removal. When a school board member has been elected to serve for a fixed term of office, he cannot be removed prior to the expiration of that term except for cause. Cause may involve a number of reasons: malfeasance, misconduct, inefficiency, incapacity, neglect of duty, absence from meetings, illegal expenditures, or financial interest in contracts.[39]

In the case of appointed school board members, the removal may be by the appointive body, or it may be by another agency designated by the statutes. Another method of removal is by a recall election in which a stated number or percentage of the elec-

---

37. People v. Becker, 112 Cal. App. 2d 324, 246 P.2d 103 (1952).

38. Commonwealth *ex rel.* Matthews v. Coatney, 396 S.W.2d 72 (Ky. 1965).

39. A case treating this issue is *In re* Cain v. Fernandez, 595 N.Y.S.2d 181 (App. Div. 1st Dep't 1993), where a board member became ineligible for office by not residing in the school district.

tors petition for a special election to determine if the member may continue in office.

For the removal of an elected board member, notice and hearing are typically required. Generally, a formalized court procedure is not held, and one is not entitled to a jury trial.[40]

---

40. For a case involving the recall of local school board members, see Brooks v. Branch, 424 S.E.2d 277 (Ga. 1993). In Russell v. Fernandez, 599 N.Y.S.2d 769 (Sup. Ct. 1993) the court held that an appointed school board member had the same right to appeal her removal as did an elected school board member. For a comprehensive article on the removal of school board members *see* Ralph Mawdsley & Clifford Hooker, *Removal of School Board Members*, 57 EDUC. LAW REP. 627 (Feb. 15, 1990).

Chapter Four

TORT LIABILITY

§ 4.0. Introduction.

A tort is a civil wrong, other than a breach of contract, for which a court will provide a remedy in the form of damages. The wrong grows out of harm to an individual by the unreasonable conduct of others. The remedy is premised on the notion that one should be allowed to recover something, usually money, from the one who harmed him.

At all levels, school personnel are faced with a potential for accidents. The educational environment cannot be made accident-proof; for despite the best efforts of all concerned, accidents do occur. An injured party may or may not be able to recover in damages for his injury; this depends on a number of factors. This chapter will treat those factors and others, including the elements of due care, the nature of immunity of various categories of school personnel, and the current status of tort law in the educational sector.

Torts involve four major categories: intentional interference, negligence, accountability, and civil rights torts. The first category involves one person's invading the rights of another intentionally. Negligence involves an individual's unintentionally injuring another person. Accountability is the tort of failure to provide proper instruction for pupil learning. A civil rights tort involves one denying to another a right protected by law. Each of these four areas will be treated in this chapter.

§ 4.1. Intentional Interference.

When one person invades the rights of another and injures that individual, he commits an intentional tort. Assault and battery fall into this category. Assault is an overt attempt to injure another person physically. Although it does not involve actual physical contact, an individual's behavior or demeanor is such as to put another in a state of peril or to threaten him. Shaking a fist menacingly may constitute assault. Battery involves actual physical contact with another. It is often used in conjunction with and may be the end product of assault.

a. *Assault and Battery.* There have been relatively few assault and battery cases in education, presumably because administrators and teachers have been given considerable discretion in the discipline of school children. Occasionally, however, a parent may sue in the belief that a teacher or principal used extreme methods in controlling student behavior. In a 1974 case from Illinois, a parent sued the school district, charging teachers and school officials with intentionally abusing, attacking, and intimidating her children. She maintained that the child's nervous system and learning abilities had been damaged. The court dismissed the suit. It held that a teacher has the right in Illinois to inflict reasonable corporal punishment as well as to chastise a student verbally. It also held that a teacher cannot be sued for liability unless there is proof of malice.[1]

In a case it was held that a teacher did not commit assault and battery on a student while restraining him in class. The student had spoken defiantly, used vulgar language, and refused to leave the classroom when ordered. The teacher then moved toward the student to evict him at which point the student threatened the teacher. The teacher immobilized the student's arms and led him toward the door at which point the student extricated himself, swung, and broke a window. His arm was cut. The court ruled that the teacher had used reasonable force and no assault and battery attached.[2] In another case, a teacher was found liable for committing unreasonable corporal punishment since ten to fifteen minutes had elapsed between the student's behavior and the teacher's "battery."[3] In a 1982 battery action initiated by one student against another, the court found for the defendant. The claim was dismissed on the ground that the defendant had been provoked by the actions of the plaintiff.[4]

b. *Defamation.* Another category of intentional interference is defamation. Defamation includes two categories: slander and libel. Slander is a spoken word which defames or injures a person's reputation. For one to be successful in a slander suit, a malicious intent to injure must be proven. Libel involves an injury to a person through the medium of printed material.

Like assault and battery, slander and libel suits occur infrequently in education. An example of a libel suit was decided by the California courts in 1975. Parents wrote a letter to their principal, charging that one of the teachers "displayed an utter lack of judg-

---

1. Gordon v. Oak Park Sch. Dist. No. 97, 24 Ill. App. 3d 131, 320 N.E.2d 389 (1974).

2. Simms v. School Dist. No. 1, 508 P.2d 236 (Ore. App. 1973). In the Commonwealth of Virginia, the law allows for the "use of incidental, minor or reasonable physical contact," . . . and the "use of reasonable and necessary force . . ." by principals and teachers. VA. CODE § 22.1-279.1.

3. Thomas v. Bedford, 389 So. 2d 405 (La. App. 1980).

4. Dixon v. Winston, 417 So. 2d 122 (La. App. 1982).

ment or respect, had been rude, vindictive and unjust, misused her authority, and had given failing grades to students she did not like."[5] The letter expressed the hope that the teacher would correct her personality defects.

The teacher countered the charges by alleging that the statements were designed to harass her. She then sued the parents for libel.

Both the trial and appellate courts held that the teacher had failed to state a cause of action for libel. Both courts recognized that the parents had used normal channels to communicate their concerns. Further, the communications were held to be privileged, that is, protected in that they had been made through official channels to responsible parties. The court recognized that a teacher may expect to receive unfavorable criticism:

> One of the crosses a public school teacher must bear is intemperate complaints addressed to school administrators by overly-solicitous parents concerned about the teacher's conduct in the classroom. Since the law compels parents to send their children to school, appropriate channels for the airing of supposed grievances against the operation of the school system must remain open.[6]

A similar case involved a defamation suit brought by three high school teachers against two parents. The suit was dismissed on the ground that parents enjoy the privilege of discussing matters of concern with the principal as long as those discussions are held in good faith.[7]

§ 4.2. Negligence.

a. *Criteria of Negligence.* A second major category of torts is negligence, a subject with which this chapter is primarily concerned. Negligence involves conduct by one person that falls be-

---

5. Martin v. Kearney, 124 Cal. Rptr. 281, 283 (Cal. App. 1975).
6. *Id.* at 283.
7. Desselle v. Guillory, 407 So. 2d 79 (La. App. 1981).

low an established or acceptable standard which results in an injury to another person. The standard is a variable one; that is, negligence under one situation may not be under another circumstance. Courts must decide such cases on the basis of the factual situation against a general set of criteria. These criteria typically include four questions: (1) Within the given situation, did one owe a standard of care, a duty, to another? That is, was the individual expected to supervise, maintain a safe environment, or give proper instruction? (2) Did one fail to exercise that standard of care or duty? That is, was the individual derelict in supervising, maintaining a safe environment, or in giving instructions? (3) Was there an accident in which a person was injured? Did one actually suffer some kind of loss or injury? (4) Was the failure to exercise due care the proximate (direct) cause of the injury? The cause of the injury must first be established; then it must be shown that there was some connection between it and one's failure to exercise due care.

b. *Defenses Against Negligence.* One should not assume that, whenever there is an injury, another person is always to blame. Many accidents occur and many tort suits are filed without the injured party recovering anything. The burden is usually upon the plaintiff (the one bringing the suit) to prove that the defendant was negligent, that is, that he actually was directly responsible for the accident. His negligence could take several forms. It could involve misfeasance — performing an act wrongfully, malfeasance — performing an unlawful act, or nonfeasance — failing to perform a required act.

Several defenses apply in tort actions. Any one, if established, will absolve the defendant of liability. Some districts may, for example, claim immunity from suit on the basis of the state legislature not allowing its agents to be sued. Individual school personnel have no such defense, for through the years they have been subject to tort suits for their negligence. The extent of school district immunity will be explored later in this chapter.

A second defense is contributory negligence. Under this defense, if it is shown that the injured individual directly and fully contributed to his injury, no one else is to blame. An example is a case in New York in which a secondary school student, against the instructions of his physical education teacher, participated in gymnastic activities without proper equipment. The appellate court held that the student had contributed directly to his injury.[8]

Closely allied to contributory negligence is a third defense, comparative negligence. Under this defense both a plaintiff and a defendant are jointly held responsible for the accident. The court settlement will properly adjust any damages to the degree of negligent responsibility of either party. This is illustrated in a case in which a defendant was held liable for one-half the costs, the school principal for one-fourth, and the board of education for one-fourth. The defendant was responsible in that he had injured another pupil at the school's pickup site before school; the other two parties were responsible for failure to supervise and for seeing that there was supervision.[9]

A New York court decided similarly with regard to the assumption of costs; however, it was overturned in that adequate screening for a baseball field had been provided to protect the spectators.[10] The district had met its responsibility of providing adequate protection and was not responsible for additional protection.

The fourth defense is assumption of risk. An individual understands, appreciates, and agrees that, in undertaking an activity, he subjects himself to a possible injury, for one cannot guarantee the safety of another. This applies particularly in activities that are considered as being potentially dangerous. For example, when an

---

8. Passafora v. Board of Educ., 353 N.Y.S.2d 178 (App. Div. 1974).

9. Titus v. Lindberg, 228 A.2d 65 (N.J. 1967). *See also* Boham v. City of Sioux City, 567 N.W.2d 431 (Iowa 1997). The school district was found to be 20 percent liable and the driver of a vehicle 80 percent liable in an accident resulting in the death of a student while crossing a street. The liability of the school district was established by the fact that a school crossing guard had directed the student to cross the street. The student was hit by a motorist who had no brakes and was unable to stop. For another case involving supervision at a school's student pickup site, see Moore v. Wood Cty., 489 S.E.2d 1 (W. Va. 1997).

10. Akins v. Glens Falls City Sch. Dist., 424 N.E.2d 531 (N.Y. 1981).

athlete tries out for the football team, he risks an injury. In any activity one assumes "normal" risks, but not those risks growing out of the negligence of another.[11]

§ 4.3. School District Immunity.

For many years school districts were held not liable for negligence suits. This action was premised on the notion that a school district is an agency of the state, and, like the state, it is not liable in its corporate capacity unless the legislature has specifically ruled otherwise. Further, it was viewed that a school district's funds are trust funds — earmarked for educational purposes and not for payment for damages.

a. *Historical Precedents.* The precedent for the long-established principle of tort immunity of school districts goes back over 200 years to a decision of an English court, *Russell v. Men of Devon.*[12] The factual situation involved a wagon broken down as a result of a bridge being out of repair. The wagon owner sued the men of the county, for they were responsible for maintaining the roads. In affixing no negligence, the court held that neither law nor reason supported the action. If a suit were allowed, it would likely lead to many such suits which would mean that all inhabitants of the county would have to pay. It also held that the legislature, not the courts, should be the source for allowing such suits. It concluded by stating that it was better for an individual to sustain an injury than the public an inconvenience.

The *Russell* decision was accepted as precedent in this country. The first real test of its application came in 1812, and it involved a similar situation to the one in *Russell.* The Massachusetts court held that public or quasi-public corporations are not liable for

---

11. Rutter v. Northeastern Beaver Cty. Sch. Dist., 423 A.2d 1035 (Pa. Super. 1980), *rev'd and remanded*, 437 A.2d 1198 (Pa. 1981). For another case supporting this notion, see Hammond v. Board of Educ. of Carroll Cty., 639 A.2d 223 (Md. Ct. of Spec. App. 1994).

12. 100 Eng. Rep. 359, 2 T.R. 667 (1788).

negligence.[13] Thus, the precedent for the immunity of school districts in this country was established and remained in effect until 1959. That year, in a case in Illinois, a state court held that a school district was liable for damages to a student injured in a school bus accident.[14] The bus had left the road, hit a culvert, exploded, and burned. The student suffered severe and permanent burns for which he sought compensation of $56,000. In its precedent-making decision, the court reasoned that liability should naturally follow negligence. The notion that "the king can do no wrong" was held to be outmoded. Further, education was viewed as being a big business, for school districts have large budgets with which to conduct their affairs.

The *Molitor v. Kaneland* decision started a movement in other states to abrogate the immunity doctrine. Several approaches have been followed since 1959. One has been for the legislature to abrogate the immunity doctrine; another has been for the courts to abrogate it. In some states it has been adhered to, modified, or found to operate on an insurance-waiver theory. Although the number of states abrogating the doctrine changes, to date several states now allow school districts to be sued.

b. *Governmental and Proprietary Functions.* One reason why courts have been reluctant to tamper with school district immunity has been because of their recognition that schools perform a governmental function. As such, they are instrumentalities of the state and, thus, act as the state itself. Some courts have distinguished, however, between what a district is required to do and what it elects to do. They have held the former to be governmental and the latter proprietary. One court characterized a proprietary function as follows: the school is not required to perform it, it can be carried out by a commercial agency, and it is used to raise money.[15] Consequently, some, but not all, courts have held school districts to a higher standard of care in performing a proprietary as opposed to a

---

13. Mower v. Leicester, 9 Mass. 237 (1812).

14. Molitor v. Kaneland, 163 N.E.2d 89 (Ill. 1959).

15. Morris v. School Dist., 144 A.2d 737 (Pa. 1958).

governmental function. Other courts have held that any such distinction is an artificial rather than a real difference.

§ 4.4. School Board Immunity.

Through the years courts have made a distinction between the immunity of school boards as corporate entities and school board members as individuals. When board members act within the scope of their legislatively prescribed or implied authority, they are acting as a corporate body. So long as they act honestly and in good faith, within their prescribed authority, they will not be held liable for an injury growing out of an error of judgment. That is, they cannot be sued for conscientious mistakes or errors in judgment. Courts have reasoned that to rule otherwise would be to deprive a community of potentially valuable civic leadership. For example, a school district, allowing the city recreation department to use a safe gymnasium facility, was not liable for an injury to a student.[16] The board of education was not responsible for providing supervision of activities in a Michigan case when a student was injured at the job site in a vocational education class.[17] However, a Connecticut board of education was held responsible, due to negligence in conducting a ministerial duty, when a student was injured after falling on an icy sidewalk at school.[18] In North Carolina a court held that participation of a school board in a risk management agreement did not waive the board's immune status.[19]

§ 4.5. School Board Member Immunity.

In contrast to the corporate action of a board of education, board members have been successfully sued as individuals. It is only

---

16. Morris v. City of Jersey City, 432 A.2d 553 (N.J. Super. 1981).

17. Weaver v. Duff Norton Co., 320 N.W.2d 248 (Mich. App. 1982).

18. Lostumbo v. Board of Educ., 418 A.2d 949 (Conn. Super. 1980). For a contrasting opinion, see Payne v. Twiggs Cty. Sch. Dist., 501 S.E.2d 550 (Ga. App. 1998).

19. Hallman v. Charlotte-Mecklenburg Bd. of Educ., 477 S.E.2d 179 (N.C. App. 1996).

when the members of a board of education exceed their authority that they may be liable — as individuals, not as a corporate body. In order to hold a member liable, it must be shown that he was motivated by malice, corrupt motive, or attempt to injure. Otherwise, board members have considerable discretion, make many decisions involving judgment, and are not subject to suit.

§ 4.6. School Employee Immunity.

The immunity traditionally enjoyed by school boards has never been extended to school employees. Superintendents, principals, and teachers have always been subject to tort suits for their own negligence. When one's actions fall below a standard of care expected of the average person, resulting in an injury, negligence is established. The behavior expected of school personnel is that which is measured against what a reasonably prudent person, one of ordinary intelligence and prudence, would do, or should have done, in the same or similar circumstances. Against that standard, a court will then determine whether liability may be imposed.

A key element in the determination of negligence is the matter of foreseeability. An administrator or a teacher is expected to "[t]ake reasonable care to avoid acts or omissions he can reasonably foresee would be likely to injure."[20] An educator is expected to foresee the possible consequences of an action or a condition and then take measures, where necessary, to remedy them. For example, in the ordinary course of a work day, it may involve removing shattered glass in a corridor, warning students to keep away from workers pruning a large tree, adding supervisors to a bus loading area where fights have recently occurred, or giving special instructions prior to undertaking an experiment in chemistry.

a. *Supervision.* Both administrators and teachers are expected to supervise students. A general charge in a tort suit is that an educator failed to supervise or failed to supervise properly.

---

20. Seitz, *Tort Liability of Teachers and Administrators for Negligent Conduct Toward Pupils,* 20 CLEV. ST. L. REV. 556 (1971).

Although no one standard of what constitutes adequate supervision exists, some generally accepted principles do prevail. For an administrator, adequate supervision involves the assignment of a qualified teacher to the activity he is directing. It includes making known to the teacher a set of general expectations. It means making periodic visits or inspections to ascertain if the teacher is meeting those conditions set for him. It also involves periodic inspection of the building, grounds, and facilities to determine that no apparent hazards exist or to see that maintenance corrects inadequacies.

For a teacher, adequate supervision involves due care commensurate with the circumstances. Older students need less direction than younger ones; mature students need less direction than less responsible ones. Low risk activities require less supervision than potentially dangerous ones. Van Der Smissen has pointed out that a teacher must "be alert to conditions which may be dangerous to participants, such as rowdyism, defective premises, lack of use of protective devices or safety equipment, and the age-skill experience of the participants in relation to the assumption of risks."[21]

Courts recognize that students cannot be held to the same degree of care as adults; consequently, less is expected of them; more is demanded of teachers who supervise them. In spite of this notion, a teacher cannot possibly supervise all students constantly at all times of the day and in all places at school. Continuous supervision is not necessarily required, but that does not imply that a teacher should not be vigilant. An Indiana court absolved a teacher of liability who was out of the room when a student was injured.

> [W]hat constitutes due care and adequate supervision depends largely upon the circumstances surrounding the incident such as the number and age of the students left in the classroom, the activity in which they were engaged, the duration of the period in which they were left without

---

21. Van Der Smissen, Legal Liability of Cities and Schools for Injuries in Recreation and Parks 115 (1975 Supp., Cincinnati: W. H. Anderson Co., 1975).

supervision, the ease of providing some alternative means of supervision and the extent to which the school board has provided and implemented guidelines and resources to insure adequate supervision.[22]

In the above case, the elementary school teacher demonstrated to the satisfaction of the court that she had properly prepared the class for independent activity, that the students were responsible, there was no evidence of previous misconduct, and the students were not engaged in any hazardous activity. She could not have predicted that a student would bring a dangerous substance to school and that it would explode.

In two different cases, teachers were found negligent in their supervisory duties. One case involved a girl who was burned when her school play costume caught on fire when it came in contact with a candle lit as part of a morning prayer.[23] In the second case, when a teacher was out of the room a student was injured by a power saw stored unsafely in the back of the room.[24] The court found for the plaintiff even though the teacher had instructed the class not to use the saw.

Courts remain in disagreement over a teacher's liability while not in the classroom. Some recognize that a teacher's mere presence is enough to discourage student misconduct while other courts recognize that a teacher's presence is no guarantee against spontaneous misbehavior. There will probably continue to be debate over this issue, especially with regard to special education teachers who have a major responsibility for preventing misbehavior, spontaneous or otherwise.

Supervision also involves the corollary of instruction. Together, they constitute the basis for many tort suits involving teachers and

---

22. Miller v. Griesel, 308 N.E.2d 701, 707 (Ind. 1974). In Dennis v. City of New York, 613 N.Y.S.2d 343 (N.Y. App. Div. 1994), where the teacher was aware that students had been playing with a classroom door shortly before an injury to a student's hand when the door was closed on it, the appeals court ruled in favor of the injured student.

23. Smith v. Archbishop of St. Louis, 632 S.W.2d 516 (Mo. App. 1982).

24. Lawrence v. Grant Parish Sch. Bd., 409 So. 2d 1316 (La. App. 1982).

administrators. Moreover, a school district may be held liable for lack of supervision of its personnel. Several court decisions, treated briefly, relate to the nature of both supervision and instruction.

Liability was established in a 1975 case in Louisiana, and the injured student was awarded damages of over $100,000.[25] He was seriously injured when his science project, a simulated volcano, exploded. The project was constructed of molded clay and mud around a glass bottle into which a metal can containing powder from a firecracker had been inserted.

While the student was waiting for the school bus, the volcano erupted and caused the boy to lose three fingers. Negligence was established in the following manner: (1) Neither the teacher nor the administration had imposed any regulations regarding the project. (2) No one had assumed any overall supervision for the display. (3) The principal had not required any reports or set any guidelines for Display Day. (4) The teacher had not determined what substances were to be used and what ones were dangerous.

A second case, decided also in 1975, established the negligence of a school district and the non-negligence of a teacher.[26] It illustrates arguments propounded by the plaintiff in establishing, and the defendant in refuting, a case of negligence. It involved a student injured in a high risk activity, a physical education class. While performing on a trampoline, she suffered severe injuries. The activity was required of all freshmen and, although the student was apprehensive about doing a "front drop," her teacher encouraged her to do so. Only one teacher supervised the twenty to twenty-five students performing on three or four trampolines; however, each trampoline was surrounded by spotters while the teacher alternated among each group. At the time of the accident the teacher was ten feet away watching another student.

---

25. Simmons v. Beauregard Parish Sch. Bd., 315 So. 2d 883 (La. App. 1975).

26. Chilton v. Cook Cty. Sch. Dist. No. 207, Maine Twp., 26 Ill. App. 3d 459, 325 N.E.2d 666 (1975).

The teacher was charged with negligence for failing to supervise closely and for forcing a reluctant student to engage in the stunt.

The school district was charged with negligence for failing to provide proper supervision for beginning students, to increase supervision as injuries increased, to require the use of a safety harness, to provide more teachers and student leaders per class, to separate beginners from experienced performers, and to test beginners on the trampoline.

In defense, the school district cited the following safety precautions: It had certified instructors present at all times. Student spotters were to be stationed around each trampoline in use. Before any student undertook an exercise, safety principles were to be taught and demonstrated. Finally, students were not to be forced to do any stunt.

The court ruled that, under the school code, the plaintiff was not bound to a standard of proof of wilful and wanton misconduct in the supervision of students in school activities before any liability can be imposed on the defendant. Using a lesser standard of care, the court took note of a number of injuries in the classes and imposed negligence on the district.

School personnel were held not to be negligent as a result of a student drowning.[27] The youth, aged eleven, was enrolled in a school-sponsored summer program. The class of seventeen was supervised by one teacher plus six helpers, some of whom could not swim. The entire class was in the swimming pool at the time of the drowning. The deceased was last seen at the shallow end of the pool; his body was found at the deep end.

The court rejected all claims by the plaintiff and held that the evidence did not support negligence on the part of school personnel. Other facts to consider were the inherent dangers of swimming, a possibility of bodily malfunction, and an individual's own negligence. In a different case, a student was killed after dashing into the street against the light. The court found for the plaintiff since only one teacher had been provided for supervising eleven

---

27. Wong v. Waterloo Community Sch. Dist., 232 N.W.2d 865 (Iowa 1975).

educable mentally retarded children. Such an action was foreseeable; more teachers should have been assigned to supervise those teenagers.[28]

In an accident in an unsupervised area of the school grounds, a Hawaiian court held that the absence of supervisory personnel was not the proximate cause of a student's injury.[29] "The duty to supervise does not require that every portion of the buildings be supervised. If certain areas are known to be dangerous, or should have been known to be dangerous, that requires supervision. There was no evidence that this area was dangerous."[30] The accident occurred when a student was hit in the eye as she was leaving school. A case was dismissed for similar reasoning when a first grader was injured when a heavy metal door was shut on his hand by a classmate.[31]

There was reasonable supervision, the court held, in that three adults supervised the bus loading area, one adult supervised the crosswalk at the street in front of the school, the vice-principal generally toured the campus, the principal stationed himself on an elevated walkway where he could see much of the campus, and teachers supervised hallways as the students left the building. These kinds of supervision were sufficient to relieve the district of any liability. The court recognized that if certain areas are known to be dangerous, they require supervision. Since there was no evidence that the area of the injury was dangerous, school officials had no duty to supervise there.

Cases against school districts involving playground supervision have been dismissed for several reasons. Two such reasons are that teachers have followed written guidelines for supervision[32] and a showing that increased supervision would not necessarily decrease unforeseeable accidents.[33]

---

28. Foster v. Houston Gen. Ins. Co., 407 So. 2d 759 (La. App. 1981).

29. Miller v. Yoshimoto, 536 P.2d 1195 (Hawaii 1975).

30. *Id.* at 1200.

31. Narcisse v. Continental Ins. Co., 419 So. 2d 13 (La. App. 1982).

32. Joseph v. Monroe, 419 A.2d 927 (Del. Super. 1980).

33. Batiste v. Iberia Parish Sch. Bd., 401 So. 2d 1224 (La. App. 1981).

Litigation has also involved supervision before and after school as well as during the lunch hour. A school is responsible for students on their way to and from school as well as while they are at school. This does not mean, however, that school personnel must supervise children several blocks away from school nor that they can ensure a safe environment away from school.[34] It does mean that authorities may set down reasonable rules and regulations to which students are expected to conform. (See, for example, *Titus v. Lindberg,* § 4.2.a.) Therefore, students may be held accountable to school authorities for misconduct occurring while on their way to and from school. A New Jersey court ruled that a principal was responsible, in part, beyond the school property itself, for providing a safe place for students in a heavily used area adjacent to school property.[35] The area was well-known and often used as a short-cut for students during the noon hour and after school. Although a hazard existed, school authorities had taken no measures to have it corrected.

Reasonable supervision is necessary also during the noon hour. However, extraordinary supervision is not required. Thus, on a cold snowy day, a teacher was not expected to remain outside the building during the noon hour in supervising students returning from lunch.[36]

In one of the largest tort settlements in history, a case in California recognized the negligence of several people, resulting in permanent disability to the injured student, and a multi-million dollar settlement.[37] The charge was failure to supervise and to diagnose and provide proper treatment for an injury.

The accident occurred on a school playground in a summer program sponsored jointly by the school district and the city. While the program supervisor was inside a building, two boys became involved in a fight. One boy hit another on the head with a

---

34. Oglesby v. Seminole Cty. Bd. of Pub. Instrn., 328 So. 2d 515 (Fla. 1976).

35. Caltavuturo v. City of Passaic, 307 A.2d 114 (N.J. 1973).

36. Lawes v. Board of Educ., 266 N.Y.S.2d 364 (N.Y. 1965).

37. Niles v. City of San Rafael, 116 Cal. Rptr. 733 (Cal. App. 1974). *See also* Meyers v. Board of Educ., 646 N.Y.S.2d 685 (N.Y. App. Div. 1996).

softball bat. When he learned of the fight, the supervisor separated the two boys. The injured one mounted his bicycle and rode home. His skull was fractured, an artery was torn, and a blood clot had formed, bringing pressure on the brain.

The boy's father took him to the hospital where various personnel acted negligently. His admission was delayed because of incorrect information given an intern. The people initially examining him had not determined correctly the severity of the injury; the suggestion was made that he should be admitted for observation. The boy exhibited the following behavior: drop of pulse, headache, swollen tissues, grogginess, sleepiness, irritability, perspiring, loss of color, and vomiting.

A staff member suggested that the father take his son home and observe him there. The father was not given any guidelines for determining change in behavior. He did, however, take the boy home but returned within three hours. The diagnosis this time was intracranial bleeding. The child remained in a coma for forty-six days. He became permanently disabled. The brain damage was irreparable, although his mental capacities were otherwise unaffected. Physically, he has only slight movements of the right hand and foot, is mute but can communicate by eye movements.

The jury awarded the boy $25,000 from the city and the school district and $4,000,000 from the hospital and the director of the outpatient clinic. The former had failed to provide proper supervision on the playground; the latter had failed to attend the plaintiff and treat him properly. That failure had aggravated the injury. Testimony revealed that, had the child been treated properly, he would have had an excellent chance of recovery.

b. *Instruction.* As mentioned in the previous section, instruction is often a part of supervision. According to Root, evidence of reasonable instruction includes:

> [E]xplaining and demonstrating how equipment operates, how materials should be used, and the proper performance of procedures or exercises; explaining the inherent dangers of equipment, materials, and procedures; instructing on methods of avoiding danger; requiring stu-

dents to use protective devices; checking that equipment and materials are being used properly; checking that students are proceeding properly; and enforcing all safety rules.[38]

The previous section on supervision pointed out that school districts, administrators, and teachers may be liable for lack of supervision. In contrast, in the area of instruction, responsibility lies more specifically with a teacher. Courts look to the sufficiency of instruction in terms of the circumstances of a case. They determine if, in view of a given learning activity or experience, there was reasonable instruction. Since this is often difficult to determine, courts often rely on the testimony of experts. These experts may be called on to testify if a given activity has educational value, was appropriate for the specific group of students in question, and if the instructions were sufficient and appropriate. Judgments are often made about the appropriateness of an activity in terms of a child's size, age, and skill.

Instructional care can also mean other things. It may include posting, demonstrating, and distributing safety regulations, reviewing and reinforcing safety measures, warning students of potential dangers, screening students before they undertake an activity, and testing students to ascertain their mastery of safety information and procedures.

The following case illustrates the liability of a teacher for failure to warn a student of a potential danger.[39] The student had constructed a cannon in a machine shop, taken it home and later loaded it, causing it to fire. The explosion blew off two fingers and part of a palm and wrist. Even though the accident did not occur at school, the teacher was negligent in not giving proper instructions to the pupil.

---

38. Suzanne Root, Administrators' and Teachers' Perceptions of the Duty of Due Care in Preventing Student Injury 70 (unpublished doctoral dissertation, Temple University, 1977).

39. Calandri v. Ione Unified Sch. Dist., 33 Cal. Rptr. 333 (Cal. App. 1963).

In another case, a teacher was charged with negligence for failing to enforce rules and regulations and for not supervising.[40] A non-class member was repairing his auto with an acetylene torch when a spark ignited the gas tank. The tank exploded, killing one student and seriously injuring another.

c. *Facilities.* Another responsibility of school authorities is to provide buildings, equipment, and grounds that are safe for students. While one cannot assure that a school environment will be accident-free, he must be prudent in lessening the possibility of an accident. Although educators have no control over building and safety codes, they are responsible for inspecting the place for defects, reporting hazardous conditions, and taking temporary measures, if necessary, in protecting people against possible harm until the hazard is removed. If considerable time elapses before a problem can be corrected, one may, for example, warn people to stay clear of an area, post signs about the hazard, close off the area completely, or station supervisors there.

Time is a key element in determining if liability exists for unsafe conditions. Courts ask how long a problem existed, how long authorities had knowledge of it, and if there has been sufficient time to correct it.

Major responsibility for providing a safe environment rests with a school board. However, this does not extend to providing supervision, such as crossing guards, after school hours.[41] It is responsible for landscaping grounds, constructing buildings, and providing equipment. Defects in those areas lie not so much with teachers and administrators as with a board. A teacher's responsibility is in the careful use of such facilities. When conditions are determined to be unsafe, a teacher should present evidence, with documenta-

---

40. Dutcher v. City of Santa Rosa High Sch. Dist., 290 P.2d 316 (Cal. 1957). For a case involving a student injured on a wood-shaper machine, see Webb v. Rogers, 750 F.2d 368 (5th Cir. 1985).

41. Plesnicar v. Kovach, 430 N.E.2d 648 (Ill. App. 1981). In a 1994 case, the court held that the school board was not liable for an injury to a mother who stepped in a hole on the side of a road. Miller v. Wadsworth City Schs., 638 N.E.2d 166 (Ohio App. 1994).

tion, to the principal who, in turn, would request that the matter be corrected. Both teacher and principal should retain a copy of the report. In the meantime, one should use good judgment in determining whether to avoid an area or discontinue using a facility or equipment considered in need of correction.

Several cases follow, which illustrate problems concerning safe facilities that arise at school and their disposition by courts. In Kentucky, a suit was brought against a board of education for allegedly permitting an excavation to remain unfilled. On the morning after a child had attended a ball game at school, his body was found at the bottom of that pit. The court ruled that governmental immunity in that state prevented any recovery.[42]

A different ruling was handed down in Pennsylvania in a case in which the immunity doctrine was abrogated.[43] The plaintiffs brought suit against the School District of Philadelphia for an injury to a student, aged fifteen, whose arm was caught in a shredding machine in an upholstery class. They alleged successfully that the district had failed to have a proper safety device for the machine, maintained defective machinery, and failed to warn children of the defective machinery. The state's supreme court agreed.

A New York court ruled, over three decades earlier than the Pennsylvania court, that, for failure to provide a protective apron for a student operating a lathe, the school district was negligent.[44] The court referred to the state statute requiring that the board of education furnish equipment necessary for the efficient management of educational activities.

A wet gymnasium floor, on which a basketball player slipped and injured his back, was held not to be dangerous.[45] Hence, the boy could not recover. The boy's coach had not questioned the condition of the floor; the opposing coaches and the referees did

---

42. Smiley v. Hart City Bd. of Educ., 518 S.W.2d 785 (Ky. 1975).
43. Ayala v. Philadelphia Bd. of Educ., 305 A.2d 877 (Pa. 1973).
44. Edkins v. Board of Educ., 41 N.E.2d 75 (N.Y. 1942).
45. Nunez v. Isidore Newman High Sch., 306 So. 2d 457 (La. App. 1975).

not think the matter serious enough to cancel the interscholastic game.

There was no requirement that a school district supervise a Saturday morning baseball game on the premises of an elementary school.[46] A child, injured by a bicycle, could not collect damages.

In another case, an injured child collected $50,000 in damages from a city and the local school board.[47] She was brain-injured when, on a swing set, a steel support pole dislodged and struck her on the head. In a similar case out of Texas when a girl was injured during school hours when a swing broke, the court dismissed the suit on the basis of the district having governmental immunity.[48] And a Georgia case involving the death of a girl when a metal soccer goal fell and struck her was dismissed since the defendants were protected by governmental immunity.

The school board had purchased used equipment on property owned by the city. The area was unsupervised. It was held that the city had a duty to exercise reasonable care in erecting and maintaining the park. It did not have to have notice of a defective condition to render it liable, for here it had actually created the hazard.

Responsibility for safe facilities includes not only grounds and classrooms, but corridors as well.[49] A loose rail on a stairway separated from the wall, causing a child to fall five or six steps on a marble stairway. The fact that the railing had been loose for several months established a *prima facie* case of negligence. Similarly, the court found for the plaintiff when a power saw with no guard was the cause of a student's losing his finger while using the saw.[50]

d. *Field Trips.* The same principles of tort law apply on field trips as they do at school. Responsibility may be shared, however, by non-school personnel who may also be involved in the activity;

---

46. Orsini v. Guilderland Cent. Sch. Dist., 46 A.D.2d 700, 360 N.Y.S.2d 288 (1974).

47. Watts v. Town of Homer, 301 So. 2d 729 (La. App. 1974).

48. Truelove v. Wilson, 285 S.E.2d 556 (Ga. App. 1981).

49. Wiener v. Board of Educ., 48 A.D.2d 877, 369 N.Y.S.2d 207 (1975).

50. McKnight v. City of Philadelphia, 445 A.2d 778 (Pa. Super. 1982).

for example, the group's host and the transportation carrier may be subject to liability. It is also possible that an injured student may have been negligent.

Liability waivers, or release forms, are often used by school authorities prior to students undertaking a field trip. Since a district or its employees cannot actually waive away their responsibilities, liability waiver forms may diminish the possibility of a suit; otherwise their essential purposes are in informing parents and securing permission for the trip.[51]

Persons on field trips are considered as being either licensees or invitees. Although courts are not in full agreement, a student on a field trip is generally considered as being a licensee. A licensee is one who is on the premises of another by permission rather than by invitation. Since a visitor is there at the convenience of the host, the host owes his guest no more than a duty to abstain from actually harming him. In contrast, an invitee is one who is on the premises of another by invitation of an owner. An owner has a greater care of duty in protecting the visitor from injury. Not only must the premises be safe, but the owner also has a duty to warn a visitor of possible dangers. This principle was stated in *Nunez:*

> An owner or occupier of lands or buildings must take reasonable and ordinary care to protect invitees from any dangerous conditions on the premises. He must also warn them of any latent dangerous defects in the premises and inspect the premises for any possible dangerous conditions of which he does not know.[52]

In a case involving a drowning on a class outing, it was held that a high school principal had given adequate instructions concerning the activity.[53] In another case, action was brought against a mu-

---

51. One example of an exception to this holding is by an appellate court in Georgia which disallowed a claim by an individual who had signed a liability waiver prior to being injured in test-driving a motorcycle. Cash v. Street & Trail, Inc., 136 Ga. App. 462, 221 S.E.2d 640 (1975).

52. Nunez, *supra* note 45, at 458.

53. Cox v. Barnes, 469 S.W.2d 61 (Ky. App. 1971).

seum, a school district, and two teachers for injuries sustained by a boy, aged twelve, who was assaulted while on tour of a museum. The court dismissed the suit, for it was the intervention of a third party, the assailant, who actually brought on the injury.[54]

e. *Medical Treatment.* To a limited extent, an educator stands in place of a parent (*in loco parentis*). One such occasion is during an emergency. Even here, however, that responsibility is limited. An administrator or teacher is not expected to, nor should he, treat a sick pupil; that is a function of one trained in medicine. An educator's responsibility is limited only to administering first aid after having determined that one needs attention. Even here, Kigin cautions:

> Whether or not to administer treatment subsequent to the injury of a pupil constitutes a risk that must be taken with the hope that the court or jury would hold the defendant blameless for what he does or does not do. This is based on prudence. By reason of the relationship of the teacher to the pupil (*in loco parentis*) the teacher is obligated to do the best he can for the pupil in the event of an injury. It is to the teacher's distinct advantage to be trained in at least the rudiments of first aid.[55]

Like Kigin, Appenzeller cautions that teachers are expected to administer lifesaving first aid when needed, but they are not expected to go beyond that. First aid is limited to giving temporary care until one can secure the services of a physician.[56]

An educator can be charged with excessive treatment of a student. A coach acted negligently in allowing an injured pupil to be

---

54. Mancha v. Field Museum of Natural History, 5 Ill. App. 3d 699, 283 N.E.2d 899 (1972).

55. DENIS J. KIGIN, TEACHER LIABILITY IN SCHOOL-SHOP ACCIDENTS 97 (Ann Arbor: Prakken Publications, Inc., 1973).

56. H. APPENZELLER, ATHLETICS AND THE LAW 208 (Charlottesville: The Michie Co., 1975).

taken off a football field without a stretcher. The movement of the player aggravated the injury.[57]

An educator can also be charged with doing too little. During football practice a boy became ill from exhaustion and began vomiting. Twenty minutes later the bus took him and his teammates to the school. The boy was placed on the floor of the cafeteria and later taken to the shower room where he was placed on a blanket. One of the coaches placed an ammonia capsule by the boy's nose. The coaches then reviewed the first aid manual but refused to call a doctor. It was a parent who noted that the boy needed professional attention immediately. The child's mother was called, she called a doctor, and he sent the boy to a hospital. He suffered heat exhaustion and irreversible shock and died the next day. The court drew two conclusions: that the delay in getting medical attention caused his death and that the coaches had attempted to administer first aid in a negligent manner.[58]

A 1942 case has long been cited over the matter of untrained people attempting to give medical treatment.[59] A boy, aged ten, had an infected finger although it did not prevent his playing ball. Two teachers decided to treat the infection. They kept the boy after school and immersed his hand for approximately ten minutes in a pan of boiling water. The hand was permanently disfigured. Since no emergency existed and neither teacher had medical training, the situation did not justify the teachers' action.

§ 4.7. Accountability.

Traditionally, courts have been reluctant to second-guess school authorities and their evaluation of a teacher's competence. More

---

57. Welch v. Dumsmuir Joint Union High Sch. Dist., 326 P.2d 663 (Cal. 1958).

58. Mogabgab v. Orleans Parish Sch. Bd., 239 So. 2d 456 (La. App. 1970). *See also* Roventini v. Pasadena Indep. Sch. Dist., 981 F. Supp. 1013 (S.D. Tex. 1997); Burden v. Wilkes-Barre Area Sch. Dist., 16 F. Supp. 2d 569 (M.D. Pa. 1998); Foster v. Estrada, 974 S.W.2d 751 (Tex. App. 1998).

59. Guerrieri v. Tyson, 24 A.2d 468 (Pa. 1942).

often than not, judges first confine their review to procedural matters by ensuring that all channels were properly followed. Then, they ascertain if the board's action was supported by sufficient evidence and whether the members' action was arbitrary or capricious.

That traditional stance of courts concerning review of school performance has been in a transitional period since the second half of the 1970s. A number of factors are responsible for this change. Many states have instituted competency-based programs which spell out instructional objectives and attempt to measure what is learned. Parents, in revolting against tax increases for education, have demanded more of schools in general and greater achievement of their children. Students have begun to sue school districts for failure to learn or achieve, and administrators are subject to increased controls in supervising teachers and in evaluating their performance.

As of 1999 it was unclear as to what legal trends will develop on the matter of teacher accountability. So far, there have been very few court decisions which provide guidance. In a 1974 decision, a teacher's dismissal was upheld for her students having scored low on standardized achievement tests. The improvement of test scores was a primary objective of the school system, and she had failed to produce the results expected of her.[60]

In a more celebrated case in California, a high school graduate sued his school district for what he deemed to be an inadequate education.[61] He filed his suit for damages on two basic tort theories: negligence and false representation. He claimed the district was negligent in teaching, promoting, and graduating him. He

---

60. Scheelhaase v. Woodbury Community Ctr. Sch. Dist., 488 F.2d 237 (8th Cir. 1973), *cert. denied,* 417 U.S. 969 (1974). As public education moves into the year 2000, more issues are likely to arise as states begin to use technology to link student achievement on statewide tests to the accreditation of individual schools, and the productivity of principals and teachers in those schools.

61. Peter W. v. San Francisco Unified Sch. Dist., 131 Cal. **Rptr.** 854 (Cal. App. 1976).

claimed the district falsely represented to his mother that he was performing at or near grade level in basic skills.

Under California law, an employer is not liable for the conduct of its employee unless it is first established that the employee would be personally liable for his conduct on some acceptable theory of liability. Further, before damages can be awarded, four conditions must exist: (1) The plaintiff must show a legal cause of action. (2) The cause must be stated in the complaint alleging facts showing a care of duty to the plaintiff. (3) The complaint must show negligence constituting a breach of duty. (4) There must be an injury to the plaintiff as a result of the breach of duty. The court concluded that it was not certain that the plaintiff had suffered injury within the meaning of the law of negligence.

In treating the complexity of the problem, the appellate court revealed the difficulty of clearly establishing negligence for a student's not learning:

> On occasions when the Supreme Court has opened or sanctioned new areas of tort liability, it has noted that the wrongs and injuries involved were both comprehensible and assessable within the existing judicial framework. . . . This is simply not true of wrongful conduct and injuries allegedly involved in educational malfeasance. Unlike the activity of the highway or the marketplace, classroom methodology affords no readily acceptable standards of care, or cause, or injury. The science of pedagogy itself is fraught with different and conflicting theories of how or what a child should be taught and any layman might—and commonly does—have his own emphatic views on the subject. The "injury" claimed here is the plaintiff's inability to read and write. Substantial professional authority attests that the achievement of literacy in the schools, or its failure, are influenced by a host of factors which affect the pupil subjectively, from outside the formal

teaching process, and beyond the control of its ministers.[62]

In a New York case on the same subject, the judge dismissed the suit.[63] Although the judge felt the matter should be reviewed by a higher court because of the issue involved, he ruled that there was no precedent in the state for attaching liability to a school district for failing to educate a student. The student, aged eighteen, and an unemployed carpenter, alleged that he could not read menus, had to take his driver test orally, and had to rely on his mother for filling out a job application. His parents claimed that teachers promoted him and although he received some special help in the lower grades, it was not until his senior year that he received special tutoring. His reading improved from second to third grade level. The parents charged the administration for failure to provide facilities and personnel, to advise them of the child's difficulty, and to take proper precautions for his condition.

In a number of other states, similar cases have been filed charging negligence for a student's not learning. To date, however the limited case law makes the legal status of accountability uncertain.

§ 4.8. Preventing Injuries.

Approximately fifty to sixty tort suits in education are decided each year by courts of record in this country. That number does not reflect the many legal actions settled before they actually reach court nor the many more accidents in which there was no suit. The real objective in being knowledgeable about tort law, however, is not so much in winning a court case but in preventing injury. An

---

62. *Id.* at 860-61.

63. Donohue v. Copiague Union Free Sch. Dist., No. 77-1122 (Sup. Ct., Suffolk Ct., New York, August 31, 1977). Twenty years after *Donohue,* the federal district court in Massachusetts held that no common law cause of action for educational malpractice existed in that state. *See* Doe v. Town of Framingham, 965 F. Supp. 226 (D. Mass. 1997).

educator should seek to provide a healthy and safe environment that lessens the likelihood of accidents.

The cases that have been treated in this chapter are very few in comparison to the thousands that courts have decided through the years. They should alert the reader to the fact that courts are not always in agreement in determining negligence. Where questions of fact are in dispute, a jury trial is held; where questions of law are involved, a judge resolves them.

How can injuries be prevented? There is no guaranteed system for doing so, but precautions can be taken. The following precautions are aimed for school board members, administrators, and teachers:

1. Employ responsible people. These people, at all levels, should be mature and safety conscious.

2. Know the extent of one's authority. Failing to act or overacting can constitute a tort.

3. Be familiar with the rights of one's subordinates. Today, denying a subordinate the exercise of his constitutionally protected rights can be the basis of a tort suit.

4. Award contracts to competent firms in doing business with the school. Responsible people should be engaged in work for the school, whether it be routine maintenance or large-scale construction.

5. Be sensitive to potential problems. One should not overlook a small problem, for it could mushroom into a very serious one.

6. Gear work to the students. A teacher should consider a student's age, maturity, and ability in making assignments.

7. Teach attitudes and responsibilities. Teaching students to be careful and to respect dangers inherent in some learning experiences may be as important as the mastery of subject matter. In like manner, an administrator should instruct teachers about their attitudes and care in helping provide a safe learning environment.

8. Make periodic inspections. The administrator should routinely inspect the entire facility; a teacher should routinely inspect his classroom.

9. Report problems promptly. First, report to the proper authorities that a condition needs correcting; then do what is wise in preventing an injury until the problem is in fact corrected.

10. Avoid overcrowding. Accidents are less likely to occur where people move freely in noncongested areas.

11. Get rid of junk. Waste materials tend to clog a facility, create sanitary and fire hazards, and invite accidents.

12. Exercise reasonable supervision. Extraordinary care is not required; the care by a reasonably prudent person is the standard.

In addition to the safety guidelines listed above, an educator is advised to be covered by liability insurance. Practices vary with respect to its availability, but it is often available to members of a union or professional association. Like administrators and teachers, school board members should also be covered. Law tends to be more exact with respect to an individual member's being covered as distinguished from a school board. There are no problems in a board's purchasing liability insurance, but some states do not state clearly that public tax funds may be used in covering individual board members.

A few states have "save-harmless" statutes. These provide that, in the event of a tort suit, a defendant's legal fees and damage claims will be paid for him.

Many tort suits that reach the courts are decided in favor of an educator, but there are enough decisions otherwise to warrant one to exercise the care by a reasonably prudent person.

§ 4.9. Civil Rights Torts.

One of the newer torts that has emerged in recent decades is the constitutional tort, also known as a civil rights tort. This tort applies to citizens who claim a deprivation of rights enumerated or implied in the Constitution by a superordinate acting under color of state law. Civil rights torts are grounded in a federal statute enacted after the Civil War as a means of ensuring that newly-freed slaves not be exploited of their rights.

Codified at 42 U.S.C. § 1983 (1871), the Act states:

> Every person who, under color of any statute, ordinance, regulation, custom or usage of any State or Territory, subjects or causes to be subjected any citizen of the United States or other person within the jurisdiction thereof to the deprivation of any rights, privileges, or immunities secured by the Constitution and laws shall be liable to the party injured in an action at law, suit in equity or other proper proceeding for redress.

The Act provides two forms of relief. An injured party may seek equitable relief, that is, removal of constraints that prompted the injury. A second form of relief may involve damages, either punitive or compensatory. Punitive damages consist of a monetary award designed to punish wrongdoers and to discourage them from denying to an injured party or to anyone else a constitutionally protected right. Compensatory damages are monetary awards to cover actual salary or other tangible assets lost.

Being a party to a § 1983 suit involves some risk, both to plaintiff and defendant. Under the Attorneys' Fees Act of 1976 (42 U.S.C. § 1988 (1976)), the prevailing party may be able to collect attorneys' fees in a § 1983 case. That determination is made by the judge presiding over a specific case. To date, § 1983 has applied to education cases involving equal right to contract, violations of protected rights, conspiracy to interfere with civil rights, racial discrimination in federally assisted programs, and discrimination in federally funded educational programs.

Section 1983 provides for concurrent jurisdiction. This means that a complainant has access to both federal and state courts. Unless a federal statute explicitly provides, a litigant may seek relief in a federal court without first having exhausted state court remedies. The Act was written, in part, to provide relief for individuals if state remedies were inadequate or ineffective.

State statutes control the time period in which § 1983 suits must be filed. To date, there has been no major court ruling which would provide any further guidance on this question. Since statutes of limitation within a state may be numerous, one would look to the statute most applicable to the suit in question.

For a number of years after its passage, § 1983 remained inactive. Before the 1960s it was largely ignored but, beginning in that decade, it began to be relied upon more frequently and to cover an increasing number of issues. The Act itself has undergone an evaluation of interpretation, and its coverage has been expanded considerably. Some of the highlights of its interpretation and expansion over a twenty-year period follow.

1. *Monroe v. Pape.*[64] In this case the Supreme Court ruled that officials of a governmental body, and not the governmental body itself, are subject to suit under § 1983. In so ruling, the Court narrowly interpreted the meaning of the phrase, "Every person," in the Act. The case involved the search of a house by police. Police had no warrant; further, they searched the wrong house. Even though narcotics were found, the search was deemed to be improper. Plaintiffs sued the police department, but were unsuccessful, for it was determined that § 1983 applies to officials of a governmental agency, but it does not apply to the agency itself.

2. *Johnson v. Branch.*[65] The Court of Appeals for the Fourth Circuit ruled that § 1983 applied specifically to a teacher in her suit against school board members. The significance of this case is twofold. First, school board members were viewed as being governmental officials under the Act and thus were not immune from suit. Second, teachers are protected in the exercise of their rights under § 1983. The case involved a black teacher who had been reassigned to a desegregated school. The teacher, with over a dozen years' experience in the district, was not rehired after one

---

64. 365 U.S. 167 (1961).
65. 364 F.2d 177 (4th Cir. 1966).

term in the reassigned position (the state at that time did not have a tenure law). Employment evaluation records were very meager, and school officials could offer only the following reasons for the teacher's nonrenewal: (1) the teacher had been tardy to school on several occasions; (2) the teacher had not always stood outside her door as classes changed; (3) the teacher had been late in turning in a twenty-day attendance report; (4) the teacher had missed one PTA meeting; (5) the teacher had allowed dust to collect in a storage cabinet in her room. The court was not persuaded that any and all of these charges related directly to the teaching-learning situation. What the court saw was that Johnson had been active in the civil rights movement and was not rehired because of that activism. Since there was no evidence that her involvement had interfered with her school assignment, she had been penalized for exercising her rights under the first amendment. The court ordered her reinstatement.

3. *Wood v. Strickland*.[66] In this case the Supreme Court set a standard for immunity of school board members. It held that school board members are entitled to qualified good faith immunity. This standard shields school officials from some kinds of tort actions, but it does not clothe them with full immunity. They are not subject to suit when they know about and respect the constitutional rights of students, when they act in the belief that what they are doing is right, and when they act with sincere beliefs and motives. They are not protected when their actions violate a student's constitutional rights, when they act in ignorance or disregard of settled law, when their decisions are based on malice or intent to injure, or when their actions are not based on good faith.

This case arose over the failure of school board members to give a due process hearing to students accused of mixing an alcoholic beverage with other liquid and serving it at a school function. The school board's disposition of the matter was judged not to consti-

---

66. 420 U.S. 308 (1975). In Laws v. Terry, 805 F. Supp. 352 (E.D. Va. 1992), a federal district court extended qualified immunity in a § 1983 suit to the Virginia Attorney General.

tute a hearing in the sense that the members were open minded and the students treated fairly. In ruling against the school board's expulsion of the students, the Supreme Court extended § 1983 by holding that the Act applies also to students whose rights have been denied them by school board members.

4. *Carey v. Piphus.*[67] *Carey* extended the *Wood* decision in that it treated the issue of students' entitlement to damages growing out of a deprivation of their rights. In resolving that issue, the Supreme Court treated two questions: the conditions that warrant the awarding of damages, and the amount of damages that can be assessed local school officials. *Carey* involved a jointure of two cases growing out of the suspension from school of two students in unrelated incidents. The common element of the two incidents was that each student was suspended without first having been given due process.

In one of the incidents, a freshman was believed to be smoking marijuana on campus. A principal viewed the boy's behavior from some distance and was unable to seize the evidence which had been tossed into some nearby shrubbery. In the other incident, the principal suspended a boy for wearing an earring, a violation of school rules. The basis for each of the students' suits was an allegation of lack of due process prior to suspension.

In speaking for the Supreme Court, Justice Powell wrote that the right to procedural due process is absolute. Failure to give students that right may be cause for legal action, including damages. The Court added a qualifier, however, when it ruled that, before students can recover substantial damages, they must prove that they were actually deprived of a right. Since in this case there was no proof of actual injury, the Court determined that the two students were entitled to $1.00 each.

The significance of *Carey* is twofold. It is an affirmation of the rights of students, but it is also a warning to them that they cannot expect to win damage awards for the mere denial of a constitu-

---

67. 435 U.S. 247 (1978).

tional right. There must also be a showing that they were actually injured by the denial of that right.

5. *Monell v. Department of Social Services of City of New York.*[68] *Monell* is significant in that it expanded the scope of possible defendants in a § 1983 suit. *Monell* reversed *Monroe* and held that municipalities and other local governmental bodies, including school boards, may be sued for a civil right tort. Previously, § 1983 had been held to be limited to governmental officials, not to governmental bodies.

Monell originated in New York City by female employees of the Department of Social Services and the City Board of Education. Plaintiffs sought injunctive relief and back pay for the defendants' actions in compelling them as pregnant employees to take unpaid leaves of absence from their jobs before they were medically required to do so.

The Supreme Court ruled that a local governmental body can be sued if its actions, whether policy or custom, inflict an injury on a person otherwise protected under § 1983. Although the Court did not define policy or custom, it stated that the action may involve persistent and widespread practices of officials, and it was the moving force behind the constitutional violation.

Monell allows individuals whose rights have been violated by government to sue the agency as well as its officials for monetary and equitable relief. This means that school boards are considered as being persons under § 1983 and can be held liable for their policies and customs if either or both of them cause an individual to be deprived of his constitutional rights.

6. *Owen v. City of Independence.*[69] This case established that local governmental bodies are not entitled to the standard of qualified good faith immunity. That standard was set for governmental officials in *Wood,* but the Court elected not to extend it to govern-

---

68. 436 U.S. 658 (1978).

69. 445 U.S. 622 (1980). The importance of an individual functioning as a "state actor" for purposes of using § 1983 can be seen in Black v. Indiana Area Sch. Dist., 985 F.2d 707 (3d Cir. 1993).

mental bodies. Further, these governmental bodies may not rely on the good faith actions of its officers as a defense to their own liability.

Owen involved the dismissal of a chief of police on four charges, none of which had been proven. The city manager, who fired Owen, based his action on an independent investigation by a city councilman, and the subsequent directive of the council that the city manager take whatever action he deemed appropriate. In actuality, the council had no authority over Owen's hiring and discharge; only the city manager possessed such authority. The council also released to the public allegedly false statements that damaged Owen's reputation. That action entitled Owen to a name-clearing hearing, a guarantee of due process.

The *Owen* decision has made it easier for an individual to sue a governmental body rather than its officers, for the former has less immunity. The upshot is that a school board member, acting in good faith and without malice, may be immune from suit while, for the same action, a school board may be liable.

7. *Maine v. Thiboutot.*[70] This case expanded the application of § 1983 by allowing individuals to claim a deprivation of rights under statutory law. Previously, § 1983 had applied only to rights insured by the Constitution. The Supreme Court stopped short, however, of holding that all federal laws come under the penumbra of § 1983. It ruled that, where a statute provides an exclusive judicial remedy, § 1983 does not apply. Conversely, the Act does apply where statutory law does not provide a remedy for individuals whose rights have been violated. The Act applies only to civil rights actions, not to other kinds of rights.

In this case, plaintiffs challenged an interpretation of the Social Security Act which would have allowed welfare benefits for three children and not for the remaining five. Parents claimed that the interpretation was incorrect and initiated a § 1983 suit.

The Supreme Court could not determine the intent of the framers of the Act and the specific phrase, "secured by the Constitution

---

70. 448 U.S. 1 (1980).

and laws." It concluded, however, that the phrase "and laws" was intended to include selective acts of Congress.

Several conditions prevail which limit individuals from flooding the courts in § 1983 suits. First, one must show that a federal statute authorizes the federal courts to entertain such a suit. Second, the suit must be premised only on a deprivation of a right secured by the Constitution or by an act of Congress involving equal or civil rights. If a plaintiff claims damages in excess of $10,000, one must assert that the claimed deprivation did not involve equal or civil rights, in which case a different statute applies.

8. *City of Newport v. Fact Concerts.*[71] This case relates to *Monell,* the decision three years earlier which had allowed compensatory damages to be assessed against a municipality. Plaintiffs in *Fact Concerts* sought to extend *Monell* by allowing punitive damages also to be assessed against a municipality. The Supreme Court declined to permit this. It held that a local governmental body could not be held responsible for the bad faith actions of its officials. To do otherwise would be to penalize unfairly all taxpayers; the appropriate remedy would be to seek relief from the tortfeasor, in this case, city officials.

The above chronology represents only a very few of the many civil rights tort cases filed in the last third of a century. These eight, plus others, have provided educators with patterns of judicial thought on civil rights torts. First, teachers have better recourse in § 1983 suits than do students. Further, teachers have a better chance of receiving monetary damages than do students. Second, suits are typically filed against the school board as the employer of teachers rather than against an administrator. Third, many people have used § 1983 as a vehicle, particularly in employment situations, with very little likelihood of their prevailing. Fourth, teachers and students have successfully applied § 1983 to key amendments: first, fourth, and fourteenth. Section 1983 has protected teachers who are critical of their superordinates or of

---

71. 453 U.S. 247 (1981).

working conditions, whether expressed orally or in print.[72] When teachers have expressed facts or opinions of public concern, courts have upheld such statements as being protected by the first amendment. It has protected teachers in determining their own lifestyle and appearance, whether in clothing or style and length of hair.[73] It has upheld teachers whose techniques of instruction may be nonconventional but accepted by experts as being related to course objectives.[74]

The fourth amendment has applied more to search of students as opposed to search of teachers. Section 1983 becomes applicable at the point that a search lacks reasonable cause and is highly invasive. Conducting a search that violates either condition may result in a student's being awarded damages.[75]

---

72. *See, e.g.,* Pickering v. Board of Educ., 391 U.S. 563 (1968); Mt. Healthy City Sch. Dist. Bd. of Educ. v. Doyle, 429 U.S. 274 (1977), *aff'd on remand,* 670 F.2d 59 (6th Cir. 1981); Givhan v. Western Line Consol. Sch. Dist., 439 U.S. 410 (1979); Swilley v. Alexander, 629 F.2d 1018 (5th Cir. 1980); Welch v. Barham, 635 F.2d 1932 (8th Cir. 1980); Lemons v. Morgan, 629 F.2d 1389 (8th Cir. 1980); Johnson v. Butler, 433 F. Supp. 531 (W.D. Va. 1977). Beginning in the late 1990s, lawyers cited § 1983, along with 42 U.S.C. § 1981 and Title 7 of the Civil Rights Act of 1964, as sources of remedy in employment discrimination cases.

73. *See, e.g.,* Lucia v. Duggan, 303 F. Supp. 112 (D. Mass. 1969); Doherty v. Wilson, 356 F. Supp. 35 (M.D. Ga. 1973); Tardif v. Quinn, 545 F.2d 761 (1st Cir. 1976); East Hartford Educ. Ass'n v. Board of Educ., 562 F.2d 838 (2d Cir. 1977); Fisher v. Snyder, 476 F.2d 375 (8th Cir. 1973). For students' rights cases involving the first amendment, see Minarcini v. Strongsville City Sch. Dist., 541 F.2d 577 (6th Cir. 1976); Sapp v. Renfroe, 511 F.2d 172 (5th Cir. 1972); Leonard v. School Comm. of Attleboro, 212 N.E.2d 468 (Mass. 1965); Gambino v. Fairfax Cty. Sch. Bd., 564 F.2d 157 (4th Cir. 1977); Thomas v. Board of Educ., Granville Cent. Sch. Dist., 607 F.2d 1043 (2d Cir. 1979).

74. *See, e.g.,* Robbins v. Board of Educ., 313 F. Supp. 642 (N.D. Ill. 1970); Knarr v. Board of Sch. Trustees, 317 F. Supp. 832 (N.D. Ind. 1970); Moore v. School Bd., 364 F. Supp. 355 (N.D. Fla. 1973); Kingsville Indep. Sch. Dist. v. Cooper, 611 F.2d 1109 (5th Cir. 1980).

75. The leading case is New Jersey v. T.L.O., 469 U.S. 325 (1985). *See also* Potts v. Wright, 357 F. Supp. 215 (E.D. Pa. 1973); Picha v. Wielgos, 410 F. Supp. 1214 (N.D. Ill. 1976).

The fourteenth amendment has been applied to both teachers and students in § 1983 cases. The due process and equal protection clauses have often been cited as having been violated.[76]

---

76. Representing a variety of issues, note particularly Valdez v. Graham, 474 F. Supp. 149 (M.D. Fla. 1979); Boykins v. Ambridge Area Sch. Dist., 621 F.2d 75 (3d Cir. 1980); Welsh v. Louisiana High Sch. Athletic Ass'n, 616 F.2d 152 (5th Cir. 1980); Hall v. Tawney, 621 F.2d 607 (4th Cir. 1970); Goss v. Lopez, 419 U.S. 565 (1975); Metzer v. Newton Special Mun. Separate Sch. Dist., 676 F. Supp. 749 (S.D. Miss. 1987); Cunningham v. Beavers, 858 F.2d 269 (5th Cir. 1988). In recent years, § 1983 has been used by students who allege sexual molestation by teachers and coaches. *See, e.g.,* Doe v. Paukstat, 863 F. Supp. 884 (E.D. Wis. 1994). Also, advocates for homeless children have won enforceable rights for homeless children under § 1983. *See* Lampkin v. District of Columbia, 27 F.3d 605 (D.C. Cir. 1994).

Chapter Five

COLLECTIVE NEGOTIATIONS

§ 5.0. Introduction.

Collective bargaining in public education is a phenomenon that began in the 1960s and 1970s and has extended to the present. Although organized labor grew rapidly in this country within the last century, its power as a body had less recognizable influence on the schools. Moreover, courts were reluctant to give unions more power, and they often ruled against strikes and picketing. However, once bargaining began in education, it grew rapidly until today, more than half the states have some kind of legislation which, in varying degree, mandates or permits some kind of bargaining between teachers and school boards.

121

Three acts by Congress have had considerable impact on organized labor in the private sector. The passage of the Wagner Act (National Labor Relations Act or NLRB) of 1935 is viewed as being a milestone in the development of organized labor. The Act, designed to limit the power of management, protects the right of employees to organize and bargain. It also grants to employees the right to strike and picket. Its constitutionality was tested and upheld in 1937.[1]

Twelve years after the passage of the NLRB, Congress attempted to reverse some of the power assumed by unions with the enactment of the Taft-Hartley Act. Another landmark statute was the 1959 Landrum-Griffin Act, designed to regulate the internal affairs of unions.

When public employees began to organize much later than private employees, they followed the pattern set by private business. Legislation authorizing bargaining in public education was first enacted by the General Assembly of Wisconsin in 1959. Other states then began to follow the Wisconsin lead.

The growth of organized labor in public education has not been universally received with approval. Some people view education as being too vital a public function to have it subjected to work stoppages or other kinds of interruptions. Other people have reasoned that a school board cannot delegate authority vested in it by the legislature to another body for decisionmaking.

A school board may bargain because the legislature authorizes it or because it agrees to. A Louisiana court held in 1974 that in the absence of specific legislation the school board had the authority to negotiate with teachers if it were determined that the process would more effectively and efficiently accomplish its objectives and purposes.[2] An Iowa court tempered the above holding when it ruled that it would be an improper delegation of authority for a

---

1. National Labor Relations Bd. v. Jones & Laughlin Steel Corp., 301 U.S. 1, 57 S. Ct. 615, 81 L. Ed. 893 (1937).

2. Louisiana Teachers Ass'n v. Orleans Parish Sch. Bd., 303 So. 2d 564 (La. App. 1974).

school board to enter into a collective bargaining agreement within the industrial context. It held that it would be acceptable to enter into an agreement based on meet-and-confer procedures since that action had no binding effect on the board. It ruled further that all decisions regarding wages, working conditions, and grievances resided with the board.[3]

It is conceded that there is no constitutional right to bargain; it exists through the will of a state legislature. Thus, laws vary considerably from state to state with respect to the degree to which collective bargaining is allowed and the scope of the issues that are bargainable. Even within a state, school districts vary considerably in sophistication of bargaining and in demands that are met. Since court decisions are based on the language of the state's collective bargaining act as well as the language of a specific contract for a school district, the reader is cautioned to be aware that a court decision in one jurisdiction may or may not be controlling in a different jurisdiction.

§ 5.1. Scope of Bargaining.

a. *Subjects in General.* Teachers' negotiations may occur under one or several conditions. One is mandatory bargaining in which a school board is required to negotiate with a representative teachers' organization. A second condition is prohibitive bargaining, which may forbid bargaining at all, or it may forbid it on specified subjects. When statutes are silent on bargaining, a school board is not obliged to enter into any collective bargaining agreement. A third condition is permissive bargaining by which a school board voluntarily agrees to bargain or to meet and confer. If a school board agrees to meet and confer, it is usually not bound to bargain to the extent that it reach an agreement. However, if a school board

---

3. Service Employees Int'l v. Cedar Rapids Community Sch. Dist., 222 N.W.2d 403 (Iowa 1975).

agrees to bargain under permissive bargaining, it is bound by the agreement it reaches.[4]

A difficulty often arises over determining just what is negotiable. Some states may spell out specific subjects while others may identify bargainable subjects in general language. It is the latter category that often precipitates court cases, particularly when a school board refuses to negotiate on any subjects other than those required. As a justification for this posture, boards often cite a potentially bargainable issue as being contrary to the statutes or against public policy.

In deciding if a particular subject is mandatory, permissible, or prohibitive, various courts take a number of factors into consideration. First, interpretation is guided by the specific wording of the collective bargaining statute; second, consideration is given to the application of other legislation to a particular issue; and third, determination is made of whether a particular topic may potentially compromise a school board or detract from its statutory requirements. Thus, depending upon the state, a given issue may fall into any one of the three categories.

1. *Mandatory Subjects.* Some courts limit mandatory subjects of bargaining to matters *significantly* related to wages, hours, and other conditions of employment. Other courts use a more flexible standard by limiting mandatory subjects of bargaining to matters *materially* related to wages, hours, and other conditions of employment. When the latter criterion is used, the courts apply a balancing test by determining if the impact of the subject outweighs its probable effect on the basic policy of the school system and by determining the impact of such subjects on wages, hours, and conditions of employment.[5]

---

4. Terms, concepts, and strategies of collective bargaining are explained in R.L. WALTER, THE TEACHER AND COLLECTIVE BARGAINING (Lincoln: Professional Educators Publications, Inc., 1975).

5. Goldschmidt, *Collective Bargaining,* 1977 YEARBOOK OF SCHOOL LAW 220 (Topeka: National Organization on Legal Problems of Education 1977). Collective bargaining in education has developed, as a legal issue, to the extent that NOLPE has included a chapter on it, beginning with the 1976 Yearbook.

Specific subjects of bargaining will be treated later in this chapter; however, a few cases will be identified here which are representative of issues that courts have been asked to resolve. In 1976, the Supreme Court of Wisconsin held that it was mandatory that the school board bargain over matters primarily related to wages, hours, and conditions of employment. It was also required to bargain on the impact of its policy which affected wages, hours, and conditions of employment.[6]

A New Jersey appellate court held that a duty-free lunch period is not a subject for mandatory negotiations but is a prerogative of management. It also held that the school board did not have to negotiate on qualifications required to fill vacancies. The court held that the following four issues were mandatorily negotiable: length of the teacher's work day, teacher's work load, pupil contact time, and teacher's facilities.[7]

A Michigan court held that, as a condition for employment, residency is not a mandatory subject of bargaining.[8]

Two other New Jersey courts ruled, in 1976, on the subject of mandatory negotiations. In one case mandatory bargaining was required over the assignment of elementary school teachers to an additional period of teaching to replace a free period they previously had.[9] In the other case, the court upheld the board's position that it was not required to negotiate the criteria or guidelines used in selecting individual teachers whose contracts were not renewed due to a reduction in force. It was also not required to negotiate over the employment rights of those teachers selected for nonrenewal.[10]

[6.] City of Beloit by Beloit City Sch. Bd. v. Wisconsin Emp. Relations Comm'n & Beloit Educ. Ass'n, 242 N.W.2d 231 (Wis. 1976).

[7.] Byram Twp. Bd. of Educ. v. Byram Twp. Educ. Ass'n, 377 A.2d 745 (N.J. App. Div. 1977).

[8.] Detroit Fed'n of Teachers v. Board of Educ., 237 N.W.2d 238 (Mich. App. 1975).

[9.] Red Bank Bd. of Educ. v. Warrington, 351 A.2d 778 (N.J. Super. 1976).

[10.] Union City Reg'l High Sch. Bd. of Educ. v. Union City Reg'l High Sch. Teachers' Ass'n, 368 A.2d 364 (N.J. App. Div. 1976).

Included among the most basic of mandatory subjects in collective bargaining is the selection, determination, and recognition of an exclusive bargaining group. Questions often arise as to who should be included and who may be excluded from the group. Generally, two categories of employees are excluded from the negotiations unit — managerial employees, usually supervisors and administrators; and the second category, defined as being confidential employees. The latter category includes people who assist the board of education in developing negotiation policies. In both instances these individuals are excluded from the bargaining group to avoid potential conflicts of interest. Those included in the bargaining unit elect their exclusive representative. In doing this, individuals give up their rights to negotiate their own terms and conditions of employment. Minority unions are given some rights, but not to the extent of the elected group; for example, the majority association may be provided with office space while a minority union may not. Further, a minority union need not get a dues check-off, while the majority union may have such an arrangement with the board of education.

Courts have ruled on topics that are considered mandatory subjects for negotiations. The New Jersey Superior Court ruled that a school board must negotiate length of school day, but it is not required to negotiate on the school calendar.[11] The Connecticut Board of Labor Relations ruled that teacher dress codes were subject to mandatory negotiations.[12]

The Kansas Supreme Court ruled that even though the merits of individual proposals are rejected by boards of education in negotiations with teacher groups, school boards must negotiate on vari-

---

11. Galloway Twp. Bd. of Educ. v. Galloway Twp. Educ. Ass'n, 384 A.2d 547 (N.J. Super. 1978).

12. Enfield Bd. of Educ. v. Enfield Teachers' Ass'n, 754 Gov't Emp. Rel. Rep. 11 (Conn. Bd. of Labor Rel. 1978). For more recent cases treating mandatory negotiations, see Tualatin Valley Bargaining Council v. Tigard Sch. Dist. 23J, 808 P.2d 101 (Ore. App. 1991); West Chicago Sch. Dist. 33 v. Illinois Educ. Labor Relations Bd., 578 N.E.2d 232 (Ill. App. 1991).

ous mandatory subjects.[13] Among such subjects cited were teacher discipline, length of school day, starting time, number of teaching periods, and the use of school facilities for union related business.[14] The Iowa Supreme Court ruled that medical insurance coverage for dependents of school district employees was a mandatory item for negotiations.[15] Other subjects for mandatory negotiations include residency requirements for new teachers.[16]

2. *Prohibitive Subjects.* It is recognized that there are some subjects over which school boards are prohibited from bargaining; that is, these subjects are inherently managerial prerogatives. Court decisions on this subject have involved the non-reemployment of teachers. For the most part, courts have ruled that a procedural question on non-reemployment is subject to bargaining; the substantive question of employment or termination is not. A New York court ruled that a board cannot bargain away its right to inspect teachers' personnel files; to do otherwise would be contrary to public policy.[17] Likewise, a decision of whether or not to promote is a managerial prerogative and not subject to negotiation.[18] A decision to abolish the position of music supervisor is a matter of educational policy, thus a prerogative of management.[19]

An Illinois court held that a just cause provision is a prohibitive subject of bargaining in that the school board cannot legally delegate such authority. Acting consistent with the school codes, the school board had nonrenewed a probationary teacher's contract.

---

13. Chee-Craw Teachers Ass'n v. Unified Sch. Dist. No. 247, 593 P.2d 406 (Kan. 1979).

14. NEA-Topeka, Inc. v. USD 501, Shawnee Cty., 592 P.2d 93 (Kan. 1979).

15. Charles City Community Sch. Dist. v. Public Emp. Relations Bd., 275 N.W.2d 766 (Iowa 1979).

16. City of New Haven v. Connecticut State Bd. of Labor Relations, 410 A.2d 140 (Conn. Super. 1979).

17. Board of Educ. v. Areman, 394 N.Y.S.2d 143 (A.D. 1977).

18. Board of Educ. v. North Bergen Fed'n of Teachers, 357 A.2d 302 (N.J. Super. 1976).

19. School Comm. of Hanover v. Curry, 325 N.E.2d 782 (Mass. App. 1975).

The teacher filed a grievance and the matter went to binding arbitration.[20]

A New York court held that it was not a violation of public policy for a school board to negotiate procedures involved in non-renewal of teachers, even when those procedures went beyond what was provided for in the statutes.[21]

The Pennsylvania Supreme Court ruled that the Philadelphia Board of Education could agree to submit a dispute over a teacher's evaluation to arbitration, even though the evaluation was the basis for the teacher's dismissal.[22]

A conflict arose over a school board's refusing to follow the recommendation of the principal and superintendent for tenure. The court ruled that the board was within its prerogative in not following the advice of the administrators. The court also ruled as void a provision in the union agreement that the board would "use as the primary basis for judgment on decisions of continuing employment for nontenured teachers the recommendation of the Administration which shall be based on classroom observation."[23]

Florida statutes do not require "just cause" for the nonrenewal of a nontenured teacher. Consequently, the state appeals court found that a school board is not permitted to negotiate such a condition in the collective bargaining contract, since such a provision would restrict the powers of the board in its managerial role.[24] The Supreme Court of Kansas identified a number of issues that were not permitted for negotiations between school boards and teacher unions; these issues included binding arbitration and class size.[25] A rule prohibiting smoking on school property was held to be a subject prohibited from negotiations, according to a Pennsylvania

20. Lockport Area Special Co-op. v. Lockport Area Special Co-op. Ass'n, 338 N.E.2d 463 (Ill. App. 1975).

21. Board of Educ., Bellmore-Merrick Cent. High Sch. Dist. v. Bellmore-Merrick United Secondary Teachers, Inc., 383 N.Y.S.2d 242 (A.D. 1976).

22. Milberry v. Board of Educ., 354 A.2d 559 (Pa. 1976).

23. Conte v. Board of Educ., 397 N.Y.S.2d 471, 472 (A.D. 1977).

24. Lake Cty. Educ. Ass'n v. School Bd., 360 So. 2d 1280 (Fla. App. 1978).

25. *Supra* note 14.

court, because the rule's enforcement was based upon educational policy which may not be delegated.[26]

3. *Permissive Subjects.* The issue of permissive subjects of negotiations will also be treated more fully in a subsequent section. However, a few cases will be given here as illustrative of the scope of permissive subjects. A Delaware statute provided that the employer and employee are required to negotiate about salaries, benefits, and working conditions but allowed agreements on other subjects as long as they were consistent with state law. Based on that act, the federal district court in Delaware held that the school board was not prohibited from negotiating a proposal by teachers calling for prior notice of administrator-school board meetings in which discussions would be held that might adversely affect a teacher's employment.[27]

The Pennsylvania Supreme Court held that just cause is a permissive subject for negotiations in that that issue is limited to procedures involved in dismissing teachers and the school board retains its authority in the actual dismissal.[28]

The Supreme Judicial Court of Massachusetts ruled as subjects for bargaining the issues of teaching load, number of substitutes hired, and class size.[29] Likewise, a New York court ruled that class size is a permissive subject of negotiations.[30]

b. *Specific Subjects.* Legislation authorizing negotiations typically specifies that the subjects of bargaining shall include "wages, hours, and terms and conditions of work." The first two terms involve less interpretation over what is specifically bargainable

---

26. Chambersburg Area Sch. Dist. v. Commonwealth, Labor Relations Bd., 430 A.2d 740 (Pa. Commw. 1981).

27. Morris v. Board of Educ., 401 F. Supp. 188 (D. Del. 1975).

28. Board of Educ. v. Philadelphia Fed'n of Teachers, 346 A.2d 35 (Pa. 1975).

29. Boston Teachers' Union v. School Comm., 350 N.E.2d 707 (Mass. 1976). In 1991, an Illinois court ruled that lesson plans are permissive bargainable subjects. *See* Alton Community Unit Sch. Dist. No. 11, Counties of Madison and Jersey v. Education Labor Relations Bd., 567 N.E.2d 671 (Ill. App. 1991).

30. Brookhaven-Comsewogue Union Free Sch. Dist. v. Port Jefferson Station Teachers' Ass'n, 385 N.Y.S.2d 318 (N.Y. 1976).

than the third one which is often the source of litigation. Seven specific issues will be treated in this section in clarification of what constitutes terms and conditions of work and thus are subject to the negotiations process.

1. *Class Size.* Courts are not in full agreement as to whether school boards have to negotiate with teachers on the size of classes.[31] In one case a school board justified its position of not negotiating on this topic because it wanted to provide for program flexibility and innovation. The teachers' union had sought to have different classes with varying numbers, and any exceptions would be by mutual agreement of teachers and the principal. The New York court agreed that the school board did not have to negotiate on this subject.[32] A second New York court modified this position when it held that, since the subject of class size was not clearly forbidden by statute, it was arbitrable. The conflict arose when the board sought to increase the size of classes as a result of a budget cut.[33] One year later another New York court held that the school board was not required to negotiate on class size, although it could voluntarily do so.[34]

A Maine school district increased the number of classes for junior high school teachers from four to five and increased the size of typing classes. The state's supreme court ruled that the provision in the contract requiring negotiations on class size and the work day does not require binding arbitration.[35]

---

31. This conclusion was reached earlier in an article by Douglas W. Howlett, *Class Size: A Mandatory Bargainable Issue?* 1, 16 NOLPE SCHOOL L.J. III (Fall, 1973).

32. West Irondequoit Teachers' Ass'n v. Helsby, 42 A.D.2d 808, 346 N.Y.S.2d 418 (1973).

33. Susquehanna Valley Cent. Sch. Dist. v. Susquehanna Valley Teachers' Ass'n, 376 N.Y.S.2d 427 (N.Y. 1975).

34. Board of Educ. v. Greenburgh Teachers' Fed'n, 381 N.Y.S.2d 517 (N.Y. 1976).

35. Superintending Sch. Comm. v. Portland Teachers' Ass'n, 338 A.2d 155 (Me. 1975).

Finally, the issue of class size was one of twenty-one issues before the Pennsylvania Supreme Court.[36] In treating this case, Hudgins reported:

> [T]he court first established criteria in determining if items were mandatory, permissive, or prohibitive subjects of bargaining. It was ruled that items are mandatory if they are of fundamental concern to the employee's interest in wages, hours, and other conditions of employment, even to the extent that the items touch on basic policy. They are mandatory where the impact of the issue on the employee in wages, hours, and other conditions of employment outweighs its probable effect on the basic policy of the system as a whole. Items are permissive where the impact of the basic policy of the system as a whole outweighs the impact of the employee's interest. If the issue is one of inherent managerial policy, the board is required to meet and discuss it, if required; however, the board is not required to bargain on such issues.[37]

The case was then remanded for a specific resolution of the question.

2. Work Load. Like the issue of class size, courts have also been divided on the issue of work load. There has been no consistent reasoning by courts whether they rule for the board or the teachers' organization. Similarly, in cases outside education that have considered this question, courts have not been in agreement. Two cases, both from New Jersey, will illustrate that point. In one, a school district tried to consolidate department chairmanships.

---

36. Pennsylvania Labor Relations Bd. v. State College Area Sch. Dist., 337 A.2d 262 (Pa. 1975).

37. H. C. Hudgins, Jr., *The Balance Between Lay and Professional Control,* in THE COURTS AND EDUCATION: THE SEVENTY-SEVENTH YEARBOOK OF THE NATIONAL SOCIETY FOR THE STUDY OF EDUCATION 69 (Clifford P. Hooker, ed. Chicago: University of Chicago Press, 1978). This last point was underscored in Overseas Educ. Ass'n v. Federal Labor Relations Auth., 961 F.2d 36 (2d Cir. 1992) when it was determined that attendance at an open house was a prohibitive bargainable issue.

The issue was whether it involved a policy decision or was subject to negotiations and/or arbitration. The state's supreme court ruled that, since it was not directly related to terms of employment, it was a decision for management.[38] In the other case, a lower court viewed the assignment of homerooms to department chairmen as being an extension of one's work load. The court felt that, since the matter was so closely tied to wages, hours, and conditions of work, it was a negotiable issue.[39]

Many cases dealing with employee working conditions have centered more or less on whether or not a particular issue was in the category of permissible or mandatory negotiations. A number of courts have ruled subjects permissible while others have taken a stronger position by ruling subjects mandatory.

3. *Financial Benefits.* Where bargaining is mandated or allowed, it is unquestioned that teachers' salaries may be negotiated. What is not as clear is the negotiability of financial benefits other than a direct salary.

Courts have upheld bargaining on dental plans,[40] health insurance,[41] and sick-leave provisions.[42]

Two cases involving disparities in bonuses or salary increments were decided, one for teachers and the other in favor of the board. In the first, a plan provided for certified teachers to receive $400.00 and provisionally certified teachers to receive $100.00, as bonuses. The court held that this issue was a term of employment and thus subject to negotiation.[43] In the other case, the court held that the school board could discriminate in awarding salary incre-

---

38. Dunellen Bd. of Educ. v. Dunellen Educ. Ass'n, 64 N.J. 17, 311 A.2d 737 (1973).

39. Board of Educ. v. West Orange Educ. Ass'n, 319 A.2d 776 (N.J. Super. 1974).

40. New Jersey Civil Serv. Ass'n v. Mayor of Camden, 343 A.2d 154 (N.J. Super. 1975).

41. State of Delaware v. AFSCME, 292 A.2d 362 (Del. 1972).

42. Allen v. Town of Sterling, 329 N.E.2d 756 (Mass. 1975).

43. Bridgeton Educ. Ass'n v. Board of Educ., 334 A.2d 376 (N.J. Super. 1975).

ments. The discrimination here was based on inefficiency or other good cause and not on the basis of certification.[44] New Hampshire court has held that the statute requiring bargaining on conditions of employment did not require a board to negotiate on money matters.[45]

Another issue involving financial considerations is the adjustment of fringe benefits. Controversy has grown out of increasing as well as decreasing such benefits. In a Massachusetts case both the school district and the teachers' association had agreed to an adjustment in salary for persons nearing retirement. Under the provision, one's salary would be adjusted upward for days worked in excess of 170. When a teacher became eligible for payments under the plan, an auditor refused to approve the allocation. The court disagreed with him and viewed the negotiated provision as being a reward for lengthy and continuous service.[46]

A Pennsylvania court upheld a school board which refused to continue to pay fringe benefits to teachers whose collective bargaining agreement had expired, although bargaining at the time was taking place.[47] An Arizona school board went further and attempted to reduce teacher compensation. The court held that the action involved a breach of contract which was being challenged unilaterally by the school board. The court held that such action was not a matter of policy.[48]

The scope of negotiated fringe benefits in recent years has expanded to include pay for extra duty assignments, medical and dental insurance, life insurance, sick leave, sabbaticals, paid personal business days, bereavement days, and tuition reimbursement, among others. A concerted effort has been made by some boards of

---

44. Clifton Teachers Ass'n v. Board of Educ., 136 N.J. Super. 336, 346 A.2d 107 (1975).

45. State Employees Ass'n of New Hampshire, Inc. v. Mills, 344 A.2d 6 (N.H. 1975).

46. Fitzburg Teachers Ass'n v. School Comm., 271 N.E.2d 646 (Mass. 1971).

47. Appeal of Cumberland Valley Sch. Dist., 376 A.2d 674 (Pa. Commw. 1977).

48. Carlson v. School Dist. No. 6, 12 Ariz. App. 179, 468 P.2d 944 (1970).

education to avoid potential litigation by distributing fringe benefits in as equitable a way as possible, for example, offering male employees parental leaves, providing married teachers family medical coverage, and offering unmarried teachers the difference in benefits.

4. *Calendar and School Days.* Several disputes about the school calendar have had to be resolved in court. The disputes have focused on whether the establishment of a school calendar is a term and condition of employment and thus negotiable or whether it is a managerial prerogative and consequently not negotiable. The courts are not in agreement as to which category a school calendar properly belongs.

The Supreme Court of Wisconsin held that a school calendar is a condition of employment and thus negotiable.[49] One year later, the Supreme Court of Connecticut was less specific. It held that "[t]he significance of calling something a 'condition of employment' is that it then becomes a mandatory subject of collective bargaining. . . . The duty to negotiate is limited to mandatory subjects of bargaining."[50]

An adjustment to a calendar was the subject of a dispute in a Missouri school district. In modifying the calendar, the school district scheduled days not originally indicated in the calendar that had been sent to teachers with their contract. In upholding the school board, the court ruled that the school calendar is not a part of the contract; thus, the board possesses unilateral power to fix three designated days not originally listed. The court observed, moreover, that the school board had initially contracted the right to fix the number of teaching days.[51]

---

49. Board of Educ. v. Wisconsin Emp. Relations Comm'n, 191 N.W.2d 242 (Wis. 1971).

50. West Hartford Educ. Ass'n v. DeCourcey, 162 Conn. 566, 295 A.2d 526, 533 (1972).

51. Adamich v. Ferguson-Florissant Sch. Dist., 483 S.W.2d 629 (Mo. App. 1972).

A California court held in 1977 that paying school teachers for a holiday before Easter was valid and any effect of that action on religious institutions was indirect and incidental.[52]

Courts have tended to rule that the length of a school day is a term and condition of employment. A New York court held that, in the absence of a statutory prohibition or countervailing public policy, a school board is free to negotiate on this subject.[53] Similarly, a New Jersey court had held three years earlier that the extension of a school day is a subject of negotiation in that it relates directly to financial and personal considerations.[54]

5. *Academic Freedom.* In labor disputes in education, the subject of academic freedom has had limited litigation. Because academic freedom is so closely allied with one's constitutional rights under the first amendment, it is not usually surrendered to a union agreement. Further, when disputes on this issue do occur, they are not usually subject to arbitration. That point was made clear in a New Jersey court decision in 1972.[55] Under the union agreement, there was a provision that a subject was deemed proper for teaching if it was appropriate for the maturation level of students. When a seventh grade teacher attempted to teach about abortion and the superintendent attempted to stop it, the court held that courses offered and subjects taught could not be a condition of employment.

Under different conditions but still involving the issue of speech, a California court held that a school board could restrict a teacher's freedom of speech.[56] The teachers' association had sought to circulate in the schools a petition on school finance

---

52. California Sch. Emp. Ass'n v. Sequoia Union High Sch. Dist., 136 Cal. Rptr. 594 (Cal. App. 1977).

53. New York City Sch. Bds. Ass'n v. Board of Educ., 383 N.Y.S.2d 208 (A.D. 1976).

54. Board of Educ. v. Englewood Teachers Ass'n, 311 A.2d 729 (N.J. 1973).

55. Board of Educ. v. Rockaway Twp. Educ. Ass'n, 120 N.J. Super. 564, 295 A.2d 380 (1972).

56. Los Angeles Teachers' Union v. Los Angeles City Bd. of Educ., 78 Cal. Rptr. 723 (Cal. 1969).

which would be forwarded to the Governor, State Superintendent of Public Instruction, and the City Board of Education. The court ruled that such action amounted to political activity and consequently had no place within the school itself.

Academic freedom was one of the issues in a Supreme Court decision in 1976.[57] The Court held that a teacher has a right to speak out at a meeting of the board of education on a subject currently under negotiations. Such statements do not constitute negotiations, the Court ruled, for the teachers had not attempted to bargain, nor were they authorized to do so. The Court saw that the teachers were exercising the first amendment right which protected them in speaking out on public issues.

The litigation arose when two teachers violated a state law that permitted only union representatives to speak out on matters of negotiation. The teachers had mailed a letter to union members on the subject of fair share, and they later circulated a petition calling for a one-year delay in implementing that provision until it could be studied more fully. The results of the questionnaire were presented to the board of education. The union then filed an unfair labor practice complaint for allowing the teachers to make the presentation.

The Supreme Court saw that the board meeting was public and to deny the teachers the right to speak would be, in effect, to inhibit all such speech since any aspect of public school operations is a potential subject of bargaining.

A case originating in Colorado concerned the legality of teachers bargaining away constitutionally protected rights to academic freedom. In this particular situation, the school board was then able to ban various controversial books from use in classes.[58]

6. *Professional Growth.* Negotiations over activities involving professional growth have included a number and variety of

---

57. City of Madison Joint Sch. Dist. No. 8 v. Wisconsin Emp. Relations Comm'n, 429 U.S. 167, 97 S. Ct. 421, 50 L. Ed. 2d 376 (1975).

58. Cary v. Board of Educ. of Adams-Arapahoe Sch. Dist. 28-J, 598 F.2d 535 (10th Cir. 1979).

issues, but one theme tends to run through all the litigation. It involves being rewarded for enhancing one's position through various kinds of professional activities or being penalized for a lack of professional growth.

In a Wisconsin case, teachers objected to loss of salary for the time they missed to attend a convention. Their petition was not upheld, for they were representing a minority union association and the school board had not agreed to pay them. Further, state law did not specifically provide for days off for teachers of a minority union to attend a convention.[59]

A Massachusetts court ruled that it was proper for an arbitrator to determine a salary position for a teacher. The teacher had added a vocational-education certificate to his regular academic certificate but was not given a salary increase. The court ruled that such action amounted to paying the teacher as little as possible and was not within the purview of educational policy.[60] The arbitrator had properly ruled that the teacher was entitled to the same salary as a new teacher with dual certification.

A New Jersey court ruled that a sabbatical leave is a term and condition of employment. As such, it was legitimate for teachers to enter into binding arbitration on such a subject.[61]

When a teacher did not enter into any professional growth activities, a school board attempted to fire her. The court held that her contract could not be terminated for that reason, although her salary could be frozen.[62]

7. Nonrenewal of Teachers' Contracts. In some sections of the country one of the current crucial issues in personnel administration is the suspension of teachers for lack of pupil enrollment. A number of school systems have already experienced the trauma of having to reduce the teaching force, an action that will likely

---

59. Board of Educ. v. Wisconsin Emp. Relations Comm'n, 191 N.W.2d 242 (Wis. 1971).

60. School Comm. v. Gallagher, 344 N.E.2d 203 (Mass. App. 1976).

61. South Orange-Maplewood Educ. Ass'n v. Board of Educ., 370 A.2d 47 (N.J. 1977).

62. Hefner v. Board of Educ., 335 N.E.2d 600 (Ill. App. 1975).

137

continue for another decade. This issue along with teacher dismissal is treated in another chapter in this book. However, it will be dealt with briefly here insofar as it touches on negotiations. Several cases will serve as examples of subjects of bargaining on termination of teachers.

Unquestionably, the authority to employ and dismiss teachers resides with the board of education, and the board cannot bargain away this right. It can, however, share this responsibility with a teachers' union in defining terms and in determining procedures that relate to employment. In doing this, the board still retains the authority to employ and dismiss.

A New York statute governed the abolition of teaching positions, but that did not prohibit the teachers' association from bargaining on a definition of seniority to include past nonconsecutive service when layoffs were contemplated.[63]

A school board cannot give up its authority to abolish teaching positions to a collective bargaining agreement. This was the essence of a 1975 decision. No charges were brought against the teachers nor had they been disciplined in any way; their release was simply a result of the abolition of positions.[64] A Washington court also held that a school district is not obligated to negotiate the nonrenewal of teachers' contracts. In this situation, the contracts of two hundred teachers were not renewed, and the teachers unsuccessfully sought relief from the courts.[65]

A New York court held that a contract provision that purported to give teachers absolute job security except in cases of unsatisfactory performance is a permissive subject of bargaining.[66]

A union agreement can provide for five additional days of notification prior to the termination of teachers, over and above what

---

63. Board of Educ. v. Lakeland Fed'n of Teachers, 381 N.Y.S.2d 515 (N.Y. 1976).

64. Schwab v. Bowen, 363 N.Y.S.2d 434 (N.Y. 1975). *See also* Carmel Sch. Dist. v. Carmel Teachers Ass'n, 348 N.Y.S.2d 665 (N.Y. 1973).

65. Spokane Educ. Ass'n v. Barnes, 517 P.2d 1362 (Wash. 1974).

66. Board of Educ. v. Yonkers Fed'n of Teachers, 386 N.Y.S.2d 657 (A.D. 1976).

is required by a statute, if the school board agrees to it.[67] It can also contain provisions for notice and termination. In so holding, the court overruled an arbitrator who had concluded that a teacher's service had been improperly terminated and that she should be reappointed and paid for lost salary.[68]

Another general subject of reduction in force relates to termination for other than lack of enrollment. For the most part, nontenured teachers have limited rights with respect to dismissal proceedings. The contract of a nontenured teacher could be terminated for absences beyond a specified three-month period of temporary incapacity. The board was also within its power in adopting a regulation defining temporary incapacity.[69]

Two nontenured teachers alleged that an agreement gave them many rights enjoyed by tenured teachers. They had been dismissed for reasons stated in the school code. The court ruled that the school board could not enter into an agreement that was in conflict with the school code.[70]

A Pennsylvania court ruled that the propriety of a teacher's dismissal was subject to arbitration on the basis that the issue dealt with wages, hours, and conditions of employment. The school board had objected to arbitration on the ground that it was an unlawful delegation of power.[71]

---

67. Associated Teachers v. Board of Educ., 60 Misc. 2d 443, 303 N.Y.S.2d 469 (1969).

68. Board of Educ., Cent. Sch. Dist. v. Harrison, 46 A.D.2d 674, 360 N.Y.S.2d 49 (1974).

69. Elder v. Board of Educ., 208 N.E.2d 423 (Ill. App. 1965). For an excellent example of a case where a local board of education's reduction in force plan for teachers was successfully implemented pursuant to a collective bargaining agreement *see* Piquard v. Board of Educ., 610 N.E.2d 757 (Ill. App. 3d Dist. 1993).

70. Wesclin Educ. Ass'n v. Board of Educ., 331 N.E.2d 335 (Ill. App. 1975).

71. Board of Educ. v. Philadelphia Fed'n of Teachers, 346 A.2d 35 (Pa. 1975). In Phoenixville Area Sch. Dist. v. Phoenixville Area Educ. Ass'n, 624 A.2d 1083 (Pa. Commw. 1993), the court held that the arbitrability of a dispute depends upon interpretation of provisions of the specific collective bargaining agreement and, where there is a question of arbitrability under the agreement has not been decided by the arbitrator, the court has no power to stay the arbitration.

§ 5.2. Required Union Membership.

Public education has not accepted a union shop which requires that employees join the bargaining unit that represents them. It has subscribed to an agency shop which requires a nonunion member to pay a fee to cover his share of the costs of the services he receives. However, in 1974, a Pennsylvania court held that agency shop agreements are illegal under the state's public employee relations act since that statute provides only for a maintenance-of-membership provision.[72] This provision means that at the time an agreement is negotiated, the members of the bargaining unit must agree to remain a member of the union for the duration of the contract.

The Supreme Court of the United States ruled in 1977 that a teachers' union could require nonunion members to pay a service charge to cover the expenses of activities related to bargaining, but it could not require them to pay for support of political and ideological activities. This, the Court held, would be in violation of the teachers' first amendment rights.[73]

A Pennsylvania court held, in 1976, that a school board could not terminate a teacher's contract for refusing to pay membership dues. That reason was not one of the enumerated causes for termination as specified in the codes.[74]

---

72. Pennsylvania Labor Relations Bd. v. Zelum, 329 A.2d 477 (Pa. 1974).

73. Abood v. Detroit Bd. of Educ., 429 U.S. 209, 97 S. Ct. 1782, 52 L. Ed. 2d 261 (1977).

74. Dauphin Cty. Tech. Sch. Educ. Ass'n v. Dauphin Cty. Area Vocational-Tech. Sch. Bd., 357 A.2d 721 (Pa. Commw. 1976). In recent years, a number of courts have entertained the question of agency fees. *See, e.g.*, Mitchell v. Los Angeles Unified Sch. Dist., 744 F. Supp. 938 (C.D. Cal. 1990); McCormick v. Labor Relations Comm'n, 588 N.E.2d 1 (Mass. 1992); Belhumeur v. Labor Relations Comm'n, 589 N.E.2d 352 (Mass. App. 1992); Ft. Wayne Educ. Ass'n, Inc. v. Aldrich, 585 N.E.2d 6 (Ind. App. 1992); and Lehnert v. Ferris Faculty Ass'n, 111 S. Ct. 1950 (1991), where the United States Supreme Court upheld *Abood, supra* note 73. This subject is treated by Charles J. Russo, William G. Gordon & Albert S. Miles, *Agency Shop Fees and the Supreme Court: Union Control and Academic Freedom*, 73 EDUC. LAW REP. 609 (June 4, 1992).

Collective bargaining agreements have authorized dues check-offs for the majority union and have on occasion allowed a similar means for collection of dues from minority unions, the intent being to prevent the majority union from imposing its will upon the minority. Some states have adopted the concept of agency shops or provisions for fair share payments, in which all employees covered by the collective bargaining agreement must help the majority union cover its expenses associated with the negotiations process. Some school districts will automatically deduct such amounts from all employees' pay; in other districts, other means for collection must be employed. In order to ensure that a checkoff serves only to defray fair share costs and not to increase membership, a Wisconsin court ruled that minority unions must be allowed dues check-offs as well.[75] In a more lenient stance, a decision from a Kansas court provided that the provisions of an exclusive bargaining agent's rights were not violated in allowing a dues check-off system for a minority union.[76]

A number of cases have involved the determination of how much of the union's dues were legitimately associated with fair share expenses. In Michigan, the portion of fees used for providing benefits that a nonmember could not avail himself from must be refunded.[77] Dues collected by the majority union in New York state must provide a means for refunding any portion of agency dues that support political activities, such as lobbying and campaign funds.[78] Religious prohibition to union membership does not free an employee from his obligation to pay agency dues. Under Oregon law, an equal amount could be donated to charity, but such religious convictions must be proven.[79] In Pennsylvania, a teacher

---

75. Milwaukee Fed'n of Teachers Local No. 252 v. Wisconsin Emp. Relations Bd., 266 N.W.2d 314 (Wis. 1978).

76. NEA-Wichita v. Unified Sch. Dist. 259, Wichita, 608 P.2d 1367 (Kan. App. 1980).

77. Garden City Sch. Dist. v. Garden City Educ. Ass'n, GERR 788:15 (MERC 1978).

78. N.Y. CIV. SERV. LAW § 208(3)(b).

79. Gorham v. Roseburg Educ. Ass'n, 592 P.2d 228 (Ore. 1979).

who refused to pay fair share dues could not be terminated, even though proscribed by an arbitrator.[80]

A New York court upheld a dues check-off system for teachers. This was in spite of an attempt by the state's Public Employment Relations Board to punish the union by revoking dues checkoff privileges.[81] This system provides for the employer to withhold dues from one's paycheck and forward them to the union.

§ 5.3. Impasse.

When the negotiating parties fail to come to an agreement, impasse results. When that situation occurs, several avenues are possible. One is the use of mediation. This involves a third party, a disinterested person, working with one or both sides in order to have someone modify a position in order to come to an agreement. A mediator cannot in and of himself impose a solution.

A second avenue is the use of a fact finder. This person conducts hearings and amasses evidence from both parties; he may collect data from others as well. At the conclusion of the hearing, the fact finder will file a report, with recommendations. Unlike a mediator, who tends to work discreetly, a fact finder helps to marshal public opinion in effecting an agreement.

Iowa permits the resolution of impasses by arbitration.[82] The arbitrator may select from final offers of both sides on an issue-by-issue basis. Thus, an arbitrator may not offer middle-of-the-road or compromise offers.

a. *Strikes.* Failure to reach an agreement through the parties to a contract, or by the intervention of a third party, can result in a strike. Although teachers' strikes are illegal in most states, a few states do allow them. In the first court opinion on this issue, the Supreme Court of Errors of Connecticut held that strikes were

---

80. Dauphin Cty. Tech. Sch. Educ. Ass'n v. Dauphin Cty. Area Vocational-Tech. Sch. Bd., 99 L.R.R.M. 3275 (Pa. 1978).

81. Buffalo Teachers' Fed'n v. Helsby, 435 F. Supp. 1098 (S.D.N.Y. 1977).

82. West Des Moines Educ. Ass'n v. Iowa Pub. Emp. Relations Bd., 266 N.W.2d 118 (Iowa 1978).

illegal, although it was legal for teachers to organize and bargain collectively over salaries and working conditions.[83] In some states where strikes are illegal, teachers have nonetheless struck.

In holding that a strike against government is illegal, the Supreme Court of Florida rejected the teachers' contention that their status constituted involuntary servitude.[84] Courts have also upheld the constitutionality of laws that specifically forbid strikes.[85]

The Supreme Court of the United States upheld the dismissal of teachers who engaged in an illegal strike.[86] Wisconsin law forbade teachers' strikes, but that did not deter teachers who struck in 1974 after negotiations had failed. After they had been reminded twice that their strike was illegal and had been invited to return to work but did not, the school board then voted to dismiss eighty-six teachers. The Court also dealt with other issues to be treated later in this chapter.

A New York court ruled that refusing to attend a back-to-school night constitutes a strike.[87] The teachers pointed out that this activity was not covered in the contract, but the court relied on the past practice of teachers' having attended these meetings, with two exceptions, for the previous seventeen years. Similarly, a New Jersey court ruled that teachers' resigning from sponsorship of extracurricular activities constituted an illegal strike.[88] The activities were not a part of the contract, and teachers refused to direct them. The court ruled that the school board could assign these activities without any extra compensation.

---

83. Norwalk Teachers' Ass'n v. Board of Educ., 138 Conn. 269, 83 A.2d 482 (1951).

84. Pinellas Cty. Classroom Teachers' Ass'n v. Board of Pub. Instruction, 214 So. 2d 34 (Fla. 1968).

85. City of New York v. DeLury, 23 N.Y.2d 175, 295 N.Y.S.2d 901, 243 N.E.2d 128 (1968).

86. Hortonville Joint Sch. Dist. No. 1 v. Hortonville Educ. Ass'n, 426 U.S. 482, 96 S. Ct. 2308, 49 L. Ed. 2d 1 (1976).

87. Bellmore-Merrick High Sch. Dist. v. Bellmore-Merrick United Secondary Teachers, Inc., 378 N.Y.S.2d 881 (N.Y. 1975).

88. Board of Educ. v. Asbury Park Educ. Ass'n, 145 N.J. Super. 495, 368 A.2d 396 (1976).

Although present at school and tending to other assigned duties, teachers boycotted a parent meeting which constituted a strike.[89] As long as services were performed, the actual preparation and discussion of a strike is in fact not a strike as ruled by an appeals court in Florida.[90]

States vary in the attitude toward strikes by public employees. Oregon permits strikes if public safety is not in danger, such as the case of firefighters and police. New York has its Taylor Law which provides for the loss of two days' pay for each day on strike.

In Pennsylvania, a decision was reached which would allow teachers to collect unemployment compensation for the extended summer vacation which resulted when the school board refused to open schools until a contract was signed.[91]

b. *Injunctions.* One tactic that a school board uses against a strike is an injunction. It is a court order that forbids an action, in this instance, a strike. It will be issued only after a school board has made a proper showing that the strike would result in grievous damage to the public. The Supreme Court of Michigan required, as a proper showing, evidence of "violence, irreparable injury, or breach of the peace."[92] The New Hampshire Supreme Court ruled that an injunction would not automatically be issued, even though it was contrary to state law for public employees to strike.[93]

In a Rhode Island case, the school district demonstrated irreparable harm to the school calendar by a strike. More specifically, it pointed out interference with student learning, inability to serve lunches to needy children, and a disadvantage to seniors entering

---

89. *In re* Suppa, 1977-78 PBC § 36,393 (N.Y.S. 1978).

90. Duval Cty. Sch. Bd. v. Florida Pub. Emp. Relations Comm'n, 363 So. 2d 30 (Fla. App. 1978).

91. Centennial Sch. Dist. v. Commonwealth Unemployment Comp. Bd. of Review, 424 A.2d 568 (Pa. Commw. 1981).

92. School Dist. v. Holland Educ. Ass'n, 380 Mich. 314, 157 N.W.2d 206 (1968).

93. Timberlane Reg'l Sch. Dist. v. Timberlane Reg'l Educ. Ass'n, 114 N.H. 245, 317 A.2d 555 (1974).

the labor market at a very late date.[94] Although a teachers' strike is a source of inconvenience, that alone is not sufficient ground to grant an injunction without allowing for the union's attorney to be present.[95]

c. *Sanctions.* A sanction is a device to punish, in some way, a party to a contract for having taken a position or engaged in some action which offended a second party. The sanction may be directed against a group or an individual. The intended effect is to get one's demands met or to punish one for what he did. This device was approved by the National Education Association in 1962. Its legality is not fully clear.

When a board of education attempted to dismiss a teacher solely for having engaged in union activity, the court held that this cannot be done.[96] Similarly, a teacher cannot be dismissed solely for being critical of the administration's posture in negotiating sessions.[97]

A New Jersey court ruled against teachers on a different matter. When a board of education decided not to rehire three nontenured teachers, one of them being the president of the local teachers' association, thirty-one of forty-seven teachers decided to resign, effective two weeks before the end of the school year. In supporting the teachers, the local and state associations imposed sanctions by sending notices to state members and to preparatory institutions within the state and in neighboring states. The state's supreme court held that the intended purpose of the resignations was to support the refusal of others to work. This action was as illegal as a strike.[98]

---

94. Menard v. Woonsocket Teachers' Guild, 363 A.2d 1349 (R.I. 1976).

95. Board of Educ., Community Unit Dist. No. 101 v. Parlor, 402 N.E.2d 388 (Ill. App. 1980).

96. McLaughlin v. Tilendis, 398 F.2d 287 (7th Cir. 1968); Muskego-Norway Consol. Schs. Joint Dist. No. 9 v. Wisconsin Emp. Relations Bd., 35 Wis. 2d 540, 151 N.W.2d 617 (1967).

97. Roberts v. Lake Cent. Sch. Corp., 317 F. Supp. 63 (N.D. Ind. 1970).

98. Board of Educ. v. New Jersey Educ. Ass'n, 53 N.J. 29, 247 A.2d 867 (1968).

d. *Picketing.* In chapter 8 *infra* it may be seen that, outside the classroom, teachers have very broad rights of free speech under the first amendment. Picketing is one form of speech, but it is not protected under the first amendment as a form of pure speech. While a teacher has a right to express himself or take a position on an issue, that right is not without limits. The exercise of that right becomes more critical when it is attached to a work stoppage.

Teachers were restrained from picketing which was designed solely to induce a breach of contract.[99] The Supreme Court of Illinois held that a court could issue a temporary injunction without notice and hearing when teachers were picketing and striking.[100] An Illinois appellate court ruled that a stop could be ordered to picketing only if it is proven that public interests would be harmed by the activity.[101] The first amendment protection of free speech was found not to apply to the picketing of the superintendent's home by striking teachers, according to the ruling of a Florida appellate court.[102]

e. *Penalties.* In spite of laws forbidding strikes, teachers have engaged in them in order to have their demands met. When a strike is settled and an agreement ratified, the parties often agree not to penalize the striking teachers. This action is viewed as a major move in "closing ranks" and proceeding with business. However, some school districts have sought and been successful in punishing teachers for striking. The punishment may take the form of dismissal, fines, or low ratings.

---

99. Board of Educ. v. Ohio Educ. Ass'n, 13 Ohio Misc. 308, 235 N.E.2d 538 (1967).

100. Board of Educ. v. Kankakee Fed'n of Teachers, 46 Ill. 2d 439, 264 N.E.2d 18 (1970), *cert. denied,* 403 U.S. 904 (1971).

101. Board of Educ., Danville Commun. Consol. Sch. Dist. No. 118 v. Danville Educ. Ass'n, 376 N.E.2d 430 (Ill. App. 1978).

102. Duval Cty. Sch. Bd. v. Florida Pub. Emp. Relations Comm'n, 363 So. 2d 30 (Fla. App. 1978).

A Kansas court upheld the right of the school district to dismiss striking teachers.[103] However, the leading case on this subject is *Hortonville District v. Hortonville Education Association,* decided by the Supreme Court of the United States in 1976.[104] The facts were previously stated in § 5.3.a. After the teachers' contracts had been terminated, three basic issues were before the High Court: bias of the school board as a hearing body, property and liberty interests of teachers, and due process in hearings. The Court held that the school board was not biased in serving as a hearing tribunal in conducting termination hearings. Although it was acknowledged that the board was familiar with the case, that fact was insufficient to disqualify it, for there had been no evidence that the board was incapable of judging the issue fairly. There had also been no evidence that the board had a personal or financial interest in the matter so as to create a conflict of interest nor was there evidence of personal animosity.

On the issue of property or liberty interests, the Court noted that the teachers had expected their jobs would remain open, and this constituted a property right.

On the third issue, due process, the Court used a balance test: the interest of the teachers in continued employment versus the interest of the school board in governmental and policy decisions. It held that the board's interest in considering alternative responses to the strike in serving the cause of education outweighed the teachers' interest in continued employment.

Some courts have upheld fines of teachers for striking. A New Jersey court held that fines as well as imprisonment were appropriate penalties for being in contempt of an anti-strike statute.[105] In 1977, a New York court upheld the imposition of fines on a teachers' union and its leaders who had defied a back-to-work order

---

103. Seamen Dist. Teachers Ass'n v. Board of Educ., 217 Kan. 233, 535 P.2d 889 (1975).

104. 426 U.S. 482, 96 S. Ct. 2308, 49 L. Ed. 2d 1 (1976).

105. *In re* Block, 50 N.J. 494, 236 A.2d 589 (1967).

during a strike.[106] A California court held that a school district can sue for monetary damages as a result of an illegal strike.[107]

The Pennsylvania Supreme Court held that formal letters of reprimand and unsatisfactory ratings for a semester constituted discipline within the meaning of the negotiated contract.[108]

§ 5.4. Arbitration.

Arbitration is a means of enforcing a contract when one grieves an action. It is a substitute for filing a court suit and is viewed as being quicker and less expensive than a law suit. It involves a third party conducting a hearing, gathering evidence, and issuing a ruling. The parties may voluntarily agree to accept the decision of the arbitrator as in advisory arbitration or agree, in advance, to accept the decision of the arbitrator as in compulsory arbitration.

Differences often exist over whether a grievance is arbitrable. The outcome often hinges on the language of the contract, and the presumption is usually in favor of a broad interpretation over the arbitrability of a dispute. Disputes over the arbitrability of grievances hinge mainly on teacher personnel problems: assignment, dismissal, and nonrenewal.

Courts are not in full agreement as to the scope of an arbitrator's authority in ruling on cases of teacher dismissal and whether an arbitrator can order reinstatement. A Maine court held that the state statutes forbade grievance arbitration on teacher dismissal and nonrenewal.[109] This ruling preceded action by the legislature which provided that just cause for permanent teachers could be negotiated by school boards.

---

106. Board of Educ. v. Lakeland Fed'n of Teachers, 399 N.Y.S.2d 61 (A.D. 1977).

107. Pasadena Unified Sch. Dist. v. Pasadena Fed'n of Teachers, 140 Cal. Rptr. 41 (Cal. App. 1977).

108. Lewisburg Area Educ. Ass'n v. Board of Sch. Dist., 376 A.2d 933 (Pa. 1977).

109. Superintending Sch. Comm. v. Winslow Educ. Ass'n, 363 A.2d 229 (Me. 1976).

Teachers in Newark, New Jersey, made a better case for arbitration when they alleged that their non-reemployment did not comply with procedural rights guaranteed under the contract. The court agreed and held that this matter was mandatorily arbitrable.[110] A Pennsylvania court held that a teacher could not be discharged for nonpayment of union dues, but that the dispute was a proper subject for an arbitration hearing.[111] A Vermont court held that an arbitrator exceeded his authority in ordering the reappointment of a teacher. The school board had not participated in the arbitration, and it was not bound to do so.[112]

A New Jersey court held that the statutory power to reduce personnel resides with a board of education, not an arbitrator. A nontenured teacher has no right to employment, and the decision not to renew is a discretionary one for the board. Thus, that issue is not subject to arbitration.[113]

For failure to appoint a local candidate as a principal despite a clause in the contract which favored local candidates if their qualifications were equal to nonlocal candidates, a school board did not have to submit its decision to arbitration.[114] Another court reversed an arbitrator's decision that had reassigned a teacher on the basis of degree requirements. The court held that, under the contract, it was intended that a master's equivalency be the same as a master's degree.[115]

Courts have also been asked to review decisions of arbitrators with respect to sabbatical leaves. The Connecticut Supreme Court upheld an arbitrator who supported a guidance counselor's claim

---

110. Newark Teachers v. Board of Educ., 373 A.2d 1020 (N.J. Super. 1977).

111. Appeal of Jones, 375 A.2d 1341 (Pa. Commw. 1977).

112. Fairchild v. West Rutland Sch. Dist., 376 A.2d 28 (Vt. 1977).

113. Board of Educ. v. Englewood Teachers Ass'n, 375 A.2d 669 (N.J. A.D. 1977).

114. Berkshire Hills Reg'l Sch. Dist. v. Gray, 369 N.E.2d 736 (Mass. App. 1977).

115. Matter of Lewisburg Area Educ. Ass'n, 371 A.2d 568 (Pa. Commw. 1977).

to a sabbatical leave.[116] In contrast, a Pennsylvania court over-turned an arbitrator's decision that had granted a teacher full salary for a half year's sabbatical leave.[117] When a school district had agreed to a broad binding arbitration provision in a negotiated contract, it could not set aside an arbitrator's ruling on a sabbatical leave, in charging that he had exceeded his powers.[118]

A Massachusetts court held that an arbitrator can fashion remedies regarding tenure, but he cannot grant it. The authority for granting tenure belongs exclusively to the school board.[119]

A collective bargaining agreement is like other contracts in that if the two parties disagree on some aspect of the agreement or one side fails to perform, the resolution of the conflict rests with the courts. Litigation has a number of drawbacks, including costs and time consumption for what often are minor issues. To avoid these disadvantages, grievance and arbitration provisions are contained in some contracts.

Most states follow the private sector in allowing, if not encouraging, the practice. Minnesota will not permit the courts to hear contract disputes until the grievance procedure has been exhausted.[120] Exceptions are made when it appears that the school district and union worked together to harm an individual teacher. New York, however, discourages public employee arbitration unless a two-pronged test can be met. First, the subject in question must be negotiable and, second, there must exist a grievance clause in the contract that covers the disputed matter. This test is called the Liverpool Rule.[121]

---

116. Board of Educ. v. Bridgeport Educ. Ass'n, 377 A.2d 323 (Conn. 1977).

117. Allegheny Valley Sch. Dist. v. Allegheny Valley Educ. Ass'n, 360 A.2d 762 (Pa. Commw. 1976).

118. Rochester City Sch. Dist. v. Rochester Teachers' Ass'n, 394 N.Y.S.2d 179 (A.D. 1977).

119. School Comm. of Danvers v. Tyman, 360 N.E.2d 877 (Mass. 1977).

120. Ellerbrock v. Board of Educ., Special Sch. Dist. No. 6, 269 N.W.2d 858 (Minn. 1978).

121. Acting Superintendent of Sch. of Liverpool Cent. Sch. Dist. v. United Liverpool Faculty Ass'n, 399 N.Y.S.2d 189 (N.Y. 1977).

Three 1992 court opinions treated three different subjects of arbitrability. They included the subject of changing a student's grade,[122] which was not allowed; the transfer of a teacher,[123] also not subject to arbitration; and awarding a teacher extra salary for teaching an extra class period,[124] which was allowable.

§ 5.5. Summary.

The law of collective negotiations hinges mainly on state statutes. This condition makes one cautious in arriving at global conclusions. Furthermore, judges have handed down what seem to be conflicting opinions involving the same or similar questions. However, their holdings have been based on an interpretation of law as it applies to a local school district contract or existing state statutes. Thus, these decisions have often been resolutions of very specific and narrowly defined issues.

The degree to which states and local school districts engage in bargaining varies greatly, ranging from no bargaining in some states to highly sophisticated unionization in others. Where bargaining is allowed, the issues subject to the negotiations process range from mandatory to permissive or prohibitive bargaining.

The Supreme Court of the United States has issued three specific rulings on negotiations in public education. It has protected teachers in exercising freedom of speech at a school board meeting, upheld the right of school boards to dismiss teachers who engage in an illegal strike, ruled that a school board can serve as an impartial tribunal in dismissing striking teachers, and held that nonunion members can be required to pay dues to cover union expenses so long as they are not routed for political purposes.

---

122. Pawtucket Sch. Comm. v. Pawtucket Teachers' Alliance, 610 A.2d 1104 (RI. 1992).

123. Board of Educ. of the Greenburgh Cent. Sch. Dist. No. 7 v. Greenburgh Teachers' Fed'n, 586 N.Y.S.2d 11 (A.D. 1992).

124. Williston Educ. Ass'n v. Williston Pub. Sch. Dist. No. 1, 483 N.W.2d 567 (N.D. 1992).

Courts have emphasized that school boards retain their authority when engaged in the bargaining process. However, decisions have made it clear that this authority is now shared with unions. Although a board has the responsibility for making policy, it must consult with a union on a variety of matters; in effect, the teachers' union does help to shape educational policy.

Chapter Six

FINANCE

§ 6.0. Introduction.

As creatures of state and local government, public schools are almost completely funded by tax dollars. Prior to the 1970s, the lion's share of money used to support public school systems came from local sources. Throughout the early history of public education in this nation, the local property tax was the major producer of public school funding. In recent years, while the federal government's share has remained small, the use of state revenues for public school funding has increased. However, the local property tax remains the backbone of public school finance.

Suffice it to say, reliance on local property tax revenues is not without problems. This "property tax dependence" has caused a certain unevenness of development throughout state educational systems, visible not only when comparing one state to another, but, even more so, when comparing one public school system to another within the same state. As the results of the National Education Finance Project (NEFP) revealed more than two decades ago, "[t]he fundamental result of heavy reliance on property taxes to

153

support public schools is that the quality of a child's education is largely determined by the wealth of the school district in which he lives."[1] This condition still exists today, and has become a major source of litigation.

To understand the problems of contemporary public school finance, one must first examine some fundamentals of school district fiscal management. A discussion of the legal prerogatives and restraints placed upon local school officials for managing the fiscal affairs of their local school districts (or divisions) is of paramount importance.

§ 6.1. Local Boards and the Power to Tax.

As stated in other sections of this book, local boards of education possess no inherent authority. They possess only authority and powers either expressly granted or implied by statute. The power to tax for school purposes is no exception to the rule.

According to *American Jurisprudence,* "school districts have no inherent power of taxation, and may exercise such power only under a valid delegation by the legislature."[2] Only a state legislature can "make a school district a taxing [entity] and delegate to the board of that district power to levy and collect a tax the object of which is the raising of a fund for school purposes."[3] Generally, the state code creates an enforcement mechanism for the collection of school taxes and empowers some agency and/or official to col-

---

1. FUTURES IN SCHOOL FINANCE (K.F. Jordan & K. Alexander eds., Bloomington, Ind.: Phi Delta Kappa, 1975). Statistics show that of the typical education dollar in revenue made available for public education expenditures in this nation during the 1991-1992 fiscal year, 47 cents came from local funds, 46 cents from state funds, and 7 cents from the federal government. National Center for Educational Statistics (Washington, D.C.; U.S.D.O.E., O.E.R.I., April, 1994).

2. 68 AMERICAN JURISPRUDENCE 2d 428 (Rochester: The Lawyer's Co-Operative Publishing Co. 1973). For a typical case demonstrating the judicial attitude that state legislatures have broad powers under the state constitution to fashion the necessary means for funding public education, see Richland Cty. v. Campbell, 364 S.E.2d 470 (S.C. 1988).

3. AMERICAN JURISPRUDENCE 2d 429.

lect from every person named on the school tax roll the sum owed in school taxes.[4]

The statutes of each state are different regarding the power of local school boards to raise and collect taxes for schools. Thus, in some states local school boards are "fiscally independent," while in other states they are "fiscally dependent." Independent school districts outnumber dependent ones.

a. *Fiscally Independent School Boards.* Fiscally independent school boards are granted legal authority by the state legislature to set the *ad valorem* tax rate on real property (not personal and intangible property) and to collect taxes for support and maintenance of the local schools. In the State of Florida, for example, local school authorities levy and collect taxes for school purposes. Local school boards need not depend on the local county or city governments for their source of local school tax revenues.[5] Likewise, in Georgia and Missouri, state law grants local public school boards authority to tax property for the support and maintenance of schools.[6]

Where school taxes are assessed and collected in violation of the constitutional authority granted to a school district, or are in some other way deemed void, taxpayers are not without remedy. Generally, remedy is available in state court to recover all money paid.[7]

---

4. *See, e.g.,* Marine Midland Bank v. Greenblatt, 465 N.Y.S.2d 587 (A.D. 1983).

5. *See, e.g.,* Gulesian v. Dade County Sch. Bd., 281 So. 2d 325 (Fla. 1973). It should be pointed out, however, that Florida state law sets a legal limit on the tax rates that can be set by local school boards.

6. *See, e.g.,* Board of Comm'rs of Newton Cty. v. Alligood, 214 S.E.2d 522 (Ga. 1975); Enright v. Kansas City, 536 S.W.2d 17 (Mo. 1976).

7. *See, e.g.,* Niagara Mohawk Power Corp. v. City Sch. Dist., 464 N.Y.S.2d 449 (A.D. 1983). For an example of a taxpayer group challenge to local school board taxing power, see Forward v. Webster Central, 526 N.Y.S.2d 870 (A.D. 1988). In North State Dev. Co. v. Pittsburgh Unified Sch. Dist., 270 Cal. Rptr. 166 (Cal. App. 1990), a public school district's levying of a "special tax" on new construction was challenged by a developer.

b. *Fiscally Dependent School Boards.* *Corpus Juris Secundum* tells us that state statutes in some jurisdictions provide "for the apportionment of school taxes to different political subdivisions possessing territory in the school district."[8] The governing board of that political subdivision, and not the local school board *(e.g., city council or county supervisors)*, "has the duty to apportion school taxes as may be designated by the statute."[9]

In the Commonwealth of Virginia, local school boards, by law, cannot levy or collect taxes for school purposes. The local county or municipal governmental agency is the tax levying authority. Local school boards also must go to their local governmental body for appropriations and budget approval.[10]

Another example of fiscal dependence can be found in a Pennsylvania court decision. According to the Pennsylvania Commonwealth Court, in that state, the power to assess or reduce assessment on property within a school district belongs to the city tax assessor and not to the local school board.[11]

Generally, state statutes require that bond issues be submitted to popular referendum. In some states, taxes for school purposes may not be raised without first receiving approval by popular vote of the community.[12] However, there have been exceptions to this pro-

---

8. 79 CORPUS JURIS SECUNDUM 183 (Brooklyn: The American Lawbook Co., 1952).

9. *Id.*

10. VA. CODE § 22.1-93 et seq. *See also* Bradley v. School Bd., 462 F.2d 1058 (4th Cir.), *motion to advance and for pendente lite relief denied,* 409 U.S. 910 (1972).

11. Leopard Indus., Inc. v. Toanone, 310 A.2d 440 (Pa. 1973). For a case in which a religious corporation (organized and existing under the laws of New York State) commenced an action to accomplish a cancellation (as a tax exempt religious organization) of the tax assessment and all local municipal taxes levied on it by the local central school district and the local governmental unit, see D'Betlan v. Town of Shandaken, 473 N.Y.S.2d 71 (App. Div. 1984).

12. Voter resistance to increases in property taxes (for school purposes) has been experienced in several states. *See also* Street v. Maries City Sch. Dist., 511 S.W.2d 814 (Mo. 1974); State *ex rel.* Daoust v. Smith, 371 N.E.2d 536 (Ohio 1977).

cedure. For example, the New Jersey Commissioner of Education certified a local school board's raising of additional school funds by taxation, when the local board found it necessary to do so because of voter reluctance to approve funds for necessary school expenditures.[13]

§ 6.2. Indebtedness and Expenditure of Funds.

Generally, state legislatures, within constitutional limitations, delegate legal authority to local school boards to incur indebtedness and to expend funds solely for the conduct and maintenance of the public schools.[14] All indebtedness and expenditures of local school boards, to be judged proper, must be made in accordance with state constitutional and statutory mandates,[15] and must be a part of an approved budget. "After the budget has once been approved by the designated reviewing body, the board of education is free to transfer amounts from one item to the other as they see fit, providing the total amount approved is not exceeded."[16] Consistently, courts of law have held that a local school board is legally bound by the funding provided and approved by the local governmental agency.[17]

---

13. *In re* Upper Freehold Reg'l Bd. of Educ., Decision of N.J. Comm. of Educ. (1978).

14. 79 C.J.S. 7 (1952). *See, e.g.,* Buse v. Smith, 247 N.W.2d 141 (Wis. 1976).

15. Northampton Area Bd. of Educ. v. Zehner, 360 A.2d 793 (Pa. 1976).

16. E.C. BOLMEIER, SCHOOL IN THE LEGAL STRUCTURE 185 (2d ed. Cincinnati, Ohio: The W.H. Anderson Co., 1973). *See, e.g.,* De Nunzio v. Board of Educ., 396 N.Y.S.2d 236 (N.Y. 1977), wherein parents challenged budgetary cuts in educational services for handicapped children.

17. *See, e.g.,* Smith Cty. Educ. Ass'n v. Anderson, 676 S.W.2d 328 (Tenn. 1984). More recently, in North Middlesex Reg'l Sch. Dist. v. Town of Townsend, 588 N.E.2d 1372 (Mass. App. 1992), a Massachusetts court held that a local school committee (school board) could submit a reduced budget to the town government even after an original budget had been submitted when the town government had not yet voted on the original budget. The Supreme Court of Missouri held that funds received from the federal government are subject to the dictates of federal law and are not considered state revenues. *See* Committee for Educ. Equity v. State, 967 S.W.2d 62 (Mo. 1998).

The administration of a school district's approved annual budget and the day-to-day fiscal management of school district matters are legal duties of local school boards. Furthermore, it is the legal prerogative of a local school board to exercise a degree of discretion it deems necessary in the performance of these duties.[18]

Local school boards are legally accountable for all debts incurred and for all funds expended during the duration of an approved budget. For example, a California appellate court held that, by state statute, taxpayers have standing to sue local school districts for "waste" of funds.[19]

An interesting case involving a school board's use of public monies was decided by an Arizona court. In *Wistuber v. Paradise Valley Unified School District,* taxpayers challenged a contractual arrangement between the school district and the teachers' association wherein the district paid the association's president to carry out certain duties as director of employee relations. To the challenging taxpayers, such a financial arrangement violated the state's constitutional prohibition of gifts or donations of public monies to a private association. In ruling against the taxpayers, the Arizona court declared that no such violation existed, since the duties performed by the president were not disproportionate to the consideration paid by the board.[20]

---

18. Weary v. Board of Educ., 360 N.E.2d 1112 (Ill. 1977). *See also* Banks v. County of Buncombe, 494 S.E.2d 791 (N.C. App. 1998).

19. Los Altos Property Owners Ass'n v. Hutcheon, 137 Cal. Rptr. 775 (Cal. 1977). *See also* Bethlehem Steel Corp. v. Board of Educ., 397 N.Y.S.2d 882 (N.Y. 1977), wherein taxpayers challenged a school board's adopted budget as exceeding the board's authority. When examining issues of expenditure, it is vital to legally define the term "cost." In Durant v. Department of Educ., 513 N.W.2d 195 (Mich. App. 1994), the court defined cost as the amount actually spent, unless established otherwise. In Virginia, as a part of the budgetary process, school boards must give notice to parents and guardians for the estimated average per pupil cost for the coming school year. VA. CODE § 22.1-92.

20. Wistuber v. Paradise Valley Unified Sch. Dist., 687 P.2d 354 (Ariz. 1984).

§ 6.3. School Property.

Generally, tax dollars pay for school property. School sites are acquired, school buildings are erected, and school supplies and equipment are purchased with funds raised through taxation. And, even though some federal funding and state funding are made available for such matters, most of these tax dollars are raised locally.

Some experts in school law adhere to the notion that all public school property is state property, regardless of the source of its funding. Since public education is legally a state function, they argue, school property is state property, to do with as the state sees fit. Others argue, however, that local school districts usually depend on local tax sources for support of new property. Therefore, school property is local property. Whether one attitude is more accurate than the other can only be determined by a careful examination of the school code of each state.

Typically, determining whether or not new school buildings are needed, whether or not existing school buildings are to be renovated, closed, or demolished, where new school buildings are to be located, and matters of supply and equipment are all decisions granted by state statute to local school boards. State law and budgetary constraints will determine the funding and the financial methods and procedures that must be adhered to by the local boards.

As Hazard said more than twenty years ago, "Funds for capital expenditures for major school plant improvement and new construction generally come from the sale of bonds."[21] And, his statement of the rule governing authority to sell bonds remains the same: authority for a local board of education to sell bonds is not implied; it must be granted by state law, and it usually requires approval by popular vote of school district residents.[22]

---

21. HAZARD, EDUCATION AND THE LAW 485 (2d ed. New York, N.Y.: The Free Press, 1978).

22. *Id.* at 485-86. *See, e.g.,* Butsche v. Coon Rapids Community Sch. Dist., 255 N.W.2d 337 (Iowa 1977); Nance v. Williams, 564 S.W.2d 212 (Ark. 1978); Cuka v. School Bd., 264 N.W.2d 924 (S.D. 1978). For a taxpayers' suit chal-

§ 6.4. Uses of School Buildings and Grounds.

Absent state law to the contrary, decisions on matters of use of school buildings and grounds are usually the local school board's to make.

As a general rule, state law grants legal authority to local school boards and their agents (for example, school principals) to prohibit the trespass upon school grounds (including all facilities) of any individual who is not a student, officer or employee, or who otherwise has no authorization to be there. A Florida court ruled that students themselves were not exempt from that state's trespass statute, when a student enrolled in one school of a particular public school system enters and remains, without permission, in another school building in which he is not enrolled.[23]

In Virginia, for example, a local school board, or the division superintendent where board policy permits, must approve the use of school buildings and grounds. And, it is the legal prerogative of the local board, or its agent, to adopt all reasonable rules and regulations necessary to protect school property when in use.[24]

According to Virginia law, local school boards may permit use of school property under their control "as will not impair the efficiency of the schools."[25] Further, local boards, by policy of the

---

lenging a state statute requiring electoral approval of certain types of bond issues and school district debt limits, see Mellinger v. Department of Comm. Affairs, 533 A.2d 1119 (Pa. Commw. 1987).

23. State v. E.N., 455 So. 2d 636 (Fla. App. 1984). In Virginia, trespass on school property during daytime is a class 1 misdemeanor. VA. CODE § 18.2-128.

24. VA. CODE § 22.1-131. Where a local board of education determines that certain property is surplus and is no longer needed for school purposes, state law will usually govern what that local board can or cannot do with the proceeds from the sale of that property. *See, e.g.,* Moore v. Wykle, 419 S.E.2d 164 (N.C. App. 1992).

25. VA. CODE § 22.1-131. In the 1990s the use of school buildings by student religious clubs caused litigation. Important cases on this issue will be discussed in a subsequent chapter of this book. *See, e.g.,* Board of Educ. of Westside Community Schs. v. Mergens, 110 S. Ct. 2356 (1990). For a case involving another type of group's request to use public school facilities opened for use by the public, see

board, may impose specific conditions for said usage. This includes use of property during school hours, after school hours, on
weekends, and during official school vacation periods.[26]

§ 6.5. Challenges to State Finance Schemes.

In the late 1960s, litigation began to appear attacking state public school financing systems.[27] The school finance cases came from
the courts in two distinct waves. One wave has been referred to as
McInnis-type cases (largely unsuccessful), while wave two became
known as the *Serrano*-type cases (largely successful).[28] Petitioners
in these actions presented similar claims saying that state educational finance schemes, based upon property-tax revenues, discriminated unfairly between classes of children, conditioning their
free access to equal educational opportunity by "accident of their
birth."

a. *McInnis-type Cases.* In 1968, a class action suit was brought
on behalf of parents and public elementary and secondary school
students in four school districts located in Cook County, Illinois.

Knights of the Ku Klux Klan v. Martin Luther King, Jr. Worshippers, 735 F.
Supp. 745 (M.D. Tenn. 1990).

26. *Id. See also* the discussion of Piele & Forsberg, *Uses of School Property,*
in THE YEARBOOK OF SCHOOL LAW 77-78 (Topeka, Kansas: NOLPE 1975). For an
excellent decision from the United States Supreme Court involving issues of local
school board control over use of school property after hours and on weekends,
and denying a local church access to school premises, see Lamb's Chapel v.
Center Moriches Union Free Sch. Dist., 113 S. Ct. 2141 (1993). *See also* Fairfax
Covenant Church v. Fairfax Cty. Sch. Bd., 811 F. Supp. 1137 (E.D. Va. 1993),
aff'd in part, rev'd in part and remanded, 17 F.3d 703 (4th Cir. 1994); Good
News/Good Sports Club v. School Dist. of City of Ladue, 859 F. Supp. 1239
(E.D. Mo. 1993), *rev'd and remanded,* 28 F.3d 1501(8th Cir. 1994), *cert. denied,*
115 S. Ct. 1240 (1995).

27. Portions of this section of the chapter are taken directly from R.S. Vacca,
The Courts and School Finance: A Reexamination, in FUTURES IN SCHOOL
FINANCE: WORKING TOWARD A COMMON GOAL 119-34 (K.F. Jordan & K. Alexan-
der eds. Bloomington, Ind.: Phi Delta Kappa, 1975).

28. J.D. Lucas, *Serrano and Rodriguez — An Overextension of Equal Protection,* 2 NOLPE SCHOOL L.J. 18-20 (1972).

Plaintiffs in the case, *McInnis v. Shapiro,*[29] claimed that the Illinois system of public school finance violated their equal protection guarantees under the fourteenth amendment. Additionally, they claimed that state statutes permitted a wide variation of expenditures per student among Illinois public school divisions. A permanent injunction was sought forbidding further distribution of tax funds in reliance on state statutes.

A three-judge United States District Court, upon hearing plaintiffs' allegations, ruled against them. The district court reached its conclusion based upon three points. First, in their opinion, the fourteenth amendment did not require that public school expenditures be made solely on the basis of "educational need." Second, "educational expenses" were not the "exclusive yardstick" for measuring the quality of a child's educational opportunity. Finally, the *McInnis* court added a further dimension to its opinion, namely, that the case presented no "judicially manageable standards" by which a federal court could determine if and when the equal protection clause is satisfied or violated.

Since the Illinois finance scheme was found to show an absence of any form of invidious discrimination, the suit was dismissed for no cause of action. In the district court's opinion, "the General Assembly's delegation of authority to school districts appears designed to allow individual localities to determine their own tax burden according to the importance which they place upon public schools." The inequity of funds between school districts, said the court, is "an inevitable consequence of decentralization."[30]

That same year, a similar action was heard by a three-judge United States District Court in Virginia. *Burruss v. Wilkerson* involved a challenge brought by parents in Bath County, Virginia, who claimed that because of the Virginia system of public school finance, their children were being denied educational opportunities

---

29. 293 F. Supp. 327 (N.D. Ill. 1968), *aff 'd mem. sub nom.* McInnis v. Ogilvie, 394 U.S. 322 (1969).

30. *Id.*

equal to those enjoyed by children attending public schools in other districts of the state.

The district court dismissed the plaintiffs' action, convinced that the deficiencies and disparities existing between public school districts in Virginia were not the results of purposeful discrimination by the state. The blame, said the court, "is ascribable solely to the absence of taxable values sufficient to produce required moneys."[31]

In both *McInnis* and *Burruss,* the courts were willing to leave it to the respective state legislatures to remedy the existing inequities. Thus, as the nation entered the decade of the 1970s, state educational finance systems remained intact as subsequent courts consistently adhered to the *McInnis* precedent.[32]

b. *Serrano-type Cases.* A new judicial attitude toward problems of school finance had its roots in a matter heard on appeal by the Supreme Court of California. In *Serrano v. Priest,* plaintiff parents and their children sought to enjoin the State of California and Los Angeles County school officials from carrying out and implementing what plaintiffs claimed was an unconstitutional school finance system.[33] Because the California school finance scheme, they argued, relied heavily on local property taxes, it caused substantial disparities in per pupil revenues available to individual school districts. Such a system was not fiscally neutral because it discriminated against poor school districts, and, ultimately, the children enrolled in those districts.[34]

---

31. 301 F. Supp. 1237 (W.D. Va. 1968), 310 F. Supp. 572 (W.D. Va. 1969), *aff'd mem.,* 397 U.S. 44 (1970).

32. *See, e.g.,* Hargrave v. Kirk, 313 F. Supp. 944 (M.D. Fla. 1970), *judgment vacated sub nom.* Askew v. Hargrave, 401 U.S. 476 (1971).

33. 96 Cal. Rptr. 601, 487 P.2d 1241 (Cal. 1971), *aff'd,* 135 Cal. Rptr. 345 (Cal. 1977). For a later decision, see Serrano v. Priest, 226 Cal. Rptr. 584 (Cal. App. 1986), where the California court discusses standards to apply in measuring or assessing educational quality.

34. *Id.* For a case involving a challenge to a state's finance system based on *ad valorem* taxes levied on real and personal property, and the resulting disparities between individual public school districts, see Fair Sch. Fin. Council, Inc. v. State, 746 P.2d 1135 (Okla. 1987).

In remanding the case for trial, the California Supreme Court opined that the California finance scheme made "the quality of a child's education a function of the wealth of his parents and neighbors."[35] Additionally, the high court found that even state grants to local school districts actually helped to widen the financial gap between poor and affluent school districts.[36]

Six weeks after *Serrano,* a United States District Court in Minnesota held, in *Van Dusartz v. Hatfield,* that the Minnesota system of public school finance (which made spending per pupil a function of school district wealth) violated the equal protection guarantee of the fourteenth amendment.[37] In reaching its decision, the district court held, as would subsequent courts in other states, that students in public elementary and secondary schools enjoy a right to have the level of spending for their education unaffected by variations in the taxable wealth of their school district or their parents.[38]

The *Van Dusartz* court did not require absolute uniformity of school expenditures. Rather, the court looked to the state legislature to remedy the situation. It encouraged the state "to adopt one of many optional financing schemes which do not violate the equal protection clause."[39]

c. San Antonio v. Rodriguez. The two-year period between 1971 and 1973 saw major changes take place in several states as legislatures and state boards worked to revise their public school finance schemes. In 1973, the United States Supreme Court, by a vote of five to four, brought an end to the *Serrano*-type attitude that depicted public education as a fundamental interest protected by the United States Constitution. *San Antonio Independent School District v. Rodriguez*[40] marked a return to a judicial standpoint that

---

35. *Id.* at 1244.

36. *Id.* at 1248.

37. 334 F. Supp. 870 (D. Minn. 1971).

38. *Id.* at 872.

39. *Id.* at 877.

40. 411 U.S. 1, 93 S. Ct. 1278, 36 L. Ed. 2d 16 (1973), *rev'g* 337 F. Supp. 280 (W.D. Tex. 1973).

public education is basically a responsibility of states and not
directly a federal matter.

Rodriguez was originally decided by a three-judge United States
District Court in Texas. The district court held for the plaintiffs,
finding the State of Texas public school finance scheme (which
relied heavily on the local property tax) unconstitutional. The
district court did not require that Texas spend equal amounts of
money on every child. What the court did advocate, however, was
that Texas establish an educational finance structure built upon
"fiscal neutrality" and not a structure where access to educational
opportunity was conditioned by local wealth.[41]

The State of Texas appealed the decision to the United States
Supreme Court, where the district court was reversed. Mr. Justice
Powell voiced the majority opinion for the High Court, which
rejected appellees' rationale on two vital points.

First, since appellees were unable to describe specifically the
class of "poor" who were being discriminated against, it must be
concluded "that the Texas system does not operate to the peculiar
disadvantage of any suspect class."[42] Justice Powell then pointed
out that the Supreme Court has never held that "wealth discrimination alone provides an adequate basis for invoking strict scrutiny . . . ."[43]

Second, the importance of public education (a service provided
by the state) does not in and of itself "determine whether it must be
regarded as fundamental for purposes of examination under the
Equal Protection Clause."[44] Further, stated Justice Powell, education "is not among the rights afforded explicit protection under our
Federal Constitution. Nor do we find any basis for saying it is
implicitly so protected."[45]

Mr. Justice Powell concluded the majority opinion by making
specific reference to the financial disparities existing among vari-

---

41. 337 F. Supp. 280 (W.D. Tex.), *rev'd,* 411 U.S. 1 (1973).

42. *Rodriguez, supra* note 40, at 93 S. Ct. 1278.

43. *Id.*

44. *Id.* at 1295.

45. *Id.* at 1297.

ous Texas public school districts. The solution to such problems, however, "must come from the lawmakers and from the democratic pressures of those who elect them."[46]

d. *Post-Rodriguez and School Finance*. In the months following *Rodriguez,* cases were decided by state appellate courts revealing a judicial trend of future litigation concerning public school finance. One such decision was handed down by the Supreme Court of New Jersey.

In *Robinson v. Cahill,*[47] the Supreme Court of New Jersey upheld a superior court ruling that New Jersey's system of financing its public elementary and secondary schools (at that time) was unconstitutional. In rendering its decision, the superior court said that the state's finance system discriminated against pupils in districts with low real property wealth, and it discriminated against taxpayers by imposing unequal burdens for a common state purpose.[48]

The New Jersey Supreme Court, Chief Judge Weintraub writing for a unanimous court, agreed with the lower court's final determination. New Jersey's educational finance system, said the high court, which relied heavily on local taxation and which led to great disparities in dollar input per pupil, had no relation to that state's own constitutional mandate to furnish "a thorough and efficient system of public schools."[49] The New Jersey Supreme Court ordered that the state legislature immediately devise a new financial scheme for public education in that state.

Milliken v. Green is a similar case from the Michigan Supreme Court. In *Milliken,* the court held that that state's system of school finance (consisting of local, general, and *ad valorem* property taxes and school aid appropriations), relied on the wealth of local school districts. That reliance resulted in substantial inequality of maintenance and support of public elementary and secondary

---

46. *Id.* at 1348.

47. 119 N.J. Super. 40, 303 A.2d 273 (1973).

48. 289 A.2d 569 (N.J. 1973).

49. *Robinson, supra* note 47, at 303 A.2d 273.

schools, denying equal protection of the laws as guaranteed by the Michigan Constitution.[50] Said the court, there is "an inherent inequality in the school district property tax bases which creates unequal support for the education of Michigan children."[51]

The Michigan Supreme Court did not require absolute equality in the distribution of state educational resources to each child in public school. No court has yet demanded that.

In December 1977, the Court of Common Pleas of Hamilton County, Ohio found that state's system of school finance in violation of the Ohio Constitution. To that court, among other things, the system which the legislature established for the financing of public elementary and secondary schools created invidious classifications among school children in violation of the equal protection clause of the Ohio Constitution.[52]

Horton v. Meskill is a 1977 decision by the Supreme Court of Connecticut. *Horton* involved an appeal of a superior court judgment declaring the Connecticut system of financing public elementary and secondary schools (in effect in 1974) violative of the state constitution, but not the Federal Constitution.[53]

The Supreme Court of Connecticut relied heavily upon *Robinson* and held, among other things, that in Connecticut the right to education is so basic and fundamental that any infringement of that right must be "strictly scrutinized." Further, stated the court, public school students in that state are entitled to equal enjoyment of the right to elementary and secondary education, and any system of financing that education which depends "primarily on a local property tax base without regard to the disparity in the financial ability . . . to finance an educational program and with no significant equalizing state support," cannot pass "strict judicial scru-

---

50. 389 Mich. 1, 203 N.W.2d 457 (1972), *amended*, Michigan Supreme Court No. 53809 (Dec. 14, 1973).

51. *Id.* at 462-63.

52. Brinkman v. Gilligan, No. C-3-75-304 (S.D. Ohio 1977).

53. 172 Conn. 615, 376 A.2d 359 (1977).

tiny." The state legislature, said the high court, is the proper body to fashion a constitutional system of educational finance.[54]

The phrase "public education is a fundamental entitlement of all children of school age" must not be interpreted generally. Thus courts will not automatically utilize the "strict scrutiny test." *Hernandez v. Houston Independent School District*[55] offers an example of a recent case wherein the interpretation of this phrase is crucial.

Appellants in *Hernandez* were several children who lived within the Houston Independent School District who, admittedly, were citizens of Mexico and who lacked any proof to support the legality of their presence in the United States. As the basis of their suit they argued that the school system's enforcement of § 21.031 of the Texas Education Code (1975), which provided for a tuition-free public education for children who are either citizens of the United States or "legally admitted aliens," constituted a violation of the due process clause and equal protection clause of the United States Constitution and the Constitution of the State of Texas.[56] As their relief appellants sought and were denied at trial, among other things, an order requiring the school district to admit *all* children between the ages of five and eighteen (who resided with a parent or guardian within the school district) and to provide them with a tuition-free education.

In affirming the lower court's decision, the Court of Civil Appeals of Texas relied on *Rodriguez* and said that a "tuition-free education is not a 'fundamental right' guaranteed by the constitution of the United States."[57] Therefore, § 21.031 of the Texas Education Code was not to be subjected to "strict judicial scrutiny." The statute in question, said the court, does bear a rational

---

54. *Id.* at 376 A.2d 374-76.

55. 558 S.W.2d 121 (Tex. 1977). For an excellent commentary discussing the importance of courts analyzing the language of a specific state's education clause, see William C. Thro, *The Role of Language of the State Education Clauses in School Finance Litigation*, 79 EDUC. LAW REP. 19 (Feb. 11, 1993).

56. *Id.* at 122-23.

57. *Id.* at 124.

relationship to a legitimate state purpose. Moreover, a "child should have no greater rights to a free education, due to his unlawful presence, than those rights he would have had if he had not come to this country."[58]

Finally, the Texas court declared that the legislature, not the judiciary, was the proper body to fashion the system of public school finance and management. And, within the limits of reason, the legislature's efforts to solve the complexity of problems should be respected.[59]

    e. *Finance Litigation in the Late-1980s and into the 1990s.* As education law moved through the 1980s and into the 1990s, issues continued to flourish. The locus of finance litigation lessened at the federal court level, but such suits continued to increase in the states.

According to experts in school finance, even though state legislative bodies continued to work to establish and define educational standards, state courts became more active in interpreting a state's mandate and its obligations to parents and children.[60] When deciding such cases, judges generally turned away from use of an equal protection rationale and looked to the explicit language of the state's own constitution, statutes, and policies.[61] *Pauley v.*

---

58. *Id.*

59. *Id.* at 124.

60. *See, e.g.,* W.E. Sparkman, *School Finance Litigation in the 1980's,* in S.B. THOMAS, N.H. CAMBRON-MCCABE & M.M. MCCARTHY, EDUCATORS AND THE LAW: CURRENT TRENDS AND ISSUES (Elmont, N.Y.: Institute for School Law and Finance, 1983). *See also* A.E. Wise, *Educational Adequacy: A Concept in Search of Meaning,* 8 J. OF EDUC. FIN. 300 (Winter, 1983); M.E. Goertz, *School Finance in New Jersey: A Decade After Robinson v. Cahill,* 8 J. OF EDUC. FIN. 475 (Spring, 1983). For a more recent commentary, see James G. Ward, *Remedies in School Finance Equity Litigation,* 36 EDUC. LAW REP. 1 (1986).

61. M.M. MCCARTHY & P.T. DEIGNAN, WHAT CONSTITUTES AN ADEQUATE PUBLIC EDUCATION (Bloomington, Ind.: Phi Delta Kappa 1983). It is interesting to note that in the decade between 1969-1970 and 1979-1980 the states' share of revenues for education increased from 39.9 percent to 46.8 percent, while the local share was reduced from 52.1 percent to 43.4 percent (federal funds made up the remainder). U.S. Department of Education, Center for Statistics, 1985-86.

Kelly (1979) offered an important example of what was to come elsewhere, when the court held the entire West Virginia State finance scheme for public education unconstitutional, and ordered sweeping reforms.[62]

f. *School Finance Litigation in the 1990s.* In the first half of the decade, more than twenty states had school finance cases before their highest courts. As was true in the 1980s, most courts treated school finance reform as a matter more appropriately handled by state legislatures than by judges.[63] However, some courts assumed jurisdiction over finance issues and ruled against the existing system of allocating dollars for the support of public education in their respective states.[64] Where this happened, state court

---

62. 255 S.E.2d 859 (W. Va. 1979). The reforms were upheld in Pauley v. Bailey, 324 S.E.2d 128 (W. Va. 1984). Comments regarding the *Pauley* case are taken directly from R. Truby, *Pauley v. Bailey and the West Virginia Master Plan,* 65 Phi Delta Kappan 284 (Dec. 1983). Recent decisions in Kentucky and Texas show a continued movement in the states to completely restructure educational finance and organizational patterns. *See, e.g.,* Edgewood Indep. Sch. Dist. v. Kirby, 777 S.W.2d 391 (Tex. 1989), where the Texas Supreme Court held that the State's school finance system, based in part on local district financing, which showed a 700 to 1 ratio between the value of taxable property in the wealthiest and poorest school districts, and school district spending per student, which varied from $2,112 to $19,333, violated the State of Texas constitutional mandate requiring an "efficient" system to achieve a "general diffusion of knowledge." The Texas Supreme Court later ruled that the State Legislature either formulate a new educational finance system by April 1, 1991 or give over the task to the courts. For a detailed analysis of the Texas decision and its implications for future litigation in other states, see William E. Sparkman & Michael P. Stevens, *Texas School Finance System Unconstitutional,* 57 Educ. Law Rep. 333 (Feb. 1, 1990). *See also* Carrollton-Farmers Branch Indep. Sch. Dist. v. Edgewood Indep. Sch. Dist., 826 S.W.2d 489 (Tex. 1992), where the Supreme Court of Texas ruled that the statute passed on April 1, 1991 to revise the State's finance system for schools was unconstitutional.

63. *See, e.g.,* Reform Educ. Fin. Inequities v. Cuomo, 406 N.Y.S.2d 44 (N.Y. 1993).

64. McDuffy v. Secretary, 615 N.E.2d 516 (Mass. 1993); Tennessee Small Sch. Sys., Inc. v. McWherter, 851 S.W.3d 139 (Tenn. 1993); Roosevelt Elem. Sch. Dist. No. 66 v. Bishop, 877 P.2d 806 (Ariz. 1994); Abbott by Abbott v. Burke, 643 A.2d 575 (N.J. 1994). As experts in school finance have concluded, judges were less inclined to focus on evidence of unequal financial support of school children. They were more persuaded by evidence of existing disparities and resulting inadequacies both in educational expenditures and programmatic opportunities available to school-aged children, when comparing one school system to others in the same state.[65]

Seeing a trend in the case law, some experts in public school law forecast the emergence of a new judicial attitude in school finance litigation. For example, Dayton predicted that the dominant judicial analysis used in the mid-1990s would involve a search for equal protection violations, coupled with an interpretation of the specific language of the state's education clause in its Constitution.[66] And, where school finance cases were heard, he predicted that the following three-pronged standard would be applied by judges: (1) a determination is made regarding the meaning of the language of the state's education clause, (2) based on that interpretation, a determination is made concerning the magnitude of the state's constitutional duty to support education for all of its school-aged children, and (3) the court must decide whether or not the state is meeting that assigned obligation.[67]

---

the restructuring of public education finance formulas, where that has occurred, is a "direct product of litigation because state legislatures have not been unanimously willing to voluntarily increase state funding to local schools." DAVID C. THOMPSON, R. CRAIG WOOD & DAVID S. HONEYMAN, FISCAL LEADERSHIP FOR SCHOOLS: CONCEPTS AND PRACTICES (New York: Longman, 1994) at 265.

65. *See* Alexandra Natapoff, *1993: The Year of Living Dangerously: State Courts Expand the Right to Education*, 92 EDUC. LAW REP. 755 (Sept. 22, 1994). In Roosevelt Elem. Sch. Dist. No. 66 v. Bishop, 877 P.2d 806 (Ariz. 1994), the Supreme Court of Arizona saw the reliance on the value of real property and certain demographic factors as personal income as producing educational disparities.

66. *See* John Dayton, *An Anatomy of School Funding Litigation*, EDUC. LAW REP. 627 (Dec. 3, 1992). *See also* James R. Hackney, *The Philosophical Underpinnings of Public School Funding Jurisprudence*, 22 J. OF LAW AND EDUC. 423 (Fall, 1992); William A. Thro, *The Role of Language of the State Education Clauses in School Finance Litigation*, 79 EDUC. LAW REP. 19 (Feb. 11, 1993); Richard Fossey, *The Constitutional Duty to "Cherish" Public Schools in Massachusetts: More than a Matter of Money*, 87 EDUC. LAW REP. 699 (Feb. 24, 1994).

67. *See McWherter, supra* note 64; Hackney, *supra* note 66.

In 1994, the Supreme Court of Virginia decided *Scott v. Commonwealth*,[68] where the above three-pronged analysis was used. A coalition of local school systems brought suit seeking a declaratory judgment that Virginia's method of financing public education violated the state Constitution. The coalition complained that Virginia's finance scheme deprived children living in poor school systems of the educational opportunities available to children living in wealthier school systems. To bolster their arguments, plaintiffs presented evidence that demonstrated major disparities both in the amount of dollars spent on student instruction and on all supplementary services provided. In addition, statistics were introduced that showed the existence of major differences in pupil-teacher ratios maintained in the poor and the wealthier systems.[69]

Both the trial court and the Supreme Court of Virginia reached the same conclusion in *Scott*. First, under the Constitution of Virginia, education is a fundamental right of all children of school age. However, said the Court, nowhere does the Constitution require either equal or substantially equal funding of programs among or within the various local school systems of the Commonwealth. Second, the constitutional duty of the General Assembly of Virginia (the state legislature) is to promulgate and fund standards of quality for the local school systems of the State. In the Court's view this was being done. Third, the Commonwealth of Virginia had met its constitutional obligation to its children. The Supreme Court of Virginia left intact the state's current system of financing public education, even though wide fiscal disparities do exist among its local school systems.[70]

---

68. 443 S.E.2d 138 (Va. 1994). Here the Supreme Court of Virginia placed the conflict within the particular political and economic context of the structure of public education in the Commonwealth of Virginia where the control of public schools has been and is within the exclusive jurisdiction of local school boards.

69. *Id. See also* Committee for Educ. Rights v. Edgar, 641 N.E.2d 602 (Ill. App. 1 Dist. 1994).

70. *Id.* As Conn has concluded, increased educational funding alone does not guarantee improved student performance; money spent wisely can make a difference in the quality of education received by children in both rich and poor school

§ 6.6. School Fees.

Over the years, the charging of fees to students attending our nation's public schools became a common practice. A look at today's schools reveals the existence of a variety of school fees that must be paid by parents and guardians. Examples of such student fees are towel fees in physical education classes, breakage fees in chemistry classes, fees for band and cheerleader uniforms, typing class fees covering supplies, and others. According to experts in school finance, the number and amount of such fees have grown in proportion to escalating costs and shrinking school system budgets. One result has been the proliferation of legal issues surrounding school fees.

Generally, to analyze the legal issues involving school fees the researcher must look to the constitution and statutes of each state. In the Commonwealth of Virginia, for example, the Constitution mandates that the General Assembly (state legislature) "provide for a system of free public elementary and secondary schools for all children of school age throughout the Commonwealth, and shall seek to ensure that an educational program of high quality is established and continually maintained."[71] The *Code of Virginia* states, "The public schools in each school division shall be free to each person of school age who resides within the school divi-

---

systems. The answer lies, he says, in the "efficient management of adequate resources." W. Lance Conn, *Funding Fundamentals: The Cost/Quality Debate in School Finance Reform*, 94 EDUC. LAW REP. 9 (Dec. 1, 1994). North Carolina's Supreme Court ruled on the legality of financing of public schools in that state. It held that the equal educational opportunities clause of the state's constitution does not require equal funding or educational advantages in all school systems. Rather, the court ignored the equity issues and focused on whether school children were receiving a sound basic education. The court set forth four indicators of what constitutes a sound basic education. Leandro v. State, 488 S.E.2d 249 (N.C. 1997). *See also* Abbott by Abbott v. Burke, 693 A.2d 417 (N.J. 1997); DeRolph v. State, 678 N.E.2d 886 (Ohio 1997); Coalition for Adequacy and Fairness in Sch. Funding, Inc. v. Chiles, 680 So. 2d 400 (Fla. 1998).

71. VA. CONST. art. VIII, § 1 (effective July 1, 1971).

sion. . . ."[72] Fees are permitted under the Code if either provided in the Code itself or permitted by the State Board of Education. The Code is clear, however, that "No pupil's scholastic report card or diploma shall be withheld because of nonpayment of any such fee or charge."[73]

As Valente pointed out fifteen years ago, an important distinction exists between fees that are charged students to cover "essential" or "basic" courses and services offered in schools, and those associated with "supportive" or "extracurricular" activities.[74] The basic principle to follow suggests that fees should not keep a student from equal access to a basic education or deprive a student of something to which he is legally entitled.

In 1988 an interesting fee issue made its way to the United States Supreme Court. In *Kadrmas v. Dickinson Public Schools,*[75] parents had challenged a North Dakota statute authorizing certain types of public school districts to charge a student fee for school bus transportation. In the parents' view this "user fee" offended the equal protection guarantee of poor children, since it deprived them of minimum access to an educational opportunity.[76]

---

72. VA. CODE § 22.1-3; and, by statute in Virginia, local school boards, with some state funding, are required to provide free of charge, to each pupil, textbooks and workbooks for required courses of instruction. Va. Code 22.1-251. For two North Carolina (decisions) involving the issue of residence and domicile of students, see Chapel Hill-Carrboro City Sch. v. Chavioux, 446 S.E.2d 612 (N.C. App. 1994); Streeter v. Greene Cty., 446 S.E.2d 107 (N.C. App. 1994).

73. VA. CODE § 22.1-6.

74. William D. Valente, *Legal Limitations on Student Fees,* 29 EDUC. LAW REP. 483 (1985). For court decisions involving issues of student fees, see Arcadia Unified Sch. Dist. v. Department of Educ., 5 Cal. Rptr. 2d 545 (Cal. 1992); Gamble v. University Sys. of New Hampshire, 610 A.2d 357 (N.H. 1992); and Rosenberger v. Rector & Visitors of Univ. of Va., 18 F.3d 269 (4th Cir. 1994), *rev'd,* 115 S. Ct. 2510 (1995).

75. 108 S. Ct. 2495 (1988).

76. *Id.* For a case involving a school district charging a student fee for school transportation, see Salazar v. Dawson, 18 Cal. Rptr. 2d 665 (Cal. App. 2 Dist. 1993).

Using a rational basis analysis, the Rehnquist Court upheld the state statute. In the Court's opinion, since education is not a fundamental right under the United States Constitution, the bus fee provision did not offend equal protection. What is more, the statutory provision was nondiscriminatory and actually encouraged local school districts to provide students with bus transportation to school.

§ 6.7. Summary.

As this nation's public school systems entered the 1970s, they faced growing financial crises. Across this country, school systems found themselves in serious financial trouble as bond issues and other tax referenda met defeat at the hands of voters. In some states the situation became so critical that whole school systems had to close early because budgets were spent.[77]

Suffice it to say, the American way of educational finance, built upon a local property tax base, had to experience change if public schools were to remain in existence. Beginning in the 1971-1972 school year, through such cases as *Serrano, Robinson,* and *Milliken,* needed reform was started.

Apparent in the post-*Rodriguez* era (since 1973) is a move among the various states to make statutory and policy changes aimed at carrying out state constitutional mandates regarding educational opportunity for all children. Clearly, the legal responsibility for ensuring financial access to a quality education for each child fell directly upon state legislatures and state boards of education.

As this nation moved into and through the decade of the 1990s, parents and other concerned citizens insisted that the quality of a child's education not be measured only by dollar input. Public school systems will be required to show that children have progressed and are "better" for what schools have done to, with, and for them. It should be noted that school choice and educational

---

77. *See* S. Landsman, *Can Localities Lock the Doors and Throw Away the Keys?,* 7 J. OF LAW AND EDUC. 431-47 (July 1978).

vouchers are again being talked about as a way to give parents a choice in sending their children to a school that they believe is their "best buy" in education. With a voucher in hand, parents will be able to choose their child's school, whether a public or private sector institution.

In their insistence on fiscally neutral systems of school finance, courts of law have never demanded that equal dollars must be spent on every child. Future courts will maintain this attitude and will insist that states be allowed latitude to provide differing resources to meet differing student needs. The responsibility will be on each state to see to it that this goal is reached. Thus, throughout the states, changes in tax policies, taxing structures, and school system organization and administration are inevitable as public education moves into the next century.

PART III

LAW AND PROFESSIONAL STAFF

Chapter Seven

EMPLOYMENT AND JOB SECURITY

§ 7.0. Types of School District Employees.

Basically, there are two types of categories of employees working within public school systems. One category includes individuals who provide support services for the system (*e.g.,* maintenance and custodial care of buildings and grounds, maintenance and operation of buses and other vehicles, operation of the cafeterias, provision of clerical and secretarial services) and is generally referred to as the nonprofessional, classified, or noncertificated staff.

The second category of school system employees comprises the professional or instructional staff members. Superintendents of schools, building principals, curriculum supervisors, guidance counselors, school psychologists, school social workers, and classroom teachers belong to this group. Typically, to be eligible for employment (full-time or part-time), in one of the aforementioned positions, an individual must initially possess a valid *certificate* issued by the state. According to some states, however, local school boards may employ individuals not holding full-force certificates in one of the above professional capacities on a temporary, substitute, or emergency basis, or through issuance of a provisional or special certificate (*e.g.,* vocational-technical teachers).

Generally, local school boards cannot legally pay professional staff members who do not hold bona fide certificates or who do not meet some special exception allowed by law. A 1977 Wisconsin case demonstrates that a school board can terminate a teacher who is not certified to teach a particular subject, even though that teacher taught that same subject for eight years prior to termination. The board's reason for termination was that the teacher was uncertified for her job.[1]

---

1. Grams v. Melrose-Midora Joint Sch. Dist. No. 1, 245 N.W.2d 730 (Wis. 1977). For another case involving the termination of a teacher who, for several years of teaching, lacked proper certification, see Chapman v. Board of Educ., 394 N.Y.S.2d (App. Div. 1977). *See also* Chambers v. Board of Educ., 397 N.Y.S.2d 436 (App. Div. 1977).

Similarly, a New York court upheld the termination of a tenured teacher who was certified only in the subject of social studies. Due to declining enrollments the school board had eliminated one social studies teaching position and selected this teacher as the one to be terminated.[2] That same year, 1983, the Supreme Court of Ohio upheld the dismissal of a continuing contract teacher when a course was eliminated and the terminated teacher was certified only in the specific course area (the teaching of electronics). Also, the Ohio court held that procedures for termination of teacher contracts for reasons relating to their conduct did not apply to termination based on the elimination of a course in which a teacher is certified to teach.[3]

§ 7.1. Certification.

Historically, the terms "certification" and "license" are synonymous. That is to say, the state by issuing a certificate to an individual is giving its formal permission to that person to practice his or her profession (teaching, administration, psychology, etc.) in the public schools of that state. Thus, a certificate legally grants entrance to practice, but does not ensure that the individual holding the certificate will gain employment. Certificates are not em-

---

2. Rappold v. Board of Educ., Cleveland Hills Union Free Sch. Dist., 464 N.Y.S.2d 240 (N.Y. 1983). For a case emphasizing the important link between certification and the subject taught by a teacher, see Tate v. Livingston Parish Sch. Bd., 444 So. 2d 219 (La. 1983). *See also* Colonial Educ. Ass'n v. Colonial Sch. Dist., 645 A.2d 336 (Pa. Commw. Ct. 1994), where a court held that declining student enrollments was not considered justification for suspension of a teacher. Here the court emphasized the need to show substantial decreases in enrollment, over a reasonable, justifiable time period.

3. State *ex rel.* Cutler v. Pike Cty. Joint Area Vocational Sch. Dist., 451 N.E.2d 800 (Ohio 1983). For a case demonstrating the interplay between teacher tenure status and teacher certification, see Bauer v. Board of Educ., 765 P.2d 1129 (Kan. 1988), where the Supreme Court of Kansas held that tenured teachers who were RIF'd be given preferred treatment for positions for which they are certified.

ployment contracts. As Bolmeier commented more than twenty-five years ago:

> The teacher's certificate is, in essence, a document indicating that the holder has met legal qualifications required by a particular state to follow the teaching profession in that state. It does not, by itself, give the holder the right to demand a teaching position.[4]

Colleges of education do not grant certificates. Local school boards do not issue certificates. Generally, state law (the legislature) delegates the legal authority to grant and issue certificates of professional practice in the public schools to the state board of education (in some states, called boards of regents).[5] Although the state board maintains legal authority for the issuance of certificates, it often delegates the administrative tasks of processing applications for certificates, evaluating transcripts, and other such matters to the state department of education (sometimes called the state department of public instruction). Thus, persons usually apply to the state department of education (or state department of public instruction), but are formally granted the certificate by the state board of education itself.

In some states, agencies other than the state board of education may be involved in the certification process. For example, school psychologists might be certificated through a state board of psy-

---

4. E.C. BOLMEIER, SCHOOL IN THE LEGAL STRUCTURE 189 (2d ed. Cincinnati, Ohio: The W.H. Anderson Co., 1973). According to *American Jurisprudence,* "teachers' licenses or certificates, like other licenses, possess none of the elements of a contract protected by the due process clause of the Fourteenth Amendment." 68 AM. JUR. 2d 462 (1973). *See also* Wardwell v. Board of Educ., 529 F.2d 625 (6th Cir. 1976); Lombard v. Board of Educ., 645 F. Supp. 1574 (E.D.N.Y. 1986). For two excellent cases treating aspects of teacher certification, see Green Bay Educ. Ass'n v. State Dep't of Pub. Instruction, 453 N.W.2d 915 (Wis. App. 1990); Hunt v. Sanders, 554 N.E.2d 285 (Ill. App. 1990).

5. As the Supreme Court of Alabama said in a 1977 decision, "The individual boards of education in Alabama have nothing whatever to do with certification of teachers. That is done by the State Board of Education." Bramlett v. Alabama State Tenure Comm'n, 341 So. 2d 727 (Ala. 1977).

chological examiners, while school nurses might receive their licensure through a state board of nursing or state board of health.

The certificate itself usually grants licensure for a specific professional position (*e.g.,* as a "teacher" in the public schools of a state). Specific *endorsements* are placed on the certificate and may be added to the certificate, as demonstrated by the person's professional training (*e.g.,* social studies, English, and reading, grades one to twelve). Generally, local school boards are encouraged not to assign professional personnel to positions for which they are neither certified nor endorsed. If such an assignment is made, the board should, within reason, see to it that the professional immediately pursue additional training for the new job. Local boards of education may prescribe additional requirements for personnel over and above state requirements.

In reversing the Tenth Circuit's decision in *Harrah Independent School District v. Martin,* the United States Supreme Court affirmed the prerogative of local school boards not to renew the contracts of teachers who refuse to comply with a school board regulation requiring all bachelor degree-level teachers to earn five semester hours of college credit every three years. To the High Court, "[t]he school district's concern with the educational qualifications of its teachers cannot under any reasoned analysis be described as impermissible . . . ."[6]

Generally, state statutes require that professional certificates be renewed after a given period of time — frequently every five or six years. During that period, professionals often return to the university to pursue the additional courses necessary to renew their certificate.[7] The Commonwealth Court of Pennsylvania has ruled that

---

6. 440 U.S. 194, 99 S. Ct. 1062, 59 L. Ed. 2d 248 (1979). It should be noted that state statutory requirements for additional training also have been legally applied to local school board members. *See, e.g.,* Warden v. Pataki, 35 F. Supp. 2d 354 (S.D.N.Y. 1999).

7. Pointek v. Elk Lake Sch. Dist., 360 A.2d 804 (Pa. 1976). For a case demonstrating the power of a legislature to constitutionally change the entire system of certification and require that teachers holding "standard certificates" (valid for life) exchange them for "professional certificates" (requiring renewal every five

a teacher who held an interim certificate, which had expired by its own terms, could be terminated prior to her obtaining recertification.[8] In the court's opinion, the lapse of the certificate caused the teacher no longer to be considered a professional employee. In the words of the court, "as of June 1, 1977, she ceased to be a professional employee since she lacked the certificate which is, by statute, fundamental to classification as a professional employee."[9]

Revocation of certification is different from removal or dismissal from employment. While a local school board can legally remove or dismiss a superintendent, principal, supervisor, counselor, teacher, or other professional employee, state commissioners and state boards are generally the only ones legally able to revoke a certificate. Additionally, state statutes usually specify grounds and procedures for certification revocation,[10] and these statutory mandates must be adhered to. Generally, courts of law will not intervene in a certificate revocation matter unless an individual has lost his certificate on grounds not specified in statute, or if mandatory procedures were not followed.[11] What is more, courts will

---

years and the accumulation of *nine* continuing education credits for renewal), see Connecticut Educ. Ass'n, Inc. v. Tirozzi, 554 A.2d 1065 (Conn. 1989).

8. Occhipinti v. Board of Sch. Dirs., Old Forge Sch. Dist., 464 A.2d 631 (Pa. 1983).

9. *Id.* at 632. *See also* Chappell v. School Bd., 12 F. Supp. 2d 509 (E.D. Va. 1998).

10. Moral unfitness, sexual misconduct, lack of requisite qualifications, willful neglect of duties, use or sale of illegal drugs, and involvement in criminal activity offer examples of grounds cited for revocation of teaching certificates by state boards. For revocation cases on point, see Startzel v. Commonwealth, 562 A.2d 1005 (Pa. Commw. 1989), where the crime of "mail fraud" was interpreted as being within the meaning of the cause "moral turpitude" as grounds for certification revocation; Roberts v. Castor, 629 So. 2d 311 (Fla. App. 1st Dist. 1993); Tenbroeck v. Castor, 640 So. 2d 164 (Fla. App. 1st Dist. 1994).

11. 68 AM. JUR. 463 (1973). For a case involving the revocation of a teacher's certificate, see Shore v. Board of Exmrs., 392 N.Y.S.2d 328 (N.Y. 1977). In Nelkin v. Board of Educ., 613 N.Y.S.2d 383 (App. Div. 1st Dep't 1994), a substitute teacher's certificate was suspended and his application for regular employment withheld pending the outcome of a medical evaluation.

also insist that plaintiffs exhaust administrative remedies available before taking their complaint into court.

§ 7.2. Legal Status of Professional Employees in Schools.

All professionals in public school systems are employees of their local school board. And, since local school boards are *quasi-municipal* corporations legally constituted to carry out a state governmental function (providing public education), professionals in local school systems are, legally, public employees.

An examination of the professional hierarchy within public school systems, however, reveals the existence of differences in legal status among professional employees. The major difference concerns those professional employees who hold legal status as school *officials* or *officers* and those who occupy legal status solely as *employees.*

According to *Black's Law Dictionary,* an officer

> is one who is invested with some portion of the functions of the government to be exercised for the public bene-fit. . . . An officer is distinguished from an employee in the greater importance, dignity, and independence of his position, in requirement of oath, bond, more enduring tenure, and fact of duties being prescribed by law.[12]

Individuals who occupy status as school officials or officers are entrusted with *authority* to do what is necessary for the well-being of the schools and to exercise independent discretion in the ad-ministration of school board policy. Decision-making authority and the possession of legal prerogatives to control the behavior of employees within the school system organization are major char-acteristics of school officialdom.

Most professionals in public school systems occupy legal status solely as *employees* of the school board and not as officers or officials. How is the term "employee" legally defined, and how

---

12. BLACK'S LAW DICTIONARY 1235 (4th ed. St. Paul, Minn: West Publishing Co., 1951).

183

does it differ from that of "officer," previously defined? As one source states,

> [T]he status of "employee" arises where one is engaged by another person to perform work or services as directed and controlled by the other person's promise to pay wages, salary, or compensation for such services, and where there is a contract between employer and employee . . . .[13]

The absence of any reference to employee decision-making authority, coupled with the notion of performance of work as directed and controlled by the employer, and the presence of a contractual agreement (including compensation for services rendered) are significant elements in understanding the differences existing between the status of an official and that of an employee.

a. *The Legal Status of Superintendents.* Legally, local superintendents of schools are both employees of the school board and administrative officers of the local school division (district). Superintendents are contracted by the school board (usually for a term fixed by state law) to serve as the board's chief administrator and educational advisor. As employees of the school board, superintendents are contracted by and work directly for the school board and they are accountable to the board for the performance of their professional tasks. Like any other board employee, they are subject to dismissal from employment.

As officers of the school system, however, superintendents are generally granted independent discretion by the board to make decisions (undergirded by board policy) on the many administrative problems that might occur in the daily operation of the school system. So long as the superintendent does not violate state law, state board regulations, or local board policy, a school board generally will not interfere with the superintendent's decisions.

---

13. WORDS AND PHRASES 531 (permanent ed. St. Paul, Minn: West Publishing Co., 1952).

In a Virginia tort case, the Supreme Court of that Commonwealth was faced with determining the legal status of a local school superintendent for purposes of judging the applicability of the doctrine of sovereign immunity.[14] Upon a complete analysis of the Code of Virginia, various state constitutional provisions, and that state's precedent cases the court determined "that a division superintendent is a supervisory official who exercises powers involving a considerable degree of judgment and discretion. Under the circumstances of this case, we hold that the division superintendent is entitled to sovereign immunity."[15]

In some states, statutory provisions have been interpreted to specifically grant "officer" status to local superintendents of schools. Ohio offers an example of one such state. According to *Ohio Jurisprudence*,

> [u]nder earlier statutes, the superintendent of schools was regarded merely as the agent or employee of the board of education. . . . But inasmuch as the statute now provides that a superintendent of schools is the executive "officer" for the board of education of the school district, and speaks of a vacancy in the "office" of superintendent, it would seem that the General Assembly had definitely characterized a superintendent of schools as a public officer, as distinguished from a public employee . . . .[16]

State statutes usually specify legal duties of local superintendents of schools,[17] with the proviso that boards of education have the prerogative to assign all other duties that they deem necessary for the overall operation of the school system.

Thus, the legal status of the local school superintendent can be determined only by examination of pertinent state law. Whether or

---

14. Banks v. Sellers, 294 S.E.2d 862 (Va. 1982).

15. *Id.* at 865.

16. 48 OHIO JURISPRUDENCE 2d 810 (1966).

17. In New York State, for example, the several powers of local superintendents of schools are specifically enumerated by statute. 52 N.Y. JURISPRUDENCE 85 (1967).

not a superintendent of schools gains tenure in that capacity is another matter that must be studied on a state-to-state basis (statutes and court decisions).[18]

Lookabill v. Board of Education is a West Virginia case involving a school superintendent who, having been assistant superintendent in the school system, accepted a nine-month contract to replace his superintendent, who had died. To accept this new position he had resigned his position as assistant superintendent, with two and one-half years remaining on his four-year contract. Following a temporary term under the new contract (approximately seven months), the board (by a vote of 3-2) appointed another man to the superintendency and reassigned the current incumbent to a position as high school principal. Citing West Virginia Board of Education Policy 5300(6) stating that an employee must have regular evaluations and a chance to improve before any change in position is made, the superintendent maintained that he could not be reassigned to the principal's position. The Supreme Court of Appeals of West Virginia did not agree with him. To the court, Policy 5300(6) refers to "employee," and the superintendent is an "officer." Thus, the policy does not apply. What is more, said the court, he never had a clear right to the office he now seeks.[19]

b. *The Legal Status of Principals.* Despite the fact that building principals are granted considerable discretion by local school boards and superintendents to conduct the day-to-day business of their individual schools, courts have consistently held that principals are not public officers. School principals are *employees* of the school board, appointed and assigned by that board to carry out administrative duties within a given school building.

---

18. In 1977, the Supreme Court of California ruled that the California Education Code provides tenure only as a *classroom teacher* and not as an administrator or supervisor. Therefore, an associate superintendent of schools for business in the Jefferson Elementary School District (with eight years of service in that position), did not have a property interest in his administrative position. Barthuli v. Board of Trustees, 139 Cal. Rptr. 627, 566 P.2d 261 (Cal. 1977). *See also* Seyfang v. Board of Trustees, 563 P.2d 1376 (Wyo. 1977).

19. 304 S.E.2d 678 (W. Va. 1983).

In 1983, the New York State Supreme Court, Appellate Division, First Department, interpreting that state's code, made it clear that the power to terminate an acting principal as of the final day of her probation lay exclusively with the district superintendent of schools.[20]

Generally, the legal status of principals is determined by interpretation of state statute. In some states (*e.g.,* the Commonwealth of Virginia), continuing contract status (tenure) as a principal is specifically enumerated in statute and is achieved after serving three probationary years in that position.[21] On the other hand, however, in states like Ohio, Tennessee, Illinois, and California, courts have interpreted state law to say that all administrative and supervisory personnel achieve tenure as teachers and not as administrators or supervisors.[22]

School boards possess the legal prerogative granted by state statute to reassign principals to any principalship or supervisory position within the school system for which they are qualified. Also, boards can reassign principals to classroom teaching positions provided the board acts in good faith and state tenure statutes are not violated. In *Lane v. Board of Education,* a principal of five years challenged his board's decision to reassign him to teaching duties, claiming that he had a property interest in his principal's position. In holding for the board, the appellate court interpreted the Illinois code and ruled that the plaintiff's property right was in his position as a certified employee and not in his administrative position. Thus, the school board could transfer him to any job for

---

20. Taylor v. Berberian, 466 N.Y.S.2d 336, 338 (N.Y. 1983).

21. VA. CODE § 22.1-294. The fact that a principal has achieved a continuing contract in that position may not preclude a school board from placing him/her back on annual contract status. *See, e.g.,* Edgar v. School Bd., 549 So. 2d 726 (Fla. App. 1989).

22. For other cases on point, see Coe v. Bogart, 519 F.2d 10 (6th Cir. 1975); Danno v. Peterson, 421 F. Supp. 950 (N.D. Ill. 1976); Barthuli v. Board of Trustees, 139 Cal. Rptr. 627, 566 P.2d 261 (Cal. 1977); Lane v. Board of Educ., 348 N.E.2d 470 (Ill. 1976). As of July 1, 1995, the State of North Carolina eliminated tenure for public school principals. *See* N.C.G.S. § 115C-325.

which he was qualified and adjust his salary accordingly.[23] The sections below discuss the legal aspects of assignment, reassignment, transfer, and demotion of administrators.

c. _The Legal Status of Supervisors._ Unlike the individual working in business and industry who holds the title "supervisor" and exercises certain _line_ (command) responsibilities, the supervisor in a public school system is generally classified (legally) as acting in a staff position possessing no administrative responsibilities. Supervisors in educational settings are usually hired to help in curriculum development and to assist teachers and administrators to improve instruction.

Legally, supervisors are generally certified by the state to practice their specialty, but they do not acquire tenure in their supervisor's position. Some states (_e.g.,_ Virginia) do allow for continuing contract status as a supervisor (after serving three years of probation in that capacity), while in other states (_e.g.,_ California) an individual acquires tenure only as a classroom teacher.

The similarities or lack thereof between an abolished supervisory position and three newly-created positions formed the basis of a New York case, _Greenspan v. Dutchess County, Board of Cooperative Educational Services._[24] To the New York court, the supervisor is entitled to appointment to one of the new positions "only if the duties of that position are similar to the duties of her former position."[25] The test to determine such a relationship, said the

---

23. 348 N.E.2d 470 (Ill. 1976). _See also_ Conte v. School Comm., 356 N.E.2d 261 (Mass. 1976). In Owen v. Board of Educ., 632 N.E.2d 1073 (Ill. App. 3 Dist. 1994), the court determined that an assistant principal was not a "teacher" for purposes of a state statute prohibiting residency requirements for teachers. _See also_ Bart v. Board of Educ., 632 N.E.2d 39 (Ill. App. 1 Dist. 1993), where the court held that reassignment of an assistant principal to a teaching position without showing cause or granting a hearing did not violate the state's school laws, and Sanders v. Delton Kellogg Sch., 530 N.W.2d 114 (Mich. App. 1995). In Diddle v. Unified Sch. Dist., 12 F. Supp. 2d 1219 (D. Kan. 1998), a local school board withstood the sex discrimination claim of an elementary school principal. The board produced evidence establishing reasons for the termination decision.

24. 466 N.Y.S.2d 430 (N.Y. 1983).

25. _Id._ at 433.

court, is whether or not the duties of the new positions are more than fifty percent of the functions performed in the former position.[26]

The legal status of supervisors in public school systems is that of an *employee* of the school board. Supervisors are not *officers* of the school system.

d. *The Legal Status of Counselors.* Generally, state education codes require that all individuals serving as guidance counselors in public school systems be certified for that position by the state. Certificates for counselors may be issued by state boards of education or, as has happened recently in some states, by boards of professional licensure (such boards also license psychologists and others who work as professional counselors).

Counselors in schools usually acquire tenure as classroom teachers and not as counselors. Such a determination is made under the control of appropriate state law and, in some situations, pertinent state court opinions.

The Supreme Court of California heard the appeal of a public school attendance counselor who, after serving two years in that position, was reassigned by his board to classroom teaching duties and was reduced in salary. The counselor held both a classroom teacher's certificate and that of a counselor in the State of California. The Supreme Court of California affirmed the decision of the lower court which was adverse to appellant's claim.[27] The California Education Code, stated the court, "provides in effect that employees holding both teaching and counseling certificates shall acquire permanent status only as a classroom teacher, and not as counselors."[28] Thus, the court continued, "[w]e hold that an employee with both teaching and counseling certificates acquires permanent status as a classroom teacher regardless of the position

---

26. *Id.*

27. Thompson v. Modesto City High Sch. Dist., 139 Cal. Rptr. 603 (Cal. App. 1977).

28. *Id.* at 607.

189

held by that employee at the completion of the probationary period."[29]

Counselors in public school systems are professional employees of the system. Legally, they in no way hold official (officer) status in school systems.

§ 7.3. Selection and Assignment of Employees.

State law provides that local school boards possess legal authority to contract and to be contracted with. Thus, all employees enter into employment contracts with local boards of education and not with administrators. It follows, therefore, that boards of education also possess legal authority to nonrenew contracts with employees and to dismiss employees under contract when cause exists to take such action (state statutes usually specify cause for dismissal).

a. *Selection of Employees.* The administrative tasks associated with recruitment and selection of personnel are usually delegated by school boards to school system personnel offices, generally under the supervision of an assistant superintendent of schools or a director of personnel. Legally, however, the ultimate selection authority of all personnel employed in public schools (certificated and noncertificated) resides with the board of education of the particular school system. To put it another way, courts have held consistently that only local boards of education (not superintendents or principals) possess legal authority (specified in state law) to contract with (hire) personnel employed by their school system.[30]

In addition to compliance with state law and their own policies, school boards must likewise comply with federal law and policy regarding recruitment, selection, and hiring of employees. Recent examples of federal laws (intended to remove any forms of discrimination) having direct impact on board employment preroga-

---

29. *Id. See also* Capella v. Board of Educ., 367 A.2d 244 (N.J. 1976).

30. Marsh v. Birmingham Bd. of Educ., 349 So. 2d 34 (Ala. 1977). *See also* School Bd. v. Goodson, 335 So. 2d 308 (Fla. 1976).

190

tives are title VII of the Civil Rights Act of 1964, title IX of the Education Amendments of 1972, § 504 of the Rehabilitation Act of 1973, and the Americans with Disabilities Act (1990). Additionally, policies and guidelines from such federal agencies as the Department of Education and the Department of Health and Human Services, and the decrees of federal courts (especially recent cases wherein 42 U.S.C. § 1983 has been applied to claims of employment discrimination) have also changed and reshaped the employment practices of local school boards.

b. *Recommendation.* Where state statutes specify that teachers and other personnel be employed by local boards of education upon recommendation of the superintendent of schools, courts of law have held that contracts are not binding absent said recommendation.[31] A statutory procedure requiring a recommendation of employees by the superintendent has been held not to constitute an illegal delegation of board authority.[32]

An example of a state statute requiring the recommendation of the superintendent is found in the Code of Virginia. According to the Code, "a school board, upon recommendation of the division superintendent, may employ principals and assistant principals."[33]

School boards are not required to accept the personnel recommendations of superintendents or building principals. Moreover, personnel recommendations of superintendents and principals are not legally binding in and of themselves. As a Florida appellate court held (interpreting the School Code of Florida) in *School Board v. Goodson*:[34]

---

31. *See, e.g.,* Bonar v. City of Boston, 341 N.E.2d 684 (Mass. 1976).

32. Hembree v. Jefferson Cty. Bd. of Educ., 337 So. 2d 9 (Ala. 1976).

33. VA. CODE § 22.1-293.

34. 335 So. 2d 308 (Fla. 1976). For a case on point, see Stanley v. Raton Bd. of Educ., 876 P.2d 232 (N.M. 1994), where the court establishes the legal authority of a local school board under appropriate state code provisions, to hire and fire without the recommendation of the superintendent. In some states this may or may not be true. The reader is advised to check appropriate state law and interpretations of that law.

The School Board is to have exclusive authority to form
contracts with the instructional personnel of the school
system. The Board may accept or reject the recommendations of the superintendent who, in turn, may accept or
reject the recommendations of the school principals.
Neither a superintendent nor a principal, acting individually or collectively, may enter into a contractual agreement with a teacher without express approval of the
School Board.[35]

Thus, it can be said that local school boards retain ultimate legal
authority to contract with (hire) professional personnel even
though authority to recommend personnel initially may be placed
by statute within the purview of school administration.

c. *Contract.* Simply stated, a contract is an agreement between
two or more parties (not merely a unilateral expectation) which is
enforceable by law. Generally, employees in public school systems
look to the written document (sometimes taking the form of a
simple salary letter) they receive from their school board, sign, and
return by a specified date as the complete embodiment of their
employment contract with the school board. Given the complexi-
ties of contract law, this may or may not be so. In reality, such a
determination can be made only after careful examination of appropriate state law, school board policies, and the specific document itself. Whether or not an agreement (oral or written) has
ripened into an enforceable contract is a question to be determined
on a case-by-case basis. As a general rule, however, once a contract exists, it is enforceable by either party and it shall not be
significantly modified or breached unilaterally by either party.

The importance of whether or not an enforceable contract exists
can be found in several school cases. *Cannon v. Beckville* involved
a superintendent of schools who did not possess a written contract
for the extension of his employment. To the Fifth Circuit, there
existed "only a unilateral and subjective expectation of a future

---

35. *Id.* at 310.

right."[36] In other words, he alone expected that at some time in the future a written contract would be executed. Such a "unilateral expectation" alone, said the court, does not create a property interest in employment "that would warrant constitutional procedural due process protection."[37] It should be emphasized, however, that the oral nature of the agreement, per se, did not defeat the superintendent's claim of extended employment. In the appellate court's view, all that existed was "a general offer of employment and a willingness to finalize the contract in writing with acceptable terms."[38]

Generally, a valid contract is enforceable whether made orally or in writing. Early in their studies, law students encounter the *statute of frauds.* Simply stated, the statute of frauds requires that certain types of contracts must be in writing. The intent of such statutes where they exist (and one must look to the appropriate state code to discover such provisions) is to prevent fraudulent claims. One type of contract that falls within the statute of frauds is any agreement that cannot be completely performed within one year. *Vail v. Board of Education*[39] is a school case wherein the *statute of frauds* came into play.

At the time he entered preliminary contract discussions with the Paris, Illinois, school board, Vail (who was at the time employed as supervisor of recreation and physical education for the Statesville Correctional Center in Joliet, Illinois), let it be known to his prospective employer that he did not want to relinquish his current position unless he could get a promise of at least two years of

---

36. Cannon v. Beckville Indep. Sch. Dist., 709 F.2d 9, 10 (5th Cir. 1983).

37. *Id.*

38. *Id.* at 11. For an excellent school case involving issues of "offer" and "intention to become bound," *see* Terrebonne v. Louisiana Ass'n of Educators, 444 So. 2d 206 (La. 1983). For a case where a teacher's failure to meet the agreed upon conditions of her contract led to the nonrenewal of her contract of employment, see Bradley v. Beach Public Schs., 427 N.W.2d 352 (N.D. 1988).

39. Vail v. Board of Educ., Paris Union Sch. Dist. No. 95, 706 F.2d 1435 (7th Cir. 1983).

employment in the new job.[40] Ultimately, the negotiating school board told its superintendent to make an offer of a one-year contract to Vail and to convey orally the board's intent (if Vail signed) to renew his contract at the end of the year.[41] Vail accepted the offer and signed a written contract with the new board. He subsequently resigned his position in Joliet and assumed his new duties as athletic director and football coach in Paris, Illinois.

In March of his first year, the board decided to nonrenew Vail's contract. No reasons were given and no hearing was held.[42] Vail took his situation into federal court seeking remedy under 42 U.S.C. § 1983. Not claiming any tenure rights under the Illinois Code, Vail simply claimed that a two-year contract existed, that the board must honor that agreement and, since he had a legitimate expectation of continued employment over that two years, the board had deprived him of that property entitlement without due process of law. Such an act by the board, he said, violated the fifth and fourteenth amendments. In response to Vail's allegations, the school board stated that such a two-year agreement was unenforceable under Illinois law, since the tenure act preempts any property interest created by an "implied contract."[43]

On the findings of fact the district court held that Vail had a constitutionally protected property interest in continued employment with the Paris school board. To the court, "the Board acting under color of state law had deprived Vail of property without due process of law . . . ."[44] Thus, Vail was awarded $19,850.99 in stipulated damages.

On appeal by the board, the Seventh Circuit focused its attention upon Vail's *detrimental reliance* on the school board's promise and held that the board worked to deny him a "legitimate expectation of continued employment."[45] In the court's opinion:

---

40. *Id.* at 1436.
41. *Id.*
42. *Id.*
43. *Id.*
44. *Id.*
45. *Id.* at 1440.

The extent of his reliance on the Board's promise is shown by the fact he left Joliet where he and his family had lived for thirteen years, left a job he had held for ten years, and even took a salary cut to take the job in Paris. The reasonableness of the reliance is illustrated by the concerns over security Vail raised from his very first meeting with Dr. Cherry to the final actions of the Board and the promises Vail received as an inducement to taking the job.[46]

To the court, the Paris board's implied promise had induced Vail to leave his position in Joliet and to take the new position.

Finally, making specific reference to the statute of frauds and the oral agreement, the court held that since there had been partial performance of the contract by parties, "the Statute of Frauds would not bar enforcement of the contract . . . ."[47]

d. *Assignment.* Courts of law have consistently held that local school boards must have enough latitude to administer effectively the operation of public school systems.[48] Assignment and reassignment of professional personnel to positions and to schools within systems are areas of school district operation wherein courts have, over the years, firmly established school board discretionary prerogatives. Absent any statutory or contractual provisions to the contrary, local boards of education are generally free to assign all personnel to any one position or combination of posi-

---

46. *Id.* In other words, Vail had relied, in good faith, to his detriment, on the conduct and statements of the Paris superintendent and board.

47. *Id. See also* Sapphire v. Board of Educ., Hastings Union Free Sch. Dist., 466 N.Y.S.2d 439 (N.Y. 1983). *Sapphire* involved a dismissed guidance counselor who was declared to have tenure and to be entitled to reinstatement by *estoppel*; and Jones v. Birdsong, 530 F. Supp. 221 (N.D. Miss. 1980), involving the contract of a counselor that the court held "never ripened into an enforceable contract." For an interesting case wherein some teachers who had already signed their new contracts but who then took steps to cancel their contracts by stating that they did not agree with the terms of the new contracts, had signed under duress, and thus had failed to *consent* to the "changing of the terms," *see Ex parte* Wright, 443 So. 2d 40 (Ala. 1983).

48. Hudson v. Independent Sch. Dist. No. 77, 258 N.W.2d 594 (Minn. 1977).

tions for which they are qualified. Said assignments must be reasonable and must be made on nondiscriminatory bases.

The power of local school boards to reassign and transfer professional personnel does not end when personnel tenure is achieved. According to *American Jurisprudence*:

> The right to continued employment in a position of the same rank or grade as that to which a teacher has been "elected" under a tenure law has been recognized, although within reasonable limits a school board has power to change the assignment of a permanent teacher so long as the work assigned is of a rank and grade equivalent to that by which the permanent status was acquired and the assignment is one for which the teacher is qualified.[49]

Additionally, suggests *American Jurisprudence*,

> tenure statutes do not guarantee to a teacher the right to continue in a particular school. . . . Employment under a continuing service contract does not prevent a board of education from transferring a teacher from one school to another or from one class of teaching position to another, unless the contract specifies the school or class of position . . . .[50]

§ 7.4. Board Authority and Teacher Personnel.

Local boards of education possess considerable legal authority in dealing with professional personnel. It has been held that local boards possess the legal prerogatives for making all personnel decisions necessary for the "best interests of the school system."[51] What is more, as the United States Supreme Court held in *Adler v. Board of Education,* "school authorities have the right and the duty to screen the officials, teachers, and employees as to their fitness

---

49. 68 AM. JUR. 2d *Schools* § 158 (1973).
50. *Id.* 157-58.
51. Morelli v. Board of Educ., 42 Ill. App. 3d 722, 358 N.E.2d 1364 (1976).

to maintain the integrity of the schools as a part of ordered society . . . ."[52]

The legal authority to employ, assign, transfer, suspend, nonrenew, and dismiss teacher personnel belongs to the local school board. Teachers in public school systems contract with the school board and not with superintendents or building principals.[53]

School board decisions in personnel matters will not be interfered with by courts of law unless it is proved that the board acted arbitrarily, capriciously, or beyond the scope of its duly constituted authority.[54] Moreover, the legal presumption is that boards of education act in *good faith* when making personnel decisions. Thus, according to Levin: "Unless the school board has dismissed, transferred, demoted, or disciplined its employees for constitutionally impermissible reasons or has failed to provide the requisite procedural safeguards, it has proved difficult for employees to challenge successfully such actions."[55]

Over the years, however, school board authority and control over teachers have received much attention as increasing numbers of complaints reached courts of law. Cases have been taken to the courts challenging almost every aspect of board regulation and censure of teacher behavior. As Hamilton observed more than four decades ago,

> [t]he list of rules and regulations affecting teachers which have been challenged is a very long one. They vary from rules concerning tenure, salary, duties, leaves of absence, and other such important matters, to the length of the teacher's skirt or where or how she will spend her time outside of school hours.[56]

---

52. 342 U.S. 485, 493, 72 S. Ct. 380, 96 L. Ed. 2d 517 (1952). *See also* Singston v. King, 340 F. Supp. 314 (W.D. Va. 1972).

53. Hart v. School Bd., 340 So. 2d 121 (Fla. 1976).

54. *Morelli, supra* note 51, at 1369.

55. B. Levin, *Employees* in THE YEARBOOK OF SCHOOL LAW 1976, at 129 (P.K. Piele ed.-in-chief, Topeka, Kan.: NOLPE, 1977).

56. 13 BI-WEEKLY SCHOOL LAW LETTERS 66 (October 15, 1953).

Local school boards continue to reassign, reprimand, discipline, and discharge teachers for a variety of reasons. Some reasons cited in litigation are as follows: admitted homosexual activity,[57] insubordination,[58] excessive and improper use of corporal punishment,[59] wearing a beard in violation of school board regulations,[60] cruelty to students,[61] persistent neglect of professional duties,[62] distributing ACLU materials and participating in ACLU activities,[63] out-of-wedlock pregnancy,[64] incompetency,[65] lack of classroom discipline,[66] below-average grades and test scores attained by students,[67] lack of tact in handling professional matters,[68] incapacity for teaching because of a sex-change operation,[69] and a variety of other causes too numerous to list. However, the employee discipline handed out by the school board and administration should not be disproportionate to the offense committed by the teacher.

---

57. Burton v. Cascade Sch. Dist., 512 F.2d 850 (9th Cir. 1975). *See also* National Gay Task Force v. Board of Educ., 729 F.2d 1270 (10th Cir. 1984). The impact of the U.S. Supreme Court's decision in Bowers v. Hardwick, 478 U.S. 186 (1986), challenging the Georgia statute criminalizing sodomy, has not been fully realized. *See also* Glover v. Williamsburg Local Sch. Dist. Bd. of Educ., 20 F. Supp. 2d 1160 (S.D. Ohio 1998).

58. Thompson v. Wake Cty. Bd. of Educ., 230 S.E.2d 164 (N.C. 1976). In Jones v. Rapides Parish Sch. Bd., 634 So. 2d 1197 (La. App. 3 Cir. 1994), a tenured teacher was dismissed for showing an "R-rated" film to his class. The school system cancelled his contract on grounds of insubordination and neglect of duty.

59. Board of Educ. v. Shank, 542 S.W.2d 779 (Mo. 1976).

60. Morrison v. Hamilton Cty. Sch. Bd., 494 S.W.2d 770 (Tenn.), *cert. denied,* 414 U.S. 1044 (1973).

61. Rolando v. School Dirs., 358 N.E.2d 945 (Ill. 1976).

62. DiLeo v. Greenfield, 541 F.2d 949 (2d Cir. 1976).

63. Woodward v. Hereford, 421 F. Supp. 93 (N.D. Tex. 1976).

64. Brown v. Bathke, 416 F. Supp. 1194 (D. Neb. 1976).

65. Gilliand v. Board of Educ., 343 N.E.2d 704 (Ill. 1976).

66. Hagerstrom v. Clay City, 343 N.E.2d 249 (Ill. 1976).

67. Klein v. Boehmer, CV75-L-70 (D. Neb. 1976).

68. Mt. Healthy City Sch. Dist. Bd. of Educ. v. Doyle, 429 U.S. 274, 97 S. Ct. 568, 50 L. Ed. 2d 471 (1977).

69. *In re* Tenure Hearing of Grossman, 321 A.2d 253 (1974), *cert. denied,* 429 U.S. 897 (1976).

The above causes are made complex in that most are not included in or defined by state statute or school board policy and "may not occur at all during the teacher's classroom work performance. They can occur on the job before school, after school, on the playground, in the halls, in the cafeteria, and during preparation periods."[70]

It is important to know that the authority of school boards to discipline and/or discharge employees applies to all workers in the school system. For example, in *Sampson v. Administrator, Louisiana Office of Employment Security* (which was actually litigated on the matter of unemployment benefits), a school bus driver was charged for failure to keep the bus in proper condition. To the school board, such behavior was termed "misconduct."[71] However, the court emphasized that the school board and administration must be able to substantiate its case with sufficient evidence to sustain the grounds specified for an employee's dismissal.[72]

When evaluating teachers' fitness, school boards are not restricted in considering teachers' in-school and in-class behavior only. As a New Jersey superior court held, local school boards have the duty of determining the general issue of "teacher fitness."[73] Regarding the actual scope of a teacher's fitness (per se), the court said: "A teacher's fitness may not be measured 'solely by his or her ability to perform the teaching function and ignore the fact that the teacher's presence in the classroom might, nevertheless, pose a danger of harm to the students for a reason not related to academic proficiency.'"[74]

---

70. 1 COLLECT. BARG. Q. (1976), at 1. In Board of Trustees v. Landry, 638 N.E.2d 1261 (Ind. App. 1st Dist. 1994), a classroom teacher was suspended for removing glossaries from school-owned textbooks.

71. 439 So. 2d 458 (La. 1983).

72. Rutan v. Pasco Cty. Sch. Bd., 435 So. 2d 399 (Fla. 1983).

73. Gish v. Board of Educ., 145 N.J. Super. 96, 366 A.2d 1337 (1976).

74. *Id.*, 366 A.2d at 1342. For two cases involving employee rights both prior to the resolution of a criminal complaint and following reversal of a conviction, see Nosik v. Singe, 40 F.3d 592 (2d Cir. 1994); Tufflie v. Governing Bd. of San Diego Unified Sch. Dist., 36 Cal. Rptr. 2d 433 (Cal. App. 4th Dist. 1994). For a comprehensive commentary on this subject, see Clifford P. Hooker, *Terminating*

In *Hardiman v. Jefferson County Board of Education* (1983), for example, a tenured junior high school teacher-coach was suspended with pay, pending a hearing before the school board, for allegedly touching the buttocks of a female student and poking her breast with a fork as she stood in the school lunch line — a charge which the teacher-coach denied.[75] That same year, in Ohio, a wrestling coach (who also served as a guidance counselor) was fired for twice telling one of his team members (during a wrestling meet) to "lie and cheat" (*i.e.,* to weigh in under someone else's name). The coach admitted the wrongdoing and voluntarily resigned as coach. Ultimately, the school board instituted proceedings to terminate him as guidance counselor.[76]

Also, use of "inappropriate language" cost a Massachusetts teacher[77] and a Nebraska teacher[78] their respective jobs. Where the former teacher lost his job for language used in a conversation with his principal, the latter teacher was dismissed for calling a black student (in a racially mixed class) a "racial name."

Teachers and Revoking their Licensure for Conduct Beyond the Schoolhouse Gate, 96 EDUC. LAW REP. 1 (Feb. 23, 1995). *See* Moore v. Johnson City Bd. of Educ., 134 F.3d 781 (6th Cir. 1998).

75. Hardiman v. Jefferson Cty. Bd. of Educ., 709 F.2d 635 (11th Cir. 1983). *See also* Sheldon Comm. Sch. Dist. Bd. v. Lundblood, 528 N.W.2d 593 (Iowa 1995). In State v. Laird, 547 So. 2d 1 (La. App. 1989), a teacher/coach was convicted of sexual molestation for an incident in which he made sexual advances toward a student in his classroom. *See* Elvin v. City of Waterville, 573 A.2d 381 (Me. 1990). In Comeau v. Board of Educ., 554 N.Y.S.2d 359 (App. Div. 1990), a supervisor of transportation was terminated for sexually harassing female subordinates. *See also* Hawkins v. Hennepin Tech Center, 900 F.2d 153 (8th Cir. 1990). In Winegar v. Des. Moines Commun. Indep. Sch. Dist., 20 F.3d 895 (8th Cir. 1994), a tenured high school teacher with an unblemished record was sanctioned for getting into an altercation with a student.

76. Florian v. Highland Local Sch. Dist. Bd. of Educ., 570 F. Supp. 1358, 1359 (N.D. Ohio 1983). *See* C.F.S. v. Mahan, 934 S.W.2d 615 (Mo. App. 1996).

77. Kurlander v. School Comm., 451 N.E.2d 138 (Mass. 1983).

78. Clark v. Board of Educ., 338 N.W.2d 272 (Neb. 1983). *See also* Logan v. Warren Cty. Bd. of Educ., 549 F. Supp. 145 (S.D. Ga. 1982), involving the dismissal of a principal after a conviction for submitting false statements to the IRS.

§ 7.5. Teachers' Tenure as Job Security.

To protect themselves from possible excessive exercises of school board authority and to establish job security, teachers have over the years relied on the existence of tenure statutes. Tenure (or continuing contract as it is called in some states) is conferred by state law and can be changed or repealed by legislative enactment only. Thus, to discover how tenure status and its specific guarantees are attained, one must examine the specific statutes of a given state. Under Texas law, for example, the decision is that of the local school board as to whether or not to adopt continuing contract provisions or to offer employees fixed term contracts.[79]

Tenure in public education systems is not a guarantee of permanent employment. Tenure laws were meant in their inception and are meant now "to give job security to certified employees who meet the necessary qualifications and who satisfactorily have served the probationary period . . . ."[80] As such, tenure restricts the legal authority of a local school board to terminate the employment of an employee (who has been awarded tenure) absent a showing of cause.[81] Once attained, therefore, tenure exists to protect competent teachers from unlawful, arbitrary, and capricious board actions and to provide orderly procedures (enumerated in state statutes) to be followed if and when cause for a teacher's dismissal is established.

It must be remembered that tenure generally is obtained in a particular school system within a given state and may or may not be honored by another school system or other educational organization within that same state. Moreover, tenure accrues to types of positions in a system (*e.g.,* teacher, principal, supervisor) and *not*

---

79. White v. South Park Indep. Sch. Dist., 693 F.2d 1163 (5th Cir. 1983).

80. Thompson v. Modesto City High Sch. Dist., 139 Cal. Rptr. 603 (Cal. App. 1977).

81. Simmons v. Drew, 716 F.2d 1160 (7th Cir. 1983). An Illinois decision has held that the purpose of tenure laws is to protect teachers from "political, partisan or capricious" school board action. Birk v. Board of Educ., Flora Community Unit Sch. Dist. No. 35, 457 N.E.2d 1065 (Ill. 1983).

to specific assignments and positions (*e.g.,* first grade teacher at Hill Elementary School).[82] In *Smith v. Board of Education* (1983),[83] the Seventh Circuit made it clear that under the statutes of Illinois two physical education teachers had tenure as teachers but not as coaches. Similarly, in *Horowitz v. Board of Education, East Ramapo Central School District* (1983),[84] a New York court held that a teacher was not entitled to tenure in a separate area (remedial reading) when her tenure was in the elementary education area.

Court decisions have placed the meaning of teachers' tenure under a federal constitutional overlay of *substantive* and *procedural due process,* as guaranteed by the fourteenth amendment. Between 1972 and 1976, courts (federal and state) consistently applied the United States Supreme Court's holdings in *Board of Regents v. Roth*[85] and *Perry v. Sindermann*[86] to matters of teacher personnel. *Roth, Sindermann,* and their progeny added a second dimension to teachers' job security. In addition to boards and administrators providing state tenure guarantees to those who qualify for them, so too were personnel decisions to be free from any constitutional violations. Thus, taken together, these two cases balanced school board personnel prerogatives with teachers' constitutional rights.

a. *The Probationary Teacher.* As previously discussed, state legislatures create tenure, and tenure guarantees and protections accrue to professional employees who qualify for them. Typically,

---

82. *See, e.g.,* Connell v. Board of Educ., City Sch. Dist., 465 N.Y.S.2d 106 (N.Y. 1983).

83. 708 F.2d 258 (7th Cir. 1983). For another case on point, separating (for tenure protection purposes) teacher from coach, see Tate v. Livingston Parish Sch. Bd., 444 So. 2d 219 (La. 1983). As a Louisiana court pointed out in a case involving a teacher, an individual must be able to show that he/she is *within the definition of the position category covered* by the state's tenure statute (*e.g.,* "teacher") to be covered by that law. Burns v. State, 529 So. 2d 398 (La. App. 1988).

84. 465 N.Y.S.2d 67 (N.Y. 1983).

85. 408 U.S. 564, 92 S. Ct. 2701, 33 L. Ed. 2d 548 (1972).

86. 408 U.S. 593, 92 S. Ct. 2694, 33 L. Ed. 2d 570 (1972).

a probationary period must be served in a given professional position before one is eligible for tenure in that position. Moreover, tenure may attach to a single position (*e.g.*, teacher, or principal, or counselor) in a particular school system within a state, and does not transfer from one position to another, or from one school system to another, or from one state to another. Also, probationary periods of teachers can be extended by local school boards,[87] and additional periods of probation can be required by state law in order for one to acquire continuing contract status in an administrative or supervisory position.[88]

The length of time that new teachers in public school systems must serve in a "probationary" classification varies from state to state, sometimes from school system to school system within a state, and sometimes from professional position to professional position within a particular school system. Generally, the period of probation required ranges from three to five years.

One cannot assume that service in a school system automatically counts as probationary time. For example, a North Dakota court held that full-time tenure was not automatic simply because a teacher had served six years in the school system under terminal contracts.[89] Similarly, in California, a temporary teacher (hired to replace a regular teacher on leave) was not entitled to statutory reemployment status.[90] Yet, in a related situation, a substitute teacher in Ohio was given one full year of salary credit for 120 days of work in one year.[91]

---

87. Graham v. Board of Educ., 15 Ill. App. 3d 1092, 305 N.E.2d 310 (1973).

88. VA. CODE § 22.1-294.

89. Sacchini v. Dickinson State College, 338 N.W.2d 81 (N.D. 1983).

90. Taylor v. Board of Trustees, Del Norte Unified Sch. Dist., 196 Cal. Rptr. 444 (Cal. App. 1983).

91. Crawford v. Board of Educ., Barbeton City Schs., 453 N.E.2d 627 (Ohio 1983). Dial v. Lathrop R-II Sch. Dist., 871 S.W.2d 444 (Mo. 1994) (en banc), involved the construction and interpretation of the 1990 amendments to the Missouri Teacher Tenure Act, allowing part-time teachers to accrue credit toward permanent status. The nonrenewal of a probationary teacher's short-term contract did not constitute a dismissal under the Arizona Teacher Tenure Act. *See* Hale v. Amphitheater Sch. Dist., 961 P.2d 1059 (Ariz. App. 1998).

Once a teacher has successfully served the probationary period in a given school district, tenure (continuing contract) status is acquired in that school district.[92] Prior to the completion of the probationary period, however, there is no "expectancy of continued employment." Thus, courts have held that *Roth* and *Sindermann* do not apply, and the probationary teacher is only entitled to notice that his or her contract will or will not be renewed for the next year,[93] unless state statutes specify otherwise.

The abolition of a position and movement of a person from one position to another may also affect the status of an employee even after a probationary requirement has been satisfied. For example, in a New York case, an assistant principal's position was abolished. She was offered a teaching position, but declined it. Subsequently, she was dropped from the preferred eligibility list for reinstatement.[94]

Probationary teachers do not possess legal entitlement to employment; theirs is a year-to-year appointment. As an Arizona court has put it, "a probationary teacher's right to remain in public service is dependent upon whether the appointing officers are satisfied with the teacher's conduct and capacity, and they are, in law, the sole judges . . . ."[95]

Termination of a probationary teacher during a contract year is different from nonrenewal of that teacher at the end of a contract year. As such, it is considered a dismissal from employment. The Supreme Court of Missouri, for example, (relying on *Roth*) held that a nontenured teacher dismissed during a contractual period is entitled to procedural due process.[96] Similarly, the Rhode Island Supreme Court held (in interpreting that state's tenure law) that

---

92. Jacob v. Board of Regents, 365 A.2d 430 (R.I. 1976).

93. Abbott v. Board of Educ., 558 P.2d 1307 (Utah 1976). *See also* Ryan v. Aurora City Bd. of Educ., 540 F.2d 222 (6th Cir. 1976).

94. Sopher v. Board of Educ., E. Ramapo Cent. Sch. Dist., 468 N.Y.S.2d 184 (N.Y. 1983).

95. School Dist. v. Superior Ct., 102 Ariz. 478, 433 P.2d 28 (1967).

96. Valter v. Orchard Farm Sch. Dist., 511 S.W.2d 550 (Mo. 1976). *See* Carey v. Aldine I.S.D., 996 F. Supp. 641 (S.D. Tex. 1998).

"[a]ny committee which dismisses a nontenured teacher during the school year is required to afford the teacher a hearing at which just cause for the committee's action must be shown."[97]

Some states mandate, by statute, that all teachers (including probationary teachers) must be notified of nonrenewal by a specific date. For example, the Code of Virginia mandates:

> If a teacher who has not achieved continuing contract status receives notice of reemployment, he must accept or reject in writing within fifteen days of receipt of such notice . . . . [W]ritten notice of nonrenewal of the contract must be given by the school board on or before April fifteenth of each year.[98]

Thus, in Virginia, if a probationary teacher is not notified of nonrenewal on or before April 15, that teacher may reasonably expect another year of employment in the same position.

Similarly, in *Ottawa Education Association v. Unified School District No. 290*,[99] the Kansas Supreme Court emphasized the importance of notifying a teacher of nonrenewal on or before April 15. Otherwise, said the court, the teacher would get a continuing contract.

b. *Tenure Guarantees*. As contrasted with a teacher's *constitutional* rights, "tenure is a statutory right imposed upon a teacher's contractual employment status . . . ."[100] Even though tenure guarantees differ from state to state, there are usually *three* basic elements contained in tenure statutes: *notice* (by a specific date), *cause* (specific statement of reasons), and *hearing* (a chance for the reasons to be discussed). All three elements have been and continue to be the subject of legal challenge.

---

97. *Jacob, supra* note 92, at 433.

98. VA. CODE § 22.1-304.

99. 666 P.2d 680 (Kan. 1983). *See also* Gillespie v. Board of Educ., N. Little Rock Sch. Dist. No. 1, 692 F.2d 529 (8th Cir. 1982).

100. 68 AM. JUR. 2d 484 (1973). Emma v. Schenectady City Sch. Dist., 28 F. Supp. 2d 711 (N.D.N.Y. 1998).

205

Since procedures to be followed in the dismissal of tenured teachers are prescribed by state statute, the wording of each statute is critical. An Arizona court overturned a local school board's dismissal of a tenured teacher, finding fault with the board's notice to that teacher. Interpreting the Arizona Code, the court held that where state law mandates that a tenured teacher be dismissed prior to April 15, that action must be made official prior to that date; mere notice of intention to dismiss is not enough.[101] Two years earlier, in a Washington case, a tenured teacher challenged a school board's action to terminate because the school board had placed a statement of its official action to dismiss within the initial notice statement sent to the teacher, rather than the notice simply containing probable cause for dismissal. The Supreme Court of Washington upheld the board, ruling that the action did not create an unfair advantage for the board.[102]

Tenured teachers can be terminated solely for cause specified in a given state statute. Cause for dismissal differs from state to state; yet, there are similarities. For example, in Pennsylvania, tenured professional employees can be dismissed only for immorality, incompetency, intemperance, cruelty, persistent negligence, mental derangement, or violation of school laws of the Commonwealth.[103] In Connecticut, cause for dismissal is specified as inefficiency, incompetency, insubordination, moral misconduct, disability as shown by competent medical evidence, elimination of position, or for other due and sufficient cause.[104] In Illinois, cause is enumerated as incompetency, cruelty, negligence, immorality, and whenever in the board's opinion a teacher is not qualified to teach or the best interests of the school require it.[105]

As stated earlier in this chapter, state statutes do not define the causes listed for dismissal of tenured employees. Definition of cause is a matter left to the courts to determine. Courts, therefore,

---

101. Board of Trustees v. Carter, 559 P.2d 216 (Ariz. 1977).
102. Martin v. Dayton Sch. Dist., 536 P.2d 169 (Wash. 1975).
103. PA. STAT. ANN. tit. 24, § 11-1102 (1962).
104. CONN. GEN. STAT. ANN. tit. 5A, § 10-151 (1977).
105. ILL. ANN. STAT. (Smith-Hurd) ch. 122, § 10-22.4 (1977).

have been placed in a position of ensuring that tenured employees are dismissed for cause only. Similarly, courts seek to ensure that teachers are not dismissed for reasons violative of their rights guaranteed under the United States Constitution. When that charge is made, the *burden of proof* is placed upon the complaining employee to show that: (1) the behavior was constitutionally protected, and (2) the exercise of that protected behavior was the "motivating factor" in the board's action to dismiss him.[106]

State law may provide tenured employees with an opportunity to have a *hearing* prior to formal *dismissal*. In some states, however, a *hearing* before the school board is not mandatory and is often not held in public. Virginia provides an example of a state statute that offers the possibility of a hearing before the school board or before a fact-finding panel.[107]

In *Morelli v. Board of Education*, a former principal sought reversal of his dismissal, claiming that his superintendent's presenting a *bill of particulars* to the school board prior to his hearing before that same board rendered the board biased to his case. He claimed that he was therefore not granted a fair, impartial hearing.[108] The Appellate Court of Illinois, Third District, disagreed with him and bolstered its opinion with the following quotation from the United States Supreme Court's decision in *Hortonville Joint School District No. 1 v. Hortonville Education Association*:[109] "[T]he initial charge or determination of probable cause and the ultimate adjudication have different bases and purposes. The fact that the same agency makes them in tandem and that they relate to the same issue does not result in a procedural violation."[110]

c. *Teacher Reassignment, Transfer, and Demotion.* State law typically grants local school boards the legal prerogatives to reassign and transfer professional personnel to any single position or

---

106. *Mt. Healthy, supra* note 68.

107. VA. CODE § 22.1-309.

108. *Morelli, supra* note 51.

109. 426 U.S. 482, 96 S. Ct. 2308, 49 L. Ed. 2d 1 (1976).

110. *Morelli, supra* note 51.

combination of positions for which they are qualified.[111] Tenure laws are interpreted as not precluding the exercise of these board prerogatives. As a United States District Court said in an Illinois case involving the reassignment of a principal to regular teaching duties, the "job security envisioned by the teacher tenure law (Illinois) is a guarantee of employment but not a guarantee of continued employment in any single capacity when the educational employee is qualified to serve in more than one capacity."[112] The court added that the Tenure Act of Illinois permits boards to make such reassignments (administrators to teaching positions) without a prior hearing, provided the board has acted in good faith.[113]

In addition to upholding the reassignment (or transfer of teachers and other professionals) to positions for which they are qualified, so too have courts insisted that the former position and the new position be "coequal"; otherwise, the reassignment might be considered a demotion. For example, in *Frank v. Arapahoe County School District*,[114] a Colorado Court opined that since a school counselor was basically a teacher under state law and not an "administrator," counselor and teacher are (for transfer purposes) coequal positions.[115] A United States District Court added, in deciding a similar case in Missouri, that there can be no demotion so long as an individual is transferred between two coequal positions.[116]

The Supreme Court of New York, Oneida County, in *Rossi v. Board of Education* (1983), broadly interpreted the New York Code and held that the principalship of a K-6 school is a "similar position" to that of a K-8 principalship. Thus, a K-8 principal

---

111. Lester v. Board of Educ., 230 N.E.2d 893 (Ill. 1967).

112. Danno v. Peterson, 421 F. Supp. 950, 953 (N.D. Ill. 1976).

113. *Id.*

114. 506 P.2d 373 (Colo. 1972).

115. *Id.* In Hightower v. State Comm'r of Educ., 778 S.W.2d 595 (Tex. App. 1989), the Court of Appeals of Texas (Austin) held that administrative officers employed as school directors of maintenance and of fiscal affairs did not qualify as teachers within the meaning of the Term Contract Nonrenewal Act; thus they were not entitled to nonrenewal procedures set out in the Act. The law does include superintendents, principals and counselors as "teachers."

116. Birdwell v. Hazelwood Sch. Dist., 352 F. Supp. 613 (Mo. 1972).

(whose position was abolished) could be transferred to a K-6 position. However, said the court, he would remain in the same salary structure such that he would receive future increments as a K-8 school principal.[117]

On the other hand, a California appellate court demonstrated the tenuous nature of the above legal point. The court was convinced that the transfer of a school counselor to a teaching position "was not a reassignment to a position of a rank and grade equal to the position of counselor . . . ."[118] Thus, the transfer was improper.

The elements of "similar rank and equal salary" also played a significant part in a Seventh Circuit decision. In *Lyznicki v. Board of Education, City School District,* the appellate court had before it a school board's nonrenewal of a principal's contract and his reassignment to a regular classroom teaching position, with no reduction in salary. To the court, looking to Illinois law, the board was well within the meaning of the Code.[119]

Generally, whether or not a transfer is voluntary is another significant element in employment decision-making cases. For example, in *Bell v. Board of Education* (1983), a New York court held that the involuntary transfer of a tenured senior high school principal to the position of a junior high school principal violated that principal's rights under the New York Code.[120]

In the past, courts of law have heard cases of several teachers who claimed that their *reassignments* to other positions were actually *demotions*. The Court of Appeals for the Fifth Circuit decided *Singleton v. Jackson Municipal Separate School District.*[121] In that case the court constructed the following definition of the term

---

117. 465 N.Y.S.2d 630 (N.Y. 1983).

118. Thompson v. Modesto City High Sch. Dist., 139 Cal. Rptr. 603 (Cal. App. 1977).

119. 707 F.2d 949 (7th Cir. 1983). *See also* Sorlie v. School Dist. No. 2, 667 P.2d 400 (Mont. 1983).

120. 468 N.Y.S.2d 85 (N.Y. 1983). *See also* Burkhart v. Board of Educ., 649 S.W.2d 855 (Ky. 1983); County Sch. Bd. v. Epperson, 435 S.E.2d 642 (Va. 1993).

121. 419 F.2d 1211 (5th Cir. 1969), *rev'd and remanded,* 396 U.S. 290 (1970). *See also* 43 MISS. L.J. 368 (1972).

209

"demotion," a definition used by subsequent courts to adjudicate such matters:

> "Demotion" . . . includes any re-assignment (1) under which the staff member receives less pay or has less responsibility than under the assignment he held previously, (2) which requires a lesser degree of skill than did the assignment he held previously, or (3) under which the staff member was asked to teach a subject and grade other than one for which he is certified or for which he has had substantial experience within a reasonably current period. In general and depending upon the subject matter involved, five years is such a reasonable period.[122]

The court added that all reassignments and discharges must be made through the application of *objective, reasonable,* and *nondiscriminatory* criteria.[123]

Regarding assignments of teachers to extracurricular duties, courts have granted discretion to local boards of education. In a New Jersey case it was held that a local board show only that the extracurricular assignments are reasonable, nondiscriminatory, are related to a teacher's interests and expertise, and do not require excessive hours.[124] And, a teacher need not be compensated for such *involuntary* assignments.

Compensation for extra assignments was one issue in a case decided by the Fifth Circuit. In this case, however, a female associate professor at a state university claimed that her heavier than

---

122. 419 F.2d at 1218.

123. *Id.* at 1218. In King v. Board of Educ., 447 S.E.2d 657 (Ga. App. 1994), the court held that a failure to reappoint a teacher as band director was not a demotion.

124. Board of Educ. v. Asbury Park Educ. Ass'n, 145 N.J. Super. 495, 368 A.2d 396 (1976). In Rapid City Educ. Ass'n v. Rapid City Sch. Dist., 442 N.W.2d 926 (S.D. 1989), the Supreme Court of South Dakota held that where a collective bargaining agreement provided no additional compensation for teachers assigned to hallway supervision during the seven periods of the day, the teachers were entitled to compensation when assigned lunchroom duty during lunch periods. *See also* Nea-Goodland v. Board of Educ., 775 P.2d 675 (Kan. App. 1989).

normal course load kept her from the opportunity to teach extra courses for pay — something which her male counterparts could do because of their normal course loads.[125] Claiming, among other things, a violation of the Equal Pay Act,[126] the plaintiff alleged that her faculty position had actually replaced two full-time professors and, as a result, she had a workload totaling eighteen to twenty-one hours per semester, while her male counterparts carried nine hours per semester. Thus, since her extra-heavy course load precluded her from working for extra pay as did male faculty, she had been placed in a position wherein she received "less money for equal work."

The United States District Court, Western District of Louisiana, dismissed her complaint and the Fifth Circuit Court of Appeals affirmed that decision. In the court's opinion, "'work load discrimination' *per se* is not actionable under the *Equal Pay Act*."[127]

d. *Procedural Safeguards: Bishop v. Wood.* In *Bishop v. Wood*,[128] the United States Supreme Court decided a nonschool case with direct bearing on teachers' tenure protections as well as on constitutional guarantees of job security.

In *Bishop,* the city manager of Marion, North Carolina terminated the employment of a policeman who claimed he had "permanent employment" as defined by city ordinance. The policeman brought suit in federal district court seeking reinstatement and back pay, claiming that he had been terminated without a "pretermination hearing" — a constitutional guarantee afforded permanent employees.[129]

The United States District Court granted a motion for summary judgment holding that, on the basis of state law (North Carolina),

---

125. Berry v. Board of Supvrs., L.S.U., 715 F.2d 971 (5th Cir. 1983).

126. 29 U.S.C. § 206(b).

127. *Berry, supra* note 125, at 982.

128. 426 U.S. 341, 96 S. Ct. 2074, 48 L. Ed. 2d 684 (1976).

129. *Id.* at 96 S. Ct. 2074. In his petition, the policeman claimed that he was told *privately,* by the city manager, that his dismissal was based upon his failure to follow orders, poor attendance at police training classes, causing low morale, and for conduct unsuited to an officer.

the policeman held his position at the "will and pleasure of the city.".[130] A three-judge panel of the Court of Appeals for the Fourth Circuit affirmed that decision,[131] and the Supreme Court of the United States granted certiorari.[132] The two questions before the high court were: (1) Was the policeman's employment status a *property* interest protected by the due process clause of the fourteenth amendment? (2) If the reasons given for his discharge were false, was that false explanation a violation of *liberty* as protected by that same clause?

In answering the first question, the Supreme Court majority looked to North Carolina state law, the Marion city ordinance under which the policeman worked, and the United States District Court's interpretation of these two. Said Mr. Justice Stevens:

> A property interest in employment can, of course, be created by ordinance, or by an implied contract. In either case, however, the sufficiency of the claim of entitlement must be decided by reference to state law. The North Carolina Supreme Court had held that an enforceable expectation of continued employment in that State can exist only if the employer, by statute or contract, has actually granted some form of guarantee.... Whether such a guarantee has been given can be determined only by an examination of the particular statute or ordinance in question.[133]

Thus, looking to the United States District Court's interpretation as controlling, the majority accepted the view that the policeman "held his position at the will and pleasure of the city," and that his only guarantees in removal were procedural.[134]

---

130. 377 F. Supp. 501 (W.D.N.C. 1973).

131. 498 F.2d 134 (4th Cir. 1974).

132. 423 U.S. 890, 96 S. Ct. 185, 46 L. Ed. 2d 121 (1975).

133. *Bishop, supra* note 128, at 426 U.S. 345. *See also* George v. Bourgeois, 852 F. Supp. 1341 (E.D. Tex. 1994), where a principal brought an action growing out of her claim to a property interest in renewal of her contract as principal under Texas law.

134. *Id.*

Regarding the *liberty* question, the Supreme Court was of the opinion that since the city manager's determination of the grounds for discharge were communicated orally to the policeman (in private), it cannot be assumed that the policeman's "'good name, reputation, honesty, or integrity' was thereby impaired."[135] And, even if the reasons for discharge stated to the policeman were false, "the reasons stated to him in private had no different impact on his reputation than if they had been true."[136]

In rendering the majority opinion, Mr. Justice Stevens concluded:

> The federal court is not the appropriate forum in which to review the multitude of personnel decisions that are made daily by public agencies. We must accept the harsh fact that numerous individual mistakes are inevitable in the day-to-day administration of our affairs. The United States Constitution cannot feasibly be construed to require federal judicial review for every such error. In the absence of any claim that the public employer was motivated by a desire to curtail or to penalize the exercise of an employee's constitutionally protected rights, we must presume that official action was regular and, if erroneous, can best be corrected in other ways. The Due Process Clause of the Fourteenth Amendment is not a guarantee against incorrect or ill-advised personnel decisions.[137]

---

135. *Id.* at 426 U.S. 348.

136. *Id.* In Geren v. Board of Educ., 650 A.2d 616 (Conn. App. 1994), the court made it clear that a teacher who claims possible injury to reputation and good name, which might impose stigma on his professional reputation, must plead a liberty violation and invoke the protections of the due process clause of the fourteenth amendment. For two decisions involving release of employee information to the public, see Beckham v. Board of Educ., 873 S.W.2d 575 (Ky. 1994), where a board released employment records to a newspaper, and Perkins v. Freedom of Information Comm'n, 635 A.2d 783 (Conn. 1993), involving the disclosure of a school psychologist's sick leave data.

137. *Id.* at 426 U.S. 349-50. In 1985, the Burger Court clarified its views on employee minimal procedural due process in Cleveland Bd. of Educ. v. Louder-

There have been several public school personnel cases heard by courts (since the Supreme Court's decision) wherein the judges saw *Bishop* as controlling.[138] An analysis of these cases reveals the emergence of a definite pattern of court attitudes toward public school personnel decision-making and teachers' rights. Some of these attitudes are: (1) a return of federal courts to a "hands off" attitude toward public school personnel decisions, (2) a renewed insistence by federal courts that aggrieved individuals seek remedies provided in state law before taking their complaint to a federal court, (3) nonintervention by a federal court in public school personnel decisions unless there clearly is present a gross violation of either constitutional law or federal statutory law, (4) the application of a more *flexible* standard of due process when school personnel decisions are heard in federal court, and (5) a look to appropriate state law and local school board policy by federal judges as controlling their decisions in school personnel cases.

Looking to the Code of Virginia, a federal district court judge, citing a procedural deficiency, overturned the decision of a local school board that had suspended a teacher without pay. In the school board's opinion, in such situations, the state statute did not require a presuspension hearing. The federal judge did not agree. As he interpreted the same state statute, a presuspension hearing was necessary in situations where a teacher would receive no pay during the period of suspension.[139]

---

mill, 1055 S. Ct. 1487 (1985), *decided on remand* at Loudermill v. Cleveland Bd. of Educ., 844 F.2d 304 (6th Cir. 1988). Also, in *Loudermill* the Court said that a pretermination hearing could assist in the process of determining whether or not charges against an employee are true and supported by evidence.

138. *See, e.g.,* Danno v. Peterson, *supra* note 22; Chamberlain v. Wichita Falls Indep. Sch. Dist., 539 F.2d 566 (5th Cir. 1976).

139. Wilkinson v. School Bd., 566 F. Supp. 766 (E.D. Va. 1983). For a similar but somewhat contrary case on point, see Jones v. Jefferson Parish Sch. Bd., 533 F. Supp. 816 (E.D. La. 1982).

§ 7.6. Antidiscrimination in Employment: *Griggs v. Duke Power Company.*

Beginning in the early 1970s, several cases were heard by federal courts challenging alleged discrimination in employment practices. A mandate emerged from these decisions requiring all employers to establish a relationship between the *purpose* of differential treatment of job applicants and employees and the *criteria* used for identification and classification of individuals who are to be placed in various categories for purposes of hiring, promotion, salary, and retention. The Supreme Court's landmark decision in *Griggs v. Duke Power Co.*[140] firmly established this element of equal protection.

Griggs was the first case to present the nation's highest court with the question of whether *Title VII of the Civil Rights Act of 1964* prohibited an employer from instituting, as a condition of employment, a high school education or achieving a passing grade on a standardized test. In deciding this issue, the Supreme Court considered several related questions, among which were the following: (1) What relationship, if any, exists between employment requirements and "job performance"? (2) What methods of evaluation are used by employers to judge the *effectiveness* of "job criteria" as they relate to job success? (3) Can employers demonstrate the "job relatedness" of "job requirements"?[141]

---

140. 401 U.S. 424, 91 S. Ct. 849, 28 L. Ed. 2d 158 (1971). For a case alleging sex discrimination under Title 7 in filling a university faculty position, see Lyford v. Schilling, 750 F.2d 1341 (5th Cir. 1985). In Department of Civil Rights *ex rel.* Peterson v. Brighton Area Schs., 431 N.W.2d 65 (Mich. App. 1988), the Michigan Court of Appeals used a disparate impact analysis and held that a school district's policy of prohibiting teachers from taking consecutive pregnancy disability and infant care leaves of absence constituted sex discrimination.

141. *Id.* According to the Supreme Court, "What is required by Congress is the removal of artificial, arbitrary, and unnecessary barriers to employment when the barriers operate invidiously to discriminate on the basis of racial or other impermissible classification." *See also* Washington v. Davis, 426 U.S. 229, 96 S. Ct. 2040, 48 L. Ed. 2d 597 (1976). In deciding this Title VII case involving black applicants for the District of Columbia police training program who were rejected

A primary effect of *Griggs* was to force employers to remove arbitrary, irrational criteria of applicant and employee selection. Also, they were to publish immediately detailed job descriptions — including not only statements describing job functions, but also including sets of qualifications necessary to obtain that job and to perform those functions.

Thus, the *Griggs* decision and a host of previous and subsequent federal laws and regulations offered civil rights lawyers the legal leverage necessary to force *equal employment opportunity* into action and to bring a halt to discrimination in employment. It became the law of the land that job applicants and employees were not to be treated arbitrarily, irrationally, or capriciously. As the Court commanded in *Griggs,* a person must be measured for the job and not measured in the abstract.

Griggs has had a profound impact on public school personnel decision-making. Shortly after *Griggs* several decisions emanated from lower federal courts striking down the use of the *Graduate Record Examination* (GRE) and *National Teachers Examination* (NTE) as means of selecting, promoting, and retaining professional personnel.

In *Armstead v. Starkville,* the Board of Education of Starkville, Mississippi had a policy that all applicants for teaching positions and in-service teachers take the GRE, General Aptitude Test, and subject area test. Attainment of specified minimum scores on these exams as a precondition of employment and retention was the board's requirement.

---

because of scores on a verbal skills test, Mr. Justice White said: "In order to violate the Constitution, an employment criterion must be used with racially discriminatory intent; racial impact alone is not sufficient." The reader is cautioned that the United States Supreme Court has shifted the burden of proof in Title 7 (*Griggs*-type) cases to employees, thus increasing the difficulty of plaintiffs prevailing in a discrimination case. *See* Wards Cove Packing Co. v. Atonio, 109 S. Ct. 2115 (1989). For a case showing the dimensions of a prima facie case of employment discrimination, see School Bd. of Leon Cty. v. Weaver, 556 So. 2d 443 (Fla. App. 1990).

A group of teachers filed suit in federal court alleging they had been denied employment because of the board's GRE requirement and that such a criterion was unreasonable and arbitrary. The court ruled in the plaintiffs' favor, holding that the GRE requirement was arbitrary and unreasonable for the following reasons:

(1) GRE tests evaluate an individual's capacity for advanced studies at the master's and doctoral levels; they are not "job related" to teacher competencies; and

(2) The school system had never conducted any empirical studies to see if the exams and required scores (combined 640 on the General Aptitude, and 50th percentile on the Advanced Test) were predictive of teacher success in that system.[142]

Chance v. Board of Examiners offers another example of a post-*Griggs* case. In *Chance,* New York City, through its board of examiners, prescribed and administered exams to candidates seeking licenses for permanent appointment to supervisory positions in the city's public school system.

A class action suit was brought challenging the constitutionality of the examination program by parties claiming a conspicuous disparity between the numbers of qualified blacks and whites who failed to pass the exams — thus the whole program was "constitutionally suspect."

A United States District Court found the examination "too subjective" and not sufficiently "job related." The exams, said the court, simply called for a "regurgitation" of memorized material, "not related" to showing necessary skills and qualifications for obtaining a principal's or supervisor's position. Also, the city

---

142. 325 F. Supp. 560 (N.D. Miss. 1971). In National Educ. Ass'n v. South Carolina, 434 U.S. 1026, 98 S. Ct. 756, 54 L. Ed. 2d 775 (1978), the United States Supreme Court upheld use of the National Teachers Examination (NTE) to hire and classify teachers in South Carolina's public schools, where plaintiffs failed to prove a racially discriminatory purpose in the state's use of that examination. *See also* Allen v. Alabama State Bd. of Educ., 164 F.3d 1347 (11th Cir. 1999).

school system made no attempt to establish the reliability or validity of the exams through empirical studies.[143]

A review of subsequent cases indicates that classroom teachers in public school systems, as well as all other professional personnel, must not be discriminated against in hiring, assignment, promotion, reassignment, and retention. These cases demonstrate that an assessment of each teacher's professional qualifications and performance, evaluated on objective criteria and compared to all other similar teachers, is a key to practicing fairness and to avoiding discrimination.

There is evidence, however, that some federal judges have sought, as their first priority, to achieve racial and sexual balance within a given school system's population of professionals. A benchmark case regarding racial balance is *Porcelli v. Titus,*[144] wherein the Court of Appeals for the Third Circuit widened the scope of faculty desegregation, making it possible to consider *race* as a factor in the selection, assignment, promotion, and retention of professionals in schools. Said the court, the integration of faculties "is as important as proper integration of schools themselves . . . ."[145] As such, "[s]tate action based partly on consideration of color, when color is not used per se, and in the furtherance of a proper governmental objective, is not necessarily a violation of the Fourteenth Amendment."[146]

---

143. 330 F. Supp. 203 (S.D.N.Y. 1971), *rev'd and remanded,* 534 F.2d 993 (2d Cir. 1976).

144. 431 F.2d 1254 (3d Cir. 1970). *See* Miles v. Board of Educ., 989 F. Supp. 1225 (E.D. Mo. 1998).

145. *Porcelli,* at 1257.

146. *Id. See also* Patterson v. American Tobacco Co., 535 F.2d 257 (4th Cir. 1976), wherein it was said that "racial quotas and preferential hiring may be an appropriate remedy where a long-standing practice of unlawful discrimination has been shown to exist." This statement was at the center of the debate on the proper role of affirmative action in making employment decisions (from hiring to firing) in the 1990s. There are those who say that employment decisions must be color-blind and must be made solely on the basis of merit, see, e.g., Smith v. Virginia Commonwealth Univ., 856 F. Supp. 1088 (E.D. Va. 1994). The United States Supreme Court, in Adarand Constr. Co. v. Pena, 115 S. Ct. 2097 (1995), held (by

Thus, out of this era of affirmative action has come an attempt by both administrative directive and judicial decree to "balance" faculties by race and by sex. Precedent was established in the early 1970s for having numerical goals in the furtherance of a proper governmental objective, namely, to move with all deliberate speed toward removal of discrimination from every sector of employment, including public school systems.

Cramer v. Virginia Commonwealth University[147] is an example of a case (among several) wherein "reverse discrimination" in employment was the plaintiff's claim. Heard by a United States District Court in Richmond, Virginia, this case involved a white male applicant for a university teaching position who "brought an action for a declaratory judgment that the university, by hiring two women to the faculty despite his own equal or better qualifications, had engaged in illegal reverse . . . discrimination."[148] In holding for the male, Judge Warriner ruled that Title VII of the Civil Rights Act of 1964 forbids the use of sex quotas or goals in employment even to overcome an existing imbalance.[149] He further opined that the university's "admittedly discriminatory hirings, having been based on sex, were unconstitutional and illegal even though they represented an attempt by the university to comply with a federally ordered affirmative action program to recruit women for faculty positions in order to compensate for alleged past deficiencies in minority hiring."[150]

To Judge Warriner, "[r]eliance upon such discriminatory practices to achieve 'quotas' or 'goals' is the use of an unconstitutional means to achieve an unconstitutional end."[151] The university's

---

a 5-4 vote) that federal affirmative action programs are subject to the same strict scrutiny standard as are racial classifications by state and local governments.

147. 415 F. Supp. 673 (1976). Subsequently, *Cramer* was vacated and remanded by the Fourth Circuit. *See* Cramer v. Virginia Commonwealth Univ., 568 F.2d 297 (4th Cir. 1978).

148. *Id.*

149. *Id.* at 679.

150. *Id.* at 673.

151. *Id.* at 680.

plan of affirmative action had been approved by federal officials under Executive Order 11246, governing all federal contractors.

Total ramifications of such cases as *Cramer* certainly have yet to be realized. Gluckman, however, sees three directions for educators as they look to possible future litigation. These are:

> (1) If the adverse effect of "affirmative action" programs on *whites* or *males* is severe enough to be regarded as actual *discrimination,* courts will likely find such affirmative action programs unacceptable.
>
> (2) If the *quality* of a program or organization is adversely affected by "affirmative action," such efforts to compensate for past discrimination will be unacceptable.
>
> (3) When preferential treatment of a race or sex approaches a level of "fixed percentages," it will likely be judged a quota system, and thus courts will deem such efforts unacceptable.[152]

In *Teaneck Board of Education v. Teaneck Teachers Association,*[153] the teachers' association had filed a grievance on behalf of a member-teacher alleging "reverse" discrimination in the failure of the school board to reappoint him as a basketball coach. Taken initially by the board of education to the Public Employment Relations Commission (P.E.R.C.) on the issue of *arbitrability,* P.E.R.C. ruled that the association's claim was within the scope of arbitration. To P.E.R.C., "the disputed issue was based upon allegations of racial discrimination that were within the scope of collective negotiations . . . ."[154]

On appeal by the board, the appellate division court reversed the P.E.R.C. ruling and held that the issue of racial discrimination was

---

152. I. Gluckman, "Affirmative Action: Is It Really Discrimination in Reverse?" (Blacksburg, Va.: unpublished paper, 1976), at 11. For two comprehensive affirmative action decisions, see Taxman v. Piscataway Twp. Bd. of Educ., 91 F.3d 1547 (3d Cir. 1996), *cert. dismissed,* 118 S. Ct. 595 (1997); Texas Educ. Agency v. Messer, 130 F.3d 130 (5th Cir. 1998).

153. 462 A.2d 137 (N.J. 1983).

154. *Id.* at 139.

preempted by the Law Against Discrimination (N.J.S.A. § 10:5-1 to 10:5-38). Therefore, said the court, the issue was not subject to collective negotiations.[155] What is more, such a matter as hiring basketball coaches was well within the legal prerogative of a school board — a prerogative that could not be "bargained away."

On certification, the Supreme Court of New Jersey held that since the board's decision on hiring implicated an "inherent managerial prerogative," the reverse discrimination claim could not be submitted to binding arbitration, where the arbitrator's decision would "trespass on managerial authority."[156] However, since the grievance of discrimination claims was permissible and to be encouraged, the matter may be referred to an appropriate forum for review and findings. Such a forum in this matter, said the court, would be the State Division of Civil Rights.[157] To the court, it was the intent of the legislature in establishing that Division that even though some interference with managerial prerogatives of public employers still might take place, "the interference is mandated to fulfill governmental policy."[158]

§ 7.7. Teacher Evaluation and Job Security.

As public education moved into the first half of the decade of the 1980s, school systems across the nation found themselves increasingly facing serious budgetary problems. In recent years declines in enrollment and decreases in revenues have forced school boards to reduce budgets and expenditures, and, since a major portion of a school system budget is for professional services (salaries), reductions in professional force (RIF) were a certainty.

Currently, there exists a growing competition between new teachers for a shrinking number of job openings and an increased feeling of insecurity among experienced teachers as programs are

---

155. *Id.*
156. *Id.* at 140.
157. *Id.* at 141.
158. *Id.*

cut from school system budgets. Local boards of education have been called upon to devise employment and retention policies and procedures to accommodate these budgetary conditions while still striving to provide job security for employees and quality education for their students.

Phillippi v. School District of Springfield[159] is a RIF-type case. Speaking to the issue of staff reductions based upon "decreases in student enrollment," the Commonwealth Court of Pennsylvania held that local school boards have the discretion to determine what is a "substantial decrease in enrollment" to justify reductions in force, absent abuse of discretion, arbitrariness, or a misconception of law.[160]

The Pennsylvania court further opined that there is a difference between a RIF of nontenured staff and a RIF of tenured staff. To the court, nontenured employees "have no rights of retention based either on efficiency rating or seniority as against tenured employees or as among themselves."[161]

a. *Fairness in Evaluation: The Ultimate Remedy.* United States District Court Judge Hoffman made the following statement in deciding a case involving Nansemond County, Virginia: "School board members are charged with the crucial task of providing the best quality education possible for all children and this duty may be discharged only if teachers are employed by ability and no other criteria."[162] In the opinion of Judge Hoffman, quality personnel produce quality instruction.

In preceding discussions of recruitment, hiring, assignment, transfer, and retention of personnel, a common thread runs through each: namely, the need to establish a standard of fairness and fair

---

159. 367 A.2d 1133 (Pa. 1977).

160. *Id.*

161. *Id.* at 1141. For some case law involving *reduction in force*, see Raben v. Board of Educ., 542 N.Y.S.2d 937 (1989); Leu v. Newton Community Sch. Dist., 441 N.W.2d 408 (Iowa App. 1989); and Harms v. Independent Sch. Dist. No. 300, 441 N.W.2d 522 (Minn. App. 1989).

162. United States v. Nansemond Cty. Sch. Bd., 351 F. Supp. 196 (E.D. Va. 1972), *rev'd,* 492 F.2d 919 (4th Cir. 1974).

treatment in evaluation. Fair evaluation procedures and fair treatment will likely yield a sense of job security. And, the more secure the competent teacher, the greater the likelihood of quality instruction.

It is imperative that procedural safeguards be built into the substantive protections of teachers. Four basic elements necessary to establish procedural rights to fair treatment in teacher evaluation have emerged from case law in point. A teacher evaluation must: (1) be directly related to the measurement of teacher effectiveness in job performance, (2) include valid, reliable, and defensible criteria as a basis for making all evaluative judgments of job effectiveness, (3) involve those individuals to be evaluated from formation of criteria to implementation of process, and (4) be developmental and not punitive in nature.[163]

A California court ruled that just because state law established a uniform system of evaluation and assessment of performance for all certified employees does not mean that local boards can no longer reassign administrators to teaching positions. Administrators serve at the pleasure of the board and can be reassigned at any time, no matter what the ratings are.[164]

---

163. 1 COLLECT. BARG. Q. 1, 3 (1976). For recent examples of cases involving issues of fair evaluation, see Dudley v. Board of Educ., 632 N.E.2d 94 (Ill. App. 1st Dist. 1994), where a teacher sought judicial relief from potential dismissal for unsatisfactory evaluation and remediation program. *See also* Trustees v. Spivey, 866 P.2d 208 (Mont. 1993), involving the termination of a teacher without a period of remediation, in light of evidence of the teacher's failure to acknowledge deficiencies upon which to improve; Schofield v. Richmond Cty. Sch. Dist., 447 S.E.2d 189 (S.C. 1994), where evaluations and instructional observations are challenged; and Shapiro v. School Dist., 637 A.2d 718 (Pa. Commw. Ct. 1994), where it was held that observation by the superintendent prior to dismissal was not required. For a case involving the nonrenewal of a probationary teacher and the importance of evaluation of classroom performance, see Alba v. Ansonia Bd. of Educ., 999 F. Supp. 687 (D. Conn. 1998).

164. Anaclerio v. Skinner, 134 Cal. Rptr. 303, 304 (Cal. 1976). *See also* Elrod v. Harrisonville Cass R-IX Schs., 555 F. Supp. 107 (W.D. Mo. 1982), wherein it was said that an assistant principal had the burden to show that his position had been eliminated for impermissible reasons.

b. *The Doctrine of Business Necessity and Teacher Evaluation.* The doctrine of business necessity (or purpose) may prove to be a viable defense for school boards whose personnel decisions are challenged in court, and, at the same time, might prove to be the tool needed to ensure both *substantive* and procedural fair treatment of teachers. Not an absolute defense of practices affecting minority employment, business necessity implies that the employment practice "is necessary to the safe and efficient operation of the business . . . ."[165] According to Urbach, "[b]usiness purpose is defined as having three criteria. First, it must be sufficiently compelling to override any racial impact. Secondly, no other available alternative having a less discriminatory impact can exist. Finally, the business practice must accomplish its stated purpose."[166]

Ideally, states Divine, business necessity as developed in *Griggs* and subsequent cases encompasses "a careful balance between merit, on the one hand, and equality, on the other."[167] Divine then cautions school personnel officials that "judgments of teacher quality are at best a very crude tool."[168] And, "when measurement of merit is not reliable, or when qualitative distinctions between candidates are not significant, the scales tip in favor of equality, requiring an appropriate representation of minority and women employees."[169]

Local school boards must retain the best qualified and most competent teachers (with proven records of competence in job performance) in an effort to provide quality education for students.

---

165. R. Urbach, *Color-Conscious Quota Relief: A Constitutional Remedy for Racial Employment Discrimination,* 11 URB. LAW ANN. 333 (1976).

166. *Id.*

167. T. Divine, *Women in the Academy: Sex-Discrimination in University Faculty Hiring and Promotion,* 5 J. OF LAW & EDUC. 429, 443 (Oct. 1976).

168. *Id.* at 442.

169. *Id.* at 443. For a case involving allegations of sex discrimination in the evaluation of applicants for a position as science department chairperson in a public school system, see Nagel v. Avon Bd. of Educ., 575 F. Supp. 105 (D. Conn. 1983).

c. *Seniority: Last-Hired, First-Fired and Job Security.* The possibility of mass teacher layoffs has raised a legal question concerning the effects of seniority rules on minority employees. The question is usually phrased as follows: Is *seniority* (last-hired, first-fired doctrine) a system that perpetuates and renews the effects of racial discrimination in the guise of job security?

For an analysis of the seniority practice as a legal issue, one must first turn to court decisions involving business and industry, (*e.g.*, *Quarles v. Philip Morris,*[170] *Franks v. Bowman Transportation Co.*[171] and several others). A review of the substance of plaintiff arguments reveals that "[m]inority and women employees are seeking legal protection from layoffs. They contend that layoffs based on length of service perpetuate past discrimination by threatening newly won jobs of groups long denied equal opportunity. These groups have been unable to accrue the necessary seniority to withstand layoffs."[172]

Seniority ("last-hired, first-fired"), says Depuy, discriminates between employees solely on the basis of "length of service." And, a system that favors older employees to new ones does not constitute a Title VII violation. Congress, states Depuy, "did *not* outlaw discrimination based on length of service. In fact, it sought to preserve it."[173]

To put it another way, seniority in employment connotes length of service (the "measure of time") as a major basis for establishing, maintaining, and protecting employee rights, duties, and benefits. As the United States Supreme Court said in *California Brewers Association v. Bryant,* a nonschool case, "A 'seniority system' is a scheme that, alone or in tandem with non-'seniority' criteria, allots to employees ever improving employment rights and benefits as their relative lengths of pertinent employment increase."[174] The

---

170. 279 F. Supp. 505 (E.D. Va. 1968).

171. 424 U.S. 747, 96 S. Ct. 1251, 47 L. Ed. 2d 444 (1976).

172. W.K. Depuy, *Last-Hired, First-Fired: Discrimination or Sacrosanct?,* 80 DICK. L. REV. 747, at 748 (Summer, 1976).

173. *Id.* at 750.

174. 444 U.S. 598, 100 S. Ct. 814, 63 L. Ed. 2d 55 (1980).

High Court emphasized, however, that a bona fide seniority system delineates how and when the "seniority time clock begins to tick," what time will or will not count toward seniority, what employment conditions are or are not influenced by seniority, and how and when seniority might be forfeited.[175]

Recognizing that opponents of seniority systems argue that the addition of § 703(h) to Title VII nullifies the "last-hired, first-fired" procedure, Depuy reaches a contrary conclusion, based on an analysis of *three* decisions from the Third, Fifth, and Seventh Circuits, wherein it was held that "use of seniority to determine the order of layoffs does not violate Title VII." [176] He warns, however, that courts will look closely at a seniority plan to be certain that it is absent of any discriminatory intent.

Depuy's analysis of the current legal scene reveals that

> [t]he last-hired, first-fired doctrine governing work force reductions is not discriminatory and not prohibited by law. To conclude otherwise would authorize preferential treatment of groups who have suffered from perpetuation of past discrimination. Preferential treatment is prohibited by Title VII because the act does not require integration, but only an end to employment discrimination. It requires "the elimination of racial barriers, not their creation in order to satisfy our theory as to how society ought to be organized." [177]

The seniority system in employment remains intact. To reach a contrary conclusion "would lead to an unwarranted remedy of a non-legal wrong that plagues one class by imposing a legal disadvantage on another." [178]

---

175. *Id.*

176. Jersey Cent. Power & Light Co. v. Local 327, Int'l Bhd. of Elec. Workers, 508 F.2d 687 (3d Cir. 1975), *vacated,* 421 U.S. 987 (1976); Watkins v. Local 2369, United Steelworkers of Am., 516 F.2d 41 (5th Cir. 1975); Waters v. Wisconsin Steel Workers, 502 F.2d 1309 (7th Cir. 1974).

177. Depuy, *supra* note 172, at 758.

178. *Id.* at 766.

The importance of local school boards taking seniority into consideration when facing a reduction in professional force (RIF) was stressed in a recent case decided in Pennsylvania. The court made it clear that boards must be free to take RIF actions at any time; however, boards "must also respect the seniority rights of tenured employees."[179] Citing a 1943 case in point, the court included the following quotation from that case:

> Seniority rights exist for the dual purposes of assuring continuity of service for faithful labor and providing efficient service to the state gained by experience.

> Seniority is a matter not to be treated lightly. The very stability of our schools depends on retaining those teachers who because of long years of experience and devotion have earned the obedience of pupils, the admiration of the parents, and the respect of the community.[180]

Seniority must be recognized by a school board as an important factor to consider when making personnel decisions, prior to implementation of any reduction plans that rely on a "last-hired, first-fired doctrine." Faced with evaluating a school system's reduction in force plan, a Washington court held that a school board may consider seniority only when it is a previously adopted criterion.[181]

Traditionally, seniority has played an important role in school cases. For example, a New York court held that a teacher was improperly dismissed where he taught appliance repair (as a part of his trade electricity courses), and another teacher was hired subsequently to teach appliance repair. In the court's opinion, since the former teacher was senior to the latter teacher, his dismissal was improper.[182]

---

179. *Phillippi, supra* note 159, at 1143.

180. Appeal of Wesenberg, 346 Pa. 438, 31 A.2d 151 (1943).

181. Black v. Joint Sch. Dist., 13 Wash. App. 444, 535 P.2d 135 (1975).

182. Nusz v. Board of Coop. Educ. Servs., Second Supervisory Dist., 459 N.Y.S.2d 889, 890 (N.Y. 1983). For examples of RIF cases, see Berry v. Kanawha Cty. Bd. of Educ., 446 S.E.2d 510 (W. Va. 1994); and Walkowski v.

The courts have been clear, however, that seniority systems cannot be used as a pretext to perpetuate illegal or unconstitutional purposes. For example, seniority systems have been under considerable attack as perpetuators of past discrimination and as plans which prevent or delay integration. As the Second Circuit said in *Arthur v. Nyquist,* "a seniority system should not be allowed to prevent or inordinately delay the achievement of a fully desegregated school system . . . ." [183]

§ 7.8. The Civil Rights Tort (42 U.S.C. § 1983).

For many years, the Civil Rights Act of 1871 was largely ignored. In 1961, the *Monroe v. Pape* decision (365 U.S. 167, 81 S. Ct. 473, 5 L. Ed. 2d 492 (1961)) initiated what has resulted in increased litigation. It was in 1961 that the provisions of the Act were made applicable to local public school board members and administrators. [184]

Emerging from the Reconstruction Era, § 1 of the Civil Rights Act of 1871 was intended to implement the language of the fourteenth amendment in an effort to bring full civil rights to the newly freed Negroes. The language of the Act itself was directed at acts of misconduct and abuse by state officials who deprived citizens of their civil rights. [185]

Now codified at 42 U.S.C. § 1983 and commonly referred to as a "§ 1983 action," the civil rights cause of action has given rise to an increasing number of both employee and student cases. In recent years, § 1983 has become an alternative action for advocates

---

Duquesne City Sch. Dist., 644 A.2d 1277 (Pa. Commw. 1994), involving issues of furlough, seniority, and recall of teachers.

183. Arthur v. Nyquist, 712 F.2d 816 (2d Cir. 1983). For a case wherein it was held that a school board could not award seniority credit to a substitute teacher who had been improperly appointed, see Daul v. Board of Educ., Mahopac Cent. Sch. Dist., 466 N.Y.S.2d 449 (N.Y. 1983).

184. Portions of this subsection are taken directly from R.S. VACCA & H.C. HUDGINS, JR., LIABILITY OF SCHOOL OFFICIALS AND ADMINISTRATORS FOR CIVIL RIGHTS TORTS (Charlottesville, Va.: The Michie Co., 1982).

185. *Id.* at 12-13.

in their attempts to take employment cases into the federal courts. Since the mid-1970s, 1983-type cases have multiplied as employees have sought remedy claiming that they have been wronged by abuses of board and administrative authority.[186]

What makes § 1983 important and popular as an alternative action is that its applicability is not dependent upon an employee holding bona fide tenure or continuing contract status.[187] What is more, the possibilities of remedy are wide and varied, from collecting compensatory damages to expungement of record, to reinstatement, and to recovery of lost wages and benefits. In other words, § 1983 has become a flexible and broad-scoped statute to restrict a wide variety of public school board and administrative actions. When acting in their official capacities, these officials are exercising state authority; thus, they cannot move to restrict or deny any person subject to them any right to which the individual is entitled under the Constitution as well as under federal laws. If a public school official acts in derogation of an employee's protected rights, that official may be charged in a court proceeding with an offense commonly known as a *civil rights tort*.

a. Generally, each state provides legislative, administrative and judicial remedies for aggrieved public school employees. The specific avenues of remedy available to aggrieved employees are too numerous to list, and "going to court with one's complaint" is but one such alternative. The establishment and implementation of state-mandated grievance procedures for employees has reduced

---

186. *Id.* at 82. To successfully sustain a section 1983 suit, the complaining party must show that the individual or individuals (be it a person, persons, or other entity) must have been functioning as a *state actor* when the alleged violation(s) took place. For a case where this was not shown by plaintiff, see Johnson v. Pinkerton Academy, 861 F.2d 335 (1st Cir. 1988).

187. *Id.* at 82-83. *See, e.g.,* McLaughlin v. Tilendis, 398 F.2d 287 (7th Cir. 1968). It must be emphasized, however, that section 1983 does not provide any *substantive rights*; it provides a remedy for violations of other federally protected rights. *See, e.g.,* McCaulley v. Greensboro City Bd., 714 F. Supp. 146 (M.D.N.C. 1987).

the need for, and therefore the number of, court cases involving administrative decisions in public school systems.

Even though the traditional rule of civil procedure holds that a litigant must exhaust existing legislative or administrative remedies before challenging the state action in federal court, interpretations of the exhaustion rule indicate flexibility when considered within the context of § 1983.[188] In fact, the possibility exists that some § 1983 matters may come into federal court after settlement in a state court. Speaking to this possibility, Levenson has suggested that

> [t]here is little reason to fear that allowing 1983 actions after state court proceedings will permit double recovery. Section 1983 was designed, in part, to provide remedies that are not available or not commonly sought in the state forum. Further, the majority of 1983 cases which follow state proceedings are brought precisely because the state judgment did not prove satisfactory.[189]

Case law seems to indicate that the general rule requiring exhaustion of state administrative or judicial remedies is considerably relaxed for actions brought under § 1983, especially when requiring such exhaustion would, in the court's view, actually leave plaintiff without remedy.[190] Thus, school officials who once believed that a matter of controversy involving an employee was settled finally and firmly by either administrative or judicial pro-

---

188. *Id.* at 24-28.

189. *Id.* at 25. *See* L.L. Levenson, *Res Judicata and Section 1983: The Effect of State Court Judgments on Federal Civil Rights Actions,* 27 UCLA L. REV. 177, 187 (October 1979).

190. *Id.* at 27. In Patsy v. Board of Regents, 457 U.S. 496, 102 S. Ct. 2557, 73 L. Ed. 2d 172 (1982), the U.S. Supreme Court held that except in cases involving prisoners and other institutionalized persons, exhaustion of state administrative remedies is not prerequisite to taking an action under 42 U.S.C. § 1983. *See also* E.J. Sarzynski, *Quackenbush v. Johnson City Central School District — The Importance of Knowing and Following Procedures in Matters Involving Handicapped Students,* 16 WEST'S EDUC. L. RPTR. 1 (April 19, 1984).

ceedings may find themselves later facing a § 1983 action taken in federal court by the same employee.

b. Generally, public school employees (especially teachers) have had success in seeking remedy under § 1983 as an alternative action.[191] As stated earlier, the applicability of this statute is not dependent upon the employee's status as either non-tenured or tenured.

A review of § 1983 litigation reveals the presence of certain "red flag," issue-producing factors. These factors are: speech and expression, association, private lives, race, and handicap. Of these "issue producers," § 1983-type cases involving basic first amendment entitlements of employees have been most numerous (verbal expression, written expression, and appearance).[192] A common thread running through such court cases is that the plaintiff employee charged that the school board and/or administrator violated his constitutional or statutory rights, the various courts granted jurisdiction and considered the merits of the allegations, and the courts (in some instances) granted remedy to the plaintiff employee.

To date, the preponderance of § 1983 suits have been filed against school boards and school board members rather than superintendents and principals. Where a clear violation can be established under law or policy, it is the body (the board) or the individuals of that body (board members) making the law or policy

---

191. *Id.* at 83. *See* K. ALEXANDER, SCHOOL LAW 629-30 (West 1980). According to the U.S. District Court, Northern District of Texas, Dallas Division, the most prominent purposes of 42 U.S.C. § 1983 are compensation and deterrence. Wells v. Dallas Indep. Sch. Dist., 576 F. Supp. 497 (N.D. Tex. 1983).

192. VACCA & HUDGINS, supra note 184, at 87-136. For a case involving § 1983 and the first amendment rights of teachers, see Renfroe v. Kirkpatrick, 722 F.2d 714 (11th Cir. 1984). *See also* Tompkins v. Vickers, 26 F.3d 603 (5th Cir. 1994), in which a teacher alleges retaliation by superintendent and others for exercising his first amendment right to speech; Shiller v. Moore, 30 F.3d 1281 (10th Cir. 1994); Cromley v. Board of Educ., 17 F.3d 1059 (7th Cir. 1994); Harris v. Victoria I.S.D., 168 F.3d 216 (5th Cir. 1999). For a case on point from higher education, see Harleston v. Jeffries, 21 F.3d 1238 (2d Cir. 1994).

who are responsible rather than the executioners of the law or policy.

c. Where exercises of constitutionally protected rights are at issue, school boards and administrative officials will need to show a direct causal link between the proscribed employee behavior and a rational basis for the board's decision to curtail that behavior, a connection supported with hard evidence. Similarly, where decisions are made to nonrenew, dismiss, transfer or suspend employees, such decisions must be made rationally and free from bias. A federal court will carefully scrutinize the merits of the school board's case, where heretofore the emphasis might have been on procedural matters.

Currently, the burden of proof in establishing a *prima facie* case of a § 1983 violation remains on the plaintiff employee. Once the *prima facie* case is made, and the case moves forward, the burden of proof remains with the plaintiff to show a connection between his or her protected conduct and the board's decision to nonrenew, dismiss, suspend, or in some other way deal with that employee. At this point, the more obvious the presence of an unlawful intent on the part of school officials, or the more arbitrary the board's decision seems, the more likely the burden of proof will split and school officials will be required to produce the evidence necessary to support the decision made regarding the employee. Where clear constitutional or statutory questions are at issue, the decisions of school boards and officials will be judged by the *preponderance of the evidence* standard. In such matters, the affirmative defense of *good faith* has been and remains relied on consistently by school officials in § 1983 actions.[193]

Clearly, where school boards and officials are held liable under § 1983, the possibilities are broad. The cases demonstrate that injunctive relief, reinstatement (sometimes with tenure), back pay, restoration of lost benefits, expungement of record, removal of letters of reprimand from personnel files, monetary damages, at-

---

193. *Id.* at 273. A determination of good faith is especially important in the issue of punitive damage awards. *See Wells, supra* note 191, at 509.

torney's fees, and payment of costs are a few possible forms of remedy available in § 1983 cases.

d. A § 1983-type case involving the nonrenewal of a nontenured male teacher in Ohio, *Mt. Healthy City School District Board of Education v. Doyle,*[194] established a judicial standard that has greatly conditioned school board and administrative authority in personnel matters. The standard, created by Justice Rehnquist, and commonly referred to as the *test of causation,* poses three questions to be asked when an employee-plaintiff alleges a § 1983 violation. These questions are: (1) Is there present in this situation some element or exercise of constitutionally or statutorily protected conduct? (2) Did this element or exercise play a "substantial or motivating part" in the board's decision (e.g., to nonrenew, dismiss, suspend, etc.) regarding this employee? (3) Absent that element or exercise, would the same decision have been made regarding this employee?[195]

To Justice Rehnquist, the above standard strikes a "balance between the interests of the teacher, as a citizen . . . and the interest of the State, as an employer, in promoting the efficiency of public services it performs through its employees."[196] Application of this causation standard, stated the Justice, helps "distinguish between a result caused by a constitutional violation and one not so caused."[197]

In *Renfroe v. Kirkpatrick* (1982),[198] both the *Doyle* causation standard and the preponderance of the evidence standard come into play in resolving a teacher-first amendment case. Cheryl Renfroe, a non-tenured teacher in her second year of employment, brought an action under § 1983 against the school board, the superintendent of schools, and her principal for their decision not to offer her a full-time position as a kindergarten teacher. Not claiming, as she could not, any protected property interest in her position as

---

194. 429 U.S. 274, 97 S. Ct. 568, 50 L. Ed. 2d 471 (1977), *aff'd on remand,* 670 F.2d 59 (6th Cir. 1981).

195. VACCA & HUDGINS, *supra* note 184, at 86.

196. *Doyle, supra* note 194, at 429 U.S. 285.

197. *Id.*

198. 549 F. Supp. 1368 (N.D. Ala. 1982).

teacher, Renfroe did claim that she had been denied even a part-time position because she had filed a grievance concerning her employment situation and the process followed by the school officials.[199] Tried before a jury, the case was presented to the jury solely on a claim that her contract's nonrenewal "was motivated because of the filing of a grievance."[200]

The jury returned a verdict for Renfroe and against all three defendants for $6,400 in compensatory damages, and punitive damages against the superintendent and principal totalling $12,500. The defendants then moved for a Judgment Notwithstanding the Verdict (JNOV) and for a new trial. Ms. Renfroe moved for an award of attorneys' fees.[201]

In this case, the district judge made it very clear that a federal court must scrutinize Ms. Renfroe's complaint to determine if there is present a "bona fide" constitutional claim — not just the assertion of a constitutional deprivation. Citing *Mt. Healthy v. Doyle* as the controlling standard, the court stated:

> Once it is established that a particular expression is protected by the First Amendment, the plaintiff must further show that the constitutionally protected conduct was a "motivating" or "substantial" factor in the Board's decision not to rehire plaintiff . . . . If plaintiff establishes by a preponderance of the evidence that her conduct was constitutionally protected, and that it was a motivating factor in the Board's decision not to rehire her, the Board must prove by a preponderance of the evidence that it would have reached the same decision as to plaintiff's reemployment even in the absence of the protected conduct.[202]

---

199. *Id.* at 1372.

200. *Id.* at 1370.

201. *Id.* at 1369.

202. *Id.* at 1373. The initial burden is placed on the plaintiff to show that his/her conduct was constitutionally protected, and that such conduct was a "substantial factor" in the board's decision not to rehire. For a case on this point taken

Upon applying the *Doyle* standard, the court granted defendant's motion for a JNOV, thus setting aside the verdict in favor of Renfroe and vacating the court's judgment. Ultimately, Renfroe's complaint was dismissed. A new trial was granted under the condition that it be held only in the event that the court's granting of a JNOV not be reversed on appeal.[203]

The *Doyle* standard, and the importance of a plaintiff being able to demonstrate (beyond a mere assertion) that his exercise of protected conduct was a motivating factor in the board's decision not to rehire him, was a major consideration in a decision out of the Eighth Circuit. The case, *McGee v. South Pemiscot School District*,[204] involved a teacher (who had been the school's track coach) who alleged that his contract was not renewed because he wrote a letter to the newspaper protesting his school board's decision to drop junior high school track. Not prevailing at the district court level, McGee appealed his case to the Eighth Circuit where that court held in his favor.

The appellate court applied the *Doyle* test and found that there was every indication that McGee's contract would have been renewed (he had received positive evaluations of his performance, his name was on the payroll, he had already been assigned classes, etc.) prior to his sending the letter to the newspaper. Referring to what it deemed "a suspicious sequence of events," the court said that it seemed "more than coincidence" that one week after the letter was sent Mr. McGee had been reevaluated as "unfit to teach," and ultimately the decision was made not to renew his

---

in state court, see Tanner v. Hazelhurst Mun. Separate Sch. Dist., 427 So. 2d 977 (Miss. 1983). *See also* Finnegan v. Board of Educ., 30 F.3d 273 (2d Cir. 1994), where a physical education teacher failed to establish that his exercise of his constitutional right to marry was the motivating factor in the board's decision to deny him tenure.

203. *Id.* at 1375. For a case (involving a school custodian's speech on behalf of a school principal subjected to a disciplinary transfer) that demonstrates the importance and use of the *Doyle* analysis, see Copp v. Unified Sch. Dist., 882 F.2d 1547 (10th Cir. 1989).

204. 712 F.2d 339 (8th Cir. 1983).

contract.[205] Thus, the judgment of the district court was reversed and the cause of action remanded.

§ 7.9. Privacy Issues: Drug Testing, and AIDS.

Of all the rights possessed by citizens in this nation, *privacy* is one of the most valued and cherished. Yet, the term itself has no clearly and narrowly defined definition.

According to *Black's, privacy* is a "generic term encompassing various rights recognized to be inherent in the concept of ordered liberty, and such right prevents governmental interference in intimate relationships or activities. . . ."[206] Other sources simply say that the term *privacy* means the right to be left alone, which includes being protected from the unauthorized, unwarranted intrusion by others, including government. Briefly stated, privacy protects citizens from unauthorized and unwarranted governmental interference in their intimate affairs.

Not specifically enumerated in the language of the United States Constitution, (*i.e.,* the word "privacy" does not appear in the document) the foundation for the right of privacy can be found in the constitutional guarantees of life, liberty, and property protected by the Constitution. The right of privacy was legitimized by the Supreme Court in *Griswold v. Connecticut.* In overturning a Connecticut birth control statute, Justice Douglas made the following pronouncement for the 7-2 majority: "the right of privacy which presses for recognition here is a legitimate one."[207] The majority opinion was premised on the ninth amendment.

In addition to possibly establishing a right of privacy on constitutional grounds, one might also argue that there exists a separate

---

205. *Id.* at 343-44. For another *Doyle*-type case, see McDonough v. Trustees of Univ. Sys., 704 F.2d 780 (1st Cir. 1983), wherein a college teacher "speaks out" on matters of public concern and is terminated from employment. For a case involving the application of the *Doyle* test to a school principal's release from employment, see Yielding v. Crockett Indep. Sch. Dist., 707 F.2d 196 (5th Cir. 1983).

206. BLACK'S LAW DICTIONARY 1195 6th ed. 1990).

207. 381 U.S. 479 (1965).

"legal right called the right of privacy, the invasion of which is a tort and gives rise to a cause of action."[208] Remedy (often in the form of damages) in a legal right of privacy action (*i.e.,* one that is statutorily based) takes the form of either a *defamation* claim or one of *mental distress.* One can go from state to state, for example, and find statutes on the books protecting the privacy of citizens.[209]

There are several employment issues in school law in which school boards and their administrators are vulnerable to potential privacy suits on both constitutional and/or statutory grounds. Two such issues are drug testing of employees and AIDS discrimination in employment. Nowhere in school law are there better examples of a complex dilemma caused by the need to balance the public's *right to know* and the *duty to protect* others, along with the concurrent responsibility to *ensure confidentiality* of sensitive personal information in an effort to protect individual employees from possible stigma and harm.

a. *Drug Testing in Employment.* The Rehnquist Court has been busy with employee drug testing cases. In 1989, the high court handed down decisions in two nonschool drug testing cases: *Skinner v. Railway Executives Ass'n*[210] and *National Treasury Employees Union v. Von Raab.*[211] In the *Railway* case the Court, by a vote of 7-2, upheld a U.S. Department of Transportation blanket drug testing (blood, urine, and breath) requirement for all workers involved in serious railroad accidents. To the majority, the requirement was premised on a "compelling interest" of government to protect the public's safety. The Court in the *Treasury Employees* case upheld mandatory drug testing as a part of a screening process of customs officials involved in certain types of safety sensitive jobs (*e.g.,* in drug interdiction). Although the testing was not based on reasonable suspicion, a 5-4 majority saw the screening require-

---

208. 62 Am. Jur. 2d, at 679.
209. *See, e.g.,* Va. Code § 2.1-377 to 2.1-386.
210. 109 S. Ct. 1402 (1989).
211. 109 S. Ct. 1384 (1989).

ment as reasonable for the affected employee category and as advancing a compelling interest of government.

At present, there are few school-related employee drug testing cases to turn to for guidance. One case of particular note, however, is *Patchoque-Medford Congress of Teachers v. Board of Education.*[212]

In *Patchoque,* school officials announced that all tenure-eligible probationary teachers (twenty-five of them) were required to submit to a urinalysis examination as a part of a full physical examination by a physician. The sole purpose of the additional exam was to determine if any of these teachers were using "illegal drugs." Those who refused to comply would not be recommended for tenure.

Challenged in court by the Congress of Teachers, the drug testing requirement was struck down. To both the trial and appellate courts, absent reasonable suspicion that any one of the probationary teachers was using illegal drugs, the urine tests could not be required as a precondition of receiving tenure.

In another school-related case, however, a federal appellate court upheld a required drug testing program for all employees "whose duties involve direct contact with young children and their physical safety." The court looked favorably on such tests so long as they "are conducted as a part of a routine employment-related medical exam — where there is a clear *nexus* between the tests and the employer's legitimate safety concern." This situation involved employees in the school system's transportation branch (which included bus drivers, bus attendants, and mechanics).[213]

Neither of the above cases rules out pre-employment drug screening, nor do they rule out required drug testing as part of an overall medical exam. Rather, the cases emphasize the need to

---

212. 505 N.Y.S.2d 888 (N.Y. 1987).

213. Jones v. McKenzie, 833 F.2d 335 (D.C. Cir. 1987). For a drug testing case involving school bus drivers and their testing positive, see Independent Sch. Dist. No. 1 v. Logan, 789 P.2d 636 (Okla. App. 1990).

justify drug testing of employees where reasonable suspicion exists and where employees are in safety-sensitive jobs.

b. *Employees and AIDS.* The United States Supreme Court used a Florida case involving a teacher with tuberculosis to create a useful standard applicable to an analysis of employee AIDS situations. In *School Board v. Arline*,[214] an elementary school teacher whose tuberculosis had been in remission for twenty years (she had contracted the disease at age thirteen) was recommended for termination by her superintendent. The superintendent's recommendation was based on the results of Arline's testing positively (once in 1977 and twice in 1978) for the presence of tuberculosis. School officials based their dismissal action on what they maintained was their duty to protect others from contagious diseases.

Claiming discrimination in violation of the "otherwise qualified" provision of the Rehabilitation Act of 1973, section 504, Arline took her case to federal district court. The federal district court did not agree with her and held for the defendant school board for two reasons. First, the court did not consider her tuberculosis condition to be within the meaning of the term "handicap," for purposes of a section 504 analysis. Second, the court saw as compelling the board's duty to protect others from contagious diseases. On appeal the Eleventh Circuit came to a different conclusion seeing Arline's condition as within the term "handicap." The trial court was reversed and the case was remanded to the district court. School officials then sought review by the Supreme Court.

In 1987 the Rehnquist Court handed down its decision in *Arline.* Remanding the case to the district court, Justice Brennan constructed the following standard which has proved helpful in the analysis of employee AIDS cases: (1) determine if the person has a condition that fits within the meaning of the term *handicapped* for purposes of section 504; and (2) determine whether the person is *otherwise qualified* for the position for which he/she is applying or for which he/she has been dismissed, transferred, or otherwise

---

214. 480 U.S. 273 (1987).

removed. Where the employee meets these two criteria, the employer must examine and weigh the reasons given for taking an adverse employment action.[215] In such situations, the court will ask the following questions: Did the employer base its actions on current medical judgments, and did the employer verify the potential risk and duration of risk of transmission of the disease to others?[216]

§ 7.10. Legal Issues in the Late 1990s.

As public education moved through the 1990s, two new legal issues emerged in employment. One area of litigation involved charges of sexual harassment in the workplace, while the other concerned the newly enacted Americans with Disabilities Act. It seems evident that both areas will continue to produce court decisions as public education enters the new century.

a. *Sexual Harassment in the Workplace.* Sexual harassment has generally been characterized as a form of employment discrimination under Title VII.[217] The United State Supreme Court's decision in *Meritor Savings Bank v. Vinson* (1986)[218] opened the way to bring sexual harassment matters to federal court. Seven years later the Supreme Court's decision in *Harris v. Forklift System, Inc.* (1993)[219] further broadened the scope of sexual harass-

---

215. *Decided on remand,* Arline v. School Bd., 692 F. Supp. 1286 (M.D. Fla. 1988).

216. For an excellent AIDS case showing the application of the *Arline* standard, see Chalk v. United States Dist. Ct., 840 F.2d 701 (9th Cir. 1988). It must first be determined whether or not an individual plaintiff qualifies before the protections of the Americans With Disabilities Act (ADA) are applied to the specific action by the board. *See* Doe v. DeKalb Cty. Sch. Dist., 145 F.3d 1441 (11th Cir. 1998).

217. 42 U.S.C. § 2000e. While not meant to replace other federal statutes that ban discrimination, Title VII is itself an antidiscrimination statute. Claims of employee discrimination based on sex can be brought under Title VII.

218. 477 U.S. 57 (1986). Following this decision, experts in employment law agreed that a plaintiff charging sexual harassment in the workplace could proceed under either, or both, of two theories: (1) *quid pro quo,* or (2) hostile work environment, as a violation of Title VII.

219. Harris v. Forklift Sys., Inc., 114 S. Ct. 367 (1993).

ment litigation and, at the same time, lessened the burden on plaintiffs to prove their case. In *Harris*, the high court stated that sexual harassment could be established from an evaluation of the totality of the circumstances in the given situation, and, more importantly, a plaintiff need not be required to show tangible psychological injury suffered because of the harassing act in order to prevail.[220]

Many sexual harassment claims have been brought by women employees against male supervisors and/or coworkers. From these cases, two categories of sexual harassment situations have emerged, and form the basis for future litigation. First there are *quid pro quo* situations where unwelcome sexual advances or requests for sexual favors are made a condition of employment, or promotion, or salary increase, or reduced workload.[221] The second type of sexual harassment situation involves the existence of a hostile work environment, where actions of a superior or coworker create an intimidating, hostile, offensive, or abusive working environment.[222] Of

---

220. *Id.* at 371. Here the Court seems to focus on the question of when comments or other actions become more than distasteful and rise to a level of severity and offensiveness that are, in fact, actionable. The Supreme Court advises that the totality of the circumstance in a specific situation must be evaluated to determine whether or not abuse or hostility exists. *See* Burlington Indus. v. Ellerth, 118 S. Ct. 2257 (1998); Faragher v. City of Boca Raton, 118 S. Ct. 2275 (1998); Hazel v. School Bd., 7 F. Supp. 2d 1349 (S.D. Fla. 1998); Matthews v. High Island I.S.D., 991 F. Supp. 840 (S.D. Tex. 1998).

221. In *Meritor Savings Bank, supra* note 218, the emphasis is placed on the presence of unwelcome requests for sexual favors linked to some term or condition placed on the victim's employment status. *See also* Babcock v. Frank, 783 F. Supp. 800 (S.D.N.Y. 1992).

222. *See Harris, supra* note 219. The frequency and severity of the conduct; the presence of humiliation; threats; verbal or physical acts; and what is voluntary or coerced behavior are a few of the factors to consider in constructing an analysis of a hostile work environment claim. It should be noted that courts will factor in the notion of the reasonable victim (woman or man) to analyze the situation from that person's view. *See, e.g.,* Ellison v. Brady, 924 F.2d 872 (9th Cir. 1991); Robinson v. Jacksonville Shipyard, Inc., 760 F. Supp. 1486 (M.D. Fla. 1991); and Chiapuzio v. B.L.T. Operating Corp., 826 F. Supp. 1334 (D. Wyo. 1993), which involved alleged verbal harassment of both male and female employees by a male

the two types of cases, the latter is the more difficult one to establish. A decision from New York State offers an excellent example. In *Locastro v. East Syracuse-Minoa Central School District* (1993), a nontenured teacher sued the school district and her principal, charging that her principal had sexually harassed her. In her complaint the teacher alleged that he had fondled her buttocks, made improper comments, and kissed her on the mouth. Even though the principal admitted the third charge, the court nevertheless ruled that the teacher had failed to establish a *prima facie* case of hostile environment sexual harassment.[223]

Sexual harassment complaints have expanded beyond the workplace and into the classroom. In the recent past there have been several cases where public school employees have lost their jobs because of sexual harassment of their students.[224] At the same time, because of the United States Supreme Court's decision in *Franklin v. Gwinnett County Public Schools*[225] (1992), school officials have been held liable for their deliberate indifference to reported behavior on the part of employees where students were either sexually, physically, or verbally abused. In *Franklin*, the United States Supreme Court declared that it was possible for

supervisor. *See* Burlington Indus. v. Ellerth, 118 S. Ct. 2257 (1998); Faragher v. City of Boca Raton, 118 S. Ct. 2275 (1998); Hazel v. School Bd., 7 F. Supp. 2d 1349 (S.D. Fla. 1998); Matthews v. High Island I.S.D., 991 F. Supp. 840 (S.D. Tex. 1998).

223. Locastro v. East Syracuse-Minoa Central Sch. Dist., 830 F. Supp. 133 (D.N.Y. 1993). *See also* Scrivner v. Socorro I.S.D., 169 F.3d 969 (5th Cir. 1999). It is interesting to note that the United States Supreme Court unanimously held that a male employee's complaint of sexual harassment and hostile work environment against his male supervisors was actionable under Title VII. *See* Oncale v. Sundowner Offshore Servs., Inc., 118 S. Ct. 998 (1998).

224. *See, e.g.,* Wexley v. Michigan State Univ., 821 F. Supp. 479 (W.D. Mich. 1993); Hastings v. Hancock, 842 F. Supp. 1315 (D. Kan. 1993); Knowles v. Board of Educ., 857 P.2d 553 (Colo. App. 1993); C.M. v. Southeast Delco Sch. Dist., 828 F. Supp. 1179 (E.D. Pa. 1993); Baldridge v. Board of Trustees, 870 P.2d 711 (Mont. 1994). *See also* Does v. Covington Cty. Sch. Bd., 884 F. Supp. 462 (M.D. Ala. 1995).

225. 112 S. Ct. 1028 (1992).

students to win money damages under Title IX where school officials failed to act on reports of a teacher's sexual harassment and abuse of a student.[226]

Case law forewarns school officials to treat all reports of alleged harassment as serious and to promptly investigate them, to have a formal policy in place that specifically deals with sexual harassment (both for employees and for students), and to follow a formalized procedure to deal with incidents when they are reported.[227] Moreover, school officials must encourage employees to report such incidents, and employers must not take adverse employment actions against any individual who reports the presence of such activities in the school system.[228]

b. *The Americans with Disabilities Act.* The Americans with Disabilities Act (ADA) makes it unlawful to discriminate in all employment practices (*e.g.,* recruitment, hiring, promotion, pay, job assignments, leave, lay-off, dismissal) against any individual covered by the Act. In addition, the ADA makes it unlawful for an employer to retaliate against an individual for asserting his or her rights and protections under the Act.[229]

---

226. *Id.* (damages available to private parties to enforce requirements of Title IX, Education Amendments of 1972, 20 U.S.C. § 1681(a)). *See, e.g.,* Doe v. Taylor, 15 F.3d 443 (5th Cir. 1994), *cert. denied sub nom.* Lankford v. Doe, 115 S. Ct. 70 (1994). *See* Mirelez v. Bay City I.S.D., 992 F. Supp. 916 (S.D. Tex. 1998); Doe v. Lago Vista Indep. Sch. Dist., 106 F.3d 1223 (5th Cir. 1997).

227. School officials are reminded to include employee-on-employee harassment in their policy and procedures. *See, e.g.,* Becker v. Churchville-Chili Central Sch. Dist., 602 N.Y.S.2d 497 (Sup. Ct. 1993); Doe v. Beaumont I.S.D., 8 F. Supp. 2d 596 (E.D. Tex. 1998); Doe v. Dallas I.S.D., 153 F.3d 211 (5th Cir. 1998).

228. *See, e.g.,* Hoeppner v. Crotched Mountain Rehab. Center, 31 F.3d 9 (1st Cir. 1994), where a special education teacher brought a Title VII retaliatory discharge action against her employer alleging that she had been fired for reporting sexual harassment incidents in her work setting; Wyatt v. City of Boston, 35 F.3d 13 (1st Cir. 1994), where a former teacher alleged that he was retaliated against for his expressed views on sexual harassment in the workplace. *See also* Ward v. Johns Hopkins Univ., 861 F. Supp. 367 (D. Md. 1994). For a major decision on point, see Gerbser v. Lago Vista Indep. Sch. Dist., 118 S. Ct. 1989 (1998).

229. AMERICANS WITH DISABILITIES ACT, 42 U.S.C. § 12101 et seq. (1990).

To be covered by the ADA, an individual must have or be perceived as having a disability. The ADA defines a disability as a physical or mental impairment that substantially limits a major life function. The Act defines major life activities as hearing, seeing, speaking, breathing, performing manual tasks, walking, caring for oneself, learning, and working.[230]

Enforced by both EEOC and the U.S. Department of Justice, the Act covers such entities as public school systems. It is expected that an individual who meets basic job requirements and can perform all essential job functions will not be discriminated against. On this last point the law requires public school employers to make reasonable accommodations so that an individual will be able to perform essential job functions. Where reasonable accommodations cannot be made, the employer is not required to make them.[231]

The ADA has major implications for day-to-day personnel practices in public school systems. For example, under the Act an employer cannot ask a job applicant if he or she has a disability, nor can a job offer be conditioned on an applicant's having to take a medical examination. However, applicants can be quizzed about their abilities to perform a specific job and can be asked to show how they can perform essential job functions. Moreover, an applicant can be asked if he or she would need any special accommodations to perform these functions. The requirements of the Act change after the person is hired. For example, an employer can request that an individual take a medical examination after he or she is hired, if all other employees in that specific job category are required to do the same.[232]

---

230. *Id.* Section 12112(a) of the ADA establishes the concept of a "qualified individual with a disability."

231. *Id.* Section 12112(b)(5)(B) requires an employer "to make reasonable accommodations to the physical or mental impairments of the employee or applicant."

232. For examples of case law involving the ADA and allegations of discrimination based upon disability, see Bombrys v. City of Toledo, 849 F. Supp. 1210 (N.D. Ohio 1993); Tyndall v. National Educ. Centers, 31 F.3d 209 (4th Cir.

The Americans with Disabilities Act also applies to private employers. In *Susie v. Apple Tree Child Care Center, Inc.* (1994), for example, a former teacher used the ADA to take her former employer into court. She contended that she was terminated from her job solely because of her epilepsy, and her employer's failure to make reasonable accommodations for her disability. The employer argued that the employee's termination resulted from her misconduct.

In denying the plaintiff's motion for summary judgment the court focused upon the issue of the employer's motivation for the discharge. To the court, "because many disabilities may worsen over time, the scope and nature of the employer's duty to reasonably accommodate the disability may also change dramatically." It can be inferred from the court's statement that because an individual is hired does not mean his or her job situation cannot change in the future in a way that may require a reevaluation of job status. And, this reevaluation may not offend the requirements of the ADA.[233]

§ 7.11. Summary.

In recent years personnel administration in public school systems has been an active area of school law. The passage of statutes (federal and state), the enactment of policy at all levels of government, and the increasing number of court decisions (federal and state) on matters of personnel management have had profound impact on the daily operation of school systems.

The importance of studying the legal status of public school personnel and the decision-making prerogatives of local school

---

1994). For a comprehensive article on the provisions and requirements of the ADA, see Allan G. Osborne, *Court Interpretations of the Americans with Disabilities Act and their Effects on School Districts,* 95 EDUC. LAW REP. 489 (Jan. 26, 1995).

233. Susie v. Apple Tree Preschool & Child Care Center, Inc., 866 F. Supp. 390 (N.D. Ind. 1994). *See also* Benedict v. Eau Claire Pub. Schs., 139 F.3d 901 (7th Cir. 1998); Figueroa v. Fajardo, 1 F. Supp. 2d 117 (D.P.R. 1998).

boards in matters of personnel administration has grown over the past decade with the proliferation of litigation involving such matters. Each year the number of court cases involving employment issues increased over that of the previous year.

Today's personnel decisions in public school systems must be the direct result of carefully planned strategies and legally defensible policies. Thus, the study of the legal dimensions of certification, recruitment, assignment, transfer, evaluation, nonrenewal, and dismissal of school personnel is a must for school boards and school administrators.

There is little doubt that, across this nation, job security is the greatest employment concern of contemporary public school teachers. As developed in previous sections of this chapter, budgetary conditions often force school systems to make reductions in instructional costs. As Levin points out, "[w]hether or not a teacher has acquired tenure, as well as his or her relative degree of seniority if tenured, has become an increasingly important and more frequently litigated issue . . . ."[234]

School boards and administrators continue to find themselves in a position of having to reduce the number of teachers and other professionals employed, as public school systems try to live within authorized budgets. Their task is no easy one as attempts are made to improve the quality of programs while pressures are felt to maintain an equitable balance among faculty in matters of sex, age, and race.

Unless contemporary local school boards implement carefully devised plans and procedures for evaluating the competence of the professional force, they will find themselves open to legal challenge from several vantage points. Evaluation systems must therefore be able to withstand strict legal scrutiny by both government agencies and courts of law.

It behooves local school boards to establish, as their primary reason for *retaining* certain teachers (while dismissing or not reappointing others), the need to keep and reward the best *qualified*

---

234. B. Levin, *supra* note 55, at 151.

and most *competent* teachers (with proven records of competence in job performance) in an effort to provide *quality* education. Thus, the need to implement a sound, reliable, and valid program of teacher evaluation becomes vital and provides a context for promoting feelings of job security.

Chapter Eight

ACADEMIC FREEDOM

§ 8.0. In General.

In this country, the concept of academic freedom grew from the influence of principles originating in 19th century German colleges and universities to the effect that scholars should be free to search for and to teach the truth without constraints imposed by their immediate superordinates or by government. Anything else would threaten the foundations of knowledge itself. Subsequent scholars and teachers have resisted efforts by others attempting to influence their teaching, its content and methodology.

The Germanic notion of academic freedom has had considerable influence on the institutions of higher learning in this country. To a lesser degree, it has had an impact on elementary and secondary schools. Unlike college students, public school pupils are subject to a compulsory attendance law and are viewed as having impressionable minds. These two distinctions justify more restraints on public school teachers than on college professors.

Academic freedom has two dimensions: a dimension of substantive freedom of a teacher to determine, within reasonable bounds, content and methodology which serve an educationally defensible purpose; and a dimension of procedure which protects a teacher from dismissal except for violation of a law, policy, or regulation clearly known.

As citizens, teachers have the same rights as anyone else. As teachers, individuals may have to forego some of those rights at given times or places. One is not entitled to exercise all his citizenship rights in a public school classroom. In 1952, the Supreme Court of the United States declared that a teacher had a choice of teaching or exercising his rights as a citizen:

> It is clear that such persons have the right under law to assemble, speak, think, and believe as they will. It is equally clear that they have no right to work for the state in a school system on their own terms. They may work for the school system under reasonable terms laid down by proper authorities. . . . If they do not choose to work under such terms, they are at liberty to retain their beliefs and associations and go elsewhere. Has the state thus deprived them of any right to free speech and assembly? We think not.[1]

The prevailing view at the time of the above decision was that, since the Constitution does not guarantee employment to anyone, a teacher agrees to work under conditions laid down for him. Yet these conditions can transgress legality. In recent years, teachers have asserted rights of academic freedom, in particular, under the first and fourteenth amendments. Increasingly, a number of these rights have been given protection by the courts. Academic freedom was first recognized as receiving constitutional protection by the

---

1. Adler v. Board of Educ., 342 U.S. 485, 492, 72 S. Ct. 380, 96 L. Ed. 2d 517 (1952).

Supreme Court of the United States in *Adler v. Board of Education* when, in dissent, Justice Douglas stated:

> I cannot for example find in our constitutional scheme the power of a state to place its employees in the category of second-class citizens by denying them freedom of thought and expression. The Constitution guarantees freedom of thought and expression to everyone in our society. All are entitled to it; and none needs it more than the teacher.[2]

The Court's majority affirmed Justice Douglas's position seventeen years later in the *Tinker v. Des Moines Independent Community School District* decision: "First Amendment rights applied in light of the special characteristics of the school environment are available to teachers and students. It can hardly be argued that either students or teachers shed their constitutional rights to freedom of speech or expression at the schoolhouse gate."[3]

The Court cautioned in *Tinker* that the rights of speech and association may be limited because of the unique nature of a school. One cannot exercise this right to the extent that it creates disruption; however, the right cannot be limited because of "a mere desire to avoid the discomfort and unpleasantness that always accompany an unpopular viewpoint."[4]

The problem is one of balance: the rights of a teacher as opposed to what is best for the students and the school community. The central focus of this chapter is to ascertain what courts have ruled to be academic freedom rights of teachers and under what conditions their rights can be curtailed for some greater good. Since procedural rights were treated in the previous chapter, only substantive rights will be considered here.

Litigation in the area of academic freedom has involved such issues as censorship of course materials, class discussions, and teacher methodology. For various reasons, particularly on the basis of certain material being offensive to individuals or groups, library

---

2. *Id.* at 342 U.S. 508.
3. 393 U.S. 503, 506, 89 S. Ct. 733, 21 L. Ed. 2d 731 (1969).
4. *Id.* at 393 U.S. 509.

materials have been removed and instructional materials have been suppressed. In addition to actual censorship of books, the showing of films and production of certain plays have been stopped.

§ 8.1. Freedom Within the School.

a. *Teaching Controversial Subjects.* Teachers have considerable freedom in organizing their classes and teaching their students. This freedom is subject, however, to some restraints. State laws may require or forbid the teaching of specific subjects or topics; similarly, local school board policy may require or forbid the teaching of specific subjects and topics. Beyond that, a teacher often can determine what specific subject matter may be incorporated into a syllabus, and a teacher often treats subjects that arise spontaneously. Determining the efficacy or wisdom of teaching such material often rests with its relevancy to the course and the restraint and objectivity with which the material is presented. When courts have difficulty in determining the appropriateness of the subject matter and the way in which it is presented, they often rely on the testimony of educational experts in determining if the matter in dispute has the general approval of the preponderance of the teaching profession.

Three cases illustrate that teaching controversial, irrelevant material can result in dismissal. In *Goldwasser v. Brown,* an Air Force officer taught basic English to foreign officers. Although his class assignment was to cover "At the Dentist" and "How to Test a Used Car," he discoursed on Vietnam and made anti-Semitic remarks. The court held that his comments bore no relevancy to his subject matter.[5]

---

5. Goldwasser v. Brown, 417 F.2d 1169 (D.C. Cir. 1969). For an interesting and related discussion demonstrating the emergence of controversy from assignments given by teachers to their class, see Eugene C. Bjorklun, *Show and Tell, the Establishment of Religion, and Freedom of Speech,* 84 EDUC. LAW REP. 601 (Oct. 7, 1993).

In the second case, the dismissal of a high school social studies teacher was upheld.[6] He had used the classroom for discussions of a number of questionable topics, including his personal opinion about union activities, approval of polygamy, criticism of marriage, castigation of fellow teachers, and proselytizing students.

A teacher who was also a minister was dismissed for insubordination for carrying his civil rights activities into the classroom. He conducted organizational meetings in class which disrupted the instructional program. Despite warnings by the administration, he persisted in this activity. The dismissal was upheld.[7]

Beyond the classroom, but still within the school itself, a teacher's restraint is still necessary. Two cases involving assembly programs point out that teachers' freedom of speech has its limits. In a 1970 case, a teacher interrupted an assembly and stated that he was walking out until a mural of Dr. Martin Luther King, Jr. was hung. The school board had decided earlier not to hang the mural in the school. The court ruled that since the teacher's speech was disruptive, it was not protected. "The interest of the State in maintaining an educational system is a compelling one. Order is necessary to accomplish this, and the First Amendment cannot be used as a device to defeat such necessity."[8]

Three years later, in a Missouri case, a court upheld the dismissal of two teachers who presented an assembly program that was profane, obscene, racially inflammatory. Although the teachers were warned after one presentation, they presented the program a second time, and it created disorder which resulted in injuries and a fire. The teachers were suspended immediately and later dismissed.[9]

1. *Sex Education.* Few issues in education create more volatile reaction than sex education. States vary considerably with respect to legislation on teaching it in the public schools. Some

---

6. Knarr v. Board of Sch. Trustees, 317 F. Supp. 832 (N.D. Ind. 1970), *aff'd*, 452 F.2d 649 (7th Cir. 1971).

7. Cooley v. Board of Educ., 327 F. Supp. 454 (E.D. Ark. 1971).

8. State v. Beeson, 266 A.2d 175, 178 (N.J. 1970).

9. Harrod v. Board of Educ., 500 S.W.2d 1 (Mo. 1973).

253

states permit and encourage such teaching, others specifically forbid it; in between those two positions others allow it provided that exacting conditions are met. The position of boards of education also varies; it often, but not always, reflects community opinion. People in favor of teaching sex education view the topic as being a natural one to treat. Opponents often cite two reasons in opposition to it: mandatory sex education classes may violate one's right to the free exercise of religion under the first amendment, and it is beyond the authority of the school board to offer such courses. There may be a third category of people reacting to the teaching of this sensitive subject merely because of its title and what it might imply. These individuals are less likely to be offended by a more neutral title such as family life education, and the more familiar sounding content that they infer from that title.

Much controversy over sex education centers on a person's religious and moral views. The controversy is frequently concerned with the context within which such subject matter is taught. Far less criticism would likely grow out of a lesson on the human reproductive system in a biology class than to the same subject being treated in a mathematics class. For example, in a 1961 case in Wisconsin, a tenured teacher was dismissed for discussing sex with a senior boys' speech class. The court ruled that the bounds of propriety had been exceeded in that the teacher had described procedures of houses of prostitution and the sex act involving the "breaking of the hymen" as if he were recalling his personal experiences, had condoned premarital relations, and told vulgar stories.[10]

The requirement that sex education have a relationship to the course was affirmed when a high school band director was dismissed for his remarks in class about sex, virginity, and premarital relations.[11] The court expressed a need for teacher restraint in talking about so sensitive an issue when it stated:

---

10. State v. Board of Sch. Dirs., 14 Wis. 2d 243, 111 N.W.2d 198 (1961).
11. Pyle v. Washington Cty. Sch. Bd., 238 So. 2d 121 (Fla. 1970).

254

It may be that topless waitresses and entertainers are in vogue in certain areas of our country and our federal courts may try to enjoin our state courts from stopping the sale of lewd and obscene literature and the showing of obscene films, but we are still of the opinion that instructors in our schools should not be permitted to so risquély discuss sex problems in our teenage mixed classes as to cause embarrassment to the children or to invoke in them other feelings not incident to the courses of study being pursued.[12]

When a course on sex education is made optional, courts tend to uphold its legality. Two cases illustrate this. In *Medeiros v. Kijosaki,* the Supreme Court of Hawaii ruled that the constitutional rights of the complaining students were not violated by sex education courses so long as the parents had the option of not permitting their children to attend. The court was also of the opinion that to forbid the showing of a sex education film in that class would be an infringement on the free speech rights of others.[13] In a New Jersey case, decided one year later, the court held that a school board violated the constitutional rights of students in that it required attendance of children at a course, "Human Sexuality." The court held that the course could be offered; however, attendance could not be required. The court noted that if the course teaches a student how to plan a future life and what conduct in life is acceptable, and if these two topics promote values that conflict with one's religious beliefs, his free exercise rights are violated.[14]

Courts have handed down conflicting opinions on allowing spontaneous discussions about sexual matters. A teacher was not rehired for making offensive sexual references in class,[15] and for

---

12. *Id.* at 123.
13. Medeiros v. Kijosaki, 478 P.2d 314 (Haw. 1970).
14. Valent v. New Jersey State Bd. of Educ., 274 A.2d 832 (N.J. 1971).
15. Robbins v. Board of Educ., 313 F. Supp. 642 (N.D. Ill. 1970).

relating personal sexual experiences and describing houses of prostitution and masturbation to a class of fifteen-year-olds.[16]

Another court decided for a teacher who, during spelling class, was asked by students, who were eighth graders, to define homosexuality. After persistence by the students, she discussed the subject in objective terms.[17]

2. *Evolution*. As an exercise of academic freedom, the teaching of evolution is less volatile than the subject of sex education. By the mid-1960s only Arkansas, Tennessee, and Mississippi had statutes that forbade such teaching. Where the issue has been raised, it has grown out of a belief that the Darwinian theory of evolution runs counter to the teaching of sacred scriptures.

The earliest court test of the legality of teaching evolution occurred in the state of Tennessee, where the real issue was often overshadowed by the stature and personalities of the opposing attorneys, William Jennings Bryan and Clarence Darrow. On trial was John Scopes, a teacher who taught that man descended from lower forms of animals. The state court held that he had no right to teach such a doctrine, although outside school he could believe it as well as oppose the law. "He had no right or privilege to serve the state except upon such terms as the state prescribed. His liberty, his privilege, his immunity to teach and proclaim the theory of evolution elsewhere than in the service of the state, was in no way touched by this law."[18]

The Supreme Court of the United States ruled on the constitutionality of an Arkansas anti-evolution statute in 1968. Passed one year after the *Scopes* trial, the act reflected a time when fundamental thinking was prevalent and when many people relied on a literal interpretation of the Bible, including the origin of man as reported in the book of Genesis. The test of the act came after a teacher taught from a text approved by the school system which

---

16. Moore v. School Bd., 364 F. Supp. 355 (N.D. Fla. 1973).

17. Brown v. Coffeeville Consol. Sch. Dist., 365 F. Supp. 990 (N.D. Miss. 1973).

18. Scopes v. Tennessee, 154 Tenn. 105, 289 S.W. 363, 364 (1927).

contained the Darwinian theory. The Supreme Court ruled that the first amendment does not permit the states to require that teaching and learning must be tailored to the principles and prohibitions of any religious sect or dogma. Speaking for the majority, Justice Fortas ruled that the statute conflicts with a given religious doctrine in the book of Genesis. He concluded:

> The State's undoubted right to prescribe the curriculum for its public schools does not carry with it the right to prohibit, on pain of criminal penalty, the teaching of a scientific theory or doctrine where that prohibition is based upon reasons that violate the First Amendment. It is much too late to argue that the State may impose upon the teachers in its schools any conditions that it chooses, however restrictive they may be of constitutional guarantees.[19]

Two years later, the Mississippi anti-evolution statute was overturned. The state's supreme court ruled that the statute violated the free exercise clause of the first amendment.[20] Finally, a federal circuit court in Texas ruled that the teaching of evolution does not violate the religion clauses of the first amendment. Although an anti-evolution statute was not the issue, a state law did permit students to leave the classroom during presentations that offended their religion.[21]

In Arkansas, a state law that required the presentation of the Biblical version of creation along with the evolutionary version was found to be unconstitutional. The court believed that this law violated the separation of church and state provisions of the first amendment.[22] On the same subject, a tenured biology teacher's dismissal was upheld by a South Dakota court. Despite several meetings with administrators and school board members, the teacher continued to devote a considerable time to discussion of

---

19. Epperson v. Arkansas, 393 U.S. 97, 107, 89 S. Ct. 266, 21 L. Ed. 2d 228 (1968).

20. Smith v. State, 242 So. 2d 692 (Miss. 1970).

21. Wright v. Houston Indep. Sch. Dist., 486 F.2d 137 (5th Cir. 1973).

22. McLean v. Arkansas Bd. of Educ., 529 F. Supp. 1255 (E.D. Ark. 1982).

evolution and creationism, almost to the exclusion of prescribed course content.[23]

3. *Assignments.* In their claim to exercise of academic freedom, teachers often make assignments that offend someone: their superordinates, students, or parents. This section will treat some such issues. It does not treat the question of procedural rights of teachers for alleged violations of law or policy; the substantive rights of teachers treated here involve only the academic freedom of teachers to make questionable assignments.

In *Parducci v. Rutland,* a court enunciated two distinct principles in determining if a questionable assignment merited a teacher's dismissal.[24] It looked at the relevancy of the material to the subject being taught and examined the fairness and balance of the teacher's presentation. Using these criteria, the court ordered the teacher's reinstatement. She had assigned *Welcome to the Monkey House* by Kurt Vonnegut as outside reading material to her eleventh grade English class. The story contained slang, vulgarity, and references to involuntary sexual intercourse. Although she was asked not to teach the story, she did anyway. The court noted that it was considered as being appropriate for the students when compared to other accepted works of literature and that school discipline was not disrupted.

When the teacher is the primary source of vulgarity rather than students being exposed to it through another means, courts look more closely to the extent of one's academic freedom. Unlike the above case, an English teacher's dismissal was upheld in a California case. The teacher maintained that it was an exercise in aca-

---

23. Dale v. Board of Educ., Lemmon Indep. Sch. Dist., 316 N.W.2d 108 (S.D. 1982). *See also* Peloza v. Capistrano Unified Sch. Dist., 37 F.3d 517 (9th Cir. 1994), *cert. denied,* 115 S. Ct. 2640 (1995). The issue still persists. In 1997 a federal district court negated a local school board policy requiring teachers to read a disclaimer of the board's endorsement of the theory of evolution before teaching the materials to students on the basis of the policy's being in violation of the establishment clause. Frieler v. Tangipahoa Parish Bd. of Educ., 975 F. Supp. 819 (E.D. La. 1997).

24. 316 F. Supp. 352 (M.D. Ala. 1970).

demic freedom to read to his tenth grade class a short story he had written and which contained vulgar language. No one complained, but the board of education advised him that he would not be retained because of this and other charges. The court ruled that the teacher's academic freedom had not been violated, and the one vulgarity charge was sufficient cause for not rehiring him.[25]

A number of circumstances taken together, rather than one isolated incident, may render a teacher unfit for teaching. A teacher allowed an alleged vulgar poem, written by a pupil, to remain on the blackboard for two weeks, approved a picture of a row of urinals for the school newspaper, and used the word "rape" before a group of girls in class. The court held that his philosophy and practices were detrimental to secondary school students.[26]

Sponseller summarized the position of the courts concerning the freedom that teachers have in making controversial assignments.

> These rights are not absolute, but have usually been extended to teachers in these areas provided the utterance or assignment was not deemed to be inappropriate for the age and maturity of the students, irrelevant to the course's objectives or such that they do not materially and substantially disrupt or threaten to disrupt the discipline of the school.[27]

---

25. Lindros v. Governing Bd. of Torrance Unified Sch. Dist., 108 Cal. Rptr. 188 (Cal. 1972).

26. Jergeson v. School Bd., 364 F. Supp. 355 (N.D. Fla. 1973).

27. Edwin H. Sponseller, Jr., *Freedom of Expression for Teachers in the Public School Classroom,* in CURRENT LEGAL ISSUES IN EDUCATION 50 (M.A. McGhehey, ed. Topeka: National Organization on Legal Problems of Education, 1977). Unified Sch. Dist. v. Hubbard, 868 P.2d 1240 (Kan. App. 1994), involved the termination of a tenured classroom teacher for his failure to intervene and stop students from making an offensive videotape. The school board was of the opinion that the teacher's failure showed his lack of classroom control. While the termination itself was ultimately overturned, the case does demonstrate the difficulties to be encountered by classroom teachers in making independent assignments to their students.

An appeals court in Connecticut upheld the dismissal of a tenured elementary school teacher.[28] The teacher had assigned students the choice of writing the alphabet or writing a letter to the teacher's fiancee. In response to the children's letters, the fiancee indicated that she and the teacher were Communists. Among the charges against the teacher were violation of the board's policy of not permitting "sectarian or partisan" instruction as well as incompetence.

4. *Discussions.* This section treats briefly the matter of the extent to which teachers can engage in class discussions which may or may not be related to the subject the teacher is assigned to teach. Only recent cases will be considered. They cover a variety of issues and reflect a degree of consistency on the part of judges' decisions. Unprofessional discussions in class about one's colleagues are not protected under the guise of academic freedom. Discussions of sex that offend one's sensibilities may not be protected. Discussions irrelevant to the subject may or may not be protected. When students initiate the topic, courts look more favorably than when teachers introduce questionable topics. Courts do not look favorably on a teacher discussing and exploiting his personal lifestyle, particularly when it deviates from conventional living. Finally, sensitive issues bearing on the topic may be protected, even though parents object.

An Illinois federal district court upheld the discharge of a teacher for using offensive sexual references and for discussing in class the action taken against a teacher for growing a beard.[29]

In spite of objections by parents, a discharged civics teacher in Texas was ordered reinstated. He had been warned not to discuss controversies and to teach from the text. Instead, he taught a unit on race relations and made comments on race and prejudice that parents found objectionable. The court held that his teaching was

---

28. Burns v. Rovaldi, 477 F. Supp. 270 (D. Conn. 1979).
29. Robbins v. Board of Educ., 313 F. Supp. 642 (N.D. Ill. 1970).

acceptable in that there had been no disruption and students had not been indoctrinated.[30]

In a case previously treated in the section on sex education, a female teacher was protected for having discussed homosexuality in an eighth grade spelling class. The subject was raised by students, and the teacher treated it carefully. This, the court found, was acceptable.[31]

A federal district court agreed with the school board's dismissal of a teacher in *Moore v. School Board*, when that teacher strayed from the subject in discussing a variety of topics: teachers' salaries, the school board and administration, his personal sexual experiences, Japanese houses of prostitution, and masturbation. The court and the school board agreed that it is acceptable for a teacher to stray occasionally from the subject, but in this instance the teacher had gone too far.[32]

The Tenth Circuit held that the liberty to structure one's courses is not unlimited; rather, community standards may dictate the extent of academic freedom. In this particular case it was held that a small community had a right to insist on an orthodox approach to teaching. Three teachers were dismissed, and they contended it was because they had played questionable records in class ("Al-

---

30. Sterzing v. Fort Bend Indep. Sch. Dist., 376 F. Supp. 657 (S.D. Tex. 1972). In a 1991 decision, the Tenth Circuit held that a teacher was not protected in repeating a rumor in class about two students having expressed affection the previous day on a tennis court. The court ruled that a classroom is not a public forum for unlimited discussion. The court ruled that the disciplinary action was justified for three reasons: the teacher had used his position of authority to confirm an unsubstantiated rumor, the teacher had not acted professionally, the teacher had embarrassed the students involved. Miles v. Denver Pub. Sch., 944 F.2d 773 (10th Cir. 1991).

31. *Brown, supra* note 17. *See also* Ward v. Hickey, 996 F.2d 448 (1st Cir. 1993). The First Circuit upheld a board's decision not to rehire a nontenured classroom teacher who claimed that her first amendment right of speech had been violated. The dispute arose out of a discussion in ninth grade biology class concerning the abortion of Down's Syndrome fetuses. While teachers retain their first amendment right to free speech, said the court, public school authorities may limit classroom speech to promote educational goals.

32. *Moore, supra* note 16.

ice's Restaurant", "Hair"), and discussed Vietnam, political matters, drugs, and hippies. The board alleged that their dismissals resulted from their creating dissension among the faculty, for being tardy, insubordinate, failing to cover material and to discipline students, and for disturbing other classes. The dismissals stood.[33]

Discussions centering around a role-playing activity dealing with students' feelings on racial matters caused complaints from parents and a warning by administrators not to deal with the issue of blacks in America nor to treat controversies. The principal and the superintendent recommended contract renewal, but the board of education refused. The court reversed the board's action and awarded damages to the teacher when it was determined that the dismissal was due to the discussions even though the activity had caused no disruption.[34]

b. *Teaching Forbidden Subjects.* Although some state constitutions have provisions with respect to teaching specific subjects, state statutes are more explicit as to what shall be taught. Statutes may even provide for how a subject shall be taught. Similarly, statutes may forbid the teaching of a specific subject, as for example, evolution which was treated in a previous section.

Local school boards are also clothed with considerable autonomy in determining curriculum, so long as their decisions are not in conflict with state rulings. More often than not, state statutes and local school board policies require rather than restrict what is

---

33. Adams v. Campbell City Sch. Dist., 511 F.2d 1242 (10th Cir. 1975); Roberts v. Rapides Parish Sch. Bd., 617 So. 2d 187 (La. App. 1993). A board's decision to suspend a tenured teacher without pay because the teacher showed an R-rated movie in class, where the movie contained violence and foul language, and where some seventh grade students were present, was upheld as rationally based upon substantial evidence. In Spurger v. Rapides Parish Sch. Bd., 628 So. 2d 1317 (La. App. 1993), a tenured teacher was suspended without pay for one semester, and placed on probation for the second semester, on charges of incompetence and willful neglect of duty, because he showed an objectionable movie to his special educational class. The movie, titled "Boss," had a "PG" rating and contained repeated racial epithets and stereotypes, and contained a brief nude scene.

34. Kingsville Indep. Sch. Dist. v. Cooper, 611 F.2d 1109 (5th Cir. 1980).

taught. In general, where a statute *requires* that a subject be taught, a complainer has less chance to win than under a statute that *forbids* the teaching of a specific subject. An elective course will usually be protected in a suit, for it is clear that an individual has the option of enrolling or not enrolling in it.

In recent years there has been more sensitivity to the portrayal of people in curriculum materials. Many states have passed laws that forbid racial stereotyping or making one class look inferior to another; they have also required that all groups of people be viewed as being equal. They have mandated programs for bilingual and bi-cultural students.

The Supreme Court ruled, in 1923, that a state law that forbade the teaching of any language other than English to elementary school students was unconstitutional.[35] A violator would be subject to a fine of $25 to $100 or 30 days in jail. The stated purpose of the act was to prevent foreigners from rearing their children in their native language and to delay the teaching of foreign language to non-foreigners until secondary school. In striking down the statute as an infringement of the rights of teachers and students, the Court stated:

> His right to teach and the right of parents to engage him so to instruct their children, we think, are within the liberty of the (Fourteenth) Amendment.
>
> That the State may do much, go very far indeed, in order to improve the quality of its citizens, physically, mentally and morally, is clear; but the individual has certain fundamental rights which must be respected. The protection of the Constitution extends to all, to those who speak other languages as well as to those born with English on the tongue.[36]

More than legislatures, courts have spoken on the degree to which religion can be taught in public schools, a subject that will be treated more fully in Chapter Twelve. The Supreme Court of

---

35. Meyer v. Nebraska, 262 U.S. 390, 43 S. Ct. 625, 67 L. Ed. 1042 (1923).
36. *Id.* at 390 U.S. 400, 401.

the United States has ruled that the Bible cannot be taught as a religion in school,[37] prayer and Bible reading as devotional exercises cannot be held in school,[38] and evolution can be taught as a theory.[39] The Court has stated that it is permissible to teach religion as literature or as history so long as it is handled objectively and without any attempt to indoctrinate one's religious thinking.

A Pennsylvania court held in a religious freedom case that a teacher's dismissal was proper.[40] By not permitting the teacher to conduct both a spoken prayer and Bible reading during class, no religious or academic freedom had been denied him. Rather, the teacher had failed to comply with an administrative order to stop this activity.

c. *Refusing to Salute the Flag.* The controversy over requiring a flag salute as a part of school activities is old. Most of the flag salute litigation has involved students; however, a few cases have also involved teachers, all decided since 1970. The courts have

---

37. Illinois *ex rel.* McCollum v. Board of Educ. of Sch. Dist. No. 71, 333 U.S. 203, 68 S. Ct. 461, 92 L. Ed. 2d 649 (1948); Doe v. Human, 725 F. Supp. 1499 (W.D. Ark. 1989).

38. Engel v. Vitale, 370 U.S. 421, 82 S. Ct. 1261, 8 L. Ed. 2d 601 (1962); School Dist. of Abington Twp. v. Schempp, 374 U.S. 203, 83 S. Ct. 1560, 10 L. Ed. 2d 844 (1963).

39. *Epperson, supra* note 19.

40. Fink v. Board of Educ., Warren Cty. Sch. Dist., 442 A.2d 837 (Pa. Commw. 1982). *See also* C.H. v. Oliva, 990 F. Supp. 341 (D.N.J. 1997). Parents of a kindergarten student sought relief from the courts for two actions involving their child. In art class he had drawn a picture of Jesus to depict something for which he was thankful. The poster was removed from display and later relegated to a less prominent place on the bulletin board. In a second incident as a first grader, the child had been allowed to read to the class a story of his choice for having attained a certain level of reading proficiency. He chose an excerpt from the Beginner's Bible. The child's teacher would not allow him to read the story in class; instead she allowed the boy to read the story to her in private. The court upheld school authority, noting that the student had no constitutional right to have his poster displayed and, in the second incident, allowing the student to read his story in private was a reasonable accommodation. To have done otherwise could have been construed as a teacher's endorsement of religion.

consistently ruled that teachers are protected in their refusal to join in the flag salute exercises.

In *Hanover v. Northrup,* a teacher notified her principal that she would not participate in the salute. Instead, a student led the exercises while the teacher remained seated with her head bowed. There was no disruption. The court overturned her dismissal for insubordination and ruled that her refusal was protected by the first amendment.[41]

A different factual situation existed in *Maryland v. Lindquist,* when a teacher objected philosophically and politically to the pledge of allegiance. He felt that he could not force patriotism on his classes, and he believed that the requirement interfered with his individual right to express his loyalty to his country. The court upheld him, holding the statute requiring the pledge to be an abridgement to his freedom of speech.[42]

The third case involved a school board policy that required all teachers to recite the flag salute at the opening of the school day. One teacher refused and instead had a second teacher, assigned to her, lead the pledge. Although the teacher had refused to participate all year, that fact was not discovered by school officials until April. Her students were not disrupted by her behavior. Although the court saw some value in the salute, it recognized that the teacher's individual rights, however obnoxious, outweighed the state's interests.[43]

The courts here have tended to look to the substantive rights that a teacher possesses as well as to the effect of the exercise of that right. When no disruption occurs and when students are not otherwise harmed or adversely influenced, there is a real burden on the school board to justify a curtailment of that teacher's freedom not to salute the flag. That justification must also be more than a mere speculation that disruption may occur.

---

41. 325 F. Supp. 170 (D. Conn. 1970).
42. 278 A.2d 263 (Md. 1971).
43. Russo v. Central Sch. Dist., 469 F.2d 623 (2d Cir. 1972).

d. *Selection of Methods of Instruction.* It is unquestioned that a state has a right to prescribe specific methods of instruction. Courts are very reluctant to substitute their judgment for that of state legislatures or local school boards. This was expressed in the early 1900s by a Massachusetts court: "The determination of the procedure and the management and direction of pupils and studies in this Commonwealth rests in the wise discretion and sound judgment of teachers and school committees, whose action in these respects is not subject to the supervision of this court."[44]

Similarly, by virtue of their training and experience, teachers have considerable freedom in determining their methods of instruction. The freedom is limited, however, by state requirements and by their local school board.

Older cases confirm that methodology rests with the wisdom of local school personnel when not in conflict with state laws. Thus, a taxpayer could not require that bookkeeping be taught by the double entry rather than the single entry method.[45] Courts have reasoned that to try to accommodate all parents who have their own notion about the best way to teach a subject would be to place teachers in an untenable position.

Newer cases on record deal with narrow issues such as teaching a specific lesson rather than a course. In *Mailloux v. Kiley,* an English class was discussing taboo words. Mailloux wrote a four-letter word on the board and asked the students to define it. Without repeating the word, he then asked students why some words were objectionable and others were not. He was later dismissed for "conduct unbecoming a teacher." The circuit court treated the question of the relevancy of the method; it did not consider the necessity of the method. It recognized that for a method to be constitutionally protected, it must have the support of the preponderant opinion of the teaching profession. Further, there was no regu-

---

44. Wulff v. Inhabitants of Wakefield, 221 Mass. 427, 109 N.E. 358, 359 (1915).

45. Neilan v. Board of Dirs. of Indep. Sch. Dist., 200 Iowa 860, 205 N.W. 506 (1925).

266

lation prohibiting the method he had used. He was reinstated and recovered his lost salary.[46]

An elementary school teacher with twenty-five years' experience, dismissed for insubordination, also recovered lost wages and was reinstated. Her class of second-graders had written letters to the cafeteria supervisor asking that raw carrots be served, had drawn cartoons showing inoperative water fountains, and had complained to the superintendent about an incinerator in the school yard. The court held that such action did not constitute protest, but was relevant to the children's study.[47]

A teacher was dismissed for allowing her students to write essays on anything they wished. Most of them treated the subjects of sex and drugs. Instead of rejecting the articles, the teacher used them as teaching devices by duplicating and distributing them to the students. The court upheld her, recognizing that her method was questionable but not unacceptable.[48]

A case that was decided against teachers was handed down in 1974. Three teachers distributed brochures of the "Woodstock" experience of 1969 that contained materials related to drugs, sex, and vulgarity. These teachers claimed that the materials were relevant to their teaching. The court ruled that they had failed to make such a case for their use as exemplary teaching tools.[49]

While a school board determines broad curriculum content and methods, it is often the teacher who best determines what is the most effective means for direct instruction. Consequently, teachers are given leeway in the preparation of lessons. The Tenth Circuit has stated:

> (A) teacher cannot be discharged for using a particular teaching method or technique relevant to the proper teaching of the subject matter involved unless the school

---

46. 448 F.2d 1242 (1st Cir. 1971).

47. Downs v. Conway, 328 F. Supp. 338 (E.D. Ark. 1971).

48. Oakland Unified Sch. Dist. v. Olicker, 102 Cal. Rptr. 421 (Cal. App. 1972).

49. Brubaker v. Board of Educ., 502 F.2d 973 (7th Cir. 1974).

district has established that the teacher was put on notice
either by regulation or otherwise before adverse action
was taken that he should not use such method or technique.[50]

A teacher in Chicago went too far in deciding what she would
and would not teach. A Jehovah's Witness, the teacher notified her
principal that she could not teach any subject dealing with patriotism, the American flag, or other such matters, for they were offensive to her religion. Efforts were made, without success, to accommodate the teacher, and she was dismissed. The court held that
the teacher's right to religious beliefs was unquestioned, but she
had no right to place her beliefs upon her students as would occur
in the absence of treating patriotic material.[51]

The claim that a teacher was nonrenewed because he refused to
submit, for administrative approval, articles for the student newspaper was unfounded. The issue was not one of academic freedom
but of the teacher's ability to perform.[52]

e. *Censorship.* The issue of censorship within a school has
arisen in a number of areas. In past years cases have involved
students and their rights to free expression in student publications,
both official and "underground." Recent issues in the area of censorship have dealt with the removal of specific books, magazines,
and other publications from the curriculum as optional or required
reading and the removal of similar items from the school library.
Regarding the removal of a particular book, some individuals have
argued that there is a distinction between the removal of a book
from the curriculum and removal from the library. In the library an
individual chooses what he reads, whereas in a course the reading
may be required. Additionally, there have been censorship cases

---

50. Simineo v. School Dist. No. 16, 594 F.2d 1353 (10th Cir. 1979).

51. Palmer v. Board of Educ., 603 F.2d 1271 (7th Cir. 1979), *cert. denied,* 444
U.S. 1026 (1980).

52. Nicholson v. Board of Educ., Torrance Unified Sch. Dist., 682 F.2d 858
(9th Cir. 1982).

involving student production of controversial plays and the viewing of objectionable films.

Obviously, the intent of the first amendment was not to require schools to include in their libraries all publications. To do so would not only be cost-prohibitive but also cumbersome. In fact, schools have the right to select and limit the number and type of books. A school library serves the students of a school by having materials appropriate for student use; as such a school library can be more selective than a public library. The control of content is not restricted just to the acquisition of library material but also to removal or replacement. Periodically, it is necessary to remove damaged, dated, or nonused materials to better serve student needs.

Bryson and Detty caution against the arbitrary selection and removal of library materials. They suggest that an official policy be adopted, but caution further:

> No school board policy or guidelines will guarantee in perpetuity the absence of litigation by individuals or groups who maintain their rights have been violated. However, school boards and school administrators can reduce the probability of having school practices litigated (and thus no financial liability) by formulating, implementing, and explicitly following a set of guidelines governing the selection and removal of library and instructional materials.[53]

Such policy should include the identification of individuals and committees which select materials, the objectives for selection, procedures for selection (including gifts), and procedures for reconsideration of materials for both inclusion and exclusion.

Censorship may be attempted by groups or individuals to restrict access to offensive material. Items have been selected for

---

53. BRYSON & DETTY, CENSORSHIP OF PUBLIC SCHOOL LIBRARY AND INSTRUCTIONAL MATERIAL (Charlottesville: The Michie Co., 1982). For a discussion of this subject, see Martha M. McCarthy, *Post-Hazelwood Developments: A Threat to Free Inquiry in Public Schools,* 81 EDUC. LAW REP. 685 (June 3, 1993), especially the subsection on Curriculum Censorship and Academic Freedom.

censorship because they may perpetrate negative ethnic or racial stereotypes, advocate offensive political positions, or contain descriptions or language that is considered obscene. The Supreme Court of the United States in *Miller v. California* issued the following definition of obscenity:

> (a) whether the average person, applying contemporary community standards would find that a work, taken as a whole, appeals to prurient interest, (b) whether a work depicts or describes, in a patently offensive way, sexual conduct specifically defined by applicable state law, and (c) whether the work taken as a whole, lacks serious literary, artistic, political, or scientific value.[54]

Censorship was the issue in an action by the Island Trees School District Board of Education in New York that resulted in a Supreme Court decision in 1992. The issue involved the removal of nine books from the school library. This action followed the demands of a parents' group in the community. The board had a committee review the nine books but refused to reinstate the books the committee had suggested. The board had objected to the books because they were anti-American, anti-Semitic, anti-Christian, and filthy. A suit was filed claiming the denial of first amendment rights to the students of Island Trees. The trial court ruled for the board; on appeal the Second Circuit reversed and ordered a reevaluation of the nine books. The Supreme Court of the United States resolved two questions: Does the first amendment restrain a school board in removing books from school libraries? If so, do students have the right to bring suit? A school board may create a curriculum designed to transmit local values consistent with the first amendment's provision of free expression. The use of the library is voluntary; the school board has discretion in library matters, but less so than in curriculum matters, including book

---

54. 413 U.S. 2415, 93 S. Ct. 2607, 37 L. Ed. 2d 419 (1973). More will be said about censorship issues in § 11.6 of this text.

removal.[55] "[L]ocal school boards may not remove books from school library shelves simply because they dislike the ideas contained in those books and seek by their removal to 'prescribe what shall be orthodox in politics, nationalism, religion, or other matters of opinion.'"[56]

In answer to the second question, the Court held that students have a right to sue for the denial of first amendment rights. In this particular case the decision regarding book removal had been made not for educational reasons but in response to political pressure. (See also § 11.6.)

In *Sheck v. Baileyville School Committee*,[57] the book *365 Days* had been in the school library for ten years but was requested to be removed because it contained an offensive word. Parents, the superintendent, and school board members had not read the book prior to its removal. They also banned students from having copies of the book while on school property. Citing *Pico,* the court ordered the book to be reinstated.

Efforts have also been made to have materials portraying violent acts removed from the curriculum. In Lake Forest, Minnesota, part of the high school English curriculum included the film "The Lottery." The film is based on the short story by Shirley Jackson in which an individual is depicted being stoned to death by townspeople. Following that film, a second film is shown discussing the previous film. Concerned residents of the district, including parents, requested that both films be removed. In response, the board of education issued a statement critical of both films, particularly their concentration on the violent aspects of the story. It further stipulated that the story itself should remain in the curriculum. The issue made its way to the Eighth Circuit. The court saw that the

---

55. Board of Educ., Island Trees Union Free Sch. Dist. No. 26 v. Pico, 457 U.S. 853, 102 S. Ct. 2799, 73 L. Ed. 2d 435 (1982).

56. *Id.* at 457 U.S. 872.

57. 530 F. Supp. 679 (D. Me. 1982).

proposed ban was an attempt to suppress a controversial presenta-tion.[58]

When it cannot be determined that the removal of books was due specifically to an attempt to impose a given moral viewpoint, the books can be removed, according to the Seventh Circuit.[59]

Much of the litigation in the area of censorship has dealt with the removal of materials currently in use. Concern has developed regarding the censorship of controversial materials through a school district's policy on acquisitions. In Mississippi, challenges were made against the State Textbook Purchasing Board regarding a state history text.[60] Only two members of the seven-member board approved the book, *Mississippi: Conflict and Change.* The book was rejected, with some of the members reasoning that it had inappropriate racial content. In deciding this case, the court found that the board in effect was preventing controversial ideas from making their way into classrooms through the texts. In the past, selected books tended to reflect the racial mores of the times. Such power vested in this group, appointed by the governor, without a review procedure, violated the first amendment. The court in-structed the legislature to change the manner in which textbooks are to be selected in the state.

§ 8.2. Freedom Outside the School.

a. *Association.* The right of association is not directly men-tioned in the first amendment; it is implied by two clauses: assem-

---

58. Pratt v. Independent Sch. Dist. No. 831, 670 F.2d 771 (8th Cir. 1982). In late 1998 the Court of Appeals for the Ninth Circuit ruled that if school officials remove controversial books from a school's curriculum on the basis of their content, children's first amendment rights would be violated. Monteiro v. Tempe Union High Sch. Dist., 158 F.3d 1022 (9th Cir. 1998). For a case involving a school board's exercise of the prerogative to select suitable materials for the school's curriculum, see Board of Educ. of Jefferson Cty. v. Wilder, 960 P.2d 695 (Colo. 1998).

59. Zykan v. Warsaw Community Sch. Corp., 631 F.2d 1300 (7th Cir. 1980).

60. Loewen v. Turnipseed, 488 F. Supp. 1138 (N.D. Miss. 1980).

bly and petition. It has been constitutionally protected from invasion by both the federal and state governments. However, like most freedoms, it is not absolute. Government may condition the exercise of that right in protecting others and in ensuring public order and safety. The question often arises as to the extent that government may set conditions that affect a teacher's right of association. That question involves two issues: the organizations with which one affiliates and the company one keeps.

1. *Affiliations.* School boards are not disposed, as they were a few decades ago, to restrict teachers in their affiliation with organizations outside school. The decade of the 1950s was a period in which school boards attempted to regulate teachers' behavior by curbing subversive influences in the schools. In the 1960s some school districts attempted to discourage teachers from engaging in civil rights activities. The decades since then have often given rise to issues involving sexual associations. A few cases in each of the first two areas will illustrate the predominant thinking of the courts on these subjects. The third area will be treated in the section on living arrangements.

The Supreme Court of the United States has handed down several decisions involving the associational freedom of teachers. One concerned a teacher who refused to answer questions about his political affiliations. His superintendent asked him to answer questions about his alleged affiliation with the Communist Party, and he refused to respond. He was discharged, not for disloyalty, but for incompetency on the basis of his refusal to cooperate with the superintendent. By a five to four vote, the Court upheld the dismissal. The majority held:

> By engaging in teaching in the public schools, petitioner did not give up his right to freedom of belief, speech, or association. He did, however, undertake obligations of frankness, candor, and cooperation in answering inquiries made of him by his employing Board ex-

273

amining into his fitness to serve as a public school teacher.[61]

One year later, the Supreme Court held that an investigation about teachers and students concerning Communist associations served the public interest to a greater extent than it intruded on one's personal liberties. In *Barenblatt v. United States,* the Court upheld the legitimacy of an associational inquiry in the field of education. The case did not involve the issue of what one teaches but rather the matter of one's associations.[62]

The *Shelton v. Tucker*[63] decision reflected a shift away from inquiry into subversive influences to an overriding concern of the 1960s: civil rights. It involved an Arkansas statute that required all public school teachers to disclose annually the names of all organizations to which they belonged or contributed within the previous five years. A teacher of twenty-five years' tenure in the Little Rock schools refused to comply. In the meantime, he testified that he was not a Communist but that he did belong to the National Association for the Advancement of Colored People. The Supreme Court reaffirmed that school boards may properly investigate the competence of people they employ. However, requiring a teacher to disclose all his affiliations restricts one's right of association. A school board may require the disclosure of some, but not all, associations, since not every association necessarily has any relevance to one's teaching.

There were a number of other cases decided in the 1960s that had a bearing on a teacher's civil rights activities. When those activities were carried on outside school and did not interfere with one's teaching, the courts consistently sustained them as being constitutionally protected by the first amendment. A leading case is *Johnson v. Branch,*[64] in which a black teacher was very active in

---

61. Beilan v. Board of Pub. Educ., 357 U.S. 399, 405, 78 S. Ct. 1317, 2 L. Ed. 2d 1414 (1958).

62. 360 U.S. 109, 79 S. Ct. 1081, 3 L. Ed. 2d 115 (1959).

63. 364 U.S. 479, 81 S. Ct. 247, 5 L. Ed. 2d 231 (1960).

64. 364 F.2d 177 (4th Cir. 1966).

civil rights work in a community experiencing racial tension. The teacher was dismissed on such pretexts as being fifteen minutes late in supervising an athletic contest, arriving a few minutes late to school, failing to stand outside her door in supervising students as classes changed, and failing to see that cabinets in her room were clean. The court agreed that the combined offenses were insufficient to merit dismissal, particularly in view of her twelve years of successful teaching. It agreed that those infractions had relevance to her teaching, but none related specifically to what transpires in the classroom.

Continuity of instruction and the desire to have employees present when school is in session have been matters of concern. Most school systems allow teachers to be absent for health reasons and may even provide a designated number of days for personal business. In some cases the observance of religious holidays may prevent a teacher from reporting for work. At issue in a New Jersey case was the dismissal of a teacher for an absence without permission for part of a school day.[65] Prior to that time the teacher had been absent eight days for religious reasons. The teacher had been informed that his absences would negatively impact his evaluation and were the basis of not granting permission for the teacher to be away from the school on the date in question. The issue before the court was one of "hardship" to the school district that resulted from the teacher's religious observances. It was established that conflicts with the school calendar occurred only between five to ten days per year, and thus the district could not prove any "undue hardship." The teacher was reinstated with back pay.

A teacher may not be dismissed because of his duties as a representative of the teachers' union, as long as such duties do not interfere with the rights of others or performance of contractual duties.[66] A teacher cannot be dismissed for friendship with former

---

65. Niederhuber v. Camden Cty. Vocational & Technical Sch. Dist. Bd. of Educ., 495 F. Supp. 273 (D.N.J. 1980).

66. Durango Sch. Dist. No. 9-R v. Thorpe, 614 P.2d 880 (Colo. 1980).

board members,[67] nor for being the political opponent of newly elected board members.[68]

   2. *Loyalty Oaths*. Government has often attempted to establish loyalty requirements for teachers during wartime. New York State, for instance, passed a law after World War I that provided for the dismissal of any teacher for "the utterance of any treasonable or seditious act." Two years later the statute was repealed. During and after World War II, many states enacted loyalty oath laws, many of which were aimed specifically at teachers.[69] In order to keep subversives out of the schools, teachers were required to execute an oath typically providing for one or two conditions: supporting the Constitution and defending the country against all enemies, and swearing that one is not, nor has been, a member of a subversive organization designed to overthrow the government. It is the latter category to which teachers have most often objected. They are wary of the potential misuse of the oath, and of having to speculate as which organizations are acceptable or forbidden.

   From 1951 to 1971, the Supreme Court of the United States handed down nine decisions involving the legality of loyalty oath laws. In 1951 it upheld the legality of a requirement that an employee list past or present membership in the Communist Party and that one swear nonaffiliation with an organization advocating overthrow of the government.[70] The next year it handed down two decisions. It overturned an Oklahoma statute requiring all state employees to subscribe to a loyalty oath. The justices distinguished between innocent and knowing membership in a subversive organization.[71] In the second case, the Court upheld New

---

   67. Burris v. Willis Indep. Sch. Dist., 537 F. Supp. 801 (S.D. Tex. 1982).

   68. Guerra v. Roma Indep. Sch. Dist., 444 F. Supp. 812 (S.D. Tex. 1977).

   69. For a study of loyalty oath laws during the period of their greatest influence, see JOSEPH E. BRYSON, LEGALITY OF LOYALTY OATH AND NON-OATH REQUIREMENTS FOR PUBLIC SCHOOL TEACHERS (Asheville, North Carolina: Miller Printing Co., 1963).

   70. Garner v. Board of Pub. Works, 341 U.S. 716, 71 S. Ct. 909, 95 L. Ed. 1317 (1951).

   71. Wieman v. Updegraff, 344 U.S. 183 (1952).

York's Feinberg Law that authorized dismissal for membership in a subversive organization advocating overthrow of the government.[72] The justices ruled, in effect, that a teacher could decide between membership and employment. They recognized the crucial role that teachers play in our society:

A teacher works in a sensitive area in a schoolroom. There he shapes the attitude of young minds towards the society in which they live. In this, the state has a vital concern. It must preserve the integrity of the schools. That the school authorities have the right and the duty to screen the officials, teachers, and employees as to their fitness to maintain the integrity of the schools as a part of ordered society, cannot be doubted. One's associates, past and present, as well as one's conduct, may properly be considered in determining fitness and loyalty.[73]

After the *Adler v. Board of Education* decision, the Court took a different turn and began to rule that a teacher's first amendment rights were paramount over any interest the state has in protecting students from possible subversive teachers. It held in 1961 that a statute requiring teachers to swear that they had not given "aid, support, advice, counsel, or influence" to the Communist Party was overly vague and could not be enforced.[74] A loyalty oath providing dismissal for enrollment in a subversive organization or for advocating overthrow of the government is too ambiguous.[75] A loyalty oath making anyone ineligible for state employment who took an oath while knowingly a member of the Communist Party or a subversive organization is also unconstitutional.[76] An oath law requiring one to swear "I am not engaged in one way or another in

---

72. Adler v. Board of Educ., 342 U.S. 485 (1952).

73. *Id.* at 493.

74. Cramp v. Board of Pub. Instr., 368 U.S. 278, 82 S. Ct. 275, 7 L. Ed. 2d 285 (1961).

75. Baggett v. Bullitt, 377 U.S. 360, 84 S. Ct. 1316, 12 L. Ed. 2d 377 (1964).

76. Elfbrandt v. Russell, 384 U.S. 360, 86 S. Ct. 1238, 16 L. Ed. 2d 321 (1964).

the attempt to overthrow the Government of the United States, or the State of Maryland, or any political subdivision of either of them, by force or violence" was declared illegal in that it placed too much surveillance on teachers and did not clearly distinguish between permissible and impermissible conduct.[77] In 1967, the Court overturned the Feinberg Law of New York, which it had upheld in 1952. The specific provisions it overturned were: advocating overthrow of the government, uttering treasonable or seditious words or committing treasonable or seditious acts. The Court invalidated the oath on the bases of vagueness, *i.e.,* a teacher not knowing what was acceptable and unacceptable and on overbreadth, *i.e.,* the law did not distinguish between knowing membership and membership actively engaged in unlawful overthrow.[78]

In two cases decided by the Supreme Court as of 1977, the Court upheld loyalty oaths containing a positive affirmation, in each instance with a *per curiam* opinion. A Colorado oath provided the teacher to "solemnly swear (affirm) that I will uphold the Constitution of the United States and the constitution of the State of Colorado, and I will faithfully perform the duties of the position upon which I am about to enter."[79]

In the other case, the Court upheld one section and overturned another of a Florida loyalty oath law. It held that one could be required to "support the Constitution of the United States and of the State of Florida." It ruled unconstitutional, however, a provision that one swear that he does not "believe in the overthrow of the government of the United States or the State of Florida by force or violence."[80]

When one examines the oath law cases more carefully, it appears that the Supreme Court recognizes that states have a respon-

---

77. Whitehall v. Elkins, 389 U.S. 54, 88 S. Ct. 184, 19 L. Ed. 2d 228 (1967).

78. Keyishian v. Board of Regents, 385 U.S. 589, 87 S. Ct. 675, 17 L. Ed. 2d 629 (1967).

79. Ohlson v. Phillips, 397 U.S. 317, 90 S. Ct. 1124, 25 L. Ed. 337, *reh'g denied,* 397 U.S. 1081 (1970).

80. Connell v. Higginbotham, 403 U.S. 207, 91 S. Ct. 1772, 29 L. Ed. 2d 418 (1971).

sibility for protecting pupils from subversive influences. However, like other citizens, teachers have a right to examine or be exposed to a variety of ideas, and membership in an unpopular or even subversive organization may not be grounds for dismissal. The right of association is basic to everyone, including teachers.

For a loyalty oath law to be upheld, it must have some standard of objective measurement. The justices have indicated that this is exceedingly difficult for negatively-stated oaths. They have looked instead to the need for protecting teachers in their practice of academic freedom.

3. *Living Arrangements.* A 1973 challenge to the right of association involved domestic lifestyles of teachers. In particular, the issue has focused on teachers having living arrangements at variance with wishes of the administration or with community thinking. These arrangements usually have sexual connotations in that cases have often involved relationships outside traditional marriage. These include both heterosexual and homosexual relations, as well as extramarital affairs. When discovered in such activities, teachers have been charged with immorality. Courts have interpreted immorality in different ways and thus offer no clear-cut standard for condoning or disapproving nonconventional living arrangements. Moreover, contemporary notions of what constitutes immorality are not the same as decades ago when, for example, a female teacher was subject to dismissal only because she married. In 1973, the Eighth Circuit overturned the dismissal of a teacher who permitted young men, friends of her son, to spend the night in her one-bedroom apartment. One such occupant was a young man engaged in student-teaching in the district. The court held that, because of the living arrangement, one could speculate as to what might have happened, but one could not infer that any immoral behavior had transpired.[81]

In contrast to the above case, the same circuit two years later upheld the dismissal of a female teacher for living with a male teacher who was not her husband. She claimed a right of privacy

---

81. Fisher v. Snyder, 476 F.2d 375 (8th Cir. 1973).

279

and freedom of association; the court recognized that a greater interest than her claimed freedom was the protection of the integrity of the schools. Although sexual immorality was not specifically established, the court held that the school board could reasonably believe that, because of the negative community reaction, her behavior could have an adverse effect on her elementary school pupils. Her conduct was seen as a violation of local community mores and was inconsistent with the community's interest in maintaining a properly moral scholastic environment.[82]

A different question on the right of association arose in the Fifth Circuit in 1975.[83] Three teachers were dismissed because they sent their children to a racially discriminatory private school. The school board argued that, because of this, the teachers would be less effective since the district was under a desegregation order. "[T]eachers who send their own children to a segregated school manifest a belief that segregation is desirable in education and a distrust in desegregated schools."[84]

A principal was reinstated and awarded punitive damages following his dismissal on the grounds of an alleged affair with his female assistant principal.[85] The dismissal had been ordered without a hearing.

The personal life of a teacher regarding such matters as not attending church,[86] the location of one's home,[87] the relationship

---

82. Sullivan v. Meade City Indep. Sch. Dist., 530 F.2d 799 (8th Cir. 1975). In 1991 the Supreme Court of Oregon upheld the dismissal of a tenured teacher based on out-of-school conduct. The teacher's husband had grown, sold, and used marijuana, activities the teacher knew had occurred. Jefferson Cty. Sch. Dist. No. 509-J v. Fair Dismissal Appeals Bd., 812 P.2d 1384 (Ore. 1991). *See also* Todd A. DeMitchell, *Private Lives Community Control v. Professional Autonomy,* 78 ED. LAW REP. 187 (Jan. 14, 1993).

83. Cook v. Hudson, 511 F.2d 744 (5th Cir. 1975).

84. Citing the district court opinion at 365 F. Supp. 855, 860 (N.D. Miss. 1973).

85. Schreffler v. Board of Educ., Delmar Sch. Dist., 506 F. Supp. 1300 (D. Del. 1981). But a female teacher who has a relationship with a fifteen-year-old boy is not protected. Elvin v. City of Waterville, 573 A.2d 381 (Me. 1990).

86. Stoddard v. School Dist. No. 1, 590 F.2d 829 (10th Cir. 1979).

with her husband, or having a child out of wedlock may not, in itself, be grounds for dismissal.[88]

b. *Residency Requirements.* A century ago, it was not unusual for teachers to live in homes in the community in which they taught. Later, as they established their own homes, it was also not unusual for them to have an understanding with the school board that they would live within the school district.

The 1970s witnessed a number of court suits attacking the legitimacy of requiring one to live in the district in which he teaches. Teachers claim that this policy is in violation of the equal protection clause.

In considering the legality of residency requirements, courts have applied the "rational interest" test. If it can be shown that there are a set of facts which support the state's interest and purposes, the statute will be upheld. Using that standard, courts have consistently upheld residency laws and policies. They have cited the fact that teachers would have a better understanding of the community in which they work, they would tend to become more involved in community activities, and they would tend to support increased tax levies in support of education.

In a 1975 court decision, a Michigan state court held that a residency regulation for administrators only was not unreasonable or arbitrary in exempting those employed before the policy was established.[89]

Five cases on this subject were decided in 1976, and these cases uniformly uphold residency requirements and also reflect a consistency of reasoning.

The Cincinnati school board was free to distinguish in a residency policy between new teachers and teachers with experience.[90] Similarly, a prospective residency requirement was upheld in Pittsburgh. The policy did not affect one's right to travel.[91] An-

---

87. Newborn v. Morrison, 440 F. Supp. 623 (S.D. Ill. 1977).

88. Avery v. Homewood City Bd. of Educ., 674 F.2d 337 (5th Cir. 1982).

89. Park v. Lansing Sch. Dist., 62 Mich. App. 397, 233 N.W.2d 592 (1975).

90. Wardwell v. Board of Educ., 529 F.2d 625 (6th Cir. 1976).

91. Pittsburgh Fed'n of Teachers v. Aaron, 471 F. Supp. 94 (W.D. Pa. 1976).

other school district's policy was found not to be in violation of the equal protection clause because the plaintiff could still properly perform his duties as a teacher.[92]

A residency policy for teachers in the School District of Philadelphia was upheld, with conditions. When adopted, it was to be applied only to teachers hired after the policy was approved; however, it was not enforced for nearly four years. The court held that, although the residency requirement was legal, it could not be enforced against those teachers employed between February 1, 1972, and May 16, 1976 (the time the policy was in effect but inoperative).[93]

The Supreme Court of the United States has also spoken on this issue. In 1976, it upheld the constitutionality of a Philadelphia ordinance requiring city employees to be residents of the city. It was challenged by a fireman who moved outside the city. The Court held the ordinance to be rational and not in violation of the employee's fourteenth amendment rights.[94]

c. *Public Statements.* Many teachers have been reluctant to speak out on public or controversial issues for fear that their jobs may be placed in jeopardy. The Constitution protects them to a considerable degree; however, the right of free speech is not unlimited. Conversely, the condition of being a teacher does not mean that one has to forego his first amendment rights as a citizen. Courts look to what is said, the forum in which it is presented, and its relationship to or effect on the school environment.

The leading case in this area is *Pickering v. Board of Education,* a 1968 decision by the Supreme Court of the United States.[95] It involved the dismissal of a teacher for making critical statements about his local board of education. He criticized the board and its emphasis on athletics, expressing his dismay over the fact that

---

92. Mogel v. Sevier Cty. Sch. Dist., 540 F.2d 478 (10th Cir. 1976).

93. Philadelphia Fed'n of Teachers, Local No. 3, AFL-CIO v. Board of Educ., No. 3583 (Ct. Common Pleas, Oct. 4, 1976).

94. McCarthy v. Philadelphia Civil Serv. Comm'n, 424 U.S. 645, 96 S. Ct. 1154, 47 L. Ed. 2d 366 (1976).

95. 391 U.S. 563, 88 S. Ct. 1731, 20 L. Ed. 2d 811 (1968).

three of four bond elections had been defeated between 1961 and 1964. Pickering's letter to the newspaper criticized the manner in which the board handled those elections, criticized the board for its priorities in allocating school funds, and criticized the superintendent for allegedly influencing teachers not to vote in the bond election.

In dismissing Pickering, the board charged that his letter contained false statements, impugned the motives of the administration, and damaged the school system.

The Court held that Pickering's speech was protected by the first amendment. It saw value in teachers speaking out on public issues, particularly as they affect their own profession. The factual errors in the letter were minor, the Court pointed out, and the data were already a matter of public record. The justices also attached no malice to the teacher's motives.

In a 1977 case, a teacher was dismissed for openly criticizing the school board and administration at a board meeting. The school board alleged that her dismissal was the result of her classroom performance, not of her statements. The court held that the public statements were protected by the first amendment.[96] The first amendment was no protection, however, to a teacher who called his superintendent a "liar" and "an autocratic administrator."[97] A teacher was ordered reinstated with lost salary after he had been dismissed for public remarks to a city council and board of trustees about his concern over community and economic problems affecting teachers and students in the district.[98]

---

96. Branch v. School Dist., 432 F. Supp. 608 (D. Mont. 1977).

97. Spano v. School Dist., 12 Pa. Commw. 170, 316 A.2d 657 (1974).

98. Lusk v. Estes, 361 F. Supp. 653 (N.D. Tex. 1973). Court opinions in the 1990s have tended to affirm the right of teachers to speak out on a variety of issues, provided they are of public concern. A high school teacher-coach claimed he was not renewed as a coach for having made negative comments about the school board in the local paper. The court ruled that the coach's comments were directed only at his team's poor performance and were not protected speech. Adkins v. Stow City Sch. Dist. Bd. of Educ., 591 N.E.2d 795 (Ohio App. 1990). In *Vukadinovich*, the cause of a teacher's dismissal was ruled to be alcoholism, not criticism of the superintendent. Vukadinovich v. Board of Sch. Trustees of

On the subject of teacher-school board negotiations, courts have distinguished between a teacher's right to talk at school and in an open forum. A school board policy was overturned which prohibited teachers from circulating petitions concerning disputed budget proposals during off-duty hours.[99] A school board policy was upheld which forbade teachers from discussing in class any aspect of a local strike. In upholding the policy, the court noted its effects on the district and the fact that fifth graders were a captive audience of children, subject to compulsory attendance laws.[100] In contrast, a nonunion teacher who spoke out at an open meeting of the school board, in opposition to an agency shop provision of a proposed collective bargaining agreement, was protected. The Court found that the teacher's statement did not constitute negotiations. The meeting was open to the public and the teacher had the same right as any other citizen under the first amendment to speak out.[101]

First amendment protection of free public expression (religion, speech, and association) does not preclude such protection for similar expression in private, ruled the Supreme Court in 1979.[102] Prior to that decision, a test had been developed in *Mt. Healthy* to determine whether a teacher's dismissal was related to the public exercise of a first amendment right or if there were other legitimate grounds for such dismissal.[103] The mere existence of alternative

---

Mich. City Areas Sch., 776 F. Supp. 1325 (N.D. Ill. 1991). A coach lost in her claim that her dismissal had resulted from her assertion of low morale in the school district. The court ruled that the teacher's comments did not relate to a matter of public concern. Sanguigni v. Pittsburgh Bd. of Pub. Educ., 968 F.2d 393 (3d Cir. 1992).

99. Los Angeles Teachers' Union v. Los Angeles City Bd. of Educ., 78 Cal. Rptr. 723 (Cal. 1969).

100. Nigosian v. Weiss, 343 F. Supp. 757 (E.D. Mich. 1971).

101. City of Madison Joint Sch. Dist. No. 8 v. Wisconsin Emp. Relations Comm'n, 429 U.S. 167, 97 S. Ct. 421, 50 L. Ed. 2d 376 (1976).

102. Givhan v. Western Line Consol. Sch. Dist., 439 U.S. 410, 99 S. Ct. 693, 58 L. Ed. 2d 619 (1979).

103. Mt. Healthy City Sch. Dist. Bd. of Educ. v. Doyle, 429 U.S. 274, 97 S. Ct. 568, 50 L. Ed. 2d 471 (1977). For a more extensive treatment of this case, see Chapter 7.

grounds is not sufficient when it is determined that the motivating factor for dismissal was based on a protected right.[104]

The circulation of a letter critical of the board of education's expenditures is not grounds for dismissal. Comments in the teachers' lounge by a teacher on school issues are protected speech.[105]

Criticism of teaching methods in the school and charges made by the superintendent that the teacher was "talking behind his back" are not grounds for dismissal.[106] Presenting grievances on television[107] and seeking the superintendent's resignation[108] are also not grounds for dismissal; neither is criticism of the board of education in public meetings[109] or at parent meetings.[110]

Obviously, not all utterances are protected speech. Although a teacher was issued a letter of reprimand and not dismissed, she still sued, claiming that her release of information to the press was protected. The court found for the school district, because the teacher's comments involved criticism of a fellow worker and could jeopardize future working relations,[111] as does calling a supervisor a scab during a strike.

Testimony given in a lawsuit by a fellow employee against the school district is not valid ground for termination,[112] nor is unsportsmanlike behavior at a school-sponsored basketball game.[113]

d. *Political Activity.* Like other citizens, teachers have the right to engage in political activity. They have the right to vote, to speak out on public issues, to participate in political campaigns, and to

---

104. Love v. Sessions, 568 F.2d 357 (5th Cir. 1979).

105. Allen v. Autauga Cty. Bd. of Educ., 685 F.2d 1302 (11th Cir. 1982).

106. McGill v. Board of Educ., Pekin Elem. Sch. Dist. No. 108, 602 F.2d 774 (7th Cir. 1979).

107. Simineo v. School Dist. No. 16, 594 F.2d 1353 (10th Cir. 1979).

108. Jordan v. Cagle, 474 F. Supp. 1198 (N.D. Miss. 1979).

109. Greminger v. Seaborne, 584 F.2d 275 (8th Cir. 1978).

110. Meyr v. Board of Educ., Affton Sch. Dist., 572 F.2d 1229 (8th Cir. 1978).

111. Swilley v. Alexander, 448 F. Supp. 702 (S.D. Ala. 1978).

112. Burnaman v. Bay City Indep. Sch. Dist., 445 F. Supp. 927 (S.D. Tex. 1978).

113. Foreman v. Vermilion Parish Sch. Bd., 353 So. 2d 471 (La. App. 1978).

run for office. The two sections that follow will treat two basic rights of engaging in political activity: campaigning for office and holding office.

1. *Campaigning for Office.* Statutes of the various states and local school board policies may restrict the rights of teachers in campaigning. They do not allow a teacher to engage in such activity at school or within the classroom. On the other hand, statutes and policies prohibiting teachers from engaging in political activity outside the school premises and outside school time have not been upheld.

An old case illustrates the prohibition of a teacher's campaigning in the school setting.[114] A teacher openly solicited students in class to inform their parents to vote for a specific candidate for superintendent. He was dismissed. Here, the court recognized that the crucial element was the place of the solicitation:

> [T]he attempt thus to influence support of such candidate by the pupils and through them by their parents — introduces into the school questions wholly foreign to its purposes and objects; that such conduct can have no other effect than to stir up strife among the students over a contest for a political office, and the result of this would inevitably be to disrupt the required discipline of a public school.[115]

It is a different matter when a school classroom is not used as a forum for teacher campaigning. In 1932, a school board policy that prohibited a teacher from engaging in a political campaign was overturned. In challenging the restriction, she campaigned against the election of a school trustee. In retaliation, the board refused her a teaching position for which she had been recommended. The court overturned the policy and held that, like any other citizen, a teacher has a right to support a candidate of one's choice.[116]

---

114. Goldsmith v. Board of Educ., 66 Cal. App. 157, 225 P. 783 (1924).
115. *Id.* at 789.
116. Board of Educ. v. Ayers, 234 Ky. 177, 47 S.W.2d 1046 (1932).

In 1976, a Kentucky court upheld this principle. Several teachers and administrators supported a candidate for school board who was opposed by the superintendent. Their candidate lost. Later, the superintendent recommended, and the school board authorized, transfer and demotion of the administrators and teachers for "the betterment of the schools." The court disallowed the action, which it interpreted as being punitive.[117]

Dismissals or transfers of employees based upon political activities and support of school board candidates running against present members are prohibited.[118]

2. *Holding Office.* By virtue of the fact that one is a teacher, he or she is not restricted in running for office. That right may be subject to conditions provided for in state statutes which may specify the kinds of offices that would be incompatible with teaching. Incompatibility exists where a superordinate-subordinate relationship exists. When the superordinate makes decisions that affect a teacher, one could not hold both positions. No problem exists if the teacher resigns his position.

State statutes also vary with respect to the point at which one becomes ineligible to teach while running for or holding an office. States may require a teacher to resign upon announcing candidacy for the office, upon being elected, or upon assuming office.

Court decisions over teachers' rights in office-holding may seem contradictory until one remembers that this litigation is based on a given state statute. Several states have held to the view of a California court decision that a teacher is not a public officer and

---

117. Calhoun v. Cassidy, 534 S.W.2d 806 (Ky. 1976). A teachers' union and its local managing agent prevailed against a principal. They had lobbied against him during an election and had charged him with being racist. The court noted that a citizen's right to speak out on issues is not limited to fair comment. Eaton v. Newport Bd. of Educ., 975 F.2d 292 (6th Cir. 1992). The Kentucky Supreme Court ruled as overly broad a statute prohibiting school employees from participating in political campaigns for members of boards of education. State Bd. for Elem. & Secondary Educ. v. Howard, 834 S.W.2d 657 (Ky. 1992).

118. Miller v. Board of Educ., 450 F. Supp. 106 (S.D. W. Va. 1978).

thus can also hold a position as legislator.[119] In contrast, both a trial court and the Supreme Court of Alaska held that a superintendent and two teachers could not serve also as legislators.[120] A like ruling was handed down in Oregon when it was charged that the separation of powers was violated by a teacher serving in the state's House of Representatives. The state's supreme court agreed:

> Our concern is not with what has been done but rather with what might be done, directly or indirectly, if one person is permitted to serve two different departments at the same time. The constitutional prohibition is designed to avoid the opportunities for abuse arising out of such dual service whether it exists or not.[121]

For the right of teachers to serve on local boards of education, see Chapter Three.

---

119. Leymel v. Johnson, 105 Cal. App. 694, 288 P. 858 (1930).

120. Begich v. Jefferson, 441 P.2d 27 (Alaska 1968).

121. Monaghan v. School Dist. No. 1, 211 Ore. 360, 315 P.2d 797, 805 (1957).

PART IV

LAW AND STUDENTS

Chapter Nine

ASSIGNMENT AND PLACEMENT

§ 9.0. Introduction.

A century ago, public education experienced rapid growth. Public school enrollments (kindergarten through grade 12) doubled, the school year was extended from 135 to 173 days, total expenditures per child increased, and attendance in public schools was legislated.[1] State governments began to assume a much more active role in providing education of their citizens.

In these early days, the prevalent judicial attitude regarding state authority over public education was that such authority was legislative. State legislatures, said the courts, possessed unrestricted prerogatives of control over educational matters, and judges would not interfere with the exercise of these prerogatives.[2]

---

1. EDWARDS & RICHEY, THE SCHOOL IN THE AMERICAN SOCIAL ORDER (2d ed. Boston: Houghton Mifflin Co., 1963).

2. Leeper v. State, 53 S.W. 962 (Tenn. 1899). Almost a century later judges show this same reluctance to interfere. For example, Pustell v. Lynn Pub. Schs.,

During the first three decades of the twentieth century, a number of cases regarding public school decisionmaking reached the courts of the various states. These early cases involved such specific matters as textbook selection, courses of study offered, and the selection of instructional materials. Throughout the early decisions, courts consistently upheld the right of state legislatures to do all things necessary to establish and control public school systems, with certain limitations.[3] As the United States Supreme Court stated in *Meyer v. Nebraska*, "that the state may do much, go very far, indeed, in order to improve the quality of its citizens, physically, mentally, and morally, is clear; but the individual has certain fundamental rights which must be respected."[4]

As indicated in previous sections of this book, the omission of any explicit mention of education in the United States Constitution and the absence of any specific provisions directing the federal government to exercise control over schools left the primary responsibility of providing education and schools to each state. Today, state constitutions and statutes generally charge the legislature with plenary authority to establish, control, and continually maintain a system of public education for all children of school age.

In most states, evidence of legal authority over public education is found in various statutes that: (1) create compulsory attendance for children of school age, (2) establish and define student classifications (*e.g.,* exceptional children), (3) mandate vaccination of school-age children as a precondition of their entrance to school, and (4) set a minimum length for the school year. Exercising their police power, states seek to bring about intellectual enlightenment

---

18 F.3d 50 (1st Cir. 1994), illustrates the reluctance of the federal judiciary to review a state law requirement that school officials conduct on-site visits of individuals who educate their children at home. The courts of other states have shown a similar attitude of abstention. *See, e.g.,* Rust v. Rust, 864 S.W.2d 52 (Tenn. App. 1993).

3. *See, e.g.,* Hardwick v. Board of Sch. Trustees, 54 Cal. App. 696, 205 P. 49 (1921); Smith v. State Bd., 10 P.2d 736 (Cal. 1932).

4. 262 U.S. 390, 43 S. Ct. 625, 627, 67 L. Ed. 1042 (1923). *See also* Flory v. Smith, 145 Va. 164, 134 S.E. 360 (1926).

and to promote the safety, welfare, and prosperity of their citizenry through enactment and implementation of such regulations.[5]

§ 9.1. Compulsory Attendance.

Over the years, courts of law have supported the notion that compulsory school attendance laws represent a valid exercise of state police power. That an enlightened citizenry is vital to ensuring the progress and stability of this nation is an established tenet of school law. Between 1918 and 1954, all states had statutes of compulsory school attendance.

An Illinois case, decided in 1901, demonstrates the historical underpinnings of compulsory school attendance laws in court precedent. In upholding the state's authority to compel school attendance (even where parents oppose said attendance), the court said:

> The welfare of the child and the best interests of society require that the state shall exert its sovereign authority to secure to the child the opportunity to acquire an education. Statutes making it compulsory upon the parent, guardian, or other person having the custody and control of children to send them to public or private schools for longer or shorter periods during certain years of the life of such children have not only been upheld as strictly within the constitutional power of the legislature, but have gen-

---

5. "The police power of a State today embraces regulations designed to promote the public convenience or the general prosperity as well as those to promote public safety, health, and morals, and is not confined to the suppression of what is offensive, disorderly, or unsanitary, but extends to what is for the greatest welfare of the state." THE CONSTITUTION OF THE UNITED STATES OF AMERICA: ANALYSIS AND INTERPRETATIONS 1089 (N.T. Small ed. Washington, D.C.: U.S. Government Printing Office, 1964). As a general rule, state law provides a legal process to terminate parental rights where the "best interests of the child" are at stake. *See, e.g., In re* B.D., 511 S.E.2d 229 (Ga. App. 1999); *In re* L.H., 511 S.E.2d 253 (Ga. App. 1999).

erally been regarded as necessary to carry out the express purposes of the constitution itself.[6]

Seventy-five years ago, the United States Supreme Court handed down a decision having a narrowing effect on the scope of legal authority of states to establish compulsory school attendance. A case involving the property rights and business interests of a group of private schools and the right of teachers to engage in their profession, *Pierce v. Society of Sisters,* was decided in 1925.

At issue in *Pierce* was an Oregon statute (Compulsory Education Act) requiring that every child (aged eight to sixteen years) attend public school only. Parents found in violation of the law would be guilty of a misdemeanor.

In declaring the Oregon statute unconstitutional (violating both the property rights of the private schools and liberty interests of parents, protected by the fourteenth amendment), the High Court declared: "[T]he fundamental theory of liberty upon which all governments in this Union repose excluded any general power of the state to standardize its children by forcing them to accept instruction from public teachers only."[7]

Over the years since *Pierce,* states have expanded the options available to parents (guardians) for providing for the education of their school age children. For example, currently in the Commonwealth of Virginia a parent is in compliance with that state's Code if the parent selects from the following options: having the child enrolled in a public, private, denominational, or parochial school; having their child taught by a tutor or teacher with qualifications prescribed by the State Board of Education and approved by the local school superintendent; or having home instruction for their

---

6. State v. Bailey, 61 N.E. 730, 731-32 (Ill. 1901). A Kentucky court showed evidence of that same attitude when it upheld a school board's attendance policy, which placed regulations on students wishing to attend school outside their attendance zones, so long as the policy was neither arbitrary nor capricious. Swift v. Breckinridge Cty. Bd. of Educ., 878 S.W.2d 810 (Ky. App. 1994).

7. 268 U.S. 510, 45 S. Ct. 510, 69 L. Ed. 1070 (1925).

child.[8] The home instruction option was added during the 1984 session of the Virginia General Assembly.[9]

It should be pointed out that contemporary local school officials have, as an alternative action, resorted to their state's child abuse and neglect statutes to prosecute parents who are not in compliance with compulsory attendance. And, more often than not, these parents are characterized in the complaint as being guilty of *educational neglect* rather than *child abuse*.

a. *Yoder and Exceptions to Compulsory Attendance.* A number of court cases involving compulsory school attendance laws as being in conflict with one's religious beliefs have involved the Amish religious order. In 1972, the United States Supreme Court heard the first case specifically challenging a state's compulsory attendance requirements. The case, *Wisconsin v. Yoder,*[10] involved a challenge by some Amish parents to the state's compulsory school attendance law which required that all children seven to sixteen years old attend a public or private school. According to their petition, the free exercise clause of the first amendment to the United States Constitution caused their children to be exempt from compulsory school attendance beyond the eighth grade, because high school attendance was contrary to Amish religious beliefs.

Initially, Jonas Yoder and Adin Yutzy, Old Order Amish members, were convicted for violating Wisconsin's compulsory attendance law. Yoder and Yutzy refused to send their children to any school after the children completed eighth grade. Both the trial court and a Wisconsin Circuit Court ruled against the parents. Each court considered the law a reasonable and constitutional exercise of governmental power.

---

8. VA. CODE § 22.1-254.

9. *Id. See also* VA. CODE § 22.1-254.1. For cases where parents challenged the constitutionality of a state's compulsory attendance statute, see Jeffrey v. O'Donnell, 702 F. Supp. 516 (M.D. Pa. 1988); Null v. Board of Educ., 815 F. Supp. 937 (S.D. W. Va. 1993); People v. DeJonge, 501 N.W.2d 127 (Mich. 1993); People v. Bennett, 501 N.W. 2d 106 (Mich. 1993); Conlara, Inc. v. Michigan State Bd., 501 N.W.2d 88 (Mich. 1993).

10. 406 U.S. 205, 92 S. Ct. 1526, 32 L. Ed. 2d 15 (1972).

On appeal to the Wisconsin Supreme Court, the lower court rulings were reversed. The state's highest court was convinced that the compulsory school attendance law unnecessarily infringed upon the parent's free exercise of their religion.[11]

The United States Supreme Court affirmed the Wisconsin Supreme Court. Convinced that the Amish parents' objection to the compulsory school attendance requirement was "firmly grounded" in Amish religious doctrine, that the Amish community does provide for the continued education and training of its children (after the eighth grade) through vocational-agricultural experiences, and seemingly impressed with the reputation of the Amish community as a "productive, self-supporting" society, the nation's Highest Court upheld the Wisconsin Supreme Court's decision favoring the parents' claim.[12]

Precedent was thus established in *Yoder* for possible future exemptions from compulsory school attendance laws being granted for children whose parents can establish a bona fide religious objection to such attendance. The onus in such lawsuits before today's courts is on the objecting parents to establish their reasons (whether for religious reasons or other reasons) for noncompliance with compulsory attendance statutes, with failure to do so subjecting the parents to possible prosecution by the state.[13]

Other religious groups or individuals have on occasion sought some modification of a state's compulsory attendance law. They have usually attempted to set up their own educational system, with varying degrees of success. Courts tend to look strictly at the way a nonpublic school is organized and maintained to ascertain if

---

11. State v. Yoder, 182 N.W.2d 539 (Wis. 1971).

12. *Yoder, supra* note 10, at 406 U.S. 212, 214.

13. *See, e.g.,* Matter of Franz, 378 N.Y.S.2d 317 (1976), involving home tutoring, and Matter of Baum, 382 N.Y.S. 2d 672 (1976), wherein parents couldn't support their charge of "racism" of their child's teacher as their reason for not sending their daughter to school. *See also* State v. LaBarge, 357 A.2d 121 (Vt. 1976). The Supreme Court of Oklahoma reaffirmed the concept of home schooling and the right of parents to direct the educational and religious upbringing of their children. *See* Martin v. Stephen, 937 P.2d 92 (Okla. 1997).

it has standards comparable to those of the public schools. It is not necessary that a nonpublic school meet all the standards and requirements of a public school, so long as the state is satisfied that a student is receiving a comparable education. A New York court ruled in 1951 that a school in which the conventional subjects were not taught was not comparable. The teacher lacked minimum qualifications and no attendance records were kept. The court ruled that the parents' stated religious beliefs that forbade formal education were not violated by the compulsory attendance statutes.[14]

In another case, a court held that it was insufficient for parents to withdraw their children from school because they felt that racial mixing was sinful.[15]

In a case based on state regulations rather than standards, the Ohio Supreme Court ruled that the regulations covering nonpublic schools were such as to eliminate all differences between them and public schools.[16] It overturned an indictment of twelve parents whose children attended a religious school. In another 1976 case, the North Carolina Court of Appeals decided a matter involving Indian parents who refused to send their children to school because the school did not teach Indian heritage and culture. As a result of their parents' actions, the children had been declared "neglected" and were thus made wards of the juvenile court.[17]

---

14. People v. Donner, 302 N.Y. 833, 100 N.E.2d 57 (1951). *See also* Blackwelder v. Safnauer, 866 F.2d 548 (2d Cir. 1989), involving a challenge to a state statute governing minimum standards of instruction of school aged children in nonpublic schools.

15. F. & F. v. Duval City, 273 So. 2d 15 (Fla. App. 1973).

16. State v. Whisner, 351 N.E.2d 750 (Ohio 1976). *See also* Murphy v. Arkansas, 852 F.2d 1039 (8th Cir. 1988) (parents challenged a state statute requiring standardized testing of children taught at home); New Life Baptist Church v. Town of East Meadow, 885 F.2d 940 (1st Cir. 1989) (religious group refused to comply with a state law permitting a town to determine the "educational adequacy" of *secular* education provided in their schools); Hubbard *ex rel.* Hubbard v. Buffalo Indep. Sch. Dist., 20 F. Supp. 2d 1012 (W.D. Tex. 1998).

17. *In re* McMillan, 226 S.E.2d 693 (N.C. 1976).

On appeal the parents claimed that the first amendment protected their prerogatives "as parents" to keep their children home from school for what they believed were legitimate reasons. In rejecting the parents' claim, the North Carolina court saw this case as being different from *Yoder.* First, the court did not treat instruction in Indian heritage or culture as a "religious" matter; thus, the first amendment protection of free exercise was not applicable. Secondly, unlike the parents in *Yoder,* there was no showing by the Indian parents that their children were being provided with sufficient "alternative" education opportunities.

In a Virginia case, *Grigg v. Commonwealth,* the parents of two school-age children (ages eleven and fourteen) withdrew their children from the public schools of the City of Chesapeake. In addition to their claim that the education their children received at home was "equal to or better than the services provided in public schools," the Griggs objected to their children being exposed to the language, violence, and lack of morality found in the schools.[18]

The chief attendance officer of the Chesapeake City school system filed separate petitions against Mr. and Mrs. Grigg and their two daughters in juvenile and domestic relations general district court. The petitions asked that an order be entered compelling the Griggs to enroll their children in public school or to make "other proper arrangements" for their education[19] and that the children be declared "children in need of services" (CHINS) under the juvenile code. The court ruled in favor of the school system and the Griggs appealed to circuit court.

The Circuit Court of the City of Chesapeake held for the school officials. Declaring the Grigg children to be CHINS, the court placed them on twelve months' unsupervised probation on the condition that they regularly attend a public, private, denominational or parochial school, or be taught at home by a tutor or

---

18. Grigg v. Commonwealth, 297 S.E.2d 799 (Va. 1982). *See also* Roemhild v. State, 308 S.E.2d 154 (Ga. 1983); Burrow v. State, 669 S.W.2d 441 (Ark. 1984).

19. *Grigg, supra* note 18, at 802.

teacher of qualifications prescribed by the State Board of Education and approved by the division superintendent.[20] The circuit court then ordered that the Grigg parents either select one of those options or arrange for home instruction by an approved tutor or teacher. The Griggs appealed to the Virginia Supreme Court.

On appeal the Grigg parents maintained that their two-student home school (called Ark II) was a private school. Thus, they said, they were actually within the law. To the high court, however, the Grigg children were receiving *home instruction,* not instruction in a *school;* and, since neither of the parents was qualified to be a tutor or teacher of qualifications prescribed by the State Board and approved by the local superintendent, the Griggs were in violation of the Code. Said the court, "in permitting home instruction only by a qualified tutor or teacher, the General Assembly has declared that such instruction by an unapproved person shall be impermissible."[21]

b. *State Law and Exceptions to Compulsory Attendance.* In recent years the compulsory attendance statutes of several states have been amended to allow for alternative education and for exemptions, while maintaining the state's authority to require education for its children. The Florida School Code, for example, mandates regular attendance at school of all children between the ages of seven and sixteen. What is more, the Code provides that parents or guardians are responsible for their child's attendance and are subject to prosecution if they are found in violation of the law.[22] The Code allows, however, that regular school attendance may be achieved through one of the following means: (1) public school, (2) parochial or denominational school, (3) private school,

---

20. *Id.* Each option available to parents or guardians was enumerated in VA. CODE § 22.1-254.

21. *Grigg, supra* note 18, at 802. In response to *Grigg,* the General Assembly of Virginia amended the Code to allow for home instruction by parents. *See* VA. CODE § 22.1-254.1.

22. 29 FLA. JURISPRUDENCE 162-63.

or (4) a private tutor who meets all requirements of state law and state board regulations.[23]

In Florida, a child may be granted a "certificate of exemption" from compulsory school attendance. The bona fide reasons specified by law are: (1) physical or mental disability, (2) distance a child would be compelled to walk to the nearest school or to the nearest publicly maintained school bus route, (3) lawful employment, and (4) upon recommendation of the juvenile and domestic relations court (accompanied by the agreement of the county superintendent of schools).[24]

§ 9.2. Vaccination.

In addition to the legality of compulsory attendance statutes, states may set conditions for children to enroll in schools. One of these conditions is the requirement that one be inoculated against specified contagious diseases. This requirement grows out of the state's police power in looking after the health and welfare of its citizens.

In recent years some states have taken a strong position regarding immunization of school-aged children as a prerequisite to public school attendance. Virginia, for example, in its Code states:

> **§ 22.1-271.2. (Effective July 1, 1990) Immunization requirements.** — A. No student shall be admitted by a school unless at the time of admission the student or his parent or guardian submits documentary proof of immunization to the admitting official of the school or unless the student is exempted from immunization pursuant to subsection C. If a student does not have documentary proof of immunization, the school shall notify the student or his parent or guardian (i) that it has no documentary proof of immunization for the student; (ii) that it may not admit the student without proof unless the student is exempted pursuant to subsection C; (iii) that the student

---

23. *Id.* at 162.
24. *Id.* at 163.

may be immunized and receive certification by a licensed physician or an employee of a local health department; and (iv) how to contact the local health department to learn where and when it performs these services. Neither this Commonwealth nor any school or admitting official shall be liable in damages to any person for complying with this section.

Any physician or local health department employee performing immunizations shall provide to any person who has been immunized or to his parent or guardian, upon request, documentary proof of immunizations conforming with the requirements of this section.

B. Any student whose immunizations are incomplete may be admitted conditionally if that student provides documentary proof at the time of enrollment of having received at least one dose of the required immunizations accompanied by a schedule for completion of the required doses within ninety days.

The immunization record of each student admitted conditionally shall be reviewed periodically until the required immunizations have been received.

Any student admitted conditionally and who fails to comply with his schedule for completion of the required immunizations shall be excluded from school until his immunizations are resumed.

C. No certificate of immunization shall be required for the admission to school of any student if (i) the student or his parent or guardian submits an affidavit to the admitting official stating that the administration of immunizing agents conflicts with the student's religious tenets or practices; or (ii) the school has written certification from a licensed physician or a local health department that one or more of the required immunizations may be detrimental to the student's health, indicating the specific nature and probable duration of the medical condition or circumstance that contraindicates immunization.

D. The admitting official of a school shall exclude from the school any student for whom he does not have documentary proof of immunization or notice of exemption pursuant to subsection C.

E. Every school shall record each student's immunizations on the school immunization record. The school immunization record shall be a standardized form provided by the State Department of Health, which shall be a part of the mandatory permanent student record. Such record shall be open to inspection by officials of the State Department of Health and the local health departments.

The school immunization record shall be transferred by the school whenever the school transfers any student's permanent academic or scholastic records.

Within thirty calendar days after the beginning of each school year or entrance of a student, each admitting official shall file a report with the local health department. The report shall be filed on forms prepared by the State Department of Health and shall state the number of students admitted to school with documentary proof of immunization, the number of students who have been admitted with a medical or religious exemption and the number of students who have been conditionally admitted.

F. The requirement for mumps immunization as provided in § 32.1-46 shall not apply to any child admitted for the first time to any grade level, kindergarten through grade twelve, of a school prior to August 1, 1981.

The requirement for Haemophilus Influenzae Type b immunization as provided in § 32.1-46 shall not apply to any child admitted to any grade level, kindergarten through grade twelve.

G. The Board of Health shall promulgate rules and regulations for the implementation of this section in congruence with rules and regulations of the Board of Health promulgated under § 32.1-46 and in cooperation with the Board of Education.[25]

The major objection to compulsory vaccination laws is that they may conflict with one's religious beliefs. Such objectors often cite scriptural passages as a basis for their beliefs. This problem was less acute prior to the enactment of compulsory attendance statutes, for parents simply had a choice of submitting their children to be inoculated or withholding them from school. However, by the end of World War I (when all states had compulsory attendance laws), courts tended to hold parents in violation of both the vaccination and compulsory attendance statutes.

When parents first challenged the vaccination laws, their objection was premised on the due process clause. Later, it was based on the first amendment. The Supreme Court ruled in 1923 that a San Antonio, Texas, ordinance requiring vaccination was not in violation of due process.[26] The ordinance was held not to be arbitrary but designed to protect public health.

Parents have objected to compulsory vaccination statutes for a variety of reasons. Non-vaccinated children of parents who objected on the basis that they believed in divine healing through faith were denied admission to public schools and then held in contempt of the compulsory attendance law in Georgia. The court held that health and safety take precedence over one's religious convictions.[27] An Arkansas court went one step further in 1964 when it ruled that parents who objected to vaccination statutes and who kept their children out of school were in violation of the state's attendance laws and ordered their children removed from their custody and placed with juvenile authorities until foster homes could be found for them.[28]

Some states have allowed a child to be exempt from the compulsory vaccination requirement if he presents supporting evidence

---

25. VA. CODE § 22.1-271.2.

26. Zucht v. King, 260 U.S. 174, 43 S. Ct. 24, 67 L. Ed. 194 (1923).

27. Anderson v. State, 84 Ga. App. 259, 65 S.E.2d 848 (1951).

28. Cude v. State, 237 Ark. 927, 377 S.W.2d 816 (1964).

of his religious convictions. The Supreme Court of North Carolina ruled in favor of a parent on this matter.[29] A Texas statute was upheld that provided for an exemption based on two criteria: possession of a doctor's certificate and the filing of an affidavit that the law conflicted with one's religious beliefs.[30] A Kentucky statute allowing exemptions for members of a nationally recognized and established church or religious denomination was upheld.[31]

Courts have looked very strictly at statutes providing for exemptions to vaccination. They have attempted to prevent an abuse of the intent of the legislation. That was an issue for a New York court which held against a parent because he was not a member of a bona fide religious organization.[32] The law exempted only children whose parents were members of a bona fide religious sect.

A Massachusetts court took a different stance when it declared a statute unconstitutional.[33] It held that the law providing for exemptions favored those who belonged to recognized religious bodies over those who might profess sincere religious beliefs outside a formally recognized church.

The Code of Virginia allows for several exemptions to that state's compulsory attendance statute. For example, a child who is suffering from contagious or infectious diseases or whose immunizations against communicable diseases have not been completed,[34]

---

29. State v. Miday, 263 N.C. 747, 140 S.E.2d 325 (1965).

30. Itz v. Penick, 493 S.W.2d 506 (Tex. 1973).

31. Kleid v. Board of Educ., 406 F. Supp. 902 (W.D. Ky. 1976).

32. Maier v. Beeser, 73 Misc. 2d 241, 341 N.Y.S.2d 411 (1972). *See also* Sherr v. Northport-East Northport Union Free Sch. Dist., 672 F. Supp. 81 (E.D.N.Y. 1987). For a case involving the exemption of a 5-year-old child from the state's immunization requirement based upon parents' religious objections, see Lewis v. Sobol, 710 F. Supp. 506 (N.D.N.Y. 1989).

33. Dalli v. Board of Educ., 358 Mass. 753, 267 N.E.2d 219 (1971).

34. VA. CODE § 22.1-271.2. Public schools have experienced situations where students have contracted the AIDS virus, and existing policies (*e.g.,* those covering infectious and contagious diseases) have proved ineffective in handling each case as it came up. Thus some states have placed mandates in their Codes to help remedy the situation. In the Commonwealth of Virginia, for example, the Code has a section speaking directly to students with AIDS. *See* VA. CODE § 22.1-

or a child who, together with his parents, by reason of bona fide religious training or belief is conscientiously opposed to attendance at school,[35] is each excused from compliance with the compulsory attendance mandate.

§ 9.3. Admission to Public School.

Children do not possess an absolute right to attend a public school. They are *entitled* to attend if they possess the qualifications specified in state law (*e.g.*, age, residence, vaccination for certain communicable diseases). Typically, matters of deciding admissibility of children to public school are left to local school boards.

Admission to a public school is one area of board authority over the pupil that has been clearly defined in judicial precedent. According to Bolmeier:

> Generally a child has a right, or at least the privilege, to attend a public school. The right of a child to be admitted to the public school, however, is not absolute. It is subject to reasonable restrictions and regulations. If the statutes do not state specifically what the restrictions and regulations are which limit admission, the board is clothed with

271.3, where the law mandates that the State Board of Education develop model guidelines for school attendance for children so infected and, in addition, requires local school systems to develop guidelines consistent with the State Board's model. For student AIDS cases, see Board of Educ. v. Cooperman, 523 A.2d 655 (N.J. 1987); Ray v. School Dist. of De Soto Cty., 666 F. Supp. 1524 (M.D. Fla. 1987); Thomas v. Atascadero Unified Sch. Dist., 662 F. Supp. 376 (C.D. Cal. 1986); Martinez v. School Bd., 711 F. Supp. 1066 (M.D. Fla. 1989).

35. VA. CODE § 22.1-254 et seq. In 1992, parents in New York were unsuccessful in seeking a religious exemption from the requirement that their child be vaccinated. The court found the policy to be rational. Lynch v. Clarkstown Cent. Sch. Dist., 590 N.Y.S.2d 687 (N.Y. Sup. Ct. 1992). In Johnson v. Prince William Cty., 404 S.E.2d 209 (Va. 1981), the Supreme Court of Virginia held that parents seeking a religious exemption from compulsory attendance must show that their beliefs constitute a bona fide religion and not merely sociological, philosophical, political, or personal beliefs. *Id.* at 213.

the discretionary authority to so determine within reasonable bounds.[36]

That local boards of education possess considerable *discretionary* authority to determine the admissibility of pupils to local public schools has been consistently upheld by courts of law.

Watson v. Cambridge[37] was an early case establishing the discretionary authority of local boards of education to determine the admissibility of children to public schools. In *Watson* it was held that a board of education has a right to deny admission to a child when the child suffers certain physical defects.

In 1913, a Massachusetts court, in *Barnard v. Shelbourne*, reinforced the prerogative of a local board to refuse admission to a student and expanded the board's discretionary authority to include retention and promotion. The court said, in part:

> The care and management of schools which is vested in the school committee includes the establishment and maintenance of standards for the promotion of pupils from one grade to another for their continuance as members of any particular class. So long as the school committees act in good faith their conduct in formulating and applying standards and making decisions touching this matter is not subject to review by any other tribunal.[38]

The legal authority of a school board to assign a pupil to a particular class and a board's legal prerogative to maintain standards of student continuance were clearly established in *Barnard*.

Courts of law were most reluctant to interfere with decision-making when deciding the early cases brought by parents who challenged board admission prerogatives. Beginning in the mid-1950s, however, a move to secure equal educational opportunities

---

36. BOLMEIER, THE SCHOOL IN THE LEGAL STRUCTURE 225 (2d ed. Cincinnati, Ohio: The W.H. Anderson Co.. 1973). There have been successful lawsuits taken on behalf of the rights of homeless children to gain free access to public school systems. *See, e.g.,* Lampkin v. District of Columbia, 27 F.3d 605 (D.C. Cir. 1994).

37. 32 N.E. 864 (Mass. 1893).

38. 102 N.E. 1095, 1096 (Mass. 1913).

for "all children" had its beginning in *Brown v. Board of Education*.[39] Decided by the United States Supreme Court, *Brown* established the principle of extending equal educational opportunities to all children of school age as a matter of constitutional entitlement. Education, said the Court, "where the state has undertaken to provide it, is a right which must be made available to all on equal terms."[40] Courts, in the years following *Brown,* consistently viewed public education as a matter of entitlement.

Two different cases out of Texas came to the United States Supreme Court in 1982 and focused attention upon the elements of residence and domicile in establishing the rights of children to attend public schools. One case, *Plyler v. Doe,*[41] involved issues of equal protection and illegal alien children while the other case, *Martinez v. Bynum,*[42] concerned school district residence as a prerequisite for attending a public school in Texas.

At issue in *Plyler* was a Texas statute that withheld from local school districts state funds for the education of any "undocumented alien children." That same statute authorized the exclusion of such children (i.e., districts were authorized to deny them enrollment in school) from an educational opportunity.

In rendering a decision in *Plyler,* the Supreme Court majority opined, for the first time, that illegal alien children are "persons" under the law and are therefore entitled to equal protection under the fourteenth amendment. Thus, held the Court, the Texas statute could not be enforced. In effect, said the Court, the Texas law imposed a lifetime hardship on a class of children not accountable

---

39. 347 U.S. 483, 74 S. Ct. 686, 98 L. Ed. 873 (1954).

40. *Id.* at 691.

41. 458 U.S. 1131, 102 S. Ct. 2382, 72 L. Ed. 2d 786 (1982).

42. 461 U.S. 321, 103 S. Ct. 1838, 75 L. Ed. 2d 879 (1982). The plight of homeless families has placed many children in a legally precarious position regarding matters of residency and domicile, causing new and perplexing legal issues to emerge. For an excellent commentary on this subject, see Patricia F. First & G. Robb Cooper, *Access to Education by Homeless Children,* 53 EDUC. LAW REP. 757 (July 20, 1989). *See also* Delgado v. Freeport, 499 N.Y.S.2d 606 (Sup. Ct. 1986).

for their disabling classification. To phrase the question differently, why cause children to suffer the deprivation of an educational opportunity solely because of their parents' violation of the law?

The *Martinez* case involved a challenge to another Texas statute. The statute at issue said, in part, that a child between the ages of five years and twenty-one years must be permitted to attend a public school in the district wherein he/she resides, or in which his/her parent or guardian, or other person having lawful control of him/her, resides at the time of application for admission to school. Where such residence was established, said the law, education must be provided tuition-free. Where a child lived apart from the parent or other lawful guardian, however, a local school board must see proof that the sole reason for the child being in the district was not to receive a "tuition free" education. This statute applied to children living apart from parents or guardians, to children moving from one Texas school district to another, to children moving into Texas from other states, and to children moving into Texas from other countries.

Roberto Martinez was born in Texas (1961), but his parents had moved to Mexico where they lived until 1977. In 1977, Roberto moved to Texas to live with his sister so that he could attend public school in Texas. Roberto's sister did not intend to legally adopt him. Roberto was denied a tuition-free education under the above described Texas law.

Taking Roberto's case to federal district court, plaintiffs claimed that the Texas statute was violative of both the due process and equal protection clauses of the fourteenth amendment. Hearing the case on the merits, the court ruled that Texas possessed a legitimate interest in protecting and preserving the quality of that state's school system for bona fide residents. Thus, the statute was constitutional. The Fifth Circuit affirmed this decision. Subsequently, the United States Supreme Court granted certiorari.

The Supreme Court upheld the Fifth Circuit, saying that a legitimate state interest is served by the Texas statute. A state, said the high court, has a right to set bona fide residency requirements

306

as a prerequisite to a child benefiting from the state's public education system, tuition free.

In the early 1970s, admission of children with handicaps to public schools and subsequent placement of these children in appropriate educational programs became issues taken by parents to federal and state courts.[43] This was also the era of massive racial integration of public schools and the ongoing battle to remove *race* as a condition of admission to or rejection from attendance in a public school.

The impact of the avalanche of court decisions from the past twenty-five years was to "open the doors" of public schools to all children, no matter what their race, socio-economic status, marital status or form of handicap. That no child of school age shall be arbitrarily or capriciously denied admission to a public school became the law of the land. Some cases in point illustrate this principle in action.

In *Cuyahoga County Association for Retarded Children and Adults v. Essex,* a federal district court held that I.Q. score alone cannot be the determiner of whether or not a child is incapable of profiting from education. Certainly, a state may consider I.Q. scores when classifying students; however, to deny children admission to school solely on the basis of I.Q. is a violation of equal protection.[44]

A 1975 Oklahoma case offers another example of limitations being placed by federal district courts on local school board admissions prerogatives. According to the court, a school board cannot prevent black students moving into the school district from attending school because the board believes that the school's educational level would decrease.[45]

---

43. *See, e.g.,* Pennsylvania Ass'n for Retarded Children v. Commonwealth, 334 F. Supp. 1257 (E.D. Pa. 1971). Final consent agreement at 343 F. Supp. 279 (E.D. Pa. 1972).

44. 411 F. Supp. 46 (N.D. Ohio 1976).

45. Board of Educ. of Indep. Sch. Dist. No. 53 v. Board of Educ. of Indep. Sch. Dist. No. 52, 413 F. Supp. 342 (W.D. Okla. 1975).

§ 9.4. Bases of Pupil Assignment to Classes and Schools.

The discretionary authority of local boards of education has been upheld relative to the assignment of pupils to special schools and to particular classrooms within those schools. For example, as early as 1936, an Iowa court upheld the authority of a school board, over parental objections, to assign a pupil with infantile paralysis, who suffered continually from pain, to a special school. In the court's opinion said assignment was a reasonable determination and did not exceed board authority.[46]

Student assessment and placement within public schools have received much attention and criticism. Ross, DeYoung, and Cohen warned public school systems that they must cease to use evaluation and placement procedures that discriminate against children on racial or socio-economic bases.[47]

The principle that pupil assignments to particular schools and classes be made on reasonable and substantial bases was of vital concern in a 1954 New York case. In *Isquith v. Levitt*[48] a New York State court ruled that the board of education could legally place children in any grade within a school based upon the "mental attainment of the child" and upon "training, knowledge, and ability."[49]

The landmark decision in the area of classification and assignment of public school pupils, however, came in 1967. In *Hobson v. Hansen*,[50] the method of testing utilized at that time by Washing-

---

46. State v. Christ, 270 N.W. 376, 379 (Iowa 1936).

47. Sterling L. Ross, Jr., Henry G. DeYoung, and Julius S. Cohen, *Confrontation: Special Education and the Law,* EXCEPTIONAL CHILDREN 38 (September, 1971). See, in particular, their discussions of the relationships between standardized test results, socio-economic background, and student grouping.

48. 137 N.Y.S.2d 493 (N.Y. 1954).

49. *Id.* at 496, 498.

50. 269 F. Supp. 401 (D.D.C. 1967). The Washington, D.C. School System placed students into either the *Honors, General,* or *Special* (educable mentally retarded) tracks based upon results from the following battery of standardized tests: *Sequential Tests of Educational Progress* (STEP) and the *School and College Ability Test* (SCAT) administered in the fourth grade, the *Stanford*

ton, D.C., public schools to place students in "ability groups" was questioned in federal district court.

Upon completion of hearing arguments in *Hobson,* District Judge J. Skelley Wright held that the tests and methods of student placement utilized by the Washington, D.C., schools were unconstitutional since they discriminated against certain children. Judge Wright was convinced that a student's chance of being enrolled in a track was directly related to his socio-economic background; and as Reutter and Hamilton have pointed out, the court found the Washington, D.C., Public School System's "tracking" method of ability-grouping not rationally explainable.[51] Thus, the system denied students equal access to educational opportunity. (On later appeal, the United States Court of Appeals for the District of Columbia upheld, among other things, the lower district court's order to abolish the "ability grouping" plan in the District of Columbia public schools).[52]

The United States Court of Appeals for the District of Columbia, offering the subsequent ruling in *Smuck v. Hobson,* did not remove or negate the District of Columbia school board's legal prerogative to make decisions concerning educational programming. In presenting a rationale for its decision the court said: "We conclude that this directive does not limit the discretion of the school board with full recognition of the need to permit the school board latitude in fashioning and effectuating the remedies for the ills of the District school system."[53]

Achievement Test (SAT) and *Otis Quick-Scoring Mental Ability Test* administered in the sixth grade.

51. *See* REUTTER, JR. & HAMILTON, THE LAW OF PUBLIC EDUCATION 142 (2d ed. Mineola, New York: The Foundation Press, Inc., 1976).

52. *See* Smuck v. Hobson, 408 F.2d 175 (D.C. Cir. 1969). A school district in Arkansas was challenged for its ability grouping of children which resulted in racial segregation. The district court ruled that the grouping was the present result of past discrimination and violated the rights of black children consigned to low ability groups. Simmons on Behalf of Simmons v. Hooks, 843 F. Supp. 1296 (E.D. Ark. 1994).

53. *Id.* at 189.

In a 1984 case, *Bester v. Tuscaloosa City Board of Education,*[54] the Eleventh Circuit was faced with a local board policy (enacted in 1981) that set minimum reading standards for promotion of students. The policy was uniformly applied to every school within the Tuscaloosa City School System.

Once operated as a racially segregated school system and subject to federal desegregation litigation from 1970-1981, the school system had only recently become integrated when the new promotion policy was put into place. As a part of a consent decree regarding the integration of schools, three of the five previously all-black elementary schools remained all-black. Prior to this, there had not been a uniform student promotion policy — each school had its own policy based upon its own standards.

The new minimum standards for promotion included an examination of a student's reading level, as measured by a student's progress in his/her reading program. All students were graded at the level at which they could read. All parents were informed of their child's reading level (via the report card), and letters were sent to parents of children reading below grade level. The latter parents were informed of the "possible retention" of their child because of a substandard reading level (minimum levels were set by the board).

The effect of the new policy on retention of black children enrolled in grades one through five was disproportionate to that of white students in the same grades. While 23.6% of black children were retained, only 5.8% of white were retained.

Parents of black children enrolled in the five all-black schools prior to the integration consent decree, all of whom received notice of their child's substandard reading level, took suit in federal district court.

To the court, the parents had no property interest in an expectation that their children would be promoted when their reading levels were substandard.

---

54. 722 F.2d 1514 (11th Cir. 1984).

The court ruled that ability grouping within the context of recently integrated public schools is permissible unless it results in resegregation of classes or schools. Here there was no violation, since the Tuscaloosa City Schools had not been resegregated because of this policy.[55]

a. *Race as a Factor.* Public school segregation has undergone a number of legal phases: application of the *Plessy* decision of 1896; modification of *Plessy* in cases involving higher education from 1938-1950; two decades of the *Brown* era, 1954-1974; and the retrenchment era, 1974 to the present.

Justification for segregation in schools was initially found in economic, political, and social policy, not to gainsay court decisions. It received great impetus from the *Plessy* decision.[56] There, the Supreme Court ruled that a Louisiana law requiring that races be segregated in public transportation facilities was reasonable, within the meaning of the fourteenth amendment. The Court held that such laws did not necessarily impute a feeling of inferiority to the black man. "If this be so," the Court observed, "it is not by reason of anything found in the act, but solely because the colored race chooses to put that construction upon it."[57] Only Justice Harlan dissented, holding that "[o]ur Constitution is color-blind, and neither knows nor tolerates classes among citizens. In respect of civil rights, all citizens are equal before the law."[58]

The origin of the phrase "separate but equal" can be found in the *Plessy* decision. The Justices cited many instances wherein the races were kept separate, schools being one such institution. Through its language, the Court looked with favor on this practice.

---

55. For another excellent case involving the retention in grade of students because of their failure to complete the requisite reading level, see Sandlin v. Johnson, 643 F.2d 1027 (4th Cir. 1981). For an excellent case involving the challenge of handicapped students to a minimum competency test as a prerequisite for receipt of their high school diploma, see Brookhart v. Illinois State Bd. of Educ., 697 F.2d 179 (7th Cir. 1983).

56. Plessy v. Ferguson, 163 U.S. 537, 16 S. Ct. 1138, 41 L. Ed. 256 (1896).

57. *Id.* at 551.

58. *Id.* at 559.

311

At any rate, the Justices indicated that they would not upset laws and long-established customs governing segregation. The Court's stance became the accepted justification for segregation of almost all public school districts in the South. Further, for almost five decades after *Plessy,* there were very few challenges in court to segregated schools.

It was higher education that first began to desegregate, and this was achieved by court order. A series of four key decisions, beginning in 1938, set the tone for the *Brown* decision that was to follow sixteen years later.[59] *Brown* was a joinder of four cases from Kansas, South Carolina, Virginia, and Delaware.[60] Each case had similar factual situations in that students had been assigned to racially segregated schools either through state constitutional mandate or legislative action. In its unanimous opinion, the Court concluded that "in the field of public education the doctrine of 'separate but equal' has no place. Separate educational facilities are inherently unequal."[61] That one decision overturned constitutional provisions or state laws in twenty-one of the then forty-eight states.[62] The same day, the Court overturned segregation in schools in the District of Columbia.[63]

---

59. *See* Missouri *ex rel.* Gaines v. Canada, 305 U.S. 337, 59 S. Ct. 65, 83 L. Ed. 233 (1938); Sipuel v. Board of Regents, 332 U.S. 631, 68 S. Ct. 299, 92 L. Ed. 247 (1948); McLaurin v. Oklahoma State Regents, 339 U.S. 637, 70 S. Ct. 139, 94 L. Ed. 1149 (1950); Sweatt v. Painter, 339 U.S. 629, 70 S. Ct. 848, 94 L. Ed. 1115 (1950). In each of these decisions, the Supreme Court ruled in favor of the black plaintiffs.

60. The following 17 states required segregation by state constitutional or statutory law prior to 1954: Alabama, Arkansas, Delaware, Florida, Georgia, Kentucky, Louisiana, Maryland, Mississippi, Missouri, North Carolina, Oklahoma, South Carolina, Tennessee, Texas, Virginia, and West Virginia. Segregation was allowed under permissive legislation in Arizona, Kansas, New Mexico, and Wyoming.

61. Brown v. Board of Educ., 347 U.S. 483, 74 S. Ct. 686, 98 L. Ed. 873 (1954).

62. *Id.*

63. Bolling v. Sharpe, 347 U.S. 497, 74 S. Ct. 693, 98 L. Ed. 884 (1954).

When the Court handed down the *Brown* decision, it asked for reargument on the question of how best to implement it. What followed those hearings was the second *Brown* decision, handed down in 1955.[64] In recognizing the complexity of dismantling dual school systems, the Court cited the following considerations: problems related to school plants, transportation systems, and personnel; revision of school districts and attendance areas; and revision of local laws and regulations. The Court then charged local school officials as being the best instruments for implementing the desegregation decrees "with all deliberate speed." Should a school district be charged with noncompliance, a person could seek relief in federal district courts.

What has followed since the two *Brown* decisions are decades of litigation over a variety of desegregation issues. That litigation and the courts' opinions have brought forth various kinds of criteria for desegregation, the major criteria being treated below. Since hundreds of desegregation cases have been handed down since 1954, only decisions by the Supreme Court of the United States will be considered initially, followed by some lower court decisions.

In its first decision following *Brown,* the Supreme Court extended its holding to make essentially private schools subject to the equal protection clause.[65] The Justices held that Girard College, an elementary and secondary school for "poor white male orphans," according to the will establishing the school, was subject to compliance under the state action doctrine because its board of trustees acted as agents of the city of Philadelphia.

On a broader scale, the Court ruled in 1958 that violence or the threat of violence was insufficient cause for delaying desegregation.[66] The case involved desegregation of the Little Rock, Arkansas, schools. The desegregation process was achieved only with

---

64. Brown v. Board of Educ., 349 U.S. 294, 75 S. Ct. 753, 99 L. Ed. 1083 (1955).

65. Pennsylvania v. Board of Dirs., 353 U.S. 230, 77 S. Ct. 806, 1 L. Ed. 2d 792, *reh'g denied,* 353 U.S. 989 (1957).

66. Cooper v. Aaron, 358 U.S. 1, 78 S. Ct. 1401, 3 L. Ed. 2d 5 (1958).

313

the assistance of and protection by the National Guard stationed at the school for one year.

In ruling that evasive plans for delaying desegregation would not be upheld, the unanimous Court saw that the legislature and the governor had been the major elements in thwarting the desegregative process.

Desegregation proceeded cautiously and slowly for a decade after *Brown,* during which time the federal courts acted with restraint and patience while, at the same time, consistently ruling that school districts must proceed with dismantling dual school systems. The Court seemed to be less concerned with the speed of desegregation than with its actually being done. It gave some indication of its patience wearing thin, however, in 1964, in a case from Virginia.[67] There, the state had shut down its public schools in Prince Edward County and set up a system of private schools for both races. At first, those schools were supported entirely by private donations; later the state subsidized them and granted tax concessions for persons who made financial contributions to the schools.

Black parents rejected the plan and sought relief in the courts. In rejecting the state's action, the Court reasoned that "[w]hatever nonracial grounds might support a State's allowing a county to abandon public schools, the object must be a constitutional one, and grounds of race and opposition to desegregation do not qualify as constitutional."[68] The Court observed further that the "all deliberate speed" criterion of *Brown II* had not been followed. One year later, the Court ruled that a grade-a-year plan could not be sustained in that it would require too long to desegregate the schools.[69]

The mid-1960s was a transitional period in the desegregation movement. There were increased federal funds available to the

---

67. Griffin v. County Sch. Bd., 377 U.S. 218, 84 S. Ct. 1226, 12 L. Ed. 2d 256 (1964).

68. *Id.* at 377 U.S. 231.

69. Rogers v. Paul, 382 U.S. 198, 86 S. Ct. 358, 15 L. Ed. 2d 265 (1965).

schools, and with those funds came guidelines requiring desegregation. With the passage of the Civil Rights Act of 1964, the federal government began to take a harder line on desegregating the schools. That stance was also reflected in the judiciary. While these changes were taking place, school districts began to use various plans and ploys to comply with federal rulings and orders but desegregate at a pace less rapidly than some people wanted. One such plan was "freedom of choice," wherein a student would actually decide which school he wished to attend. In three separate opinions, the Supreme Court in 1968 ruled that freedom of choice is constitutional, provided it works.[70] Thus, the Court began to look not at the legality of a plan in the abstract but to the effect that the plan had in accomplishing the intended purpose of creating a unitary school system. In each of the three cases, that purpose had not been met. In *Green v. County School Board of New Kent County,* the lead case, the Court noted that the plan, in operation for three years, had resulted in no white children being assigned to the all-black school and only fifteen percent of the black children being assigned to the former all-white school.

Busing became a legal issue in the early 1970s when the Supreme Court entertained the question of its being required to achieve a racial balance. Several lower court opinions had produced conflicting and inconclusive legal standards prior to 1971. In the *Swann v. Charlotte-Mecklenburg Board of Education* decision, the Court ruled that busing is a legitimate tool for desegregating schools and courts are within their power in requiring it.[71] The Court observed that state-imposed segregation must be eliminated "root and branch." However, the Justices acknowledged the complexity of desegregating schools and made three concessions: (1) Not every school in every community must reflect the racial

---

70. Green v. County Sch. Bd., 391 U.S. 430, 88 S. Ct. 1689, 20 L. Ed. 2d 716 (1968); Raney v. Board of Educ., 391 U.S. 443, 88 S. Ct. 1697, 20 L. Ed. 2d 727 (1968); Monroe v. Board of Comm'rs, 391 U.S. 450, 88 S. Ct. 1700, 20 L. Ed. 2d 733 (1968).

71. 402 U.S. 1, 91 S. Ct. 1267, 28 L. Ed. 2d 554, *reh'g denied,* 403 U.S. 912 (1971).

composition of the entire district. (2) A small number of one-race or virtually one-race schools within a district does not necessarily imply a dual school system. (3) There are no rigid, fixed guidelines as to how far a court can go in ordering desegregation. The Court recognized that school officials are not required to make year-by-year adjustments in racial composition once a district has been desegregated. Within the context of those guidelines, the Court ordered the school district to bus students, for the state had been guilty of *de jure* segregation.

In *Swann* the Court implied that the difference between *de facto* and *de jure* segregation is minimal. Had it ruled specifically that there was no difference, then *Brown I* would have been applicable to all states where *de facto* segregation existed. The Court did not go that far, however, as was evident in the first real school desegregation case outside the South.[72] The case arose in Denver, Colorado, which had no law requiring segregation. The school board there adhered to a neighborhood school plan, although there was some evidence of gerrymandered attendance zones which had resulted in one section of the city being essentially all-white. The Court did not hand down a substantive ruling on the constitutionality of *de facto* segregation; rather it remanded the case and asked the local school board to establish that it was not actually responsible for the racial imbalance. Since the board was unable to do this, the district court ordered further desegregation.

The Court dealt more directly with *de facto–de jure* segregation in 1974 in a case in Detroit.[73] In deciding the case, the Justices used as a criterion the intent of a condition that establishes segregation rather than the actual existence of it. At issue was the legality of a court-imposed merger of the city schools of Detroit with fifty-three suburban school districts. The Supreme Court overturned the lower court's order and held that the suburban districts

---

72. Keyes v. School Dist. No. 1, 413 U.S. 189, 93 S. Ct. 2686, 37 L. Ed. 2d 548 (1971).

73. Milliken v. Bradley, 418 U.S. 717, 94 S. Ct. 3112, 41 L. Ed. 2d 1069 (1974).

were not responsible for the segregative condition existing in the city. Further, although there was evidence of *de jure* segregation in Detroit, there was no evidence of it in the surrounding school districts. The Justices then ruled that "Before the boundaries of separate and autonomous school districts may be set aside by consolidating the separate units for remedial purposes or by imposing a cross-district remedy, it must first be shown that there has been a constitutional violation within one district that produces a significant segregative effect in another district." That is, "it must be shown that racially discriminatory acts of the state or its local school districts have been a substantial cause of inter-district segregation. Thus, an inter-district remedy might be in order where the racially discriminatory acts of one or more school districts caused racial segregation in an adjacent district, or where district lines have been deliberately drawn on the basis of race." Consequently, "without an inter-district violation and inter-district effect, there is no constitutional wrong calling for an inter-district remedy."[74]

In a later ruling involving the Detroit schools, the Court held that federal courts can order compensatory programs for children who have been victims of *de jure* segregation.[75] Further, the agency responsible for the segregation can be ordered to bear the costs of the program.

The distinction that exists between *de jure* and *de facto* segregation is no longer as clear as it once was. Thus, to carry their initial burden, plaintiffs in desegregation cases might gather the necessary data and prove that school officials *intended* to create segregated schools. Where such intent is established at the prima facie level and the matter goes forward in court, the burden will shift to the defendant school board to show that its actions were not the product of an intent to create segregation in its schools.[76]

---

74. *Id.* at 418 U.S. 744-45.

75. Milliken v. Bradley, 433 U.S. 267, 97 S. Ct. 2749, 53 L. Ed. 2d 745 (1977).

76. J.J. Harris, III, et al., *Desegregation Litigation in the Aftermath of Brown: Overcoming the Inertia of the Status Quo,* EDUCATORS AND THE LAW (Elmont,

To the Sixth Circuit, showing segregative *intent* is constitutionally required in matters of de facto school segregation. If such *intent* is not established, said the court, a public school board otherwise innocent could not be held liable for nor be compelled to eliminate de facto school segregation that might have been caused by some other government agency.[77]

In 1974, the Supreme Court also held that special programs could be offered to Chinese students whose native language was not English.[78]

In relying on its earlier *Swann* decision, the Supreme Court held that the Pasadena, California, schools did not have to adjust their black-white pupil ratio which had become more disparate after an initial program balancing the schools.[79] There was no evidence that school officials were in any way responsible for the resegregation which had resulted in five of thirty-two schools having a black population of over fifty percent, a condition at variance with the lower court's order.

N.Y.: The Institute for School Law and Finance, 1983). *See, e.g.,* Price v. Denison Indep. Sch. Dist., 694 F.2d 334 (5th Cir. 1982).

77. Bell v. Board of Educ., Akron Pub. Schs., 683 F.2d 963 (6th Cir. 1983). For an excellent case in point, where the burden of showing intent was not placed on plaintiffs, see Dowell v. Board of Educ., 795 F.2d 1516 (10th Cir. 1986). The possibility of a local school system gaining the prerogative to either modify or gain release from an existing court-ordered desegregation plan was reaffirmed by the United States Supreme Court in Oklahoma Pub. Schs. v. Dowell, 111 S. Ct. 630 (1991). In sending the matter back to federal district court, Chief Justice Rehnquist (for a 5-3 majority), underscored the importance of determining that a local school board has, over a reasonable period of time, made a good-faith effort to eliminate the vestiges of past discrimination to the extent practicable. *See* Missouri v. Jenkins, 115 S. Ct. 2038 (1995); Pennsylvania Human Relations Comm'n v. School Dist. of Philadelphia, 658 A.2d 470 (Pa. Commw. 1995); Palmer v. Board of Educ., 46 F.3d 682 (7th Cir. 1995). *See also* United States v. Yonkers Bd. of Educ., 7 F. Supp. 2d 396 (S.D.N.Y. 1998); Manning v. School Bd., 28 F. Supp. 2d 1353 (M.D. Fla. 1998).

78. Lau v. Nichols, 414 U.S. 563, 94 S. Ct. 786, 39 L. Ed. 2d 1 (1974).

79. Pasadena City Bd. of Educ. v. Spangler, 427 U.S. 424, 96 S. Ct. 2697, 49 L. Ed. 2d 599 (1976).

The element of purposeful or intentional discrimination played an important role in a decision from a federal district court in Virginia. In July, 1984, District Judge MacKenzie (who had presided over the original desegregation case involving the Norfolk Public Schools and who in 1975 declared that school system unitary) approved a new school board desegregation plan that ended mandatory busing (mandatory busing had been in effect since 1970). Even though the new plan would leave ten of thirty-five neighborhood schools with an enrollment that was ninety percent black, Judge MacKenzie declared that the plan was a reasonable one fashioned without discriminatory purpose or intent. In this case, he said, the burden was on the plaintiffs (challenging the new school board plan) to show the presence of the intent factor, and they failed to carry that burden. The case, *Riddick v. School Board*,[80] was affirmed by the Fourth Circuit in 1986, and the Supreme Court denied certiorari.

Riddick is an example of a growing attitude in the federal courts to reevaluate the appropriateness of busing as the remedy of choice. Today's judges focus instead upon the progress made in a specific school system since that system was declared unitary. In doing so the judicial analysis focuses upon the past history of segregation in that school system and asks: Did the school system carry out its affirmative duty, under court supervision, to work toward the removal of all vestiges of segregation in the system?

In a 1976 Virginia decision, the United States Supreme Court ruled that a commercially operated, nonsectarian private school

---

80. 627 F. Supp. 814 (E.D. Va. 1984), *aff'd*, 784 F.2d 521 (4th Cir. 1986). For a comparison case, see Oklahoma Pub. Schs. v. Dowell, *supra* note 77. *See also* Flax v. Potts, 864 F.2d 1157 (5th Cir. 1989), where the court of appeals agreed with the district court below that returning greater local control would assist in preserving the overall racial composition of a school district. The discontinuance of busing was an important part of that process. Two cases reveal a trend of the 1990s that courts will not hold jurisdiction indefinitely over school systems that have been declared to be unitary. Reed v. Rhodes, 1 F. Supp. 2d 705 (N.D. Ohio 1998); United States v. Unified Sch. Dist. No. 500, 974 F. Supp. 1367 (D. Kan. 1997).

319

discriminated under 42 U.S.C. § 1981 when it refused to admit black students.[81] The Court reasoned that a contractual agreement was involved wherein the school offered instructional services in exchange for tuition. The state's interest in and control over these schools stem from its having to exact assurance that constitutional and statutory regulations are followed.

The Supreme Court ruled that the Dayton, Ohio, schools did not have to reflect, within fifteen percent, the city's black-white population.[82] In affirming its position in the Detroit case, the Court held that the existence of segregation is not so critical as the source or intent of it. Where no intentional action of the board to segregate exists, there is no compelling reason to order that the board desegregate.

In 1982, the U.S. Supreme Court's decision in *Washington v. Seattle School District No. 1*[83] seemed to lessen the burden of plaintiffs to show the presence of *intent* in equal protection violations through a demonstration of what the Court said were "blatant acts" and "subtle actions" by school officials. In declaring a state-wide initiative (known as Initiative 350) unconstitutional (Initiative 350 was drafted in response to a desegregation plan enacted by the Seattle School Board making extensive use of busing and mandatory reassignment of students and intended to prohibit local school boards from reassigning any student to attend a school other

---

81. Runyon v. McCrary, 427 U.S. 160, 96 S. Ct. 2586, 49 L. Ed. 2d 415 (1976). Section 1981 of Title 42 of the U.S. Code provides: "All persons within the jurisdiction of the United States shall have the same right in every State and Territory to make and enforce contracts, to sue, be parties, give evidence, and to the full and equal benefit of all laws and proceedings for the security of persons and property as is enjoyed by white citizens, and shall be subject to like punishment, pains, penalties, taxes, licenses, and exactions of every kind, and to no other." During its 1988-89 term, the U.S. Supreme Court declined to overrule its earlier decision regarding suits by private persons for racial discrimination under section 1981, but seemed to limit its use to employment cases. *See* Patterson v. McLean, 109 S. Ct. 2363 (1989).

82. Dayton Bd. of Educ. v. Brinkman, 433 U.S. 406, 97 S. Ct. 2766, 53 L. Ed. 2d 851 (1977).

83. 458 U.S. 457, 102 S. Ct. 3187, 73 L. Ed. 2d 896 (1982).

320

than one geographically nearest his/her home), the Court focused upon what it saw as a reallocation of decisionmaking authority to redress a racial problem from local school boards to the state legislature and said, "the Equal Protection Clause not only protects against blatant attempts to deny racial minorities full participation in the political life of a community, but also prevents subtle actions which place special burdens on the ability of minority groups to achieve beneficial legislation."[84]

Thus, *subtle actions* of any type which result in the placement of *special burdens* on racial minorities might now exist as another standard to apply in cases where courts are looking for a type of *constructive intent* to segregate or to maintain a segregated situation.[85]

In a much-publicized ruling concluding the Court's work in its 1977-1978 term, the Justices ruled for the first time on reverse discrimination.[86] The case involved a suit by a white student who was rejected by the medical school at the University of California at Davis. The applicant was bypassed under a program in which 16 of 100 first-year slots were designated for minority students, a number of them less qualified than plaintiff Bakke, a Caucasian, who did not qualify. The Court divided five to four on two key rulings. In one, the Justices ruled that race was the key reason by which Bakke had been rejected; thus the admissions program operated on unconstitutional grounds. Bakke was ordered admitted to the medical school. In the other ruling, the Court approved the concept of affirmative action, in which a variety of criteria in-

---

84. *Id.*

85. *Id. See also* Mills v. Polk Cty. Bd. of Pub. Instr., 993 F.2d 1485 (11th Cir. 1993). The court ordered the school district to desegregate racially identifiable schools. As late as 1994, a federal district court in Illinois held that a school district had violated equal protection by separating public school students on the basis of race. People Who Care v. Rockford Bd. of Educ., 851 F. Supp. 909 (N.D. Ill. 1994). For two cases where courts have dealt with race-conscious student admission programs, see Vaughns v. Board of Educ., 980 F. Supp. 834 (D. Md. 1997); Wessman v. Gittens, 160 F.3d 790 (1st Cir. 1998).

86. Regents of Univ. of Cal. v. Bakke, 438 U.S. 265, 98 S. Ct. 2733, 57 L. Ed. 2d 750 (1978).

volving both objective and subjective data, including race, can be employed in admissions. The Court did not approve of rigid quotas based on race. It remains to be seen what effect this decision will have on public school desegregation, on faculty employment, and on admissions in higher education.

Regarding faculty desegregation, the Sixth Circuit held that students do not have a constitutional right to attend a school where the teaching staff reflects a specific racial composition, and that flexible affirmative action programs, rather than hiring quotas, are appropriate to remedy disadvantages suffered by students as a result of past racial discrimination in faculty hiring.[87]

The above cases catalog briefly a chronology of desegregation activity by the nation's Highest Court. Initially, the Court was unequivocally resolute in affirming a plaintiff's complaint of discrimination in school assignments by race. The Court consistently and unanimously upheld a student seeking admission to a desegregated school. A decade later, it became even firmer in ordering immediate desegregation. It showed a lack of patience with plans that did not desegregate and which attempted to evade or forestall desegregation. Beginning in 1974, the Court began to retreat when it realized that there are limits beyond which courts cannot go in desegregating schools. It has recognized that other avenues may be as successful as court edicts.

Whether state courts are required to fashion a greater remedy than are federal courts in desegregation matters was an issue in *Crawford v. Board of Education. Crawford* began as a state court action in which the trial court (on both state and federal court grounds) declared that the Los Angeles School District was "substantially segregated." The trial court was upheld by the Supreme Court of California (on grounds that the Constitution of the State of California prohibits both de jure and de facto segregation). Subsequent to that decision, the voters of California ratified Proposition I, which amended the California Constitution to prohibit state courts from requiring busing except to remedy viola-

---

87. Oliver v. Kalamazoo Bd. of Educ., 706 F.2d 757 (6th Cir. 1983).

tions of the U.S. Constitution and where a federal court would so order. Proposition I ultimately was applied to the Los Angeles situation, thus halting any further busing of students.[88]

The California Court of Appeal declared that since Los Angeles had not intentionally segregated its students, Proposition I applied, and there was no reason to require a greater remedy in state court than is required by a federal court under the federal Constitution. This decision was then taken to the U.S. Supreme Court.[89]

To Justice Powell, Proposition I did not violate the equal protection clause of the fourteenth amendment. The majority did not see this Proposition as embodying a racial classification scheme. Nor did the majority see any unfair burden being allocated to any group on the basis of a discriminatory principle. What is more, the Court reiterated the point of law that in cases where a neutral law causes a disparate impact, then intentional discrimination must be proved to establish a violation of equal protection.[90]

In *NAACP v. California,*[91] a post-*Crawford* case, appellants (who unsuccessfully had taken suit in federal district court seeking declaratory and injunctive relief) alleged that Proposition I violated the equal protection clause. Appellants sought a declaration that Proposition I was unconstitutional and an order enjoining state officials and state courts from implementing and enforcing the provisions of the Proposition. The Ninth Circuit denied relief.

Numerous cases have also been resolved in lower courts in which the bases of classification and assignment of pupils were challenged on racial grounds. In such cases, as in those previously cited, courts have neither denied nor negated the legal prerogatives of school officials. However, they have insisted that all subsequent classifications and assignments of pupils be based on objective, nonracial standards. A Florida case and a Mississippi case (decided in 1970) both illustrate this point. Significantly, each case

---

88. Crawford v. Board of Educ., 458 U.S. 527, 102 S. Ct. 3211, 73 L. Ed. 2d 948 (1982).

89. *Id.*

90. *Id.*

91. 711 F.2d 121 (9th Cir. 1983).

involved assignment of public school students to special educational settings.

In the first case, *Wright v. Board,* the Court of Appeals for the Fifth Circuit directed that assignment of students to schools offering compensatory or remedial training be made on objective and nonracial grounds.[92] In the second case, *United States v. Hinds,* the Fifth Circuit approved assignment of students to a reading clinic when those assignments were made on "sound education and administratively feasible grounds."[93]

Spangler v. Board[94] is another important decision involving special grouping of students, from a federal district court out of California. It offers a similar ruling to those cited above in *Wright* and *Hinds.* The court in *Spangler* found for the plaintiffs, for it was convinced that the degree of racial segregation present within the integrated public schools of Pasadena, California, was "a result of interclass grouping. . . ."[95] Three factors influenced the court's decision: (1) The school system's achievement test and intelligence test scores were acknowledged as "racially discriminatory" by the Assistant Superintendent of Schools. (2) Teachers and counselors, whose recommendations were considered in evaluating student placement, admitted assuming that blacks, particularly those from lower socio-economic backgrounds, would achieve lower than others if placed in upper groups. (3) Parents were allowed to make requests for placement of their children in higher groups; thus children of more assertive parents would have an advantage of placement.[96] In the opinion of Judge Real, the racial effect of these grouping procedures was to increase segregation in the schools.

---

92. Wright v. Board of Pub. Instr., 431 F.2d 1200, 1202 (5th Cir. 1970).

93. United States v. Hinds Cty. Sch. Bd., 433 F.2d 602, 605 (5th Cir. 1970).

94. Spangler v. Board of Educ., 311 F. Supp. 501 (C.D. Cal. 1970).

95. *Id.* at 519. Two systems of grouping students were in general use in the Pasadena schools. At the elementary school level, students were grouped as *gifted* or *below-average;* at the secondary level as *fast, regular,* or *slow.*

96. *Id.* at 519-20, at the discussion of "Interclass Grouping."

The Fifth Circuit, ruling in a 1971 Louisiana case, held that a public school district which operated as a unitary system for only one semester could not assign students to schools within that district on the basis of achievement test scores.[97] Relying heavily on *Singleton v. Jackson Municipal Separate School District*,[98] the court made it clear that "regardless of the innate validity of testing, it could not be used until a school district had been established as a unitary system."[99]

Precedent does exist, however, allowing local boards of education to assign special students (specifically, handicapped children) to particular schools "without respect to unitary zones." A case in point, decided by a federal district court in Tennessee, is *Robinson v. Shelby County Board of Education.*[100]

Over the decade of the 1970s, court-ordered desegregation plans (generally calling for the massive busing of public school students) dominated the legal scene in all sections of the nation — Wilmington, Louisville, Indianapolis, Boston and Los Angeles, among other cities. The net effect of such plans has seriously diminished the once plenary power of local school boards to assign pupils to schools within their school districts. With the primary emphasis placed on achieving acceptable racial and ethnic mixes of student populations, federal judges and federal governmental agencies maintained constant checks on school system enrollments, by individual schools, and overruled any school board assignment plan that fell below the court's or agency's standard.[101]

---

97. Lemon v. Bossier Parish Sch. Bd., 444 F.2d 1400 (5th Cir. 1971). *See also* United States v. Sunflower Cty. Sch. Dist., 430 F.2d 839 (5th Cir. 1970).

98. Singleton v. Jackson Mun. Separate Sch. Dist., 419 F.2d 1211 (5th Cir. 1969), *rev'd and remanded,* 396 U.S. 290 (1970).

99. *See Lemon, supra* note 97, at 1401.

100. 311 F. Supp. 97, 105 (C.D. Cal. 1970).

101. For some cases on point, see, e.g., Northside Indep. Sch. Dist. v. Texas Educ. Agency, 410 F. Supp. 360 (W.D. Tex. 1975); United States v. Texas Educ. Agency, 532 F.2d 380 (5th Cir. 1976); Morgan v. Kerrigan, 530 F.2d 401 (1st Cir. 1976); Acree v. County Bd. of Educ., 533 F.2d 131 (5th Cir. 1976).

Some federal judges took the prerogative away from local boards and placed the entire student assignment plan under the supervision of court-appointed experts.[102] In other jurisdictions, state courts directed state boards of education to mandate the implementation of "magnet school programs" to attract white and non-Hispanic students back to public schools.[103]

b. *Sex as a Factor.* In the past, there have been situations wherein sex has been considered as a criterion for determining a student's eligibility to public school and in making assignment to given schools. As with other admissions criteria previously discussed, local school boards, traditionally, were generally presumed correct in their judgment as to the qualifications of a student for said admission or assignment, and courts of law were reluctant to review these matters. The passage and implementation of federal statutes[104] regarding discrimination based upon sex, however, forced several cases into the courts.

Vorchheimer v. School District involved a challenge brought by a female high school student (Susan Vorchheimer) who had been denied admission to an all-male academic high school. In a class action suit originally brought in the Federal District Court for the Eastern District of Pennsylvania, the plaintiff, who had graduated with honors from a junior high school, sought relief under 42 U.S.C. § 1983, from alleged unconstitutional discrimination. Upon completion of the trial, the district court granted her an injunction, ordering that plaintiff and other qualified female students be admitted to the all-male (Central) academic high school.[105]

In November, 1973, while completing her ninth grade year, Susan Vorchheimer's parents received a communication from the junior high school principal listing the four types of senior high schools available to their daughter. These types were *comprehensive* (providing a wide range of courses and courses of study, with

---

102. *Morgan, supra* note 101.

103. Board of Educ. v. School Comm., 345 N.E.2d 345 (Mass. 1976).

104. *See, e.g.,* tit. 6, C.R.A. 1964, 42 U.S.C. § 2000d, and tit. 9, Education Amendments 1972, 20 U.S.C. § 1681 et seq.

105. 532 F.2d 880 (3d Cir. 1976), *aff'd,* 430 U.S. 703 (1977).

the criterion for enrollment being residency within a designated area of Philadelphia), *technical, magnet,* and *academic.* For the academic high schools (all-male Central High and all female Girls High) certain admissions requirements were specified. These requirements were *tests* (a minimum score in the eighty-second percentile, national composite score in the most recent Iowa Tests) and *achievement* (a record of all A's and B's with not more than one C in any major subject taken). Only seven percent of the students in the entire Philadelphia School District were able to attend either high school.

After visiting a number of senior high schools in the city, Susan decided that she wished to attend Central High School. Subsequently, her father submitted her application for admission and it was rejected, solely on the basis of her sex.[106]

Finding no congressional enactments which authoritatively addressed the problem before the court, the district court reviewed the line of recent sex discrimination cases from the other federal courts. As a result of his analysis, District Judge Newcomer held that the result of the school board policy excluding young women from attending Central High School "is to deny them the opportunity to attend a coeducational, academically superior, high school."[107] To Judge Newcomer, the denial was significant enough to have an "adverse impact on her and on other women."[108]

On appeal, the United States Court of Appeals, Third Circuit, reversed Judge Newcomer. The high court held that when attendance at either of the two single-sex high schools was voluntary and when the educational opportunities at both schools were basically equal, the regulations which established admission based on

---

106. 400 F. Supp. 326 (E.D. Pa. 1975).

107. *Id.* at 328. Central High School was founded in 1836 as the first public high school in Philadelphia and was the second public high school in the United States. Girls High School was organized as an academic high school for females, in 1893. These two were not the only single-sex schools in Philadelphia. Edison High School and Benjamin Franklin High School admitted only males, and Kensington High School admitted only females.

108. *Id.* at 342.

gender classification did not offend the equal protection clause. As Circuit Judge Weis said for the majority:

> It is not for us to pass upon the wisdom of segregating boys and girls in high school. We are concerned not with the desirability of the practice but only its constitutionality. Once that threshold has been passed, it is the school board's responsibility to determine the best methods of accomplishing its mission.[109]

Judge Weis' attitude toward maintaining school board decision-making in this matter is quite clear.

The United States Court of Appeals for the Fifth Circuit had an opportunity, in 1977, to hear an appeal from a federal district court in Mississippi involving a county school district's sex-segregated student assignment plan.[110] The district court had recommended that the Amite County School District be permitted to maintain a sex-segregated student assignment plan among the four schools which comprise the district.

County school officials argued that their sex-segregated assignment plan was not racially motivated. Further, they stated that sex segregation within schools is not a denial of federal statutory rights.[111] Finally, school officials maintained that the continued operation of sex-segregated schools would aid in keeping whites in the racially desegregated public school system.[112]

Regardless of Amite County's educational reasons using gender as a basis for assigning students to schools within the district, the Fifth Circuit Court considered the assignment plan as prohibited by federal statutory law. It remanded the case back to district court

---

109. *Vorchheimer, supra* note 105, at 888.

110. United States v. Hinds Cty. Sch. Bd., 560 F.2d 619 (5th Cir. 1977). *See also* United States v. Georgia, 466 F.2d 197 (5th Cir. 1972); Moore v. Tangipahoa Parish Sch. Bd., 421 F.2d 1407 (5th Cir. 1969).

111. *Hinds County, supra* note 110, at 623.

112. *Id.* at 624.

where a remedy was to be fashioned "in light of the best educational interests of the children and parents involved."[113]

In a case out of higher education law, a male registered nurse applied for admission to a bachelor degree program at the state-supported Mississippi University for Women. Otherwise qualified for admission to the program, the applicant (Mr. Hogan) was denied admission because of his gender.[114]

Claiming that the school's gender-based admission policy violated the equal protection clause under the fourteenth amendment, Hogan took the matter into federal district court. The district court, however, granted defendant's motion for summary judgment and held that a rational relationship existed between the university being maintained as a single-sex school and the state's legitimate interest of providing the greatest practical range of educational opportunities for women students. This decision was appealed to the Fifth Circuit.[115]

The Fifth Circuit reversed the district court on grounds that the court had improperly applied the rational basis test to a gender-based situation. The case was remanded. The Fifth Circuit subsequently reversed the district court and concluded that Hogan had been denied equal protection of the law. The case went to the U.S. Supreme Court.[116]

In a five-to-four decision, the Supreme Court affirmed the court of appeals. According to Justice O'Connor, for the majority, Hogan was a victim of discrimination based upon his sex. To uphold a classification based upon gender, said the court, an important governmental objective must be present and the means used (in this case the exclusion of males from admission to the University)

---

113. *Id.* at 625.

114. Mississippi Univ. for Women v. Hogan, 458 U.S. 718, 102 S. Ct. 3331, 73 L. Ed. 2d 1090 (1982).

115. *Id.*

116. *Id.* On rehearing the state argued that the University was exempt from the requirements of title 9.

must be related to achieving that objective. In *Hogan* the University could not carry the burdens of this standard.[117]

c. *Marriage or Pregnancy as a Factor.* Over the years, public school systems have generally discouraged, and in some instances excluded, married or pregnant students from attending school. Some past reasons specified by school officials for such decisions are: (1) marriage emancipates children from their parents, therefore married students are exempt from compulsory attendance statutes,[118] (2) married students may cause turmoil and therefore their presence is detrimental to the other students,[119] (3) pregnancy and parenthood at school age are socially unacceptable, and (4) unwed pregnancy is an example of "immoral" behavior.[120] In today's public schools a student cannot be excluded solely on the basis of pregnancy.

In *Carrollton-Farmers Branch Independent School District v. Knight,* students were suspended from high school because of their marriage. They filed suit in county court seeking reinstatement and were successful. The school board then appealed to the Court of Civil Appeals of Texas.

In upholding the lower court ruling for the students' reinstatement, the appellate court based its decision on three points. First,

---

117. *Id.* In 1994-1995 the battle continued, involving the possible admission of women to historically all-male public military institutions. *See, e.g.,* Faulkner v. Jones, 858 F. Supp. 552 (D.S.C. 1994), involving the Citadel military school in South Carolina, where, under a U.S. District Court order, a female student was allowed to attend day classes but not participate in the regular Cadet program. The decision to admit the student was affirmed by the Fourth Circuit, and subsequently the Citadel was ordered to admit Faulkner to the Corps of Cadets without delay. *See* Faulkner v. Jones, 51 F.3d 440 (4th Cir. 1995). For an earlier and similar case on point, see United States v. Commonwealth of Va., 976 F.2d 890 (4th Cir. 1992), involving the Virginia Military Institute (VMI), and the establishment of a parallel leadership program in conjunction with the private, all female Mary Baldwin College. The Fourth Circuit approved the women's leadership program in United States v. Commonwealth of Va., 44 F.3d 1229 (4th Cir. 1995).

118. State v. Priest, 270 So. 2d 173 (La. 1946).

119. McLeod v. State, 122 So. 737 (Miss. 1929).

120. Nutt v. Board of Educ., 278 P. 1065 (Kan. 1928).

the presence of the married students had not caused disorder in the high school. Second, there was no evidence that marriage had impaired the study habits of the couple. Finally, the suspension policy for marriage had not been uniformly applied to other students.[121]

More recently, a federal district court in Georgia heard a complaint filed by a fifteen-year-old girl who was seeking readmission to regular (day) school. School officials had denied her admission to regular school, invoking a school board policy that required students who married or became parents to attend night school.

Even though the court found a rational basis for the school board's "night school" policy, it nevertheless opined that the plaintiff student had been denied equal protection of the law and she should be readmitted. The major determining factor for the court's decision was that night school students were required to pay tuition and buy their own textbooks, but regular day school students were not required to do the same.[122]

In 1969, a federal district court in Mississippi heard *Perry v. Grenada Municipal Separate School District.* At issue was a school board policy automatically excluding unwed mothers from high school admission. Ruling in the student's favor, the court held that unwed mothers could not be excluded solely because they were "unwed mothers." Moreover, a charge of "lack of moral character" would have to be clearly established and substantiated through a fair hearing process. The court was also of the opinion that before any such exclusion could be upheld, a link must be established between the unwed pregnancy and a harmful effect on other students.[123]

Ordway v. Hargraves[124] is a similar case and was heard by a federal district court in Massachusetts. The matter involved an unmarried senior (Fay Ordway) at Middlesex Regional High

---

121. 418 S.W.2d 535 (Tex. 1967).
122. Houston v. Prosser, 361 F. Supp. 295 (N.D. Ga. 1973).
123. 300 F. Supp. 748 (N.D. Miss. 1969).
124. 323 F. Supp. 1155 (D. Mass. 1971).

School. In 1971, Fay became pregnant and was told by her principal that she must cease attending regular classes at the high school, citing a school regulation that stated "whenever an unmarried girl . . . shall be known to be pregnant, her membership shall be immediately terminated."[125]

Deciding in the student's favor, and ordering her reinstatement to classes, the court reasoned:

> No danger to petitioner's physical or mental health resultant from her attending classes during regular hours has been shown; no likelihood that her presence will cause any disruption of or interference with school activities or pose a threat of harm to others has been shown; and no valid educational or other reason to justify her segregation and require her to receive a type of educational treatment which is not the equal of that given to all others in her class has been shown.[126]

The court went on to say:

> It would seem beyond argument that the right to receive a public school education is a basic personal right or liberty. Consequently, the burden of justifying any school rule or regulation limiting or terminating that right is on the school authorities.[127]

Apparent in the above cases is the legal principle that students of school age possess an entitlement to public school attendance. As such, they shall not be denied admission or placement in appropriate classes and schools *solely* because of their marital status or because they are pregnant.

    d. *Disability as a Factor.* Court decisions and legislative enactments (federal and state) of the past have mandated that *all* children, including those with disabilities, are entitled to admission to school and placement in an appropriate, meaningful, and quality

---

125. *Id.* at 1156.
126. *Id.* at 1158.
127. *Id.*

program. As one writer has summarized, "the 'right to education' means that the school systems must provide all children equal opportunities to develop their own capabilities; the school systems thus are required to provide different programs and facilities for pupils with different needs, according to their needs."[128] Certainly implied in the above statement is the mandate that students of legal age of attendance in public school systems shall not be denied admission or appropriate school and classroom placement solely because they are disabled. They must be provided for.

Beginning with *Pennsylvania Ass'n for Retarded Children v. Commonwealth* (1972),[129] the federal courts have firmly brought the due process and equal protection guarantees of the fourteenth amendment into the field of special education. Even though the final consent agreement in *P.A.R.C.* was binding only on the parties involved, the case served to generate several subsequent class actions, brought on behalf of all types of exceptional children (*e.g.,* mentally retarded, autistic, gifted, language impaired), each of which ensured them access to an appropriate, meaningful, and effective public education, whatever their unique needs.

Lau v. Nichols was decided by the United States Supreme Court in 1974. A class action, *Lau* was originally brought in a United States District Court by parents of non-English speaking Chinese students in the San Francisco public schools. The plaintiffs sought relief claiming that officials operating the public schools were responsible for their children's "unequal educational opportunities" by failing to provide courses in the English language, which parents alleged violated the equal protection clause of the fourteenth amendment. The district court denied relief, and the circuit

---

128. Turnbull, *Legal Aspects of Educating the Developmentally Disabled* in CONTEMPORARY LEGAL PROBLEMS IN EDUCATION 183 (Topeka, Kansas: NOLPE, 1975).

129. 334 F. Supp. 1257 (E.D. Pa. 1971); final consent agreement at 343 F. Supp. 279 (E.D. Pa. 1972).

court of appeals affirmed that holding, finding no violation of equal protection.[130]

In a decision overturning the circuit court's holding, the United States Supreme Court (Mr. Justice Douglas, speaking for the majority) focused upon the necessity of a public school system providing equal access to a meaningful educational opportunity. In Douglas' words, "there is no equality of treatment merely by providing students with the same facilities, textbooks, teachers, and curriculum."[131]

With Chief Justice Burger, and Justices White, Stewart, and Blackmun concurring, Mr. Justice Douglas rendered the following opinion regarding the notion of an "effective educational program":

> Basic English skills are at the very core of what these public schools teach. Imposition of a requirement that, before a child can effectively participate in the educational program, he must already have acquired those basic skills is to make a mockery of public education. We know that those who do not understand English are certain to find their classroom experiences wholly incomprehensible and in no way meaningful.[132]

Serna v. Portales Municipal Schools[133] involved a 1974 class action for declaratory and injunctive relief against a school district in New Mexico, alleging that school officials discriminated against Spanish surnamed students. A United States district court held for the plaintiff parents and created a bilingual-bicultural school program as relief. The school board appealed this action to the United States Circuit Court of Appeals for the Tenth Circuit.

---

130. 483 F.2d 791 (9th Cir. 1974). The case law discussions beginning with this footnote and ending with footnote 147 are adapted from a lengthier discussion prepared by Professor Vacca, the author of this chapter, that appears in FINANCING PUBLIC SCHOOLS IN VIRGINIA (S.B. Thomas ed., 1976).

131. 414 U.S. 563, 94 S. Ct. 786, 39 L. Ed. 2d 1 (1974).

132. *Id.*

133. 499 F.2d 1147 (10th Cir. 1974), *aff'g* 351 F. Supp. 1279 (D.N.M. 1972).

In their behalf, appellee parents claimed and showed: (1) very little English was spoken by many Spanish surnamed children when they entered school; (2) these children also grew up in a culture totally alien to the one thrust on them in public school; (3) these children were subjected to intelligence tests and achievement tests given totally in English; (4) no bilingual instruction was available in the schools; (5) there were no Spanish surnamed teachers or administrators in any of the individual schools; (6) nothing in the curriculum reflected the historical contributions of people of Mexican and Spanish descent; and, as a direct result (7) there was a higher rate of failure and drop-out among Spanish surnamed children as compared to the other children.

In affirming the lower court decision granting relief to the parents and children, Circuit Judge Hill saw *Serna* as "strikingly similar" to *Lau,* and reiterated the emphasis of the Supreme Court on "meaningful educational opportunity." Said Judge Hill, "we believe the trial court, under its inherent equitable power, can properly fashion a bilingual-bicultural program which will assure the Spanish surnamed children receive a meaningful education."[134]

Berkelman v. San Francisco Unified School District was a 1974 civil rights action taken in a district court, challenging the San Francisco Unified School District's standards for admitting students to Lowell High School (an academic, college preparatory high school). A school system policy existed which stated that only applicants whose prior academic achievement placed them in the top fifteen percent of all junior high school graduates in San Francisco would be accepted to Lowell High School. The district court denied relief, and plaintiffs appealed.[135]

In upholding the district court's decision (denying relief), Circuit Judge Goodwin was of the opinion that a disproportion of black and Spanish-American students attending Lowell High School did not create a suspect classification, and did not render the system's admissions standards unconstitutional. The school

---

134. *Id.* at 1154.
135. Appealed at 501 F.2d 1264 (9th Cir. 1974).

system's legitimate interest in establishing an academic, college preparatory high school outweighed any harm "imagined" or "suffered" by "students whose achievement had not qualified them for admission to that school."[136]

Judge Goodwin then focused on the circuit court's need to ensure that the end product of the admission standards created a meaningful educational setting at Lowell High School when he said:

> The task is to examine the school district's assertion that the standard of past academic achievement substantially furthers the purpose of providing the best education for the public school students in the district. If the past achievement standard does substantially further that purpose, then the district has not unconstitutionally discriminated in its . . . admission policy.[137]

Significantly, Judge Goodwin's notion of meaningful educational opportunity did not equate equality with sameness; rather, he emphasized the need to provide effectively for individual differences in students, as evidenced by the following quotation from his opinion:

> The student whose best performance has demonstrated ability to move at an advanced rate in an advanced program will receive a "better" education than he or she would receive if required to work in subject matter and at a pace which does not provide as great an educational challenge. Likewise, a student with an interest in vocational training receives a "better" education if permitted to take vocational courses than if required to continue against his wishes with the "traditional" high school program.[138]

---

136. *Id.* at 1264. It should be noted, however, that the circuit court struck down as unconstitutional the requiring of higher admission standards for girls than for boys.

137. *Id.* at 1267.

138. *Id.*

Davis v. Page was a civil rights action (not a class action) brought in a district court in New Hampshire in 1974. In *Davis,* a father brought action on behalf of his elementary school children on grounds that a local board policy requiring that his children remain in school classrooms where religiously offensive activities and discussions were taking place was unconstitutional. The district court denied relief.[139]

Ruling against plaintiff's claim of exclusive control of his children, District Judge Bownes stated most emphatically that the interests of children "are not coterminous with that of their parents." Nor, he said, are children's rights and interests "limited to those which their parents assert."[140] In Judge Bownes' opinion:

> The balance is a most precarious one. The parents' right to freely exercise their religion and their inherent right to control the upbringing of their children must be weighed against the state's interest in providing its youth with a proper and enabling education and the children's right to receive it.[141]

In summary, Judge Bownes said that parents do not possess a constitutional right to stand between their children and an "effective" education.[142] What is more, "[t]he state has an interest in maintaining and sustaining a coherent and comprehensive educational program."[143]

In re G.H. was a 1974 decision of the Supreme Court of North Dakota. This was an appeal from a juvenile court involving obligations to pay for the education of a school-aged, handicapped girl. Several references to *Rodriguez* and its implications for the rights of children to equal access to a meaningful educational program

---

139. 385 F. Supp. 395 (D.N.H. 1974).
140. *Id.* at 398.
141. *Id.* at 399.
142. *Id.* at 400-01.
143. *Id.* at 404.

are contained in the North Dakota court's decision. Examples of such references follow.[144]

"We are satisfied," said Judge Vogel, "that all children in North Dakota have the right, under the State Constitution, to a public school education. Nothing in *Rodriguez* ... holds to the contrary."[145] Therefore, failure to provide educational opportunity for handicapped children (except those, if there are any, who cannot benefit at all from it) is a constitutional violation.[146] As such, depriving the handicapped girl of a "meaningful educational opportunity would be just the sort of denial of equal protection which has been held unconstitutional in cases involving discrimination based on race and illegitimacy and sex."[147]

In *Brookhart v. Illinois State Board of Education,* the Seventh Circuit reversed the district court below and ordered that diplomas be issued to eleven students who met all requirements for high school graduation but had not achieved acceptable scores on the Peoria, Illinois Minimal Competency Test (M.C.T.). The plaintiff students (each of whom was classified as handicapped under the Education for All Handicapped Children Act) claimed that they were being denied a "free appropriate education" without due process of law. More specifically, they had been denied notice of and exposure to the requirements tested through the administration of the M.C.T. The Seventh Circuit agreed with plaintiffs.[148]

There is no doubt that court decisions similar to those cited above, coupled with emerging federal[149] and state statutes, have given birth to a movement in public school systems across this nation. The intent of this movement is for states and their schools

---

144. 218 N.W.2d 441 (N.D. 1974).

145. *Id.* at 446.

146. *Id.*

147. *Id.* at 447.

148. Brookhart v. Illinois State Bd. of Educ., 697 F.2d 179 (7th Cir. 1983). For another case on point, see Johnson v. Sikes, 730 F.2d 644 (4th Cir. 1984).

149. *See, e.g.,* P.L. 94-142, The Education for All Handicapped Children Act (a revision to Part B, Education of the Handicapped Act), enacted in November, 1975. *See also* P.L. 93-112, 29 U.S.C. § 794, § 504 of Rehabilitation Act of 1973.

to provide an appropriate educational opportunity for all children of school age (whatever their unique needs) — an opportunity that ensures basic, minimal quality education for each child. As a New York court said recently, where the New York State Constitution mandates a right for *all* children to obtain a free public education, that mandate includes handicapped children.[150]

Four years later, in a 1980 federal case out of Illinois, a parents' organization (Parents in Action on Special Education) challenged the Chicago school system's use of standardized intelligence tests (I.Q. tests) to determine the placement of students into special classes for the educable mentally retarded. The parents' group (PASE) alleged that the tests used were racially and culturally biased. As such, they claimed that the tests violated the equal protection clause of the fourteenth amendment, § 504 of the Rehabilitation Act of 1973, title 6 of the Civil Rights Act of 1964, the Equal Education Opportunities Act of 1974, and the Education for All Handicapped Children Act of 1975.

Not convinced by the testimony of either side's experts, the federal judge personally examined the tests on an item-by-item basis. Based upon his analysis, the judge declared that (with the exception of a few items) the tests used by the school system were constitutional as administered. The tests in question, he said, did not discriminate against black children.[151]

§ 9.5. State Testing of Student Competencies.

In recent years, states have moved through legislative enactment to ensure that all graduates of public schools in that state have received an effective education. These legislative acts have not been without challenge in court.

---

150. Matter of Wagner, 383 N.Y.S.2d 849 (N.Y. 1976).

151. Parents in Action on Special Educ. (PASE) v. Hannon, 506 F. Supp. 831 (N.D. Ill. 1980). For a case where a court focused upon socioeconomic background, rather than race, in evaluating the distribution of students in achievement groups, see Montgomery v. Starkville, 854 F.2d 127 (5th Cir. 1988).

In 1978, the Florida legislature amended that state's law to require all students in Florida public schools to pass a functional literacy examination (state competency test) as a precondition of receiving a high school diploma. Subsequently, some present and future high school seniors, who had failed or would fail the new test, brought suit in federal district court challenging the constitutionality of using the test to deny diplomas. More specifically, these students alleged that the use of the test in this way had an unconstitutionally disproportionate impact on black students (ultimately it was shown that the failure rate of blacks was approximately ten times greater than that of whites.) The district court agreed with plaintiffs that the use of the test as a diploma sanction violated both the due process and equal protection clauses of the Constitution. Thus the court enjoined any use of the test for diploma issuance until the 1982-1983 school year. However, the court did not find fault with the test content and did allow the test to be used for remedial purposes.[152]

In deciding to grant the four-year injunction the district court cited two basic reasons. First, the immediate use of the test as a diploma sanction would, in effect, serve to perpetuate past discrimination against black students who had attended segregated schools for the first four years of their education (these would be among the first group of students subject to the sanction in 1979). Second, the test's implementation schedule provided insufficient notice regarding the skills to be tested. Four to six years (of integrated schools) between announcement of the test and the test's implementation would be needed to develop the student skills to be tested.

The case was appealed to the former Fifth Circuit, where the district court's injunction was upheld, but the case was remanded for further findings on two issues. First, the Fifth Circuit wanted the State of Florida to show that the competency test itself was "a fair test of what is taught." The court stressed the need to show sufficient proof that the test measured "what was actually taught in

---

152. Debra P. v. Turlington, 474 F. Supp. 244 (M.D. Fla. 1979).

the schools of Florida." Second, if the above could be demonstrated, the State of Florida would then need to show either that the test's racially discriminatory impact "was not due to the present effects of past intentional discrimination, or that the test's use as a diploma sanction would remedy those effects."[153]

On remand, the district court found that the State of Florida had met its burden on the first issue in demonstrating by the preponderance of the evidence that the competency test was instructionally valid. Regarding the second issue, the court found that there was no causal link between the disproportionate failure rate of black students and the present effects of past segregation.[154]

The case was appealed to the new Eleventh Circuit. The appellate court held that the district court below was not clearly erroneous in its finding that the competency test itself was instructionally valid. What is more, the district court was not clearly erroneous in its finding that vestiges of past intentional segregation did not cause the test's disproportionate impact on blacks, and that the use of the test as a diploma sanction would help remedy vestiges of past segregation.[155]

Some states have allowed local school systems to establish and implement a community service requirement as a precondition for graduation from a public high school. Such a requirement has been upheld under the United States Constitution.[156]

§ 9.6. Summary.

The legal authority to determine the admissibility of children to public school systems and to place them in appropriate schools and classes is, within the bounds of state law, the local school board's

---

153. Debra P. v. Turlington, 644 F.2d 397 (5th Cir. 1981).

154. Debra P. v. Turlington, 564 F. Supp. 177, 186 (M.D. Fla. 1983).

155. Debra P. v. Turlington, 730 F.2d 1405 (11th Cir. 1984). For a decision involving Hispanic students and their claim that they were "disproportionately burdened" by a desegregation plan in effect in their school system, see Diaz v. San Jose Unified Sch. Dist., 861 F.2d 591 (9th Cir. 1988).

156. *See, e.g.,* Immediato v. Rye Neck Sch. Dist., 73 F.3d 454 (2d Cir. 1996).

to exercise. Provided the board acts in good faith and does not violate either state or federal law, courts of law will not interfere with board decisions on admission and placement of students.

As demonstrated in this chapter, court decisions and legislative enactments (federal and state) have mandated that all children, whatever their race, religious belief, socioeconomic background, or disability, are entitled to a meaningful, appropriate, and quality educational opportunity. Contemporary public school boards, administrators, and professional staff members must therefore accept their legal responsibilities to carry out these mandates.

There are also many responsibilities that must be accepted by parents. This chapter also demonstrates that parents are not completely free to stand between their child and a meaningful educational opportunity. Parents must possess a bona fide reason for refusing to send their child to school, and they have a legal responsibility to see to it that acceptable educational alternatives are offered when their child is kept out of school.

Chapter Ten

CONTROL AND PUNISHMENT

§ 10.0. In Loco Parentis.

When students are at school, they are expected to submit to school authority. This is necessary in order that teachers may teach and students may learn. In establishing and maintaining a climate conducive to teaching and learning, educators have considerable discretion in controlling student conduct. The legal term for the relationship of educator to pupil is *in loco parentis* (in place of the parent). It was explained by Blackstone in his *Commentaries:*

> A parent may also delegate part of his parental author-ity, during his life, to the tutor or schoolmaster of his child; who is then *in loco parentis,* and has such a portion of the power of the parents *viz.* that of restraint, and cor-rection as may be necessary to answer the purposes for which he is employed.[1]

As originally conceived, the doctrine of *in loco parentis* was intended to treat discipline matters; however, it was later expanded to include other areas of the school program.

In its original state, *in loco parentis* clothed school personnel with almost unlimited authority in disciplining children. The right extended not only to the time that students were in school, but also while they were en route to and from school and at school-sponsored activities away from school. Teachers and administra-tors were consistently upheld in using questionable methods of exacting student obedience, and courts only interfered when it was clearly shown that educators had acted arbitrarily, capriciously, or unreasonably. As a result of this almost unlimited authority, school officials sometimes acted imprudently but with reasonable assur-ance that their actions would be upheld.

The concept of *in loco parentis* has undergone considerable modification since the Blackstone statement. As a result of court decisions, school authorities now cannot make arbitrary decisions

---

1. BLACKSTONE, COMMENTARIES ON THE LAWS OF ENGLAND 453 (T. Cooley ed., 1884). That principle was reaffirmed more than a century later in Hamilton v. Unionville-Chadds Ford Sch. Dist., 714 A 2d 1012 (Pa. 1998).

regarding student discipline without being challenged. Further, courts have set conditions that must be met if boards, administrators, and teachers are to be upheld.

This chapter will include an examination of the doctrine of *in loco parentis* as it applies to two basic areas of school control: discipline and search and seizure. Both substantive and procedural aspects of discipline will be studied, and the more recent issue of the application of *in loco parentis* in searching students will also be examined.

§ 10.1. Corporal Punishment.

Corporal punishment denotes the infliction of physical pain upon a student for misconduct. The legal justification for it is found in state statutes. Some states specifically authorize it, some states specifically forbid it, other states do not mention it but by implication authorize or allow it. As of 1993, twenty-five states now forbid corporal punishment either by state statute or local school board policy. This number represents a significant increase in the number of states now forbidding this age-old disciplinary practice.

Where corporal punishment is allowed, it must conform with the law of reasonableness. That law has been derived from lower court decisions through the years.

a. *Supreme Court Decisions.* In 1975 and 1977, the Supreme Court of the United States spoke for the first time on the legality of corporal punishment. Each time it upheld the practice. In the first case, *Baker v. Owen,*[2] the Court affirmed without comment a decision of a federal district court out of North Carolina that allowed teachers to administer corporal punishment. Further, it was allowable in spite of an objection by the child's parents. However, for a teacher or administrator to be protected, four guidelines must be observed: (1) Students must be warned in advance as to the kinds of behavior punishable by paddling. (2) It must not be used as a

---

2. 395 F. Supp. 294 (M.D.N.C.), *aff'd mem.,* 423 U.S. 907 (1975).

first-line of punishment for misbehavior. (3) A second school official must be present to witness the paddling. (4) Parents, on request, must be furnished a written statement of the paddling, including the reasons for it and the names of the witnesses.

This opinion should not be construed as meaning that it is applicable to all states when, in fact, it applied only to North Carolina.

In another case, out of Florida, the Supreme Court in 1977 ruled that, since the eighth amendment is applicable only in criminal matters, it does not protect one who has been corporally punished, even when it is severe.[3] The Court held further that a student is not entitled to notice and a hearing prior to corporal punishment in that both require time, personnel, and a diversion of attention from normal school pursuits.

b. *Legal Guidelines.* Where corporal punishment is allowed, it must conform to the laws of a state as well as to the law of reasonableness. Through the years, courts have spelled out some general guidelines as to what constitutes reasonable corporal punishment. A few relevant cases are discussed below to illustrate each guideline.

1. *It Is Consistent with Statutory Law.*[4] Where statutes authorize or allow corporal punishment, a student has little chance of overturning the legislation. Where it is forbidden, a teacher will not be protected unless it was used in self-defense or in protecting the lives and property of others.

In a 1973 case out of Vermont, a student was charged with sending a vulgar note to a fellow classmate, and for that he was spanked. He challenged the law as being vague, overbroad, and in violation of his fourteenth amendment rights. The court upheld the law and rejected each of the student's contentions.[5] In contrast, a 1976 decision out of Missouri upheld the dismissal of a teacher for

---

3. Ingraham v. Wright, 430 U.S. 651, 97 S. Ct. 1401, 51 L. Ed. 2d 711 (1977). *See* Harris v. Tate Cty. Sch. Dist., 882 F. Supp. 90 (N.D. Miss. 1995).

4. This guideline and the six others that follow are adapted, in part, from EDWARD C. BOLMEIER, LEGALITY OF STUDENT DISCIPLINARY PRACTICES 63 (Charlottesville: Michie Co., 1976).

5. Gonyaw v. Gray, 361 F. Supp. 366 (D. Vt. 1973).

repeatedly resorting to corporal punishment outside the scope of school board policy. Specifically, and in spite of warnings, she had slapped students on the face, a violation of the local policy. The state's supreme court upheld the dismissal.[6]

2. *It Is for Correction.* Like a parent, a teacher may occasionally need to resort to corporal punishment as the best means of bringing a child to obedience. When one acts with the same kind of authority and in the same manner that a parent would, the teacher will be upheld. An example is a 1975 case out of Louisiana.[7] It initially involved a fight by two eighth-grade students and, although the teacher separated them, they resumed fighting. The teacher then grabbed the boys and threatened to send them to the principal, whereupon one of the boys cursed him and threatened reprisal by his father. The teacher then paddled the boy with a wooden paddle, the boy cursed him again, and the teacher turned him over his knees and paddled him again. The court held for the teacher, recognizing that, like parents, teachers have the right to administer corporal punishment for good cause.

3. *It Is Not Cruel or Excessive.* If educators use excessive force in disciplining students, they will not be upheld. Further, they may be subject to criminal liability. The determination of what constitutes cruel or excessive punishment is determined by the factual situation. A classic example is a 1967 court decision which did not uphold a teacher.[8] The teacher, who stood 6' 2" and weighed 230 pounds, subdued a student in his physical education class who was 4' 9" and weighed 101 pounds. In squeezing the boy's chest and shaking him, the teacher broke the boy's arm. The

---

6. Board of Educ. v. Shank, 542 S.W.2d 779 (Mo. 1976).

7. Roy v. Continental Ins. Co., 313 So. 2d 349 (La. App. 1975). The Fifth Circuit ruled in 1988 that the use of corporal punishment may have a rational basis, in spite of research to the contrary. Cunningham v. Beavers, 858 F.2d 269 (5th Cir. 1988).

8. Frank v. Orleans Parish Sch. Bd., 195 So. 2d 451 (La. 1967). For a contrasting case, see Daniels v. Gordon, 503 S.E.2d 72 (Ga. App. 1998). For a decision involving the qualified immunity defense in a corporal punishment case, see Saylor v. Board of Educ., 118 F.3d 507 (6th Cir. 1997).

court did not accept the teacher's actions as being necessary to his self-defense but rather saw him as exerting excessive force on his pupils.

Subsequent allegations have involved not so often charges of excessive punishment but, rather, unusual punishment. Persons bringing such complaints have attempted to protect students from paddling by elevating students' rights to protection under the eighth amendment. Although there have been a few decisions to the contrary, lower courts have, for the most part, been reluctant to give students this protection. A 1974 decision out of the Eighth Circuit held that excessive corporal punishment may be cruel and unusual.[9] That same year the Seventh Circuit held that pupils who were administered corporal punishment in a state correctional institution were subjected to cruel and unusual punishment in violation of the eighth amendment.[10]

That specific question was answered by the Supreme Court of the United States in 1977,[11] when it ruled, five to four, that two junior high school students spanked for misconduct were not subject to eighth amendment protection. Although there was evidence that the students had been badly whipped, corporal punishment, no matter how severe, was insufficient to create a violation of the eighth amendment. The Court ruled that it was the intent of the eighth amendment to apply only to situations involving criminal punishment. Regarding the issue of excessive punishment, the Court stated:

> If the punishment inflicted is later found to have been excessive — not reasonably believed at the time to be necessary for the child's discipline or training — the school authorities inflicting it may be held liable in damages to the child and, if malice is shown, they may be subject to criminal penalties.[12]

---

9. Bramlet v. Wilson, 495 F.2d 714 (8th Cir. 1974).

10. Nelson v. Heyne, 491 F.2d 352 (7th Cir. 1974).

11. *Ingraham, supra* note 3.

12. *Id.*, 97 S. Ct. at 1415.

The four dissenting Justices felt that the eighth amendment should apply. Speaking for the minority, Justice White observed that if the same beatings had been inflicted on a criminal, they likely would not have passed constitutional muster.

4. *It Leaves No Permanent or Lasting Injury.* This standard implies that a student may have a temporary injury and still have no case against a teacher or administrator who disciplined him. Courts have consistently ruled this way. However, where the reverse is true and lasting injuries do occur, one may be liable. The testimony of experts is often called on for analysis and verification of one's injuries. In one case, a doctor who examined a boy testified that the spanking was excessive, and he prescribed tranquilizers for him. The teacher had paddled the child, age eleven, for defiance on the playground. The court agreed that the punishment was excessive.[13] In another case, a student charged a teacher with assault and battery when, while being removed from class, the boy shoved his hand in a glass window and sustained severe cuts. Here the court ruled in favor of the teacher, whose actions had been reasonable in attempting to correct the obstreperous pupil.[14] A Pennsylvania court decided for a student who was struck on the head, knocked against the blackboard and furniture, and subjected to ridicule during class.[15]

5. *It Involves No Malice.* If a teacher is angry when administering corporal punishment, that individual's actions will not be upheld. The object of corporal punishment is correction of the child, not revenge on the part of the teacher. A court ruled in 1961 that a teacher's discipline was in anger[16] when the student was told to remove gloves belonging to another student and, before he could do so, the teacher struck him on the ear, bursting an eardrum.

6. *It Suits the Age and Sex of the Child.* The law of reasonableness applies to these criteria. It would be unreasonable to

---

13. People v. Ball, 58 Ill. 2d 36, 317 N.E.2d 54 (1974).

14. Simms v. School Dist. No. 1, 508 P.2d 236 (Ore. App. 1973).

15. Landi v. West Chester Area Sch. Dist., 353 A.2d 895 (Pa. 1976); Caffas v. Board of Sch. Dirs., 353 A.2d 898 (Pa. 1976).

16. Tinkham v. Kole, 110 N.W.2d 258 (Iowa 1961).

paddle an eighteen-year-old senior, for other forms of discipline may serve better. It would also be unreasonable for a female teacher to paddle a high school male; likewise, for a male teacher to paddle a high school female. However, in a 1963 case, a male teacher slapped a fifteen-year-old girl twice — lightly and without anger — and was protected. He did this after persuasion had been unsuccessful. Although he had been given orders not to spank students at the school, a psychiatric hospital, the court upheld him, ruling that his authority can be no more questioned than that of parents.[17]

A Texas court considered a student's weight, among other factors, in upholding school officials who had spanked a boy for unexcused absences.[18]

7. *It Involves an Appropriate Instrument.* Various kinds of implements have been used to paddle students, and the efficacy of them has been considered by the courts. The use of a wooden paddle has been upheld.[19] A twelve-inch ruler has been held to be a reasonable instrument.[20] A paddle three inches wide and twenty inches long, used excessively, creating psychological trauma involving medication, was not upheld.[21] Striking a student on his ear was not upheld.[22] Slapping a student on his face has not been upheld.[23] For the most part, it has not been the instrument itself that is questionable but rather the part of the person to which it is applied, the degree to which it is used, and the end result of the spanking. If the punishment results in more than temporary pain or injury, the teacher will not be upheld.

---

17. Indiana State Personnel Bd. v. Jackson, 192 N.E.2d 740 (Ind. 1963).

18. Coffman v. Kuehler, 409 F. Supp. 546 (N.D. Tex. 1976).

19. *Roy, supra* note 7. In 1988 the Eighth Circuit also upheld the use of a paddle which resulted in hurt feelings and minor discomfort to the child. Wise v. Pea Ridge Sch. Dist., 855 F.2d 560 (8th Cir. 1988).

20. People v. DeCaro, 17 Ill. App. 3d 553, 308 N.E.2d 196 (1974).

21. *Ball, supra* note 13.

22. *Tinkham, supra* note 16.

23. *Landi, supra* note 15.

Through the years courts have upheld corporal punishment as a legitimate means of disciplining students. That position has not changed in recent years.[24] Attempts to give constitutional protection to students against its use have failed. Students do, however, have recourse against its excessive use, and those avenues have always been available. Otherwise, the *in loco parentis* doctrine still applies with respect to the use of corporal punishment. More states now disapprove of the use of corporal punishment.

§ 10.2. Sanctions.

Like corporal punishment, a sanction is an administrative device used to punish students for unacceptable behavior and to try to effect compliance with school rules. It is designed to deny a student a privilege or to take from an individual what he has otherwise earned. It may take such forms as declaring one ineligible to participate in an activity, retaining one after school hours, assigning one special duties, being denied special privileges — all for the purpose of changing a student's behavior. Although there are unofficial reports of its use in a number of schools, there are very few cases that have been litigated in the courts. These cases have in-

---

24. In the 1970s the courts have upheld and protected teachers and administrators in the use of corporal punishment in the following cases: Ware v. Estes, 458 F.2d 1360 (5th Cir. 1972); Sims v. Board of Educ., 329 F. Supp. 678 (D.N.M. 1971); Gonyaw v. Gray, 361 F. Supp. 366 (D. Vt. 1973); People v. DeCaro, 17 Ill. App. 3d 553, 308 N.E.2d 196 (1974); Gordon v. Oak Park Sch. Dist. No. 97, 24 Ill. App. 3d 131, 320 N.E.2d 389 (1974); Roy v. Continental Ins. Co., 313 So. 2d 349 (La. App. 1975); Baker v. Owen, 395 F. Supp. 294 (M.D.N.C.), *aff'd mem.*, 423 U.S. 907 (1975); Coffman v. Kuehler, 409 F. Supp. 546 (N.D. Tex. 1976); Sims v. Waln, 536 F.2d 686 (6th Cir. 1976); Jones v. Parmer, 421 F. Supp. 738 (S.D. Ala. 1976); Ingraham v. Wright, 430 U.S. 651, 97 S. Ct. 1401, 51 L. Ed. 2d 711 (1977). During the same time the courts have not upheld teachers and administrators in their use of corporal punishment in the following cases: Johnson v. Horace Mann Mut. Ins. Co., 241 So. 2d 588 (La. 1970); Nelson v. Heyne, 491 F.2d 352 (7th Cir. 1974); Bramlet v. Wilson, 495 F.2d 714 (8th Cir. 1974); People v. Ball, 58 Ill. 2d 36, 317 N.E.2d 54 (1974); Hogenson v. Williams, 542 S.W.2d 456 (Tex. App. 1976); Board of Educ. v. Shank, 542 S.W.2d 779 (Mo. 1976).

volved denying a person the right to participate in graduation exercises and lowering a student's grade. For the most part, school officials have not been upheld in applying such sanctions. A major justification is that what a student has already earned, he is entitled to.

The earliest case involved three girls who refused to wear graduation caps and gowns because of their alleged odors.[25] The girls were punished by not being allowed to participate in graduation exercises and their diplomas were withheld. The court ruled that the students could be prohibited from participating in graduation exercises, but the diplomas could not be withheld since all requirements for graduation had been completed.

In a 1971 case involving graduation, a New York court ruled that a girl should be allowed to participate in graduation exercises[26] when she had been excluded for having allegedly assaulted the principal. The court viewed the punishment as unrelated to the offense and not suited for attaining desirable educational results of the school system.

Several cases, primarily in the 1970s, have treated the subject of lowering grades as a sanction. Since there are limited decisions, one is cautioned against making global conclusions; however, they do support the general proposition that what one has earned academically should not be taken from him if the offense was unrelated to the grade earned. The courts in Illinois are not in agreement on this issue. A 1976 decision upheld a school board policy that provided for the reduction of a student's grades as punishment for unexcused absences.[27] The specific penalty involved a drop of

---

25. Valentine v. Independent Sch. Dist., 191 Iowa 1100, 183 N.W. 434 (1921).

26. Ladson v. Board of Educ., 323 N.Y.S.2d 545 (N.Y. 1971).

27. Knight v. Board of Educ., 38 Ill. App. 3d 603, 348 N.E.2d 299 (1976). Smith v. School City of Hobart, 811 F. Supp. 391 (N.D. Ind. 1993), offers an excellent example of a case where a student's grades were reduced, as a disciplinary measure, for alcohol-related misconduct. The federal district court invalidated, as a violation of substantive due process, a rule that provided for a 4% reduction in grades for each day that a student was suspended.

one letter grade for each class missed. The court reasoned that the sanction was helpful in discouraging truancy, which is itself an indication of a lack of effort. Conversely, good grades are dependent on effort, including class attendance.

Two years later an Illinois court reasoned differently when it invalidated a school board policy that automatically lowered a student's grades for unexcused absences. The court saw that the school board could enact a policy for treating disciplinary infractions, but it lacked the power to employ academic sanctions for student misbehavior.[28]

A Kentucky court decision is in agreement with the second opinion above. The case grew out of a policy providing for a five-point reduction of a grade for each unexcused absence during a nine-month period. In declaring the regulation invalid, the court held that the school was justified in suspending the student but not in lowering the grade.[29] The court refused to decide the constitutionality of such a rule, but it held that the board was without power to authorize the punishment since it was not provided for in the statutes governing student conduct.

A different issue concerned a student who wore a black armband to graduation exercises. A letter of recommendation to a college contained that information, and the student sought to have it omitted from his permanent record. The court allowed the information to stay, for the data had been recorded objectively and no punitive intent could be ascertained from the school having recorded it.[30]

---

28. Hamer v. Board of Educ., Twp. High Sch. Dist. No. 113, 383 N.E.2d 231 (Ill. App. 1978).

29. Dorsey v. Bale, 521 S.W.2d 76 (Ky. App. 1975). *See also* T.H., Jr. v. Board of Trustees, 681 So. 2d 110 (Miss. 1996); Casey v. Northport Sch. Comm., 13 F. Supp. 2d 242 (D.R.I. 1998); Mazerski v. Horseheads Cent. Sch. Dist., 950 F. Supp. 69 (W.D.N.Y. 1997).

30. Einhorn v. Maus, 300 F. Supp. 1169 (E.D. Pa. 1969).

§ 10.3. Exclusion From School.

a. *Substantive Due Process.* Through the years courts have not interfered with the substantive right of school officials to exclude students. They have recognized the value of an education and of a child's remaining in school. This issue was addressed in the *Brown* decision of 1954 when the Supreme Court stated:

> Today, education is perhaps the most important function of state and local governments. Compulsory school attendance laws and the great expenditures for education both demonstrate our recognition of the importance of education to our democratic society. It is required in the performance of our most basic responsibilities, even service in the armed forces. It is the very foundation of good citizenship. Today it is a principal instrument in awakening the child to cultural values, in preparing him for later professional training, and in helping him adjust normally to his environment. In these days it is doubtful that any child may reasonably be expected to succeed in life if he is denied the opportunity of an education. Such an opportunity, where the state has undertaken to provide it, *is a right* which must be made available to all on equal terms. (Emphasis added.)[31]

The reference to education as being a "right" has not consistently been accepted by the Court. For instance, in the 1973 *Rodriquez* school finance decision, discussed in Chapter Six, the justices held that education is not a right under the federal Constitution that is explicitly or implicitly guaranteed to anyone. Two years later in *Goss v. Lopez*, discussed later in this section, the Court observed that education is neither a right nor a privilege, rather it is an entitlement. Further, in 1982 in ruling on the right of illegal alien

---

31. Brown v. Board of Educ., 347 U.S. 483, 493, 74 S. Ct. 686, 98 L. Ed. 873 (1954).

children to attend public schools, the Court held that these children had a right to attend public schools at state expense.[32]

In spite of a clear statement from the Supreme Court on whether education is a right, an entitlement, or a privilege, that Court, as well as lower courts, has recognized and accepted the necessity of suspending or expelling students for very serious misbehavior. The nature of the misbehavior warranting exclusion may vary, as is revealed in a study of a number of court decisions on this subject. The three cases that follow serve as examples.

Judicial thinking consistently holds that not all proscribed behavior has to be spelled out specifically in a student code before one can be punished. A student is entitled, however, to be informed about questionable or "gray areas" of conduct which may lead to exclusion. Such regulations as "flagrant disregard of teachers," "loitering in areas of heavy traffic," and "rowdy behavior in areas of heavy traffic" were specific enough to justify thirty-day suspensions, according to a federal district court in Pennsylvania.[33] The Supreme Court of Connecticut held that a state statute authorizing expulsion of students for "conduct inimical to the best interests of the school" was vague and unenforceable because no

---

32. Plyler v. Doe, 458 U.S. 1131, 102 S. Ct. 2382, 72 L. Ed. 2d 786 (1982).

33. Alex v. Allen, 409 F. Supp. 379 (W.D. Pa. 1976). In Nicholas B. v. School Comm. of Worcester, 587 N.E.2d 211 (Mass. 1992), the court upheld the expulsion of a student for the remainder of the school year for an assault occurring away from school. The fight had started at school, prompting the conclusion of a clear link to the need for control of student behavior. Similarly, a Delaware student was expelled for selling cocaine to an undercover policeman. The transaction had not occurred at school, but the court concluded that there was cause for concern in having a known drug dealer among the student body. Howard v. Colonial Sch. Dist., 605 A.2d 590 (Del. Super. Ct. 1992). A New York court upheld a three-day suspension of a student for having stolen muffins from a school cafeteria but ruled that removing the child from the wrestling team was excessive. Manico v. South Colonie Cent. Sch. Dist., 584 N.Y.S.2d 519 (Sup. Ct. 1992). In the late 1990s the courts still uphold school officials in their suspension of students for behavior at school activities held after school and away from school. *See* Pirschel v. Sorrell, 2 F. Supp. 2d 930 (E.D. Ky. 1998), in which a student was seen disposing of beer in a parking lot where his school was involved in a basketball tournament.

standards had been set for implementing it.[34] The permanent expulsion of two girls who deliberately planned and attacked a fellow pupil was upheld. The victim was kicked, beaten, and stabbed in the head with scissors.[35]

Often accompanying the exclusion of a student is the obligation of the school district to provide him with the opportunity for alternative instruction if the child and his parent cannot afford to pay the costs themselves. This position was underscored by the Fifth Circuit in 1974:

> In our increasingly technological society getting at least a high school education is almost necessary for survival. Stripping a child of access to educational opportunity is a life sentence to second class citizenship unless the child has the financial ability to migrate to another school system or enter private school.[36]

b. *Procedural Due Process.* Courts have been more active with respect to the procedural rights of students who are to be excluded from school rather than with the authority of the school to exclude them. Although some states have had statutes on their books for many years that guaranteed to students certain elements of procedural due process, the matter was not seriously challenged in courts until the 1960s. *Dixon v. Alabama State Board of Education,* the precedent-making decision, involved a case in higher education where students were expelled or placed on probation for a sit-in at a lunch counter.[37] The students were disciplined without

---

34. Mitchell v. King, 363 A.2d 68 (Conn. 1975). Kulbany v. School Bd. of Pinellas Cty., 839 F. Supp. 1544 (M.D. Fla. 1993), demonstrates the authority of school officials to enforce school discipline against a student who was suspended from school for consuming an alcoholic beverage, off school grounds, and prior to attending a high school football game. For another decision regarding a school district's policy on possession or consumption of alcohol, drugs, or other such substances, see Martinez v. School Dist. No. 60, 852 P.2d 1275 (Colo. App. 1992).

35. Fortnam v. Texarkana Sch. Dist., 514 S.W.2d 720 (Ark. 1974).

36. Lee v. Macon Cty. Bd. of Educ., 490 F.2d 458, 460 (5th Cir. 1974).

37. 294 F.2d 150 (5th Cir.), *cert. denied,* 368 U.S. 930 (1961).

any notice of charges, nor were they granted a hearing. This case established the right of students in a public institution of higher education to notice and a hearing prior to suspension or expulsion, a right protected by the due process clause of the fourteenth amendment. Specifically, a student was entitled to (1) the names of witnesses against him, (2) an oral or written report on the facts to which each witness testified, (3) an opportunity to present his defense to the charges against him, and (4) an opportunity to produce oral or written testimony of witnesses in his behalf.

The question of the applicability of *Dixon* to the elementary and secondary school setting was not answered for several years. In the meantime, the Supreme Court of the United States ruled on the procedural due process rights of young people with respect to juvenile court proceedings. That landmark 1967 case, *In re Gault*, established the right of young people to due process rights under the fourteenth amendment prior to being committed to a juvenile home.[38] The case began with a complaint by a neighbor that Gerald Gault, age fifteen, had made an obscene telephone call to her. Based on that complaint, Gerald was arrested. What followed was a series of steps that the Supreme Court found not to be consistent with the fourteenth amendment. No notice was left for Gerald's parents, who were at work and later learned from a neighbor where he was. At the juvenile detention home where Gerald was detained, his parents were informed of a hearing to be held the following day. The arresting officer filed a petition with the court; the parents saw it after two months had elapsed.

At the initial hearing, the complainant was not present, no one was sworn, no transcript was made, and the only testimony given was by the presiding judge. At the formal hearing approximately one week later, the parents asked that the complainant be present, but the request was denied. A conflict developed over who said what. Nonetheless, the judge found Gerald guilty based on his using vulgar, obscene language and for being habitually involved

---

38. 387 U.S. 1, 87 S. Ct. 1428, 18 L. Ed. 2d 527 (1967).

357

in immoral matters. The latter finding grew out of Gerald's being, at the time, on six months' probation for stealing.

The Supreme Court of the United States decided the case in 1967. It held that a minor in juvenile court was entitled to the following constitutional protection: (1) specific notice of charges against him with time to prepare for a hearing, (2) notification of the right to counsel or, if counsel cannot be afforded, the right to court-appointed counsel, (3) privilege against self-incrimination, and (4) right to confrontation and cross-examination of witnesses. The Court expressed concern for, but did not rule specifically on, the constitutional right of appellate review and a transcript of the proceedings.

Gault did not apply specifically to school exclusions, but a number of lower courts began to clarify the procedural due process rights of students in exclusionary hearings. That matter was treated specifically by the Supreme Court in 1975 in *Goss v. Lopez.*[39] *Goss* involved the suspension of nine students at several schools in Columbus, Ohio, for a variety of reasons. Under Ohio law, a principal was empowered to suspend a pupil for up to ten days. He was required to notify the student's parents within twenty-four hours and state the reasons for the suspension. If a pupil or a parent appealed to the board of education, a hearing for the student was then required.

Some of the students denied the misconduct, and the matter was eventually appealed to the Supreme Court. The Court held that in suspensions of less than ten days a student must be given at least informal notice of the charges against him and the opportunity for some sort of hearing. If he denies the charges, he must be informed of the evidence against him and be given the opportunity to present his side of the story.

The Court did not extend all the standards of *Gault* to a public school exclusion hearing. It held that a school does not have to allow a student to be represented by counsel, to have witnesses, or to confront and cross-examine witnesses against him.

---

39. 419 U.S. 565, 95 S. Ct. 729, 42 L. Ed. 2d 725 (1975).

The Court ruled that a student has an entitlement to a public education, a property right protected by the fourteenth amendment. That right can be taken away only by adhering to minimum procedural standards. In school suspensions, due process is flexible and is to be determined by the nature of the misconduct and the severity of the penalty. The more serious the misconduct and the stricter the penalty, the greater adherence to procedural due process is required. The Court held that school officials may remove a student from school prior to a suspension if his presence is a danger to persons or property or is disruptive to teaching and learning. The Court did not rule on the elements of due process for suspensions of longer than ten days but observed that more may be needed for students.

One month after *Goss,* the Supreme Court handed down another decision that also had some bearing on due process.[40] The case involved the issue of a student's being allowed to sue school board members for damages for a denial of constitutional rights. In this case, the right denied was procedural due process in an expulsion hearing. The Court held that individual school board members could be sued when they denied to students their constitutional rights. On remand to a lower court for a determination of whether due process had been followed in informing students and parents about a hearing, the Eighth Circuit held that the inadequate notice was a violation of procedural due process.[41]

A 1978 decision by the Supreme Court clarified further the above decision. The Court held that, where students have been suspended from school without procedural due process, the students, if not injured, are entitled to recover nominal damages, which the Court set as being $1.00.[42]

That decision grew out of two cases that arose over the suspension of a pupil for allegedly violating a school rule against use of drugs and of another pupil for violation of a rule against males

---

40. Wood v. Strickland, 420 U.S. 308, 95 S. Ct. 992, 43 L. Ed. 2d 214 (1975).
41. Strickland v. Inlow, 519 F.2d 744 (8th Cir. 1975).
42. Carey v. Piphus, 435 U.S. 247, 98 S. Ct. 1042, 55 L. Ed. 2d 252 (1978).

wearing earrings. The two cases were consolidated before the
Supreme Court. The Court ruled that before damages are awarded,
one must first submit proof that actual injury was caused by a
denial of procedural due process.

Another ruling by the Supreme Court in 1978 clarified the rights
of students in exclusion hearings. This case, involving higher education, reaffirmed that academic discipline is the province of
scholars, not courts.[43] A student dropped from a medical program
for lack of progress in the clinical work was not entitled to due
process protection granted to students in exclusions for behavior
reasons. The Court recognized that the breaking of school rules
was not an issue; rather, the discipline hinged on the perceptions of
the student's supervisors about her progress in the program. Their
judgment was sufficient to support a cause for removal.

The Supreme Court has handed down several decisions as to
what constitutes minimal due process for students. It has required
some schools to afford students more rights than they had and to
require some schools to do less than they were then doing. Beyond
the Supreme Court guides, a local administrator is bound also by
state law. Thus, requirements may be compatible with the fourteenth amendment and still vary from state to state. They may also
vary depending on the circumstances of a given situation. Given
those conditions, the following standards generally apply.[44]

1. *Notice of Charges.* It is accepted now that, before a student can be excluded from school, he must first be given notice of
the charges against him. The notice may be oral if there is no
question or disagreement about the student clearly having been
engaged in the misconduct. For the most part, written notice is

---

43. Board of Curators of Univ. of Mo. v. Horowitz, 435 U.S. 78, 98 S. Ct. 256,
54 L. Ed. 2d 171 (1978). For a discussion of the case, see Thomas J. Flygare, *The
Horowitz Case: No Hearing Required for Academic Dismissals,* 626-27 Phi
Delta Kappan 59 (May, 1978).

44. For a more thorough treatment of the elements of procedural due process,
see Robert E. Phay, The Law of Procedure in Student Suspensions and
Expulsions (Topeka: National Organization on Legal Problems of Education,
1977).

preferred and should state the specific charges against the student, the school policy or rule that was broken, and the date, time, and place of the hearing. The student should be advised of his rights in the hearing, although a Miranda[45] warning need not apply. He should also be advised that he can waive a hearing and have an informal conference with the principal for a disposition of the matter. Although it is not formally required, a copy of the notice should be given to both the student and his parents. Specific state statutes or local board policies may require procedures with respect to the content and delivery of the notice.

2. *Right to a Hearing.* Courts have consistently ruled that a court-like atmosphere does not have to govern a disciplinary hearing.[46] A school disciplinary hearing is an administrative hearing, not a trial. Thus, it may be conducted with a degree of informality. It must be conducted, however, with fairness. At a minimum, this requires that a student be given the opportunity to present his case, after he has had sufficient time to prepare for it. Although courts have not spelled out what constitutes sufficient time, presumably from one to five days is adequate. The difference in time would depend on the complexity and severity of the incident.

Most hearings might be held in the principal's office with the student, his parents, and witnesses present.

3. *Right to Counsel.* Courts are divided on the question as to whether a student can have counsel. It is understood that parents may be present to advise their child; it is less clear that legal counsel are entitled to represent him. Some courts have ruled that an attorney may be present, but he may not engage in an adversarial relationship; that is, he may be available to counsel his client but not cross-examine or refute testimony.

---

45. Miranda v. Arizona, 384 U.S. 436, 86 S. Ct. 1602, 16 L. Ed. 2d 694 (1966). In this case the Court held that, at the time of his arrest, a suspect was entitled to be informed of his constitutional right to remain silent and to have legal counsel.

46. Madera v. Board of Educ., 267 F. Supp. 356 (S.D.N.Y.), *rev'd on other grounds,* 386 F.2d 778 (2d Cir.), *cert. denied,* 390 U.S. 1028 (1967).

There is some legal weight that in an expulsion hearing in which the school board attorney plays a prominent role, a student should also be entitled to have an attorney represent him.

4. *Weight of Evidence.* Again, the formal rules of evidence that govern a court trial do not apply in an exclusion hearing.[47] Prior to suspension of a student, the student should have the opportunity to examine the evidence against him, question the individual conducting the hearing, and refute testimony of witnesses. Only when it is ascertained that the charges can be supported by substantial evidence or guilt beyond a reasonable doubt, should one be declared guilty of the charges.[48] That standard eliminates a lesser one of changes to be supported by circumstantial evidence or a preponderance of the evidence. It also implies that an administrator may no longer take as accepted or unquestioned fact the statement of a person reporting a student for violation of school rules, if the student denies it.

5. *Call of Witnesses.* Court decisions are not in full agreement with respect to the right of a student to confront, cross-examine, and compel witnesses to appear. In some states, school

---

47. Boykins v. Fairfield Bd. of Educ., 492 F.2d 697 (5th Cir. 1974), *cert. denied,* 420 U.S. 962 (1975). *See also In re* Stratton, 526 N.E.2d 201 (Ill. App. 1988). In this case the expulsion of a student was overturned because of inadequate notice. The student's attorney was given notice of charges against the student the night of the hearing. The notice did not contain any specific charges. The school board refused a continuation of the hearing. Such notice was deemed inadequate, for the student lacked adequate time to prepare for the hearing. The weight-of-evidence standard does not give a school board the right to introduce new evidence in deliberations involving a student's expulsion. In another case, a student had been expelled for drug possession. Following the hearing and in closed session the superintendent of schools advised the board that a drug counselor had told him the student had confessed guilt to her. Based on that added information, the school board expelled the student for the remainder of the semester. Newsome v. Batavia Local Sch. Dist., 842 F.2d 920 (6th Cir. 1988). In 1999, the Fifth Circuit Court warned that a school administrator speaking with a student's parent will not in every case create a "meaningful opportunity" for a student to tell his/her side of the story. Meyer v. Austin I.S.D., 167 F.3d 887 (5th Cir. 1999).

48. *In re* Winship, 397 U.S. 358, 90 S. Ct. 1068, 25 L. Ed. 2d 268 (1970).

boards have subpoena power while it is lacking in others. A number of recent court decisions have held that confronting and cross-examining witnesses is fundamental to due process.[49]

6. *Privilege Against Self-Incrimination.* The fifth amendment protection against self-incrimination does not apply to school disciplinary proceedings; it applies only to criminal proceedings. The testimony given by a student in a school disciplinary hearing can later be used in a criminal proceeding, although a student may then object to the use of statements made at the school hearing.

Courts have also held that disciplining a student for breaking a school rule by school officials and trying that individual for the same offense in a court case does not constitute double jeopardy, a concept which applies only to criminal proceedings.[50]

7. *Right to a Transcript.* Courts are not in agreement as to whether a student, as a matter of right, is entitled to a transcript of the proceedings.[51] It would seem proper to supply him with one, the cost to be borne by him.

8. *Right to Appeal.* A number of states provide some mechanism for a student to appeal an adverse exclusionary decision. Typically, it may go through the Department of Education or directly into the courts. Increasingly, students have resorted to federal rather than state courts and sought an exclusionary reversal on the basis of a denial of due process under the fourteenth amendment.

Procedural due process rights accorded students in school disciplinary hearings have undergone clarification. This clarification has resulted essentially in placing restrictions on administrative and school board authority before a student can be suspended or expelled. Unquestionably, students have due process rights, and the nature and extent of these rights vary with the circumstances. The key elements that have guided judicial decision-making have

---

49. Givens v. Poe, 346 F. Supp. 202 (W.D.N.C. 1972); Smith v. Miller, 514 P.2d 377 (Kan. 1973).

50. State *ex rel.* Fleetwood v. Board of Educ., 252 N.E.2d 318 (Ohio 1969).

51. Buttny v. Smiley, 281 F. Supp. 280 (D. Colo. 1968); Pierce v. School Comm., 322 F. Supp. 957 (D. Mass. 1971).

been fairness and reasonableness. Where both have been applied, school officials have usually been upheld. Where they have not been applied, students have usually won.

§ 10.4. Search and Seizure.

a. *The Constitutional Issue.* Beginning in the 1970s one of the areas involving the control of student behavior has been the matter of search and seizure. School administrators have been called upon to search students and their property, principally for harboring or dealing in drugs. These searches have prompted the question of the applicability of the fourth amendment to the United States Constitution to the school setting. That amendment provides:

> The right of the people to be secure in their persons, houses, papers, and effects, against unreasonable searches and seizures, shall not be violated, and no Warrants shall issue, but upon probable cause, supported by Oath or affirmation, and particularly describing the place to be searched, and the persons or things to be seized.

The amendment does not define what constitutes a legal search, nor does it specify what constitutes an unreasonable one. Consequently, the courts have been asked to clarify these two questions. The amendment guarantees to citizens the right to be secure against governmental intrusion with respect to their property and possessions. A citizen is protected to the extent that limitations are placed upon government in order to insure unwarranted intrusion by it into a person's property and possessions. This restriction does not insulate a citizen from any and all searches; rather he is protected only from unreasonable searches and seizures. The amendment at least requires that three elements be present in order for a search to be legal: the issuance of a warrant based upon probable cause, an oath supporting the necessity of the search, and specific identification of the elements to be searched.

Initially, the fourth amendment restricted the federal government only. It was not until 1949 that it was made applicable to the states through the incorporation, by implication, of the fourth amendment, into the fourteenth.[52]

The fourth amendment applies specifically to law enforcement officials and criminal cases. Less vigorous and exacting standards apply to school officials when they engage in a search. In order for a search to be legal, it must be directed toward maintaining a climate in which the school can function as an educational institution. Unquestionably, a school official may search a school in the normal course of his duty, such as insuring the safety of the building from fire hazards and in insuring that the premises are free of unsanitary conditions and hazardous materials.

A more serious question arises with respect to the application of the fourth amendment to a school official's search of a student, his possessions, and areas normally under his personal control. To date, most courts have distinguished between the rigid standards governing search by law enforcement officials and the standards governing search by school officials. This distinction has been enunciated in clarifying school disciplinary proceedings and criminal indictments. That is, a penalty exacted by a school administrator is less severe than that handed down by a court; consequently an educator is not subject to all the standards of justice that courts must observe.

One of the reasons for the lack of understanding of the fourth amendment and its application to juveniles has stemmed from the actual role of an administrator in a search. That issue was resolved, in large measure, in *New Jersey v. T.L.O.,*[53] a major decision by the Supreme Court of the United States in 1985. In that case the justices ruled, in the first instance, that school personnel are subject to the fourth amendment's ban on unreasonable searches and seizures. Having decided that, the justices then ruled that school personnel are bound by exceptions to the amendment's requirements. Thus, in undertaking a search, school officials are subject

---

52. Wolf v. Colorado, 338 U.S. 25, 69 S. Ct. 1359, 93 L. Ed. 1782 (1949).
53. 469 U.S. 325 (1985).

to a standard of "reasonable cause" rather than "probable cause." Further, they are not required to have a warrant.

"Reasonable cause" does not appear in the fourth amendment. The Court used this less rigid standard in recognition that the school's interest in preserving order outweighs a student's expectations of privacy and personal security. The necessity for maintenance of discipline requires some flexibility, thus the use of the less exacting standard of "reasonable cause."

The Supreme Court acknowledged that students have an expectation of privacy, even at school. However, this expectation must be balanced against an administrative need for maintaining discipline. Whether a search is legal depends on its reasonableness under all circumstances of the search. Reasonableness is determined by two considerations. First, is the action justified at its inception? It is justified when there are reasonable grounds to suspect that the search will turn up evidence that the student is in violation of the law or of school rules. Second, is the search reasonably related to the circumstances which justified an intrusion on the student's privacy? This consideration is met when the search process is reasonably related to the objectives of the search and is not excessively intrusive in terms of the student's age, sex, and the nature of the infraction.

T.L.O. dealt with a restricted area of search, that of a student's purse. It did not involve, and the Supreme Court did not treat, such issues as the search of a student's person, locker, or desk. Also, it did not treat the question of admissibility of illegally obtained evidence in court by school officials.

Lower courts have consistently followed the *T.L.O.* decision. The same year that *T.L.O.* was handed down, a California court relied on it in upholding the search of a student.[54] Reasonable cause existed when the student was in a restroom without a pass and was acting suspiciously. Reasonable cause also existed for the search of a student's locker when the student had earlier been seen in the principal's office where a clock was later reported as being

---

54. *In re* Bobby B., 281 Cal. Rptr. 253 (1985).

missing. The student had also been seen with a pot of honey reported as missing from the school's home economics department.[55] Reasonable cause did not exist for the search of a student simply because that person possessed a package of cigarettes. That fact did not lead one to the conclusion that the student would also possess marijuana.[56] Reasonable cause did not exist for the search of a student who was tardy or truant.[57] Search of a student's car was reasonable, even though evidence produced cocaine rather than alcohol, the initial reason for the search.[58]

As a non-law enforcement official and, arguably, a private individual acting *in loco parentis*, a school official has considerable autonomy in conducting searches and seizures. In doing this, it is expected that he exercise initiative and reasonable judgment in determining if a student is harboring illegal or unsafe materials, has broken a school rule, or is creating problems inimical to the safety and welfare of others. When there has been reasonable cause to believe that a student meets one of the above conditions, the administrator has been upheld in conducting a search; furthermore, he has been expected to do it as a duty. The legal question has centered around the circumstances under which the search was conducted and the admissibility of evidence growing out of the search.

---

55. R.D.L. v. State, 499 So. 2d 31 (Fla. 1986). In *In re* Ronnie H., 603 N.Y.S.2d 579 (App. Div. 2d Dep't 1993), an assistant principal's complying with a student's request to return to him the contents of a pocket in a jacket that did not belong to that student, but one that he was wearing at the time and in which the assistant principal found drugs, was not considered a search and was considered reasonable by the court. To the court, the assistant principal had cause to suspect a violation of school policy and rules regarding illegal substances.

56. In Interest of Dumas, 515 A.2d 984 (Pa. 1986). In contrast, see State v. Harris, 623 N.E.2d 1240 (Ohio App. 8th Dist. 1993), which involved the prosecution and ultimate conviction of an individual for possession and sale of cocaine within 1,000 feet of a school, even though that person did not know, at the time of the transaction, that she was near a school.

57. *In re* William G., 709 P.2d 1287 (Cal. 1987).

58. Johnson v. State, 762 P.2d 493 (Alaska App. 1988).

In some court decisions a school administrator has been held not to be acting *in loco parentis* when engaging in a search. Several conditions have prompted such rulings. One is when a school official searches a student, finds narcotics, and turns the evidence as well as the student over to police for prosecution rather than limit disciplinary action to school-imposed sanctions. A second condition is when a search goes beyond what is deemed to be reasonable. This has generally been true when school officials require that students undress or when searches are made of a student's personal effects, such as a wallet or a purse, without the student's presence. A third condition is when a school official lacks reasonable suspicion for engaging in a search in the first place. It is then that the *in loco parentis* doctrine does not fully support an administrative search.

When school officials engage in searches, they have been challenged most often on two matters. One involves the circumstances under which the search was conducted; the other involves the admissibility of evidence growing out of the search.

b. *Consent to Search.* In a number of instances school officials have searched students, their possessions, and areas normally under their personal control with or without the student's consent. In some cases a search has been made without the student's knowledge. When consent has been freely and knowingly given, one cannot later challenge the evidence seized in the search.[59]

When consent has not been given, courts have had to determine if the search was valid. Two cases are illustrative. A California court held that a search without consent was legal,[60] asserting that a greater interest accrued to society by protecting itself from drug users and possessors than in upholding an individual's rights. In this case, the vice-principal conducted a search of a student's locker after he received information that one could purchase

---

59. *In re* State in Interest of G.C., 121 N.J. Super. 108, 296 A.2d 102 (1972), citing State v. King, 44 N.J. 346, 209 A.2d 110 (1965); Schaffer v. State, 55 Del. 115, 184 A.2d 689 (Del. Super.), *cert. denied,* 374 U.S. 834 (1962); People v. Fahrner, 213 Cal. App. 2d 535, 28 Cal. Rptr. 926 (1963).

60. *In re* Donaldson, 269 Cal. App. 2d 509, 75 Cal. Rptr. 220 (1969).

Methedrine pills from her. The search was upheld on the grounds that the administrator was acting as a private individual, preserving order, and functioning *in loco parentis.*

The other case involved the search of a student's person.[61] After receiving information that the boy had marijuana, the principal summoned the student to the office and directed that his pockets be emptied. At first the student refused but later complied. The court held that the principal's conduct was necessary and proper in maintaining order and discipline.

To date, courts have not required that, in the search of lockers, students must first give consent. In the search of a student's person, administrators have usually refrained from actually coming into physical contact with the individual but instead have directed that he empty his pockets or other effects. That strategy, in effect, when complied with by the student, constitutes student consent.

c. *Reasonable Cause.* A reasonable school search is one conducted by a superior charged with the responsibility for maintaining discipline and order and security. A student's rights must yield when there is danger of the institution's being undermined as an educational enterprise. When there is a reasonable belief that a student has narcotics in his possession, this constitutes reasonable cause for a search.

In determining whether or not a particular search is reasonable when conducted by school officials, one must consider two factors: the nature of the place to be searched and the purpose for which the search is conducted.

1. *The Nature of the Place.* School property is state property whose title rests with the local board of education. Although schools often supply lockers to students, the state retains control of them. One reasonable stipulation restricting the use of a locker is that it must not contain anything in violation of law. "Not only have the school authorities a right to inspect, but *this right be-*

61. M. by Parents R. and S. v. Board of Educ., 429 F. Supp. 288 (S.D. Ill. 1977).

comes a duty when suspicion arises that something of an illegal nature may be secreted there."[62]

In *State v. Stein,* the court differentiated between school property and other kinds of property. A school locker is not like a house, a car, or a private locker which connote private possession. A student may have exclusive control of his locker as opposed to fellow students, but that possession is not exclusive against the school and its officials.[63]

A different kind of possession relates to the search of an individual and his own property, but that fact has not altered the holdings of the courts concerning a school official's search. In two cases the courts extended the same reasoning applied to locker searches to searches of automobiles. In *Keene v. Rodgers,* the question first arose as to the legality of the search of a student's automobile on campus.[64] The car was draped with flags, and desecration was suspected. On orders from their superordinates, two campus officers searched the vehicle. The owner assisted by unlocking the car without protest. Inside were found frayed flags, a can of beer, and a bag of marijuana, all in violation of the school's code of behavior. The search was deemed to be proper, and this decision extended the jurisdiction of an administrative search from school-owned property to student-owned property on campus.

This principle extends, for the most part, to the search of a student's person. In large measure this has amounted to a student searching himself. When this issue is examined in more detail later in this chapter, some exceptions will be noted.

2. The Purpose of the Search. A principal is responsible for the safety and welfare of students in his school. He is expected to protect a student from harm to himself as well as to the greater school population. Whenever an administrator has reasonable

---

62. People v. Overton, 301 N.Y.S.2d 479, 249 N.E.2d 366, 367 (1969).

63. State v. Stein, 203 Kan. 638, 456 P.2d 1 (1969), *cert. denied,* 397 U.S. 947 (1970).

64. Keene v. Rodgers, 316 F. Supp. 217 (D. Me. 1970). *See also* Speake v. Grantham, 317 F. Supp. 1253 (S.D. Miss. 1970).

suspicion that a student may be harboring something illegal or harmful, he has the authority to make a search.

A search conducted by a principal is not without limits. There must be reasonable suspicion to believe that a student is in possession of something illegal or harmful. This standard will not uphold an administrator engaging in a "fishing expedition" or conducting a search without good reason. When he is acting within the scope of his authority and with good cause, a school administrator does not have to have his search measured legally against that of a police officer.

The standard governing the source of information leading to a search is not as rigid as that which applies to information given a policeman. The source of information need not be corroborated for purposes of reliability.[65]

Reasonable suspicion exists when one has knowledge of or information about the existence of illegal or dangerous materials on campus. For example, the following set of facts gave an administrator sufficient cause to search a student: (1) He had information that the student had sold drugs on campus earlier in the day. (2) He had observed bulges in the student's pockets. (3) He had observed a pouch tied to the student's belt. (4) The student had shown the contents of the pouch (money) but not the contents of his pockets. The student initially resisted a search of his pockets, and all these circumstances provided sufficient cause for the search.[66] Reasonable cause existed when a student, caught smoking, was ordered to empty his pockets, which held marijuana.[67]

---

65. *In re* C., 26 Cal. App. 3d 403, 102 Cal. Rptr. 682 (1972); People v. Young, 12 Cal. App. 3d 878, 90 Cal. Rptr. 924 (1970). School systems do not have to reveal the names of student informants in search and seizure. *See, e.g.,* Commonwealth v. Snyder, 597 N.E.2d 1363 (Mass. 1992). *See also* State v. Moore, 603 A.2d 513 (N.J. Super. Ct. 1992).

66. *In re* C., *supra* note 65. School officials are protected in engaging in searches for items that look like dangerous weapons or illegal materials, even if later it is determined that the materials are not dangerous or illegal. *See, e.g.,* Breeding v. Driscollett, 82 F.3d 383 (11th Cir. 1996).

67. Nelson v. State, 319 So. 2d 154 (Fla. App. 1975). In a 1997 case involving a medical search of a student suspected of having used drugs, reasonable cause

In contrast, a New York court agreed that school officials lacked sufficient reason for engaging in a particular search.[68] A teacher had observed a teen-age boy entering a restroom twice within an hour and leaving each time within five to ten seconds. The student had been under observation for six months for possibly dealing in drugs. During this time he had also been seen eating with a student, also under suspicion. In the judgment of the teacher, these circumstances constituted unusual behavior. The teacher then reported the matter to a second teacher, the coordinator of security. The coordinator then reported the matter to the principal, who ordered that the boy be brought to the office. Before the boys' dean and the principal, the security officer searched the boy. After finding thirteen glassine envelopes in the boy's wallet, the coordinator then had the boy stripped. A vial containing nine pills was uncovered.

While recognizing that school authorities have broad authority in maintaining discipline, the court resolved the immediate issue by weighing the interest of society against the individual's rights. In this case, the individual's rights were deemed to be paramount. Reasonable cause did not exist. The limited information had failed to make a sufficient case for the search. The court also deplored the indignity done the student by forcing him to strip by pointing

---

was found to exist. The search involved a nurse taking the student's blood pressure and pulse based on the child's erratic behavior. Bridgman v. New Trier High Sch. Dist. No. 203, 128 F.3d 1146 (7th Cir. 1997). The District Court of Rhode Island upheld a pat-down search of all students in the cafeteria in an attempt to locate a knife used for slicing pizza. The knife was not found during the search but was later seen in a dumpster behind the school. The court ruled that the search was minimally intrusive in that the pat-down involved only the areas about the ankle and the students' pockets and no items were removed from the students. Brousseau v. Westerly, 11 F. Supp. 2d 177 (D.R.I. 1998). *See also* Des Roches v. Caprio, 156 F.3d 571 (4th Cir. 1998); Smith v. McGlothin, 119 F.3d 788 (9th Cir. 1997); and Thompson v. Carthage, 87 F.3d 979 (8th Cir. 1996), all involving a mass search of students, the intrusiveness of the search, and the element of individualized suspicion.

68. People v. D., 34 N.Y.2d 483, 315 N.E.2d 466 (1974).

out the possible psychological damage that can be done to a sensitive young person.

Teachers of a fifth grade class went too far in conducting a strip search for $3.00 reportedly stolen from another student. The court held that the search was unreasonable in subjecting all students to it.[69]

d. *Administrative Versus Police Searches.* For a number of decades courts have differentiated between searches by private individuals and those by governmental officials. The Supreme Court ruled more than seven decades ago that the fourth amendment was designed to restrain governmental authority and no one else.[70] Searches by governmental officials must comply with considerably stricter standards than those done by persons not acting in a governmental capacity. The general rule has been that evidence obtained in an illegal search and seizure by a private individual is admissible in a criminal proceeding. In marked contrast, evidence taken in an illegal search by law enforcement officials is inadmissible.

Courts have looked to the initiator of the search in determining the degree to which one is bound by the fourth amendment. It has been established that school administrators do not need a warrant when acting *in loco parentis*. When they initiate a search but later call on a policeman for assistance, the policeman does not need a warrant. However, if the policeman initiates a search, he needs a warrant, even if school officials cooperate with him.

It has been held that where police or security officers are regularly assigned to a school, they are less subject to the requirements of the fourth amendment than are policemen not attached to the school. They are, however, not as free as school officials. This point was underscored in *Walters v. United States,* when the court held that the search authority of a school security officer was not

---

69. Bellnier v. Lund, 438 F. Supp. 47 (N.D.N.Y. 1977). *See also* Jenkins by Hall v. Talladega City Bd. of Educ., 95 F.3d 1036 (11th Cir. 1996).

70. Burdeau v. McDowell, 256 U.S. 465, 41 S. Ct. 574, 65 L. Ed. 1048 (1921).

as extensive, without a warrant, as that of a school administrator. It was also reaffirmed in *People v. Guillermo.* In this case the court upheld a security officer's search of a student carrying knives on his person. It recognized that such officers do not have power coextensive with those of police; rather, the power is supplementary to that of local law enforcement officials.[71]

As of this date the courts are not in full agreement as to when a school administrator is a governmental official for purposes of a search. The distinction is acute in terms of its application to the school setting, for it dictates the degree of autonomy that an administrator has under or outside the fourth amendment. Courts have tended to hold an administrator not acting as an agent of the state where there is clear justification (reasonable suspicion) for the search and when it operates within the bounds of necessity and propriety. On the other hand, when searches have been recklessly and carelessly undertaken and when the student and evidence have been turned over to police, a school administrator may be acting more nearly as an agent of the state.[72]

---

71. Waters v. United States, 311 A.2d 835 (D.C. 1973). People v. Guillermo, 181 Cal. Rptr. 856 (Cal. App. 1982). A security guard had reasonable cause for searching a student's book bag after hearing a dull thud when the bag hit a metal cabinet. In re Gregory, M., 587 N.Y.S.2d 731 (A.D. 1992). In another case out of New York, a security guard was upheld in conducting a search after having brushed up against a gun tucked in the student's waistband. In re Keving P., 587 N.Y.S.2d 730 (A.D. 1992). *See also* State *ex rel.* Juvenile Dep't of Wash. Cty. v. DuBois, 821 P.2d 1124 (Ore. App. 1991).

72. New Jersey v. T.L.O., 469 U.S. 325, 105 S. Ct. 733, 83 L. Ed. 2d 19 (1985). *See, e.g.,* People v. Stewart, 63 Misc. 2d 601, 313 N.Y.S.2d 253 (1970); Moore v. Student Affairs of Troy State Univ., 284 F. Supp. 725 (N.D. Ala. 1968); Piazzola v. Watkins, 316 F. Supp. 624 (M.D. Ala. 1970). Contrast with State v. Baccino, 282 A.2d 869 (Del. Super. 1971); People v. Jackson, 65 Misc. 2d 909, 319 N.Y.S.2d 731 (1971); State v. Young, 234 Ga. 488, 216 S.E.2d 568, *cert. denied,* 423 U.S. 1039 (1975). A Pennsylvania court upheld the search by an undercover police officer of a student seen holding a plastic bag in one hand and money in the other. The search uncovered thirty vials of narcotics. The court used the reasonableness test of T.L.O. rather than rely on the standard of probable cause. In re S.F., 607 A.2d 793 (Pa. Super. Ct. 1992).

e. *Searches Involving Dogs.* One of the legal questions involving searches of students has been the use of dogs. Animals especially trained in sniffing out drugs have been brought into schools for the purpose of alerting administrative personnel as to who has drugs or where the drugs are stored. This technique has raised questions of legality that have been examined in court decisions. The first case, out of the Seventh Circuit, involved several legal questions, one of them being the use of dogs in a school that had experienced problems with drugs. The school officials, in cooperation with police, secured the services of a private agency that used dogs specifically for detecting drugs. Several teams of searchers went through each room of the building where the dogs patrolled the aisles. If a dog alerted before a given student, that student was asked to remove all personal effects and to lay them on the desk. If the dog alerted a second time before that student, he was then searched by school officials. A thirteen-year-old girl was one of seventeen students so searched. Although she protested against the search and maintained that she did not have drugs nor had she used them, she was subjected to a strip search. No drugs were found.

The court held that the use of the dogs was legal and no fourth amendment rights had been violated. It was established that the work of the dogs was actually preliminary to the search itself. The court ruled further that the strip search violated the student's fourth amendment rights. The court characterized such a search as outrageous and rejected the notion that school personnel were subject to good-faith immunity for such actions.[73]

A federal district court out of Texas spoke more forcefully against the use of dog teams as drug sniffers. It held that such a practice violated a student's right of privacy because of the threatening physical presence of the animals.[74]

---

73. Doe v. Renfrow, 631 F.2d 91 (7th Cir. 1980).
74. Jones v. Latexo Indep. Sch. Dist., 499 F. Supp. 223 (E.D. Tex. 1980).

The Fifth Circuit, in 1982,[75] held that the use of dogs in sniff-searching students is unconstitutional. It ruled, however, that dogs searching automobiles and lockers is constitutional.[76]

f. *Illegal Searches*. In consistently upholding the searches that school administrators make, courts have clothed principals with considerable discretion. With very few exceptions, the courts have seen the officials as acting responsibly, based on information they had, and displaying reasonableness in the search itself.

It is possible, however, for a search to go beyond the limits that a court will accept as being reasonable. When that happens, an injured party may properly have recourse against the administrator. More specifically, he may sue under the Civil Rights Act of 1871, 42 U.S.C. § 1983, referred to in Chapter Four. Under this act, several junior high school students in Pennsylvania brought action against school officials, the city, and city police for what they claimed was an illegal search.[77] After a child complained of a ring having been stolen, the principal and assistant principal initiated a search of eight girls. They were unsuccessful and called the police. When the police were unsuccessful in questioning the girls, they

---

75. Horton v. Goose Creek Indep. Sch. Dist., 677 F.2d 471 (5th Cir. 1982).

76. More cases treating the issue of dog searches include Bellnier v. Lund, 438 F. Supp. 47 (N.D.N.Y. 1977); M.M. v. Anker, 607 F.2d 588 (2d Cir. 1979); Zamora v. Pomeroy, 639 F.2d 662 (10th Cir. 1981). The holdings in the limited number of school searches involving dogs have tended to apply reasonableness standards. Searches of inanimate objects involving dogs are reasonable, but searches of persons involving dogs tend to be viewed as invasive of one's privacy. *See* Sutton v. Kathy I.S.D., 961 S.W.2d 216 (Tex. App. 1997).

77. Potts v. Wright, 357 F. Supp. 215 (E.D. Pa. 1973). In Cornfield by Lewis v. Consolidated High Sch. Dist. No. 230, 991 F.2d 1316 (7th Cir. 1993), a student enrolled in a behavior disorder program was subjected to a strip search, his naked body visually inspected, and his clothes physically inspected by a teacher and an administrator. Even though no drugs or other contraband were found, the court used the *T.L.O.* standard and upheld the search as reasonable under the circumstances. In State of West Virginia *ex rel.* Cathy Galford v. Mark Anthony B, 433 S.E.2d 41 (W. Va. 1993), a strip search of an eighth-grade student by a school social worker was found to be not reasonable in scope.

376

brought in a police matron who subjected the girls to a strip search. The search did not uncover the ring.

The court could not determine to what degree the school administrators were possibly liable for the search, for although they had initiated it, they relinquished the task to police. What was not clear was whether the school officials had made threats to the girls which forced them to succumb to the searches. Similarly, suit against the city chief of police and the superintendent of schools was not dropped, for it had not been determined whether these two persons had had knowledge of the incident and failed to take action to prevent it. The court held that the nature of the act rather than the status of individuals governed the action taken under color of law.

What the court did hold was that the search had exceeded the bounds of necessity. Although the court did not say so, presumably a stolen ring is not so serious a problem as the use of narcotics on campus. A more likely reason was the nature of the search itself. The students were submitted to an indignity not commensurate with the gravity of the problem.

Before the case could be resolved on remand, an out-of-court settlement was made. Each of the girls was awarded $800.00 in damages, to be paid in part from the city, county, and school district.

In an interesting case involving Louisiana law only, the state's supreme court held that a student is afforded the same fourth amendment rights as adults when a search results in a criminal prosecution.[78] Unlike earlier cases, the court here ruled that a student does not shed his fourth amendment rights when he enters the school campus. The case grew out of a teacher's searching a boy's oversized wallet locked in safekeeping while the student was engaged in physical education. The teacher had suspected that the student had narcotics based on his having turned his back while filling the storage bag with his wallet, furtive actions, and diffi-

---

78. State v. Mora, 330 So. 2d 900 (La. 1976).

377

culty in placing his wallet in the bag. Subsequent examination of the wallet revealed narcotics.

In a 1976 Illinois case, a court held that the search of junior high school students was illegal.[79] Similarly, policemen who had joined in the search on the basis of a request by the principal were also held in violation of the students' constitutional rights. The court ruled that reasonable cause did not exist; no drugs were found in the search.

Courts have been consistent in upholding administrators in their search of lockers and student vehicles on campus. It is recognized that neither should harbor something harmful or illegal. Courts are not in complete agreement about the search of a student's person. It is acceptable for a student to search himself but having him undress completely or to his underwear exceeds the bounds of necessity and prudence.

Searches have been upheld where reasonable suspicion existed. The circumstances of each case determine if reasonable cause applied. The benefit of the doubt is given to the administrator. However, in the few cases where he is viewed as functioning as an agent of the state, he is held to requirements of the fourth amendment.

§ 10.5. AIDS.

A phenomenon of the 1980s that has affected society at large, including schools, was the identification of a new disease, AIDS (Acquired Immune Deficiency Syndrome). Even though the disease has been prevalent in this country for more than a decade,

---

79. Picha v. Wielgos, 410 F. Supp. 1214 (N.D. Ill. 1976). In a 1992 case school officials were similarly not upheld. Several searches of a student had been unsuccessful, but based on a tip, the principal ordered the student to submit to a pat-down search, empty his pockets, remove his shoes, and lower his trousers. No drugs were found. A week later, the student was subjected to a search that revealed nothing. That same day a search of the student's automobile trunk revealed drugs. The original pat-down search was not upheld because it was deemed to be excessively intrusive. Coronado v. State, 835 S.W.2d 636 (Tex. Crim. App. 1992).

little is yet known about it. It is known to be caused by a virus, HIV, that is spread by sexual contact, blood transfusions, and intravenous drug use. No cure has yet been found, and efforts to stabilize the disease have been only moderately successful. Many people die within two years after discovering they have AIDS.

Fear and paranoia have often characterized reactions to the problem of AIDS; AIDS victims have not uncommonly been treated as lepers were centuries ago, in spite of the conclusion by both the Public Health Service and the Center for Disease Control that the disease is not highly contagious. Generally, AIDS victims or those individuals testing positive for it tend not to pose a health risk to other students or employees in a school setting. To date, there is no evidence that an AIDS victim poses a risk to other persons living in the same house, individuals caring for an AIDS victim, persons eating food prepared by an infected person, persons kissing, sneezing, or coughing, persons swimming in the same pool, or using facilities such as telephones, toilets, showers, or water fountains.

A real problem for school personnel addressing the problem of AIDS involves openness. Can AIDS victims be excluded from school, isolated at school, or identified openly as having the disease?

Case law to date is limited on the rights of AIDS victims versus the authority of school officials. As of now, however, court decisions have tended to favor students with AIDS. Judges have reasoned that the potential for transmitting AIDS is not great enough to justify the exclusion of an AIDS victim from school. In a 1987 case out of Florida, a federal district court ruled that three brothers, carriers of the AIDS virus, were entitled to attend school in a regular classroom setting.[80] The school district had attempted to provide homebound instruction for the boys, but the strategy violated section 504 of the Rehabilitation Act. In *Thomas v. Atasca-*

---

80. Ray v. School Dist. of De Soto Cty., 666 F. Supp. 1524 (M.D. Fla. 1987).

379

dero Unified School District,[81] a federal district court in California ruled that a kindergarten AIDS victim was entitled to attend a regular kindergarten class. The child had been removed from the class after having been bitten by another student on the leg without breaking any skin. The court determined that the child's needs and rights outweighed any threat of safety to other students.

§ 10.6. Substance Abuse.

In the late 1990s educational personnel have increasingly had to contend with pervasive substance abuse in schools. It is a problem that surfaced in secondary schools and has since expanded to include lower grades as well. No school-age group is immune from the problem, and no section of the country has escaped it. For school officials, the problem is two-fold: Prevention and dealing with those in possession of or who use drugs.

With respect to prevention, no school system can really claim to be free of drugs and alcohol. It can, however, take measures to reduce the problem. Suggested strategies involve a comprehensive study of the extent of the problem and enactment of policies regarding penalties for possession and use of drugs and alcohol.

Testing of students for drugs has been litigated less often than testing of employees. One of the first cases involving students was decided by a New Jersey court in 1985. It involved a challenge to the school board policy requiring all secondary school students to submit to a urinalysis test. The court invalidated the testing. Basing his opinion on *T.L.O.,* which had been decided by the Supreme Court earlier in the year, the judge concluded that the urinalysis testing constituted a search. Requiring students to submit to such testing interfered with the student's privacy and did not meet the standard of a reasonable search as stated in *T.L.O.* The search also violated due process in that the results of the test could lead to a

---

81. 662 F. Supp. 376 (C.D. Cal. 1986). *See also* Robertson v. Granite City Community Unit S.D. No. 9, 684 F. Supp. 1002 (S.D. Ill. 1988); Doe v. Dalton Elem. Sch. Dist. No. 148, 694 F. Supp. 440 (N.D. Ill. 1988); Doe v. Belleville Pub. Sch. Dist. No. 118, 672 F. Supp. 342 (S.D. Ill. 1987).

student's exclusion from school without attendant due process requirements. The court also rejected the school district's claim that the testing was medical, not disciplinary.[82]

In 1985, a federal court in Arkansas ruled on the legality of testing by urinalysis. At issue was a school board policy that required individuals to submit to urinalysis if suspected of using drugs. One girl suspected of smoking marijuana in the restroom was allowed to withdraw from school, for which she lost all credits for the semester. Through her parents, the girl later sued, charging that she had been coerced to withdraw and that the testing policy was unreasonable.[83]

The court found the test to be useless. The test could detect the presence of marijuana in one's urine for weeks after its use, but it could not detect how much or when it was used. The court rejected the notion of need as justification for a urinalysis test. The search became unreasonable when school officials required a student to disrobe from the waist down and urinate in the presence of an adult.

---

82. Odenheim v. Carlstadt-East Rutherford Sch. Dist., 510 A.2d 709 (N.J. Super. Ct. 1985). Drug testing of athletes was upheld in Schaill v. Tippecanoe Cty. Sch. Corp., 864 F.2d 1309 (7th Cir. 1989). The United States Supreme Court, in Vernonia Sch. Dist. v. Acton, 115 S. Ct. 2386 (1995), upheld a school district's random drug testing program involving athletes. *Vernonia* was extended in 1998 when the Seventh Circuit upheld a school district policy requiring students to submit to random, unannounced urinalysis before they could participate in any extracurricular activity. The same policy applied to students who drove their cars to school. The court justified such searches on the basis that school officials serve as guardian or custodian of children in their care. Todd v. Rush Cty. Schs., 133 F.3d 984 (7th Cir.), *cert. denied*, 119 S. Ct. 68 (1998). For a contrasting decision, see Willis v. Anderson Commun. Sch. Corp., 158 F.3d 415 (7th Cir. 1998), *cert. denied*, 119 S. Ct. 1259 (1999).

83. Anable v. Ford, 653 F. Supp. 22 (W.D. Ark. 1985). In Student Alpha ID Number GUJA v. School Bd. of Volusia Cty., 616 So. 2d 1011 (Fla. App. 5th Dist. 1993), a student's suspension for possession of marijuana was upheld even though she contended that her due process rights had been violated. The student actually had been charged with distribution of drugs on campus, but was ultimately suspended for a lesser charge of possession of drugs.

School officials have considerable autonomy in disciplining students for consumption of alcohol as well as possession of drugs. This autonomy extends to their right to suspend students for consumption of alcohol off-campus.[84]

§ 10.7. School Violence.

One of the notable concerns of school personnel of the 1990s was the increase in violence at schools. The problem affected all regions of the country at all levels of school organization, and went beyond what was once perceived as an inner city problem. It has reached into suburban as well as rural schools. The cost in money for damages is very high, and the loss of lives of both young people and adults has had a profound effect on society. School officials report an increasing climate of fear in which young people and their teachers wonder if, on a given day, they will be victims of unforeseen violent acts.

As education moved into the mid-1990s, both the federal and state governments began to take drastic steps to curb acts of violence on school campuses. The federal government has as one of its goals in America 2000 the elimination of violence in schools. In 1990, Congress passed the Gun-Free School Zones Act which made it unlawful for any individual to possess knowingly a firearm in a school zone. The Act extended a school's territory to a distance of 1,000 feet from the campus proper. In 1995, however, the United States Supreme Court struck down that statute. The High Court's view was that this is a matter better left to the various states.[85] An example of state action in addressing the problem may be found in the legislative response of Virginia. The legislature

---

84. Douglas v. Campbell, 116 S.W. 211 (Ark. 1909); Board of Educ. v. McCluskey, 458 U.S. 966 (1982); Pirschel v. Sorrell, 2 F. Supp. 2d 930 (E.D. Ky. 1998).

85. In 1995, the United States Supreme Court, by a vote of 5-4, ruled that the Gun Free Schools Act of 1990 (18 U.S.C. § 922q (1)(A)) constituted an invalid exercise of federal authority (under the Commerce Clause) to control weapons on public school grounds. *See* United States v. Lopez, 115 S. Ct. 1624 (1995); *See, e.g.*, VA. CODE § 18.2-128.

toughened its statute and increased the penalty for trespass on school grounds,[86] increased the penalty for making threats against school personnel,[87] drafted new restrictions on the possession of firearms by minors, and empowered school officials to exclude students for violence and weapons violations.[88]

Massachusetts has made it possible for principals to suspend a student who is charged with a felony or is the subject of a felony delinquency complaint if the principal determines that the student's continued presence in school would be deleterious to the school population.[89]

In North Carolina the General Assembly enacted a statute, effective December 1993, which requires school officials to report to law enforcement officials the possession or suspected possession of weapons or drugs. It also provides for automatic suspension of students who violate the Act.[90]

While legislators have wrestled with the problem, courts have also been called upon to resolve conflict. One area of controversy has involved the question of liability of school officials for the protection of students and their liability for injury to the school population. To date, courts have been reluctant to place an affirmative duty on teachers and principals for the protection of each

---

86. *See, e.g.,* VA. CODE § 18.2-60.

87. *See, e.g., id.*

88. *See, e.g.,* VA. CODE § 22.1-277.2.

89. MASS. GEN. LAWS 71-37H (1994).

90. G.S. 115 C-288 (1993). Recent cases from other states support automatic suspension. A high school student in West Virginia was suspended for carrying two knives on the school bus, a violation of the state's Safe Schools Act. Cathe A. v. Doddridge Cty. Bd. of Educ., 490 S.E.2d 340 (W. Va. 1997). A Virginia court upheld the expulsion of a student for possession of a knife on a field trip. The student had violated school board policy which prohibited possession of knives at school-sponsored events. Wood v. Henry Cty. Pub. Schs., 495 S.E.2d 255 (Va. 1998). A Minnesota court upheld the suspension and expulsion of two high school students who drove a pick-up truck onto school grounds displaying a BB gun. Peterson v. I.S.D. No. 811, 999 F. Supp. 665 (D. Minn. 1998).

student from possible harm from third parties.[91] The key determination is whether a special relationship exists between school officials, employees, and students. Recently, the Fifth Circuit broke with precedent and recognized the existence of a special relationship;[92] however in this instance, the injured individual, a deaf student, attended a residential school for the deaf. Because the school had custody of the student for twenty-four hours each day, that circumstance created the special relationship and imposed a different degree of responsibility.

Society in general recognizes the severity of the problem of violence at school. People agree that affirmative steps must be taken to reduce acts of violence. The task of school administration in the new century is a daunting one, but law enforcement officials and courts have empowered them to take firm steps. Nevertheless, it is not likely that schools will soon be free of drugs and violence, which is a stated objective in the statement of national goals, America 2000.

§ 10.8. Peer Sexual Harassment.

The extent of the duty to protect students from sexual harassment by other students remains a debatable point of law. The United States Supreme Court *in DeShaney v. Winnebago Department of Social Services*[93] (a non-school case) held that nothing in the fourteenth amendment requires a state to protect the life, liberty, or property of citizens against invasion by private actors, unless a special relationship exists between a state agency and a citizen (*e.g.*, a person is in the custody of or incarcerated by the

---

91. *See* B.M.H. v. School Bd. of Chesapeake, 833 F. Supp. 560 (E.D. Va. 1993); D.R. v. Middle Bucks Area Vocational & Tech. Sch., 972 F.2d 1364 (3d Cir. 1992); Dorothy J. v. Little Rock Sch. Dist., 7 F.3d 729 (8th Cir. 1993).

92. Walton v. Alexander, 20 F.3d 1350 (5th Cir. 1994). For a case involving the issue of liability under § 1983 for injury to a student who was hit and killed by a stray bullet shot by a trespasser, see Johnson v. Dallas Indep. Sch. Dist., 38 F.3d 198 (5th Cir. 1995).

93. 489 U.S. 189 (1989).

state). Post-*DeShaney* courts have, as a general rule, applied the special relationship test to public school cases.

In *B.M.H. v. School Board of Chesapeake (Virginia)*, a female student unsuccessfully sued school officials and teachers following a sexual assault on school grounds by a male student. Three days before the incident she said that she reported to school officials that the same student had threatened her with sexual assault. A federal district court held that neither the state's compulsory attendance statute nor its child abuse statute created a special relationship giving rise to a special duty to protect B.M.H. from harm.[94]

Walton v. Alexander involved a male student at the Mississippi School for the Deaf who had been sexually assaulted by a fellow student. The assault was reported to school officials, parents were notified, and an investigation was conducted as required by school policy. The students were suspended from school. Upon return to school, both received psychological counseling and were reassigned to separate dormitories. Subsequently, however, the two students were reassigned to the same dormitory where a second sexual assault occurred. The victim's parents sued in federal district court, claiming that the school's superintendent failed to protect their son from harm. While the parents prevailed at trial, the Fifth Circuit Court on appeal reached a different conclusion. In the appellate court's view, the district court was correct in finding that a special duty did exist (the assaulted student was in 24-hour residential care, dependent on the school for his needs, and he was not free to leave). However, the attack was found to be the result of "mere negligence" and "carelessness" on the part of school officials, and not the direct result of their "deliberate indifference."[95]

---

94. *B.M.H.*, *supra* note 91. *See also* Rowinsky v. Bryan, 80 F.3d 1006 (5th Cir.), *cert. denied*, 117 S. Ct. 165 (1996).

95. Walton v. Alexander, *supra* note 92. The court offered the following definition of "deliberate indifference": where a school official knows about, or willfully avoids knowing about, the possibility of serious harm to a student, fails to take appropriate action, and the student is harmed. *See also* Doe v. Petaluma City Sch. Dist., 949 F. Supp. 1415 (N.D. Cal. 1996), where the court held that a plaintiff must show that she was subjected to unwelcome harassment, it was so perva-

The Fifth Circuit held in another case, *Doe v. Taylor*,[96] that private individuals can seek money damages if it is shown that school officials learned of a student being abused but failed to do something about it. In *Doe v. Taylor*, school officials are reminded that simply because a special relationship does not exist they are not free from liability when acts of assault, sexual harassment, or molestation are committed on school property. School officials may be held liable if nothing is done to prevent or correct a situation where dangerously aggressive and disruptive behavior exists.

The most significant decision to date is *Davis v. Monroe County Board of Education*.[97] In *Davis*, a female fifth-grade student (hereafter referred to as L.D.) was sexually assaulted in a public school classroom. Even though she had reported the matter (and subsequent behavior) to her teachers, the male student continued to harass her. Subsequent reports were made after each incident. One teacher changed the students' seats to remedy the situation. Another teacher told L.D.'s mother that the principal had been made aware of the problem. The assaultive behavior continued. After the eighth incident, L.D. and her mother met with the principal. Ultimately the perpetrator was charged with and pled guilty to sexual battery.

L.D.'s mother filed suit in federal district court,[98] alleging that school officials were responsible for her daughter's emotional distress. Relying on 42 U.S.C. § 1983 and Title IX, she charged that the failure of the Monroe County School Board to have a student-against-student sexual harassment policy, and the failure of

---

sive and severe as to create a hostile educational environment, school officials knew of or should have known of the problem, and they failed to take prompt and appropriate action.

96. 15 F.3d 443 (5th Cir.), *cert. denied*, 115 S. Ct. 70 (1994). *See also* Dorothy J. v. Little Rock Sch. Dist., 7 F.3d 729 (8th Cir. 1993); Nicole v. Martinez Unified Sch. Dist., 964 F. Supp. 1369 (N.D. Cal. 1997); Monteiro v. Tempe Union High Sch. Dist., 158 F.3d 1022 (9th Cir. 1998).

97. 120 F.3d 1390 (11th Cir. 1997).

98. Aurelia D. v. Monroe Cty. Bd. of Educ., 862 F. Supp. 363 (M.D. Ga. 1994).

school officials to do something about the sexual battery situation, were the proximate causes of her daughter's suffering. The trial court dismissed the suit, but a three-judge panel of the Eleventh Circuit reinstated the Title IX complaint.[99] On appeal by the school board, the Eleventh Circuit reheard the case *en banc*.

The Eleventh Circuit rejected the Title IX arguments. While condemning the harm done to L.D., the court was nonetheless of the opinion that school officials could not be held liable for the tortious conduct of a non-employee, private person (in this case a student). At no time in this case, said the court, was it ever alleged that any employee directly participated in this matter. While acknowledging that school officials were on notice of the situation, to ask that they be held directly liable for the wrongdoing of a student is to argue for an extension of liability under Title IX not intended by Congress.[100]

---

99. Davis v. Monroe Cty. Bd. of Educ., 74 F.3d 1186 (11th Cir. 1996). *See* Doe v. Oyster River Coop. Sch. Dist., 992 F. Supp. 467 (D.N.H. 1997), where the court held that a school system may be held liable for peer sexual harassment if (1) school officials knew or should have know of the matter but failed to correct the problem, (2) a special relationship or duty existed to protect students from harm by private persons, and (3) the harassment was severe and pervasive.

100. *Davis, supra* note 97, at 1395. On May 24, 1999, however, the United States Supreme Court handed down a decision in *Davis*. In a 5-4 decision (Justice O'Connor writing for the majority), the Court reversed and remanded the case and, in doing so, set a high standard in peer sexual harassment situations. School officials may be liable where the harassment is so severe and pervasive that it limits the student victim's ability to learn; where school officials know of the harassment; where school officials show deliberate indifference to the matter; and where school officials fail to take reasonable steps to remedy the situation. Davis v. Monroe Cty. Bd. of Educ., 119 S. Ct. 1661 (1999).

Chapter Eleven

EXPRESSION

§ 11.0. Introduction.

Throughout the early history of public education in this nation, students usually played a submissive role within their schools. With few exceptions, the general rule was that students were to express themselves in ways deemed "unacceptable" by their administrators and teachers. Typically, students dressed in particular ways prescribed by a school dress code, spoke out in class only when encouraged to do so by their teachers, and usually abstained from placing any items in school publications which had not received prior approval of the school administration or their faculty sponsor.

Beginning in the 1960s, however, the scene began to change. At first, the college campus served as a base for launching a new breed of more activist students, determined to express their beliefs on current political and social issues, and to express their individuality as persons.[1] Gradually, this activist spirit and behavior began to filter down to high schools and even to elementary schools across this country. A new era of student expression was born, resulting in an avalanche of litigation challenging school policies and rules governing student expression.

The period of the mid-1970s through the early 1980s opened the way for public school students to challenge dress codes, hairstyle regulations, publication control, and other like matters based on an old piece of civil rights legislation enacted by Congress more than a century earlier. Referred to as the "constitutional or civil rights tort" law, Section 1983 of Title 42 (Civil Rights Act of 1871) is considered the most significant malpractice law for people engaged in public education in this country.[2]

To date, the expression freedoms allowed public school students have not been fully and comprehensively tested in a § 1983 context. As the following sections will illustrate, however, more and more cases (especially the cases since 1975) came into the courts premised on § 1983 grounds.[3]

§ 11.1. Expression Defined.

According to *Black's Law Dictionary*, to express is to make something known (in words) distinctly and explicitly so as not to be left to inference or implication.[4] Generally, individuals in our society express themselves in a variety of ways. Some of these ways are: the written word, pictures and drawings, gestures, symbols, and the spoken word. Given a particular situation, one or a

---

1. *See, e.g.,* Dixon v. Alabama State Bd. of Educ., 294 F.2d 150 (5th Cir.), *cert. denied,* 368 U.S. 930 (1961).

2. For a comprehensive treatment of § 1983 as it applies to public school matters, see R.S. VACCA & H.C. HUDGINS, JR., LIABILITY OF SCHOOL OFFICIALS AND ADMINISTRATORS FOR CIVIL RIGHTS TORTS (Charlottesville, Va.: Michie Co., 1982).

3. The benchmark case granting public school students standing to sue school officials for damages under § 1983 is Wood v. Strickland, 420 U.S. 308, 95 S. Ct. 992, 43 L. Ed. 2d 214 (1975).

4. BLACK'S LAW DICTIONARY 691 (4th ed. 1968).

combination of these means might prove more effective than the others in making an individual's feelings, beliefs, or wishes known to others.

The first amendment to the United States Constitution contains the following language: "Congress shall make no law . . . abridging the freedom of speech, or of the press; or the right of the people peaceably to assemble, and to petition the government for a redress of grievances."[5] Nowhere in the above statement is the word "expression" used — nor does that word, itself, appear elsewhere in the body of the Constitution. Thus, over the years, mainly through the process of selective incorporation, the federal courts have acted to create the substantive right to freedom of expression.

In the era of the 1960s, federal courts expanded the first amendment's free speech clause. In addition to covering such matters as students speaking out on campus, also included were such matters as student attire (dress), students wearing symbolic armbands, buttons, and badges, and student hairstyles. All such actions by students came under the purview of the constitutional protection of free speech.[6] Add to that the application of the free press, assembly, and redress for grievances guarantees (also made applicable to public school systems through the fourteenth amendment), and it becomes obvious that student expression in schools underwent radical change. It must be stated at the outset, however, that the right of expression available to students in public schools has never been judged as absolute, nor has it been equated to freedom of expression available to adults in the community.

---

5. Passed by Congress, September 25, 1789; ratified December 15, 1791.

6. For an excellent article on point, see C. Smith, *The Constitutional Parameters of Student Protest,* 1 J. OF LAW & EDUC. 39 (Jan. 1972). For an excellent commentary containing a comprehensive update of the issues, see Ralph D. Mawdsley & Alice L. Mawdsley, *Free Expression in Public Schools: A Trend Toward Greater Control Over Students,* 48 EDUC. LAW REP. 305 (Sept. 28, 1989). *See also* William D. Valente, *Student Freedom of Speech in Public Schools,* 46 EDUC. LAW REP. 889 (July 21, 1988). School officials are cautioned that they may be subject to a suit for damages under 42 U.S.C. § 1983 when student first amendment speech rights are at issue. *See, e.g.,* Guidry v. Broussard, 897 F.2d 181 (5th Cir. 1990).

§ 11.2. Student Appearance as Expression.

For many years, most public school systems in this nation maintained strict rules and regulations concerning student appearance while in the school and in attendance at school functions. Generally, these rules and regulations were the responsibility of building principals to enforce and were justified as necessary to protect the school's learning environment from disruptive reactions of the majority of students to nonconventional modes of dress and attire worn by other students. Additionally, some school boards and administrators justified codes governing student appearance as necessary to inculcate proper moral, spiritual, and civic values in public school students.

In the past, courts of law were reluctant to substitute their judgments for those of school officials in matters of student appearance. *Pugsley v. Sellmeyer* (1923),[7] offers a good example of this early attitude.

The Clay County, Arkansas, school board had a policy that read: "The wearing of transparent hosiery, low-necked dresses or any style of clothing tending toward immodesty in dress, or the use of face paint or cosmetics, is prohibited."[8] Pearl Pugsley, then 18 years old, who knew of the school policy, came to school one day with talcum powder on her face. A teacher told Pearl to wash her face and not to come to school again with powder on. Pearl disobeyed the mandate, refused to comply with the school policy, and showed up again wearing face powder, whereupon she was denied admission to school. Pearl's father brought suit challenging the reasonableness of the school policy.

Convinced that the school board policy was reasonably calculated to promote school discipline, the Supreme Court of Arkansas denied Pugsley's appeal for remedy. What is more, the Arkansas Supreme Court was convinced that Pearl Pugsley should demon-

---

7. 158 Ark. 247, 250 S.W. 538 (1923). For another early case on point, see Stromberg v. French, 143 So. 2d 629 (Ala. 1931).

8. *Pugsley, supra* note 7, at 250 S.W. 538.

strate obedience and respect for duly constituted authority, "an essential lesson to qualify one for the duties of citizenship . . . ."[9]

The judicial attitude of noninterference expressed in *Pugsley* was, with few exceptions, generally held by subsequent courts through the late 1960s. For example, in *Leonard v. School Committee*,[10] a 1965 case involving a student hair length regulation, the Supreme Judicial Court of Massachusetts held that school officials had the right to order a student to get his hair cut. The student's parents had claimed in court that school officials could not bar their son from attending classes solely because his hair was grown well over his ears. The hair appearance of a student, they argued, is in no way connected to the successful operation of a public school.

In holding for the school system, the Massachusetts court was convinced that family privacy rights of personal appearance must give way to reasonable school regulations calculated to protect the rights of other students, teachers, administrators, and the community. Because of this, the high court would not substitute its judgment for that of the school committee unless it was shown that the committee acted arbitrarily or capriciously.

Ferrell v. Dallas Independent School District (1968),[11] offers another example of judicial noninterference in school regulations proscribing student appearance. In *Ferrell,* three male students were denied enrollment in a Dallas, Texas, high school because of their "Beatle-type" haircuts. Members of a musical group, the students claimed that their hairstyle was a necessity to their role as musicians and was acceptable as judged by standards within their field of entertainment.

The principal of the high school required that the three boys have their hair trimmed before they could be admitted to his

---

9. *Id.* at 539.

10. 212 N.E.2d 468 (Mass. 1965).

11. 392 F.2d 697 (5th Cir. 1968). More recently, in Colorado Indep. Sch. Dist. v. Barber, 864 S.W.2d 806 (Tex. App. 1993), male students successfully challenged enforcement of a school's dress code which prohibited male students from having long hair or from wearing earrings. Among other things, the court saw the code prohibitions as discriminatory, based on sex.

school. He was of the opinion that the length and style of the boys' hair, unless cut, would be so distractive as to cause a disturbance in school.

Taking their case ultimately to the United States Court of Appeals for the Fifth Circuit, the boys argued that the school regulation was not only unlawful under the constitution and statutes of their state, but was also violative of the fourteenth amendment to the United States Constitution. The substance of their claim was that they were being discriminated against because of their hair length.

Upholding the school regulation and the principal's ultimatum, the Fifth Circuit Court opined that the Constitution does not establish an absolute right to free expression and that this right can be infringed upon by the state where a compelling reason exists to do so. In *Ferrell,* the compelling reason for the hair regulation and the principal's haircut order was obvious, namely, the maintenance of an effective and efficient school.

The Fifth Circuit reiterated its attitude regarding the importance of school boards protecting a school system's educational and disciplinary needs through the implementation of a "hairstyle regulation." The case, *Domico v. Rapides Parish School Board,*[12] actually involved the application of a school board's student dress code (more specifically the application of a policy prohibiting students from wearing beards) to all employees, as well as to students.

Finding a rational basis for the regulation limiting the liberty interest of choice in matters of appearance, the court said that a school board has a legitimate concern and an undeniable interest in "teaching hygiene, instilling discipline, asserting authority, and compelling uniformity."[13]

---

12. 675 F.2d 100 (5th Cir. 1982).

13. *Id.* at 102. Here the court cites its earlier decision in Karr v. Schmidt, 460 F.2d 609 (5th Cir.), *cert. denied,* 409 U.S. 989 (1972). For a case where male Native American students took issue with enforcement of a hair length restriction on grounds that it violated their liberty to freely exercise their religious beliefs,

The Fifth Circuit does remind us of the difference between college-level, elementary, and secondary schools. Hairstyle regulations at the college-level, says the court, "cannot, absent exceptional circumstances, be justified."[14] In a high school environment, however, a person's appearance may have an adverse impact on the educational process and, as such, barring any arbitrary or capricious acts, can be regulated.

a. ***Tinker v. Des Moines Independent Community School District.*** Beginning in the late 1960s, court attitudes regarding student appearance began to change. Two important cases marking the emergence of a new judicial standard are: *Burnside v. Byars* (1966),[15] and the landmark case from the United States Supreme Court, *Tinker v. Des Moines Independent Community School District* (1969).[16]

In *Burnside,* students in an all-Negro high school in Mississippi sought injunctive relief against the enforcement of a school regulation forbidding the wearing of freedom buttons in school. Their principal mandated that they could not wear the buttons in school. He based his order on two reasons. First, because the buttons (which read: "One Man One Vote," "SNCC") did not have any bearing on their education. Second, the wearing of the buttons would "cause commotion" in the school.

Losing their case before the trial court, the students appealed to the United States Court of Appeals for the Fifth Circuit. In their

---

see Alabama and Coushatta Tribes of Texas v. Trustees, 817 F. Supp. 1319 (E.D. Tex. 1993).

14. *Id. See also* Miller v. School Dist. No. 167, 495 F.2d 658 (7th Cir.), *reh'g denied,* 500 F.2d 711 (7th Cir. 1974).

15. 363 F.2d 744 (5th Cir. 1966). It should be noted that the same court, on the same day, reached the opposite result when presented with different facts in a similar case, Blackwell v. Issaquena, 363 F.2d 749 (5th Cir. 1966). In a student button case, Chandler v. McMinnville Sch. Dist., 978 F.2d 524 (9th Cir. 1992), the court held that school officials do not have limitless discretion to suppress political speech. Here the students wore buttons containing the word "scab" in connection with a teachers' strike. No disruption could be tied to the wearing of the buttons.

16. 393 U.S. 503, 89 S. Ct. 733, 21 L. Ed. 2d 731 (1969).

appeal the students argued that wearing the buttons was an exercise of free speech, protected by the first amendment of the United States Constitution. The appellate court agreed with them and reversed the trial court with directions to invalidate the rule.

Convinced that children in public schools do have a first amendment right to express ideas (a substantive right), the Fifth Circuit Court was of the opinion that school authorities must therefore show a compelling reason for violating that right. Since it could not be shown by school authorities that the wearing of the buttons had actually and materially disrupted the school, the principal's prohibition and ultimate action were unreasonable.

In 1969, the United States Supreme Court heard *Tinker v. Des Moines,* an Iowa case involving student appearance, in the form of symbolic expression. This time, however, the matter involved students wearing black armbands to protest the Vietnam War.

A group of adults and parents had decided to publicize their objections to the war in Vietnam and their support of a truce by wearing black armbands during the holiday season and by fasting on December 16 (1965), and New Year's Eve. Hearing of the plan, the principals of the Des Moines schools met and adopted a policy that any student wearing an armband to school would be asked to remove it, and if he refused, he would be suspended until he returned without the armband.

Aware of the regulation, John Tinker, Mary Beth Tinker, and Christopher Eckhardt wore black armbands to school and were sent home until they would come back without their armbands. They did not return to school until after the planned period of protest had expired.

Claiming civil rights deprivations under 42 U.S.C. § 1983, the students (through their fathers) sought nominal damages and injunctive relief in a United States District Court. Holding that the action of the school authorities was reasonable in order to prevent disturbance, the district court dismissed the complaint.[17] On ap-

---

17. *See* 258 F. Supp. 971 (D. Iowa 1966).

peal, the United States Court of Appeals for the Eighth Circuit affirmed the lower court decision.[18]

The United States Supreme Court reversed the lower courts and remanded the case. In the opinion of this nation's court, "undifferentiated fear or apprehension of disturbance is not enough to overcome the right to freedom of expression."[19] The school regulation in question, said Mr. Justice Fortas, violates the constitutional rights of students if it cannot be justified "by a showing that the students' activities would materially and substantially disrupt the work and discipline of the school."[20] Thus, the *Tinker* test of "material and substantial disruption" came into being and became the major tool for judicial analysis when working to settle student expression litigation.

The impact of the *Tinker* test was far-reaching. Cases continued to come before the courts (federal and state), involving issues of student expression.

A 1974 decision from the Supreme Court of Virginia offers an example of the *Tinker* test being applied to determine material and substantial disruption in a non-appearance case. The case, *Pleasants v. Commonwealth*,[21] involved the Hanover County, Virginia, public school system.

The defendants and thirty-four other students were arrested, charged with unlawful trespass, and ultimately convicted in County Court for their activities while engaged in a protest on the grounds of Patrick Henry High School. The protestors were demanding that the principal immediately readmit to school some recently suspended students. The principal refused to meet the demand and the protest became progressively noisier and more disruptive.

The students appealed their conviction to the Supreme Court of Virginia, presenting two arguments. First, as bona fide students at

---

18. 383 F.2d 988 (8th Cir. 1967).

19. 393 U.S. 503, 507.

20. *Id.* at 740.

21. 203 S.E.2d 114 (Va. 1974).

Patrick Henry High School they had a right to be on school grounds during the school day, absent the violation of some written regulation of the school board. Second, they argued that their protest on school grounds was constitutionally protected by the first amendment, citing the *Tinker* decision as controlling.

Regarding their first point, the Virginia Supreme Court was of the opinion that the school principal acts as a duly authorized agent of the school board. As such, he is charged with the duty of maintaining order and discipline in the school. In doing so, said the court, "he was vested with the inherent power to revoke, for good cause, the right of any student to remain on school property when that student alone or in concert with others, disrupted regular school activities or the maintenance of good order and discipline."[22] That the principal is duty bound to take reasonable measures to restore order was the opinion of the court.

Appellants' reliance on *Tinker* was likewise not acceptable to the Virginia Supreme Court. After reiterating the importance of first amendment rights of students in school, the court focused on the facts presented in *Pleasants*. Certainly, said the Virginia court, students can freely express themselves. They may not, however, "do so in a manner which would materially and substantially interfere with discipline and good order in the operation of the school or with the rights of others." Such behavior, it concluded, is not immunized by the guarantee of free speech.[23]

b. *Student Appearance Post-Tinker*. Not too long after the *Tinker* decision came down, a United States District Court in Connecticut was faced with a dress code challenge in *Crossen v. Fatsi*.[24] The code at issue required that all students be neatly dressed and groomed, maintain standards of modesty and good taste conducive to an educational atmosphere, and refrain from wearing "extreme" styles of clothing and grooming.[25]

---

22. *Id.* at 116.

23. *Id.* at 116-17. Judge Harmon quotes directly from *Tinker* at 393 U.S. 503 (1969).

24. 309 F. Supp. 114 (D. Conn. 1970).

25. *Id.* at 115-16.

The plaintiff-pupil claimed that his beard and mustache were not prohibited under the code, because he did not consider it to be an "extreme style or fashion." And, among other things, his appearance was a matter of privacy and personal expression, protected by the United States Constitution, ninth and fourteenth amendments. At no time, however, did plaintiff claim that his appearance was an exercise of free expression or symbolic speech.

In holding the school dress code unconstitutional, the district court made several important determinations, each of which furnishes workable guidelines for school boards and administrators. The court first considered the wording of the regulation, then the purpose of its existence.

The wording of the school code in question, said the court, is too vague and overbroad. "It leaves to the arbitrary whim of the principal, what in fact constitutes extreme fashion or style in the matter of personal grooming . . . ."[26] Thus, the existing rule is "too imprecise to be enforceable . . . ."[27]

Regarding the purpose of the rule, the court resorted to *Tinker*-type language. A code, said the court, "must clearly define the standards and it should be reasonably designed to avoid the disruption of the classroom atmosphere and decorum, prevent disturbances among students, avoid the distraction of other pupils or interference with the educational process of the school."[28] In the instant case the above condition did not exist.

The school district was thus enjoined from suspending or disciplining the student-plaintiff, using the existing dress code. Additionally, the student's record was to be expunged of any notations referring to the disciplinary incident.[29]

Massie v. Henry (1972)[30] is another case in point that involved some male high school students in Haywood County, North Carolina. In *Massie*, plaintiff-students had worn their hair and/or side-

_____

26. *Id.* at 117.
27. *Id.* at 118.
28. *Id.*
29. *Id.* at 119.
30. 455 F.2d 779 (4th Cir. 1972).

burns at a length in direct violation of a school rule (recommended by a student-faculty-parent committee and adopted by the high school principal). A district court found for the school system, declared the regulation justified, and found that none of plaintiffs' constitutional rights had been denied.[31]

In rendering a decision to reverse the district court, the United States Court of Appeals for the Fourth Circuit was convinced by three factors. First, there was no evidence shown that anyone's health was impaired by the length of the students' hair. Second, no sufficient proof was shown of any "disruptive effect" caused by the plaintiffs' actions. Third, school officials insisting on conformity of students for conformity's sake alone, without having any more compelling reason, was not enough to substantiate the grooming code.

In sum, the Fourth Circuit Court was of the opinion that school officials bear the burden of establishing the necessity of infringing upon a student's freedom. There must be sufficient proof, said the Court, that the necessity for the school action (school rule and its enforcement) outweighs the protection of student rights. As a district court said in deciding a 1973 Massachusetts dress code case, school authorities must show a countervailing interest sufficient to justify intrusion into an area of constitutionally protected rights.[32] Absent a clear showing of a connection between the compelling reason or reasons for implementing a dress code and the requirements of the code itself, the code will fail in court.[33]

---

31. District Court decision unreported.

32. Bishop v. Cermenaro, 355 F. Supp. 1269 (D. Mass. 1973). For a decision upholding a student grooming code (regulating hairstyle), see Royer v. Board of Educ., 365 N.E.2d 889 (Ohio 1977). *See also* Mercer v. Board of Trustees, 538 S.W.2d 201 (Tex. 1976). Recently, the Seventh Circuit held that a student's right to wear an expressive T-shirt was not clearly established in Baxter by Baxter v. Vigo Cty. Sch. Corp., 27 F.3d 728 (7th Cir. 1994). *See also* Broussard by Lord v. School Bd., 801 F. Supp. 1526 (E.D. Va. 1992).

33. Independent Sch. Dist. No. 8 v. Swanson, 553 P.2d 496 (Okla. 1976). A few dress code violations still wind up in court. In 1997 the Supreme Court of Texas upheld school officials for disciplining an eight-year-old boy for wearing his hair in a ponytail five inches below the collar. The punishment involved a

Student and employee appearance as a constitutionally protected right again was made clear in 1982 in the *Domico* case.[34]
Citing both *Landsdale v. Tyler Junior College*[35] and *Handler v.
San Jacinto Junior College*,[36] the Fifth Circuit made it clear that
all citizens have a right to choose their mode of personal hair
grooming, and that this right falls as a liberty interest within the
protection of the fourteenth amendment, a protection that guards
against *arbitrary* state action.[37]

The key to a board's success in defending an appearance regulation in a public school system, however, lies in establishing a
compelling reason for the prohibition. To the Fifth Circuit in deciding the *Domico* case, if a board concludes that an employee's
mode of dress or appearance has "an adverse impact on the educational process," the employee's interest in selecting his own style
becomes "subordinate to the public interest."[38]

§ 11.3. Student Publications as Expression.

While federal and state courts have been faced with numerous
cases involving student appearance (dress, hair, and other symbolic
expression), so too have cases been brought challenging school
rules and procedures governing student publications. These "free-

---

suspension of three days and the requirement that he attend an in-school suspension for four months. Board of Trustees of Bastrop v. Toungate, 958 S.W.2d 365
(Tex. 1997). See also a decision from a federal district court in Texas, where the
court held that students wearing rosaries did not equate with a gang-related activity and, thus, school officials acted without authority in seeking to stop the practice. Chalifoux v. New Canay Indep. Sch. Dist., 976 F. Supp. 659 (S.C. Tex.
1997).

34. *Supra* note 12.

35. 470 F.2d 659 (5th Cir.), *cert. denied,* 411 U.S. 986 (1972).

36. 519 F.2d 273 (5th Cir. 1975).

37. *Domico, supra* note 12, at 102. Here the court cites Kelley v. Johnson, 425
U.S. 238, 96 S. Ct. 1440, 47 L. Ed. 2d 708 (1976).

38. *Domico, supra* note 12, at 102. *See* Phillips v. Anderson Cty. Sch. Dist.
Five, 987 F. Supp. 488 (D.S.C. 1997).

dom of the press-type cases" have involved both school-sponsored and nonschool-sponsored publications.

a. *School-Sponsored Publications*. Schools officials have legal responsibility for all school-sponsored publications. Generally, school authorities may be held accountable for what is said or otherwise depicted in school publications. Thus, school boards and school administrators usually exercise more control over school sponsored publications than they do over nonschool-sponsored publications. As Reutter and Hamilton have stated,

> [p]ublications paid for with school funds or produced as a part of the curriculum of a school are subject to more controls than are papers produced by students off premises. . . . However, the fact that a newspaper is financed by the school does not give the school authorities either the duty or the right to determine content per se.[39]

The authors' last point referring to determinations of *content* has, in recent years, become a very sensitive and litigious issue.

Requiring public school students to submit written material to school authorities for their review, prior to publication in a school-sponsored periodical, is not necessarily unreasonable or unconstitutional, per se. Several factors must be taken into consideration before such a determination can be made. For example, one must first identify the presence of or lack of a compelling reason stated by school officials for having a "prior submission" policy. Second, one must ask if students and faculty know of the existence of such a policy and whether the policy has ever been explained to all

---

39. REUTTER, JR., & HAMILTON, THE LAW OF PUBLIC EDUCATION 554 (2d ed. New York, N.Y.: Foundation Press 1976). It should also be said that school officials may not use the power to "cut off funding" to a school publication as a tool of censorship. *See* Joyner v. Whiting, 341 F. Supp. 1244 (M.D.N.C. 1972). *See also* Mississippi Gay Alliance v. Goudelock, 536 F.2d 1073 (5th Cir. 1976), where it was held that even though a university student newspaper was supported in part by student fees collected by the state university, the first amendment was applicable only if school officials had also exercised direct control over student publication of material. Financial support alone is not enough to establish "state action." *Id*. at 1074-75.

students and faculty. A third issue to probe concerns the purpose of the school publication itself. Another area to consider is the language of the school policy. Is the policy definitive and clear in the types of material that are prohibited, or is the policy too broad and vague? Finally, are there procedural safeguards built into the implementation of the prior-submission policy?

Gambino v. Fairfax County School Board[40] involved the contents of portions of an article submitted for publication, entitled "Sexually Active Students Fail to Use Contraceptives," in *The Farm News*, a newspaper published in the Hayfield Secondary School (a public school in Fairfax County, Virginia).

The article in question was submitted to the school principal for prior review and possible publication in the school paper, a procedure followed (by prior agreement) when material was thought to be potentially controversial. After reviewing the material, the school principal ordered that the students not publish the article as written. The principal considered the portions of the article dealing with information on contraceptives to be in violation of School Board Notice 6130, in effect at the time, which prohibited the schools from offering sex education until a decision had been reached on a proposed program. She said, however, that the rest of the article (containing results obtained from a canvass of Hayfield student attitudes toward birth control) could be published. The students insisted on printing the whole article as written. The U.S. District Court (Eastern District of Virginia) held for the students and enjoined the school authorities from prohibiting publication of the entire article in the school newspaper.

On appeal, the school board's major contentions were:

> (1) The first amendment does not apply to *The Farm News* because it is an in-house organ of the school system, funded and sponsored by the Board, and therefore cannot be viewed as a public forum; (2) the school's students are a captive audience because the newspaper is solicited for and distributed during school hours, and

---

40. 429 F. Supp. 731 (E.D. Va.), *aff'd,* 564 F.2d 157 (4th Cir. 1977).

students cannot avoid exposure to the controversial article — therefore the public forum doctrine does not apply;
and (3) even if the newspaper itself is subject to the first
amendment protection, the article is not protected because
its publication would undermine a valid school policy
which prohibits the teaching of birth control as a part of
the curriculum.[41]

In affirming the lower court's decisions, the Fourth Circuit
Court reiterated the district court's opinion that the Fairfax County
School Board's general policy toward student publications caused
The Farm News to be a newspaper established as a "public forum
for student expression," thus it came under the first amendment's
protection. What is more, students are not a captive audience simply because they are compelled to attend school. Finally, since the
school newspaper was established as a "public forum" and not as
an "official school publication," it cannot be viewed as a part of
the curriculum. Thus, "the general power of the Board to regulate
course content does not apply."[42]

Trachtman v. Anker[43] is another decision involving prior disapproval by school officials of publication of a sex survey in a student publication. This controversy began when a staff member on
The Stuyvesant Voice, a student publication at Stuyvesant High
School in New York City, submitted a plan to the school's principal to survey the sexual attitudes of students and publish the results in the *Voice.* The principal denied the request. On appeal to
the Chancellor of the New York City Schools and to the school
board, the students were subsequently advised that they could not
conduct the survey.[44]

Taking their case into federal district court, plaintiff students
claimed that the school authorities' actions in prohibiting the distribution of the questionnaire and preventing publication of the

---

41. *Id.* at 564 F.2d 157.
42. *Id.* at 158.
43. 426 F. Supp. 198 (S.D.N.Y.), *aff'd,* 563 F.2d 512 (2d Cir. 1977).
44. *Id.* at 563 F.2d 512, 514-15.

results violated the first amendment. Upon hearing the evidence, the district court judge was convinced that distribution of the questionnaire and information might prove "psychologically harmful" to thirteen- and fourteen-year-old students (ninth and tenth grade) who were "emotionally immature"; therefore, permission to distribute the questionnaire to them could be denied consistent with the first amendment.[45] However, school authorities could not take such actions when said survey and information was to be made available to "older students." Thus, the psychological and educational benefits to be gained from distribution of the questionnaire to this group of students (eleventh and twelfth grade) and the publishing of the results in the "Voice" for this same group to read could not be prohibited.[46]

On appeal, the case was remanded to the district court with instruction to dismiss the complaint. According to the United States Court of Appeals for the Second Circuit, "The first amendment right to express one's views does not include the right to importune others to respond to questions when there is reason to believe that such importuning may result in harmful consequences."[47] School officials need only show a reasonable basis to justify restraints on secondary school publications distributed on school property. Reason to believe that "harmful consequences might result to students" offers such a reasonable basis for action and meets the "forecast" requirements set forth in *Tinker.*

Nicholson v. Board of Education, Torrance Unified School District[48] is a case out of the Ninth Circuit in which the following question was asked: "Must students and their faculty advisor submit to the principal for prior review all articles designated for publication in the student newspaper?"[49] The appellate court said

---

45. *Id.* at 515.

46. *Id.*

47. *Id.* at 519-20. Supreme Court *review denied,* 435 U.S. 925 (1978).

48. 682 F.2d 858 (9th Cir. 1982).

49. *Id.* The primary first amendment issue in this case involved the matter of whether or not a teacher could bypass the express orders of the principal that all

yes. In the court's opinion, so long as the school rules on prior review are reasonable and the principal's intent in his review is to ensure accuracy and a more responsible student press, then pre-publication review is not offensive to the first amendment.[50]

b. *Nonschool Publications.* Courts have consistently held that school authorities have the power to reasonably regulate the time, place, and manner of distribution of nonschool publications on school property during the school day. School officials have had legal difficulties, however, with prohibitive actions regarding the control of content of nonschool publications.[51]

Even though student publications may be nonschool in origin, school officials still bear the burden of showing compelling reasons for interfering with student first amendment rights. Usually, rules and regulations for controlling nonschool publications on school grounds built upon the need to protect the school's educational environment from disruption will withstand judicial scrutiny when put to the test.[52]

---

articles to be placed in the school newspaper be reviewed by him prior to their publication.

50. *Id.* See the Supreme Court's decision in Hazelwood v. Kuhlmeier, 108 S. Ct. 562 (1988), where the high court upheld a school principal's removal of two articles from the school newspaper. In the opinion of the majority, ". . . educators do not offend the First Amendment by exercising editorial control over the style and content of student speech in school-sponsored expressive activities so long as their actions are reasonably related to legitimate pedagogical concerns." *Id.* at 571. *See also* DeNooyer v. Livonia Public Sch., 799 F. Supp. 744 (E.D. Mich. 1992).

51. 16 A.L.R. Fed. 189.

52. *Id.* at 196. *See, e.g.*, Eisner v. Stamford Bd. of Educ., 440 F.2d 803 (2d Cir. 1971). For a case showing the importance of school officials having a compelling reason to ban the distribution of nonstudent literature on campus, see Rivera v. East Otero Sch. Dist. R-1, 721 F. Supp. 1189 (D. Colo. 1989). More recently, in Hedges v. Wauconda Community Unit Sch. Dist. No. 118, 9 F.3d 1295 (7th Cir. 1993), the court held that a school principal could lawfully and constitutionally control the time, place, and manner of distribution of written material in school, even where the material is religious in nature.

Thomas v. Board of Education, Granville Central School District[53] offers a perfect example of a court's insistence that school officials establish a "sufficient nexus" between school authority to maintain discipline and control on school grounds and their actions involving a student activity that took place almost exclusively off school grounds. In the opinion of the Second Circuit, when a proper *nexus* does not exist, school officials have no legal right to interfere with student first amendment expression.

The case out of New York State involved the suspension of four high school students who had put together a publication called *Hard Times.* The publication was produced almost exclusively off-campus (with an occasional article written or typed at school). The publication was not printed on school property, and the editorial staff did not utilize school paper and ink in producing it.

It seems that the President of the Granville Board of Education learned of the publication from her son. She reported it to the school principal and he conducted an investigation. Ultimately the principal and superintendent suspended the editors for five days. They cited as their reason the "production of a 'morally offensive, indecent, and obscene publication'."[54]

Seeking remedy under 42 U.S.C. § 1983, the students asked a federal district court for both preliminary and permanent injunctive relief. Denying their request, the district court opined that (1) the plaintiff-students had not shown a sufficient likelihood of achieving success on the merits, and (2) *Hard Times* was not within the purview of the first amendment because of its "potential damage to school discipline." The students appealed.[55]

The Second Circuit distinguished *Thomas* from *Tinker* — thus, the *Tinker* standard did not apply here. Since the student activities had occurred almost entirely off school grounds, school administrators had "ventured out of the school yard and into the general community where the freedom accorded expression is at its ze-

---

53. 607 F.2d 1043 (2d Cir. 1979), *cert. denied,* 222 U.S. 1081 (1980).
54. *Id.* at 1050. *See* n.12, court opinion.
55. 478 F. Supp. 114 (N.D.N.Y. 1979).

nith . . . ." The actions of the school administrators therefore "must be evaluated by the principles that bind government officials in the public arena."[56]

In reversing the district court below, the appellate court concluded that off-campus, community-based student expression must be evaluated by an "independent, impartial decisionmaker," not by school officials. Since this was not the case here, the punishment of these students was violative of the first amendment.[57]

Where school officials have reasonable rules and regulations setting requirements for time, place, and manner of distribution of nonschool publications, students are expected to comply with those requirements. Direct disrespect for and disobedience of these reasonable requirements may result in disciplinary actions being taken against the student violators.[58]

In drafting reasonable time, place, and manner prohibitions, school officials must keep in mind that "expression" is involved. Therefore, the statements must be narrowly tailored to further the school system's compelling interest for having the regulations.[59]

School officials must be cautious when establishing rules requiring administrative review and approval of contents of nonschool publications prior to their possible distribution on school grounds. In recent years, courts have been reluctant to give unlimited authority to school officials for deciding on the acceptability of materials contained in nonschool publications.[60]

There have been several cases wherein school officials have attempted to forbid the distribution of nonschool materials because they found the contents to be libelous, vulgar, obscene, repulsive, or otherwise objectionable. A review of the court decisions on

---

56. *Thomas, supra* note 53, at 1050.

57. *Id.* It should be noted here, however, that even though the *Tinker* standard was inapplicable, school officials had done nothing about *Hard Times* for over a week after its discovery, and there had been no disruption.

58. *See, e.g.,* Schwartz v. Schuker, 298 F. Supp. 238 (E.D.N.Y. 1969); Graham v. Independent Sch. Dist., 335 F. Supp. 1164 (S.D. Tex. 1970).

59. McCall v. State, 354 So. 2d 869 (Fla. 1978).

60. Fujishima v. Board of Educ., 460 F.2d 1355 (7th Cir. 1972).

point reveals that the judges themselves cannot agree on the degree of specificity needed to define such terms, and thus to sustain the administrative actions taken.[61] There is general agreement, however, that students must be made aware of a school system's definitions of such terms as "obscene," prior to the enforcement of the rule.[62]

Also necessary to establish the reasonableness of prior approval policies is the existence of procedural guidelines for implementation in school situations. *Quarterman v. Byrd* (1971) is an important decision emphasizing the need for procedural safeguards to implement school policy.[63]

In *Quarterman,* a tenth grade student at Pine Forest High School, North Carolina, was suspended from school for ten days and placed on probation. He had violated a school rule which prohibited the distribution of "any advertisements, pamphlets, printed material, announcements or other paraphernalia" without express permission of the school principal.[64]

Two months later, the same student distributed an "underground" paper in which one of the articles concluded with the following statement (in capital letters):

WE HAVE TO BE PREPARED TO FIGHT IN THE HALLS IN THE CLASSROOMS, OUT IN THE STREETS BECAUSE THE SCHOOLS BELONG TO THE PEOPLE. IF WE HAVE TO — WE'LL BURN THE BUILDINGS OF OUR SCHOOLS DOWN TO SHOW THESE PIGS THAT WE WANT AN EDUCATION THAT WON'T BRAINWASH US INTO BEING RACIST. AND THAT WE WANT AN EDUCATION

---

61. Baker v. Downey City Bd., 307 F. Supp. 517 (C.D. Cal. 1969); Papish v. Board of Curators, 464 F.2d 136 (8th Cir. 1971); Antonelli v. Hammond, 308 F. Supp. 1329 (D. Mass. 1970); Koppell v. Levine, 347 F. Supp. 456 (E.D.N.Y. 1972).

62. *See* Vought v. Van Buren, 306 F. Supp. 1388 (E.D. Mich. 1969); Baughman v. Freienmuth, 478 F.2d 1345 (4th Cir. 1973).

63. 453 F.2d 54 (4th Cir. 1971).

64. *Id.* at 55.

THAT WILL TEACH US TO KNOW THE REAL
TRUTH ABOUT THINGS WE NEED TO KNOW, SO
WE CAN BETTER SERVE THE PEOPLE!!![65]

He was again suspended from school for ten school days.

The United States Court of Appeals for the Fourth Circuit was
not called upon to assess the language in the student publication.
Rather, the court was called upon to decide the constitutional validity of the regulation for violation of which plaintiff student was
disciplined.[66]

Early in the court's opinion it is made clear that "school officials may, by appropriate regulation, exercise prior restraint upon
publications distributed on school premises . . . ."[67] Specifically,
said the court, "where they can 'reasonably forecast substantial
disruption of or material interference with school activities' on
account of the distribution of such printed material."[68]

Lacking in the school's regulation, however, and thus making
the regulation invalid, was the presence "of any criteria to be followed by the school authorities in determining whether to grant or
deny permission"[69] to distribute certain materials. Procedural safeguards are needed, said the court, "in the form of 'an expeditious

---

65. *Id.* at 55-56.

66. *Id.* at 57. *See also* Riseman v. School Comm., 439 F.2d 148 (1st Cir.
1971).

67. *Quarterman, supra* note 63, at 58.

68. *Id.,* In Jacobs v. Board of Sch. Comm'rs, the United States Court of Appeals for the Seventh Circuit made it clear that the occasional presence of "earthy"
words in a student publication cannot be found to be likely to cause substantial
and material disruption of the educational objectives of a school. 490 F.2d 601,
610 (7th Cir. 1973), *cert. denied,* 417 U.S. 928 (1974). The Seventh Circuit
applied both *Tinker* (1969) and *Hazelwood* (1988), and upheld the disciplining of
a student who wrote an article encouraging other students to "hack" into the
school's computer network. The court was convinced that school officials had
made a reasonable forecast of a substantial disruption of school activities. *See*
Boucher v. School Bd., 134 F.3d 821 (7th Cir. 1998).

69. *Quarterman, supra* note 63, at 59.

review procedure'"[70] to reach the school authorities' decision to prohibit the distribution.

In 1973, the Fourth Circuit Court applying the *Quarterman* test in *Baughman v. Freienmuth,*[71] set forth specific requirements for establishing reasonable prior regulations. In the statement were the following items:

> (1) Prior restraints must contain precise criteria sufficiently spelling out what is forbidden so that reasonably intelligent students will know what they may or may not write.
>
> (2) A definition of the term "distribution" and its application to different kinds of material must be included.
>
> (3) There must be *prompt* approval or disapproval of what is submitted to school officials for their review.
>
> (4) The results of failure to act promptly must be specified.
>
> (5) An adequate and prompt appeals procedure must be included.[72]

Hernandez v. Hanson[73] is a 1977 decision from a United States District Court in Nebraska. In this case, plaintiffs brought a class action challenging the policies and regulations of the Omaha Public School District which required students to obtain prior approval before distributing literature in the schools on behalf of nonschool-sponsored organizations. It was board policy that students, staff members, or the school facilities could not be used in any way to advertise or promote the interests of any community or nonschool agency or organization without prior board approval. Certain procedures were spelled out for individuals to use to gain the necessary prior approval, beginning with submitting a written request to

---

70. *Id.*

71. *Supra* note 62.

72. *Id.* at 1351. The need for "reasonably clear" screening procedures is also emphasized in Shanley v. Northeast Indep. Sch. Dist., 462 F.2d 960 (5th Cir. 1972).

73. 430 F. Supp. 1154 (D. Neb. 1977).

the principal of the school.[74] Also included in the procedures were several reasons why a request might be acted upon unfavorably, for example, when the content of the material is commercial in nature, or sectarian, or obscene (which was defined in detail).[75]

At no time did plaintiffs challenge the prerogative of the board to regulate time, place, and manner of distribution. At issue was the board's right to require prior approval of all material.[76]

In deciding the case, District Judge Denney held that there is nothing, per se, unreasonable in requiring prior approval of written distributions by students so long as procedural safeguards are in effect. What is more, the board's outright prohibition of literature that is "sectarian in nature" was valid.[77]

District Judge Denney found fault with the school board's policy to screen all literature meant for distribution to "several students" and not to "all students," since it was not likely that "disruption" of the school would occur from such limited distributions. He also was of the opinion that prohibiting material just because it was "commercial" in nature was at odds with the first amendment.[78]

Concern for possible "harmful consequences" suffered by students was the basis of extending the authority of a building principal to decide on the acceptability of material in a case out of the Fourth Circuit. *Williams v. Spencer*[79] involved the actions of a Maryland school principal to restrain the distribution on school property of a nonschool-sponsored publication, the *Joint Effort* (Issue No. 2). Designed as a "self-styled underground newspaper," the *Joint Effort* was promoted among students as "an alternative for student expression."[80]

---

74. *Id.* at 1157.
75. *Id.* at 1157-58.
76. *Id.* at 1158.
77. *Id.* at 1155.
78. *Id.*
79. 622 F.2d 1200 (4th Cir. 1980).
80. *Id.* at 1202.

The first issue of the paper had been distributed on school property with the express permission of the school principal. Since this first issue met with great success, a second issue was put together.[81] Issue 2 contained various literary contributions, cartoons, and advertisements. Advance approval of the contents (prepublication and predistribution) was not required. Thus, school officials were not aware of the contents of this issue of the paper.[82]

The *Joint Effort* (Issue No. 2) was distributed within the school building. Twenty minutes after the distribution began, a building monitor (Mr. Patterson) halted the process and confiscated all remaining copies (approximately 80 copies had been sold at that time). It seems that Mr. Patterson took exception to a cartoon depicting him as a cowboy holding a pistol and saying (in a dialect): "Don' Smoke Dat Evil Weed, I'll Bust Yo Ass!"[83]

Citing as his intent the enforcement of the *Publication Guidelines of Montgomery County,* the principal upheld the monitor's seizure of the newspaper and the halting of its distribution on school property. All confiscated copies were returned to the student editors. As required by the school system's policy, the principal (within two days) stated in writing his reasons for his actions. These reasons were: (1) a member of the school staff was depicted in the newspaper in "derogatory terms with clear racial overtones"; and (2) there appeared in this issue an advertisement for "drug paraphernalia," which encourages action that "endanger the health and safety of students."[84]

After unsuccessfully taking an administrative appeal, the students filed suit in federal court. Ultimately the district court entered judgment for the school officials and an appeal was taken.

Applying the mandates of such cases as *Tinker* (1969),[85] *Jacobs*

---

81. *Id.*

82. *Id.* at 1203.

83. *Id.*

84. *Id.* Regarding the second reason, Issue 2 carried an advertisement for the Earthworks Headshop, a store specializing in the sale of drug paraphernalia.

85. *Tinker, supra* note 16.

(1975),[86] *Quarterman* (1971),[87] and *Baughman* (1973),[88] the Fourth Circuit concluded that "The First Amendment rights of the students must yield to the superior interest of the school in seeing that materials that encourage actions which endanger the health and safety of students are not distributed on school property."[89] As such, the court held: "[b]ecause the only type of material regulated by the guideline is material that must yield to the school's superior interest, we think the guidelines do not prohibit constitutionally protected conduct of the students. Thus, the guideline is not unconstitutional on its face."[90]

In such situations as found in this case, school officials would not need to demonstrate that the newspaper's contents would "materially and substantially disrupt" the school. Thus, the banning of the *Joint Effort* (Issue No. 2) did not violate the first amendment.[91]

In 1981,[92] a Federal District Court in Indiana upheld the suspension and expulsion of some high school students who had distributed leaflets advocating a student "walk-out." Distributed in the school halls prior to classes and as students passed to their classes, the leaflets advocated a walk-out in protest against the way in which certain school disciplinary procedures were enforced.

To the district court, the students' leaflet activity clearly fell within the protection of the first amendment, and the suspensions and expulsions constituted an infringement of the students' right to expression. However, the fact that a prior walk-out of fifty-four students had occurred, coupled with the administration's appre-

---

86. *Jacobs, supra* note 68.

87. *Quarterman, supra* note 63.

88. *Baughman, supra* note 62.

89. *Williams, supra* note 79, at 1205. The advertisement in the *Joint Effort* primarily promoted the sale of a waterpipe used to smoke marijuana and hashish. The advertisement also promoted paraphernalia used in connection with cocaine. Under Maryland law (as in federal law) marijuana, hashish, and cocaine are all classified as "controlled substances."

90. *Id.*

91. *Id.* at 1206.

92. Dodd v. Rambis, 535 F. Supp. 23 (S.D. Ind. 1981).

hension that another and larger walk-out would occur in response to the leaflet distribution, justified the disciplinary actions.[93]

In reaching its decision, the district court applied the *Tinker* standard. Thus, the question in *Dodd* was: could the student's conduct (in distributing the leaflets) "reasonably have led school authorities to forecast substantial disruption of or a material interference with school activities . . . [or] intru[sion] in the school affairs or the lives of others."[94] Applying the *Tinker* standard to the circumstances of this case, the court answered in the affirmative, and the court added that it was not necessary to show that serious and substantial disruption stemmed directly from the distribution activity.[95]

Considering all the factors of this case, said the court, "the distribution of the leaflets by plaintiffs would result in a substantial disruption or material interference with the activities of the school unless appropriate action was taken . . . . As such, . . . the school officials . . . could properly discipline the plaintiffs for their actions in distributing the . . . leaflets. . . ."[96]

The district court warned however, that this decision is not intended to give school officials either an invitation or a license to prohibit constitutionally protected conduct.[97] Care and caution still must be used when dealing with the right of expression.

§ 11.4. Freedom of Association and Assembly.

Americans have long cherished the right to gather together and assemble with others in whom they find a common bond. In our society there exist many kinds of clubs, associations, societies, and other formal organizations (both public and private) joined by people who share a common interest or cause. Historically, some organizations have been more acceptable to the greater social

---

93. *Id.* at 29.
94. *Id.* Here the court quotes directly from *Tinker, supra* note 16, at 740.
95. *Id.*
96. *Id.* at 30.
97. *Id.* at 31.

system than have others, creating numerous court battles fought to establish and clarify what have come to be called the freedom of association and the right peaceably to assemble.

In recent years, formal clubs and associations of students have become a part of the daily life of the public school, with some even having a formal designation as co-curricular. From time to time, however, other student organizations and groups have come into existence without the expressed sanction of school officials. In these situations the battles for formal recognition within the school's program have been taken into the courts on first and fourteenth amendment grounds. As in other matters discussed in this chapter, the federal courts have been faced with the problem of determining where, in fact, the student's rights to association and assembly begin and the school's prerogatives to infringe upon these guarantees begin.

a. *Association.* *Gay Alliance of Students v. Matthews* is a 1976 decision of the United States Court of Appeals for the Fourth Circuit.[98] In that case, student leaders of the Gay Alliance of Students had submitted to Virginia Commonwealth University officials an application for registration as a student organization with all the rights and privileges granted to bona fide student organizations. Their application was ultimately turned down by the Board of Visitors (the university's governing board).

Even though the board did not state any reasons for its disapproval action, it was stipulated by the parties that the board was motivated by the following: (1) recognizing the Alliance as a campus organization would increase opportunities for homosexual contacts, (2) students who otherwise might not have joined would tend to do so if the group was recognized, and (3) recognition of the Alliance by the university would tend to attract other homosexuals to the university.[99] The district court found that no cognizable constitutional deprivation was imposed by withholding recognition. However, the district court did order that the university

---

98. 544 F.2d 162 (4th Cir. 1976).

99. *Id.* at 164.

provide the Alliance with access to school facilities, access to the school newspaper, access to school bulletin boards, and many other privileges. On appeal, the Fourth Circuit Court held that the university's refusal to register the association on the same terms as those applied to other student organizations violated the first and fourteenth amendments. Said Judge Winter, "[t]he very essence of the first amendment is that each individual makes his own decision as to whether joining an organization would be harmful to him, and whether any countervailing benefits outweigh the potential harm."[100] If individuals have a right, said Judge Winter, to associate with others in furtherance of their mutual beliefs, that right is furthered where registration of a group by a university encourages such association.

Regarding the existence of student societies, fraternities, associations, and clubs in public secondary schools, the courts have also attempted to ensure the free association of students. However, state legislatures and local school boards have over the years demonstrated considerable control over student organizations, both school sponsored and nonschool sponsored (but existing on school grounds) as an exercise of their authority to protect the educational environment from disruption.

Courts of law have been reluctant to interfere with school board authority and have consistently held that student organizations found to be inimical to the good government of the school, to discipline, and to student morale must be prohibited within the school. Likewise, the judges have stated that student organizations that cause disruption of the learning environment may be prohibited.[101] As the Court of Civil Appeals of Texas said in deciding a 1968 case in point, "while the last thing we would wish to do is to interfere with the right of freedom of association or the civil rights

---

100. 544 F.2d at 166-67.

101. *See, e.g.*, Holroyd v. Eibling, 188 N.E.2d 797 (Ohio 1962); Robinson v. Sacramento City Unified Sch. Dist., 53 Cal. Rptr. 781 (Cal. 1966).

of students involved, we must maintain an orderly system of administration of our public schools."[102]

A recent example of federal court action that expands the parameters of freedom of expression came from a U.S. District Court in Rhode Island. In *Fricke v. Lynch,*[103] the court was faced with the complaint of a male homosexual student who had asked for but was denied the principal's permission to bring a male escort to the senior dance.[104] Meeting again with the principal to ask his permission, plaintiff Fricke explained his commitment to homosexuality and indicated that he was (at that time) exclusively homosexual and could not conscientiously date girls.[105] This time the principal gave Fricke written reasons for his denial, with his prime concern being "the fear that disruption would occur."[106]

There is little doubt that the principal was genuinely concerned for the safety of Fricke and his male escort. In fact, at least one incident had already occurred in which another student, unprovoked, shoved and hit Fricke necessitating his receiving five stitches to close an eye wound.[107] Also, it should be pointed out that one year earlier another male student had requested permission to bring a male escort to the junior prom, resulting in other students taunting him, spitting at him, and even slapping him.[108]

In the present instance, Fricke argued that his first amendment right of association, his right to free speech, and his fourteenth amendment right to equal protection were violated by the principal's refusals. What is more, to Fricke, he had a right to attend and participate in the event just like all other students. Yet, because of his honesty about his sexual preferences, "his attendance would

---

102. Passel v. Fort Worth Indep. Sch. Dist., 429 S.W.2d 917 (Tex. 1968).
103. 491 F. Supp. 381 (D.R.I. 1980).
104. *Id.* at 383.
105. *Id.*
106. *Id.* at 383-84.
107. *Id.* at 384.
108. *Id.* at 383.

have a certain political element and would be a statement for equal rights and human rights." [109]

In resolving the issues presented in this case, the district court focused upon Fricke's free speech claim and relied upon such cases as *Tinker*, [110] *Shanley*, [111] and *Burnside*, [112] each recognizing and enforcing "students' rights to free expression inside and outside the classroom." [113] However, the district court recognized the balance created in these same cases placing limits on first amendment rights in the school where student conduct materially and substantially disrupts the school. [114]

After careful analysis of the facts presented in this case, the court concluded that "a violent reaction is not sufficient reason to restrain such speech in advance, and an actual hostile reaction is rarely an adequate basis for curtailing free speech." [115] In the matter of Fricke, the court could not see where any disturbance would interfere with the main business of the school — education. No classes would be disrupted. [116] In such a context, said the court, "the school does have an obligation to take reasonable measures to protect and foster free speech, not to stand helpless before unauthorized student violence." [117] Meaningful security measures were possible to protect the students.

Fricke's conduct was quiet and peaceful. "Any disturbance that might interfere with the rights of others," said the court, "would be caused by those students who resort to violence, not by Aaron (Fricke) and his companion, who do not want to fight." [118]

---

109. *Id.* at 385.
110. *Tinker, supra* note 16.
111. *Shanley, supra* note 72.
112. *Burnside, supra* note 15.
113. *Fricke, supra* note 103, at 386.
114. *Id.*
115. *Id.* at 387.
116. *Id.*
117. *Id.*
118. *Id.* at 388.

b. *Assembly*. The United States Supreme Court has long declared that holding a peaceful public meeting to conduct a lawful discussion is a constitutionally protected right of all citizens.[119] Equally clear, however, is that public gatherings that become less than peaceful or at which speakers incite groups to riot are not protected and are therefore subject to governmental control and regulation to preserve law and order.[120]

Lawrence University Bicentennial Commission v. City of Appleton[121] is a 1976 decision of a United States District Court in Wisconsin. In this case an association of college students had applied for permission to rent the Appleton High School East gymnasium for purposes of a public lecture by Angela Davis. Their application was disapproved by the board of education by a vote of four to two. According to the board, their policy stated that school buildings were not to be used for religious or political activities unless the activity is nonpartisan or nondenominational.[122]

Plaintiffs argued that Ms. Davis' lecture was to be nonpartisan and not political in nature. They also contended that the board had, in the past, allowed other groups to assemble in school buildings (for example, the League of Women Voters) where candidates and holders of political office gave speeches.

No evidence was ever presented to the board of education that violence and disruption accompanied any of Ms. Davis' previous lectures. Nor was there any evidence that any violence would occur at the proposed lecture.[123]

In granting plaintiffs' request for a preliminary injunction and ordering that the student association be permitted to use the school's facilities for their lecture, Chief Judge Reynolds found fault with the words "political" and "religious" used in the board

---

119. *See* De Jonge v. Oregon, 299 U.S. 353, 57 S. Ct. 255, 81 L. Ed. 278 (1937).

120. *See* Feiner v. New York, 340 U.S. 315, 71 S. Ct. 303, 95 L. Ed. 295 (1951).

121. 409 F. Supp. 1319 (E.D. Wis. 1976).

122. *Id.* at 1322-23.

123. *Id.*

policy. The distinctions drawn by such words, he said, "are impermissible because they have the effect of regulating speech on the basis of its content, and this state officials may not do."[124]

No additional evidence was presented by the board to show that the students' use of the gym would interfere with any other scheduled activities. Nor was the format of the lecture anything unusual or different from that of any other groups using the facility.

Judge Reynolds did not remove the prerogatives of school authorities to control the use of school buildings by groups. He did warn, however, that there are limitations on this authority.

> It is true that the state need not open the doors of a school building as a forum and may at any time choose to close them. Once it opens the doors, however, it cannot demand tickets, of admission in the form of convictions and affiliations that it deems acceptable.[125]

In *People v. Witzkowski,*[126] some university students had received permission from school officials to conduct an "antiwar demonstration" in the south lounge of the student union building. Instead of remaining in the authorized area, the students moved, on their own, to a lobby area where they seated themselves on the floor blocking the entrance to a room where the Marine Corps was recruiting. When university security officers ordered them to leave, they refused to do so. After repeated warnings, the protestors were ultimately arrested.[127]

The student demonstrators were convicted of violating an Illinois statute prohibiting interference with public institutions of higher learning. The Appellate Court of Illinois upheld that conviction. In the opinion of that court, the purpose of the statute was to protect the institutions from disruption and not to suppress free expression. The student protestors had been given adequate notice

---

124. *Id.* at 1323.
125. *Id.* at 1324-25.
126. 357 N.E.2d 1348 (Ill. 1976).
127. *Id.* at 1350.

and ample time, prior to their arrest, to vacate the university building.[128]

The Fifth Circuit heard an appeal from the U.S. District Court, Middle District of Louisiana, involving the Iranian Student Organization at Southern University.[129] The case had been taken into district court under 42 U.S.C. § 1983 (naming as defendants the Governor of Louisiana and University officials), where the student organization sought a temporary restraining order, preliminary and permanent injunctive relief, and declaratory relief against enforcement of state and local ordinances and University regulations which they said "interfered with the exercise of (their) first amendment rights."[130] The ordinances and regulations at issue required posting a $10,000 bond, prohibited "chanting and using amplifiers in public demonstrations," and forbade marches by "unrecognized student organizations" such as the Iranian Student Association.[131]

Subsequently, the parties entered a consent decree which "amended the University rules by deleting official recognition of an organization as a prerequisite to obtaining permission to march and by adding a provision that recognizes the students' right to engage in peaceful protests."[132]

Upon acquiring the above relief, the students sought to recover attorney's fees as the "prevailing party" in the action. The district court denied the motion and the case was appealed to the Second Circuit.[133] The appellate court upheld the denial of the motion.

c. *Time and Place Regulations.* In *Grayned v. City of Rockford*,[134] the United States Supreme Court upheld the prerogative of school officials to forbid deliberately noisy or diversionary

---

128. *Id.* at 1353.

129. Iranian Students Ass'n v. Edwards, 604 F.2d 352 (5th Cir. 1979).

130. *Id.* at 353.

131. *Id.*

132. *Id.*

133. *Id.* The district court denied the motion on the ground that "plaintiffs had shown neither probable success on the merits, nor a 'compelling reason' to justify the imposition of attorney's fees on the defendants."

134. 408 U.S. 104, 92 S. Ct. 2294, 33 L. Ed. 2d 222 (1972).

activities by students that disrupt or are about to disrupt normal school activities. According to the Court, school officials do not offend the first amendment by fixing times and places for such activity.

In judging the reasonableness of time and place regulations regarding student assembly, four factors will be considered by the courts. First, the nature of the place where prior control of assembly is made applicable will be considered (the school). Second, the special characteristics of the people present in that place will be examined (the students). Third, the normal pattern of activities conducted in the place will be established (education). Finally, the impact of the assembly activity on those normal activities will be assessed (disruption).[135]

§ 11.5. Flag Salute.

Over the years, there have been incidents in public school systems involving students who refuse to participate in a salute to the American flag and in the recitation of the Pledge of Allegiance. In these situations students have expressed their defiance of such exercises (most of which were required either by state law or school board policy) for a variety of reasons.

In the early cases, deprivation of religious freedom was often cited by those who refused to participate in flag salute ceremonies. The Jehovah's Witnesses organization was one group that took exception to the flag salute exercises in public schools.

---

135. *Id.* Whether or not the school has become a limited open *forum* for student expression or for the expression of outside (community) groups must be determined by examining the *nature of the activity* (curricular or noncurricular), the *nature of the place* (gym, auditorium, classroom, etc.), *policy statements* of school officials (dealing with use of school facilities), and *the past pattern and usage* of the specific place. This has become an issue of critical importance to contemporary public school systems. *See, e.g.,* Bender v. Williamsport Area Sch. Dist., 475 U.S. 534 (1986); Students Against Apartheid Coalition v. O'Neil, 838 F.2d 735 (4th Cir. 1988); Garnett v. Renton Sch. Dist., 865 F.2d 1121 (9th Cir. 1989); Searcey v. Harris, 888 F.2d 1314 (11th Cir. 1989); Board of Educ. of Westside Community Schs. v. Mergens, 110 S. Ct. 2356 (1990).

Minersville v. Gobitis,[136] decided in 1940, was the first flag salute case decided by the United States Supreme Court. In that case, involving Jehovah's Witnesses who saw the local school board's requirement that all students participate in the flag salute as an expression of belief and worship contrary to their religion's dictates, this nation's highest court did not consider the requirement of saluting the flag in any way repugnant to the United States Constitution.

Three years later, however, in *West Virginia State Board of Education v. Barnette*,[137] the Supreme Court had another chance to review a flag salute case involving Jehovah's Witnesses. This time the West Virginia State Board of Education required that the salute to the flag become a regular part of the day's activities in every public school of the state, with refusal to participate considered an act of insubordination, dealt with accordingly. Students who were expelled from school for their refusal to salute the flag were denied readmission to the school until they complied with the requirement.

The Supreme Court in *Barnette* held the flag salute requirement an unconstitutional exercise of governmental authority. To the Court's majority such a requirement "invades the sphere of intellect and spirit which it is the purpose of the First Amendment to our Constitution to reserve from all official control."[138]

In the years following *Barnette*, public school districts enacted policies meant both to preserve the requirement that students salute the flag and to protect the right of students who wish not to participate in the exercise. These policies usually allowed students who objected to the exercise either to leave the room or to stand silently while the pledge of allegiance was said. There have been court cases brought by students challenging such policies.

Generally, courts have held that school boards cannot require students to salute the flag. What is more, school authorities cannot

---

136. 310 U.S. 586, 60 S. Ct. 1010, 84 L. Ed. 1375 (1940).
137. 319 U.S. 624, 63 S. Ct. 1178, 87 L. Ed. 1628 (1943).
138. *Id.*

require that students who refuse to participate in the salute to the flag either leave the place where the exercise is held or stand silently during the exercise. So long as the student who refuses to participate is quiet and is nondisruptive of the exercise itself or of the rights of those participating in the exercise, he or she cannot be chastised or in some other way punished.[139]

§ 11.6. The Right to Receive Expression.

Freedom of expression in public schools has taken a new path, opening another avenue of litigation in the courts. Instead of dealing with the right of students to give, exhibit, or project their ideas, opinions, information, and beliefs (expressions), the new category of cases deals with the reciprocal right of students "to receive" the ideas, information, and beliefs (expressions) of others.[140] *Bicknell v. Vergennes Union High School Board of Directors*[141] offers a good example of this type of case.

a. *Books and Instructional Materials.* Decided by the Second Circuit in 1980, *Bicknell* involved a Vermont public school board's decision to remove certain books from the school library, in response to an ongoing controversy. It seems that certain parents

---

139. *See, e.g.,* Holden v. Board of Educ., 216 A.2d 387 (N.J. 1966); Frain v. Baron. 307 F. Supp. 27 (E.D.N.Y. 1969); Goetz v. Ansell, 477 F.2d 636 (2d Cir. 1973). Two nonschool related events might prove to have a profound impact on future flag salute policies within public schools. First, during the 1988-89 term, the Rehnquist Court rendered a decision in Texas v. Johnson, 109 S. Ct. 1486 (1989), wherein the Court saw the first amendment as protecting a protestor's flag burning as "expressive conduct." Second, the various legislative initiatives (in Congress and the States) to protect the American flag from any form of desecration have been under attack. In United States v. Eichman, 110 S. Ct. 2404 (1990), the U.S. Supreme Court struck down the federal Flag Protection Act, 18 U.S.C. § 700 (Supp. 1990).

140. On this specific point of law, see Virginia State Bd. of Pharmacy v. Virginia Citizens Consumer Council, 425 U.S. 748, 96 S. Ct. 1817, 48 L. Ed. 2d 346 (1976). For an excellent book offering a comprehensive treatment of this subject, see J.E. BRYSON & E.W. DETTY, CENSORSHIP OF PUBLIC SCHOOL LIBRARY AND INSTRUCTIONAL MATERIAL (Charlottesville, Va.: Michie Co., 1982).

141. 638 F.2d 438 (2d Cir. 1980).

objected to what they referred to as the "vulgarity and indecency of language in the books."[142]

Some months before the board removed the books, a policy governing the selection and removal of books had been adopted. In reaction to the parent complaints, however, the board altered its policy and voted to remove the books from the library shelves and to place them on a "restricted shelf." The board also voted to prohibit the school librarian from purchasing any additional major works of fiction, and that any book purchases other than those in a certain specified category be reviewed by the school administration in consultation with the board.[143]

A group of students, their parents, library employees, and an unincorporated association known as the Right to Read Defense Fund brought suit to enjoin removal of the books and any alteration of the school library policy. The plaintiffs alleged that (1) their first amendment rights were violated, primarily because the board's action was motivated solely by the "personal tastes and values" of board members, and (2) the board's action denied them due process because the board violated its own internal policies and procedures.[144]

A federal district court had dismissed the complaint. In affirming that decision, the Second Circuit held that: (1) There is no first amendment violation in removing books on the basis of vulgarity and indecency of language, where this determination is not made on the basis of the board members' "own standards of taste . . . ."[145] Also, these books were not removed because of their ideas, nor were they removed because of some political motivation. (2) The students and librarian had no due process right to a hearing before the removal of the books took place. Here there was no requisite

---

142. *Id.* at 440. The books involved were *Dog Day Afternoon,* by P. Mann, and *The Wanderers,* by R. Price. *See also* Fleischfresser v. Directors, 15 F.3d 680 (7th Cir. 1994), where parents challenged use of an elementary school reading series.

143. 638 F.2d 438, 441.

144. *Id.*

145. *Id.*

"particularized and personal interest on the part of the person asserting the right."[146] (3) Even though the school librarian had a more particularized claim, the board had not dismissed her or reprimanded her; it just removed certain functions from her job assignment. And, in general, "an employee of a governmental agency has no constitutionally protected interest in the particular duties of a job assignment."[147] (4) Regarding the board's not following policy, state procedural requirements do not create interests entitled to due process protection.

In dissent, Judge Sifton was in favor of reversing and remanding the matter for discovery and trial to examine more closely the board's procedural irregularities, and to explore in depth the board's reasons for wanting the books removed. The merits of the board's rationale for doing what it did were not considered.[148]

That same year, 1980, the Seventh Circuit heard the appeal of some plaintiff students who claimed first and fourteenth amendment violations of their "right to know" and their "right to read literary works in their entirety," because of the acts of public school officials in (1) removing certain books from English courses and the high school library, (2) eliminating certain courses from the high school English curriculum, and (3) failing to rehire certain English teachers. Claiming that the official's actions had "a chilling effect on the free exchange of knowledge," the students in *Zykan v. Warsaw Community School Corporation*[149] brought suit in federal district court under 42 U.S.C. § 1983. Subsequently, the district court dismissed an amended complaint and plaintiff students appealed.[150]

---

146. *Id.* at 442.

147. *Id.*

148. *Id.* at 443.

149. 631 F.2d 1300 (7th Cir. 1980).

150. The amended complaint cited six separate incidents. The first four incidents involved the removal of certain books from certain courses and the school library, without proper consultation with teachers, parents, or students, or without steps taken to determine literary value or scholastic value; another incident involved the elimination of some courses from the curriculum because "the teaching

At the outset, the Seventh Circuit established as clear and settled law that (1) students do not "shed their constitutional rights at
the school house gate," and (2) the first amendment's guarantees
are sufficiently broad to provide some protection for "academic
freedom." What was less than clear and settled law, however, were
the precise contours of academic freedom and its appropriate role
in secondary schools, as opposed to colleges and universities.[151]

To the court, even though secondary school students "retain an
interest in some freedom of the classroom, if only through the
qualified 'freedom to hear'," two factors tend to limit that freedom. These factors are: (1) the student's right to and need for such
freedom is bounded by the level of his or her intellectual development, and (2) the importance of secondary schools in the development of intellectual faculties is only one part of a broad formative
role. This latter factor, said the court, also encompasses "the encouragement and nurturing of those fundamental social, political,
and moral values that will permit a student to take his place in the
community."[152] As such, "the community has a legitimate, even a
vital and compelling interest in 'the choice [of] and adherence to a
suitable curriculum for the benefit of our young citizens . . . .'"[153]

That local school boards must have broad discretion to regulate
the specifics of the classroom (a part of their task being the transmission of the mores of the community), subject only to limited
constitutional constraints, is both appropriate and permissible. But,
the court warns, this does not mean that a board is free to "fire a
teacher for every random comment in the classroom," nor can
boards insist upon "instruction in a religiously-inspired dogma to
the exclusion of other points of view,"[154] or from placing a "flat

---

methods and content . . . offended their (school officials') social, political and
moral beliefs"; while the other incidents involved certain decisions not to rehire
two English teachers who had been involved in the above matters. *Id.* at 1302-03.

151. *Id.* at 1304.

152. *Id.*

153. *Id.* Here the court cites Palmer v. Board of Educ., 603 F.2d 1271 (7th Cir.
1979), *cert. denied,* 444 U.S. 1026 (1980).

154. *Id.* at 1305.

prohibition on the mention of certain relevant topics in the classroom."[155]

The appellate court also could not conceive of how a student could "assert a right to have the teacher control the classroom when a teacher herself does not have such a right."[156] In the court's opinion, a student's appreciation of a teacher's skills could not "invest a teacher with a constitutionally based tenure when the actions of the school board have given that teacher none."[157]

Regarding the school library, the court saw it as "a general resource the purpose of which is to foster intellectual curiosity and serve the intellectual needs of its users."[158] This purpose, the court suggests, is not without limitations imposed by budgetary constraints and by the fact that materials provided in that resource must "properly supplement the basic readings assigned through the standard curriculum."[159] As such, "[a]n administrator would be irresponsible if he or she failed to monitor closely the contents of the library and did not remove a book when an appraisal of its content fails to justify its continued use of valuable shelf space."[160]

To the court, however, this does not mean that administrators can "purge" material offensive to a single, exclusive perception of the way things should be, nor can administrators prohibit students from buying or reading a particular book or from bringing it to school and discussing it there.[161] In the court's opinion, the amended complaint contained no such allegations.

Thus, the judgment of the district court was vacated and remanded for further proceedings. Since the principles and issues in the case were "sufficiently novel and important," the plaintiffs were given leave to amend their complaint again, "to allege the

---

155. *Id.* at 1305-06.
156. *Id.* at 1307.
157. *Id.* at 1308.
158. *Id.*
159. *Id.*
160. *Id.*
161. *Id.*

kind of interference with secondary school academic freedom that has been found to be cognizable as a constitutional claim."[162]

b. *Theatrical Production and Films*. Decided on December 29, 1981, *Seyfried v. Walton*[163] involved a § 1983 suit brought by some secondary school students and their parents who contended that their first amendment rights to expression were violated when the school district superintendent determined that a proposed school-sponsored production of "Pippin" would be inappropriate, and therefore must be cancelled. The superintendent had declared that his decision was based on the fact that "Pippin" had a sexual theme.

It seems that several months prior to the play's production the director (also an English teacher at the school) consulted with the assistant principal, edited the script (since there were certain "sexually explicit" scenes), revised the scenes, and finally reached agreement with the principal that the preparation for the production should go forward.

In March of 1981, shortly after rehearsal had begun, a father of a "Pippin" cast member complained to his brother, the school board's president, that the play "mocked religion." The board president directed the superintendent to look into the matter. After reviewing the script, the superintendent determined that the play did not mock religion, but it was "inappropriate for a public high school because of its sexual content."[164] Subsequently, he directed the school principal to stop the play.

Some interested parents appeared before the school board to express their views on the play. The board refused to overturn the superintendent's decision. The play was not presented in the spring of 1981.

Suing under § 1983, the parents of three "Pippin" cast members claimed that the students' first amendment rights had been

---

162. *Id.* at 1309.
163. 668 F.2d 214 (3d Cir. 1981).
164. *Id.* at 215-16.

abridged. After a two-day trial the district court entered judgment for the defendants.[165]

On appeal the Third Circuit held that the superintendent's decision to cancel the play did not violate the students' first amendment rights. To the appellate court, "the district court properly distinguished student newspapers and other 'non-program related expressions of student opinion' from school-sponsored theatrical productions."[166] The critical factor in this case, said the Third Circuit, "is the relationship of the play to the school curriculum."[167] The school staff and administration viewed the play as an integral part of the school's educational program; and even though voluntary for students, the play "was considered a part of the curriculum in theater arts."[168]

Based upon the above rationale, the appellate court agreed with the district court, "that those responsible for directing a school's educational program must be allowed to decide how its limited resources can be best used to achieve the goals of educating and socializing its students."[169] In such matters (said the court) courts are reluctant to interfere, especially in "the resolution of conflicts which arise in the daily operation of school systems and which do not directly and sharply implicate basic constitutional values."[170] The conflict in *Seyfried,* in the Third Circuit's opinion, did not

---

165. 512 F. Supp. 253 (D. Del. 1980).

166. 668 F.2d 214, 216.

167. *Id.*

168. *Id.* For a different point of view, see Boring v. Buncombe Cty. Bd. of Educ., 136 F.3d 364 (4th Cir. 1998). The court ruled that a drama teacher's choice for a play to be presented in statewide competition did not involve a matter of public concern. The court upheld the principal's decision not to allow "Independence" to be presented because of the play's strong sexual themes. The court also opined that school officials and not classroom teachers should make curricular decisions.

169. *Id.* at 217.

170. *Id.* Here the Court is quoting from the Second Circuit's opinion in Pico v. Board of Educ., Island Trees Union Free Sch. Dist. No. 26, 638 F.2d 404 (2d Cir. 1980), which was pending before the U.S. Supreme Court.

"'directly and sharply implicate' the first amendment rights of the students." [171]

In 1982, the Eighth Circuit decided *Pratt v. Independent School District No. 831.* [172] In *Pratt,* some junior and senior high school students in Minnesota brought an action in federal district court to compel school officials to reinstate the film version of a short story ("The Lottery") and a trailer film (which discusses the story and its themes) to the school's curriculum. It seems that a group of parents and other citizens became concerned about the use of the films in American literature classes (taught at the senior high school), sought to have the films removed from the school district's curriculum (on grounds that the films were too violent and would have a destructive impact on the religious and family values of students), and pursued their complaint through the appropriate procedures for review and selection of instructional materials. Subsequently, the school board acceded to the group's demands and removed the films.

After a hearing, the district court found that the school board's objections to the films had "religious overtones" and that the films had been banned because of their "ideological content." [173] As such, the court held that the local board's decision violated the first amendment and ordered the films reinstated in the curriculum.

Affirming the district court, the Eighth Circuit held that the school board "cannot constitutionally ban the films because a majority of its members object to the films' religious and ideological content and wish to prevent the ideas contained in the material from being expressed in school." [174]

In its opinion, the Eighth Circuit reiterated the case-hardened tenets of school law which establish (1) that local school authorities are the principal policymakers for public schools, (2) that local school boards are accorded comprehensive powers and substantial

---

171. *Id.*
172. 670 F.2d 771 (8th Cir. 1982).
173. *Id.* at 773.
174. *Id.*

discretion to discharge their tasks, (3) that within this comprehensive authority is the discretion to determine the curriculum most suitable for students and the teaching methods to be employed, and (4) that such curricular decisions may properly reflect the local community's views and values as to content and methodology.[175] But, the appellate court cautions, "school boards do not have an absolute right to remove materials from the curriculum."[176]

In *Pratt*, the plaintiff students carried their burden of establishing that the board banned the films because the majority of its members objected to the ideas expressed in them. Therefore, said the court, "to avoid a finding that it acted unconstitutionally, the board must establish that a substantial and reasonable governmental interest exists for interfering with the student's right to receive information."[177] Bare allegations that such a basis exists, said the court, are not sufficient.[178]

Since the board failed to carry its burden of establishing a substantial governmental interest, the student's first amendment rights were violated, and the district court decision was affirmed.[179]

c. *Pico*. Less than five months after the Eighth Circuit's decision in *Pratt*, the United States Supreme Court decided a case on point from the Second Circuit. The case, *Board of Education, Island Trees Union Free School District No. 26 v. Pico*,[180] presented this nation's Highest Court with two basic questions: (1) Does the first amendment impose limitations on a local public school board's prerogatives to remove books from the school library? (2) If question one is answered in the affirmative, did the school board in this case exceed those limitations?[181]

---

175. *Id.* at 775-77.
176. *Id.* at 776.
177. *Id.* at 777.
178. *Id.*
179. *Id.* at 779-80.
180. 457 U.S. 853, 102 S. Ct. 2799, 73 L. Ed. 2d 435 (1982).
181. *Id.*, 457 U.S. at 863.

The major incident that formed the basis of this suit involved the school board's removal of *eleven*[182] books from the school library. Alleging that the removed books were anti-American, anti-Christian, anti-Semitic, and "just plain filthy,"[183] the board claimed that it had the same prerogative to remove library books as it does to place books on the library shelves. Moreover, in the opinion of some board members, when school library books contain vulgarities, explicit descriptions of sexual relations, and disparaging comments about religious and ethnic groups (all matters that offend that community's moral and social values) a public school board must act to remove those books from possible student consumption.

It seems that in September 1975, the school board president, vice president, and one other board member attended a conference sponsored by PONYU (Parents of New York United), a politically conservative organization, where they obtained a list of "objectionable" books. Subsequently, it was found that the high school library housed *nine* of the listed books, while another listed book was found in the junior high school library.[184]

In February, 1976, the board met with the school superintendent and the school principals and gave an "unofficial direction" that the listed books be removed from the library shelves and taken to the board offices so that members could read them. The directive was carried out, even though the superintendent objected.[185] In a press release to justify its actions the board said: "It is our duty, our moral obligation, to protect the children in our schools from this moral danger as surely as from physical and medical dangers."[186]

---

182. *Id.*, at 858. The books in question were *Slaughterhouse Five, The Naked Ape, Down These Mean Streets, Best Stories of Negro Writers, Go Ask Alice, Laughing Boy, A Hero Ain't Nothing But a Sandwich, Soul on Ice, A Reader for Writers,* and *The Fixer.*

183. *Id.* at 857.

184. *Id.* at 856.

185. *Id.* at 857.

186. *Id.* This is a direct quotation from the district court's opinion.

Subsequently, the school board appointed a book review committee (four parents and four staff members) to read the listed books and recommend to the board whether it should or should not retain the books. The committee was to take into account such factors as "educational suitability," "good taste," "relevance," and "appropriateness to age and grade level."[187] The committee ultimately recommended that *five* of the books be retained and *two* others be removed from the school libraries. The committee took no position on *one* other, could not agree on a recommendation on *two* others, and recommended that the last of the nine be made available to students whose parents approved.[188]

Soon after the committee made the above recommendations, the board rejected its report. Adopting its own stand on the books, the board decided to (1) return one book to the high school library without restriction, (2) make another available subject to parental approval, and (3) remove the remaining books from the elementary and secondary school libraries and from use in the curriculum.[189] The board gave no reasons for its actions.

Pico, et al., brought suit in federal district court under 42 U.S.C. § 1983. The board's actions, said plaintiffs, "denied them their rights under the First Amendment."[190] As remedy, plaintiffs requested a declaration that the board's actions were unconstitutional and injunctive relief ordering the board to return the nine books to the school libraries and ordering that the board not interfere with the use of the books in the curriculum.[191]

The district court granted summary judgment in favor of the school officials.[192] Pico, et al., appealed. A three-judge panel for the Second Circuit reversed the district court and remanded the

---

187. *Id.*

188. *Id.* at 858.

189. *Id.* at 859.

190. *Id.*

191. *Id.*

192. Pico v. Board of Educ., Island Trees Union Free Sch. Dist. No. 26, 474 F. Supp. 387 (E.D.N.Y. 1979).

case for trial on the factual issues raised in the allegations.[193] In the opinion of the appellate court, the board was "obliged to demonstrate a reasonable basis for interfering with the respondent's First Amendment rights."[194] Thus, the key question to be answered at trial concerned whether the board's removal of the books "was motivated by a justifiable desire to remove books containing vulgarities and sexual explicitness, or rather by an impermissible desire to suppress ideas."[195] Certiorari was granted by the U.S. Supreme Court.[196]

Justice Brennan wrote for a majority that saw the issues as narrow, both substantively and procedurally.[197] Citing *Meyer*,[198] *Epperson*,[199] *Tinker*,[200] and *Ambach*,[201] the Court made it very clear at the outset that (1) local school boards have broad discretion in the management of school affairs, (2) federal courts should not ordinarily intervene in the day-to-day decisionmaking of school officials, (3) school officials have comprehensive authority to prescribe and control conduct in schools, and (4) there is a legitimate and substantial community interest in promoting respect for authority and traditional values (social, moral, and political).[202] However, warned Justice Brennan, these prerogatives "must be exercised in a manner that comports with the transcendent imperatives of the First Amendment."[203]

The majority's rationale in reaching a decision seems to be built on three specific points of view: (1) the right of a student to re-

---

193. Pico v. Board of Educ., Island Trees Union Free Sch. Dist. No. 26, 638 F.2d 404 (2d Cir. 1980).

194. *Id.* at 414-15.

195. *Pico, supra* note 180, at 457 U.S. 861.

196. Certiorari granted at 454 U.S. 891 (1981).

197. 457 U.S. at 856.

198. Meyer v. Nebraska, 262 U.S. 390, 43 S. Ct. 625, 67 L. Ed. 1042 (1923).

199. Epperson v. Arkansas, 393 U.S. 97, 89 S. Ct. 266, 21 L. Ed. 2d 228 (1968).

200. *Tinker, supra* note 16.

201. Ambach v. Norwick, 441 U.S. 68, 99 S. Ct. 2806, 60 L. Ed. 2d 49 (1979).

202. 457 U.S. 864.

203. *Id.*

ceive ideas is a necessary predicate to the student-recipient's "meaningful exercise of his own rights of speech, press, and political freedom,"[204] (2) school officials "cannot suppress expressions of feeling with which they do not wish to contend,"[205] and (3) the school library is the principal locus of free inquiry and study, protected by the first amendment.[206]

In the opinion of this nation's Highest Court, a public school board does not have absolute discretion to decide what books should or should not be in the school library for student consumption. Thus, in removing books from school library shelves a board cannot base its decision to do so solely on its "dislike" of the ideas contained in the removed books. Nor could the board base its removal decision solely on the fact that the books were objected to by PONYU, when the board members themselves had not reviewed the contents of the books.[207] The Second Circuit decision was affirmed.

§ 11.7. Freedom of Expression in the 1990s.

As demonstrated in previous subsections of this chapter, the Supreme Court's decision in *Tinker* (1969)[208] ushered in a new era, the "era of student rights." In effect, application of the *material and substantial disruption* standard by the courts below opened up more rights for students, while decreasing the disciplinary authority of school administrators. On matters of student speech and expression, the 1970s and early 1980s were character-

---

204. *Id.* Here the court uses a direct quotation from Burnside v. Byars, 363 F.2d 744 (5th Cir. 1966).

205. *Id.* at 457 U.S. 868.

206. *Id.* at 457 U.S. 868-69.

207. *Id.* at 457 U.S. 874-75. For a case on point, see Del Carpio v. St. Tammany Parish Sch. Bd., 865 F. Supp. 350 (E.D. La. 1994), where a federal district court held that a school board's decision to remove a book from the system's libraries was not content neutral. In the court's view, the removal denied students access to ideas solely because the ideas were not consistent with board members' values and concepts of morality.

208. *Tinker, supra* note 16.

ized by some experts as a time when school officials were reluctant to act, out of a "fear of being sued."

By the mid-1980s, however, the judicial pendulum began to swing back in the opposite direction. Two decisions from the United States Supreme Court were instrumental in setting this trend in motion. The benchmark decisions were *Bethel School District v. Fraser* (1986) (involving student speech),[209] and *Hazelwood v. Kuhlmeier* (1988) (involving school newspapers).[210]

The controversy in *Fraser* began with a brief speech by a 17-year-old honor student in the high school auditorium. The student, Matthew Fraser, was giving a nominating speech on behalf of a classmate who was running for vice president of the student government. In his speech Fraser used, according to school officials, sexual innuendo and metaphors.[211]

Following his speech Fraser was disciplined, based on a school policy which said that "conduct which materially and substantially interferes with the education process is prohibited, including the use of obscene, profane language or gestures."[212] Fraser unsuccessfully appealed his discipline to a school grievance officer who, after hearing the evidence concluded that the speech was "indecent, lewd, and offensive to the modesty of the students and faculty in attendance at the assembly."

Fraser took the matter to federal district court where he prevailed. To the trial court, Fraser's rights under both the first and fourteenth amendments had been violated by school officials.[213] On appeal to the Ninth Circuit, the trial court decision was affirmed. The school board then sought review by the Supreme Court.

---

209. 478 U.S. 675 (1986).

210. *Hazelwood, supra* note 50.

211. *Fraser,* at 687. The speech does not appear in Chief Justice Burger's majority opinion, but does appear in Justice Brennan's concurring opinion.

212. *Id.* at 685.

213. The district court awarded Fraser $278 in damages and $12,750 in costs and attorney fees.

The Supreme Court ruled, by 7-2, in favor of the school district. According to Chief Justice Burger for the majority, children's rights are not coextensive with those of adults. Moreover, the first amendment does not protect students in the use of vulgar and offensive language in public discourse.[214] Focusing on the content of Fraser's speech, the Court said that the determination of what manner of speech in the classroom or in an assembly is appropriate rests with school officials and not with students. In the Chief Justice's words, "A high school assembly or classroom is no place for sexually explicit monologue directed towards an unsuspecting audience of teenage students."[215]

In 1988, the Rehnquist Court decided the *Hazelwood* case, which involved a student newspaper. The controversy actually began in 1983, when two articles written by students were removed from publication in the school newspaper (*Spectrum*) by direction of the school principal. The principal acted because he objected to the content of the articles. One article dealt with pregnancy experiences of three of the school's students, while the second article explored the impact of divorce on kids.[216]

Believing that there was no time to make necessary changes in the stories prior to publication, the principal eliminated the two pages on which the articles appeared, without informing the student authors of his decision. Subsequently, three student staff members from *Spectrum* filed suit in federal district court seeking a declaration that their first amendment free speech rights had been violated, an injunction, and money damages. The district court denied the students' request. To the court, school officials may impose restraints on student speech in activities that are an integral part of the school's educational function.[217]

The students appealed to the Eighth Circuit, where the trial court decision was reversed. Even though the appellate court

214. *Id.* at 683.
215. *Id.*
216. *Hazelwood, supra* note 50.
217. Kuhlmeier v. Hazelwood, 607 F. Supp. 1450 (E.D. Mo. 1985).

agreed that *Spectrum* was a part of the school's curriculum, it said that the newspaper was, because of prior practice, a *public forum* "intended to be operated as a conduit for student viewpoint." As such, school officials could not censor the newspaper's contents except when "necessary to avoid material and substantial interference with school work or discipline . . . or the rights of others."[218]

Subsequently, the United States Supreme Court took the case and, by a vote of 5-3, reversed the Eighth Circuit. To the majority, the principal had acted reasonably in his response to certain pedagogical concerns regarding the two articles. Moreover, the Court drew a distinction between *symbolic speech* (as protected in *Tinker*) and "speech sponsored by the school and disseminated under its auspices."[219]

The *Hazelwood* standard of "reasonable exercise of legitimate pedagogical concerns" extends beyond the issue of student newspapers, especially when linked to the *Fraser* opinion. These two decisions taken as a whole grant school officials considerable discretion in deciding all matters of student expression where the school's official imprimatur is present, whether the context of the activity is curricular in nature or where the school's sponsorship of the activity is obvious.[220] Thus, in the 1990s, school boards and their administrative officers (especially building principals), relying on *Hazelwood* and *Fraser*, have set more stringent requirements into place on matters of student speech (where what is said is vulgar or obscene), student dress and attire, and student expression in school publications (especially where subjects covered are sensitive in nature).

In recent years a new generation of student expression cases has come before the courts involving religious issues within the con-

---

218. Kuhlmeier v. Hazelwood. 795 F.2d 1368 (8th Cir. 1986). Here the Eighth Circuit was echoing *Tinker.*

219. *Hazelwood, supra* note 50.

220. For some examples, see Bystrom v. Fridley. 686 F. Supp. 1387 (D. Minn. 1987); Crosby v. Holsinger. 852 F.2d 801 (4th Cir. 1988); Poling v. Murphy, 872 F.2d 757 (6th Cir. 1989); Desilets v. Clearview Reg'l Bd. of Educ., 647 A.2d 150 (N.J. Super. A.D. 1994).

text of public schools. In these situations student groups have requested access to the school (facility, publications, etc.) as "a forum" for student religious expression. The United States Supreme Court has decided a case on point.[221] A more complete discussion of student religious groups can be found in Chapter 12 of this text.

§ 11.8. Assaultive Speech.

In the mid-1990s, in a variety of school settings, the mere utterance of offensive words, by one student to another, by a teacher to a student, or by a student to a teacher has called forth an official administrative action.[222] As demonstrated in earlier sections of this chapter, the traditional rule is that language which is obscene, profane, threatening, or in some other way disruptive shall not be tolerated in a school or at a school sponsored function. More recently, however, speech considered intimidating, hostile, insensitive, or in some way socially or culturally biased has formed the basis of several court cases involving public school systems and colleges. As such, courts have had to differentiate between student or employee speech that is merely distasteful and speech, no matter how distasteful, that is either inherently or actually threatening or in some other way harmful.[223]

School administrators found themselves confused by what seemed to be conflicting directives from the courts. In some situations, judges maintained the traditional view that focused on the effects of speech. In other situations judges focused their judicial analysis on the content of one's expressive act. In both situations, however, the focus changed from the rights of the speaker (i.e., the

---

221. *Mergens, supra* note 135. *See also* Rivera v. East Otero, *supra* note 52.

222. *See* Boulton v. Morgan, 643 So. 2d 1103 (Fla. App. 4 Dist. 1994), where a teacher used racial slurs in class. In such situations the age of the students is a legitimate concern of school administrators. *See, e.g.,* Berger v. Rennselaer Cent. Sch. Corp., 982 F.2d 1160 (7th Cir. 1993).

223. Lovell v. Poway Unified Sch. Dist., 847 F. Supp. 780 (S.D. Cal. 1994). *See also* IOTA XI Chapter of Sigma Chi v. George Mason Univ., 993 F.2d 386 (4th Cir. 1993).

one expressing himself/herself) to the rights of the receivers or
listeners receiving that expressive act and to the harm the expressive act causes to others.[224]

In general, the law on expression in public schools, whether
applied to slogans on wearing apparel, to colors of wearing apparel, or to buttons worn, or to words printed on signs, or to words
spoken, or to the use of gestures, grew in scope. While the mere
forecast of harm was not enough, where expressive acts become
conduct and that conduct brings harm to someone else, or to school
property, school administrators can punish individuals for their
words or gestures, or other expressive activity. Thus, school system policies on expression must be more conduct-focused, especially where the intent of the expression is to do actual harm, or
where actual harm is legitimately forecast.[225]

§ 11.9. Summary.

While student expression remains a sensitive area of school law,
the possibility of large numbers of situations reaching the courts is

---

224. Richard S. Vacca & H.C. Hudgins, Jr., *Student Speech and the First
Amendment: The Courts Operationalize the Notion of Assaultive Speech*, 89
EDUC. LAW RPTR. 1 (April 21, 1994). The authors define assaultive speech as
those expressive acts (spoken, written, or gestures) of one or more persons that
either cause actual harm to another person or persons, or, at a minimum, place
another person or persons in imminent fear of harm. The reader should keep in
mind that context must be a factor in the analysis, plus the likelihood that the
message will be understood by the receiver of the expressive act.

225. As Burke reminds contemporary school administrators,

> If it can be shown that gang-related clothing causes a disruption or
> interferes with the rights of other students, it is very likely that its pro-
> hibition or reasonable restriction will be upheld . . . Consequently, if
> students wearing gang clothing were to behave as the Tinker students
> did without causing any material disruption, regulatory gang clothing
> dress codes would obviously fail. However, if wearing gang clothing
> causes violence, fear, or intimidation . . . , then regulation will be up-
> held.

N. Denise Burke, *Restricting Gang Clothing in the Public Schools*, 80 EDUC. LAW
RPTR. 513 (April 8, 1993), at 521.

now greatly reduced. Beginning with *Tinker*, the United States Supreme Court developed a manageable judicial standard to be applied by subsequent courts as they adjudicate student expression cases.

Out of the litigious 1960s came the legal mandate that public school students shall not be deprived of their first amendment protections while in attendance at school, unless school authorities can show a compelling reason for infringing upon those guarantees. Clearly, student expression that materially and substantially interferes with or disrupts the school's educational environment is not immunized from disciplinary action.

In exercising any form of control over student expression (dress, symbolic expression, oral expression, publications, association, or assembly), contemporary school officials must, in addition to establishing a compelling reason, establish fair procedures for implementing their control action. Students must know of these procedures before they are applied to their particular matter.

Finally, school authorities are not at liberty to censure student expression solely because they consider the mode of attire or contents of the publication or speech distasteful. The courts require that preferences of style and taste not be primary motivating factors in making decisions involving the first amendment. School officials in the new century must base their decisions on reasonable exercises of pedagogical concerns, as set forth in both *Fraser* and *Hazelwood*.

As this chapter demonstrates, contemporary public school boards and administrators must be cognizant of the fact that they are subject to a suit for damages under 42 U.S.C. § 1983 if they knew or should have known that their actions violated a student's right to expression. Thus, where the first amendment clearly is implicated in a student's exercise of behavior, school officials must proceed with care and caution.

Chapter Twelve

RELIGION

§ 12.0. Introduction.

The framers of the Federal Constitution included two provisions in the first amendment that treat religion: the free exercise clause and the establishment of religion clause.

The free exercise clause provides that a person may believe what he wishes. He may believe in his God or no God, and government will not interfere with that belief. Government may, however, restrict the practice of one's belief if it harms or abuses the rights of others.

The establishment clause requires that government be neutral in matters of religion. It does not favor one religion over another, many religions over some, or all religions over none. It does not promote one religious activity over another, nor does it compel participation in a religious activity. What many people do not understand is that the United States is not a government of religion; rather, it is a nation of essentially religious people.

In spite of government's professed neutrality in religion, the fact remains that it has not been, nor can it be, completely separated from religion. If it were, policemen and firemen employed by the state or its agents would not answer an emergency call from a parochial school or church. Government does respond to such a call, not in terms of aiding religion but under the umbrella of its police power in which it looks after the health, safety, and welfare of all its citizens.

When this country was in its colonial and early constitutional periods, its schools were largely nonpublic, and their mission was largely theocratic. The aim of many of them was preparing young men for the ministry and all students for personal salvation. However, as states began to organize public schools, the question arose as to the church-state relationship in education. The issue was not as hotly debated then as now, for communities were essentially homogeneous and compulsory attendance was not universal.

When there were early challenges to government and to religion or religious practices in the schools, they were based on violations of state constitutions and state statutes. It was not until this century that the Federal Constitution was cited in contesting religious practices in schools. Initially, these cases were premised on the fourteenth amendment, for it restricted state action, unlike the Bill of Rights, which restricted actions of the federal government. Over a period of years, however, through a number of Supreme Court decisions, the Justices have used clauses in the Bill of Rights to act as a restriction on states as well. This expansion of jurisdiction is known as the incorporation doctrine. The free exercise clause was incorporated in 1940[1] and the establishment clause in 1947.[2]

The incorporation doctrine has also made it easier for people to bring suit against government in matters of religion and education. As a result, in the last four decades people have brought an in-

---

1. Cantwell v. Connecticut, 310 U.S. 296, 60 S. Ct. 900, 84 L. Ed. 1213 (1940).
2. Everson v. Board of Educ., 330 U.S. 1, 67 S. Ct. 504, 91 L. Ed. 711 (1947).

creasing number of suits against school districts based on the religion clauses.

Another reason for an increase of suits involving religion and education has been an increase in the religious heterogeneity of school communities. Justice Clark pointed out in 1963 that there were 83 sects in this country having over 50,000 members.[3] As of 1982 that number was 96, and there were 113 others having a membership of 1,000 to 50,000.[4]

This chapter will focus on the major issues involving religion in the public schools. To a limited degree, older state court decisions will be reviewed. For the most part, emphasis will be on decisions of the Supreme Court of the United States with lesser emphasis on recent representative state court decisions.

§ 12.1. Finance of Religious Activities.

a. *Textbooks*. The first real test of the constitutionality of using tax funds in support of education in nonpublic schools culminated in a decision by the Supreme Court of the United States.[5] The action was cited as a violation of the fourteenth amendment, since the first amendment had not yet been made applicable to state action. The litigation arose when the state of Louisiana passed a statute that provided for free textbooks for children in nonpublic schools, the cost to come from public tax funds. The practical effect of the legislation was to help those children enrolled in Roman Catholic schools.

---

3. School Dist. of Abington Twp. v. Schempp, 374 U.S. 203, 83 S. Ct. 1560, 10 L. Ed. 2d 844 (1963).

4. INFORMATION PLEASE ALMANAC 1982, 412-18 (New York: Information Please Publishing Inc., 1982). The 1990 Almanac and the World Almanac 1990 give data by religions in a broad context, but not by specific denominations. The 1999 edition of the World Almanac lists sixty different religious groups in this country. It also includes subgroups, bringing the total to 161. Of that number, 81 list memberships of 50,000 or more. Several groups elected not to reveal their membership total.

5. Cochran v. Louisiana State Bd. of Educ., 281 U.S. 370, 50 S. Ct. 335, 74 L. Ed. 1157 (1930).

Chief Justice Hughes rendered the decision of the Supreme Court. The Court refuted the argument that the state was taking public property for private use. The Court reasoned that the child and his parents, not the church, reaped the benefits of the legislation; consequently this action did not relieve the parochial schools of any obligations. Further, the state also benefited since it had an interest in the education of all students.

The Court stated its rationale as follows:

> One may scan the acts in vain to ascertain where any money is appropriated for the purchase of school books for the use of any church, private, sectarian, or even public school. The appropriations were made for the specific purpose of purchasing school books for the use of the school children of the state, free of cost to them.[6]

It was from this decision that the term "child benefit theory" originated. That term has been used to designate the use of public money, directly or indirectly, in support of a child in attendance at a nonpublic school. The legal reasoning is that a distinction can be made between a child and his school as the beneficiary of state funds. Where it can be shown that the child, not the school, benefits, it is sometimes acceptable. However, if the school is the primary beneficiary, the action will not be upheld. It is this theory upon which a justification has been made for use of tax funds in support of parochial education. Court rulings have differed on the subject.

The *Cochran v. Louisiana State Board of Education* decision has spawned a number of court decisions involving not only the textbook issue but also a variety of welfare legislation as a challenge to the child benefit theory. The Supreme Court has ruled on the specific issue of the legality of a state supplying books for nonpublic school students on three occasions since *Cochran*. Each time it has upheld the practice. The second ruling involved a practice of the state of New York which, in a 1975 amendment to a

---

6. *Id.* at 374.

statute, required the state to loan textbooks at no cost to children enrolled in grades seven to twelve in both public and nonpublic schools. The Supreme Court held that the statute neither advanced nor inhibited religion.[7] The books were furnished to children, not to schools. Public school authorities selected them, and the state retained ownership of them.

In a decision treated more fully later in this chapter, the Court upheld the loan of textbooks to nonpublic school children in Pennsylvania.[8] In a 1977 decision out of Ohio, the Court dealt with a variety of issues, the loan of textbooks being only one. It ruled that a state may lend textbooks to parochial school children.[9]

State courts have also ruled on the constitutionality of using tax funds for textbooks for children in parochial schools. More often than not, they have taken a position contrary to the nation's Supreme Court and ruled against the legality of such legislation. These cases have been based on the narrow issue of whether the statute was in violation of the state's constitution and did not consider whether it contravened the Federal Constitution. In Oregon the supreme court held in 1961 that the child benefit theory could conceivably be modified to include any kind of expenditure for the benefit of the child.[10] It ruled that the concept should be modified; consequently a statute providing for free textbooks to nonpublic school pupils was held to be in violation of the state's constitution.

The Missouri Supreme Court held that it was counter to the state's constitution to require school boards to loan textbooks to teachers and pupils in parochial schools.[11] It was also unconstitutional to provide texts to children in private schools. It ruled that when a sect establishes a religious school to promote its tenets, a

---

7. Board of Educ. of Cent. Sch. Dist. No. 1 v. Allen, 392 U.S. 236, 88 S. Ct. 1923, 20 L. Ed. 2d 1060 (1968).

8. Meek v. Pittenger, 421 U.S. 349, 95 S. Ct. 1753, 44 L. Ed. 2d 217, *reh'g denied,* 422 U.S. 1049 (1975).

9. Wolman v. Walter, 433 U.S. 229, 97 S. Ct. 2593, 53 L. Ed. 2d 714 (1977).

10. Dickman v. School Dist., 232 Ore. 238, 366 P.2d 533 (1961).

11. Paster v. Tussey, 512 S.W.2d 97 (Mo. 1974).

sectarian purpose is evident. Further, individuals can have and do promote a sectarian purpose.

In *Gaffney v. State Board of Education,* the Supreme Court of Nebraska ruled against a textbook loan statute.[12] It was held to be in violation of the state's constitution which forbade any aid or appropriation to any educational institution not exclusively owned by the state.

The Illinois Supreme Court ruled in 1973 that a textbook loan program to nonpublic school students was unconstitutional.[13] Under the legislation, parents could request specific books from a list maintained by the Superintendent of Public Instruction. These books were to be loaned to parents of nonpublic school students who requested them, provided the district loaned them to public school students. The court held that parents were not entitled to the books as a matter of course, nor had the state a duty to provide them. The court ruled the legislation unconstitutional on the ground that the taxpayers of the local school district pay for the texts of public school students while the state pays for the texts for nonpublic school students.

A 1978 decision by the Massachusetts Supreme Judicial Court invalidated a state law mandating textbook loans to private school students. The court declared that an amendment to the state constitution clearly prohibited any kind of aid to private schools.[14] The first amendment tests established in *Lemon v. Kurtzman* notwithstanding, a California textbook loan program still was found to be in violation of various provisions of the state constitution.[15]

In contrast to the above five state court decisions outlawing texts for parochial school students at public expense, a decision by the Supreme Court of Rhode Island upheld such action.[16] That court ruled that the state statute providing for texts for children in

---

12. 192 Neb. 238, 220 N.W.2d 550 (1974).

13. People *ex rel.* Klinger v. Howlett, 56 Ill. 2d 1, 305 N.E.2d 129 (1973).

14. Bloom v. School Comm., 379 N.E.2d 478 (Mass. 1978).

15. California Teachers Ass'n v. Riles, 176 Cal. Rptr. 300 (Cal. 1981).

16. Bowerman v. O'Connor, 247 A.2d 82 (R.I. 1968).

nonpublic schools was not in violation of either the state or federal constitutions.

b. *Transportation.* The second area of aid to children in non-public schools to get into the federal courts involved transportation. Although this subject has prompted litigation since 1912, the first major federal court decision occurred in 1947.[17] It grew out of a statute in New Jersey that authorized local school districts to make rules and contract for bus transportation. Ewing Township authorized reimbursements to parents of children attending both public and parochial schools. This statute was challenged as being in violation of the first and fourteenth amendments.

In a five to four ruling, the Supreme Court of the United States held that no denomination could be excluded from the benefits of public welfare legislation because of their faith or lack of it. Writing for the majority, Justice Black based the Court's decision on the establishment clause of the first amendment. He gave his definition of that clause:

> The "establishment of religion" clause of the First Amendment means at least this: Neither a state nor the Federal Government can set up a church. Neither can pass laws which aid one religion, aid all religions, or prefer one religion over another. Neither can force nor influence a person to go to or to remain away from church against his will or force him to profess a belief or disbelief in any religion. No person can be punished for entertaining or professing religious beliefs or disbeliefs, for church attendance or non-attendance. No tax in any amount, large or small, can be levied to support any religious activities or institutions, whatever they may be called, or whatever form they may adopt to teach or practice religion. Neither a state nor the Federal Government can, openly or secretly, participate in the affairs of any religious organizations or groups and vice versa. In the words of Jefferson, the clause against establishment of religion by law was

---

17. *Everson, supra* note 2.

intended to erect a "wall of separation between church and state."[18]

The majority held that, against that standard, the establishment clause had not been violated. The bus legislation was viewed as amounting to a welfare measure in seeing that children arrive to and from school safely. In doing this, the Court held that there was no violation of the Federal Constitution. The issue of a violation of the state's constitution was not before the Court. It is significant to note that the decision did not require that transportation be furnished; it held only that a state may provide it.

The Supreme Court refused to hear a federal court decision out of Missouri and thereby upheld the lower court's decision which ruled that a state is not required to furnish transportation to nonpublic school students.[19] More recently, in the *Wolman v. Walter* decision of 1977, the Court held that it was unconstitutional for the state to finance field trips for parochial school students.[20] Like *Everson,* the Court ruled five to four on this specific issue. The rationale of this holding was that field trips could presumably be financed for children to go to religious centers or to engage in religious study.

Two other lower federal court decisions also invalidated legislation providing transportation for parochial school students. A federal district court in Iowa held that the school district option of providing transportation outside the school district lines advances religious activity and is thus unconstitutional.[21] The federal district court in Rhode Island ruled unconstitutional a state statute which provided transportation costs for parochial school students.[22]

---

18. *Id.* at 330 U.S. 15.

19. Leukemeyer v. Kaufmann, 364 F. Supp. 376 (W.D. Mo. 1973), *cert. denied,* 419 U.S. 888 (1974).

20. *Wolman, supra* note 9.

21. Americans United for Separation of Church & State v. Benton, 413 F. Supp. 955 (S.D. Iowa 1976).

22. Members of Jamestown Sch. Comm. v. Schmidt, 427 F. Supp. 1338 (D.R.I. 1977).

State court rulings have tended to disallow the use of tax funds in support of pupil transportation to nonpublic schools. The controlling case, decided before *Everson*, was *Judd v. Board of Education*, a 1938 decision out of New York.[23] Here, the court rejected the child benefit theory. It took the position that free transportation for children in parochial and private schools encouraged attendance at those schools. Over three decades later an appellate court in New York extended *Judd* when it disallowed field trip transportation for parochial students.[24]

The child benefit theory as applied to transportation was also rejected by the Alaska Supreme Court in 1961.[25] It voided a statute authorizing transportation by holding that the constitution prohibited the appropriation of public money for the support or benefit of any sectarian, denominational, or private school. To hold otherwise would be for the state to give a direct benefit to the schools excluded by the constitution. The Supreme Court rejected a similar statute again in 1968 as it applied to transportation of children in private schools.[26]

Two transportation decisions have been rendered by Wisconsin courts. The Supreme Court held in 1968 that if transportation were provided for some children, it would have to be provided to all equally.[27] The issue was whether it was mandatory to transport students to a parochial school. Eight years later, the second decision held that, because a parochial school was situated 130 feet beyond a designated limit, transportation was not required.[28] The statute had allowed for transportation of parochial school students five miles beyond the public school district boundaries.

Two state courts have specifically upheld the payment of transportation for nonpublic school students. A Massachusetts court ruled that elementary school children in both public and nonpublic

---

23. 278 N.Y. 200, 15 N.E.2d 576 (1938).

24. Cook v. Griffin, 364 N.Y.S.2d 632 (A.D. 1975).

25. Matthews v. Quinton, 362 P.2d 932 (Alaska 1961).

26. Spears v. Honda, 449 P.2d 130 (Alaska 1968).

27. Cartwright v. Sharpe, 40 Wis. 2d 494, 162 N.W.2d 5 (1968).

28. Young v. Board of Educ., 74 Wis. 2d 144, 246 N.W.2d 230 (1976).

schools must be given free transportation.[29] The Illinois Supreme Court upheld a statute requiring local school boards to provide the same transportation for nonpublic school pupils as it did for public school pupils.[30]

In 1980 the U.S. Supreme Court refused to hear an appeal of a decision by the Pennsylvania Supreme Court affirming a directive by the Secretary of Education. Pennsylvania law (Act 372) required that nonpublic school children be bused within ten miles to their schools. Several school districts had followed this law only to the extent that they bused nonpublic school students as far as they bused public school students, usually distances much less than ten miles and within school district boundaries. The Pennsylvania Supreme Court indicated that no first amendment violation occurred, that the law in question was designed to transport nonpublic school students to their schools only in an attempt to provide services similar to those for public schools and that crossing district lines was irrelevant.[31] A final point was that Act 372 did not aid private schools, but rather students. The same statute was challenged unsuccessfully on the basis of disproportional costs for transporting nonpublic school children.[32]

The Federal District Court in Connecticut found the state's program for transporting private and parochial school children not to be in violation of the establishment clause. Plaintiffs' argument that most of the nonpublic schools were run by the Roman Catholic Church was not relevant.[33]

Child safety was the reason behind the enactment of the Nebraska Pupil Transportation Act, and the legislation was determined not to constitute an aid to nonpublic schools.[34] By modify-

---

29. Quinn v. School Comm., 332 Mass. 410, 125 N.E.2d 410 (1955).

30. Board of Educ. v. Bakalis, 54 Ill. 2d 448, 299 N.E.2d 737 (1973).

31. Springfield Sch. Dist. v. Department of Educ., 397 A.2d 1154 (Pa. 1979), *cert. denied,* 443 U.S. 901 (1980).

32. Bennett v. Kline, 486 F. Supp. 36 (E.D. Pa. 1980).

33. Cromwell Property Owners Ass'n v. Toffolon, 495 F. Supp. 915 (D. Conn. 1979). *See also* Helms v. Picard, 151 F.3d 347 (5th Cir. 1998).

34. State *ex rel.* Bouc v. School Dist., 320 N.W.2d 472 (Neb. 1982).

ing a 1956 statute, the Rhode Island legislature enacted a law which was upheld by the Court of Appeals for the First Circuit. The court found that the section of the statute in question would not require that public school administrators, in coordinating the program, become excessively entangled in sectarian matters.[35] A West Virginia school district allowed nonpublic school students to use school buses on regular runs or receive money to cover their transportation costs. Despite different ways of distributing transportation services, the court ruled that equal treatment was provided.[36]

Public school districts need not go out of their way to provide busing for nonpublic school students. Such busing is required only as far as it is provided for public school children. Thus, district-set boundaries are permissible, even if no nonpublic schools are within those boundaries.[37] The court denied a parent's request to transport beyond the five-mile busing limit, for the district policy was uniformly followed throughout the system.[38]

This issue is still not resolved as can be seen by the court opinions above. Based on the preponderance of court rulings, federal courts have tended to uphold transportation of nonpublic school students on the ground that it is not in violation of the Federal Constitution. State courts have tended to negate statutes on the ground that it violates the state's constitution. Thus, a state statute may be legal according to the Federal Constitution and illegal within the jurisdiction of the state's constitution.

c. *Teachers' Salaries.* The use of public tax funds to pay for salaries of teachers in nonpublic schools has not resulted in the amount of litigation as have the two previous issues. This plan was novel in that it did not aid students directly but expanded the concept of child benefit to teachers. This question has reached the Supreme Court of the United States where decisions were handed

---

35. Members of Jamestown Sch. Comm. v. Schmidt, 699 F.2d 1 (1st Cir. 1983).

36. Janasiewicz v. Board of Educ., 299 S.E.2d 34 (W. Va. 1982).

37. Murphy v. School Comm., 389 N.E.2d 399 (Mass. App. 1979).

38. Finkel v. New York City Bd. of Educ., 474 F. Supp. 468 (E.D.N.Y. 1979).

down in 1971 and 1973. The litigation involved cases out of Rhode Island and Pennsylvania. In each instance the Court declared unconstitutional the payment of teachers' salaries from tax funds.[39]

Rhode Island's statute authorized the expenditure of state funds to supplement salaries of elementary school teachers in nonpublic schools. These supplements, not to exceed fifteen percent of a teacher's current salary, were to be paid directly to the teachers. Other terms of the legislation were that a parochial school teacher's salary, including the supplement, could not exceed that of a public school teacher. The teacher had to be certified by the state and had to teach courses and use materials that were found in the public schools.

Pennsylvania's act authorized the Secretary of Education to purchase specified secular services from nonpublic schools. Among other services, the state would reimburse a nonpublic school for teachers' salaries. This case was combined with the one from Rhode Island for a hearing.

The Supreme Court relied initially on a two-part test, devised in 1963, in determining whether the legislation was legal: (1) Does the act have a secular legislative purpose? (2) Does the primary effect of the act either advance or inhibit religion? The Court then added a third test: (3) Does the act excessively entangle government and religion? The Court concluded that the program did not meet this test under the three guidelines it propounded: the character and purposes of the institutions that are benefited, the nature of the aid the state provides, and the resulting relationship between government and the religious authority.

Kuser states that excessive entanglement exists when "a religious institution is required to yield to governmental supervision, regulation, or inspection in exchange for a state-provided benefit, usually financial assistance in some form. These controls are re-

---

39. Lemon v. Kurtzman, 403 U.S. 602, 91 S. Ct. 2105, 29 L. Ed. 2d 745, *reh'g denied,* 404 U.S. 876 (1971).

quired to assure the use of the benefits provided for secular purposes, not for sectarian purposes in any form."[40]

The Court distinguished how books differ from teacher salaries in terms of child benefit: "Unlike a book, a teacher cannot be inspected once so as to determine the extent and intent of his or her personal beliefs and subjective acceptance of the limitations imposed by the First Amendment. These prophylactic contracts will involve excessive and enduring entanglement between state and church."[41]

In a decision two years later, the Court ruled that reimbursement due the nonpublic schools prior to the *Lemon I* ruling of 1971 were to be paid. However, no funds were to be transmitted to the schools for services after that ruling.[42]

d. *Tuition.* Following the Supreme Court's decision in *Lemon I,* the Pennsylvania legislature enacted the Parent Reimbursement Act. It was designed to overcome the constitutional infirmity of *Lemon* by aiding parents rather than teachers. It provided for an annual tuition reimbursement to parents of children enrolled in nonpublic schools. It amounted to $75.00 for each elementary school pupil and $150.00 for each secondary school pupil.

The Supreme Court disallowed the plan.[43] The majority saw the state as promoting rather than being neutral in religion. For the majority, Justice Powell noted that the establishment clause does not allow for novel forms of aid.

The *P.E.A.R.L.* decision, also in 1973, involved the legality of three provisions of the legislature of New York, two of them

---

40. Edwin Charles Kuser, "Public Education and the First Amendment under the Burger Court" 69 (unpublished doctoral dissertation, Temple University, 1977).

41. *Lemon, supra* note 39, at 403 U.S. 619.

42. Lemon v. Kurtzman, 411 U.S. 192, 93 S. Ct. 1463, 36 L. Ed. 2d 151 (1973).

43. Sloan v. Lemon, 413 U.S. 825, 93 S. Ct. 2982, 37 L. Ed. 2d 939, *reh'g denied,* 414 U.S. 881 (1973).

treating tuition.[44] One provision was for a cash reimbursement of $50.00 per elementary school child and $100.00 per secondary school child to parents of low income. The second provision was for tax relief for parents who did not otherwise qualify for tuition payments. Parents could deduct a specified amount per child, depending on their taxable income. The Court ruled that the plan was unconstitutional in that it aided religious education. Again, the Court used the three-part test of *Lemon I*. It then concluded that the aid was indirect — to parents rather than to schools — but that did not lessen the fact that it promoted religion.

A state court decision from Illinois in 1973 also invalidated a tuition grant to parents for children attending nonpublic schools.[45] The grant was designed to equalize the per pupil amount contributed by the state to a local school district and was limited to parents whose income was less than $3,000 per year. The state's highest court ruled that this amounted to an establishment of religion.

In an apparent change of direction in 1983, the Supreme Court of the United States ruled that a Minnesota statute permitting deductions on state income tax returns for expenses relating to attendance in secondary and elementary schools was constitutional.[46] In particular, such a law allowed deductions for tuition, books, and transportation for parents who paid tuition for private or parochial school attendance. Applying *Lemon v. Kurtzman,* the justices observed that secular interests are served by an educated population. The deduction, one of many available, did not create excessive entanglement in religious matters. A key factor that made this legislation different from previous attempts at such deductions was that parents of public school students could also deduct certain educational expenses.

---

44. Committee for Pub. Educ. & Religious Liberty v. Nyquist, 413 U.S. 756, 93 S. Ct. 2955, 37 L. Ed. 2d 948 (1973). This decision will hereafter be referred to as *P.E.A.R.L.*

45. *Klinger, supra* note 13.

46. Mueller v. Allen, 463 U.S. 388, 103 S. Ct. 3062, 77 L. Ed. 2d 721 (1983).

Prior to the Minnesota ruling, an almost identical statute was declared unconstitutional in the First Circuit.[47] Further, a New Jersey tax deduction program was found to favor religion, since most nonpublic school students attend sectarian schools.[48]

A not-for-profit private school or college which practices discrimination based on race does not qualify for tax exempt status. Contributions to such institutions may no longer be deductible from federal income tax.[49]

e. *Maintenance.* The only significant case to date treating the legality of direct grants from tax funds for maintenance and repair services in public schools is *P.E.A.R.L.,* a 1973 decision by the Supreme Court of the United States.[50] The grants were designed to serve schools whose children were from low income areas. An allocation of $30 to $40 per pupil for a building more than 25 years old could not exceed 50 percent of the average per pupil cost of similar services in public schools. The Court held that the plan was unconstitutional in that it advanced religion. There was no safeguard in the statute to prevent schools from using the grant money for facilities furthering religious purposes.

f. *Special Services.* Yet another issue of the use of tax funds in support of parochial schools has been that of financing specialized kinds of services. These services have involved a variety of programs. The Supreme Court has upheld some and overturned others.

In *Levitt,* the Court ruled that New York's reimbursement to nonpublic schools for costs involved in testing, records, and reports constituted an impermissible aid to religion.[51] Of the $28 million originally earmarked for this program, most of it went for the administration of teacher-made tests. Since the Court had no

---

47. Rhode Island Fed'n of Teachers, AFL-CIO v. Norberg, 630 F.2d 855 (1st Cir. 1980).

48. Public Funds for Pub. Schs. v. Byrne, 444 F. Supp. 1228 (D.N.J. 1978).

49. Bob Jones Univ. v. United States, 461 U.S. 574, 103 S. Ct. 2017, 76 L. Ed. 2d 157 (1983).

50. *P.E.A.R.L., supra* note 44.

51. Levitt v. P.E.A.R.L., 413 U.S. 472, 93 S. Ct. 2814, 37 L. Ed. 2d 736 (1973).

assurance that the tests were free of religious instruction, the Court invalidated the plan.

Two years later the Court invalidated two acts of the Pennsylvania legislature.[52] One act provided for auxiliary services for nonpublic school pupils in their schools. These services included counseling, testing and psychological services, speech and hearing therapy, and teaching services for exceptional, remedial, and educationally disadvantaged students. These services were provided by public school teachers employed by the intermediate unit. The Court held that they constituted an excessive entanglement in that there existed a potentiality for fostering religion. It would have required continual surveillance to insure that religion was not involved in the activities. The second act, which provided for aid for teaching materials and audiovisual equipment, was also invalidated in that it had the primary effect of advancing religion.

In *Wolman,* decided in 1977, the Court ruled specifically on the legality of six kinds of services to nonpublic school pupils in Ohio.[53] Two of those services, field trips and books, have already been treated in earlier sections of this chapter. In its ruling, the Court treated each issue separately and looked to the link between the use of public funds and its direct or indirect fostering of religion.

Issue 1. The Court held that states may finance therapeutic, remedial, and guidance counseling services for parochial school children so long as they are not offered at the parochial school. The fact that these services had been offered in parochial schools had invalidated the Pennsylvania plan. The Court recognized that providing these services at neutral sites does not advance religion nor create an excessive entanglement.

Issue 2. States may provide certain diagnostic services — speech and hearing — at parochial schools. These are viewed as being general health services and are unlike some kinds of teach-

---

52. *Meek, supra* note 8.
53. *Wolman, supra* note 9.

ing and counseling which could be tied in more closely with religion.

Issue 3. States may provide parochial schools with standardized tests and test scoring if that service is made available to public schools. Since these tests were prepared and scored commercially, they were not subject to religious influence, and local parochial teachers were not involved, unlike the New York plan. The Court saw that the state has an interest in the quality of instruction at both public and parochial schools, and standardized tests give some indication of that quality.

Issue 4. States may not lend wall charts and slide projectors for use in parochial schools. Here, the Court could not separate the secular from the sectarian function of such materials.

Of the six issues, only two Justices, Stewart and Blackmun, voted in the majority on all questions. A total of 16 dissents were recorded, an indication of the lack of agreement of the Justices.

The Illinois case, treated in the previous section, also involved the issue of the validity of state grants for auxiliary services. They included health, guidance, counseling, psychological, remedial, and therapeutic services for children in nonpublic schools. The Court recognized that the health services were secular, but the legislation did not treat all students alike. It reasoned that the state paid for the costs for parochial school students while the local taxpayers paid for the costs of public school students. The Court held that the other kinds of services were susceptible to sectarian activities. Consequently, both kinds of services were ruled unconstitutional.[54]

---

54. *Klinger, supra* note 13. In 1997, the United States Supreme Court reversed Aguilar v. Felton, 473 U.S. 402 (1985). In Agostini v. Felton, 117 S. Ct. 2010 (1997), the high court upheld the use of Title I funds in parochial schools. To the court, the mere presence of a publicly paid teacher on the grounds of a sectarian school does not violate the *Lemon* test. One year later (1998), the Supreme Court of Wisconsin upheld the Milwaukee voucher program that allowed state funds to be used at private sectarian schools. No first amendment violation was found. Jackson v. Benson, 578 N.W.2d 602 (Wis. 1998).

§ 12.2. Activities Involving Religion.

a. *Prayer and Bible Reading*. The practice of Bible reading and having prayers in the public schools has been challenged in lower courts for decades. In a majority of nine cases decided from 1884-1962, the courts upheld the practice of saying prayers. Even more cases were litigated in state courts on the issue of Bible reading, most of them occurring from 1880 to 1930, and the courts divided on its constitutionality. It was not until the 1950s that these issues got into the federal courts and the 1960s that the Supreme Court ruled on their legality, beginning with *Engel v. Vitale*.[55] That case grew out of a recommendation of the Board of Regents of New York State that the following prayer be recited at the opening of the school day:

> Almighty God, we acknowledge our dependence upon Thee,
> and we beg Thy blessings upon us, our parents,
> our teachers and our country.[56]

Parents objected to the prayer and brought suit. The Supreme Court ruled in 1962 that the state had no business in carrying on any program of government-sponsored prayer. For precedent, it cited history: the persecution of individuals in European countries and subsequent coercion of colonists to subscribe to a given religious model. The Constitution was written to prevent this from occurring, the Court stated through Justice Black, and it was designed so that government would be neutral in matters of religion.

Whereas, in the narrowest sense, *Engel* treated a specific prayer written by a state, it did not deal with the larger question of the legality of other kinds of prayers. That question was decided the following year in *School District of Abington Township v. Schempp*.[57] The case involved the legality of both prayer and

---

55. Engel v. Vitale, 370 U.S. 421, 82 S. Ct. 1261, 8 L. Ed. 2d 601 (1962).

56. *The Regents Statement on Moral and Spiritual Training in the Schools,* 38 THE UNIVERSITY OF THE STATE OF NEW YORK BULLETIN TO THE SCHOOLS, 94 (Dec. 1951).

57. *Schempp, supra* note 3.

Bible reading as devotional exercises at the opening of the school day. The decision was a joinder of two cases, one out of Pennsylvania, the other out of Baltimore. The Pennsylvania case was a challenge to the state statute requiring the reading of ten verses of scripture, without comment. Reciting the Lord's Prayer was optional but taken for granted. There was no provision for children not wishing to participate.

The Maryland case was a challenge to the Baltimore ordinance requiring the reading of a chapter of the Bible and reciting the Lord's Prayer daily. At first there was no excusal privilege; later one was made.

The two criteria the Supreme Court used in determining the legality of the practice were also used in subsequent rulings: "[W]hat are the purpose and the primary effect of the enactment? If either is the advancement or inhibition of religion then the enactment exceeds the scope of legislative power as circumscribed by the Constitution."[58]

The Court ruled that the exercises were religious ceremonies and the fact that they took a very small amount of time was irrelevant. "The breach of neutrality that is today a trickling stream may all too soon become a raging torrent and, in the words of Madison, 'it is proper to take alarm at the first experiment on our liberties.'"[59]

The Court made it clear that it was outlawing a religious practice, but it was not forbidding the study of religion. Objective study of religion as history or literature or the study of comparative religions would be acceptable.

One year after *Schempp* the Supreme Court was presented with a case involving a variety of issues implicating religion in schools. The case was remanded in light of the *Schempp* holding. At its second consideration, the Court ruled that devotional Bible reading and the recitation of prayers were unconstitutional.[60] The Justices

---

58. *Id.* at 222.

59. *Id.* at 225.

60. Chamberlin v. Dade Cty. Bd. of Pub. Instr., 377 U.S. 402, 84 S. Ct. 1272, 12 L. Ed. 2d 407 (1964).

dismissed the appeal on the other issues, which included observance of religious celebrations, singing religious songs, displaying religious symbols, holding baccalaureate services, and conducting a religious census.

In an opinion by the Second Circuit in 1965, voluntary prayers for kindergarten students were invalidated.[61] Although many parents wanted the prayers, the principal objected. The students had been reciting the following prayer in the morning:

> God is Great, God is Good and we
> Thank Him for our Food, Amen!

In the afternoon, students had been reciting the following prayer:

> Thank You for the World so Sweet,
> Thank You for the Food we Eat,
> Thank You for the Birds that Sing —
> Thank You, God, for Everything.

The court held that there is no constitutional duty for a state to permit public prayer in state-owned buildings.

In spite of the Supreme Court decisions on prayer and Bible reading, the practice has not ended. It has continued in many school systems, sometimes in open defiance of the Courts' rulings or in other places in subtle ways. Some of these practices have also been challenged. A federal district court ruled in 1971 that Alabama's statute requiring daily Bible reading violated the establishment clause, and all public schools in the state were ordered to stop the exercise.[62] The Fifth Circuit disallowed a statute commanding the inculcation of Christian virtues in schools.[63] The

---

61. Stein v. Oshinsky, 348 F.2d 999 (2d Cir. 1965), *cert. denied,* 382 U.S. 957 (1965). In August, 1995, President Clinton reaffirmed his support of the rights of students in public schools to say grace before meals, pray individually, and to organize student initiated religious clubs.

62. Alabama Civil Liberties Union v. Wallace, 371 F. Supp. 966 (M.D. Ala. 1971). *See* Metzl v. Leininger, 57 F.3d 618 (7th Cir. 1995), where the Court struck down the recognition of Good Friday as an official public school holiday.

63. Meltzer v. Board of Pub. Instr., 548 F.2d 559 (5th Cir. 1977).

practical effect of the statute was that Bible verses were read over the public address system and Gideon Bibles were distributed. The court held that these exercises advanced or inhibited religion. It had been held twenty-four years earlier that the distribution of Gideon Bibles to children in public schools was a violation of the Constitution in that it favored one religion over another.[64]

Courts have also looked askance at ingenious efforts to use public schools for activities forbidden by the *Schempp* holding. The Third Circuit prohibited a school district in Pennsylvania from permitting voluntary Bible readings and nondenominational mass prayers in school.[65] In rejecting the argument that the prayers were neutral and that the activity was voluntary, the court held neither qualification really changed the legality of the activity.

A court also upheld a school board in refusing to allow high school students to use the school premises for voluntary group meetings.[66] Initially, students met before school and offered group prayers. The meetings were begun without the knowledge or permission of the faculty and administration. No one sponsored the group. After the principal learned of these meetings, he advised the students that their action violated public policy. The court upheld the principal and ruled that disallowing the practice would not deny the students any of their constitutional rights. The court did not wish to sanction an ingenious effort of students to countermand *Schempp,* and it cited a concurring opinion by Justice Frankfurter: "Separation means separation, not something else. Jefferson's metaphor in describing the relation between Church and State speaks of a 'wall of separation,' not a fine line easily overstepped."[67]

---

64. Tudor v. Board of Educ., 100 A.2d 857 (N.J. 1953), *cert. denied,* 348 U.S. 816 (1954). *See* Schanou v. Lancaster Cty. Sch. Dist., 863 F. Supp. 1048 (D. Neb. 1994), in which the court allowed the distribution of Bibles to students after school hours and at designated sites.

65. Mangold v. Albert Gallatin Sch. Dist., 438 F.2d 1194 (3d Cir. 1971).

66. Hunt v. Board of Educ., 321 F. Supp. 1263 (S.D. W. Va. 1971).

67. Illinois *ex rel.* McCollum v. Board of Educ. of Sch. Dist. No. 71, 333 U.S. 203, 68 S. Ct. 461, 92 L. Ed. 2d 649 (1948).

Courts have entertained a variety of issues around the common theme of having prayers in some form in the schools. Invariably, courts have ruled that such practices conflict with the establishment clause. For example, a state statute permitting teachers to have student volunteers lead the class in prayers violated the establishment clause even though students could leave the room.[68] A similar program was disallowed in Massachusetts.[69] The Court of Appeals for the Ninth Circuit ruled that in spite of their being voluntary, assemblies could not be held because school officials had granted permission for prayers to be uttered.[70]

In addition to affirming the Fifth Circuit's ruling disallowing a school board policy requiring prayer and Bible reading, the Supreme Court ruled that Bibles could not be distributed on school grounds.[71]

b. *Meditation.* Since courts have made it clear that public schools cannot be used as vehicles for sponsoring prayer and Bible reading as part of devotional exercises, some states and school systems have sought to accommodate individuals and groups advocating some kind of reflective thought at the opening of the school day. The plans have varied but have been similar in that they provide for an individual to engage in prayer and/or meditation as he wishes. The full impact of these kinds of legislation and policies is yet to be examined fully by the courts, but so far they have often been looked upon favorably, provided the state's role is clearly neutral. That test was not met in a New Jersey case when a court disallowed a plan whereby students went to the gymnasium at the opening of school, listened to remarks of the Congressional Chaplain as recorded in the *Congressional Record,* and meditated silently on any subject they wished. The court ruled that since the

---

68. Karen B. v. Treen, 653 F.2d 897 (5th Cir. 1981).

69. Kent v. Commissioner of Educ., 402 N.E.2d 1340 (Mass. App. 1980).

70. Collins v. Chandler Unified Sch. Dist., 644 F.2d 759 (9th Cir. 1981).

71. Meltzer v. Board of Pub. Instr., 577 F.2d 311 (5th Cir. 1978), *cert. denied,* 439 U.S. 1089 (1979). Contrast that case with Peck v. Upshur Cty. Bd. of Educ., 155 F.3d 274 (4th Cir. 1998), in which the Fourth Circuit upheld a school board policy allowing limited distribution of Bibles to very young children.

"remarks" were actually the prayer of the Chaplain, the school was sponsoring a religious service.[72]

A Tennessee statute providing for meditation in the schools was held to be in violation of both the first and fourteenth amendments. According to the statute, each school day would begin with one minute of silence in which students were instructed to meditate, pray, or reflect.[73] Similar legislation in New Mexico was ruled to be unconstitutional. The plan was viewed as being an indirect means of providing prayer in the schools.[74] Citing the *Abington* case, the Supreme Judicial Court of Massachusetts found that a proposed bill permitting one minute of voluntary prayer or meditation was unconstitutional.[75]

A different situation occurred in a Massachusetts case. There, the court held that a statute requiring a period of silence at the opening of school is not in violation of the first amendment.[76] The statute, with its 1973 amendment, provided for meditation or prayer, as the individual wished, although neither was actually required. The court ruled that the exercise neither advanced nor inhibited religion and there was no coercion for students to participate. "A state statute which mandates a moment of silence in a public school setting is not *per se* an invalid exercise of police power. All that the statute requires students to do is be silent."[77]

In an advisory opinion by the Supreme Court of New Hampshire, the justices agreed that a statute authorizing silent meditation was legal.[78]

---

72. State Bd. of Educ. v. Board of Educ., 108 N.J. Super. 564, 262 A.2d 21 (1970).

73. Beck v. McElrath, 548 F. Supp. 1161 (M.D. Tenn. 1982).

74. Duffy v. Las Cruces Pub. Schs., 557 F. Supp. 1013 (D.N.M. 1983).

75. Opinions of Justices to House of Representatives, 440 N.E.2d 1159 (Mass. 1982).

76. Gaines v. Anderson, 421 F. Supp. 337 (D. Mass. 1976).

77. *Id.* at 342.

78. Opinion of the Justices, 307 A.2d 558 (N.H. 1973). The Supreme Court had an opportunity to hand down a definitive ruling on this issue in 1987 but declined to do so. The justices ruled that New Jersey legislators who challenged the prohibition lacked standing to sue. The plan by the legislature provided that

467

c. *Voluntary Prayer During Non-instructional Time.* In a school district in New York, students wishing to hold voluntary prayer sessions before school and on school property were denied permission by school officials. Students contended that this denial violated the free exercise clause. The district court used the three-pronged test from *Lemon* and found aid would be given to a religious group in the form of free rent. This was affirmed by the Second Circuit, which also noted that the school day began when buses arrived, not when classes commenced.[79]

A Bible club can constitutionally meet on school grounds during an activity period. That was the ruling of the Supreme Court in the *Mergens* decision of 1990. In deciding on the legality of the club, the Court upheld the Equal Access Act passed by the Congress in 1984. It provided that public secondary schools receiving federal funds and which operate a limited open forum could not discriminate against students wishing to meet on the basis of religious, political, philosophical, or other content. (20 U.S.C. § 4071 (1984)) The Court determined that a limited open forum existed when a public secondary school allows noncurriculum-related student groups to meet on school premises during noninstructional time. In determining if a club related directly to the curriculum, the justices propounded four questions: (1) Is the subject matter of the club taught, or will it soon be taught in a regularly scheduled course? (2) Does the subject matter of the club concern the body of courses as a whole? (3) Is participation in the club required for a particular

---

public school students should observe a minute of silence at the opening of the school day. The statute did not specify how the time was to be spent except that it should be used "for quiet and private contemplation and introspection." Both the district and circuit courts held that the statute breached the separation of church and state. The legality of this practice still remains in doubt. May v. Cooperman, 780 F.2d 240 (3d Cir. 1985); Karcher v. May, 108 S. Ct. 388 (1987). For a decision from the Eleventh Circuit upholding the Georgia Minute of Quiet Reflection in Schools Act, see Bown v. Gwinnett Cty., 112 F.3d 1464 (11th Cir. 1997).

79. Brandon v. Board of Educ., Guilderland Cent. Sch. Dist., 487 F. Supp. 1219 (N.D.N.Y.), *aff'd,* 635 F.2d 971 (2d Cir. 1980), *cert. denied,* 454 U.S. 1123 (1981).

course? (4) Does participation in the club result in academic credit?

The Court also ruled that a faculty member could act as sponsor for the club, although that individual's role would be limited to clerical and supervisory functions and would not involve active participation with respect to discussion of religious topics.[80]

Bible reading over the school's public address system, recitation of classroom prayers, distribution of Bibles, and supervised religious meetings before and after school hours were contested by a local chapter of the American Civil Liberties Union. The Fifth Circuit ruled that these activities were unconstitutional, even though the practices had been stopped before the decision was made.[81]

d. *Graduation Exercises.* Since the prayer and Bible reading decisions by the Supreme Court, some individuals have challenged the tradition of having religious activities at secondary school graduation exercises. Two cases have treated the matter of having an invocation and a benediction. Both were decided in 1974, and both held that the prayers could be said. In a case out of Pennsylvania, a court ruled that no substantial federal question was presented and there was no evidence that religion was advanced.[82]

---

80. Board of Educ. v. Mergens, 496 U.S. 226 (1990).

81. Lubbock Civil Liberties Union v. Lubbock Indep. Sch. Dist., 669 F.2d 1038 (5th Cir. 1982).

82. Weist v. Mt. Lebanon Sch. Dist., 320 A.2d 363 (Pa.), *cert. denied,* 419 U.S. 967 (1974). The courts have handed down mixed opinions on the legality of prayers at graduation exercises. A federal district court upheld the practice in Graham v. Central Community Sch. Dist. of Decatur Cty., 608 F. Supp. 531 (S.D. Iowa 1985). Oregon's Supreme Court held that the issue was moot in that the girl who protested the activity had already been graduated. Kay v. David Douglas Sch. Dist. No. 40, 738 P.2d 1389 (Ore. 1987). That same year a California court ruled that an invocation at high school graduation exercises violated both the state and federal constitutions. The fact that prayers may be nondenominational and graduation exercises may be voluntary does not establish the activity's legitimacy. Bennett v. Livermore Unified Sch. Dist., 238 Cal. Rptr. 819 (Cal. App. 1987). Two years later a California court upheld prayers at graduation exercises. The court saw that the issue was not whether the activity was religious, but whether it

The ceremony was held to be more of a public ritual than a religious exercise.

In the other case out of Virginia, the court held that any infringement of the establishment clause was minimal.[83] Like the previous case, the judge ruled that the service was ceremonial, not educational or religious. There was no calculated indoctrination in the prayers. "The event, in short, is so fleeting that no significant transfer of government prestige can be anticipated."[84]

The controversy over graduation exercises has been centered specifically in having prayer as part of the ceremony. As recently as early 1995 the controversy has not been fully settled, so that some confusion remains. The nation's Supreme Court provided some guidance in 1992 when it ruled that a public school could not provide for a nonsectarian prayer to be given by clergymen selected by the Rhode Island school.[85] School officials attempted to

---

was being used for secular purposes. An activity need not be exclusively secular. The court saw that the prayer added dignity and decorum to the ceremony. Any religious effect of the prayers was remote and incidental. Sands v. Moronzo Unified Sch. Dist., 262 Cal. Rptr. 452 (Cal. App. 1989). More recently, however, the Fifth Circuit saw a school district's policy of permitting student-selected, student-given prayers as not serving a secular purpose (of solemnizing the event). Doe v. Santa Fe I.S.D., 168 F.3d 806 (5th Cir. 1999).

83. Grossberg v. Deusebio, 380 F. Supp. 285 (E.D. Va. 1974).

84. *Id.* at 289.

85. Lee v. Weisman, 112 S. Ct. 2648 (1992). Note that the Fifth Circuit handed down a ruling contrary to the Supreme Court's *Weisman* decision, one year later. In Jones v. Clear Creek Indep. Sch. Dist., 977 F.2d 963 (5th Cir. 1992), the court upheld the use of graduation prayers. The distinction here was that the prayer was student-initiated and student led. The U.S. Supreme Court declined to hear the *Jones* case. *See, e.g.,* Goluba v. School Dist., 45 F.3d 1035 (7th Cir. 1995). For a similar and more recent case where the Ninth Circuit reached a contrary conclusion to that found in *Jones,* see Harris v. Joint Sch. Dist. No. 241, 41 F.3d 447 (9th Cir. 1994). For a recent article on this issue, see Richard S. Vacca & H.C. Hudgins, Jr., *Pomp and Controversy,* 181 AM. SCH. BD. J. 29 (May 1994). In Ingebretsen v. Jackson Pub. Sch. Dist., 88 F.3d 274 (5th Cir. 1996), the court struck down a state statute allowing student-initiated prayers during compulsory events on school property. Conversely, in Doe v. Madison Sch. Dist. No. 321, 7 F. Supp. 2d 1110 (D. Idaho 1997), the court held that permitting students chosen by academic standing to give uncensored presentations, including prayers,

avoid any church-state controversy by providing clergy with a pamphlet which recommended guidelines considered appropriate for prayer. The Supreme Court determined, however, that the process was flawed. "The government involvement with religious activity in this case is pervasive, to the point of creating a state-sponsored and state-directed religious exercise in a public school." For example, the principal decided that an invocation and a benediction would be given; the principal chose the clergyman to deliver the prayers; and the principal provided the clergyman with a copy of the school's guidelines and advised him that prayers should be nonsectarian. The above involvement of the principal clearly demonstrated that the state was engaged in a religious exercise.

A different question was raised in a 1974 case when parents challenged the legality of holding a graduation exercise in a Roman Catholic church. They took the position that their children could not attend without violating their conscience. The school board's defense was that the ceremonies were the responsibility of the seniors who determined where they would be held and who the speakers would be. It also added that attendance was voluntary. The court decided that the board could not delegate those kinds of decisions to students. It also held that it was cruel to force some students not to participate because of their religious beliefs.[86]

§ 12.3. Study of Religion.

a. *At School.* After the Supreme Court incorporated the religion clauses of the first amendment into the fourteenth amendment as a protection for citizens from state government, individuals began to challenge long-standing practices involving religious study in schools. They objected to public schools allowing their facilities to

---

as part of graduation programs did not violate the constitution. The Third Circuit disallowed graduation prayers in a case out of New Jersey. At the school in question, students voted whether or not to have graduation prayers. ACLU of N.J. v. Black Horse Pike Reg'l Bd. of Educ., 84 F.3d 1471 (3d Cir. 1996).

86. Lemke v. Black, 376 F. Supp. 87 (E.D. Wis. 1974).

be used for the study of religion in general and the Bible in particular. The landmark case that clarified the state-church relationship on this question was *McCollum*, decided in 1948.[87] The Supreme Court invalidated a plan whereby a local Council on Religious Education provided for religious instruction for students from the three major faiths in the community: Catholics, Jews, and Protestants. The Council selected and paid for teachers who went into the schools once a week and taught students whose parents requested the course. The denominations were kept separate and nonparticipants studied in another part of the building.

An avowed atheist challenged this practice, and the Supreme Court ruled eight to one in her favor. The Court saw that tax-supported property was being used to support religious instruction and the state's compulsory education law assisted with the program of religious instruction.

The *McCollum* case did not address the issue of allowing students to leave public schools for religious study, a matter to be treated in the next section. It merely held that teaching of religion within a public school during the day violated the first amendment.

A case with a similar factual situation was decided in Virginia in 1970. Teachers from a private organization came into the Martinsville elementary schools during school hours to provide religious instruction for children of parents requesting it. The district court held that this created an establishment of religion.[88] It reasoned that if the class were taught within constitutional limits, every student should be required to attend; if the study were necessary for the education of one child, it should be necessary for all.

In a 1977 decision, a California court held that a student Bible club could not meet on school campus during the day.[89] The club's

---

87. *McCollum, supra* note 67.

88. Vaughn v. Reed, 313 F. Supp. 431 (W.D. Va. 1970).

89. Johnson v. Huntington Beach Union High Sch. Dist., 137 Cal. Rptr. 43 (Cal. App. 1977). In the 1980s, the Supreme Court entertained the question of the legality of Bible Clubs on two occasions. The first involved the right of college students to have such a club at a state-supported institution. The justices found no problem with this arrangement where they saw that an open forum had been

stated purpose was for students to know God better by prayerfully studying the Bible. Its membership was open to those genuinely interested in the club's purpose. The court held that this activity constituted a breach of the establishment clause.

The study of the Bible as literature is permissible; but when a supplemental text was used which supported a particular sect, such a program violated the first amendment.[90] Two such Bible study programs in neighboring Tennessee districts were contested and one was found to be constitutional and the other unconstitutional. Listening to tape recordings of class sessions in each of the programs preceded the decision. At issue was not the program but rather how individual teachers presented the material.[91]

Despite the secular message implied, the Ten Commandments are of a religious nature and the requirement of their posting in all classrooms was held to be unconstitutional.[92] Even where no state funds are used, the mandate of posting the Ten Commandments is unconstitutional.[93]

---

created on campus and where students could freely express their views. Widmar v. Vincent, 454 U.S. 263 (1981). Five years later, in 1986, the Court declined to rule on the legality of a Bible Club in a secondary school, for it determined that the appellants lacked standing to sue. Bender v. Williamsport Area Sch. Dist., 475 U.S. 534 (1986). That club had sought to organize, consistent with the Equal Access Act passed by the U.S. Congress in 1984. The Act provided that secondary schools could not refuse recognition to an extraclass club that met during noninstructional time where the school had created a limited open forum. In 1990 the Supreme Court sanctioned Bible Clubs in public schools. Board of Educ. of Westside Community Schs. v. Mergens, 496 U.S. 226 (1990). That ruling upheld the legality of the Equal Access Act. The Court ruled that, since the school maintained a limited open forum, school officials were prohibited from discriminating against students who wished to meet at school during noninstructional time.

90. Hall v. Board of Sch. Comm'rs, 656 F.2d 999 (5th Cir. 1981).

91. Wiley v. Franklin, 497 F. Supp. 390 (E.D. Tenn. 1980). *See also* Gibson v. Lee Cty. Sch. Bd., 1 F. Supp. 2d 1426 (M.D. Fla. 1998).

92. Ring v. Grand Forks Pub. Sch. Dist. No. 1, 483 F. Supp. 272 (D.N.D. 1980). In Washegesic v. Bloomingdale, 33 F.3d 679 (6th Cir. 1994), the location of a picture of Jesus Christ on a wall in a public high school was challenged, and the Court upheld the student's suit to have it removed.

93. Stone v. Graham, 449 U.S. 39, 101 S. Ct. 192, 66 L. Ed. 2d 199 (1980).

b. *Outside School.* Four years after *McCollum,* the Supreme Court, in *Zorach v. Clauson,*[94] ruled on the legality of dismissing students from public schools during the day for study at religious centers. The Court upheld this plan, pointing out that public schools were not being used to promote religion; it merely involved cooperation with religious authorities. The cooperation amounted to an adjustment of pupil schedules and keeping attendance records. The fact that the activities were not held at public schools distinguished it from the *McCollum* decision.

Two lower courts upheld dismissal plans similar to the one above. The Wisconsin Supreme Court upheld a state statute allowing a school board to dismiss children, with parental approval, for religious instruction.[95] The court was satisfied that the plan met its three-part test: (1) *Location.* The teaching was done at churches, not in public schools. (2) *Use of funds.* The only expenditure of public funds involved public school teachers checking monthly attendance reports supplied by the religious instructors, a very minimal cost. (3) *Participation.* Looking at the overall operation of the program, the court was satisfied that the school was not involved in promoting religion.

The Fourth Circuit held in 1975 that a school's scheduling of classes to accommodate pupils interested in religious training sessions was insufficient to create an endorsement of the program.[96] In doing so, it overruled the district court. The circuit court recognized that the key test had an indirect rather than a primary effect on the program. Like *Zorach,* the court saw the program as involving an element of cooperation whereby the students were released to a trailer parked near the school.

A cooperative plan between public and parochial schools involving religious instruction was invalidated by an Oregon court in 1973.[97] This case was based on the state's constitution. The plan

---

94. 343 U.S. 306, 72 S. Ct. 679, 96 L. Ed. 954 (1952).
95. State *ex rel.* Holt v. Thompson, 66 Wis. 2d 659, 225 N.W.2d 678 (1975).
96. Smith v. Smith, 523 F.2d 121 (4th Cir. 1975).
97. Fisher v. Clackamas Cty. Sch. Dist., 507 P.2d 839 (Ore. App. 1973).

consisted of two parts. Seventh and eighth grade children attended public school for four periods and parochial school for three periods. Fifth and sixth grade children were released for four thirty-minute periods per week for religious instruction. The court's main objection to the program was that the students in the two public schools were selected solely from students from the religious school. Thus, religious affiliation was the prerequisite for attendance at the public schools. What the court saw was a public school really being operated within the context of a parochial school. In effect, the state was paying for the salaries of teachers who taught only parochial school students.

Parts of a release program in Utah were found to be unconstitutional, including the granting of elective credit for participation in such programs.[98] The particular program was viewed as creating an excessive involvement between the school and a church group.

§ 12.4. Religion in the General Curriculum.

A state may unquestionably require that specified courses be taken by all students. A state possesses this authority in the interest that it has for all students to become good citizens. A local school board may also require subjects, but that authority is more limited than the state's, particularly when parents object. The right to select courses for children coexists with both school and parents. Some parents have objected to required or elective courses and learning activities that clash with their religious beliefs. It is their contention that the school is sponsoring religion in offering the courses and experiences. Related issues such as teaching evolution and saluting the flag are treated elsewhere in this book.

Two cases have involved a challenge to activities in required physical education courses as being in conflict with one's religious beliefs. In a case from the 1920s a parent objected to dancing as being a required part of physical education. The court held that a

---

98. Lanner v. Wimmer, 463 F. Supp. 867 (D. Utah 1978).

student could not be required to take dancing if the parents objected to its being in violation of their freedom of religion.[99]

In a required physical education course, a student refused to wear a prescribed uniform and to engage in certain exercises. She believed that the gym shorts were immodest and the exercises were sinful. The parents refused to allow the girl to participate, even though school authorities made certain adjustments for her, including not wearing the uniform and waiving certain exercises. The court ruled that she was required to take the course, she was not required to wear the uniform, and she could be excused from exercises deemed immodest or sinful.[100]

In 1974, the federal district court in New Hampshire ruled that the state's interest in providing students with a proper education outweighed the first amendment rights of parents.[101] The issue arose over parents objecting to students watching movies and television, play acting, and singing or dancing to worldly music. Until 1971, the school board had accommodated the parents' wishes, but the board then nullified its policy as a result of discipline problems, for the excusal involved approximately twenty percent of the students. The parents had also sought exemption from music and health courses for their children. The court saw that to excuse the children from all classes they objected to would cripple their education.

A court held that children of the Jehovah's Witnesses faith could not be required to stand and participate in the singing of the National Anthem.[102] Although the court saw the anthem as being a patriotic rather than a religious exercise, it held that students could

---

99. Hardwick v. Board of Sch. Trustees, 54 Cal. App. 696, 205 P. 49 (1921).

100. Mitchell v. McCall, 273 Ala. 604, 143 So. 2d 629 (1962).

101. Davis v. Page, 385 F. Supp. 395 (D.N.H. 1974). For a more recent opinion, see Guyer v. School Bd. of Alachua Cty., 634 So. 2d 806 (Fla. Dist. Ct. App. 1994). In a decision from the Tenth Circuit, a Jewish student unsuccessfully challenged the appropriateness of her high school choir director's selections of sectarian songs and the use of Christian churches as sites for choir performances. *See* Bauchman v. West High Sch., 132 F.3d 542 (10th Cir. 1998).

102. Sheldon v. Fannin, 221 F. Supp. 766 (D. Ariz. 1963).

legitimately be excused from singing it, based on their religious beliefs.

Parents have also objected to the choice of books that schools use. As a general principle, their right to select them is more limited than their decision as to their child enrolling in a course. In 1975, in a highly publicized situation in West Virginia, a federal district court held that the use of controversial textbooks does not violate the constitutional principle of separation of church and state.[103] Parents in Kanawha County had objected to the books, stating that they discouraged Christian principles and good citizenship. The court conceded that some materials in the texts were offensive to the parents' religious beliefs; however, the school board had not abused its authority in selecting the texts. The court recognized that the first amendment "does not guarantee that nothing about religion will be taught in the schools."[104]

Parents in New York objected to the use in secondary schools of *Oliver Twist* and *The Merchant of Venice* because they viewed them as being offensive to their Jewish faith in that Jewish characters were portrayed in a bigoted manner. The court held that the books could be used.

> Except where the book has been maliciously written for the apparent purpose of promoting and fomenting a bigoted and intolerant hatred against a particular racial or religious group, public interest in a free and democratic society does not warrant or encourage the suppression of any book at the whim of any unduly sensitive person or group of persons merely because a character described in such book as belonging to a particular race or religion is portrayed in a derogatory or offensive manner. The necessity for the suppression of such a book must clearly depend upon the intent and motive which has actuated the author in making such a portrayal.[105]

---

103. Williams v. Board of Educ., 388 F. Supp. 93 (S.D.W. Va. 1975).
104. *Id.* at 96.
105. Rosenberg v. Board of Educ., 196 Misc. 542, 92 N.Y.S.2d 344, 346 (1949).

Two cases from the Eleventh Circuit in 1987 brought considerable attention to the issue of how far people may go in challenging the use of textbooks in public schools. Both decisions refuted parental objections to the books. In the first case, parents in Tennessee objected to the assignment of books whose content offended their religion. They claimed that exposure to the books might cause a child to adopt "feminist, humanist, pacifist, anti-Christian, vegetarian, or one-world government views." Such a perspective, they claimed, was incompatible with their Christian faith. The district court found that the textbooks were required reading and that the plaintiffs' free exercise rights had therefore been burdened. The court of appeals reversed.[106] It rejected parental claims that their free exercise rights had been violated. It noted that the parents really objected to objectionable ideas rather than to an inculcation of those ideas. There was no evidence that students were ever called upon to say or do anything that required them to affirm or deny a religious belief or engage in or refrain from engaging in any activity forbidden by their convictions.

In the second case, a district court in Alabama banned 44 texts from public schools for failure to treat religion fully and for promoting what it termed to be secular humanism. The Eleventh Circuit reversed.[107] It found that the texts conveyed no message of endorsement of secular humanism. It used the effect test of *Lemon* and ruled that the content encouraged independent thought, tolerance of diverse views, self-respect, maturity, self-reliance, and logical decisionmaking, all appropriate activities. The court noted that some of the texts contain ideas that are consistent with secular humanism, but they also contain ideas consistent with theistic religion. Mere consistency with religious convictions does not constitute an establishment of religion.

---

106. Mozert v. Hawkins Cty. Pub. Schs., 827 F.2d 1058 (6th Cir. 1987). *See also* Fleischfresser v. Directors, 15 F.3d 680 (7th Cir. 1994), where parents challenge use of the Impressions series with elementary school children.

107. Smith v. Board of Comm'rs of Mobile Cty., 827 F.2d 684 (11th Cir. 1987).

The teaching of Darwin's theory of evolution has long been controversial, and two recent cases indicate that the controversy will continue for some time. A South Dakota teacher was terminated for not conforming to a series of remediation guidelines, which included a provision that he spend more instructional time on general biology than on evolution and creation science.[108] In Arkansas, an injunction was sought and granted by the federal court for the Eastern District of Arkansas preventing the enforcement of a state statute which required "equal time" for the teaching of evolutionary theory and the Biblical version of creation.[109]

A more definitive ruling on this issue was handed down by the Supreme Court in 1987.[110] At issue was the legality of a Louisiana statute that required any public school teaching evolution to also teach creation science. At the time Louisiana was the only state with a creation science law on the books. Both the district and circuit courts struck down the law. Speaking for the Supreme Court majority, Justice Brennan ruled that states may not require public schools to teach creation science. The statute violated the principle of separation of church and state in that it was written to advance religion. The Court recognized further that creationism is a religious theory, but it is not a scientific theory.

In dissent, Justice Scalia charged that the majority had adopted a "repressive" policy toward Christian fundamentalism. He argued that the people of the state were entitled to have whatever scientific evidence there might be against evolution presented in their schools.

§ 12.5. Religion and Extracurricular Activities.

Litigation over the place of religion in the general curriculum has also spilled over into its involvement in extracurricular activi-

---

108. Dale v. Board of Educ., Lemmon Indep. Sch. Dist., 316 N.W.2d 108 (S.D. 1982); Anable v. Ford, 653 F. Supp. 22 (W.D. Ark. 1985). For a recent case on point, see Peloza v. Capistrano Unified Sch. Dist., 37 F.3d 517 (9th Cir. 1994).

109. McLean v. Arkansas Bd. of Educ., 529 F. Supp. 1255 (E.D. Ark. 1982).

110. Edwards v. Aguillard, 482 U.S. 578 (1987).

ties. People have objected to the promotion of religion in required or elective courses; similarly, they have objected to its use in clubs or extracurricular activities.

The key case bearing on this subject is *Board of Education v. Mergens*, a 1990 decision by the Supreme Court of the United States. *Mergens* involved a question of the legality of a secondary school allowing a Bible Club to organize and meet during the school day.[111] The case hinged on an interpretation of the Equal Access Act, a law passed by the United States Congress in 1984. The Act provides:

> It shall be unlawful for any public secondary school which receives Federal financial assistance and which has a limited open forum to deny equal access or a fair opportunity to, or discriminate against, any students who wish to conduct a meeting within that limited open forum on the basis of the religious, political, philosophical, or other content of the speech at such meetings.[112]

Local school officials denied the students' request to organize, and a suit followed. Before the Supreme Court, eight justices agreed that school district recognition of the Bible Club was consistent with the Equal Access Act. In speaking for the majority, Justice O'Connor used four key standards in determining if a school club is directly related to the curriculum. (1) Is the subject matter of the club taught or soon will be taught in a regularly scheduled course? (2) Does the subject matter of the club concern the body of courses as a whole? (3) Is participation in the club required for a particular course? (4) Does participation in the club result in academic credit? The Court ruled that the role of the faculty sponsor should be limited to custodial responsibilities. It also noted that the school should make clear that recognition of a

---

111. 496 U.S. 226 (1990). *See also* Pope v. East Brunswick Bd. of Educ., 12 F.3d 1244 (3d Cir. 1993); Garnett v. Renton Sch. Dist., 987 F.2d 641 (9th Cir. 1994).

112. The Equal Access Act (EAA), 20 U.S.C. § 4071 (1990).

club does not mean endorsement of that club's views, whether it be religious, political, or philosophical.[113]

The lesson for school officials is that, if a secondary school receives federal funds and has at least one noncurriculum-related student group, it is required to provide equal access to all groups regardless of the philosophical, political, religious, or other content of the members' speech.

§ 12.6. Accommodating the Needs of Religious Sects.

In a different vein, the Supreme Court in 1994 ruled on a different kind of special service. It involved the legality of the creation of a special school district composed entirely of a religious sect. Kiryas Joel was created as a special school district by the legislature of New York in response to special needs of children of that village. A community of Orthodox Jews moved to Monroe, New York, and they formed the village of Kiryas Joel. The children were educated in parochial sex-segregated schools with religion being at the core of their study. Children in need of special education were forced to attend public school, and that created psychological problems for them. Accordingly, the state legislature created the village of Kiryas Joel as a separate school district in 1989.

The Supreme Court ruled 6-3 against the legality of the state legislation.[114] The majority ruled that the Act conflicted with the Constitution in that the state had created a school district and then delegated its authority to manage it to a religious body. In fact, the population of the district was composed only of one religious sect.

---

113. *Mergens, supra* note 111. For use of public tax funds in support of a student religious group's publication, see Rosenberger v. Rector & Visitors of Univ. of Va., 115 S. Ct. 2510 (1995).

114. Board of Educ. of Kiryas Joel v. Grumet, 114 S. Ct. 2481 (1994). The New York State Legislature then rewrote the statutes to permit all communities inside larger school districts to secede and organize their own school districts. This was then tested in court by a taxpayer group. The taxpayer group did not prevail. *See* Grumet v. Cuomo, 617 N.Y.S.2d 620 (Sup. Ct. 1994); Grumet v. Pataki, 675 N.Y.S.2d 662 (N.Y. App. Div. 1998).

The creation of the new district ran counter to the trend of consolidating school districts.

By implication, the problem could have been resolved by the state's being more sensitive to the special population. It could have created a more isolated environment where the children would have likely experienced considerably less trauma.[115]

---

115. Courts have been asked to resolve the issue of equal access to public school facilities by religious groups for special-purpose programs. *See, e.g.,* Lamb's Chapel v. Center Moriches Union Free Sch. Dist., 113 S. Ct. 2141 (1993); Good News/Good Sports Club v. School Dist. of City of Ladue, 28 F.3d 1501 (8th Cir. 1994). *See also* Bronx Household of Faith v. Community Sch. Dist. No. 10, 127 F.3d 207 (2d Cir. 1997), in which a school's refusal to allow a church to hold religious services once a week at the school was upheld. A different ruling was handed down in Liberty Christian Center v. Board of Educ., 8 F. Supp. 2d 176 (N.D.N.Y. 1998). For a comprehensive commentary on this subject, see Ralph D. Mawdsley, *Extending Lamb's Chapel to After School Religious Meetings*, 96 EDUC. LAW REP. 17 (Feb. 23, 1995).

Chapter Thirteen

SPECIAL EDUCATION

§ 13.0. Introduction.

The principle that all children, including those with disabilities, have protected rights (legal and constitutional) to receive appropriate, nonarbitrarily determined educational opportunities is a recent phenomenon. As Singletary reminded us,

> [h]istorically, public education in our country has been based on the assumption that all people should be given an adequate education at public expense — all people, that is, except the handicapped and various minority populations. Just recently has the concept of *all* been interpreted to its fullest extent. . . . This recent period may be characterized as striving to guarantee an education for all and a special education for some.[1]

---

1. E. E. Singletary, *The Law and Special Education*, LEGAL ISSUES IN EDUCATION 22 (M.D. Alexander et al., eds. Blacksburg, Virginia, 1974).

"We have come to recognize," continued Singletary, "that those individuals who need the educational opportunity the most have, in the past, been afforded it the least."[2]

As emphasized earlier in Chapter 9, the move to secure equal access to educational opportunities for all children actually had its formal beginning forty years ago when the United States Supreme Court rendered its benchmark decision in *Brown v. Board of Education* (1954).[3] In *Brown,* a case known more for its impact on racial integration of public schools and not for its applicability to issues involving the rights of disabled children, this nation's Highest Court established the principle of extending *equal* access to educational opportunities to all children of school age, as a basic constitutional entitlement.

In the years immediately following *Brown,* courts (federal and state) consistently viewed public education, where the state undertook to provide it, as a basic entitlement of *all* children of school age. Consequently, judges began strongly to insist that state legislatures, state boards of education, and local boards of education (within the scope of their respective state constitutions and state code provisions) do all that was necessary to provide for the *unique* needs of every child.

In the early challenges by parents, courts of law took the traditional view that granted local school boards the prerogative both to deny disabled children admission to public school and the authority to set standards for student progress and continuance in school. Beginning in the early 1970s, however, admission of children with disabilities to public school systems and the placement of these admitted children into appropriate education programs (programs wherein the child would make progress) became issues taken by parents to federal and state courts. As Ross, DeYoung, and Cohen suggested in the early 1970s, the results of such litigation caused public school systems of various states to cease to employ pro-

---

2. *Id. See also* H. R. TURNBULL, III, LEGAL ASPECTS OF EDUCATING THE DEVELOPMENTALLY DISABLED (Topeka, Kan.: NOLPE, 1975).
3. 347 U.S. 483, 74 S. Ct. 686, 98 L. Ed. 2d 873 (1954).

grams of student evaluation and placement that discriminated against certain children and denied those children their constitutional right to equal access to an appropriate and meaningful educational opportunity.[4]

§ 13.1. The Impact of *P.A.R.C.* and *Mills.*

In 1972, Thomas K. Gilhool, the attorney for the plaintiffs in the landmark case of *Pennsylvania Association for Retarded Children v. Commonwealth* (better known as *P.A.R.C.*),[5] suggested that the federal court's decision in that case would mark the beginning of a long line of similar decisions. His judgment was correct in that numerous court cases (involving almost every state and the District of Columbia), each with the primary purpose of securing for *all* exceptional children their constitutionally guaranteed "right to education," were brought in an "avalanche of litigation."[6]

Because *P.A.R.C.* was taken as a class action by parents of retarded children and ultimately settled by a consent decree, the actual legal value of the *P.A.R.C.* decision is found in what the district court suggested, since the consent agreement itself was binding solely on the parties in that case. In sum, the *P.A.R.C.* agreement itself did not create law; it simply set forth a plan to provide for retarded children in Pennsylvania who, up to that time, had been excluded from receiving educational opportunities in the schools of that Commonwealth. Also, as Burgdorf has said, "[t]he legal analysis and argument contained in the complaint in *P.A.R.C.*

---

4. S. L. Ross, Jr., et al., *Confrontation: Special Education and The Law,* 38 EXCEPT. CHILD. 5 (1971). For a case involving a challenge to use of I.Q. testing for the placement of African-American children in special education classes, see Crawford v. Honig, 37 F.3d 485 (9th Cir. 1994).

5. 334 F. Supp. 1257 (E.D. Pa. 1971), final consent agreement, 343 F. Supp. 279 (E.D. Pa. 1972).

6. T.K. Gilhool, *Education: An Inalienable Right,* 39 EXCEPT. CHILD. 598 (1973).

have been employed as a touchstone in the drafting of later complaints."[7]

Mills v. Board of Education of the District of Columbia expanded and extended several of the principles set down in the *P.A.R.C.* case. *Mills* (1972) involved a challenge from parents (of Peter Mills and six other children with a variety of handicaps) to what they alleged were "exclusionary practices" (the "culprit" they claimed was the labeling of their children) actually affecting some 18,000 exceptional children. In the plaintiff-parents' view, such acts by the local board denied such children equal access to a public education in violation of their constitutional rights to due process. More specifically, the parents in *Mills* alleged that their children (who were classified as behavior problems) had been denied public education benefits. At the time of the litigation the District of Columbia mandated a free public education for all children between the ages of seven and sixteen. The plaintiff parents claimed that their children had been labeled without a fair and impartial hearing (a violation of their due process rights under the fifth amendment).[8]

Actually expanding the notions created in *P.A.R.C.* beyond the entitlements of retarded children, the *Mills* court emphasized the entitlement (under the District of Columbia School Board's regulations, as well as the United States Constitution) of all children, including children with disabilities, to a publicly supported education and the importance of providing *due process* (especially an impartial hearing) prior to any classification, exclusion, or termination of students. As the court stated in *Mills,*

> no child eligible for a publicly supported education in the District of Columbia public schools shall be excluded from a regular public school assignment by a rule, policy, or practice of the board of education or its agents unless

---

7. THE LEGAL RIGHTS OF HANDICAPPED PERSONS: CASES, MATERIALS, AND TEXT 90-91 (R.L. Burgdorf, Jr. ed. Baltimore, Md.: Paul H. Brooks Publishers, 1980).

8. Mills v. Board of Educ., 348 F. Supp. 866 (D.D.C. 1972).

> the child is provided with an adequate alternative suited
> to the child's needs, which may include special educa-
> tion.[9]

Additionally, the district court described the education process as "continuous," a notion that persisted throughout subsequent special education litigation.

Taken together, *P.A.R.C.* and *Mills* set the stage for the development of comprehensive plans at the local and state levels to provide education opportunities for *all* children with disabilities. For example: (1) generally, states (and their local education agencies) began to extend access to a publicly supported educational opportunity to all children of school age, and mandated that no school age child shall be *arbitrarily* excluded from or denied access to such an opportunity; (2) where such mandates were implemented, states (and their local education agencies) had an obligation to make reasonable efforts to tailor educational programs to the unique needs of children with disabilities and not simply deny program opportunities to children with disabilities without making such efforts; (3) parents or guardians of children with disabilities (as well as the children themselves) were accorded procedural due process rights intended to ensure direct involvement in and continuous information concerning their child's status and program; and (4) generally, financial assistance (*e.g.,* tuition, transportation costs, etc.) was made available to eligible parents in an effort to ensure that each child should have access to an appropriate education program, wherever it existed.

P.A.R.C., Mills, and several decisions that followed (1972-1976) also broadened the definitions of such terms as *disabled, exceptional,* and *handicapped.* As a result, states and local school districts began to realize that potentially all children, no matter what the nature of their exceptionality, might be encompassed by state constitutional and statutory provisions.[10] Thus, massive efforts were undertaken to find children who, heretofore, had been educa-

---

9. *Id.* at 878.

10. TURNBULL, *supra* note 2, at 2-6.

tionally neglected, or who had been excluded from an educational program because of faulty testing and placement procedures.

§ 13.2. The Right to Education: Redefinition and Redirection.

Within two years following *P.A.R.C.* and *Mills,* and up to the United States Supreme Court's benchmark decision in *Rodriguez* (a challenge to the State of Texas' system of financing its public schools, and not a case involving special education),[11] a significant change took place with regard to the concept of the "right" of all children to a publicly established and maintained education. As quoted in previous chapters, the Warren Court's attitude in *Brown* declared that the *importance of education* in our society made it imperative to provide every child of school age with access to an education opportunity, without discrimination. From 1954 to 1973 (with the United States Supreme Court's decision in *Rodriguez*) the emphasis was on making certain, by application of fourteenth amendment guarantees of equal protection and due process, that the "doors to equal educational opportunity" were opened to every eligible child.

Contrary to the opinions of some legal scholars, the *Rodriguez* decision (1973) did not negate the *Brown* (1954) decision. In both decisions the Supreme Court enunciated the principle that equal education opportunity, where the state itself mandates it, is a matter of *entitlement* guaranteed and protected by state constitution and state statute. As one expert concluded, the Supreme Court's ruling in *Rodriguez* "need not necessarily impede a state court's finding with regard to the fundamentality of education based on its own constitution."[12]

The primary focus of attention in the post-*Rodriguez* era, however, was redirected away from efforts to "open public school

---

11. San Antonio Indep. Sch. Dist. v. Rodriguez, 411 U.S. 1, 93 S. Ct. 1278, 36 L. Ed. 2d 16 (1973).

12. B. Levin, *School Finance Reform in a Post-*Rodriguez *World,* CONTEMPORARY PROBLEMS IN EDUCATION 165 (M.A. McGhehey ed. Topeka, Kan.: NOLPE, 1975).

doors" to all children, and courts of law turned their attention to the issue of ensuring *quality* educational programs for children once they enter the school. As Turnbull commented two years after *Rodriguez*, "the 'right to education' means that the school systems must provide all children equal opportunities to develop their own capabilities; the school systems thus are required to provide different programs and facilities for pupils with different needs, according to their needs."[13] School practices, he concluded, could not deny students "a meaningful opportunity for education. . . ."[14]

Beginning in the second half of the 1970s, parents and other concerned people sought to ensure equal access to *appropriate* and *meaningful* educational opportunities for all children with disabilities and did so by directing their efforts toward the individual states and state code provisions (or the lack thereof). In the post-*Rodriguez* era the onus continued to be on each state, under its own constitutional and statutory mandates, to provide an educational opportunity to every child of school age. As a result, concerned and assertive advocates for children with special needs began to search out appropriate state mandates and to insist that they be interpreted and made to apply to public school systems within the boundaries of the particular state.

With greater frequency, post-*Rodriguez* courts (mostly state courts) were asked by parents and other advocates to force state and local school boards to implement legislation affecting exceptional children. Concurrently, efforts were made in our nation's capital to bring into being some national legislation for the rights of all handicapped children. As Alexander and Alexander have commented, "with the awareness created by the litigation in *P.A.R.C.* and *Mills* and emergent cases from the states, the Congress moved rapidly to provide federal legislation and funding which would assist in educating the handicapped."[15]

---

13. TURNBULL, *supra* note 2, at 19.

14. *Id.* at 20.

15. K. ALEXANDER & M.D. ALEXANDER, THE LAW OF SCHOOLS, STUDENTS, AND TEACHERS 184 (St. Paul, Minn.: West Publishing Co., 1984).

§ 13.3. The Emergence of Statutes at the Federal Level.

Generally regarded as the first national civil rights statute to protect the rights of people with disabling conditions, the Rehabilitation Act (P.L. 93-112) was passed by Congress in 1973.[16] Section 504 of that statute contains the following language: "No otherwise qualified handicapped individual in the United States, as defined in section 706(6) of this title, shall solely by reasons of his handicap, be excluded from the participation in, be denied the benefits of, or be subjected to discrimination under any program or activity receiving Federal financial assistance."[17]

In essence, states Shrybman, § 504 "deals with nondiscrimination on the basis of handicap and basically requires that recipients of federal funds provide equal opportunities to disabled persons."[18] A broad-based statute, § 504 covers such items as "barrier-free facilities and program accessibility; employment; post-secondary education; and health, welfare, and social services."[19]

As the regulations were implemented, the key phrase in § 504 quickly became the "solely by reason of his handicap" language. The intent of this language was that an *otherwise qualified* handicapped person could not be excluded from or in some other way *discriminated* against in any federally funded activity or program, *solely* because of his or her disability. According to Valenti, feder-

---

16. *See* 29 U.S.C. § 794 (1973), and the federal regulations for implementing the law at 34 C.F.R. § 104.

17. *Id.* The requirement that no student be discriminated against solely on the basis of his/her disability has been applied to extracurricular activities. *See, e.g.,* University Interscholastic League v. Buchanan, 848 S.W.2d 298 (Tex. App. 1993); Hoot by Hoot v. Milan Area Sch., 853 F. Supp. 243 (E.D. Mich. 1994); State *ex rel.* Lambert v. West Virginia State Bd., 447 S.E.2d 901 (W. Va. 1994).

18. J.A. SHRYBMAN, DUE PROCESS IN SPECIAL EDUCATION 50 (Rockville, Md.: Aspen Systems Corp., 1982). Under § 504, he states, "a handicapped person is one who has a physical or mental impairment that substantially limits one or more major life activities, has a record of that type of dysfunction, or is regarded as having that disability."

19. *Id.* at 51.

ally aided school districts could no longer *presume* a lack of qualification in a person (an applicant or a continuing employee) solely because of the presence of a handicap and had to show where and how that handicap related in fact to a disqualification.[20] What is more, a finding of *intentional* discrimination was not necessary to establish a *prima facie* violation of § 504. The impact and effects of a discriminatory act were enough to make such a case.[21]

The United States Supreme Court, in a 1979 decision made it clear, however, that the language of § 504 did not limit the prerogatives of an educational institution to require reasonable physical qualifications of students who wish to enter certain training programs. In *Southeastern Community College v. Davis,*[22] the High Court upheld the denial of admission of a student to a nursing program because of that student's serious hearing difficulty. To the Court, such a denial was not a violation of § 504, since there would exist a risk to the safety of the patients during her training period. Speaking directly to the college's unwillingness to make any major adjustments in its nursing program that would make it possible to admit the applicant and accommodate her hearing disability, the Court said: "It is undisputed that respondent could not participate in Southeastern's nursing program unless the standards were substantially lowered. Section 504 imposes no requirement upon an educational institution to lower or to effect substantial modifications of standards to accommodate a handicapped person."[23] It is important to note the Court's statement that § 504 does not require that program requirements or standards be lowered or substantially modified to accommodate an applicant's disability. In other words, other situations might exist wherein it will be necessary to make *reasonable* modifications of programs and program

---

20. W.D. VALENTI, LAW IN THE SCHOOLS 327 (Columbus, Ohio: Charles E. Merrill Publishing Co., 1980). *See* Michael U. *ex rel.* K.U. v. Alvin I.D.S., 991 F. Supp. 599 (S.D. Tex. 1998).

21. *See, e.g.,* New Mexico Ass'n for Retarded Citizens v. New Mexico, 495 F. Supp. 391 (D.N.M. 1980).

22. 442 U.S. 397, 99 S. Ct. 2361. 60 L. Ed. 2d 980 (1979).

23. *Id.* at 442 U.S. 413.

requirements (without lowering standards) so that disabled persons (who are otherwise technically and academically qualified) can gain admittance to and demonstrate success in an educational program.

The courts have created a three-pronged standard to apply in § 504 cases. Under this standard the following questions must be answered to determine if the aggrieved individual is otherwise qualified under the law: (1) Is the plaintiff a handicapped person under the law? (2) Is the activity involved one that receives federal assistance? (3) Is the plaintiff a person who has been excluded from that activity solely because of his/her handicap?[24]

In a subsequent § 504 case, a federal district court in New York ruled against a high school senior, classified as neurologically impaired, who had been prohibited from participating in inter-scholastic athletics solely because he had reached age nineteen. The court found that he had not been treated any differently from nonhandicapped students and, thus, he could not prevail in a handicap discrimination and equal protection action.[25]

Finally, § 504 does allow for lawsuits seeking monetary damages. Such remedy may be possible even before an administrative hearing is held.[26]

Passage of the Education Amendments of 1974 (P.L. 93-380) extended due process protections to parents of children with disabilities (between ages thirteen and twenty-one) in such matters as

---

24. *See, e.g.,* Wolff v. South Colonie Cent. Sch. Dist., 534 F. Supp. 758 (N.D.N.Y. 1982).

25. Cavallaro v. Ambach, 575 F. Supp. 171 (W.D.N.Y. 1983).

26. *See, e.g.,* Miener v. Missouri, 673 F.2d 969 (8th Cir. 1982). Regarding the Education for All Handicapped Children Act and suits for damages under 42 U.S.C. § 1983, the Second Circuit has said that damages "would not be recoverable in cases . . . where the parent has (1) been properly notified of the procedural remedies available to consider such complaints and (2) not been hindered in pursuing them." Quackenbush v. Johnson City Sch. Dist., 716 F.2d 141 (2d Cir. 1983). Also, it must be kept in mind that as a general rule damages for basic education claims under the Rehabilitation Act of 1973 must be premised on a claim of either *bad faith* or *intentional discrimination. See, e.g.,* Barnett v. Fairfax Cty. Sch. Bd., 721 F. Supp. 757 (E.D. Va. 1989).

testing, identification, placement, record examination, and program finance.[27] Where parents or guardians are dissatisfied with such matters, the option of a due process hearing, binding on the parties, was created by law.

In November, 1975, Congress passed P.L. 94-142, The Education for All Handicapped Children Act (EAHCA).[28] To experts writing at that time, P.L. 94-142 represented an enforceable civil rights act for children with disabilities. The new law was intended to make certain that children with disabilities receive appropriate special education and related services. In 1980, Bryson and Bentley reflected on this new law and its implementation. In their view, the statute established the legal principle that no child may be excluded from school and assigned to a special education class without first being granted all appropriate due process procedures.[29]

Some of the major features of the EAHCA and its implementing regulations were:

(1) that all handicapped children (as defined in the law) be provided access to a free, nonarbitrarily determined education and related services (first priority given to find and identify children not receiving such programs and services, and second priority given to upgrade and expand programs and services for children already identified and provided for);

---

27. 88 Stat. 484 (1976).

28. *See* 20 U.S.C. § 1401 et seq. (1976), and the federal implementing regulations at 34 C.F.R. § 300. The Act was reenacted and retitled as the Individuals with Disabilities Education Act (IDEA), 20 U.S.C. § 1401 et seq. (1990).

29. J.E. BRYSON & C.P. BENTLEY, ABILITY GROUPING OF PUBLIC SCHOOL STUDENTS 78-79 (Charlottesville, Va.: Michie Co. 1980). As P. Manville reminded us, "[a] handicapped child's right to an appropriate education has been guaranteed since 1975 with the Education for All Handicapped Children Act (EAHCA) and Section 504 of the Rehabilitation Act of 1973." 18 WEST'S EDUC. LAW RPTR. 9 (Aug. 23, 1984) *But see* Sellers v. Manassas Sch. Bd., 141 F.3d 524 (4th Cir. 1998), for a decision denying a FAPE (Free Appropriate Public Education).

(2) that these programs and related services be designed to meet the unique needs of the child;

(3) that all handicapped children (as defined in the
law) be educated in the "least restrictive environment"
(even if that environment might exist in a nonpublic setting);

(4) that an I.E.P. (individualized educational program)
be designed for each child (subject to annual reevaluation); and

(5) that all children covered under the law and their
parents (guardians) were entitled to procedural due process protections at all stages of the law's implementation.[30]

Responsibility for administering the new law was placed in the
Bureau of Education for the Handicapped (BEH). Thus, BEH
became the primary federal agency responsible for monitoring the
states and local agencies to see to it that the intent of the law was
carried out.[31]

§ 13.4. Recent Litigation Involving Special Education.

For more than two decades now, the courts have been busy with
a variety of special education cases, since Congress did not clearly
define every aspect and guarantee of the above-mentioned federal
mandates, especially P.L. 94-142. Some examples of issues before
the courts are: (1) issues focusing upon the *right to education* itself
(*e.g.,* allegations that certain eligible children have not been identified for special services, or that eligible children who have been
identified are not being appropriately placed); (2) issues involving
the law's evaluation process and procedures (*e.g.,* allegations that
parents or guardians have not been properly notified and informed,
or that school officials failed to secure parental consent prior to

---

30. This summary of the highlights of the 1975 Act is gleaned from H.
APPENZELLER, THE RIGHT TO PARTICIPATE 55-66 (Charlottesville, Va.: The Michie
Co., 1983). For the federal regulations implementing the Act, see 34 C.F.R. § 300
et seq. (1999).

31. *Id.*

evaluation of their child); (3) questions concerning the I.E.P. (Individualized Education Program) itself (*e.g.*, allegations of improper committee composition; or that improper procedures were followed in formulating the Plan; or that necessary related services were not included in the Plan); (4) allegations of *improper placement* of children and *improper program administration* (*e.g.*, charges that a child had not been placed in the least restrictive environment, or that improper and unauthorized changes in placement have taken place, or that a child's public school program placement is not appropriate and, therefore, a private placement should be implemented, at no cost to the parents); and (5) questions stemming from the *misbehavior* of some exceptional children who have been mainstreamed into regular school classrooms and activities (*e.g.*, claims by parents that exceptional children should not be subject to the same policies, rules, and procedures of student control and discipline as are other children).

Over the past twenty-five years, the struggle to implement the Act (now retitled as IDEA) and its regulations has resulted in parents obtaining necessary leverage in a public school system's decision-making process and, as the Supreme Court said in *Smith v. Robinson* (1984), P.L. 94-142 has become the exclusive avenue through which petitioners assert equal protection claims to publicly financed special education.[32] As such, the Act legitimized the active participation of parents (guardians) in their child's educational program, from the initial planning to the final implementation phase. According to the federal judiciary, as a general rule, monetary damages are not possible as a remedy for violations of the Act. The comprehensive administrative process within the statute (plus the possibility of court injunctions) forms adequate remedy for plaintiff parties.[33]

---

32. Smith v. Robinson, 468 U.S. 992, 104 S. Ct. 3457, 79 L. Ed. 2d 304 (1984). This leverage is not unlimited, as demonstrated in two decisions from the late 1990s. *See* Devine v. Indian River Cty. Sch. Bd., 121 F.3d 576 (11th Cir. 1997); Wenger v. Canastota Cent. Sch. Dist., 146 F.3d 123 (2d Cir. 1998).

33. *See Miener, supra* note 26, wherein the court held that remedy under the Education for All Handicapped Children Act should be limited to non-monetary

a. *Right to an Appropriate Educational Program.* As stated earlier in this chapter, implicit in the language of P.L. 94-142 was the mandate that all children (as defined in and covered under the Act) be evaluated and placed as needed to gain access to a free, appropriate education and necessary related services. What was not clear, however, was the meaning of the word *appropriate* and the meaning of the term *related services.* Did these two concepts imply that an educational opportunity be designed to meet (at least minimally) the unique needs of a child? Or did these terms contain an implicit requirement that a local education agency must provide

relief. For a case wherein parents of a handicapped child were entitled to an award of attorney's fees, see Blazejewski v. Board of Educ., 599 F. Supp. 975 (W.D.N.Y. 1985). *See also* Barnett v. Fairfax, *supra* note 26. For a comprehensive commentary on the subject, see Perry A. Zirkel & Allan G. Osborne, *Are Damages Available in Special Education Suits,* 42 EDUC. LAW REP. 491 (Dec. 23, 1987). The reader should be aware, however, that in 1986 Congress passed the Handicapped Children's Protection Act. As an amendment to the EAHCA, the HCPA (20 U.S.C. § 1415(e)(4) *et seq.*) allows for parents who prevail in either the administrative processes of the EAHCA or court procedures to seek attorney fees and costs. For some excellent cases on point, see Fontenot v. Board of Elem. & Secondary Educ., 805 F.2d 1222 (5th Cir. 1986); Eggers v. Bullitt Cty., 854 F.2d 892 (6th Cir. 1988); Neiz v. Portland, 684 F. Supp. 1530 (D. Ore. 1988); Holms v. District of Columbia, 680 F. Supp. 40 (D.D.C. 1988); Howley v. Tippecanoe Sch. Corp., 734 F. Supp. 1485 (N.D. Ind. 1990); Massachusetts Dep't of Pub. Health v. School Comm., 841 F. Supp. 449 (D. Mass. 1993); E.M. v. Millville Bd. of Educ., 849 F. Supp. 312 (D.N.J. 1994). For two cases where parents were not considered prevailing parties, see S-1 and S-2 v. North Carolina State Bd., 21 F.3d 49 (4th Cir. 1994); Brown v. Griggsville Community Union, 817 F. Supp. 734 (C.D. Ill. 1993). For a comprehensive commentary on attorney fees, see David L. Dagley, *Prevailing Under the HCPA,* 90 EDUC. LAW REP. 547 (June 30, 1994). *See also* D.H. v. Ashford Bd. of Educ., 1 F. Supp. 2d 154 (D. Conn. 1998) (parents entitled to attorney fees based on their status as prevailing parties); Eirschele v. Craven City Bd. of Educ., 7 F. Supp. 2d 655 (E.D.N.C. 1998) (parents denied award of expert witness fees as a part of attorney fees); Nicholas v. Taylor Cty. Bd., 7 F. Supp. 2d 789 (N.D. W. Va. 1998) (parents failed to show that they were prevailing parties for purposes of recovering attorney fees under IDEA); Mr.& Mrs. B. *ex rel.* W.B. v. Watson Bd. of Educ., 34 F. Supp. 2d 777 (D. Conn. 1999); Board of Educ. of Harford Cty. v. Thomas, 36 F. Supp. 2d 256 (D. Md. 1999).

the "best possible educational opportunity" for the child and one designed to enable a child to develop to his or her full potential?

In 1981, a United States District Court, Eastern District of Virginia, heard a case involving the King George County, Virginia, school system.[34] Plaintiff-parents in *Bales v. Clarke* sought reimbursement for various expenses incurred by them in providing education and training for their child. In *Bales,* the child was one who, at age nine years, had received a serious head injury in an automobile accident. The child was tested at the University of Virginia and by the King George County School System and subsequently placed in a self-contained class for speech and language therapy. A major issue in *Bales* had its origin in a request by the parents that they be reimbursed for summer programs provided for their child and for their travel expenses while their child was a patient-student in the Home for Crippled Children in Pittsburgh, Pennsylvania. School officials did not agree and the parents took their case to federal court.

Expressing the opinion that the handicapped child in this case was not entitled to year-round schooling without a showing of irreparable loss during the summer months and that the provision of psychological counseling in this case was not an entitlement in the absence of serious behavior problems, the district court ruled against the parents.[35] To the district judge, the statutory requirement of an *appropriate education* is not synonymous with the "best possible education," nor is it synonymous with an education which enables a child to achieve his or her full potential. Such a mandate would be unrealistic, said the court, as even the best schools lack the resources to enable every child to reach that goal.[36]

One year later, the United States Supreme Court decided *Hendrick Hudson Central School District v. Rowley.*[37] The *Rowley*

---

34. Bales v. Clarke, 523 F. Supp. 1366 (E.D. Va. 1981).

35. *Id.* at 1370-72.

36. *Id.* at 1370.

37. 458 U.S. 176, 102 S. Ct. 3034, 73 L. Ed. 2d 690 (1982).

case presented the High Court with its first opportunity to interpret the 1975 Education for All Handicapped Children Act, especially its mandate that an "appropriate education" be provided each child covered under the Act.

Amy was a hearing-impaired student (she had minimal residual hearing) enrolled in regular classes since kindergarten. An intelligent student (an I.Q of 122) and an excellent lipreader, Amy had passed from grade to grade with above average grades (she received help every day from a tutor and help three hours a week from a speech therapist). Amy's parents had requested that school officials provide the additional services of a sign language interpreter. In the parents' view, the related services of an interpreter would enable Amy to develop to her maximum potential. School officials, on the other hand, questioned whether such services were required since Amy was functioning at or above grade level (in other words, Amy was benefiting from her educational opportunity).[38]

Ruling in the school system's favor, the Supreme Court majority focused upon the "benefit" received by Amy, which they saw as meeting the standards of the Act. To put it another way, the Court was convinced that Amy had "access" to a "meaningful educational program" which resulted in her making progress at or above grade level.

In the majority's opinion, once a court determines that the *requirements* of the Act are met (i.e., both compliance with procedures required by law and student access to a program designed to deliver educational benefit to that student), judges should not look beyond that.[39]

---

38. *Id.* at 3039-40.

39. *Id.* at 3046. For a case where the importance is placed on a student receiving "a meaningful educational benefit" from his educational placement, see Swift v. Rapides Parish Sch. Bd., 812 F. Supp. 666 (W.D. La. 1993). In Mohawk Trail Reg'l Sch. Dist. v. Shawn D. *ex rel.* Linda D., 35 F. Supp. 34 (D. Mass. 1999), the court held that providing a student with an "adequate education" did not meet the requirements of IDEA.

To the majority, the intent of the Act is not to ensure that a handicapped child be provided with the "best" educational program or that the program ensure maximum development of his or her full potential. Rather, the Act is meant to provide free access to a "basic floor opportunity" for each child, resulting in some benefit to that child.[40]

Litigation post-*Rowley* continued to focus upon three issues. These issues were: (1) guaranteeing student access to (placement in) *appropriate* educational programs (including necessary *related* services) designed to bring about some benefit to the child; (2) where such programs (including services) should be offered and by whom they should be offered; and (3) who (local education agency or parent) is obligated to pay for such programs and related services (wherever they exist). In a 1983 decision from a federal district court in Tennessee, the following definition is offered for the phrase "free appropriate education": "instruction and support services designed to meet the unique needs of the handicapped child which are provided at public expense, meet state educational standards, approximate grade levels used in the State's regular education program and comport with the child's individualized educational program."[41]

In *Rettig v. Kent City School District,* the Sixth Circuit was faced with the issue of a school system's obligation to the development of a handicapped child's potential. In that court's opinion the Education for All Handicapped Children Act does not require that a state (here it was Ohio) maximize the potential of handi-

---

40. *Id.* at 3048-52.

41. Clevenger v. Oak Ridge Sch. Bd., 573 F. Supp. 349 (E.D. Tenn. 1983). The Ninth Circuit used the following four-pronged standard to apply in determining the appropriateness of a student's placement and educational program: (1) determine the academic benefits to the special education student; (2) determine the nonacademic benefits to that student (such as language and behavior models provided him/her by the other students present); (3) evaluate the negative effects of that student's presence on the teacher and other students; and (4) figure the costs for educating that student in a mainstreamed environment. *See* Clyde K. v. Puyallup Sch. Dist., 35 F.3d 1396 (9th Cir. 1994). *See also* Wirta v. District of Columbia, 859 F. Supp. 1 (D.D.C. 1994).

capped children commensurate with opportunity provided to other children.[42]

In 1984, the United States Supreme Court decided a case out of Texas having a direct bearing upon the issue of related services necessary to assist a handicapped child to "benefit from special education." Originally decided pre-*Rowley* by the United States District Court, Northern District of Texas,[43] and later reversed and remanded by the Fifth Circuit,[44] *Irving Independent School District v. Tatro*[45] put the following question before this nation's Highest Court: Does the Education for All Handicapped Children Act require that a school district provide for the *clean intermittent catheterization* of a handicapped child during school hours, as a *related* and *supportive* educational service required to assist a handicapped child to benefit from education?[46]

Turning to the language of the Education for All Handicapped Children Act, the Court answered the above question in the affirmative. It was clear to the Court that without having catheterization services provided to her, the student in this case could not attend school and, therefore, would not benefit from special education. Like other supportive services specifically provided for in the Act (*e.g.*, transportation), catheterization (which is not specifically mentioned in the Act) enables this particular student to have access to and remain at school during the school day and, accordingly, receive the benefits of educational programs.[47]

---

42. Rettig v. Kent City Sch. Dist., 720 F.2d 463 (6th Cir. 1983).

43. Tatro v. Texas, 481 F. Supp. 1224 (N.D. Tex. 1979).

44. Tatro v. Texas, 625 F.2d 557 (5th Cir. 1980).

45. 48 U.S. 883, 104 S. Ct. 3371, 82 L. Ed. 2d 664 (1984), *on remand,* Tatro v. Texas, 741 F.2d 82 (1984).

46. *Id.* at 82 L. Ed. 2d 672.

47. *Id.* at 672-73. For examples of cases involving issues of related services, see Bevin H. v. Wright, 666 F. Supp. 71 (W.D. Pa. 1987); Corbett v. Regional Center, 676 F. Supp. 964 (N.D. Cal. 1988); School Dist. of Philadelphia v. Department of Educ., 547 A.2d 520 (Pa. Commw. 1988); Liscio v. Woodland Hills, 734 F. Supp. 689 (W.D. Pa. 1989). In Detsel v. Sullivan, 895 F.2d 58 (2d Cir. 1990), it was held that a student was entitled to obtain Medicaid payment for private-duty nursing services provided while attending a public school. *See also*

In 1984, the Ninth Circuit affirmed the prerogative of a local school district to transfer a physically handicapped, female, elementary school student (she had cerebral palsy), over the objection of the student's parents, from the school where she was enrolled to another school.[48] The primary motivating factor in the board's transfer decision was the fact that the student, who was evaluated as a student of "at least normal intelligence," was not making "satisfactory progress" in reading and writing in her current placement.[49] In the opinion of school officials, in the new placement, assistance could be provided from an instructor especially qualified to work with students who had that particular disability, with the primary objective being the student's making progress, and this was well within the bounds of both federal and state law.[50]

In upholding the school district, the court was of the opinion that the transfer was reasonably calculated to furnish the student with an educational opportunity *appropriate* to her individual needs. Citing *Rowley* (and acknowledging the parents' sincere interest in their child), the Ninth Circuit emphasized its reluctance to interfere with the discretion of school officials.[51] Said the court:

Clovis v. Office of Admin. Hearings, 903 F.2d 635 (9th Cir. 1990); Schonfeld v. Aetna Life, 593 N.Y.S.2d 250 (N.Y. App. Div. 1st Dep't 1993); and Kathy Dye Spaller & Stephen B. Thomas, *A Timely Idea: Third Party Billing for Related Services*, 86 EDUC. LAW REP. 581 (Jan. 13, 1994). *See also* Cedar Rapids Commun. Sch. Dist. v. Garret F., 106 F.3d 822 (8th Cir. 1997), *aff'd*, 119 S. Ct. 992 (1999), where the United States Supreme Court interpreted narrowly the *medical exemption* of IDEA and underscored the role played by necessary, related, and supportive services. For additional decisions on point, see DeBord v. Board of Educ., 126 F.3d 1102 (8th Cir. 1997); Morton Community Unit Sch. Dist. v. J.M., 152 F.3d 583 (7th Cir. 1998); Nieuwenhuis v. Delavan-Drien, 996 F. Supp. 855 (E.D. Wis. 1998).

48. Wilson v. Marana Unified Sch. Dist. No. 6, 735 F.2d 1178 (9th Cir. 1984).

49. *Id.* at 1180.

50. *Id.* The *Wilson* plaintiffs appealed a state administrative decision made pursuant to both the Education for All Handicapped Children Act and the Rehabilitation Act of 1973, and a judgment on the pleadings was rendered in federal court for the school officials.

51. *Id.* at 1183. Said the court: "[W]e must grant deference to the sound judgment of various state education agencies."

> We are equally convinced that the Marana Unified School District is greatly concerned with the welfare of all the children that pass through its system. Since the school district is acting within the bounds of federal and state law, we must grant deference to its sound judgment concerning the education of Jessica Wilson.[52]

The fact that the transfer was for the purpose of ensuring that the student would make progress was the key factor in this case.

b. *The Individualized Educational Program (I.E.P.).* As demonstrated above, the implementation of the Education for All Handicapped Children Act in 1975 fostered numerous lawsuits throughout the country. Many of these suits involved the development, implementation, and evaluation of the Individualized Educational Program (I.E.P.).

Intended to be a written statement for each child, the I.E.P. remains the *sine qua non* of the Act. It sets and controls the goals of the student's unique educational program, the educational setting (in the "least restrictive environment"), the length of the program, the instructional methodologies to be employed, the evaluation system to be used, the extracurricular activities to be included, the modes of discipline, the related services, and the standards of progress to be met. In other words, all aspects of a child's free, appropriate educational program should be included and detailed in the written I.E.P. for that child — a written agreement reached through total participation of parents, designated school personnel, and (where appropriate) the student.[53]

---

52. *Id.* at 1184. For more decisions upholding the placement decisions of local school boards, see Doyle v. Arlington Cty., 953 F.2d 100 (4th Cir. 1992); Livingston v. DeSoto, 782 F. Supp. 1173 (N.D. Miss. 1992); and Lewis v. School Bd. of Loudoun Cty., 808 F. Supp. 523 (E.D. Va. 1992).

53. 20 U.S.C. § 1401(19) et seq. Portions of this subsection are taken directly from E.T. Connors & R.S. Vacca, *IEP's — Gateway for Legal Entanglement,* in COMING OF AGE: THE BEST OF ACLD (W.M. Cruickshank & J.W. Lerner eds., Syracuse, N.Y.: Syracuse University Press, 1982). In 1997, the newly enacted IDEA amendments specified that the I.E.P. team developing the plan shall be composed of the parent(s), at least one general educator, at least one special

The particulars of the Individualized Education Program are detailed in IDEA (1997). IDEA mandates that an I.E.P. must be in writing and signed by the child's parents.

IDEA specifies that the child's progress (or lack thereof) should be reviewed at least annually. What is more, any adjustments made to the I.E.P. (intended to provide for the increase or furtherance of the educational goals) must be approved by all parties to the initial agreement.

Generally, the recorded *causes of complaints* regarding the I.E.P. fall into seven distinct categories. These categories of complaint are generally stated as allegations of (1) improper committee composition, (2) improper development procedures followed, (3) timelines for development not observed, (4) required portions omitted, (5) included services not provided, (6) implementation delayed, and (7) included services not provided on a cost-free basis to parents or guardians.

Accountability regarding the content of the I.E.P. represents another area of potential litigation. According to the Act's original implementing regulations,

> Each public agency must provide special education and related services to a handicapped child in accordance with an individualized education program. However, Part B of the Act does not require that any agency, teacher, or other person be held accountable if a child does not achieve the growth projected in the annual goals and objectives.[54]

It should be noted that the above section *did not state* that an agency or teacher *is not accountable*. It merely suggested that such agencies and personnel are not necessarily accountable if the child

---

educator, a representative of the local education agency (LEA), an individual who can interpret the implications of evaluation results, other knowledgeable professional personnel (related services personnel, school psychologist, etc.), and whenever appropriate, the child. *See, e.g.,* IDEA 1997: LET'S MAKE IT WORK (Reston, Va. Council for Exceptional Children, 1998), and 34 C.F.R. § 300 et seq. (1999).

54. 45 C.F.R. § 121a.349 (Aug. 23, 1977).

does not achieve the growth projected in the annual goals and objectives.

Since the enactment of P.L. 94-142, the crucial role of the I.E.P. has been consistently emphasized by courts of law. For example, the Third Circuit in *Battle* (a class action challenge to a Pennsylvania statute which set as a limit 180 days of instruction per year for all children, handicapped or not), depicted the I.E.P. as the "heart" of the federal mandate to meet each child's unique needs. In the words of that court:

> The I.E.P. is the statutory vehicle for formulating the educational objectives and the educational program for each child. We consider it most persuasive that at this fundamental point in the educational decision making process, the statute required consideration of each individual child.... Moreover, as difficult as it is to define the scope of the "unique needs" which must be met by special education . . . , there can be little doubt that by requiring attention to "unique needs," the Act demands that special education be tailored to the individual.[55]

Hayes and Higgins remind us that not only is the I.E.P. the "cornerstone" of the law and the "management tool" for resources and goals, it is also "one way to document assurance of an appropriate education."[56] Moreover, these authors clearly state that the requirements of P.L. 94-142 (and the key element of the I.E.P.) make "teachers responsible and accountable for assuring that each handicapped child receive the required special education and related services set forth in the I.E.P."[57]

Hayes and Higgins suggest that the accountability of teachers rests on the *delivery* of education and related services to handicapped children placed in their classrooms. This represents a sig-

---

55. Battle v. Pennsylvania, 629 F.2d 269, 280 (3d Cir. 1980). *See also* Crawford v. Pittman, 708 F.2d 1028 (5th Cir. 1983).

56. J. Hayes & S.T. Higgins, *Issues Regarding the IEP: Teachers on the Front Line*, 44 EXCEPT. CHILD. 267 (Jan. 1978).

57. *Id.*

nificant point, since accountability in the mid-1980s was expressed and measured in terms of "student progress and achievement."[58] As public education enters the year 2000, the burden falls squarely on the shoulders of classroom teachers, responsible for implementing I.E.P.'s, to demonstrate that children are better for what has been done to, with, and for them. A review of the 1990s case law in this chapter reveals that parents and other advocates of children with disabilities are now insisting that public school officials and their teachers are legally responsible for *results* of educational programmatic decisions, as measured by actual student achievement (or the lack thereof).

It should be kept in mind, however, that the I.E.P. does not constitute a guarantee that a child will progress at a specified rate. School officials and teachers are obligated only to make good-faith efforts to assist each child in achieving the objectives and goals listed in that particular child's individualized education program.

To protect themselves from legal action regarding an I.E.P., there are some suggested guidelines for school officials and teachers to follow. First, school people must follow (to the letter) every step in the I.E.P. planning procedures (*e.g.*, identification, testing, evaluation, parent involvement). Second, all goals and objectives should be stated in broad terms, allowing for needed flexibility. Third, guarantees regarding student progress and timetables should not be made if they cannot be accomplished. Finally, it should be made clear that every effort will be made (in good faith) to carry out the educational program outlined in the I.E.P.[59]

School officials must keep in mind that judges are reluctant to interfere with such matters as evaluating, placing, and teaching students. To allow such actions would put the courts in the position of overseer of the day-to-day operation of the schools.

In reviewing decisions made by educational agencies regarding the I.E.P., courts most likely will take the approach taken by the Second Circuit in *Karl v. Board of Education* (1984). First, the

---

58. *Id.*
59. Connors & Vacca, *supra* note 53.

505

court will determine whether or not the agency has complied with the procedural requirements of the law. If the answer to the first inquiry is positive, then the court will undertake a substantive review of the I.E.P. itself.[60]

A private school case from New York offers an interesting alternative regarding the I.E.P. that might affect public schools, especially if public school people lead parents to believe that they are going to provide specific services that guarantee student progress to specific levels of learning. In *Pietro v. St. Joseph's School,* the New York Supreme Court, Suffolk County, heard the complaint of parents who charged that their son was a victim of educational malpractice. The complaint alleged that the young man attended St. Joseph's School from 1978 to 1979, and that the school authorities "failed to ascertain whether the child was capable of learning, failed to evaluate him, failed to provide him with special education facilities, failed to hire proper personnel, and failed to teach in a manner the child could understand."[61]

Deciding against the parents and their attempt to recover tuition costs, the New York court said, however, that it could conceive of a future successful malpractice suit by parents (in private sector schools), "if an express agreement had been entered between a parent and school in which the school contracted that the student would reach a certain proficiency after pursuing certain studies."[62] The authors believe that public schools might increase their vulnerability to a similar educational malpractice suit argued on a contract theory, if school officials in some way orally guarantee

---

60. Karl v. Board of Educ., Genesco Cent. Sch. Dist., 736 F.2d 873 (2d Cir. 1984). For a decision where, among other things, formulation of the I.E.P. was an issue, see Lachman v. Illinois State Bd., 852 F.2d 290 (7th Cir. 1988). For a decision from the United States Supreme Court, where parents successfully challenged the appropriateness of the goals set for their daughter, in her I.E.P., see Florence Cty. Sch. Dist. v. Carter, 114 S. Ct. 361 (1993). For other I.E.P. case law decisions, see Amann v. Stow Sch. Sys., 982 F.2d 644 (1st Cir. 1992); Lewis v. School Bd. of Loudoun Cty., 808 F. Supp. 523 (E.D. Va. 1992); Evans v. Evans, 818 F. Supp. 1215 (N.D. Ind. 1993).

61. Pietro v. Saint Joseph's Sch., 48 U.S.L.W. 2229 (N.Y. 1979).

62. *Id.*

that certain student competencies will result from the successful completion of a particular curriculum, and then write these guarantees into the formal I.E.P.

c. *Tuition Reimbursement and Transportation.* Generally, as suggested in prior sections of this chapter, federal and state law mandates that every local school district must establish free, appropriate programs to meet the specific needs of handicapped students (*i.e.,* those who meet the statutory definition). When the local district cannot meet these needs, tuition reimbursement shall be made to parents (within certain statutory limitations) who must then send their child to a program maintained by another school district or private organization within or outside the state (*e.g.,* a private facility meeting state-approved criteria).[63] It has been held that financial reimbursement must go to parents (within certain statutory limitations) for the transportation of their handicapped children to public or private facilities (in-state and out-of-state) when no *appropriate* program is available for that child in his or her local public school district.

In *Hanes v. Pitt County Board of Education* (1980), a federal district court ordered that an emotionally handicapped child be placed in a residential state school and that the local school district pay tuition costs. According to the court, the school board was required to spend an amount necessary to ensure that the child was not entirely excluded from receiving an education.[64] Similarly, in 1981, a federal district court in Connecticut ordered the state to pay for an emotionally disturbed student enrolled in an out-of-state

---

63. *See, e.g.,* Hark v. School Dist., 505 F. Supp. 727 (E.D. Pa. 1980); McNair v. Cardimore, 676 F. Supp. 1361 (S.D. Ohio 1987); Fisher v. District of Columbia, 828 F. Supp. 87 (D.D.C. 1993); Fagan v. District of Columbia, 817 F. Supp. 161 (D.D.C. 1993); Peterson v. Hastings Public Sch., 31 F.3d 705 (8th Cir. 1994); School City of Mishawaka v. Family and Children's Ctr., Inc., 13 F.3d 1052 (7th Cir. 1994); Doe v. Board of Educ., 9 F.3d 455 (6th Cir. 1993), *cert. denied,* 114 S. Ct. 2104 (1994).

64. Hines v. Pitt Cty. Bd. of Educ., 497 F. Supp. 403 (E.D.N.C. 1980).

facility. To that court the facility provided the environment that the child needed to gain necessary educational skills.[65]

A federal district court in Massachusetts ordered a local school committee to pay the day tuition of a handicapped student. In the court's view, the school committee had failed to design an appropriate program for that handicapped student.[66]

It must be emphasized, however, that parents, as a general rule, cannot *unilaterally* move their child to a private placement and expect to automatically recover tuition costs. For example, in *Stemple v. Board of Education* (1980), the Fourth Circuit declared that parents were not entitled to reimbursement for tuition when they *unilaterally* moved their handicapped child to a private school prior to an administrative hearing.[67] In 1982, the Second Circuit, in a similar case, held that a public agency is not required to pay for parent-initiated handicapped placements.[68] Also, in 1982, the Fourth Circuit held that a premature § 1983 suit for relief could not be maintained under P.L. 94-142.[69]

As a general rule, when a public school district is furnishing a child a free appropriate education and his parents unilaterally withdraw him from it and enroll him in a private school, a local

---

65. Papacoda v. Connecticut, 528 F. Supp. 68 (D. Conn. 1981). For a comprehensive commentary on specialized locations and related services, see Ronald D. Wenkart, *Does EHCA Require Residential Placement in Psychiatric Hospitals,* 40 EDUC. LAW REP. 1111 (October 1, 1987).

66. Bloomstrom v. Massachusetts Dep't of Educ., 532 F. Supp. 707 (D. Mass. 1982).

67. Stemple v. Board of Educ., 623 F.2d 893 (4th Cir. 1980), *cert. denied,* 450 U.S. 911 (1981). *See also* Padilla *ex rel.* Padilla v. School Dist. No. 1, 35 F. Supp. 2d 1260 (D. Colo. 1999), where the court held that exhaustion of administrative remedies under IDEA is not required where the process would prove futile.

68. Zvi D. v. Ambach, 694 F.2d 904 (2d Cir. 1982). *See also* Rowe v. Henry Cty. Sch. Bd., 718 F.2d 115 (4th Cir. 1983).

69. McGovern v. Sullins, 676 F.2d 98 (4th Cir. 1982). For an excellent up-date on parents' legal prerogatives to remove their children from an approved public school program, place them in private settings, and request tuition reimbursement, see Alan G. Osborne, *Reimbursement for Unilateral Parental Placements in Unapproved Private Schools under IDEA,* 90 EDUC. LAW REP. 1 (June 16, 1994).

school district is not required to pay tuition. However, the United States Supreme Court did create a possibility of exceptions to this rule when it decided the *Burlington* case in 1985. If the public school program is shown not to be appropriate, and parents move their child to an appropriate program, then reimbursement is possible.[70] However, a local school board is not automatically obligated to pay tuition costs if parents first have not exhausted procedural remedies available to them prior to their decision to withdraw their child from his current school placement. Such a request might be declared premature, since the statutory procedures available to parents for placement challenges and placement appeals are readily available and are so specific and extensive. Finally, tuition reimbursement is not possible when the student is removed from a public school program and placed in one that is a nonapproved facility.

Transportation of children with educational disabilities to and from appropriate educational programs also has been the subject of litigation. By federal statute, "related services" should be made available at no cost to parents. Transportation is considered to be a related service, and transportation includes: travel to and from school and between schools, travel in and around school buildings, and specialized equipment.[71] The implementing regulations of

---

70. Burlington Sch. Comm. v. Department of Educ., 105 S. Ct. 1996 (1985). *See also* Cain v. Yukon Pub. Schs., Dist. I-27, 556 F. Supp. 605 (W.D. Okla. 1983). For two more cases involving parents who unilaterally placed their child in a private setting and then requested tuition and other costs, see Florence Cty. Sch. Dist. v. Carter, 114 S. Ct. 361 (1993); and Hall v. Shawnee Mission Sch. Dist., 856 F. Supp. 1521 (D. Kan. 1994). *See also* Board of Educ. Dist. No. 200 v. State, 10 F. Supp. 971 (N.D. Ill. 1998); Joshua v. Board of Educ., 13 F. Supp. 2d 1199 (D. Kan. 1998); Springer v. Fairfax Cty. Sch. Bd., 134 F.3d 659 (4th Cir. 1998). In Babicz v. Broward Cty. Sch. Bd., 135 F.3d 1420 (11th Cir. 1998), parents failed to show that they had exhausted their administrative remedies under IDEA.

71. In Felter v. Cape Girardeau Sch. Dist., 810 F. Supp. 1062 (E.D. Mo. 1993), transportation services from the sidewalk of a parochial school to special education classes at a public school were made a part of a student's I.E.P.

§ 504 of the Rehabilitation Act (1973) also provided for transportation. In the language of these regulations,

> If a recipient places a handicapped person in or refers such person to a program not operated by the recipient as a means of carrying out the requirements of this subpart, the recipient shall ensure that adequate transportation to and from the program is provided at no greater cost than would be incurred by the person or his or her parents or guardian if the person were placed in the program operated by the recipient.[72]

The issues of transportation and transportation costs are now and have been the subject of litigation.

A general tenet of school law holds that public school systems have no inherent obligation to provide transportation for students. The obligation does not exist unless otherwise required by statute or court decree. For example, as stated earlier in this chapter, from the start P.L. 94-142 mandated that local education agencies have an "[o]bligation to provide a related service at no cost to the parents if the related service is necessary for the child to benefit from special education."[73] Thus, in a given situation, if transportation is established as such a "necessary related service," one that gives a student with educational disabilities *access* to an education, the local public school system is required to provide this service, or in some other way make it possible.[74] To put it another way, "[t]rans-

---

72. 45 C.F.R. § 84.33.

73. SHRYBMAN, *supra* note 18, at 140.

74. *Id.* at 141. On March 3, 1999, the United States Supreme Court, in a 7 to 2 decision, held that the medical exemption (under IDEA's related services requirement) only applies to services performed by a physician, and not to the nursing services needed. Writing for the majority, Justice John Paul Stevens opined that the intent of IDEA is to guarantee that students like the individual in this case are integrated into public schools. The services required by the student in order for him to function in his classes and activities included urinary catheterization, suctioning of his tracheotomy, feeding him, repositioning him in his wheelchair, monitoring his blood pressure, and responding to alarms from his ventilator. These services had been provided by a licensed practical nurse and paid for by his

portation is a mandatory related service if it is included in the I.E.P. as necessary to provide part of an appropriate program or if it is necessary for a child to receive other related services, to get to and from a residential or special school, or to participate in extra-curricular activities."[75]

It should be emphasized that a claim of budgetary constraints may not work to deny services to a child with disabilities. As one court said, budgetary constraints could not be an excuse from the obligation to provide a free appropriate education to handicapped children.[76] In the year 2000, this judicial attitude remains the same.

§ 13.5. Discipline and Children with Disabilities.

The inclusion of children with educational disabilities into general education classes and activities has spawned numerous legal issues. In recent years, a growing problem in public school systems involves the discipline and control of "mainstreamed" children with educational disabilities. However, a nagging legal question remains unanswered. Are children with educational disabilities subject to the same school policies, rules, regulations, and punishments as are all other children?

Generally, public school boards and school officials may exclude from school, a class, or any school activity any student whose conduct disrupts the educational environment, or who willfully defies school board policy or school rules, or who poses a threat of harm to himself/herself or to others, or who defaces or destroys school property. As District Judge Warriner said in a student discipline case out of Virginia (a non-special education

---

parents through an insurance policy. Under the Supreme Court's ruling, however, the school system would have to pay the costs of the nursing services and for those of a teacher assistant. Cedar Rapids Commun. Sch. Dist. v. Garret F., *supra* note 47.

75. S. Howard, *P.L. 94-142: What Constitutes a Related Service*, SCHOOLS AND THE LAW OF THE HANDICAPPED 76 (E.H. Malakoff ed., Washington, D.C.: National School Boards Association Council of School Attorneys, 1981).

76. Kerr Center Parents Ass'n v. Charles, 581 F. Supp. 166 (D. Ore. 1984).

case), "No school child has a constitutional right to be free from discipline. Indeed, discipline is a boon, not a curse."[77]

Nowhere in either the Rehabilitation Act of 1973 or IDEA (prior to 1997) is discipline specifically mentioned. Beginning in 1978, however, decisions have been rendered by both federal and state courts (all involving misbehaving special education students) from which some direction could be taken. Basically, these court cases in some way involved one or more of the following issues: (1) the relationship, if any, between a student's misbehavior and his/her disability; (2) the appropriateness, or lack thereof, of school policies, rules, and disciplinary methods and procedures employed in a particular case; (3) allegations that school board members and school administrators are in direct violation of the Rehabilitation Act and/or IDEA through the enforcement of school disciplinary policies, rules and procedures; (4) the possibility that the removal of misbehaving disabled students from a class, activity, or from school represents a deprivation of a disabled student's entitlements under both federal and state law; and (5) the charge that the I.E.P. has been violated (breached) by the disciplinary action taken.

Generally, school officials do not lose their prerogatives to discipline and control disruptive students solely because they are disabled. However, there are additional considerations to be made in matters involving such students. For example, school officials must strive to maintain and not interrupt (or deviate from) a student's I.E.P.

Where a student with a disability disrupts a general education class, activity, or the school itself, or poses a threat of harm to himself/herself or to others, he or she should be dealt with immediately and not ignored. As with all students, however, there should be a strict adherence to due process procedures. But, as Cambron-McCabe has suggested, "[c]ourts have interpreted the Education for All Handicapped Children Act (EAHCA) and § 504 of the Rehabilitation Act as providing additional protection for

---

77. Bernstein v. Menard, 557 F. Supp. 90 (E.D. Va. 1982).

handicapped students. In effect, a second procedural layer has been superimposed on the discipline process for these students."[78]

As a *first step* (in a nonemergency situation), possible changes in program and placement should be considered (employing the procedures mandated by IDEA) in an attempt to alleviate the need to take disciplinary action.[79] As a part of this process an attempt should be made to determine if the misbehavior is or is not related to the student's disability. This is referred to as a *behavioral manifestation determination review*. No one person should make this determination.[80] It should be made by the I.E.P. team and other specialized personnel, as needed.

If no behavioral manifestation exists that connects the student's disability with his/her misbehavior, the student generally may be subject to the same disciplinary procedures as are all other students. If a behavioral manifestation is established, however, then the procedures for reevaluating the student's placement and pro-

---

78. N.H. Cambron-McCabe, *Disciplinary Handicapped Students: Legal Issues and Implications*, in S.B. THOMAS, N.H. CAMBRON-MCCABE, & M.M. MCCARTHY, EDUCATORS AND THE LAW: CURRENT TRENDS AND ISSUES 1 (Elmont, N.Y.: Institute for School Law and Finance, 1983).

79. *See, e.g.*, Frederick L. v. Thomas, 408 F. Supp. 832 (E.D. Pa. 1976); Cain v. Yukon Pub. Schs., Dist. I-27, 556 F. Supp. 605 (W.D. Okla. 1983).

80. *See, e.g.*. Stuart v. Nappi, 443 F. Supp. 1235 (D. Conn. 1978); Howard S. v. Friendswood Indep. Sch. Dist., 454 F. Supp. 634 (S.D. Tex. 1978); Doe v. Koger, 480 F. Supp. 225 (N.D. Ind. 1979); Sherry v. New York State Educ. Dep't, 479 F. Supp. 1328 (W.D.N.Y. 1979); S-1 v. Turlington, 635 F.2d 342 (5th Cir.), *cert. denied*, 454 U.S. 1030 (1982); Kaelin v. Grubbs, 682 F.2d 595 (6th Cir. 1982); *Cain, supra* note 70. *See also* Metropolitan Sch. Dist. v. Daila, 969 F.2d 485 (7th Cir. 1992), *cert. denied*, 122 L. Ed. 2d 740 (1993); Robbins v. Maine Sch. Dist., 807 F. Supp. 11 (D. Me. 1992); Big Beaver Falls Area Sch. Dist. v. Jackson, 624 A.2d 806 (Pa. Commw. 1993); Louisiana *ex rel.* B.C. Jr., 610 So. 2d 204 (1993); Parents of Student W. v. Puyallup Sch. Dist., 31 F.3d 1489 (9th Cir. 1994); M.P. by D.P. v. Governing Bd., 858 F. Supp. 1044 (S.D. Cal. 1994); Thomas By and Through Thomas v. Davidson Academy, 846 F. Supp. 611 (M.D. Tenn. 1994). For a complete listing of the key participants in the decision-making process, see C.E.C. document, *supra* note 53, and 34 C.F.R. § 300 et seq. (1999).

gram (as specified in IDEA) should be followed.[81] Parents should be informed of and involved in every phase of a disciplinary action.

As a general rule, in *emergency* situations (i.e., where a student becomes totally uncontrollable and violent, or presents an actual danger to himself or herself, or poses a threat of harm to others, or in some other way disrupts the school or classroom or activity) immediate removal of the student is permissible, within the procedural requirements of IDEA. However, a due process procedure must be implemented as soon thereafter as possible.[82]

In 1988, the Rehnquist Court brought some degree of clarity to disciplinary matters involving disruptive children with educational disabilities when it decided *Honig v. Doe*.[83] A California case, *Honig* involved the indefinite suspensions and proposed expulsions of two emotionally disturbed public school students who had exhibited violent and disruptive behavior in school. Both students were suspended from school indefinitely, pending completion of expulsion proceedings. School officials had determined that the students' disruptive behavior established their "dangerousness," which necessitated their immediate removal from school.

Taking the disciplinary matter into federal district court, plaintiffs complained that the indefinite suspensions and expulsion

---

81. *See* note 80 *supra.* For commentaries on point, see David L. Dagley, Michele D. McGuire & Charles W. Evans, *The Relationship Test in the Discipline of Disabled Students*, 88 EDUC. LAW REP. 13 (March 10, 1994); Brenda T. Williams & A. Katsiyanis, *The 1997 IDEA Amendments: Implications for School Principals,* 82 NASSP BULL. 12 (Jan. 1998).

82. *Id.* In recent years school officials have become aware of their potential liability for injury to students caused by the behavior of disruptive and/or dangerous students placed in their classes, especially where weapons are involved. For a recent case on point, see Hunter v. Carbondale Area Sch. Dist., 829 F. Supp. 714 (M.D. Pa.), *aff'd*, 5 F.3d 1489 (3d Cir. 1993), *cert. denied*, 114 S. Ct. 903 (1994); Spivey v. Elliott, 29 F.3d 1522 (11th Cir. 1994); Virginia Dep't of Educ. v. Riley, 23 F.3d 80 (4th Cir. 1994). For a recent case involving parents who alleged acts of verbal and physical harm to their child with cerebral palsy by a teacher's aide, see Franklin v. Frid, 7 F. Supp. 2d 290 (W.D. Mich. 1998).

83. 108 S. Ct. 592 (1988).

proceedings violated the "stay put" provision of the Education for All Handicapped Children Act (EAHCA). The Act's "stay put" provision provides that a child (covered under the Act) "shall remain in (his or her) then current educational placement" pending the completion of any review proceedings, unless parents and the state or local educational agency otherwise agree.[84] Also, the Act directs that parents must be given prior notice of any changes in their child's placement.[85] The district court entered a summary judgment for the students and issued a permanent injunction.

On appeal to the Ninth Circuit, the trial court was affirmed with modifications. The Court reiterated that students covered by the EAHCA may not be expelled for behavior related to their disability. However, in the Court's view a suspension of 10 school days did not constitute a prohibited change in placement, even where the misbehavior is handicap-related.[86]

The United States Supreme Court granted certiorari and decided *Honig*. With Justice Brennan writing for the majority, the high court held, among other things, that the "stay put" provision of the EAHCA prohibits state or local school authorities from *unilaterally* excluding disabled children from the classroom for dangerous or disruptive conduct *growing out of their* disabilities during the pendency of a review proceeding.[87] However, the majority opinion made it clear that school officials are not left "hamstrung."[88] School officials may use procedures to deal with students who endanger themselves or others. According to Justice Brennan, "[s]uch procedures may include the use of study carrels, timeouts, detention, or the restriction of privileges. More drastically, where a

---

84. 20 U.S.C.A. § 1415(e)(3).

85. *Honig, supra* note 83, at 594; 20 U.S.C.A. § 1415(b)(1)(c). For a case on point, see M.P. by D.P. v. Governing Bd., *supra* note 80.

86. Doe v. Maher, 793 F.2d 1470 (9th Cir. 1986).

87. *Honig, supra* note 83, at 604-05.

88. *Id.* at 605. *See* Gadsden City Bd. of Educ. v. B.P., 3 F. Supp. 2d 1299 (N.D. Ala. 1998), where a board was granted a temporary restraining order against two students and allowed to use an expedited hearing mechanism under IDEA to remove the students from school.

student poses an immediate threat to the safety of others, officials may temporarily suspend him or her for up to 10 school days."[89] The Court saw the 10-day rule as reasonable and as a period when school officials and parents could come together to decide on what to do with the child, which might necessitate a change in placement.[90]

Because *expulsion* (by its very nature) is legally an exclusion from school, it must be considered a change in placement of the student. As such, *expulsion* should be considered only where the student's behavior is irremediable, and all other alternatives have been exhausted. If ultimately implemented, expulsion of a student with disabilities does not negate the obligation of school officials to provide access to an educational opportunity and related services.

Because expulsion is so serious a mode of discipline, it will behoove school officials to follow the procedures for change of placement mandated by IDEA and not follow the regular procedures for expulsion of students as mandated by local school board policy.[91]

---

89. *Id.* There has been some confusion over the meaning of the 10-day *Honig* rule. It is the judgment of the authors that the intent of the rule is to prevent prolonged or indefinite out-of-school suspensions of students with educational disabilities.

90. *Id.* Under the 1997 IDEA Amendments, a student may not be suspended from school for a total of more than 10 days without receiving services and the procedural protections stipulated in IDEA. Students may be placed in an interim alternative education setting (IAES) for 45 days (for such offenses as weapons and drugs). A student may be placed in an IAES for more than 45 days or have his/her existing program changed, but the procedural requirements of IDEA must be followed. Where a behavioral manifestation determination reveals that the student's misbehavior and disability are not linked, a student may be disciplined in the same manner as other students in general education. However. at no time shall a student's education and related services be terminated. 20 U.S.C. § 1415 et seq.

91. For an excellent treatment of the potential implications of the *Honig* decision, see Edward J. Sarzynski, *Disciplining a Handicapped Student.* 46 EDUC. LAW REP. 17 (June 23, 1988). For a comprehensive treatment of student discipline under the new IDEA 1997 Amendments, see Allan G. Osborne, Jr., DISCIPLINARY

In all disciplinary procedures involving students with disabilities (short-term and long-term suspensions, expulsions, etc.), confidentiality and security must be emphasized. All reports and recommendations must be kept confidential and secure from scrutiny of unauthorized third parties. However, parents of students with disabilities must be afforded an opportunity to inspect, review, and challenge the accuracy of all records regarding their children.[92]

§ 13.6. Emerging Legal Issues in Special Education in the 1990s.

As special education moved through the late-1990s, the scene continued to change as new statutes came into being, and new legal issues emerged. Coupled with a growing philosophy that no disability is too severe to keep any student out of the school's mainstream, and a growing ability to accommodate students with educational disabilities in the regular classroom through the use of assistive technology, the total or full inclusion movement came into being and spawned numerous law suits.

a. *Inclusion*. As a general rule, inclusion means the integration (not separation) of all students into the mainstream of a school to the maximum extent possible. No student should be excluded from participation in any class or activity solely because of a disability.[93]

In 1989, the Fifth Circuit decided *Daniel R. R. v. State Board of Education,* a case involving a child with Down's syndrome (he was six years old) who had been attending a half-day regular education pre-kindergarten program. After experiencing some problems, the school district recommended that the placement be changed to a segregated special education program. In its view, the regular classroom curriculum would need drastic modifications to

---

OPTIONS FOR STUDENTS WITH DISABILITIES, and Supplement (Education Law Ass'n 1997).

92. In Belanger v. Nashua, 856 F. Supp. 40 (D.N.H. 1994), a mother of an E.D. student sought her son's school records to gain information relating to his juvenile court proceedings.

93. *See, e.g.*, Roncker v. Walter, 700 F.2d 1058 (6th Cir. 1983).

make the placement effective. The parents disagreed and took the matter to a hearing officer. The hearing officer agreed with the school system. Subsequently, a federal district court agreed with the hearing officer, and the Fifth Circuit affirmed that decision.[94]

In characterizing the situation as a balancing of the interests of the student with the decision-making prerogatives of the school system, the Fifth Circuit created the following four-pronged standard of analysis: (1) a determination must be made regarding the best interests of the student and the benefits of the placement to that student, (2) the benefits to the other students in the classroom must be considered and evaluated, (3) the degree to which the classroom curriculum must be modified to accommodate the student with disabilities must be considered, and (4) the possible overall disruption to the classroom environment must be analyzed.[95]

Three years later, a similar case was decided in New Jersey. In *Oberti v. Board of Education,* the parents of a Down's syndrome child took issue with a proposal made by school officials to place their child in a segregated special education setting. The parents wanted a regular education placement. An administrative judge agreed with the school system and the parents went to federal district court, where the court ruled in favor of the parents.[96] The court emphatically said that the inclusion of a student with disabilities in the mainstream of the school is a right and not a privilege. However, that presumption can be rebutted if the following factors can be demonstrated by school officials: (1) the mainstreamed student would receive little or no benefit from the inclusion; (2) the student would be so disruptive that the education of the other students would be impaired; and (3) the cost of providing

---

94. Daniel R. R. v. State Bd., 875 F.2d 1036 (5th Cir. 1989). *See also* Timothy v. Rochester Sch. Dist., 875 F.2d 954 (1st Cir. 1989), where the court added that the receipt of special services is not contingent upon a child's first demonstrating that he/she will benefit from an educational program.

95. *Id.*

96. District Court decision as cited in Oberti v. Board of Educ., 995 F.2d 1204 (3d Cir. 1993).

related services would negatively impact on the other students. In other words, the inclusion of the student with disabilities would be required, absent a showing of undue burden on the school's operations. The lack of funds is not, in and of itself, enough to prevent the implementation of the decision to include the student in a regular education placement.

Over the five years between 1989 and 1994, the courts were busy deciding disputes where inclusion was the major issue. While the emphasis in these special education cases remained on satisfying the procedural provisions of federal and state statutes, the more recent decisions looked at more substantive questions, including the affirmative obligation of school officials to first consider general education placements for students with disabilities (and the need to provide supplementary aid and services in those settings), prior to making a decision to place students in more segregated settings.[97] One such case was *Sacramento City Unified School District v. Holland.*[98]

Holland involved a moderately mentally retarded student who had been attending special education programs under an I.E.P. Subsequently, Holland's parents requested a full-time regular classroom placement. School officials countered with a proposed placement that divided their daughter's time between special education (for her academic subjects) and regular education (for her nonacademic subjects).[99]

Claiming that the school system's placement would violate the least restrictive environment requirement of IDEA, the parents appealed to a hearing officer. The hearing officer ordered the school system to place Holland in a regular education class and to provide the teacher with support services and assistance. This

---

97. *Id.* In other decisions, emphasis was placed on providing necessary supplementary services to classroom teachers in general education classrooms where inclusion has taken place. *See* Green v. Rome, 950 F.2d 688 (11th Cir. 1991).

98. 14 F.3d 1398 (9th Cir. 1994).

99. *Id.*

decision was affirmed by a federal district court, and that court's judgment was affirmed on appeal to the Ninth Circuit.[100]

In rendering its decision, the Ninth Circuit Court adopted the following standard of analysis ultimately used by the district court. To evaluate the appropriateness of a regular education placement for a student with disabilities: (1) compare the benefits to the special education student of a placement in a segregated setting with the benefits of a regular classroom placement, supplemented with appropriate aids and services; (2) determine the nonacademic benefits of interaction with regular education children; (3) evaluate the effect of the presence of the special education student on the regular education teacher and on the other students in the class; and (4) figure the cost of the mainstreaming decision.[101]

b. *Americans with Disabilities Act (ADA)*. The Americans with Disabilities Act (ADA) is another source of litigation that emerged in the mid-1990s. With the passage of the Americans with Disabilities Act (1990),[102] school boards and administrators began to reexamine their daily operations in an effort to provide all individuals meeting the statute's qualifications with equal access to facilities, programs, activities, and services provided by their schools. Because of its initial intent, the impact of the ADA was first experienced in employment. While very little legal activity has been experienced regarding student rights, that situation is beginning to change.

In *Thomas By and Through Thomas v. Davidson Academy* (1994),[103] for example, a seventeen-year-old female student (who had been enrolled in the Academy since the first grade) was ex-

---

100. *Id.*

101. *Id.* For more recent inclusion cases, see B.K. v. Toms River Bd. of Educ., 998 F. Supp 462 (D.N.J. 1998); Hartmann v. Loudoun Cty., 118 F.3d 996 (4th Cir. 1997), *cert. denied*, 118 S. Ct. 688 (1998); Moubry v. I.S.D. 696, 9 F. Supp. 2d 1086 (D. Minn. 1998).

102. AMERICANS WITH DISABILITIES ACT, 42 U.S.C. § 12101 et seq. (1990). The date of implementation of the ADA was set at January 2b, 1992.

103. Thomas By and Through Thomas v. Davidson Academy, 846 F. Supp. 611 (M.D. Tenn. 1994).

pelled from school because of her misbehavior. Thomas, who suffered from a serious blood disorder, had fulfilled all academic requirements, had been active in extracurricular activities, and had only one other disciplinary sanction during her entire enrollment at Davidson Academy.[104]

In November of her senior year, Thomas was diagnosed with the serious blood disorder and school officials were notified of her condition. While not a contagious condition, people with Thomas' disorder are required to avoid situations where injury might occur, and to seek immediate medical treatment if injury is sustained.

That January, Thomas was cut while working in art class. Her teacher described her as "hysterical." The teacher took her to the principal's office where Thomas remained very upset emotionally. A school nurse was called in to help Thomas and her mother was summoned to school. Throughout the entire episode Thomas remained very excited, and she was not very cooperative. Subsequently, after meeting with Thomas and her mother, the principal decided that expulsion was the appropriate disciplinary action to take.[105] Thomas' mother took her daughter's case to a federal district court.

Citing the ADA, and its precursor Section 504, the trial court held for Thomas. As the court reasoned, Thomas' condition is one that substantially limits her ability to perform one or more life activities; thus, she is covered by the ADA. Moreover, she is an otherwise qualified person who meets all of her school program's necessary requirements. In other words, but for her disability, she is academically qualified to remain in school and complete her program of study. Finally, the court was convinced that her behavior (or misbehavior) in the art class and the principal's office was directly related to her disability.[106]

The principal's expulsion action was not appropriate. In the court's words, the action resulted from a blind adherence to poli-

---

104. *Id.*
105. *Id.*
106. *Id.*

cies and standards resulting in a "failure to accommodate" Thomas' disability. The court enjoined school officials from carrying out the expulsion, and warned officials and employees from "retaliating, coercing, intimidating, threatening, or interfering with Thomas" in the exercise and enjoyment of her rights under the ADA and Section 504.[107]

§ 13.7. Summary.

It is apparent that court decisions and legislative enactments over the past decade have created constitutional and legal mandates (on both the federal and state levels) that *all* children, especially those with educational disabilities, have an entitlement to a free, appropriate, nonarbitrarily determined educational opportunity (including related services). What is more, such opportunities (designed to meet the unique needs of each child) should result in progress made by each student. A careful examination of the contemporary legal scene reveals that the specific mandate is for children with educational disabilities to be granted free access to *quality* educational opportunities.

Local public school systems, now and in the future, must demonstrate that methods of identification, assessment, placement, and special programming of children with disabilities comply with the law, and that all requirements and procedures be followed to the letter of the law. On the other hand, courts (federal and state) will not interfere with or overturn public school officials relative to special educational programs unless it is clearly shown that mandated policies, regulations, or procedures have been either ignored or circumvented.

---

107. *Id.* For an excellent commentary summarizing the requirements of the ADA, see Ronald D. Wenkart, *Americans with Disabilities Act and the Impact on Public Education*, 82 EDUC. LAW REP. 291 (July 1, 1993). For a recent decision demonstrating the breadth of rights extended to public school students under the ADA, see Bingham v. Oregon Sch. Activities Ass'n, 37 F. Supp. 2d 1189 (D. Ore. 1999), where a student-athlete successfully challenged an eight semester eligibility rule. The court considered the waiver to be a "reasonable accommodation" enabling him to participate in sports.

As the new century begins, the due process rights of children with educational disabilities and their parents (from evaluation and programming to disciplinary questions) must be of critical concern to school officials. And, where no appropriate public school program exists, state and local educational agencies must share in the financial obligations with parents of providing viable alternatives. However, parents (guardians) cannot, as a general rule, ignore or circumvent the law (federal or state) and unilaterally place their children in another setting without first exhausting administrative remedies available to them.

Appendix

CONSTITUTION OF THE UNITED STATES

WE THE PEOPLE of the United States, in Order to form a more perfect Union, establish Justice, insure domestic Tranquility, provide for the common defence, promote the general Welfare, and secure the Blessings of Liberty to ourselves and our Posterity, do ordain and establish this CONSTITUTION for the United States of America.

ARTICLE I

SECTION 1. All legislative Powers herein granted shall be vested in a Congress of the United States, which shall consist of a Senate and House of Representatives.

SECTION 2. [1]The House of Representatives shall be composed of Members chosen every second Year by the People of the several States, and the Electors in each State shall have the Qualifications requisite for Electors of the most numerous Branch of the State Legislature.

[2]No Person shall be a Representative who shall not have attained to the Age of twenty five Years, and been seven Years a Citizen of the United States, and who shall not, when elected, be an Inhabitant of that State in which he shall be chosen.

[3]* [Representatives and direct Taxes shall be apportioned among the several States which may be included within this Union, according to their respective Numbers, which shall be determined by adding to the whole Number of free Persons, including those bound to Service for a Term of Years, and excluding Indians not taxed, three fifths of all other Persons.]. The actual Enumeration shall be made within three Years after the first Meeting of the Congress of the United States, and within every subsequent Term of ten Years, in such Manner as they shall by Law direct. The Number of Representatives shall not exceed one for every thirty

---

NOTE. — The superior numbers preceding the paragraphs designate the number of the clause.

* The part included in brackets was repealed by section 2 of amendment XIV.

Thousand, but each State shall have at Least one Representative; and until such enumeration shall be made, the State of New Hampshire shall be entitled to chuse three, Massachusetts eight, Rhode-Island and Providence Plantations one, Connecticut five, New-York six, New Jersey four, Pennsylvania eight, Delaware one, Maryland six, Virginia ten, North Carolina five, South Carolina five, and Georgia three.

[4]When vacancies happen in the Representation from any State, the Executive Authority thereof shall issue Writs of Election to fill such vacancies.

[5]The House of Representatives shall chuse their Speaker and other Officers; and shall have the sole Power of Impeachment.

[1]SECTION 3. *The Senate of the United States shall be composed of two Senators from each State, [chosen by the Legislature thereof,] for six Years; and each Senator shall have one Vote.

[2]Immediately after they shall be assembled in Consequence of the first Election, they shall be divided as equally as may be into three Classes. The Seats of the Senators of the first Class shall be vacated at the Expiration of the Second Year, of the second Class at the Expiration of the fourth Year, and of the third Class at the Expiration of the sixth Year, so that one-third may be chosen every second Year; [and if Vacancies happen by Resignation, or otherwise, during the Recess of the Legislature of any State, the Executive thereof may make temporary Appointments until the next Meeting of the Legislature, which shall then fill such Vacancies].**

[3]No Person shall be a Senator who shall not have attained to the Age of thirty Years, and been nine Years a Citizen of the United States, and who shall not, when elected, be an inhabitant of that State for which he shall be chosen.

[4]The Vice President of the United States shall be President of the Senate, but shall have no Vote, unless they be equally divided.

---

* The part included in brackets was repealed by section 1 of amendment XVII.

** The part included in brackets was changed by clause 2 of amendment XVII.

[5]The Senate shall chuse their other Officers, and also a President pro tempore, in the absence of the Vice President, or when he shall exercise the Office of President of the United States.

[6]The Senate shall have the sole Power to try all Impeachments. When sitting for that Purpose, they shall be on Oath or Affirmation. When the President of the United States is tried, the Chief Justice shall preside: And no Person shall be convicted without the Concurrence of two-thirds of the Members present.

[7]Judgment in Cases of Impeachment shall not extend further than to removal from Office, and disqualification to hold and enjoy any Office of honor, Trust, or Profit under the United States: but the Party convicted shall nevertheless be liable and subject to Indictment, Trial, Judgment, and Punishment, according to Law.

SECTION 4. [1]The Times, Places and Manner of holding Elections for Senators and Representatives, shall be prescribed in each State by the Legislature thereof; but the Congress may at any time by Law make or alter such Regulations, except as to the Places of chusing Senators.

[2]The Congress shall assemble at least once in every Year, and such Meeting shall [be on the first Monday in December,] unless they shall by Law appoint a different Day.*

SECTION 5. [1]Each House shall be the Judge of the Elections, Returns, and Qualifications of its own Members, and a Majority of each shall constitute a Quorum to do Business; but a smaller Number may adjourn from day to day, and may be authorized to compel the Attendance of absent Members, in such Manner, and under such Penalties as each House may provide.

[2]Each House may determine the Rules of its Proceedings, punish its Members for disorderly Behavior, and, with the Concurrence of two thirds expel a Member.

[3]Each House shall keep a Journal of its Proceedings, and from time to time publish the same, excepting such Parts as may in their Judgment require Secrecy; and the Yeas and Nays of the Members

---

* The part included in brackets was changed by section 2 of amendment XX.

of either House on any question shall, at the Desire of one fifth of those Present, be entered on the Journal.

[4]Neither House, during the Session of Congress, shall, without the Consent of the other, adjourn for more than three days, nor to any other Place than that in which the two Houses shall be sitting.

SECTION 6. [1]The Senators and Representatives shall receive a Compensation for their Services, to be ascertained by Law, and paid out of the Treasury of the United States. They shall in all Cases, except Treason, Felony and Breach of the Peace, be privileged from Arrest during their Attendance at the Session of their respective Houses, and in going to and returning from the same; and for any Speech or Debate in either House, they shall not be questioned in any other Place.

[2]No Senator or Representative shall, during the Time for which he was elected, be appointed to any civil Office under the Authority of the United States, which shall have been created, or the Emoluments whereof shall have been increased during such time; and no Person holding any Office under the United States, shall be a Member of either House during his Continuance in Office.

SECTION 7. [1]All Bills for raising Revenue shall originate in the House of Representatives; but the Senate may propose or concur with Amendments as on other Bills.

[2]Every Bill which shall have passed the House of Representatives and the Senate, shall, before it become a Law, be presented to the President of the United States; if he approve he shall sign it, but if not he shall return it, with his Objections to that House in which it shall have originated, who shall enter the Objections at large on their Journal, and proceed to reconsider it. If after such Reconsideration two thirds of that House shall agree to pass the Bill, it shall be sent, together with the Objections, to the other House, by which it shall likewise be reconsidered, and if approved by two thirds of that House, it shall become a Law. But in all such Cases the Votes of both Houses shall be determined by Yeas and Nays, and the Names of the Persons voting for and against the Bill shall be entered on the Journal of each House respectively. If any Bill shall not be returned by the President within ten Days (Sun-

days excepted) after it shall have been presented to him, the Same shall be a Law, in like Manner as if he had signed it, unless the Congress by their Adjournment prevent its Return, in which Case it shall not be a Law.

[3] Every Order, Resolution, or Vote to which the Concurrence of the Senate and House of Representatives may be necessary (except on a question of Adjournment) shall be presented to the President of the United States; and before the Same shall take Effect, shall be approved by him, or being disapproved by him, shall be re-passed by two thirds of the Senate and House of Representatives, according to the Rules and Limitations prescribed in the Case of a Bill.

SECTION 8. [1] The Congress shall have Power To lay and collect Taxes, Duties, Imposts and Excises, to pay the Debts and provide for the common Defence and general Welfare of the United States; but all Duties, Imposts and Excises shall be uniform throughout the United States;

[2] To borrow money on the credit of the United States;

[3] To regulate Commerce with foreign Nations, and among the several States, and with the Indian Tribes;

[4] To establish an uniform Rule of Naturalization, and uniform Laws on the subject of Bankruptcies throughout the United States;

[5] To coin Money, regulate the Value thereof, and of foreign Coin, and fix the Standard of Weights and Measures;

[6] To provide for the Punishment of counterfeiting the Securities and current Coin of the United States;

[7] To Establish Post Offices and post Roads;

[8] To promote the Progress of Science and useful Arts, by securing for limited Times to Authors and Inventors the exclusive Right to their respective Writings and Discoveries;

[9] To constitute Tribunals inferior to the Supreme Court.

[10] To define and punish Piracies and Felonies committed on the high Seas, and Offenses against the Law of Nations;

[11] To declare War, grant Letters of Marque and Reprisal, and make Rules concerning Captures on Land and Water;

[12]To raise and support Armies, but no Appropriation of Money to that Use shall be for a longer Term than two Years;

[13]To provide and maintain a Navy;

[14]To make Rules for the Government and Regulation of the land and naval Forces;

[15]To provide for calling forth the Militia to execute the Laws of the Union, suppress insurrections and repel Invasions;

[16]To provide for organizing, arming, and disciplining the Militia, and for governing such Part of them as may be employed in the Service of the United States, reserving to the States respectively, the Appointment of the Officers, and the Authority of training the Militia according to the discipline prescribed by Congress;

[17]To exercise exclusive Legislation in all Cases whatsoever, over such District (not exceeding ten Miles square) as may, by Cession of particular States, and the acceptance of Congress, become the Seat of the Government of the United States, and to exercise like Authority over all Places purchased by the Consent of the Legislature of the State in which the Same shall be, for the Erection of Forts, Magazines, Arsenals, dock-Yards, and other needful Buildings; — And

[18]To make all Laws which shall be necessary and proper for carrying into Execution the foregoing Powers, and all other Powers vested by this Constitution in the Government of the United States, or in any Department or Officer thereof.

SECTION 9. [1]The Migration or Importation of Such Persons as any of the States now existing shall think proper to admit, shall not be prohibited by the Congress prior to the Year one thousand eight hundred and eight, but a tax or duty may be imposed on such Importation, not exceeding ten dollars for each Person.

[2]The privilege of the Writ of Habeas Corpus shall not be suspended, unless when in Cases of Rebellion or Invasion the public Safety may require it.

[3]No Bill of Attainder or ex post facto Law shall be passed.

[4]*No Capitation, or other direct, Tax shall be laid, unless in Proportion to the Census or Enumeration herein before directed to be taken.

[5]No Tax or Duty shall be laid on Articles exported from any State.

[6]No preference shall be given by any Regulation of Commerce or Revenue to the Ports of one State over those of another: nor shall Vessels bound to, or from, one State be obliged to enter, clear, or pay Duties in another.

[7]No money shall be drawn from the Treasury, but in Consequence of Appropriations made by Law; and a regular Statement and Account of the Receipts and Expenditures of all public Money shall be published from time to time.

[8]No title of Nobility shall be granted by the United States: And no Person holding any Office of Profit or Trust under them, shall, without the Consent of the Congress, accept of any present, Emolument, Office, or Title, of any kind whatever, from any King, Prince, or foreign State.

SECTION 10. [1]No State shall enter into any Treaty, Alliance, or Confederation; grant Letters of Marque and Reprisal; coin Money; emit Bills of Credit; make any Thing but gold and silver Coin a Tender in Payment of Debts; pass any Bill of Attainder, ex post facto Law, or Law impairing the Obligation of Contracts, or grant any Title of Nobility.

[2]No State shall, without the Consent of the Congress, lay any Imposts or Duties on Imports or Exports, except what may be absolutely necessary for executing its inspection Laws; and the net Produce of all Duties and Imposts, laid by any State on Imports or Exports, shall be for the Use of the Treasury of the United States; and all such Laws shall be subject to the Revision and Control of the Congress.

[3]No State shall, without the Consent of Congress, lay any duty of Tonnage, keep Troops, or Ships of War in time of Peace, enter into any Agreement or Compact with another State, or with a for-

---

* See also amendment XVI.

eign Power, or engage in War, unless actually invaded, or in such imminent Danger as will not admit of delay.

ARTICLE II

SECTION 1. [1] The executive Power shall be vested in a President of the United States of America. He shall hold his Office during the Term of four Years, and, together with the Vice-President, chosen for the same Term, be elected, as follows:

[2] Each State shall appoint, in such Manner as the Legislature thereof may direct, a Number of Electors, equal to the whole Number of Senators and Representatives to which the State may be entitled in the Congress: but no Senator or Representative, or Person holding an Office of Trust or Profit under the United States, shall be appointed an Elector.

*[The Electors shall meet in their respective States, and vote by Ballot for two Persons, of whom one at least shall not be an Inhabitant of the same State with themselves. And they shall make a List of all the Persons voted for, and of the Number of Votes for each; which List they shall sign and certify, and transmit sealed to the Seat of the Government of the United States, directed to the President of the Senate. The President of the Senate shall, in the Presence of the Senate and House of Representatives, open all the Certificates, and the Votes shall then be counted. The Person having the greatest Number of Votes shall be the President, if such Number be a Majority of the whole Number of Electors appointed; and if there be more than one who have such Majority, and have an equal Number of Votes, then the House of Representatives shall immediately chuse by Ballot one of them for President; and if no Person have a Majority, then from the five highest on the List the said House shall in like Manner chuse the President. But in chusing the President, the Votes shall be taken by States, the Representation from each State having one Vote; A quorum for this Purpose shall consist of a Member or Members from two thirds of

---

* This paragraph has been superseded by amendment XII.

the States, and a Majority of all the States shall be necessary to a Choice. In every Case, after the Choice of the President, the Person having the greatest Number of Votes of the Electors shall be the Vice President. But if there should remain two or more who have equal Votes, the Senate shall chuse from them by Ballot the Vice President.]

[3]The Congress may determine the Time of chusing the Electors and the Day on which they shall give their Votes; which Day shall be the same throughout the United States.

[4]No person except a natural born Citizen, or a Citizen of the United States, at the time of the Adoption of this Constitution, shall be eligible to the Office of President; neither shall any Person be eligible to that Office who shall not have attained to the Age of thirty-five Years, and been fourteen Years a Resident within the United States.

[5]In case of the removal of the President from Office, or of his Death, Resignation or Inability to discharge the Powers and Duties of the said Office, the same shall devolve on the Vice President, and the Congress may by Law provide for the Case of Removal, Death, Resignation or Inability, both of the President, and Vice President, declaring what Officer shall then act as President, and such Officer shall act accordingly, until the Disability be removed, or a President shall be elected.

[6]The President shall, at stated Times, receive for his Services, a Compensation, which shall neither be encreased nor diminished during the Period for which he shall have been elected, and he shall not receive within that Period any other Emolument from the United States, or any of them.

[7]Before he enter on the Execution of His Office, he shall take the following Oath or Affirmation: — "I do solemnly swear (or affirm) that I will faithfully execute the Office of President of the United States, and will to the best of my Ability, preserve, protect and defend the Constitution of the United States."

SECTION 2. [1]The President shall be Commander and Chief of the Army and Navy of the United States, and of the Militia of the several States, when called into the actual Service of the United

States; he may require the Opinion, in writing, of the principal Officer in each of the executive Departments, upon any subject relating to the Duties of their respective Offices, and he shall have Power to grant Reprieves and Pardons for Offences against the United States, except in Cases of Impeachment.

[2]He shall have Power, by and with the Advice and Consent of the Senate, to make Treaties, provided two-thirds of the Senators present concur; and he shall nominate, and by and with the Advice and Consent of the Senate, shall appoint Ambassadors, other public Ministers and Consuls, Judges of the supreme Court, and all other Officers of the United States, whose Appointments are not herein otherwise provided for, and which shall be established by Law; but the Congress may by Law vest the Appointment of such inferior Officers, as they think proper, in the President alone, in the Courts of Law, or in the Heads of Departments.

[3]The President shall have Power to fill up all Vacancies that may happen during the Recess of the Senate, by granting Commissions which shall expire at the End of their next Session.

SECTION 3. He shall from time to time give to the Congress Information of the State of the Union, and recommend to their Consideration such Measures as he shall judge necessary and expedient; he may, on extraordinary Occasions, convene both Houses, or either of them, and in Case of Disagreement between them, with Respect to the Time of Adjournment, he may adjourn them to such Time as he shall think proper; he shall receive Ambassadors and other public Ministers; he shall take Care that the Laws be faithfully executed, and shall Commission all the Officers of the United States.

SECTION 4. The President, Vice President and all civil Officers of the United States, shall be removed from Office on Impeachment for, and Conviction of, Treason, Bribery, or other high Crimes and Misdemeanors.

ARTICLE III

SECTION 1. The judicial Power of the United States, shall be vested in one supreme Court, and in such inferior Courts as the Congress may from time to time ordain and establish. The Judges, both of the supreme and inferior Courts, shall hold their Offices during good Behavior, and shall, at stated Times, receive for their Services a Compensation which shall not be diminished during their Continuance in Office.

SECTION 2. [1] The judicial Power shall extend to all Cases, in Law and Equity, arising under this Constitution, the Laws of the United States, and Treaties made, or which shall be made, under their Authority; — to all Cases affecting Ambassadors, other public Ministers and Consuls; — to all Cases of admiralty and maritime Jurisdiction; — to Controversies to which the United States shall be a Party; — to Controversies between two or more States; — between a State and Citizens of another State;* — between Citizens of different States; — between Citizens of the same State claiming Lands under Grants of different States, and between a State, or the Citizens thereof, and foreign States, Citizens or Subjects.

[2] In all Cases affecting Ambassadors, other public Ministers and Consuls, and those in which a State shall be Party, the supreme Court shall have original Jurisdiction. In all the other Cases before mentioned, the supreme Court shall have appellate Jurisdiction, both as to Law and Fact, with such Exceptions, and under such Regulations as the Congress shall make.

[3] The trial of all Crimes except in Cases of Impeachment shall be by Jury; and such Trial shall be held in the State where the said Crimes shall have been committed; but when not committed within any State, the Trial shall be at such Place or Places as the Congress may by Law have directed.

SECTION 3. [1] Treason against the United States shall consist only in levying War against them, or, in adhering to their Enemies, giving them Aid and Comfort. No Person shall be convicted of

---

* This clause has been affected by amendment XI.

Treason unless on the Testimony of two Witnesses to the same overt Act, or on Confession in open Court.

[2]The Congress shall have power to declare the Punishment of Treason, but no Attainder of Treason shall work Corruption of Blood, or Forfeiture except during the Life of the Person attainted.

ARTICLE IV

SECTION 1. Full Faith and Credit shall be given in each State to the public Acts, Records, and judicial Proceedings of every other State. And the Congress may by general Laws prescribe the Manner in which such Acts, Records and Proceedings shall be proved, and the Effect thereof.

SECTION 2. [1]The Citizens of each State shall be entitled to all Privileges and Immunities of Citizens in the several States.

[2]A Person charged in any State with Treason, Felony, or other Crime, who shall flee from Justice, and be found in another State, shall on demand of the executive Authority of the State from which he fled, be delivered up, to be removed to the State having Jurisdiction of the Crime.

[3]*[No Person held to Service or Labour in one State, under the Laws thereof, escaping into another, shall, in Consequence of any Law or Regulation therein, be discharged from such Service or Labour, but shall be delivered up on Claim of the Party to whom such Service or Labour may be due.]

SECTION 3. [1]New States may be admitted by the Congress into this Union; but no new State shall be formed or erected within the Jurisdiction of any other State; nor any State be formed by the Junction of two or more States, or parts of States, without the Consent of the Legislatures of the States concerned as well as of the Congress.

[2]The Congress shall have Power to dispose of and make all needful Rules and Regulations respecting the Territory or other Property belonging to the United States: and nothing in this Con-

---

* This clause has been affected by amendment XIII.

stitution shall be so construed as to Prejudice any Claims of the United States, or of any particular State.

SECTION 4. The United States shall guarantee to every State in this Union a Republican Form of Government, and shall protect each of them against Invasion; and on Application of the Legislature, or of the Executive (when the Legislature cannot be convened) against domestic Violence.

ARTICLE V

The Congress, whenever two-thirds of both Houses shall deem it necessary, shall propose Amendments to this Constitution, or, on the Application of the Legislatures of two-thirds of the several States, shall call a Convention for proposing Amendments, which, in either Case, shall be valid to all Intents and Purposes, as part of this Constitution when ratified by the Legislatures of three-fourths of the several States, or by Conventions in three-fourths thereof, as the one or the other Mode of Ratification may be proposed by the Congress; Provided that no Amendment which may be made prior to the Year One thousand eight hundred and eight shall in any Manner affect the first and fourth Clauses in the Ninth Section of the first Article; and that no State, without its Consent, shall be deprived of its equal Suffrage in the Senate.

ARTICLE VI

[1] All Debts contracted and Engagements entered into, before the Adoption of this Constitution shall be as valid against the United States under this Constitution, as under the Confederation.

[2] This Constitution, and the Laws of the United States which shall be made in Pursuance thereof; and all Treaties made, or which shall be made, under the Authority of the United States, shall be the supreme Law of the Land; and the Judges in every State shall be bound thereby, any Thing in the Constitution or Laws of any State to the Contrary notwithstanding.

[3] The Senators and Representatives before mentioned, and the Members of the several State Legislatures, and all executive and

judicial Officers, both of the United States and of the several States, shall be bound by Oath or Affirmation, to support this Constitution; but no religious Test shall ever be required as a Qualification to any Office or public Trust under the United States.

ARTICLE VII

The Ratification of the Conventions of nine States, shall be sufficient for the Establishment of this Constitution between the States so ratifying the Same.

———

AMENDMENT I

Congress shall make no law respecting an establishment of religion, or prohibiting the free exercise thereof; or abridging the freedom of speech, or of the press; or the right of the people peaceably to assemble and to petition the Government for a redress of grievances.

AMENDMENT II

A well regulated Militia, being necessary to the security of a free State, the right of the people to keep and bear Arms, shall not be infringed.

AMENDMENT III

No Soldier shall, in time of peace be quartered in any house, without the consent of the Owner, not in time of war, but in a manner to be prescribed by law.

AMENDMENT IV

The right of the people to be secure in their persons, houses, papers, and effects, against unreasonable searches and seizures, shall not be violated, and no Warrants shall issue, but upon probable cause, supported by Oath or affirmation and particularly describing the Place to be searched, and the persons or things to be seized.

AMENDMENT V

No person shall be held to answer for a capital, or otherwise infamous crime, unless on a presentment or indictment of a Grand Jury, except in cases arising in the land or naval forces, or in the Militia, when in actual service in time of War or public danger; nor shall any person be subject for the same offence to be twice put in jeopardy of life or limb; nor shall be compelled in any criminal case to be a witness against himself, nor be deprived of life, liberty, or property, without due process of law; nor shall private property be taken for public use, without just compensation.

AMENDMENT VI

In all criminal prosecutions, the accused shall enjoy the right to a speedy and public trial, by an impartial jury of the State and district wherein the crime shall have been committed, which district shall have been previously ascertained by law, and to be informed of the nature and cause of the accusation: to be confronted with the witnesses against him; to have compulsory process for obtaining witnesses in his favor, and to have the Assistance of Counsel for his defence.

AMENDMENT VII

In suits at common law, where the value in controversy shall exceed twenty dollars, the right of trial by jury shall be preserved, and no fact tried by jury, shall be otherwise reexamined in any Court of the United States, than according to the rules of the common law.

AMENDMENT VIII

Excessive bail shall not be required, nor excessive fines imposed, nor cruel and unusual punishments inflicted.

AMENDMENT IX

The enumeration in the Constitution, of certain rights, shall not be construed to deny or disparage others retained by the people.

AMENDMENT X

The powers not delegated to the United States by the Constitution, nor prohibited by it to the States, are reserved to the States respectively, or to the people.

(Ratification of first ten amendments was completed December 15, 1791.)

AMENDMENT XI

The Judicial power of the United States shall not be construed to extend to any suit in law or equity, commenced or prosecuted against one of the United States by Citizens of another State, or by Citizens or Subjects of any Foreign State.

(Declared ratified January 8, 1798.)

AMENDMENT XII

The electors shall meet in their respective states and vote by ballot for President and Vice-President, one of whom, at least, shall not be an inhabitant of the same state with themselves; they shall name in their ballots the person voted for as President, and in distinct ballots the person voted for as Vice-President, and they shall make distinct lists of all persons voted for as President, and of all persons voted for as Vice-President, and of the number of votes for each, which lists they shall sign and certify, and transmit sealed to the seat of the government of the United States, directed to the President of the Senate; — The President of the Senate shall, in presence of the Senate and House of Representatives, open all the certificates and the votes shall then be counted; — The person having the greatest number of votes for President, shall be the President, if such number be a majority of the whole number of Electors appointed; and if no person have such majority, then from the persons having the highest numbers not exceeding three on the list of those voted for as President, the House of Representatives shall choose immediately, by ballot, the President. But in choosing the President, the votes shall be taken by states, the representation from each state having one vote; a quorum for this purpose shall consist of a member or members from two-thirds of the states, and a majority of all the states shall be necessary to a choice.* [And if the House of Representatives shall not choose a President whenever the right of choice shall devolve upon them, before the fourth day of March next following, then the Vice-President shall act as President, as in the case of the death or other constitutional disability of the President.] — The person having the greatest number of votes as Vice-President, shall be the Vice-President, if such number be a majority of the whole number of Electors appointed, and if no person have a majority, then from the two highest numbers on the list, the Senate shall choose the Vice-President; a quorum for the purpose shall consist of two-thirds of the whole number of Senators, and a majority of the whole number shall be necessary to a choice. But no person constitutionally ineligible to the office of President shall be eligible to that of Vice-President of the United States.

(Declared ratified September 25, 1804.)

AMENDMENT XIII

SECTION 1. Neither slavery nor involuntary servitude, except as a punishment for crime whereof the party shall have been duly convicted, shall exist within the United States, or any place subject to their jurisdiction.

SECTION 2. Congress shall have power to enforce this article by appropriate legislation.

(Declared ratified December 18, 1865.)

---

* The part included in brackets has been superseded by section 3 of amendment XX.

541

AMENDMENT XIV

SECTION 1. All persons born or naturalized in the United States, and subject to the jurisdiction thereof, are citizens of the United States and of the State wherein they reside. No State shall make or enforce any law which shall abridge the privileges or immunities of citizens of the United States; nor shall any State deprive any person of life, liberty, or property, without due process of law; nor deny to any person within its jurisdiction the equal protection of the laws.

SECTION 2. Representatives shall be apportioned among the several States according to their respective numbers, counting the whole number of persons in each State, excluding Indians not taxed. But when the right to vote at any election for the choice of electors for President and Vice-President of the United States, Representatives in Congress, the Executive and Judicial officers of a State, or the members of the Legislature thereof, is denied to any of the male inhabitants of such State, being twenty-one years of age, and citizens of the United States, or in any way abridged, except for participation in rebellion, or other crime, the basis of representation therein shall be reduced in the proportion which the number of such male citizens shall bear to the whole number of male citizens twenty-one years of age in such State.

SECTION 3. No person shall be a Senator or Representative in Congress, or elector of President and Vice-President, or hold any office, civil or military, under the United States, or under any State, who, having previously taken an oath, as a member of Congress, or as an officer of the United States, or as a member of any State legislature, or as an executive or judicial officer of any State, to support the Constitution of the United States, shall have engaged in insurrection or rebellion against the same, or given aid or comfort to the enemies thereof. But Congress may by a vote of two-thirds of each House, remove such disability.

SECTION 4. The validity of the public debt of the United States, authorized by law, including debts incurred for payment of pensions and bounties for services in suppressing insurrection or rebellion, shall not be questioned. But neither the United States nor any State shall assume or pay any debt or obligation incurred in aid of insurrection or rebellion against the United States, or any claim for the loss or emancipation of any slave; but all such debts, obligations and claims shall be held illegal and void.

SECTION 5. The Congress shall have power to enforce, by appropriate legislation, the provisions of this article.

(Declared ratified July 28, 1868.)

AMENDMENT XV

SECTION 1. The right of citizens of the United States to vote shall not be denied or abridged by the United States or by any State on account of race, color, or previous condition of servitude

SECTION 2. The Congress shall have power to enforce this article by appropriate legislation.

(Declared ratified March 30, 1870.)

AMENDMENT XVI

The Congress shall have power to lay and collect taxes on incomes, from whatever source derived, without apportionment among the several States, and without regard to any census or enumeration.

(Declared ratified February 25, 1913.)

AMENDMENT XVII

The Senate of the United States shall be composed of two Senators from each State, elected by the people thereof, for six years; and each Senator shall have one vote. The electors in each State shall have the qualifications requisite for electors of the most numerous branch of the State legislatures.

When vacancies happen in the representation of any State in the Senate, the executive authority of such State shall issue writs of election to fill such vacancies: *Provided,* That the legislature of any State may empower the executive thereof to make temporary appointments until the people fill the vacancies by election as the legislature may direct.

This amendment shall not be so construed as to affect the election or term of any Senator chosen before it becomes valid as part of the Constitution.

(Declared ratified May 31, 1913.)

AMENDMENT XVIII

[SECTION 1. After one year from the ratification of this article the manufacture, sale, or transportation of intoxicating liquors within, the importation thereof into, or the exportation thereof from the United States and all territory subject to the jurisdiction thereof for beverage purposes is hereby prohibited.

[SECTION 2. The Congress and the several States shall have concurrent power to enforce this article by appropriate legislation.

[SECTION 3. This article shall be inoperative unless it shall have been ratified as an amendment to the Constitution by the legislatures of the several States, as provided in the Constitution, within seven years from the date of the submission hereof to the States by the Congress.]*

(Declared ratified January 29, 1919.)

AMENDMENT XIX

The right of citizens of the United States to vote shall not be denied or abridged by the United States or by any State on account of sex.

Congress shall have power to enforce this article by appropriate legislation.

(Declared ratified August 26, 1920.)

---

* Repealed by section 1 of amendment XXI.

AMENDMENT XX

SECTION 1. The terms of the President and Vice-President shall end at noon on the 20th day of January, and the terms of Senators and Representatives at noon on the 3d day of January, of the years in which such terms would have ended if this article had not been ratified; and the terms of their successors shall then begin.

SECTION 2. The Congress shall assemble at least once in every year, and such meeting shall begin at noon on the 3d day of January, unless they shall by law appoint a different day.

SECTION 3. If, at the time for the beginning of the term of the President, the President elect shall have died, the Vice-President elect shall become President. If a President shall not have been chosen before the time fixed for the beginning of his term, or if the President elect shall have failed to qualify, then the Vice-President elect shall act as President until a President shall have qualified; and the Congress may by law provide for the case wherein neither a President elect nor a Vice-President elect shall have qualified, declaring who shall then act as President, or the manner in which one who is to act shall be selected, and such person shall act accordingly until a President or Vice-President shall have qualified.

SECTION 4. The Congress may by law provide for the case of the death of any of the persons from whom the House of Representatives may choose a President whenever the right of choice shall have devolved upon them and for the case of the death of any of the persons from whom the Senate may choose a Vice-President whenever the right of choice shall have devolved upon them.

SECTION 5. Sections 1 and 2 shall take effect on the 15th day of October following the ratification of this article.

SECTION 6. This article shall be inoperative unless it shall have been ratified as an amendment to the Constitution by the legislatures of three-fourths of the several States within seven years from the date of its submission.

(Declared ratified February 6, 1933.)

AMENDMENT XXI

SECTION 1. The eighteenth article of amendment to the Constitution of the United States is hereby repealed.

SECTION 2. The transportation or importation into any State, Territory, or possession of the United States for delivery or use therein of intoxicating liquors, in violation of the laws thereof, is hereby prohibited.

SECTION 3. This article shall be inoperative unless it shall have been ratified as an amendment to the Constitution by conventions in the several States, as provided in the Constitution, within seven years from the date of the submission hereof to the States by the Congress.

(Declared ratified December 5, 1933.)

AMENDMENT XXII

SECTION 1. No person shall be elected to the office of the President more than twice, and no person who has held the office of President, or acted as President, for more than two years of a term to which some other person was elected President shall be elected to the office of the President more than once. But this article shall not apply to any person holding the office of President when this Article was proposed by the Congress, and shall not prevent any person who may be holding the office of President, or acting as President, during the term within which this Article becomes operative from holding the office of President or acting as President during the remainder of such term.

SECTION 2. This article shall be inoperative unless it shall have been ratified as an amendment to the Constitution by the legislatures of three-fourths of the several States within seven years from the date of its submission to the States by the Congress.

(Declared ratified March 1, 1951.)

AMENDMENT XXIII

SECTION 1. The District constituting the seat of Government of the United States shall appoint in such manner as the Congress may direct:

A number of electors of President and Vice President equal to the whole number of Senators and Representatives in Congress to which the District would be entitled if it were a State, but in no event more than the least populous State; they shall be in addition to those appointed by the States, but they shall be considered, for the purposes of the election of President and Vice President, to be electors appointed by a State; and they shall meet in the District and perform such duties as provided by the twelfth article of amendment.

SECTION 2. The Congress shall have power to enforce this article by appropriate legislation.

(Declared ratified April 3, 1961.)

AMENDMENT XXIV

SECTION 1. The right of citizens of the United States to vote in any primary or other election for President or Vice President, for electors for President or Vice President, or for Senator or Representative in Congress, shall not be denied or abridged by the United States or any State by reason of failure to pay any poll tax or other tax.

SECTION 2. The Congress shall have power to enforce this article by appropriate legislation.

(Declared ratified February 4, 1962.)

AMENDMENT XXV

SECTION 1. In case of the removal of the President from office or of his death or resignation, the Vice President shall become President.

SECTION 2. Whenever there is a vacancy in the office of the Vice President, the President shall nominate a Vice President who shall take office upon confirmation by a majority vote of both Houses of Congress.

SECTION 3. Whenever the President transmits to the President pro tempore of the Senate and the Speaker of the House of Representatives his written declaration that he is unable to discharge the powers and duties of his office, and until he transmits to them a written declaration to the contrary, such powers and duties shall be discharged by the Vice President as Acting President.

SECTION 4. Whenever the Vice President and a majority of either the principal officers of the executive departments or of such other body as Congress may by law provide, transmit to the President pro tempore of the Senate and the Speaker of the House of Representatives their written declaration that the President is unable to discharge the powers and duties of his office, the Vice President shall immediately assume the powers and the duties of the office as Acting President.

Thereafter, when the President transmits to the President pro tempore of the Senate and the Speaker of the House of Representatives his written declaration that no inability exists, he shall resume the powers and duties of this office unless the Vice President and a majority of either the principal officers of the executive department or of such other body as Congress may by law provide, transmit within four days to the President pro tempore of the Senate and the Speaker of the House of Representatives their written declaration that the President is unable to discharge the powers and duties of his office. Thereupon Congress shall decide the issue, assembling within forty-eight hours for that purpose if not in session. If the Congress, within twenty-one days after receipt of the latter written declaration, or, if Congress is not in session, within twenty-one days after Congress is required to assemble, determines by two-thirds vote of both Houses that the President is unable to discharge the powers and duties of his office, the Vice President shall continue to discharge the same as Acting President; otherwise, the President shall resume the powers and duties of his office.

(Declared ratified February 10, 1967.)

AMENDMENT XXVI

SECTION 1. The right of citizens of the United States, who are eighteen years of age or older, to vote shall not be denied or abridged by the United States or by any State on account of age.

SECTION 2. The Congress shall have power to enforce this article by appropriate legislation.

(Declared ratified July 1, 1971.)

AMENDMENT XXVII

No law varying the compensation for the services of the Senators and Representatives shall take effect, until an election of Representatives shall have intervened.

(Declared ratified May 7, 1992.)

TABLE OF CASES

A

551

553

B

C

TABLE OF CASES

D

582

E

F

G

H

I

K

O

P

625

Pierce v. School Comm., 322 F. Supp. 957 (D. Mass. 1971) —
§ 10.3, n. 51

Pierce v. Society of Sisters, 268 U.S. 510, 45 S. Ct. 510, 69 L. Ed.
1070 (1925) — § 1.5, n. 27; § 9.1, n. 7

Pietro v. Saint Joseph's Sch., 48 U.S.L.W. 2229 (N.Y. 1979) —
§ 13.4, nn. 61, 62

Pike Cty. Joint Area Vocational Sch. Dist., State *ex rel.* Cutler v.

Pinellas Cty. Classroom Teachers' Ass'n v. Board of Pub. Instruction, 214 So. 2d 34 (Fla. 1968) — § 5.3, n. 84

Pinkerton Acad., Johnson v.

Piphus, Carey v.

Piquard v. Board of Educ., 610 N.E.2d 757 (Ill. App. 3d Dist. 1993)
— § 5.1, n. 69

Pirschel v. Sorrell, 2 F. Supp. 2d 930 (E.D. Ky. 1998) — § 10.3,
n. 33; § 10.6, n. 84

Piscataway Twp. Bd. of Educ., Taxman v.

Pitt Cty. Bd. of Educ., Hines v.

Pittenger, Meek v.

Pittman, Crawford v.

Pittsburgh Bd. of Pub. Educ., Sanguigni v.

Pittsburgh Fed'n of Teachers v. Aaron, 471 F. Supp. 94 (W.D. Pa.
1976) — § 8.2, n. 91

Pittsburgh Unified Sch. Dist., North State Dev. Co. v.

Plantation Residents Ass'n v. School Bd., 424 So. 2d 879 (Fla.
App. 1982) — § 3.2, n. 10

Pleasants v. Commonwealth, 203 S.E.2d 114 (Va. 1974) — § 11.2,
nn. 21-23

Plesnicar v. Kovach, 430 N.E.2d 648 (Ill. App. 1981) — § 4.6,
n. 41

Plessy v. Ferguson, 163 U.S. 537, 16 S. Ct. 1138, 41 L. Ed. 256
(1896) — § 9.4, nn. 56-58

Plyler v. Doe, 458 U.S. 1131, 102 S. Ct. 2382, 72 L. Ed. 2d 786
(1982) — § 9.3, n. 41; § 10.3, n. 32

Poe, Givens v.

Pointek v. Elk Lake Sch. Dist., 360 A.2d 804 (Pa. 1976) — § 7.1,
n. 7

Q

R

S

646

T

651

Y

INDEX

A

ACADEMIC FREEDOM.
Association.
    Freedom of association, §8.2 (a).
Censorship, §8.1 (e).
Class discussions.
    Controversial subjects, §8.1 (a).
Collective bargaining.
    Subjects of bargaining, §5.1 (b).
Controversial subjects.
    Teaching controversial subjects, §8.1 (a).
Elections.
    Political activity, §8.2 (d).
Evolution.
    Teaching controversial subjects, §8.1 (a).
Flags.
    Refusal by teacher to salute flag, §8.1 (c).
Forbidden subjects.
    Teaching forbidden subjects, §8.1 (b).
Freedom of association, §8.2 (a).
Generally, §8.0.
Historical background, §8.0.
Loyalty oaths.
    Freedom of association, §8.2 (a).
Methods of instruction.
    Selection, §8.1 (d).
Political activity.
    Out-of-school activities, §8.2 (d).
Public statements, §8.2 (c).
Religion.
    Teaching controversial subjects, §8.1 (a).
    Teaching forbidden subjects, §8.1 (b).
Residency requirements, §8.2 (b).
Sex education.
    Teaching controversial subjects, §8.1 (a).

ADMINISTRATIVE LAW.
Forms of law, §1.2.

661

B

BOARDS OF EDUCATION.
Generally. (*See* SCHOOL BOARDS).

C

CANINE SNIFFS.
Searches, §10.4(e).

CENSORSHIP, §8.1(e).

CIVIL RIGHTS.
Jurisdiction.
    Civil rights torts, §4.9.
Torts.
    Deprivation of civil rights, §4.9.
        School employees, §7.8.

CLASS SIZE.
Collective bargaining.
    Subjects of bargaining, §5.1 (b).

COLLECTIVE BARGAINING.
Academic freedom.
    Subjects of bargaining, §5.1 (b).
Arbitration, §5.4.
    Impasse resolution, §5.3.
Class size.
    Subjects of bargaining, §5.1 (b).
Contracts.
    Arbitration agreements, §5.4.
Dues.
    Union dues.
        Required payment, §5.1.
Financial benefits.
    Subjects of bargaining, §5.1 (b).
Generally, §§5.0, 5.5.
Historical background, §5.0.
Hours of work.
    Subjects of bargaining.
        Mandatory subjects, §5.1 (a).
Impasse resolution, §5.3.
Injunctions.
    Impasse resolution, §5.3 (b).

COLLECTIVE BARGAINING—Cont'd

COMMON LAW.
Forms of law, §1.2.

COMPARATIVE NEGLIGENCE, §4.2 (b).

COMPULSORY ATTENDANCE, §9.1.
Exceptions, §9.1 (a).
   State law, §9.1 (b).

COMPUTER RESEARCH, §2.11.

CONFLICTS OF INTEREST.
School boards.
   Restrictions on office-holding, §3.4 (b).

CONGRESS.
Role in public education, §1.4.

CONSENT.
Searches and seizures.
   Students, §10.4 (b).

CONSTITUTIONAL LAW.
Academic freedom generally, §§8.0 to 8.2. (*See* ACADEMIC
    FREEDOM).
Civil rights.
   Generally. (*See* CIVIL RIGHTS).
Equal protection clause.
   Finance.
      Challenges to state finance schemes, §6.5.
Finance.
   Constitutional challenges to state finance schemes, §6.5.
Searches and seizures.
   Students.
      Constitutional issues, §10.4 (a).
Students.
   Exclusion from school.
      Due process.
         Procedural due process, §10.3 (b).
         Substantive due process, §10.3 (a).
   Freedom of association and assembly.
      Generally, §11.4.
   Freedom of expression.
      Generally, §§11.0 to 11.8. (*See* STUDENTS).

INSURANCE.
Collective bargaining.
    Subjects of bargaining.
        Financial benefits generally, §5.1 (b).

J

JURISDICTION.
Civil rights torts, §4.9.
Federal courts, §1.4 (c).

JURISPRUDENCES.
Legal research, §2.6.

L

LABOR RELATIONS.
Collective bargaining.
    Generally, §§5.0 to 5.5. (*See* COLLECTIVE BARGAINING).

LAW LIBRARIES, §2.0.

LEGAL DICTIONARIES.
Research tools, §2.8.

LEGAL ENCYCLOPEDIAS.
Research tools, §2.6.

LEGAL RESEARCH.
Tools of legal research, §§2.0 to 2.12. (*See* RESEARCH TOOLS).

LEXIS, §2.11.

LIBEL.
Tort liability, §4.1 (b).

LOYALTY OATHS.
Academic freedom.
    Freedom of association, §8.2 (a).

M

MARRIAGE.
Students.
    Assignment to classes and schools.
        Marriage as factor, §9.4 (c).

SCHOOL DISTRICTS—Cont'd

Immunities.
    Tort immunity, §4.3.
        Employees.
            School employee immunity. (*See* TORTS).
        Governmental and proprietary functions, §4.3 (b).
        Historical precedents, §4.3 (a).
Powers, §3.1.
Religion, §12.6.
State legislatures.
    Powers as to school districts, §3.1.
Status, §3.1.
Torts.
    Immunity, §4.3.
        Employees.
            School employee immunity. (*See* TORTS).
        Governmental and proprietary functions, §4.3 (b).
        Historical precedents, §4.3 (a).
    Teacher accountability.
        Generally, §4.7.

SEARCHES AND SEIZURES.

Consent.
    Students, §10.4 (b).
Constitutional issues.
    Students, §10.4 (a).
Dogs.
    Students.
        Searches involving dogs, §10.4 (e).
Students.
    Administrative v. police searches, §10.4 (d).
    Consent to search, §10.4 (b).
    Constitutional issues, §10.4 (a).
    Dogs.
        Searches involving dogs, §10.4 (e).
    Illegal searches, §10.4 (f).
    Reasonable cause, §10.4 (c).

SEX DISCRIMINATION.

Employment discrimination generally. (*See* EMPLOYMENT DISCRIMINATION).

SEX DISCRIMINATION—Cont'd
Students.
    Assignment to classes or schools.
        Sex as factor, §9.4 (b).

SEX EDUCATION.
Academic freedom.
    Teaching controversial subjects, §8.1 (a).

SEXUAL HARASSMENT IN THE WORKPLACE, §7.10.

SEXUAL HARASSMENT OF STUDENTS BY STUDENTS, §10.8.

SHEPARD'S CITATIONS.
Research tools, §2.4.

SICK LEAVE.
Collective bargaining.
    Subjects of bargaining.
        Financial benefits generally, §5.1 (b).

SLANDER.
Tort liability, §4.1 (b).

SPECIAL EDUCATION, §§13.0 to 13.6. (*See* STUDENTS).

STANDING DOCTRINE, §1.3.

STATES.
Attorneys general.
    Role in public education, §1.5 (d).
Courts.
    Role of state judiciaries in public education, §1.5 (c).
Governors.
    Role in public education, §1.5 (b).
Legislatures.
    Role in public education, §1.5 (a).
    School districts.
        Powers as to, §3.1.
Role of state governments in public education, §1.5.
Statutes.
    Tools of legal research, §2.1 (c).

STATUTES.
Forms of law, §1.2.

STUDENTS—Cont'd
Vaccination.
    Compulsory vaccination, §9.2.
Witnesses.
    Exclusion from school.
        Procedural due process.
            Call of witnesses, §10.3 (b).
            Self-incrimination, §10.3 (b).

SUBSTANCE ABUSE.
Students.
    Drug testing, §10.6.
    Searches and seizures.
        Generally, §10.4.
Teachers.
    Privacy issues involving professional staff employees.
        Drug testing, §7.9 (a).

T

TAXATION.
School board's power to tax, §6.1.
    Fiscally dependent school boards, §6.1 (b).
    Fiscally independent school boards, §6.1 (a).

TEACHERS.
Academic freedom.
    Generally, §§8.0 to 8.2. (*See* ACADEMIC FREEDOM).
AIDS.
    Privacy issues involving school employees, §7.9 (b).
Assault and battery.
    Tort liability generally, §4.1 (a).
Assaultive speech, §11.8.
Assignment of professional staff employees, §7.3 (d).
    Reassignments of tenured teachers, §7.5 (c).
    School board authority, §7.4.
Certification, §7.1.
Collective bargaining.
    Generally, §§5.0 to 5.5. (*See* COLLECTIVE BARGAINING).
Contracts.
    Employment contracts generally, §7.3 (c).
Defamation.
    Parental criticism of teachers, §4.1 (b).